# The
# Great
# Divide

# The
# Great
# Divide

The Challenge of

U.S.-Mexico Relations

in the 1990s

## Tom Barry

## Harry Browne

## Beth Sims

**Grove Press    New York**

*Published simultaneously in Canada*
*Printed in the United States of America*

FIRST EDITION

Library of Congress Cataloging-in-Publication Data

Barry, Tom, 1950–
The great divide: the challenge of US–Mexico relations in the
1990's / Tom Barry.
Includes bibliographical references and index.
ISBN 0-8021-1559-4
1. United States—Relations—Mexico.    2. Mexico—Relations—United
States.    I. Title.
E183.8.M6B37   1994      303.48'273072—dc20      93-33080

*Design by Laura Hough*

Grove Press
841 Broadway
New York, NY 10003

1 3 5 7 9 10 8 6 4 2

132715

# Contents

# Maps and Tables

## Maps

## Tables

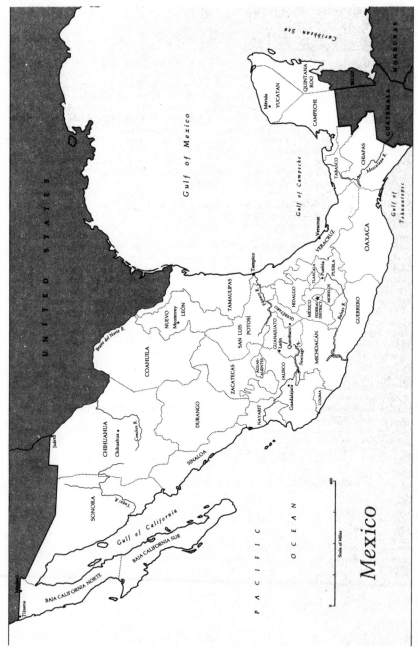

# Mexico

Scale of Miles

# U.S.–Mexico Border Region

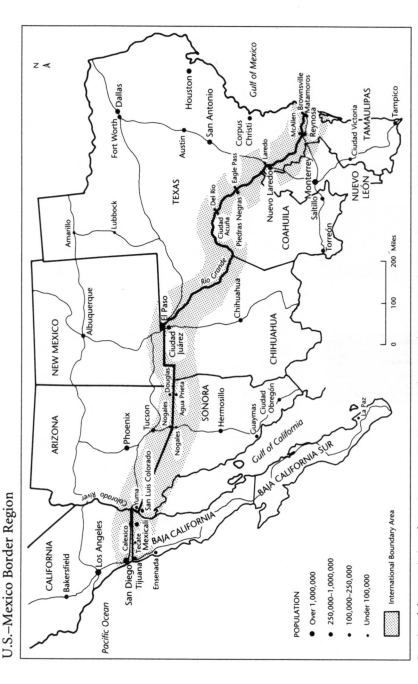

Reprinted, by permission, from Lawrence A. Herzog, *Where North Meets South: Cities, Space, and Politics on the U.S.–Mexico Border* (Austin: Center for Mexican American Studies, University of Texas at Austin, 1990), 34.

# Introduction

The border between the United States and Mexico is an arbitrary line drawn straight through desert sage and sand. The Rio Grande defines more than 1,200 miles of this 1,952-mile line, but from El Paso–Ciudad Juárez to San Diego–Tijuana the international division has no natural dimension.

To cross this line is to enter not only a different nation but also another part of the world. Immigrants from Latin America leave the third world and underdevelopment for an encounter with the "developed" world. The U.S.-Mexico border is the dividing line between the south and the north, the great divide that separates colony from imperium, desperation from hope. At no other international border are the contrasts so striking. The desert is no different; the sky is the same impenetrable blue. But from one side to the other, the human landscape is foreign.

All international borders are at once fascinating and disconcerting. They awaken and challenge one's sense of national identity. But it is not the contrasting cultures, the differences between political systems, or even the sudden change in language that makes crossing the U.S.-Mexico line so shocking. Instead, it is the experience of passing so rapidly between economic worlds. The line is the edge of a third world society that reaches ever farther south, beyond Juárez to the teeming barrios of Mexico City and into the Central American isthmus. The line divides the industrial North from the misery of the Southern Hemisphere. Crossing north to south, paved streets, auto insurance, and the American dream are left behind for a part of the world—the largest part—where one-room hovels, economic misery, and the lack of basic public services are the norm.

The dividing line is stark and unmistakable. But it is not impermeable. In fact, its ability to keep the two worlds apart has steadily diminished. Those living in the borderlands, that stretch of territory paralleling the boundary on either side, have long recognized and exploited the porous

1

border. Many have family on both sides, and the respective economies, although dramatically different, have always been interdependent. Crossing the line is as routine as visiting relatives, shopping, or going to work.

Most U.S. citizens, however, have had no personal or economic links south of the border. The U.S.-Mexico boundary underlined their privilege while isolating them from the political turmoil and economic desperation of their southern neighbors. Mexico, a nation of eighty-six million, was part of an unknown world that did not touch their lives.

Yet slowly the borderlands have been inching northward. No longer are immigrant foreign workers confined to the agriculture of the Southwest; over the past two decades they have become an integral part of the low-paid service sector throughout the United States. Mexican boys are selling flowers on the streets of New York City, Salvadorans are working in the restaurants of Washington, D.C., Mexican women are serving as maids and nannies from Portland to Atlanta. Latin Americans are of course not the only foreigners crossing into the United States, but it is the new wave of Spanish speakers predominantly from Mexico, Central America, and the Caribbean that has alerted U.S. citizens to the fact that the dividing line between the United States and Latin America is no longer so clearly demarcated.

The cross-border movement has by no means been in one direction. The self-proclaimed Manifest Destiny of the United States justified the habitual expansion of U.S. boundaries in the nineteenth century. Recognizing that the days of filibusters and colonialism were over, twentieth-century America relied on its new economic might backed by an Open Door policy of free trade to push its way past foreign borders in industrial capitalism's aggressive search for new markets and raw materials. With the United States the undisputed capitalist center at the close of World War II, U.S.-based transnational corporations began crisscrossing international boundary lines with increasing ease.

At first the search was mainly for sources of raw materials and new foreign markets. But U.S. firms soon began relocating "offshore" to take advantage of inexpensive and passive labor forces to work on their global production lines. Gradually manufacturing became globalized, meaning that corporations started placing parts of their production process overseas. As U.S. firms relocated outside the country, U.S. workers lost jobs and saw their bargaining power shrink. The globalization of production has been developing since the late 1950s, and it has involved Mexico since the mid-1960s. With the 1965 creation of the Border Industrialization Program, the export-oriented *maquila* sector was born in Mexico.

Relocating to sites with cheaper workforces has been a manufacturing tradition in the United States. At first, firms in the industrial belt looked to the nonunionized southern and southwestern states. Hoping to boost wider economic development, Sun Belt states competed with each other by offering relocating companies special tax exemptions, free warehouse facilities, and unorganized workforces. Crossing state lines to find more profitable manufacturing locations readied the U.S. corporate sector for international border-hopping. Tennessee or New Mexico could compete with Connecticut and Michigan but not with the dollar-an-hour wages of Mexico and other foreign locations.

Many businesses and free-trade proponents regard the border line as part of the bottom line of company balance sheets. Crossing the international border is essential to keeping U.S. firms competitive and profitable, they argue. Free trade and capital's ability—indeed its right—to seek higher return across international borders have become part of the new ideology of global capitalism. National borders, the public welfare, and governments, it is said, all must align themselves with this imperative of global trade and investment. There is a mathematical logic and beauty to this ideology of the global bottom line that does not leave room for consideration of nonbusiness questions concerning social equity and environmental sustainability.

*The Great Divide* is a book about the challenges that face the United States and Mexico in the 1990s. These range from transboundary and immigration issues to the evolving economic and foreign policy relations between the two nations. While looking specifically at U.S.-Mexico relations, we found that much of the discussion was relevant to the broader concerns of North-South relations.

In many ways, the border line separating the southern United States and Mexico is a metaphor for the economic future of America. In attempting to bridge this international divide, U.S. and Mexican citizens alike face choices and challenges that arise from living in an increasingly global economy and society.

The disparities, tensions, and common interests of these two neighbors illustrate the development dilemma posed by the global economy. Can Mexico or any other undeveloped nation achieve prosperity if it opens its borders to foreign competition and puts its workforce on the global assembly line? Can the United States retain prosperity if its workforce competes directly with those of third world nations? Can impoverishment and economic decline be avoided by following the direction of international traders and investors?

The book is divided into four parts. In the first section we focus on the border region for a close-up of the social and economic face of U.S.-Mexico relations. Included here are chapters on immigration and narcotics as well as an examination of the *maquila* industry. The second section discusses the environmental repercussions of the cross-border relationship. The third reaches into the heart of U.S.-Mexico economic relations. Finally, we look at the official relations between Washington and Mexico City, and follow with our conclusion.

# Part I

# Life on the Line

# Beginning at

# the Border

Geography brings the United States and Mexico together. It is along their common border that many of the challenges that face the two nations are most acutely felt. The society and economy of the borderlands reflect historic tensions and divisions between the two nations. At the same time, the increasing interdependence of the neighboring countries is most apparent in the border region. Just as obvious is the asymmetry that characterizes binational relations. Although many U.S. border cities are deeply dependent upon their larger Mexican twin cities for retail trade, the disparity between the two countries in wealth, welfare, and productive infrastructure is clear to anyone traveling through the borderlands.

At the border the two societies stand side by side, and their economic interactions highlight the benefits and problems of having a poor nation rub shoulders with a wealthier one. As the barriers to foreign imports and investment fall, the border is less a dividing line between two economies and more a wall between two societies. For the most part, it serves to obstruct northbound migration while raising few barriers for U.S. citizens wanting to visit or live in Mexico. Retirees and other "snowbirds" looking for a warm climate and a less expensive place to live have established expatriate enclaves throughout Mexico. But there is no corresponding freedom of movement for those seeking jobs and new lives north of the border.

The borderlands are the place where one best sees the problems of crossing the great economic and social divide between the two neighbors. Here the two societies are meshing, and economic integration is a daily occurrence. But the border is also a battleground where the U.S. authorities have mobilized their defenses against the advances of northbound immigration and narcotics flow.

## Defining the Border

Politics, war, and economic expansion carved the border line that separates Mexico and the United States. At first no fences or opposing flags marked this line crossing the largely uncharted and unpopulated region now known as the U.S.-Mexico borderlands. Today, however, the border is no longer just a mapmaker's creation. It is firmly fixed by concrete channels, steel walls, barbed wire, boundary markers, cattle fences, and the understanding that life is decidedly different on the other side.

The secession from Mexico of the Lone Star Republic of Texas in 1836 marked the beginning of the erosion of Mexico's northern territories. A decade later the Treaty of Guadalupe Hidalgo, which closed the Mexican-American War of 1846–48, virtually reduced Mexico by more than a third. This new territory became the province of eight new U.S. states.[1]

Superior U.S. military power proved decisive in drawing the new international boundary, but the border line was also the result of financial dealings between a wealthy, expansionist nation and an unscrupulous leader of a poor one. As compensation for its severed lands, Mexico under General Santa Ana received fifteen million dollars from Washington in 1848 and another ten million for the Gadsden Purchase in 1853. The Gadsden Purchase, which placed a strip of land along the bottom of what is now Arizona and New Mexico in U.S. hands, was the last major alteration in the international border.

For 1,254 miles the international boundary follows the Rio Grande on its path southeast from El Paso del Norte (now the site of El Paso and Ciudad Juárez) to the Gulf of Mexico. But west of the Rio Grande (known in Mexico as the Río Bravo del Norte) no natural features define the border, with the brief exception of the Colorado River. Until the Boundary Commission got to work placing stone boundary markers, the border was just a phantom line through the Chihuahuan and Sonoran deserts. From the Rio Grande to the Pacific the border stretches 698 miles, including a 24-mile jog along the Colorado River. Altogether—from the Gulf of Mexico to the Pacific Ocean—the U.S.-Mexico international boundary extends 1,952 miles.

Although the borderlands have long been a focus of tensions between the two nations, the definition of the actual border line has since 1854 been largely undisturbed by disputes between the two nations, and the one major territorial wrangle that arose was settled amicably.[2] The chief difficulty in maintaining the boundary has been the willful Río Bravo del

Norte. The official boundary line followed the river's midpoint; when the river shifted course, so did the U.S.-Mexico border. Silt accumulations in the shallow channel have caused the river to overflow its banks and establish new channels. To keep Mexico south of the river and the United States north, the U.S. Army Corps of Engineers "rectified" the erratic Rio Grande by constraining it within concrete channels as it turns southeast at El Paso.

Other than a scattering of missions, forts, and ranches, what are now the borderlands were sparsely populated until after the Mexican-American War. A series of twin border towns emerged gradually in the last half of the century. Some had their origins as frontier military posts or old Spanish ranchos while others developed primarily to satisfy the demands of north-south trade, but slowly the border region began taking shape. From a line traced through empty horizons, the border became a zone of development. Established as a boundary to keep two nations apart, over time the border drew the neighboring economies and societies together. The centers of this mutual attraction are the interdependent twin cities that serve as the hubs for the expanding border economy.[3]

The Prohibition era (1918–33) and the associated cross-border vice business sparked the initial boom in the Mexican border towns. Later the war economy of the 1940s and in particular the siting of new U.S. military bases in such border towns as El Paso and San Diego greatly boosted economic development along the border. In the 1960s the Border Industrialization Program, the Mexican government program that opened the country's northern frontier to export-oriented factories called *maquiladoras* (or *maquilas*) and the rising importance of the U.S. Sun Belt served to foster economic and population growth in the borderlands.

There is little confusion about where one nation ends and the other begins, but a definition of the borderlands region is more problematic. Certainly the fourteen twin cities that straddle the border are included, although there is some debate about whether San Diego is really a border city since its economic center lies seventeen miles from Tijuana. Proud of their border home, El Paso residents complain that their city is the largest U.S. border town—not the pretentious San Diego. Not too long ago there were few who really cared about how far north or south the borderlands extended. But with recent national attention—and the prospect of new business and increased federal spending—the borderlands debate has heated up.

In Mexico the borderlands have generally been defined two ways: The broader definition includes the entirety of the six northern states, while the narrower refers only to a zone extending about thirteen miles south of the border to the customs checkpoints or encompassing the thirty-five *municipios* or municipalities that parallel the border.[4] Generally, when Mexicans speak of the *frontera norte* (northern border) or of the *fronterizos*, they are referring to this narrow strip along the border and the people who live there. But *el norte* refers to all six border states—Tamaulipas, Nuevo León, Coahuila, Chihuahua, Sonora, and Baja California—as well as Durango and Sinaloa, and sometimes even Zacatecas.[5]

In the United States there is no official border zone that hugs the boundary and is subject to special customs regulations as in Mexico. Unlike the Mexican side, all customs stations are at the port of entries, although the U.S. Border Patrol has inspection stations as far as 75 miles from the border. In the 1970s the Southwest Border Regional Commission developed a definition based on the twenty-five counties that skirt the border.[6] Another definition has the borderlands extending 62.5 miles (100 kilometers) in either direction of the border. This would include San Diego and Las Cruces, New Mexico, but exclude such other cities as San Antonio, Tucson, and Monterrey in Mexico that share in the border society and economy. For purposes of discussing environmental issues, both the U.S. and Mexican governments use the 100-kilometer definition of the borderlands as established by the La Paz Treaty in 1983.

With population or culture used as a guideline, the borderlands could be said to extend much farther north into the United States. After all, there are more people of Mexican descent living in San Francisco than in Nogales, Arizona. Waxing philosophical, some say the border is pushing its way into the Midwest, the Southeast, or wherever immigrants from Latin America are found. In the context of regional economic integration, there is much pondering about the fading of borders, and *American Demographics* magazine even heralds a new "hypernation" emerging out of the North American nations. Similar speculation revolves around an ever-expanding "third nation," which some call MexAmerica, being shaped around the cultural and social integration of Mexico's *el norte* and the U.S. Southwest.

No clear consensus exists as to where the borderlands begin and end. For different purposes, a broader or more strict spacial definition of the borderlands may be more fitting. But as border scholar Jorge Bustamante has observed, two fundamental concepts are crucial in defining the borderlands. One is a recognition of internationality as a definitive characteristic of border life, and the second is that border societies and economies are continually interactive.[7]

## Mixing and Matching

International social and economic crisscrossing does make the borderlands special. In some U.S. border towns, Spanish is more common than English. Cross-border baseball teams, marathons, and Lions Clubs are common, especially in smaller border towns. At one point the mayors of both Columbus, New Mexico, and Palomas, Chihuahua, had wives from the other side of the line. Retail trade and tourism tightly link border economies, and city planners and border scholars are beginning to talk of transfrontier metropolises that cross the international border. Los Dos Laredos and Ambos Nogales have long existed in the parlance of those border towns.

Historically, formal cross-border cooperation has occurred mostly on a federal level. The prototype of a transboundary organization is the International Boundary and Water Commission (IBWC), which has counterpart organizations on both sides. Although eminently successful in carrying out its main mission—maintaining a trouble-free international demarcation—the binational commission does not have the mandate to address the multitude of environmental, infrastructure, development, and public health problems that now plague the border. In fact, its overly technical view of the border (seeing the Rio Grande first as an international boundary and only secondarily as a river or ecological system, for instance) obscures the larger problems that confront this heavily urbanized and industrialized region.

City governments and agencies have begun to work together formally to solve specific problems and to begin to address their joint status as twin cities. San Diego and Tijuana are leading the way in this regard, having established regular communications between police departments and even hosting joint city council meetings. The binational health councils along the border also illustrate the benefits of transboundary cooperation. Rather than risk violating international protocol, the border towns sometimes have found that informal channels work best, each side helping out the other when special needs arise.

The economic interdependence and social integration of the borderlands can be overemphasized. Although the judges and city officials in Laredo speak Spanish, few on the U.S. side of the border would trade in their U.S. citizenship for a Mexican passport. San Diego promotes itself as "America's Finest City," while Tijuana advertises that it is the "Most Visited City." More evident than the integrated character of the twin cities is the fact that they belong to two different worlds and realities: One side is the edge of the developed world, the industrialized north, while the cities on the other side are the outposts of the underdeveloped south.

Borderlands unity is also undermined by east-west differences. On both sides of the international line, the borderlands are highly segmented. East-west relations have been hampered by geography and the lack of a transportation network paralleling the border. Historically, the predominant social and economic interactions have been in a north-south direction. On neither side of the border is there a shared identity as a borderlands population, but this lack of a homogeneous border community is particularly evident on the U.S. side because of the differences among the white, Mexican-American, and native Mexican population groups.[8]

Ambiguity pervades border life. Socially and economically the border barely exists, but the border is real enough when it comes to labor mobility, customs and immigration checks, and as a dividing line between two markedly different systems of social and political organization. Even though the Mexican twins are generally much larger and even more industrialized than the U.S. border towns, the greater wealth, social organization, and power of the United States are readily evident. On one side, most of the streets are paved; on the other side, most are rutted and dusty. On one side, the tap water is drinkable; on the other, one doesn't dare. On one side of the line, there are adequate sewage and drainage systems, but on the other side, one does not flush paper down the toilet, and raw sewage drains through open canals. Looking over from the dusty *colonias* of Juárez toward the shimmering banks and office buildings of downtown El Paso shatters any wild notions about a third transboundary nation being born. A tortilla in the north or a Pizza Hut in the south does not necessarily mean that the two sides are merging.

This tension between unity and division is evident in the cultural mix of the borderlands. Mexican food and the Spanish language are part of the character of the U.S. Southwest. On the Mexican side, many prefer hamburgers to burritos, and English words have been incorporated into border slang. For the most part, this cultural interpenetration is not a matter of conquest or reconquest but an internationalization process common to all international borders. Mexican officials and intellectuals in the country's interior have long criticized the *anglicismos*, like *puchear* (to push) or *la troca* (truck), that pepper the language of *fronterizos*, complaining that *el norte* was letting its cultural heritage slip away. Certainly English-language music, movies, and advertising are common throughout the northern borderlands, but not as common as in the elite circles of Mexico City. As in most cross-border interactions, there is a marked asymmetry that arises from the economic imbalance between the two nations. Not only are Mexicans consuming more hamburgers, but they are eating them at McDonald's and Burger King. Fueled by a larger consuming public and powered by a flood of advertising, the U.S. business/cultural complex is gradually eating away at Mexico's cultural core.

In an epoch of globalization and international communications, too much can be made of cultural imperialism. But identity is important. Is a new international borderlands identity being shaped, or is Mexico's border region just another colony falling into the grasp of U.S. shopping-mall and fast-food imperialism? It is true that the cultural landscape of Mexican border towns has long been influenced by the United States. But the economic liberalization policies of the Mexican government combined with the forces of globalization have accelerated this process.[9]

## Borderlands Development

Once known as the land of sunshine, silence, and adobe, the borderlands are now one of the world's most urbanized border zones.[10] International border scholar Lawrence Herzog called the U.S.-Mexico border boom the greatest demographic and economic transformation of any border zone in the world.[11] In 1900 there were fewer than a hundred thousand people living in the borderlands. Today there are approximately ten million living in border *municipios* and counties, nearly three million more than in 1980, and virtually all the population is concentrated in the twenty-eight main twin cities, outside of which the borderlands remain a largely desolate and lonely region.[12]

On the U.S. side, border growth rates have been two to three times the national average over the past three decades. The population explosion has been even more dramatic on the Mexican side—about 1 percent higher than the national rate of population growth—doubling the population in the northern border zone over the past two decades and rapidly converting small border towns into major metropolises. Juárez and Tijuana, both with more than 1.2 million people, are among the largest cities in Mexico. About 100 new immigrants are thought to come to live in Juárez every day, and Colonia Libertad in Tijuana is among the world's most densely inhabited urban ghettos. Sun Belt migration in the United States and northward migration in Mexico probably account for about half the population growth in the borderlands.[13]

The prospect of a regional free trade agreement has spurred new interest in the U.S.-Mexico border as a commercial and transport district. Free trade, however, is not a new concept in the borderlands. Mexico has a long history of creating special tariff zones along its northern border to bolster population and commercial growth, and in the mid-1980s the U.S. Congress considered a proposal to create a coproduction/free trade zone along both sides of the border. Declared or not as free trade zones, the borderlands, particularly on the Mexican side, have long benefited from free trade in the form of contraband merchandise, or *fayuca* as it is called in Mexico. In their thirst for consumer goods unavailable on their own side, border residents have found ways to avoid all tariff and nontariff barriers to free trade. They have been assisted by a thriving sector of professional smugglers.

Ever since the launching of the Border Industrialization Program in 1965 the border as a barrier dividing national economies has become more porous. The program, which took advantage of U.S. tariff provisions facilitating international production-sharing investment, opened the northern border region to U.S. export-oriented investment. Tariffs, taxes, investment controls, and other barriers to trade were waived for companies locating along the border. More than a quarter of a century later some two thousand *maquiladoras* employing a half million workers are assembling duty-free materials into goods for export back to the United States. By the late 1980s the *maquila* sector—for so long treated as the exception to Mexico's protectionist economic development strategy—became the model for future export-oriented growth.

This evolution from a remote outback to a zone of mutual development has occurred in fits and starts. It has been directly tied to the economic development patterns of the two nations, but it has also paralleled the history of many other international borders. The explosive development along the U.S.-Mexico border is not an isolated case; as global economic integration advances, international borders that were once buffer regions far from metropolitan centers become dynamic economic corridors. Once regarded as peripheral to mainstream society and economy, borders are now leading the way toward new models of international commerce and investment as their functions are reconceptualized. With the transformation of global markets and financial systems, increased international migration, and the rise in production-sharing strategies, the line between the United States and Mexico has become increasingly open to economic penetration.[14]

## The Old Trickle-Down Problem

The boom in the *maquila* industry, a dramatic rise in cross-border traffic, and the social and economic integration of the U.S. and Mexican borderlands have spurred economic growth. But all is not well in the borderlands, despite this surge in investment and trade. Increased economic activity has not automatically translated into prosperity for the region. On the U.S. side, job growth has fallen far short of population growth and wages remain far below national levels. Economic, environmental, and social infrastructure is manifestly inadequate, and many fear that trade liberalization will aggravate this already severe infrastructure shortfall.

Industrial development councils in U.S. border cities have been promoting the Border Belt since the 1950s as a low-wage region without unions and with an array of tax breaks and subsidies for relocating companies. Promoters of U.S. border development have encouraged companies to relocate to their cities because of their proximity to Mexico but also because of the inequality of living standards on either side of the border. Companies could set up manufacturing facilities in Mexico to take advantage of the low wages while having their offices and homes of managers located on the U.S. side.

Even as some of the apparel and electronics firms that had relocated to the U.S. borderlands once again picked up stakes to set up *maquilas* on the other side, these same promotional groups stuck to this development strategy of attracting runaway plants to the region. More recently, business and government officials have become eager for free trade even though it might further threaten the welfare of the region's low-wage and unskilled population while escalating the infrastructure crisis. Similarly, the Mexican border region has rushed into a development strategy based on *maquilas* and low wages with little thought given to social and city planning and infrastructure. Dollars have trickled across the border and into the local economy—but not enough to pay for the social and economic infrastructure costs of development and not enough to lift the region out of poverty.

With the exception of San Diego, the U.S. borderlands are among the poorest regions in the United States. A full quarter of families there fall below the poverty line.[15] Unemployment is also higher than the U.S. average, ranging from a low of 8 percent in San Diego to 14 percent in Brownsville at the border's eastern extremity. Generally, poverty levels increase from west to east, with the Texas border cities of McAllen, Laredo, and Brownsville having the highest unemployment rates in the nation in 1989 and El Paso ranking among the top ten.

In 1993 the average salary in El Paso was 72 percent of the U.S. national average. Distributing that below-average wage among the larger-than-average families of the El Paso area meant that the average per capita income was only 55 percent of the national average. In 1960, before the *maquila* program began, about 20 percent of El Paso residents had incomes below the national average. By 1991 that figure swelled to 42 percent.[16] Most of the city's population of Mexican descent is crowded into the blighted south side of the city, whereas the one-third of the population that is white inhabits the suburban subdivisions north of Interstate 10. In 1979, 29 percent of El Paso's Latino population lived below the poverty line; the figure rose to 43 percent by 1989.[17] The poverty is most evident in downtown El Paso in an area dubbed Little Chihuahua. Only a few blocks from the Westin luxury hotel and the border crossing, families crowd into small rooms in downtown tenement buildings and have no private baths.

Per capita income, low by U.S. standards, is still three to seven times higher than on the Mexican side. Even the poorest U.S. communities enjoy per capita income two to three times higher than most Mexican *municipios*. The economic disparity between the U.S. and Mexican sides of the border is especially striking when one realizes that the economic gap is much narrower at the border than for the two nations as a whole. Whereas the U.S. borderlands are among the poorest regions in the United States, Mexico's northern border is that country's wealthiest region.

With 16 percent of Mexico's population, the border states account for 22 percent of national income. Unemployment is minimal, although the low figures are misleading because the government counts as employed all who work at least one hour a week. Employment and wage statistics can also vary widely. In 1986, for example, 24 percent of workers in Matamoros received less than the minimum wage, while only 7 percent of Tijuana workers were under the minimum.[18] Although illiteracy for the border states is about a third of that found in the other states, this does not always translate into improved employment opportunities.

As in the United States, the poorest areas are found in the eastern border states (with the prominent exception of Nuevo León), while Baja California is the state with the highest socioeconomic indicators.[19] Although the standard of living is generally much better than in the rest of

Mexico, the differences from the U.S. borderlands in most socioeconomic indicators are still staggering. While a majority of the residents of the U.S. borderlands have completed high school, only about 10 percent on the Mexican side have completed twelve years of schooling.[20] Although substantially below the national average, infant mortality in Mexico's northern zone is approximately five times that of the U.S. borderlands, where infant mortality approximates the U.S. national average.[21]

The northern border has Mexico's highest minimum wage but also the country's highest cost of living.[22] An import-dependent economy, the border strip suffers more than any other part of Mexico from peso devaluations. Reductions in the peso's value constitute a boon to *maquila* owners, who pay their workers in the devalued pesos, but the devaluations have caused dramatic decreases in workers' spending power in this region where the cost of living is 90 percent of the U.S. level.

Despite their proximity to the United States and their higher-than-average socioeconomic indicators, the Mexican border cities are not unlike most third world cities. The lack of decent and affordable housing is the most salient problem. Women and men who work all day as maids or gardeners on the U.S. side or in modern factories owned by companies like GE and Zenith come home at night to the desperate conditions of life in the *colonias perdidas*. The land and housing shortage has pushed families onto hillsides, floodplains, and the slopes of arroyos to build their homes. At first they erect their shelters using heavy cardboard, scrap lumber, and tin sheets. Gradually they manage to construct small concrete-block homes. It takes about a day's wage to purchase a dozen cement blocks, and four months' wages to buy enough for a basic twelve-by-twelve-foot house.[23]

The absence of proper housing is not a one-sided problem. An estimated five thousand homeless live in El Paso, and as many as fifty thousand live in nearby *colonias*. The communities referred to as *colonias* on the U.S. side are uncharted rural subdivisions of substandard housing in which families own their own plots but generally lack water, sewerage, adequate drainage, and paved roads.[24] Most *colonia* residents buy or haul their own water, but many of the *colonia* residents have septic tanks, which contaminate not only the Rio Grande and underground aquifers but also their own personal wells.

The larger Mexican border cities are infrastructure wastelands. Spreading out from the city centers, each new subdivision or squatters' settlement has assumed its own grid pattern, creating endless transportation and planning headaches. Social services fall far short of the needs of the exploding population. Every summer hundreds of dehydrated children are brought to the Juárez general hospital, which is only several minutes away from El Paso, for treatment of gastrointestinal problems resulting from severe water shortages in the *colonias*. But during the summer of 1989 the hospital's cooling and heating system was not working, as was frequently the case. Trying to find some relief from the heat, the children and other patients took to sleeping on dirty floors. In a two-month period in 1989 more than a dozen children died as a result of the intense heat and inadequate treatment for dehydration.[25] At the same time, hospital workers had to carry patients and bodies up and down the stairs because the elevators also were out of service and there was no money with which to fix them.

## Norteños and Fronterizos

In Mexico, *el norte* has long been a hotbed of change and influence. For that reason, Mexico's leaders have regarded the northern borderlands with some apprehension. After all, the Mexican Revolution did come sweeping down from the north. A 1906 strike at the U.S.-owned Cananea copper mine in northern Sonora sparked the popular opposition against the *porfiriato* dictatorship, and the first skirmish between the *federales* and Madero's revolutionaries bloodied the frontier town of Juárez in 1911. Francisco Madero, the intellectual author of the revolution, came from the border state of Coahuila, while Pancho Villa and his followers hailed from Durango and Chihuahua. Three of the country's early postrevolutionary presidents (de la Huerta, Obregón, and Elías Calles) were Sonorans.

The Spanish never had a strong presence in the north. This rugged mountain and desert domain was the land of miners and ranchers. No major prehispanic civilization arose from the north, and the native peoples that did make a home here (the Yaquis in the Pacific lowlands and the Tarahumaras in the Sierra Madre) had few relations with the *norteños*. From the beginning it was a land of tough and self-reliant Mexicans who tended to think and act more independently than those from the interior.[26]

Not only have they been more affected by the modernizing winds of the north, but these people have also had a long history of contact with U.S. companies—the railroads, mines, and agribusinesses. It was no coincidence that Monterrey, Mexico's industrial center, rose in the north, only 140 miles from the border.

Since the mid-1800s the Mexican government has been seeking ways

18

to keep its remote northern border tied to the country's center. During the Cárdenas administration (1934–40) the government sought to develop and populate the northern border with irrigation and land-distribution programs. Worried that the *fronterizos* were losing their language and culture, the government sponsored special educational and civic programs to keep the language pure and patriotism strong.

In the early 1980s there seemed to be a new revolution stirring in the north as the National Action party (PAN) began building a strong anti-PRI (Institutional Revolutionary party) movement there. It was both a civic rebellion against the PRI dictatorship and a declaration that the time had come for the private sector to be put in the driver's seat. The PRI's wholehearted embrace of free-market economic policies took some of the wind out of PAN's sails, but widespread public disgust with the PRI bureaucracy has kept PAN strong.

Improved communication and transportation links as well as its own economic strength mean that the region is no longer so isolated from the centers of power in Mexico. Today the *fronterizos* and *norteños* are increasingly following U.S. political and economic models. The people here look not to Mexico City but to the north for their styles, culture, and ideology. *Norteño* ballads and rancheras are still popular in the cantinas, but *fronterizos* are also rooting for the Dallas Cowboys and Los Angeles Dodgers. Along the border the demand for U.S. goods is evident, but for most they are not affordable. Advertising, proximity to the United States, and the increasing presence of U.S. retail outlets in Mexico are importing U.S. consumer habits to a people who cannot afford U.S. consumer goods.

The northern borderlands have also become the destination for used vehicles, clothes, tires, appliances, and just about everything else discarded by the United States. Downtown stores in U.S. border cities advertise *Ropa americana por libra* (American clothes by the pound). A baled bundle of used clothes cost $5.98 at one El Paso outlet. "We're becoming a secondhand society living off the waste of the U.S.," lamented Víctor Clark Alfaro, a human rights activist in Tijuana.[27]

At the border, U.S. visitors enter Mexico to seek the old—street vendors, posed photographs in donkey carts, and handicrafts from Old Mexico. Heading north—legally or illegally—are those who seek the new. They want part of the future and think they will be able to find it only across this magical line. As Carlos Monsiváis wrote: "The heart of the Mexican dream is Los Angeles."[28] It is the land where dreams wait to be realized.

## The Latinization of the United States

You do not have to be a demographer to know that the ethnic and cultural composition of U.S. society is rapidly changing. The predominance of an English-speaking population of European descent persists, but this majority is diminishing in the face of a more rapidly expanding population of immigrants and ethnic minorities. Bilingual signs in airports and government buildings, Spanish-language billboards and media, and the emergence of strong but insular Guatemalan, Cuban, Vietnamese, South Korean, Salvadoran, and Mexican communities in U.S. cities are among the most obvious signs of this demographic change. The rise of "English only" campaigns and immigration-control movements, boosted by widespread fears of a declining U.S. economy, are signs of a popular reaction to this population shift that is redefining U.S. society.

Most prominent, especially in the U.S. Southwest, has been the rise of that part of the U.S. population labeled Hispanic by the U.S. Census Bureau but increasingly referred to as Latinos by community leaders. In 1950, 2.6 percent of the U.S. population was Hispanic; it rose to 4.7 percent by 1970 and 9 percent by 1990.[29] Hispanics are increasing in number about five times faster than whites and are expected to constitute about 13 percent of the U.S. population by the year 2010.[30]

Between 1980 and 1990 the Latino population in California increased from 19 percent of the state to 26 percent. Most dramatic was the increase in Los Angeles, where the number of Latino residents rose 62 percent in the 1980s. If this trend continues, more Latinos than Anglos will reside in Los Angeles by 2010.[31] Buoyed by such statistics, State Senator Art Torres proclaimed: "The legacy of Los Angeles left by its founding fathers and mothers—Spanish, Indian, and Mexican—is now being reclaimed by a new generation of leaders."[32] Indeed, the population statistics are auspicious for Latino politicians hoping to capture the new Latino vote and to put forward a Latino political agenda.[33]

Immigration is a major factor in the Latino population growth, with the U.S. Census Bureau estimating in 1990 that more than 40 percent of Latinos were born outside the United States. About half of California's Latino growth in the past decade came from legal and undocumented immigration.[34] Because immigrants tend to be young and because Latinos have higher fertility rates, the Latino population is much younger than the U.S. average—a median age of 25.3 years compared with 33.6 years for the balance of the U.S. population. Just 5 percent of Latinos in the United States are over age sixty-five compared with more than 13 percent for non-Latinos. Immigrants compose only about 7 percent of the U.S. labor force but have accounted for 22 percent of the growth in the workforce since 1970 and are expected to constitute 25 percent of that growth in the 1990s.[35]

Immigrant Latinos may share a Latin-American birthplace (Mexico, Central America, South America, and the Spanish-speaking Caribbean— Puerto Rico, Cuba, and the Dominican Republic) and their language, but they share little else. Their cultures, lifestyles, class backgrounds, race, language cadences and accents, and political inclinations differ sharply. The cultural mix within the United States can be truly grasped only through an understanding of what each of the twenty nationalities brings to this society.

In the effort to establish a common political agenda, and in recognition of some social commonalities (such as being Spanish speaking and having familial origins in Latin America), many politicians and academics have nonetheless found the need to resort to such generic terms as *Hispanic* and *Latino*. In recent years the term *Latino* has gained increased acceptance, especially in political and academic circles. Nationalists, radicals, and progressives within Spanish-speaking communities have long frowned on the use of *Hispanic*, charging that those who prefer that label are trying to whiten or Europeanize their identities by accenting their Spanish rather than Latin-American, mestizo, or African heritage.

The term *Latino* is regarded as more race-neutral. Although useful for political, marketing, and census purposes, the Hispanic and Latino labels disguise the many racial, ethnic, and class differences among the different communities. Such panethnic terms also fail to distinguish between the native- and foreign-born.[36]

In the U.S. census after 1980, Mexican origin is a subcategory of Spanish or Hispanic origin. Mexican-origin residents represented 2 percent of the population in 1970, rising to 5 percent by 1990. Census figures show that 80 percent of Hispanic-origin Californians were of Mexican descent, and 91 percent of Hispanic-origin Texans were of Mexican descent.[37] Two border states, California and Texas, were home to 54 percent of Latinos, followed by New York, Florida, Illinois, New Jersey, Arizona, New Mexico, and Colorado.[38] Mexicans and Mexican Americans are the largest population group in most border towns—San Diego being the usual exception to border generalizations, with the Latino share being just 20 percent. The largest majorities are found along the Texas border, ranging from 69 percent in El Paso to 97 percent in Starr County. Persons of Mexican origin are the fastest-growing minority in the United States and are projected to be the "majority minority" in California by the year 2030.[39] In 1990 U.S. residents of Mexican origin constituted 64 percent of all Latinos in the United States.

Except for the self-labeled Hispanos of northern New Mexico (whose ancestors lived in the area long before Mexico declared its independence from Spain), well over 90 percent of the Latinos of the borderlands could be aptly termed Mexican Americans, meaning Americans of Mexican descent. However, because of the negative stereotyping by the Anglos of the region, it was not until the late 1950s that the term *Mexican American* became an accepted self-designation. Especially in the nineteenth century the term *Mexican*—or "Messcan," as it was commonly pronounced—connoted half-breed, intellectually inferior, indolent, dishonest, backward, and treacherous.[40] By calling themselves Spanish, Mexican Americans established some distance between themselves and their Mexican roots. They sought to avoid the negative stereotyping while at the same time benefiting from the European or white connotation of Spanish ancestry.[41]

In the late 1950s, and especially in the 1960s, the term *Mexican American* came into widespread use with the founding of the Mexican American Political Association, United Mexican American Students, and other groups that wanted to affirm their Mexican ancestry. Other Mexican-origin Latinos, especially university students and militant community organizers, adopted the term *Chicano*—a derivative of *mexicano*—in the spirit of the new nationalism that was building throughout the Southwest.[42] In fact, the increasingly common use of *Chicano* eased the acceptance of Mexican American as a self-identifier.[43]

Closely associated with the "brown power" nationalist sentiment of the early Chicano movement was a conception that the mestizos of the Southwest together with the Mexican people formed part of the mythical nation of Aztlán.[44] They were all part of the "Cosmic Race," the utopian term first used in 1920 by Mexican intellectual José Vasconcelos in a reference to a "fifth race" or a *raza de bronce* (bronze race) that melds other races together.[45] Colloquially they were *La Raza*—a term meaning "our people." The cultural nationalism of the early Chicano leaders was clearly expressed in the Plan de Santa Barbara, the manifesto of the 1960s Chicano movement, which asserted there was a "crucial distinction in political consciousness between a Mexican American and a Chicano mentality. The Mexican American is a person who lacks respect for his cultural and ethnic heritage. . . . In contrast, Chicanismo reflects self-respect and pride in one's own heritage and cultural background." Gradually the less restrictive definition of a Chicano as a person of Mexican ancestry but not an immigrant gained acceptance throughout the Southwest particularly among students, militants, and progressives.

Together with the cultural nationalism of the 1960s there arose many illusions about how culturally pure and politically correct Mexico was. But this idealism was soon shattered as romantic notions of Mexico clashed with the reality of the widespread oppression, racism, and exploitation that existed in Mexico. For many Chicanos, the green, white, and red colors of the Mexican flag—once appropriated as their own cultural banner—faded as a symbol of their own ethnic pride because of their rising confusion and disillusionment about Mexico.

The struggle over terminology reflects the long-running identity crisis faced by Mexican Americans. Racism and negative stereotyping certainly lie at the heart of this cultural crisis, but the search for self-identity has also been complicated by the conflicting attitudes about Mexico, assimilationist ambitions, internalized repression, and the economic and political marginalization of the Mexican-American people.

The positioning of Mexican Americans with regard to Mexico and Mexican immigrants has long been a source of tension and conflict. This has been seen most clearly in the debate over immigration laws. Although there exists broad sympathy for immigrants, Latino concern that immigration flows threaten hard-won social and economic progress is also widespread. In recessionary times, anti-immigrant sentiment tends to rise.

The stagnant U.S. economy in recent years has stalled the economic progress of Latinos. In 1990, 23 percent of all Latino families and 20 percent of all Mexican-origin families existed below the poverty line, compared with 9 percent for all U.S. families.[46] According to a 1990 report on the status of U.S. Latinos, two-thirds of all Latinos "lack the skills required for stable employment that pays a reasonable wage." Furthermore, the study found that 40 percent of those aged twenty-five to thirty-four had not completed four years of high school, and that the real median income of Latinos had fallen between 1979 and 1987 in all but four of the thirteen metropolitan areas surveyed.[47]

But one must be careful in making cultural, social, and economic characterizations based on generic labels. Generalized descriptions of the socioeconomic status of Latinos point to the inexactitude of such umbrella terms as *Latino* or *Hispanic*. This standardized terminology also leads to racial and cultural stereotyping when in fact there exist major differences between the socioeconomic status of the various U.S. minority (mainly Mexican Americans and Puerto Ricans) and immigrant groups

(Cubans, Dominicans, Central Americans, Mexicans, and South Americans) of Latin American descent. Most obvious is the privileged economic status of the middle- and upper-class Cuban-American community. But sharp class distinctions also exist within the various ethnic groupings, and the large influx of poor immigrants from Mexico and Central America tends to obscure the socioeconomic advances being made by the native-born Latinos.

Although it is often argued that free trade would boost economic growth in the Southwest, virtually all the studies of the probable impact of the North American Free Trade Agreement (NAFTA) have concluded that the sector of the population likely to be most adversely affected and displaced are low-skilled, low-wage workers, a sector in which Latino workers are disproportionately represented.[48]

Latino organizations such as the National Council of La Raza and MALDEF provided strong initial support for NAFTA, including backing "fast track" negotiations. But in response to rising concerns about trade liberalization with Mexico and other less developed countries, some Latino organizations later took more even handed although still largely supportive positions with respect to the proposed free trade agreement. According to Antonio González, a project director for the Southwest Voter Research Institute, the predominant attitude (among Latinos) is "compassion for Mexico but don't take my job."[49]

For Latinos, political power may not necessarily be proportionate to their numbers. Dramatic increases in the number of Latino public officials, especially at the state and local levels, do indicate that the tables are turning. But voter registration and turnouts far below national averages continue to frustrate Latino politicians. Hispanic turnout in the 1992 elections was 29 percent, compared to 54 percent for Blacks. Voter registration rates for Hispanics have not improved over the past two decades. In fact, there has been a decline in the percentage of Hispanics that are registered, dropping from 44 percent and 38 percent in 1972 and 1976 respectively, to 35 percent in both the 1988 and 1992 elections.

The low registration and turnout rates for Hispanics are partly explained by the large noncitizen population. Omitting noncitizens from the population base would raise Hispanic turnout in 1992 to 48 percent.[50] Another factor explaining low voter participation is the higher percentage of Hispanics that are in their late teens and early twenties—a group that shows low participation rates in most ethnic categories. Language barriers and the traditional marginalization of Hispanic communities also help explain low voter participation. However, the fact that voter registration has held steady since 1988 indicates that efforts by groups such as the Southwest Voter Education Project have prevented further decline despite the rapid increase in the number of eligible Hispanic voters.

A monolithic Latino voting bloc can not be assumed by Latino politicians.[51] Latino support for Democratic candidates is likely but can no longer be counted on. Not only are Latino voters increasingly split between Democratic, Republican, and independents, but they are also divided by their diverse countries of origin, cultures, class backgrounds, and divergent aspirations.[52] Shaping a common political agenda for Latinos has proved difficult not only because the various communities of Latin American descent do not share a common sense of identity but because of diverse political views and class status both within and between the different ethnic groups. This is especially true on foreign policy issues but also extends to such domestic issues as affirmative action, immigration reform, and abortion.[53] Among most groups there does, however, exist a strong support for bilingual education and generally for increased government services.[54]

Conservative immigration-reform groups, some environmental organizations, and population control groups all raise concerns about the effect of "Latinization" on the quality of life in the United States. They suggest that the large immigrant population, legal and illegal, is contributing to social fractionalization while taking jobs from native-born citizens and overtaxing the country's social services.[55] The influx of Latino immigrants in recent decades has given rise to large ethnic factions of Mexicans, Salvadorans, and Guatemalans that do not speak English, do not participate in the U.S. political process, and do not make it through the educational system. Although they are gradually assimilating, their social isolation and lack of personal resources hinder this process.

Others celebrate the immigrant presence, pointing out that the United States has long been a nation of immigrants and arguing that immigrants are actually good for the U.S. economy. Furthermore, the percentage of U.S. residents who are foreign-born—about 6 percent—is far below the 14 percent of the high point of immigration in the 1900–20 period. Not only are today's immigrants generally younger than the average population, but they tend not to use social services (except for education) as much as native-born citizens.[56] Immigration proponents also argue that immigrant workers make the U.S. economy more competitive, have only a slight impact on wage levels, and do not cause massive job displacement.[57]

Mexican immigration—and by extension all south-north immigration into the United States—is a national and international phenomenon that goes to the heart of U.S.-Mexican relations. It involves, as we will examine in the next chapter, such larger questions as the economic imbalances between nations, the failure of economic development models in third world countries, and the impact of free trade and globalization of production on international labor mobility. Especially for borderlands communities, these are more than abstract questions: They are features of everyday life.

# Crossover Dreams—and

# Nightmares

On an average day, between seven thousand and nine thousand people enter the United States illegally over its border with Mexico. The crossings are surprisingly visible. Standing on the Paso del Norte bridge in El Paso, one can watch passengers unload from cars in Juárez in broad daylight, walk down the southern bank of the Rio Grande, cross over either by foot or on rafts run by entrepreneurs, climb up the northern bank, pay a small entrance fee to thugs or scouts, and enter the United States through holes in the Cyclone fence. In and near San Diego, where nearly half the crossings occur, hundreds of people gather at nightfall in a few areas. Along the few lighted stretches of the border, or with the help of night vision equipment, one can view their subsequent dash through the fence and over the scrub brush. At times television-news viewers have seen terrifying footage of large groups of immigrants sprinting north through San Diego's southbound border crossing, directly into oncoming freeway traffic.

Images such as these have contributed to a feeling among many Americans that the country has lost control of its borders. Headlines describing "floods" or "tidal waves" of illegal immigrants, political rhetoric about a "silent invasion," and greatly exaggerated estimates of the numbers of undocumented foreigners have had a similar effect. Perceptions that they take jobs from legal U.S. residents or at least undercut wages and working conditions add to the resentment of undocumented immigrants. Throughout the United States there is also widespread concern that they burden the social welfare and education systems and that some cross into the United States to commit crimes, returning to Mexico to escape capture.[58]

These issues are not new.[59] They have been the subject of popular debate since the 1920s, when Mexican migration first became an important national issue in this country. The negative perceptions of illegal immigration have exerted considerable pressure for action on legislators—especially those from border states. Historically, this pressure has produced periodic deportation campaigns—generally corresponding to U.S. economic downturns—and a variety of immigration reforms.[60] But none of these efforts has put a stop to illegal immigration, and their deterrent effect has generally been short-term. The United States has proved unable to design or unwilling to enforce policies that would "seal the borders," as some have hoped.

## Criminals or International Workers?

Near the fetid green water of the Tijuana River, a graffiti artist has tagged the south side of the wall with a message: "Neither illegals nor criminals—international workers." The sentiment of the message is accurate even if undocumented immigrants do commit the misdemeanor of "entry without inspection." By far the majority of Mexican immigrants are workers who cross the boundary in search of decent jobs or family members of those workers. These international workers have made significant contributions to the development of the United States and the profitability of U.S. business.

The demand for labor by U.S. railroad companies and later by agribusinesses began to pull Mexican workers into the western United States in the 1880s. Expanding rapidly into the Southwest, the Southern Pacific and Santa Fe railroads developed a rapacious appetite for cheap labor. Realizing that Mexicans would be much more convenient than the then-favored Chinese coolies, the railroad companies began recruiting from the south. Mexicans lived much closer than the Chinese, were almost as desperate, and could easily be sent home when no longer needed.

By 1910 approximately twenty thousand Mexicans were being recruited each year by agents for the railroad companies. Other industries also began recruiting in Mexico or illegally paying labor contractors and smugglers to bring workers across the border. Mexican labor formed the backbone of the westward spread of cotton plantations and for the proliferation of large-scale vegetable, fruit, and sugar beet plantations. To a lesser extent, Mexican workers contributed to the development of copper mining in the Southwest.[61] During World War I, when native-born labor was in especially short supply, Mexicans played a critical role in sustaining the U.S. economy.

When World War I ended, however, the United States expressed little gratitude for the contributions of Mexican labor. Deep schisms began to develop within U.S. society around the issue of Mexican immigration. Businesses fought to defend their access to the cheap and abundant Mexican labor supply. Opposing them were labor unions and a growing anti-immigrant sentiment among the general public. This division set the stage for seventy years of policy debate and international conflict.

The return of the doughboys and the postwar recession of 1921–22 made Mexicans personae non gratae, especially among workers threatened with or suffering from unemployment. With the encouragement of labor leaders and some politicians, mobs attacked Mexicans at work, at home, and in the streets. But at the same time, U.S. employers—particularly growers, railroads, and the auto and steel industries—continued to recruit Mexicans. Their agents sought cheap labor both in Mexico itself and in the vast Mexican labor pool that had accumulated in Texas. The Mexican workers they hired lived in fear of deportation because of the heightened anti-immigrant atmosphere.

Unable to seek justice from the authorities, workers were unlikely to complain about common abuses, ranging from unsafe working conditions and underpayment of wages to beatings and robberies. As continued to be true in the coming decades, efforts to rid the country of undocumented residents did not prevent employers from hiring them. Instead, anti-immigrant measures actually increased the benefits to employers of hiring undocumented workers by increasing workers' vulnerability to abuse.[62]

The Great Depression dealt an even harsher blow to Mexican immigrant workers. Hundreds of thousands were rounded up and deported. Unemployment in manufacturing and mining eliminated those jobs, and by the late 1930s the Dust Bowl migration to California meant that growers there no longer needed Mexicans to perform stoop labor.

Mexican migration entered a new cycle with the onset of World War II. Again the country faced a labor shortage, and U.S. recruiters were back in Mexico looking for temporary farmworkers. Washington assisted the recruitment effort by negotiating an executive agreement with Mexico in 1942 called the Emergency Farm Labor Program. Under the bracero program, as it became known, the U.S. government hired Mexicans chosen by the Mexican government and then subcontracted the workers out to growers. The U.S. government guaranteed transportation and the payment of a minimum wage. The bracero program continued in a variety of forms until 1964.[63] In the late 1950s more than four hundred thousand braceros worked legally each year on U.S. farms and orchards.

The Mexican government had serious misgivings about sending its citizens abroad and about the vulnerability of braceros to abuse by their employers. But the money the workers sent back was so valuable to the Mexican economy that the country never decided to halt the program. In the end the U.S. government called it off. In part this was due to the growing civil rights and farmworker-organizing movements, which increased the nation's concern over the living and working conditions of immigrant workers. The program's cancellation was also due to decreased demand for legal braceros that stemmed from mechanical innovations such as the tomato harvester, introduced in the early 1960s.

The bracero program failed to halt undocumented immigration from Mexico to the United States. Many more illegal immigrants crossed the border from 1942 to 1964 than did legally contracted braceros, the large majority to work in seasonal agriculture. But when the program was combined with an enforcement campaign launched in 1954 called Operation Wetback, there was a large drop in the number of Mexicans apprehended crossing the border illegally. In 1953 the Immigration and Naturalization Service (INS) apprehended nearly 900,000 undocumented foreigners; this figure dropped to 250,000 in 1955 and to 88,000 in 1956. Upon the termination of the bracero program, illegal immigration accelerated rapidly. In 1976 INS apprehensions passed 1 million.[64]

From the railroads to modern agribusiness, U.S. employers and Mexican workers established a seasonal migratory pattern that continued for decades. Very few immigrants crossed with the intention of staying in the United States. Migrant workers usually came from small, often isolated towns and villages concentrated heavily in the poor agricultural states of central Mexico. And earning enough to support their families was the nearly universal motive behind migration.

Dramatic changes in the Mexican economy during the 1980s produced a shift in the nature of migration. Drastic cuts in government services, huge outflows of capital, and the loss of export markets meant soaring unemployment and an end to most government support for small farmers. Within Mexico millions of people migrated from the countryside to large cities, no longer able to eke out a living from barely arable land. Hundreds of thousands migrated to Mexico's northern border, seeking employment in the burgeoning *maquiladora* assembly plants. In the cities millions were forced into the informal economy, as street vendors, window washers, and beggars. The call of the north became more persuasive than ever. Increasingly, migrants came from and headed to large urban centers, rather than to farming communities. These migrants were looking for jobs in the service sector—with restaurants, hotels, car washes, and construction firms—or in manufacturing. Although some of them were coming only temporarily, more appeared to have given up hope of ever earning a living in Mexico and came planning to stay.[65]

The overall economic effect on Mexico of the migration of its citizens to the United States is unclear. On the one hand, Mexican nationals in the United States—with and without documents—send huge sums of money to their families relative to what they could earn in Mexico. This is extremely important for the Mexican economy, possibly surpassing the country's income from either tourism, the *maquiladora* program, or foreign direct investment. A 1992 study placed the amount between $2 billion and $6.2 billion for 1990, and strongly suggested that the actual amount was closer to the upper limit than the lower.[66]

On the other hand, the exodus of people represents a loss of human capital, and because immigration requires planning and fortitude, emigrants tend to be the ambitious, entrepreneurial individuals that the Mexican government is counting on to revitalize the country's economy as the state's role shrinks. Many studies indicate that the money sent to Mexico by workers in the United States does not contribute to long-term economic development. Instead it goes to the purchase of consumer goods, many of which are imported.[67]

## Like It or Not, Here We Come

The swath of land where the United States meets Mexico is both the place where the interdependence and integration of the two countries are most apparent and the scene of the most determined efforts to keep a strict dividing line between them. Deployment of military troops, the use of high-tech detection systems, and the imposition of forbidding physical barriers at the border have undoubtedly succeeded in turning back some of the immigrant stream. But they fall far short of being long-term solutions.

Perhaps nobody knows this better than the Border Patrol agents themselves. Every day they get a dose of global economic and political reality: peasants with no productive land and no hope of getting any, workers with no decent jobs and no hope of getting them, Central Americans frightened and tired of living under repressive governments, and Mexicans who simply want a better life for their families and children. Put in the position of the "aliens" they chase, these custodians of the border would probably make the same choice to take the big trip north.

31

For the most part, it comes down to economics. No matter how frustrating or unrewarding, many Border Patrol agents keep their jobs because the pay is good. The United States may be in a state of economic decline and the standard of living is slipping, but it still looks like the land of opportunity to millions living outside its borders. Immigration scholars have long discussed the "push" and "pull" factors contributing to international migrant streams. Generally these refer to the conditions of poverty and political repression that push people out of their own homes and the higher wages and increased opportunities that pull them toward another country.

The poorest of the poor are not the main immigrants; rather, they tend to be community members who are better off than their neighbors and have the savings to afford the necessary bus tickets, bribes, and "coyotes" (immigrant smugglers). They are also the "risk takers" of their communities in their willingness to chance failure and unknown hardships. Clearly, the closer one is to the United States, the less expensive and less arduous the migration. That explains, at least partially, why Mexico has historically lost more of its citizens to the United States than have more distant Latin American countries.

But the economics of immigration are not that simple. Domestic factors such as overpopulation, increasing poverty, and political repression are not the only forces pushing international migration flows. Saskia Sassen, an expert on global restructuring at Columbia University, has concluded that capital mobility and foreign intervention also fuel labor mobility. When the political and economic systems of nations become interconnected, labor tends to flow to the country where there is less social stratification and higher standards of living.[68] Just as the advance of European capitalism and technology resulted in migration to Europe from the affected African and Asian countries, so, too, has the U.S. global reach set off migratory flows from countries like the Philippines, Vietnam, South Korea, the Dominican Republic, Haiti, El Salvador, Nicaragua, and Mexico.

Economic expansionism (foreign trade, investment, and financial dealings) together with an interventionist foreign policy helps establish the context for international migration. According to Sassen, "The central role played by the United States in the emergence of a global economy over the past 30 years lies at the core of why people migrate here in ever-increasing numbers. U.S. efforts to open its own and other countries' economies to the flow of capital, goods, services, and information created conditions that mobilized people for migration, and formed linkages between the United States and other countries that subsequently served as bridges for migration."[69]

One of the earliest and clearest examples of economic integration that sparked immigration to the United States was seen in Puerto Rico, where U.S. investment in export-oriented manufacturing and U.S.-led agricultural modernization established the international context for migration. Peasants who found they no longer had a vital place in the domestic economy because of U.S. investment in sugar plantations or nontraditional agroexports saw the folly of working at home for third world wages when they might be able to find the same kind of job in the United States for much higher ones. In the case of Mexico, the bracero program established a strong link between Mexican labor and U.S. capital, forming a migratory pattern that to a certain extent still exists in U.S. agriculture. Likewise the *maquila* program did create jobs, but it also caused many Mexicans from the interior to look north for opportunity.

Economic growth does not necessarily stem out-migration. Although their own economies were booming, many Taiwanese and South Koreans chose to leave for the United States, which they judged would offer more possibilities for upward mobility. Uneven development, often a product of modernizing economic growth, also results in international migration. As Sassen has observed, "Measures commonly thought to deter emigration—foreign investment, or the promotion of export-oriented agriculture and manufacturing in poor countries—have had precisely the opposite effect. Such investment contributes to massive displacement of small-scale agricultural and manufacturing enterprises, while simultaneously deepening the economic, cultural, and ideological ties between recipient countries and the United States."[70] These factors all encourage migration—something to consider when evaluating claims that U.S.-Mexico free trade will slow the tide of migration from Mexico.

Global economic restructuring and integration have clearly raised the levels of international migration. But these same economic forces are also changing the labor market in the United States. At a time when traditional highly paid manufacturing jobs have become scarce, new immigrants are finding a place in the expanding informal and low-skilled services economy. Moreover, the postwar collaboration of capital and labor is breaking down as U.S. companies have become transnational ones and U.S. workers have been forced to compete with foreign workers employed by U.S.-owned firms.[71] As union shops disappear, low-wage jobs in nonunion workplaces expand. Technological development has created a narrow sector of highly paid technicians, consultants, and information specialists.

But they depend on armies of poorly paid women and men working dead-end jobs assembling parts, pushing paper, entering data, and cleaning office buildings.

The restructuring of capital-labor relations has resulted in increased economic polarization, with those at the top experiencing the "need" for more personal services—dog walkers, errand runners, restaurant workers, and gardeners—to maintain their lifestyles. Hard-working immigrants struggling for economic footholds often fill these slots. The restructuring of the U.S. family has contributed to this demand. With the rise of the two-income family, U.S. workers do not have time for household work traditionally performed by housewives; child care becomes a necessity when both parents are working, and in many areas there is a ready supply of Mexican women willing to take children into their own homes for as little as one dollar an hour. No longer are maids, nannies, and other household help the exclusive province of the very wealthy. Professional couples are finding that they too can join the garden economy by paying (in cash with no taxes) Mexican immigrants to do their shopping, gardening, and cleaning. Also forming part of this expanding informal ("off-the-books") economy of immigrant labor are skilled workers who do dry-walling, electricity, car repair, sewing, and construction work for low fees.

Many immigration experts and economists argue that the entry of recent immigrants into the manufacturing sector, especially small-batch producers with flexible production strategies, is helping keep the U.S. economy competitive.[72] Agribusiness, although increasingly mechanized, remains heavily dependent on immigrant and other Latino labor. Seventy percent of migrant farmworkers are Mexican men, and only 3 percent of migrants are non-Latino U.S.-born workers.[73]

A strong argument can also be made that the aging U.S. society needs the injection of largely young immigrants. During the 1990s the number of U.S. citizens age eighty-five and older is projected by the Census Bureau to grow by 42 percent—about six times the rate of overall population growth. At a time when the U.S. workforce is growing older, Mexico is a young society—half the population being under the age of fifteen—and provides a continual supply of young workers willing and able to do jobs unwanted by U.S. citizens. In a *Wall Street Journal* article Peter Francese, president of American Demographics, advised, "The United States needs to admit more immigrants now to get us out of the demographic bind we put ourselves in by restricting immigration in the first place."[74] Immigrants, it is argued, can fill the rising need for workers to care for the elderly, the sick, children, and the handicapped. As the slow-growing U.S. population ages, all these needs will become more acute.

Clearly the "pull" factors still exist within the U.S. economy. Despite its overall crisis, immigrant labor is still in high demand, not just by business but also by households. But labor market forces alone do not fully explain the character of the pull north. Also critical are the social factors, or what immigration experts call "social networks."

## To Cross Is to Die

*Cruzar es morir un poco*, according to a Mexican ballad. "To cross is to die a little" captures the tragedy of leaving one's home and being forced to leave one's culture, family, and even style of dress behind. For peasants, *Cruzar es morir un poco* also evokes the sadness of leaving the rancho and the life of the campo.

But in its romanticism for Mother Mexico, the ballad may paint a false picture of immigration. Migration to the United States is in many communities a rite of passage for young men. Upon their return, with new clothes and a new sense of themselves, they establish themselves as eligible bachelors capable of providing for a family.

Until the 1980s most Mexican immigrants were what sociologists call sojourners, not permanent settlers. They supplied the seasonal labor needed to harvest the citrus of Arizona, the lettuce of California, and the cucumbers and chili peppers of Lower Rio Grande Valley in Texas. Today, however, only 10 to 15 percent of the Mexicans in California, Arizona, and Texas work in seasonal agriculture. Instead they are found throughout the formal economy and constitute a major element in the booming informal economy in the United States. Increasingly Mexicans come to the United States to stay. They are settlers, and while often sad about leaving Mexico, they are hopeful about finding a new and better home in the United States.

Easing their entry into and adjustment to the new society are far-reaching social networks that make the new arrival feel at home. The most important networks are those formed by relatives and members of the same communities back home in Mexico or deeper in Latin America. Rarely does the immigrant enter the United States completely alone. Usually he or she comes with a phone number or address of some acquaintance and perhaps even instructions about how to negotiate the way there. Most head for Los Angeles or other traditional destinations, not because these are necessarily the places of most opportunity but rather because that is where their social networks lead them.

These social networks make immigration a self-perpetuating process. Each new settler in the United States becomes a magnet drawing others north. As the immigrants settle in, creating their own ties of kinship and friendship in the United States, they are no longer temporary sojourners in U.S. society but permanent residents. But each new settler creates a host of potential immigrants who dream of repeating his or her success.[75]

Immigrants from the south also rely on networks of social-justice activists who provide assorted services, such as immigration counseling and temporary housing, and organize on behalf of this vulnerable population. Some immigrant communities have also begun establishing their own mutual assistance networks with the help of sympathetic U.S. citizens. One such organization is the Mixtec Civic Committee, a group of Indians from the southern Mexican state of Oaxaca who work on the truck farms north of San Diego but who also have strong links with the Mixtec Indians who live and work in Baja California. Campesino Families is another mutual aid organization based in Bakersfield, California, which sponsors cooperative schools and child-care centers.

The existence of social networks established in the United States has been one reason for the changing character of the migrant stream. No longer is the stereotype of the lone Mexican campesino immigrant accurate. Entire families are coming north at the same time, and it is now common for women to cross the border alone. Over the past three decades the immigrant community has become steadily more heterogeneous, but it was Mexico's economic crisis of the early 1980s that really sparked the nontraditional immigration of urban residents and women and children. Determining that there were no prospects for economic betterment in either the campo or the city, they counted their savings, packed their bags, and hopped on a bus for the border.[76] As the workforce in Mexico has become more integrated and as gender stereotypes slowly break down, women have decided that they, too, want a chance for a better life that crossing the line might give.

## Fear and Loathing on the Border

Entering the United States has always been a risky proposition for the undocumented. Without legal status, they are particularly vulnerable to extortion, police brutality, economic exploitation, and racist violence.

Lately the victimization of undocumented immigrants has worsened. Economic downturn in the United States, the rise of burglaries in U.S. border communities, and the increased flow of narcotics across the land border have all aggravated border tensions, leading to a rise in violence directed at the immigrants. Also contributing to the climate of hostility that emerged in the 1980s were alarmist warnings from the CIA, INS, and White House about the "invasion" of our borders.[77] In 1984 President Reagan summarized this rising preoccupation with the immigrant flow from Mexico, Central America, and other Latin American nations: "The simple truth is that we've lost control of our borders, and no nation can do that and survive."[78]

Even before crossing *la linea* separating Mexico from the United States, northbound migrants must be constantly on the lookout for police and thieves. The Federal Judicial Police, the *federales*, have long preyed on migrants intent on crossing to the United States. Reforms by the Salinas administration have cut down on police corruption and human rights abuses. But those Mexicans, and especially Central Americans, heading to *el otro lado* still commonly find themselves victims of police corruption and violence.[79] The government's Paisano project, which is part of the president's social services program called PRONASOL (National Solidarity Program) encourages Mexican citizens to report cases of police abuse. However, a survey in Nogales, Sonora, found that a year after the Paisano campaign was launched four out of ten migrants interviewed reported they had been victims of police misconduct.[80] When asked, most illegal immigrants say they would rather be picked up by the U.S. Border Patrol than face the brutality of the Mexican police.[81]

On their journey north the immigrants next pass through the gauntlet of thieves and rapists that haunt the border zone. In some cases the assailants are the very men hired to guide the frightened travelers into the United States. These are the coyotes or *polleros* (chicken keepers) whose business is smuggling their *pollos* or human contraband into the United States. Although many are dishonest and ruthless, most are dependable and fear the *bandidos* who stalk the border as much as their clients do.

Depending on how and where the immigrants choose to cross, different risks and dangers await them. For many Mexican peasants traveling every year to the United States for seasonal farmwork, the best route is the physically exhausting trip through the deserts and mountains of the Southwest. For those who know the way, there is little risk of encounters with the U.S. Border Patrol, the border enforcement arm of the INS. But for those with less experience and endurance, these cross-country entries often lead to severe dehydration, sunstroke, and often death. Drownings are also common—eighty-seven deaths in 1988—for those who attempt crossing the 164-foot-wide All-American Canal, which courses through the blistering desert near Yuma, Arizona.

Drownings are also frequent along the Rio Grande. Suddenly finding themselves in water over their head or in swift current, the immigrants often panic, and their bloated bodies later turn up downstream. In 1989, 117 drowning victims were recovered from the banks of the Lower Rio Grande, 53 of whom were never identified.[82] Lately, however, freeway crossings claim more victims than river and canal crossings. Between 1987 and 1991, 127 immigrants died and 96 more were injured trying to scurry across the north-south freeways in San Diego County.

What most of these immigrants have in their minds as they prepare to cross the border are not the physical risks but their prospects for avoiding the Border Patrol, commonly known as *La Migra*. In the major twin cities, women and men—sometimes entire families—stop at the line that marks the last of Mexico, reviewing their strategies before this critical stretch of their journey. Getting to the other side of the border fence is usually no problem. Conveniently there are usually holes cut into the fence or sometimes dug under it. On the outskirts of some cities there are gashes large enough to drive a truck through—and sometimes people do. The informal economy prevails at *la linea*: Vendors sell plastic bags to keep feet dry at shallow river and canal crossings, human *mulas* will carry people across, microentrepreneurs sell hot dogs and burritos for the last meal in Mexico, and for a small fee, scouts will check ahead for signs of the Border Patrol.

In their dark green uniforms and light green Chevy Blazers, Border Patrol members wait—and then strike, putting the EWIs (Entering Without Inspection) in the back of their "war wagons" and taking them to the *Corralón* (corral) for processing. For those who see this drama for the first time, it shocks, absorbs, amazes, and disgusts. It is a tragedy of human relations, but there is also a comic aspect, especially if you are not part of the action. Looking from the downtown bridge between Juárez and El Paso, you can see coiffured and high-heeled young women, probably *maquila* workers, being floated over to the other side of the Rio Grande channel for a day of shopping and socializing in El Paso. In Tijuana hundreds of prospective undocumented immigrants line up along the border fence, facing a couple of beleaguered Border Patrol agents who know that most of them will probably make it to their destination. In Nogales a couple of elderly men, members of the flourishing informal economy, can be seen making regular trips back and forth across the border, carrying bags of aluminum cans for recycling in the United States.

As twilight descends, floodlights flash on at a few popular crossing spots, a sign that the action will continue trough the night. Some prefer crossing by cover of night, but others say that it is easier to blend into the crowd and escape the clutches of the Border Patrol during the daytime. With night goggles amplifying the starlight, the Border Patrol is also ready for the night shift. Overhead in Tijuana a Border Patrol helicopter circles, its powerful spotlight scouring the border and looking for large groups trying to make it across. The regulars, those who frequently cross into the United States for jobs and shopping, call the helicopter *el mosco* (the mosquito) for its pesky character and persistent buzzing.

Most residents of the U.S. border cities take little notice of all this activity. A green van screeches around the corner, a Border Patrol agent hops out and scoops up a couple of "illegal aliens," and no one seems to notice. It is part of the accepted background of life on the line. But this type of law enforcement that makes some human beings illegal outrages an increasingly vocal minority of human rights, church, and immigration activists. Rubén García, who now runs the Annunciation House for immigrants in El Paso, said that when growing up in El Paso he never noticed that he was living in a virtual police state.[83]

This perception has been borne out by recent human rights reports by Americas Watch and the American Friends Service Committee. In its 1992 report *Brutality Unchecked*, Americas Watch concluded that beatings, rough physical treatment, and verbal abuse by the INS and its agents were routine and that the border agents go beyond apprehending undocumented immigrants to judging and punishing them.[84] According to the AFSC's 1992 report, *Sealing Our Borders: The Human Toll*, the Border Patrol's involvement in drug interdiction has "injected a higher level of paramilitary readiness in immigration control," thereby confusing the patrol's mandate.[85]

Such attitudes and practices have resulted in serious injuries and deaths. Between 1980 and 1992, Border Patrol agents shot dozens of people, killing at least eleven and permanently disabling another ten in the San Diego area alone.[86] Particularly appalling is the impunity that has protected implicated Border Patrol agents from prosecution. Americas Watch found the INS was willing "to cover up or defend almost any form of egregious conduct by its agents," including murder, beatings, torture, and sexual abuse.

The brutality against undocumented immigrants, while certainly not justifiable, is understandable to some degree. Border Patrol agents perform a thankless, impossible job. Each day they know that they will be able to catch only about a third of those crossing the border illegally, and almost all of those whom they do detain will eventually make it safely into the United States. Low morale and frustration combined with the increase of violence by drug traffickers and border bandits contribute to their often brutal response.

The state-of-siege mentality that characterizes the INS is in part a product of the increasing number of illegal immigrants it incarcerates rather than simply deposits on the other side of the border, as it usually does with Mexicans without a criminal record. As the number of OTMs (Other Than Mexicans) has risen, the INS has steadily increased the size of its detention centers, which are filled with Haitians, Central Americans, and other OTMs whose deportation process often drags on for months. As the U.S. General Accounting Office (GAO) reported in 1992, the number of "criminal aliens" requiring detention has increased dramatically, while the "flow [of OTMs] has become a torrent" in recent years.[87]

Crime is a serious problem along the border—both for the migrants themselves and for the communities that hug the border. In San Diego approximately a quarter of those arrested for auto theft and burglary are undocumented persons.[88] Most of the crime by the undocumented, however, is committed not by the millions of undocumented people seeking work in the United States or even by the coyotes who guide them across the border but by what police call "the rob and return bunch" and the "border bandits."[89]

As one researcher noted, "Despite the awareness that migrant workers as a group are not responsible for much serious crime, police nevertheless lump the crimes committed by this group—'public order misdemeanors' and nonviolent 'survival crimes'—with the statistics for the major crimes (robbery, rape, and murder) committed by border bandits, usually against the migrant workers themselves."[90] Moreover, the high proportion of "aliens" in INS and border-town jails does not necessarily reflect an equally high proportion of alien crimes. Although certainly a matter of concern for border communities, alien crime may actually be less than commonly believed since the undocumented resident is more likely to be arrested and held without bail than a citizen. Although the extent of immigrant crime may be exaggerated and most immigrants unfairly stereotyped as criminals, there is no denying that crime by undocumented immigrants—those labeled EWIs—has increased dramatically and has become an acute concern for border communities. As a result, some citizen coalitions are calling for stricter immigration-law enforcement and new barriers (ditches, walls, floodlights, etc.) at the border to obstruct the illegal flow.

In the heated public debates along the border over what to do about cross-border crime, there is little attention to or concern about crime committed against undocumented residents of their communities. Generally such crime goes unreported, mostly because of the fear of victims that they will be deported but also because of the widespread distrust and fear that most Mexicans and Central Americans have of the police. A Border Patrol information officer estimated that nine of every ten crimes committed against undocumented people are left unreported.[91]

Symptomatic of the rising border tensions was the 1990 appearance in San Diego County of a citizen program to stop the flow of immigrants. Organizers of the "Light Up the Border" campaign called on supporters to park their cars in strategic areas while training their high beams on the border. The hundreds of people who gathered on the hills and in the canyons of northeast Tijuana each evening waiting to dash into the United States faced yet another obstacle to reaching *el otro lado*. Although frightening, the lights of some five hundred cars were not able to turn the tide of this determined immigrant force, proving no more ominous than the INS helicopters circling overhead, the threat of border bandits, or the deep fear of passing unprotected into a foreign land.

The "Light Up the Border" campaign was only one case of a nativist backlash against the economic and political refugees streaming into the United States from the south. More alarming was the appearance of vigilante squads, ranging from the Ku Klux Klan to a group of skinheads called the White Aryan Resistance, that began patrolling the border. Such organized citizen immigration-control efforts proved short-lived, but they created a climate in which the abuses of immigrants multiplied. In north San Diego County, an agricultural area where many migrant workers live in appalling squalor in narrow canyons that skirt the coast, the backlash has assumed shocking dimensions. In January 1990 a Carlsbad store owner and his brother, tired of Mexicans loitering around his store, bound Candido Gayoso with duct tape, put a paper bag with no holes over his head, and wrote on the bag *"No más aqui"* ("No more here") as a warning. Aficionados of war games have hunted undocumented immigrants with paint bullets, but there have also been numerous cases of real shootings simply because the gunmen did not like Mexicans.

As if to assure border residents that the government is on their side, the Army Corps of Engineers announced plans in 1992 to mount searchlights on more than 150 concrete poles, each some sixty feet high, along thirteen miles of the California border below San Ysidro. The plan gratified immigration-control activists but alarmed those concerned that the border is turning into a war zone. Another ominous sign was the construction by army reservists of a steel wall along the same stretch of border, replacing the highly porous chain-link fence. Defying immigrants to cut holes in this mother of all fences, the new twelve-foot-high rust-colored barrier is made of 180,000 metal sheets originally intended for use in the Persian Gulf War to establish temporary landing fields in the desert sands.

## The Search for an Immigration Policy

The latest U.S. attempt to restrict illegal immigration from Mexico, the 1986 Immigration Reform and Control Act (IRCA), strengthened the shift from temporary to permanent immigration. The product of nearly two decades of legislative wrangling, IRCA made two dramatic changes in immigration law: It imposed sanctions on the employers of undocumented migrants, and it granted legal status to more than three million qualifying undocumented immigrants of all nationalities.[92]

Both these changes contributed to the permanence of Mexican immigrants. First, employer sanctions made it somewhat more difficult for undocumented immigrants to find jobs. This meant that once immigrants had secured positions, they were less likely to leave them for a long trip home. This in turn meant it was preferable to bring family members illegally to the United States than to visit in Mexico. Second, the legalization of the status of 2.3 million Mexicans in the United States increased their security and their ability to house and support undocumented family members.

IRCA's employer sanctions provision followed from the recognition that preventing immigrants from finding jobs when they arrived at their destinations was a key to reducing illegal immigration. Until IRCA it was illegal for undocumented immigrants to reside in the United States, but it was legal to employ them.[93] Not surprisingly, many employers—especially those in seasonal and labor-intensive businesses like vegetable farming and construction—took advantage of this situation to hire undocumented workers, almost all of whom came from Mexico.

One obvious reason for hiring Mexican workers is that their fear of deportation makes them unlikely to defend their rights in the case of abuses of wage or occupational health and safety laws. Some employers seem also to have believed that undocumented workers were less likely to vote to join a union. That labor and human rights abuses are widespread is clear from the number of complaints filed by undocumented workers and their advocates, despite the threat of being returned to Mexico. The Los Angeles–based Center for Human Rights and Constitutional Law reported in 1992 that "in our experience representing thousands of [undocumented] workers, approximately 25 percent are paid below the legal minimum wage, they are regularly penalized (including arrests and deportation) for engaging in union activities to improve working conditions, over 35 percent work under conditions which violate health and safety laws . . . , women are often subject to sexual abuse, and instances of physical beatings and other anti-Mexican 'hate crimes' are on the rise."[94]

But research has shown that the most important reasons for hiring undocumented workers are not related to their legal status so much as to their relatively low expectations of working conditions and job benefits. Over the years immigrants have proved willing to perform hard labor in uncomfortable settings and to work temporarily with no job security. These characteristics, employers argue, mean that undocumented workers do jobs that legal residents will not do, and that therefore they do not take jobs away from citizens. In fact, the argument continues, undocumented workers actually *save* jobs for legal residents by keeping companies profitable that would otherwise go under.

Numerous mainstream economic analyses support the idea that undocumented labor makes a positive contribution to the national economy. They argue that even if some displacement of U.S. workers *does* occur, the low wages and high productivity of undocumented workers mean cheaper goods and services for consumers. Cheap foreign labor also means a more efficient economy overall, greater investment, and eventually jobs for those who were displaced.[95]

Union officials and many labor economists dispute this view of the impact of undocumented workers on the U.S. economy. They suggest that the proper question is not "Who would do these jobs in the absence of illegal immigrants?" but "What would these jobs look like if employers had to hire legal employees?" Those companies competing directly with firms in other nations might well find themselves forced out of business by having to pay higher wages or offer steadier jobs. Light manufacturing and some seasonal agriculture are industries in this position. But many— probably most—undocumented workers are employed in other areas, such as food service, retailing, construction, and temperate-climate agriculture, which face little or no international competition.[96]

In those sectors somewhat insulated from international competition, employers would be forced to automate, restructure, or improve wages and working conditions. But since all employers would face the same labor shortage, none would be undercut by competitors' employing cheap labor. Effectively prohibiting the hiring of undocumented workers might slightly increase the cost of certain goods and services, but the amounts would be barely noticeable: Only five cents of the price of a head of lettuce goes to farmworkers, for example, so a 20 percent wage hike would add a penny to the cost.[97] And proponents of ensuring that employers hire only documented workers argue that there is a moral dimension to economics and that efficiency should be balanced by equity. Protecting the rights and the jobs of those at the lowest end of the economic scale makes sense morally and in terms of long-term political stability.

A more fundamental criticism of the mainstream perspective that undocumented immigration has a positive economic effect attacks the theory itself as irrelevant to the real world. Mainstream economists use models that assume full employment, a smooth labor market, and no racial discrimination. The fact that none of these assumptions holds—and certainly not in the lower-income areas where new migrants tend to settle—means that immigrants compete directly with a pool of low-wage and unemployed workers who face great obstacles in finding replacement jobs if they lose out. In this case the benefits of greater economic "efficiency" go exclusively to employers, and tension is created between the new settlers and the groups—often largely African-American—with which they compete.[98]

The debate over immigrants, jobs, and the economy stymied IRCA's predecessor bills for eighteen years. Employers pressured their representatives to stop any law that would endanger their access to temporary low-wage immigrant labor. Unions and immigrant-rights groups opposed any bill that might lead to increased abuse of labor laws and of undocumented workers. Latino leaders joined employers in opposing penalties for hiring undocumented workers, fearful—with some reason, it turned out—that employers would discriminate against foreign-looking job applicants in order to protect themselves against prosecution.[99]

In the end employers were given a big loophole: They had to "knowingly hire" an undocumented worker to be subject to penalties; this meant that any decently forged document could be accepted by employers as proof of legality. In addition, farm employers were assured a supply of low-wage, flexible labor by the creation of two new immigration categories: Special

Agricultural Workers (SAWs) and Replenishment Agricultural Workers (RAWs). SAW status was to be granted to immigrants who had worked at least ninety days during 1986 or at least ninety days during both 1984 and 1985. The number of applicants far exceeded expert predictions, and studies of farm employment data indicate that at least half the SAW applications were almost surely fraudulent.[100] RAWs were intended to supplement SAWs if the U.S. Department of Labor certified a farm labor shortage, but this provision was never put into effect.

The SAW and RAW provisions were a large part of IRCA's second major change, legalizing the status of certain qualifying immigrants. But the legalization debate had focused largely on IRCA's "amnesty" provision, which offered legal status to people who had illegally entered the country before January 1982 and could show they had lived here until at least May 1987 with only brief absences. Mexicans submitted 1,229,016 applications for legalization, nearly all of which were accepted.

The amnesty provision responded not to the debate over jobs but to the broader question of the effect of undocumented immigrants on U.S. society. For many, the presence of millions of "illegals" represents a loss of national sovereignty because of their violation of the country's borders. Immigrants are also seen as a threat to the U.S. national character. It is argued that there are too many to assimilate effectively into the American way of life and that their proximity to Mexico means that they retain ties that other immigrants have to cut upon arrival.

Others believe that the undocumented population represents a time bomb of social unrest that is fueled by the labor and human rights abuses the foreigners are subject to. The undocumented immigrants' lack of trust in and access to the legal system compounds the problem. In the 1980s these concerns were fed by evidence of rapidly increasing illegal crossings—both from Mexico and Central American nations—and what turned out to be wild estimates of the total number of undocumented immigrants living in the United States.

Most estimates of illegal crossings are based on the number of people apprehended by the INS, which runs the Border Patrol. In 1980 the INS reported 910,361 apprehensions; in 1986 this figure peaked at 1,767,400. The INS estimates that 2 to 3 persons are successful in entering the country for every 1 person who is caught and that between 90 and 95 percent of those apprehended are Mexicans. These figures mean that estimates for the total number of Mexicans illegally entering the United States increased from roughly 2.5 million in 1980 to roughly 4 million in 1986.

But calculating what fraction of these undocumented entrants stayed in the United States was much more difficult, so estimates of the population of undocumented immigrants were subject to much greater political manipulation. In 1976, for example, the INS commissioner, Leonard Chapman, told the U.S. Senate that some 4 to 12 million foreigners resided illegally in the United States. He later wrote that the number of undocumented Mexicans was roughly 6 million. The actual number was probably less than 2 million, since five studies by academics and researchers at the U.S. Census Bureau estimated the total population of undocumented Mexicans in 1980—four years later—at between 1.5 and 2.5 million.[101] Nevertheless, Arthur Corwin, an immigration-control proponent, asserted in 1985 that in 1981 between 8 and 10 million undocumented foreigners lived here. Very high estimates such as these continued to make the news and to be used by legislators in debating IRCA.

By 1991 it was clear that IRCA had failed to stem illegal immigration. The Border Patrol reported apprehending 1.2 million undocumented immigrants that year, nearly as many as in pre-IRCA 1985. In part this failure is due to the inability of the INS to enforce employer sanctions; this in turn is related to the ease with which documents are forged. One highly controversial proposal would create a nationwide computerized system that could instantly verify an applicant's eligibility to work. According to Daniel Stein, executive director of the Federation of American Immigration Reform (FAIR), "We're moving toward a greater national consensus on the need for a national work document, a national registry of births and deaths, and ultimately a national health-care card, a Social Security card issued at birth, and a national birth certificate."[102] This proposal for a national ID has been attacked as an infringement of the constitutional right to privacy and as more likely to change how fraud occurs than to eliminate it. According to the INS itself, a computerized ID system would be far too expensive.

The difficulties of enforcing employer sanctions have led many immigration-control proponents to pay more attention to those activists and academics who have long argued that the only long-term answer is the economic development of Mexico. Presidents Bush and Salinas made use of this argument to support the conclusion of a North American free trade agreement (NAFTA). Such an agreement, they argued, would generate economic growth in Mexico, producing jobs and raising wages so that Mexicans would have less reason to emigrate.

Though pleased with the attention being paid to the root cause of

Mexican-U.S. migration, many immigration observers are skeptical that free trade is the answer. In the short term the economic and social changes stemming from the adoption of NAFTA would very likely produce a rapid increase in migration, as hundreds of thousands of small farmers and their families are forced out of work by imports of much cheaper corn and other grains from the United States and Canada.[103] And in the long term, even if NAFTA does produce more jobs than it eliminates in Mexico, the jobs are likely to be similar to those already available in foreign-owned *maquiladoras*. Hundreds of "Help Wanted" signs and very high levels of employee turnover testify to the inability of these jobs to retain workers and halt emigration to the United States during the 1980s. In fact, even when the Mexican economy was growing at 6 percent per year from 1945 to 1980, migration continued apace.[104] Furthermore, the current plan for NAFTA includes no provisions for improving labor standards, so that Mexican wages and working conditions are very likely to remain far below those in the United States and Canada.

Another source of skepticism toward claims that NAFTA will reduce long-term migration is an alternative view of migration that traces the root cause to social linkages between advanced and developing countries and to the disruption of traditional lifestyles. Both foreign investment and trade work to reduce the cultural gap between countries, making immigration easier to contemplate. A free-trade agreement would accelerate both the process of social integration between the United States and Mexico and the disintegration of Mexico's traditional patterns of work and life. Both these effects can be expected to increase the flow of migrants from Mexico to the United States.

On a more fundamental level, fair-trade activists questioned the exclusion of labor-related questions from the NAFTA negotiations. Why should the conditions under which goods and capital cross borders be discussed, but not those surrounding the movement of workers? Why not address the question directly, instead of hoping for an indirect resolution through investment and growth? Jorge Bustamante, Mexico's leading authority on immigration, has long questioned U.S. motives for not bilaterally negotiating a solution to the immigration problem. According to Bustamante, "For us, this thing about the U.S. losing control of the border is kind of a joke. They don't want to have control of the border. It would be uneconomic."[105] In his view, undocumented immigrants should be called "commodity immigrants" since they constitute a self-transportation of labor as a commodity to where the capital owner demands it. Pointing to widespread violation of immigrant rights in the United States, the Salinas administration briefly advocated that immigration and labor mobility issues be discussed within the framework of the free trade agreement.

For the most part, however, calls by progressives for "open borders" for migrant flows and demands by Mexican leaders for binational immigration accords ignore the social and economic challenges that increasing immigration from Latin America represents for the United States. Recognizing that realistic, not utopian, solutions are needed, some U.S. Latino leaders have started discussing the possibility of a new temporary worker program. Unlike the bracero program, the new program would extend beyond the agricultural sector and would ensure that workers' rights to organize and receive the minimum wage would be respected. Unfortunately no national group has formulated and proposed a specific plan for such an international agreement on migration. Memories of the abuses stemming from the bracero program remain vivid, leading most immigrant advocates to shy away from any similar contractual agreement.[106] Community activists, immigrant-rights groups, and labor unions are making admirable efforts to organize undocumented workers, to inform immigrants of their rights, and to enforce those rights in court. But few of these groups are truly interested in pursuing the questions of how to discourage illegal immigration or how to enforce immigration limitations. The same is true of the Mexican government, which has declined to discuss the possibility of controlling immigration flows either through a program of economic incentives or through a law-enforcement program to limit migrant flows across its northern border. Unless a migration agreement includes completely open borders, some restriction on border crossings and an enforcement mechanism will always be necessary.

Although unpalatable and complex, the need to control U.S. borders and to manage cross-border labor flows must form part of an alternative policy proposal. To ignore them is to assure continued widespread U.S. fears of an uncontrolled "invasion," continued scapegoating of undocumented workers as causing economic hardship, and continued abuse of immigrants' human and labor rights.

# The Drug

# Connection

The long, mostly open border between the United States and Mexico invites all types of transboundary relationships. Along with migrants, tourists, winter vegetables, manufactured goods, and pollutants, there is trade in *mercancía noble*, contraband. From car stereos and microwave ovens to marijuana, heroin, and cocaine, the porous border permits a bustling, cross-boundary trade that falls outside the law.

In the case of drugs, this trade undermines governing structures, fuels violent crime, distorts vulnerable economies, and bolsters well-organized and well-armed interests whose tools for influencing the authorities range from bribery to murder. To get a handle on these problems and on the social disruption of drug abuse, the United States and Mexico have over the years mounted a number of on-again, off-again initiatives. Relishing an on-again stage over the past few years, the two countries are lauding the productive and cooperative relations of the upgraded, binational drug war. Lurking behind the friendly rhetoric, however, the drug trade continues to flourish. It is fed by the same ingredients that helped it grow to its current stature: astounding profits, Mexico's economic needs, the unquenchable U.S. demand for drugs, and a history of backdoor trading relationships that laid the infrastructure for the current drug traffic.

*Contrabandistas* have traveled the isolated canyons, dusty roads, and shallow waterways of the U.S.-Mexico border since the 1800s. Capitalizing on the legal, geographic, and cultural differences between the two countries, the smugglers have crisscrossed the border, providing consumers in each country with goods not readily available—or legally restricted—on their own side of the line.

During the Civil War, for instance, steamboats puffed up the Rio Grande into the little ports that dotted the river to load up with Confederate cotton. They were supposed to head overseas with the cargo and bring back foreign exchange for the Confederacy. But they often never made it that far. Instead they funneled cotton into Mexico, lining the pockets of the traders with riches they poured into fancy homes along the "Gold Coast" in what is now the infamous—and still dirt-poor—Starr County, Texas.[107]

In the twentieth century Prohibition and the Mexican Revolution stimulated another burst of illicit trade. Thirsty gringos who couldn't care less about federal restrictions paid hard cash for bootlegged Mexican liquor and a powerful cactus moonshine called *sotol*.[108] About the same time, U.S. traffickers were funneling weapons and ammunition to revolutionary factions in northern Mexico. And during World War II, many Mexicans with an entrepreneurial spirit headed north with loads of tires, coffee, and other goods that were rationed or just unavailable in the United States.

Nowadays the contraband that most preoccupies U.S. and Mexican officials is drugs. But drugs are not the only goods that have been peddled back and forth between the two countries in recent years. Until Mexico liberalized its import policies, entrepreneurs with a little front money and a vehicle with some cargo space also transported *fayuca*—black-market electronic equipment, appliances, and other consumer goods. Car stereos, VCRs, whiskey, and bolts of fabric were shuttled into Mexico on cargo planes. Stolen cars were—and still are—driven down to Mexico in large numbers. There they are sold, given away as bribes, or used in drug trafficking. Before Mexico eased its import restrictions, even medical and dental equipment found its way to Mexican practitioners who could not or would not wade through the bureaucratic red tape required for import authorization.[109] Up from Mexico came fake Rolex watches, Levi's, designer jeans, folk crafts, and counterfeit money. With the new trading rules, such traffic has slowed considerably, but U.S.-bound runners still smuggle semiprecious metals, archaeological artifacts, and exotic birds.

Unauthorized traffic in such merchandise represents merely lost tax revenues to the U.S. and Mexican governments, but trade in illegal drugs is increasingly seen as a national security threat in both countries. Under the Salinas and Bush administrations, the two countries sharply stepped up their drug control efforts, responding in part to an upsurge in drug traffic from Mexico during the mid-1980s. But controlling the flow of substances such as marijuana, heroin, and cocaine is not a new aspect of U.S.-Mexico relations. It has been an objective of their binational policies for decades, achieving greater or lesser importance depending on the volume of drugs crossing the border and the intensity of U.S. concern.

## Ebb and Flow of the Mexican Connection

Ironically the modern, illegal drug trade between the United States and Mexico began back in the 1800s as a legal transaction. Marijuana, which grows wild in Mexico, was long considered a traditional folk drug in that country. In the nineteenth century the intoxicating weed was welcomed into the United States, which was then experimenting with a pharmaco-poeia of unregulated, narcotics-laced medicines for a variety of ailments. Unwary of the habit-forming effects of some of these substances, the medical profession promoted, and Americans freely purchased, opiates, coca-based products, and marijuana.[110]

Because of its proximity and availability, Mexican marijuana virtually monopolized the U.S. market, and Mexican exports of marijuana and heroin were legal until Mexican President Plutarco Elías Calles banned them in 1927.[111] Even so, small-scale shipments of marijuana continued to flow into the United States through the 1950s. This traffic caused no friction between the two governments, however, possibly because mari-juana consumption by that time was largely concentrated among Mexi-can-origin populations in the United States.[112] The ballooning demand for drugs in the United States during the 1960s pushed Mexican produc-tion of marijuana to new heights. By 1975 cheap Mexican pot was meeting nearly 90 percent of the U.S. demand.

Besides marijuana, Mexico is a major producer of heroin for the U.S. market. Opium poppies rode the rails into Mexico at the turn of the century, brought in by Chinese laborers building the country's railway system. Adapting well to the mountainous regions in northern Mexico, the poppy was cultivated in Sonora, Chihuahua, Sinaloa, and Durango. The smokable form of opium became so popular that "opium dens" sprang up in urban centers like San Francisco and Ciudad Juárez. Proc-essed into morphine and heroin, the drug supplied a small market in Mexico—which stimulated Mexican government concerns about addic-tion as far back as the 1920s—but most was shipped to the United States.[113]

Unlike marijuana, Mexican heroin made up only a small portion of the U.S. market, as most consumers preferred the more potent and readily available products smuggled in from Italy, France, Asia, and the Middle East.[114] World War II, however, cut off traditional sources and simulta-neously created a need for morphine to treat wounded soldiers. With official U.S. encouragement, the Mexican government legalized the pro-duction of opium to meet the needs of the U.S. military. After the war, when traditional suppliers muscled their way back into the business, Mexican "brown" heroin mostly supplied addicts in the U.S. Southwest. Only when the "French Connection" was severed in the early 1970s did Mexican heroin enter the U.S. market in force. From a 10 to 15 percent market share in 1972, Mexican "brown" claimed a full 87 percent of the U.S. market by 1975.[115]

Mexico beefed up its eradication programs during the 1970s and brought production of opium poppies back under control. Renewed foreign competition also helped edge Mexican heroin out of the U.S. market. Mexico began a wide-scale aerial eradication program aimed at marijuana, while traffickers in prime growing areas like Colombia and Jamaica began shipping high-potency marijuana such as "Colombian gold" and "ganja" to eager U.S. buyers. Just as important, the Mexican government began spraying large marijuana fields with paraquat, a dangerous herbicide that can cause permanent lung damage. The move, highly publicized by the U.S. media, drew fire in Congress and from the U.S. public because of the potential for harm to U.S. consumers. It also temporarily shattered the U.S. market for Mexican pot, which could be cut and sold before the herbicide had a chance to kill off the leaves, endangering unwary smokers.

The combination of these factors sharply reduced the amount of drugs entering the United States from Mexico. Going into the 1980s, Mexico was supplying about a quarter of the U.S. market for heroin. Likewise, in 1980 less than 10 percent of the marijuana consumed in the United States came from Mexico.[116] Since cocaine had not yet become widely popular in the United States, the drug trade receded as a priority issue in U.S.-Mexico relations.

But not for long. Mexico's economic collapse of the early 1980s coincided with favorable weather conditions, an expanding U.S. market for drugs, and a burst of consumer interest in cocaine. Production and trafficking of opiates and marijuana increased accordingly, and by the mid-1980s these drugs were reclaiming Mexico's market share in the United States. Despite several decades of eradication programs and an intensified antidrug program over the past few years, Mexico is a top supplier of drugs to the United States in the early 1990s. The National Narcotics Intelligence Consumers Committee estimates that more than 70 percent of the foreign marijuana consumed in the United States during 1991 came from Mexico.[117] Likewise, available evidence suggests that about 20 percent of the heroin used in the United States comes from Mexico, a drop from the 1986–87 high of about 40 percent.[118] What is more, most of the heroin provided by Mexico is now a potent variety known as "black tar."

The 1980s saw another trend develop in U.S.-Mexico drug relations: the use of Mexico as a major transshipment route for South American cocaine. Mexico does not grow coca or produce cocaine, but it has been a transit route for cocaine for as long as there has been a market for it in the United States. Demand for cocaine surged in the United States in the 1980s, stimulating increased traffic through Mexico. Also pushing Mexico into a transshipment role was the U.S. crackdown on cocaine traffic through the Caribbean and the southeastern United States. Mexico's long, undefended border with the United States attracted South American cocaine cartels that found entry through their more traditional routes obstructed by U.S. interdiction operations. By the 1990s it was estimated that more than half the cocaine entering the United States passed through Mexico first.[119]

## Big Money in Hard Times

Vast sums drive the drug trade. As of 1989, the U.S. State Department reported that a full 60 percent of the world's illegal drug supply was consumed in the United States.[120] In 1986 the U.S. House of Representatives Select Committee on Narcotics Abuse and Control estimated that the value of the drug trade in the United States could be as high as $110 billion, although others put the total closer to $60 billion.[121] Even the lower figure is staggering, but if the higher sum is accurate, the money poured into the U.S. drug trade exceeded 2 percent of the U.S. gross domestic product at the time of the study. Other comparisons are just as startling. If the committee was on target, the amount U.S. citizens spent on drugs in the mid-1980s represented twice what the United States paid for oil, half of U.S. military expenditures, and about three-quarters of the Mexican gross national product.[122]

Reliable figures on the money involved in the drug trade are as difficult to get in Mexico as they are in the United States. In 1991, however, Jorge Tello Peón, chief of the "crimes against health" department of the Mexican attorney general's office, gave a jarring estimate of the value of the trade in Mexico. He said that traffickers in Mexico were earning nearly as much as the country's total export earnings.[123]

These huge dollar flows are especially crucial during times of economic downturn, when the juxtaposition of poverty and profit spurs more people to take part in the illicit economy. Production and trafficking centers often are located in communities where economic opportunities are rare. Isolated growing areas friendly to poppies and marijuana or proximity to the border and a network of drug-running contacts are the only assets some communities can boast.

Even though some 90 percent of the value of illegal drugs is added in the United States at the wholesale and retail levels, growing marijuana and opium poppies nets Mexican campesinos far more cash than cultivating legal crops.[124] When Mexico's economy went into its tailspin in 1982, drug production climbed. Small-scale farmers produce the majority of the marijuana and opium poppy grown in Mexico, and after *la crisis*, marijuana and poppy plots cropped up more frequently alongside fields of corn and beans grown by subsistence farmers. Intercropping with legal crops had been common since the 1970s, partly because the Mexican government is reluctant to spray herbicides on such plots owing to the political and human costs that result when the spray drifts onto food crops. But the increased production of illegal drugs by campesinos also reflected the stranglehold poverty had on Mexico's rural population. In 1987 the U.S. State Department's Bureau of International Narcotics Matters pointed to Mexico's economic stagnation and high inflation rate as serious push factors behind campesino production of illicit crops: "[F]inancial rewards for a peasant to grow marijuana or opium poppy far outweigh those to be received through cultivating legitimate crops. Peer pressure from other peasants growing illicit crops adds to the incentive. Even peasants who work the fields of others growing such crops earn at least twice the prevailing minimum wage. Thus, the growing of narcotics represents a buffer from the economic crisis."[125]

What the State Department found in 1987 paralleled the reality that existed a full decade before. At that time a campesino in the Sierra Madre could earn about four hundred dollars a year raising traditional crops. If he grew opium poppies, however, that income climbed to between two and four thousand dollars per year.[126] In view of inflation, inadequate credit, periodic drought, and the paltry size of peasant landholdings, the money from drug production offered welcome relief to many poor campesinos.

Grinding rural poverty still plagues small farmers in Mexico. In fact, social disruption and economic pressure from free-market reforms have intensified in rural areas, fueling the tendency to grow illicit crops as a household survival strategy. According to the U.S. State Department, that is one explanation why, in the face of enhanced eradication and interdiction programs, producing areas in Mexico have expanded, not shrunk.

Whereas the tristate region of Sinaloa, Durango, and Chihuahua remains the primary source of most illegal drugs from Mexico, the area devoted to regular cultivation of these crops has grown over the years. A significant amount of marijuana for export is now produced in Jalisco, San Luis Potosí, Sonora, Zacatecas, Chiapas, Guerrero, Michoacán, and Oaxaca.[127]

Opium poppy cultivation has also expanded. Once largely confined to Sinaloa, Durango, Chihuahua, and Guerrero, opium poppies are now grown in a zone that starts at the northern tip of the Sierra Madre Occidental in Sonora and Chihuahua and continues down to Chiapas and the Guatemalan border. As the State Department explains, "Adverse agricultural and economic conditions have forced farmers in nontraditional areas to turn to cultivating illicit crops."[128]

Not only campesinos find work in the drug trade. *La droga* spawns a multifaceted industry, requiring a wide range of skills and employees. Those who produce and process the drugs are only the first links in the chain. Someone must package the product. Others devise and craft the contraptions—like hollow fence posts or hidden compartments in propane tanks—in which the substances are concealed. Bodyguards, "enforcers," and armed squads protect the shipments, guard the ringleaders, and make sure people pay up or otherwise follow through on their commitments. There are "mules" to run the drugs across the border; there are lookouts, drivers, and pilots. Some of the most sophisticated organizations rely on communications experts to set up secure phone lines and radio hookups to their sources, distributors, and partners. And of course, there are accountants, money launderers, and in some cases even financial advisers.

The unemployed are common recruits for the less skilled of these jobs, and the incomes they make from drug-running can have a dramatic effect on shaky economies. In a little place like Douglas, Arizona, the fifteen hundred dollars a driver makes running a load of dope to Tucson can make a big difference to local businesses. As one observer described the economic effects of the drug trade on a small town along the south Texas border, "[The drivers are] all unemployed, but after two weeks they're buying pickups and ostrich-skin cowboy boots with matching belts. Pretty soon there's money all around town. The car dealers are selling trucks, gas sales go up, so do groceries and clothes. The bank deposits are up—but no one says anything. And no taxes are paid. It creates a false economy."[129]

Aside from the employment networks, there are investments. Because of the illegality of the trade, there are no figures describing the extent of these investments or their impact on local economies. Most observers, in fact, question the real effect of drug money in Mexico, pointing to the diversified nature and large size of the economy as factors that tend to dilute the significance of drug revenues. But drug money is invested in Mexico—and in the United States. It is known that traffickers have put money into tourist hotels, restaurants, movie theaters, shopping centers, and luxury homes. "The traffickers are the only ones investing money in Mexico," a Mexican businessman complained to a reporter in 1986. "The rest take their dollars out. They are building roads, drainage, restaurants, and hotels, which creates jobs."[130]

Real estate booms and bank deposit surpluses in places like Mazatlán, Durango, Phoenix, and San Diego are fed in part by drug money, although the size of their economies hides the full extent of trafficker involvement. In some communities, however, the drug trade involves wide sectors of the population and leaves visible marks on the economy. One observer estimated that 15 to 20 percent of the population in the Sonoran border town of Agua Prieta depended on drugs in 1991, a trend that began in the early 1980s.[131] During its drug-running heyday in the mid-1980s, the "Gold Coast" in Starr County, Texas, boasted million-dollar homes and luxury cars bought with cash in an area where half the workforce was unemployed.[132] In 1990 a controversial study in Douglas, Arizona, sampled residents and found that they believed 30 to 60 percent of the town's economy was based on the drug trade.[133]

But profits from the drug trade do not have the strong multiplier effect these examples suggest. As with junk bond speculation and other get-rich-quick schemes, drug profits pay for personal consumption more than for productive investments or improvements in infrastructure. Trafficking and production centers tend to show no lasting benefits as a result of the drug trade even though individuals may have profited and helped support the local economy in critical ways. "The big traffickers piss the money away," observed Mike Gallagher, a reporter who has studied the drug trade for nearly two decades. "They buy big cars, they buy elephants and tigers and make zoos on their mountain estates," Gallagher explained. "They may build a clinic or two, but these guys are crooks. They don't care about their communities and add nothing to them."[134]

### Networks of Violence

What does have a multiplier effect is the violence. Trafficking in illegal drugs provides the economic backbone for organized crime. A bilateral commission studying U.S.-Mexico relations reported that drugs represented almost 40 percent of the economic activity of powerful criminal organizations in the United States.[135] In both Mexico and the United States the strongest of these organizations are vertically structured networks with international links. Most of them are "polydrug" organizations, controlling production, transportation, and wholesale distribution of a number of drugs simultaneously. Their capacity for corrupting officials and imposing their will on society expands along with their profits, presenting immense challenges to elected officials.

Intergang rivalries spill across the border, and trafficking organizations from Sonora and Sinaloa have settled scores with rivals and turncoats in U.S., as well as Mexican, cities. Drug-related murders, sometimes accompanied by torture and mutilation, have hit border communities and nearby cities. Execution killings, to ensure loyalty and prevent theft within smuggling rings, have also become more common in border communities. In 1989, for example, both Tucson and Agua Prieta suffered gruesome execution-style mass murders carried out by groups involved in the drug trade.[136]

The violence is not confined to the border. Mexicans called the mountain city of Culiacán, Sinaloa, "Little Chicago" during the 1970s because the gunfights between rival drug gangs resembled those of Chicago's mobsters during Prohibition. Others thought the Chicago comparison far too generous. "Culiacán," journalist Craig Pyes observed, "has only 350,000 inhabitants and the equivalent of a St. Valentine's Day Massacre every two weeks."[137] By 1986 Culiacán's murder rate climbed to five a day, accompanied by widespread rape and other assaults on the general public. As in some of the inner cities in the United States, residents in Culiacán were afraid to sit near their windows because they feared being struck by stray bullets.[138]

The increased antidrug efforts of the United States and Mexico have not reduced the violence. In 1992 Guadalajara's drug-related murder rate was three per day. Violence is up in Culiacán and in Sonora as well. Quick to fight with machine guns, hand grenades, and semiautomatics, their arsenals purchased with the huge profits of drug sales, traffickers are much better armed than in the 1980s.

The weapons trade worries both the U.S. and Mexican governments, as well as affected communities. Flowing exclusively from north to south, these arms include high-caliber assault weapons and military-issue armaments like grenades, rocket launchers, and, in one case, even a fully armed combat assault helicopter.[139] Trafficker arsenals often have greater firepower and are more sophisticated than those of the military forces and law-enforcement agencies responsible for stemming the drug trade. This is especially so at the local level, where police forces and drug agents in both Mexico and the United States are likely to find themselves out-gunned in confrontations with traffickers.

In towns where traffickers hold sway, the weapons contribute to a climate of fear and intimidation that aids corruption and makes a shambles of daily life. In Ojinaga, a dusty border town just a few miles upstream and across the border from Big Bend National Park in Texas, traffickers with AK-47s slung across their shoulders walked the streets in broad daylight as recently as 1987. Shoot-outs on street corners and at convenience stores, ice-cream stands, and restaurants threatened innocent bystanders and rivals alike, while traffickers received protection from federal agents, local police, and the military in exchange for monthly payoffs.[140]

In addition to these specific forms of violence, trafficking networks have the potential to become alternative centers of power, threatening constitutional structures.[141] To some extent, this distortion of the governing system has already occurred in Mexico. It has been visible in corruption that has sometimes penetrated to top levels of the government and that has riddled certain governing, military, and security structures. Corruption in Mexico has been described as the "glue that holds the Mexican system together and the oil that makes it work." The "oil" makes the "wheels of bureaucracy turn," while the "glue . . . seals political alliances."[142]

Corruption is so much a part of the way things have historically been done in Mexico that bribery, kickbacks, and buyoffs often do not have the unethical taint such deeds acquire in the United States. It is not surprising then that drug-related corruption has penetrated nearly all aspects of Mexico's drug-war machinery at one time or another.[143] In November 1991, for example, an army unit guarding a Colombian drug shipment near Veracruz killed seven Mexican antidrug agents in a shoot-out that lasted nearly three hours.[144]

Aside from being a public embarrassment to the Salinas government—the whole event was videotaped from an antidrug aircraft flying overhead—the involvement of military troops and early government attempts to downplay the Veracruz incident demonstrated the continued role of corruption in perpetuating the drug trade in Mexico. The Mexican press reported that the November gunfight was the third time over the preceding few months that local military had blocked police from intercepting drug shipments, allowing the traffickers to escape.[145] Not only a threat to antinarcotics efforts, military involvement in trafficking schemes is an internal security issue that jeopardizes government authority as well as law-enforcement operations.

The major Mexican trafficking organizations have historically been dominated by family groups, such as the Herreras, who have controlled the most important economic and government functions in the state of Durango for four decades.[146] But the family-based operation is gradually being blended with cartel-like organizational structures based on megadollar monetary relationships and specialized functions. The Guadalajara cartel, involved in the torture-murder of U.S. Drug Enforcement Agent Enrique Camarena, was one of the first examples of this phenomenon in Mexico. This form of organization amplifies the power and reach of the trafficking networks, posing the potential for the kind of national disruption and violence seen in Colombia and Peru over the last decade. This potential seems to have been an important factor behind President Salinas's declaration that drug trafficking is a matter of national security in Mexico.

## Foundations of the Drug War

Mexico has been conducting its own eradication campaigns since 1948. In the highlands Mexican soldiers met *mano a mano* with marijuana stalks and opium poppies, beating them with sticks until the fields were mangled piles of weeds. These search-and-destroy missions were reasonably effective, but they failed to keep pace with production. So in 1961 Washington gave Mexico Korean War–vintage aircraft and military equipment to use in its *gran campaña* against marijuana and poppy fields.[147] U.S. advisers also went to Mexico to help with drug control efforts. Production continued to climb, however, encouraged by the decade's expanding market for mind-altering substances in the United States.

By 1969 the drug trade and the drug consumption habits of U.S. young people had so annoyed the "law-and-order" administration of Richard Nixon that the United States launched a surprise border search-and-seizure effort called Operation Intercept.[148] The three-week operation—which involved searching every vehicle and individual crossing into the United States from Mexico—was intended to squeeze Mexico economically by snarling legitimate trade and tourist traffic. The operation netted no major drug shipments but did push Mexico into stepping up its own antidrug programs and working with the United States on a joint effort known as Operation Cooperation.[149]

Operation Cooperation ensured the United States a strong voice in Mexican drug policy, but it failed to put a dent in the rapidly expanding marijuana and opium supply, and U.S. advisers pressed Mexican counterparts to use herbicides against the crops.[150] When Mexico began an aerial eradication program in 1975, the United States was there with money, advice, and other support.

Washington's financing enabled Mexico to buy or lease U.S. planes and helicopters for the *campaña permanente* against drug crops. Other U.S. aid was provided so that Mexico could construct field air bases, train pilots, and install communications systems.[151] The aircraft, used both for spraying herbicides and transporting troops, were maintained largely with U.S. funding, with maintenance and advisory services provided in part by U.S. corporations.

Mexico's commitment to the eradication campaign was particularly strong for a number of reasons. These ranged from the desire to regain control of highland areas where campesinos—receiving their first good incomes ever—were thumbing their noses at Mexico City to concerns about domestic drug abuse to the country's need to maintain good relations with the United States.[152] As a consequence, Mexico's working relationship with U.S. drug-control forces was at an all-time high during the mid- and late 1970s. Information exchanges were numerous, and U.S. drug enforcement agents worked closely with Mexican counterparts. Joint investigations of traffickers and their organizations also went forward. By the end of the decade drug control enthusiasts in the United States were pointing to Mexico as a model of antinarcotics policy. Eradication was up, arrests were up, production was down, and Mexico's share of the U.S. drug market plunged.

When the program fell apart at the end of the López Portillo administration, the United States was so used to holding up Mexico as an example of good drug policy that at first U.S. policymakers did not know there was a problem. Although U.S. support for Mexico's aerial eradication program continued, it had dropped to modest levels of annual support: around eight million dollars a year. But the eradication program was suffering from inefficiency, low salaries, maintenance failures, and rising corruption.[153] The new government of Miguel de la Madrid—saddled with an economic disaster and opposed to the Reagan administration's Cold War policy in Central America—did not make the drug fight a high priority. Weather conditions were favorable, and peasants caught in an economic tailspin turned to illicit crops to pull out of it.

The traffickers themselves regrouped, stronger than ever, from the campaigns of the 1970s. Polydrug organizations, sometimes linked in cartel-type structures, funneled heroin, marijuana, and cocaine to the

United States. Supported by networks of corruption, some of them—like the Sinaloan traffickers who moved south and became the Guadalajara cartel—became ostentatious, greedy, and overconfident. They began investing in state-of-the-art multiacre marijuana plantations that were based on agribusiness management and production techniques. Well-irrigated emerald islands popped up even in the Chihuahua desert, with fields worked by campesinos trucked in for premium wages (in Mexican terms) from destitute rural areas miles away. Drug production and trafficking to the United States surged, while cooperation between antidrug forces in the two countries fell off.

These years marked the low point of recent U.S.-Mexico antidrug efforts. Because many other issues drive the U.S.-Mexico relationship, however, the two countries remained on generally decent terms as far as the broader picture was concerned. Problems such as debt management and Washington's strong support for the economic reforms begun under de la Madrid tied the two countries together in powerful bonds that drug control failures could not sever. Washington's pressure on Mexico to get into step with the drug war intensified, and U.S. antidrug assistance climbed, especially after President Reagan signed a secret directive in 1986 declaring the international drug trade a threat to U.S. national security.

## Current Initiatives

After the Salinas and Bush administrations took office, collaboration on drug-control activities intensified, and by the early 1990s cooperation between the two countries was at its strongest since the 1970s. Because of Mexican sovereignty concerns and the fact that antidrug efforts are considered law-enforcement operations, it is difficult to get detailed information about current U.S.-Mexico drug-control activities. Totals on the amount of U.S. funding or good descriptions of the types of activities on which the two countries work together are closely guarded by the responsible agencies. According to one DEA agent who asked to remain anonymous, some initiatives that would be public information if they occurred in other countries are classified with regard to Mexico because of that country's nationalist sensitivities.

What is clear, however, is that until 1993 Mexico traditionally received the largest amount of U.S. annual expenditures for foreign drug control. From 1978 to 1990 the State Department's Bureau of International Narcotics Matters (INM) provided $150.3 million to Mexico as assistance for drug-control activities, with more than half of that amount provided after 1986.[154] In 1991 the INM contributed nearly $20 million to Mexico with a similar amount provided in 1992. As with other U.S. government aid programs, however, direct aid to Mexico was cut back in 1993. The INM currently funds only U.S. activities related to the drug war in Mexico, and the Mexican government has picked up its own share of the tab.[155]

Until 1993, INM provided about a quarter of the Mexican Attorney General's annual budget for drug control, according to Elizabeth Carroll, Mexico desk officer at INM. Even with cutbacks in government-to-government aid, official U.S. assistance is likely to continue in the form of contracts with private firms. Such contracts are already in force in both eradication and high-tech communications activities and could be expected to climb if government-to-government aid drops.[156]

Besides INM, other U.S. government agencies have helped Mexico's anti-drug activities. One of the U.S. agencies supporting Mexico's drug war is the Department of Defense (DOD). Much of U.S. security assistance to Mexico is used for antinarcotics activities. Most of this aid goes for trainings through the International Military Education and Training program, which has averaged just under a half million dollars a year since the mid-1980s. Some of these trainings teach Mexican personnel how to operate and maintain equipment used in antinarcotics activities.

The DOD has donated surplus equipment to Mexico for the drug war under presidential drawdown authority granted by the Foreign Assistance Act of 1961. In 1991 the department transferred twenty-one UH-1H Huey helicopters to Mexico, boosting the year's antinarcotics aid to forty-eight million dollars.[157] And in early 1992 President Bush authorized the Defense Department to donate helicopters, spare parts, support equipment, and technical assistance valued at twenty-six million dollars to the Mexican government.[158] Besides the defense contributions, agencies such as DEA and the Agency for International Development (AID) provide services that support antidrug work in Mexico, but they are not included in the INM budget figures.

All aspects of the drug war, including detection, eradication, intelligence, and interdiction, have been supported by U.S. antidrug assistance. Over the years the aid has boosted the technological capabilities and professional skills of Mexican law-enforcement and military forces with training and equipment. The INM has funded trainings, usually offered through U.S. law-enforcement agencies like the FBI, DEA, and Customs, that focus on everything from sniffer-dog training to techniques for combating money laundering. Cessna Citation surveillance aircraft from the U.S. Customs Service track cocaine smugglers as they fly north from Colombia to landing strips in Mexico. The information is then relayed to Mexican law-enforcement agencies to help them interdict the traffickers. Law-enforcement agencies in each country work together on joint investigations, sharing information and evidence needed to disrupt trafficking networks.

Demand reduction is financed, too, through the Agency for International Development and U.S. Information Service (USIS). The AID, for example, spent nearly two million dollars on demand-reduction programs in Mexico in 1991.[159] Working with Mexican private organizations, the AID supported antidrug education and research programs. Some of these programs were aimed at youth—AID-sponsored dance performances dramatizing problems relating to drug abuse, for instance. Likewise, one USIS project supported the creation of an antidrug music video and record album aimed at young people in Mexico.

Most of the direct aid from the INM supported the aerial eradication program. After the 1970s the U.S. program expanded to include several components besides procurement and maintenance of aircraft. By the late 1980s the INM was providing funds to purchase herbicides and fuel for the Mexican air fleet. For a time it also paid salary supplements for Mexican pilots, mechanics, and other technicians, although that program was discontinued and the salary boosts are now paid by the Mexican government. During the early 1990s INM support to the eradication program was primarily used for a maintenance contract with Bell Helicopter Services to keep the air fleet in good running condition.[160] Even so, Mexican drug-interdiction planes and helicopters have been plagued by mechanical problems, and in at least one case a helicopter crashed as the result of engine failure.

Mexico's Office of the Attorney General coordinates the drug-control efforts in the country, and most U.S. aid was funneled through that office. But the Mexican armed forces also participate in the programs, with about a quarter of the hundred-thousand-strong army involved in eradication activities at any one time. Like the police agencies, Mexico's military has received support for equipment purchases, training, and other aspects of force modernization under the antidrug programs.

Under U.S. law, aid cannot be provided to police or law-enforcement officials in foreign countries in order to support or train them in programs involving internal intelligence or surveillance. But the DEA and the FBI are exempt from these restrictions if they are helping foreign law-enforcement officials fight the drug trade.[161] Under the Administration of Justice program—a hemisphere-wide U.S. aid program aimed at police and judicial structures—the FBI has taught forensic courses and basic law-enforcement skills to Mexican officers.[162]

Despite restrictions, Mexico's police forces have received support from agencies besides the DEA and FBI. The U.S. Army, for instance, has provided technical assistance to the Mexican Office of the Attorney General.[163] And training sessions sponsored by the Customs Service and Coast Guard have helped law-enforcement and military forces learn investigative skills. Customs, for instance, conducted a course in financial enforcement programs for investigators from the Mexican Treasury and Central Bank. According to a cable from the U.S. Embassy in Mexico City to the secretary of state, Customs also "supports [the antinarcotics] intelligence and training needs" of Mexico's Customs Service and the Federal Judicial Police and has helped Mexican drug interdiction officers in the fields of "search, seizure, and evidence collection" under the Administration of Justice program.[164] Likewise, the Coast Guard has trained Mexican Navy personnel in interdiction and vessel-boarding procedures.

Another example is U.S. aid to Mexico's Northern Border Response Force (NBRF). Known as Operación Halcón in Mexico, the force was established in the late 1980s to enhance Mexico's aerial interdiction capability in northern border regions. As interdiction efforts became more successful, cocaine traffickers began following new air routes and started using airstrips in different parts of the country, not just along the northern border. As a result, the NBRF now serves a nationwide area.

A rapid response team composed of agents from the Mexican Federal Judicial Police, the NBRF has sharply increased cocaine busts in Mexico. It has also received a large amount of high-tech support from the United States. Much of its equipment came from the United States, bringing a need for U.S. technical assistance at the same time. A U.S. Customs program, for instance, trained the team's pilots to use sophisticated radar equipment and communications devices. Customs also taught Mexican team members how to fly and repair the U.S.-made aircraft used to track the smugglers' planes as they come up from South America. Similarly, the U.S. Embassy in Mexico City set up a counternarcotics Tactical Analysis Team to relay U.S. Air Force intelligence to Mexican drug authorities about trafficking activities. The embassy team also helps Mexican officials coordinate operations and plan activities.

In addition to programs like these, the U.S. and Mexican governments are conducting negotiations and devising bilateral agreements to advance the drug war. A new Mutual Legal Assistance Treaty, for example, provides mechanisms for sharing evidence needed for prosecutions in each country. Another instrument, the Tax Information Exchange Agreement, provides means by which the two countries can exchange information on criminal and tax cases against traffickers and money launderers. Under the U.S.-Mexico Binational Commission, working groups meet periodically to discuss thorny issues like extradition and draw up frameworks for agreements. In a related vein, the two countries are working together to provide demand-reduction programs to Central American governmental and nongovernmental organizations. And in recognition of Mexico's own expertise, the Organization of American States (OAS) has used Mexican trainers and epidemiologists to carry out demand-reduction programs under its auspices.

## The Frictions of Asymmetry

Despite cooperative efforts, the drug trade has been a lasting source of friction between Mexico and the United States, often overshadowing other areas of disagreement such as immigration and foreign policy. Finger-pointing and chicken-and-egg arguments over the relative influence of U.S. demand versus Mexican supply on stimulating and maintaining drug traffic have been as typical of U.S.-Mexico antidrug relationships as have periods of cooperation. Richard Craig, an expert on the drug trade and drug policy, describes those relations as "cyclical in nature, often unilateral, incident-prone, and highly acrimonious."[165]

As with other policy areas, the tensions of the antidrug relationship stem partly from the overall asymmetry between the United States and Mexico. Although, as noted above, Mexico has its own good reasons for fighting the drug trade, it has pursued antidrug strategies framed mostly by U.S. wishes and needs since the early part of the century.[166] When drug use and abuse surge in the United States, domestic pressures rise to cut off the flow of drugs into the country. If Mexico's share of the U.S. market happens to be high at the time, the pressure is aimed at Mexico.

Because of the United States' importance as a trading partner and as a source of tourist and investment dollars, Mexico generally responds by cranking up its own antidrug activities. This factor was the main reason the Nixon and Reagan administrations chose in effect to shut down the border through enhanced customs inspections when they wanted to push Mexico toward "cooperation" on the drug war in 1969 and 1985.[167]

In the 1980s U.S. influence grew even greater because Mexico needed

Washington's help with debt management strategies and its okay on loans from international financial institutions like the World Bank. That type of much-needed support was directly threatened by U.S. congressional restrictions on aid to countries that did not cooperate "fully" on antinarcotics activities. Because of these restrictions, Mexico had to meet "certification" requirements in order to continue receiving U.S. backing on other economic issues. The U.S. president and State Department repeatedly certified Mexico as fully cooperating on antidrug efforts, an assessment that some members of Congress strongly contested until the late 1980s. But the fact that Mexico's drug control activities had to be given a U.S. stamp of approval set off waves of anti-U.S. criticism in Mexico whenever certification time rolled around.

This pattern of U.S. pressure and Mexican compliance—with all its corresponding negative foreign policy effects—results partly from the supply-sided focus of U.S. antidrug strategies. Historically U.S. policies put the greatest emphasis on curtailing production and severing trafficking routes in source and transit countries, while neglecting effective prevention and treatment programs to reduce demand at home. To implement international antidrug programs, the United States deploys U.S. drug enforcement agents in supplier countries. U.S. intelligence agencies float satellites overhead and take surveillance photos of the territories of U.S. allies, sometimes without permission. Washington pushes countries involved in the supply network to draw up laws and devise policies compatible with U.S. antinarcotics objectives. In some places, notably the Andean countries, the United States has even sent its military to join in antinarcotics operations.

Mexico is considered a "crucial component" of U.S. drug-control strategies, so the antidrug activities of the United States are especially pronounced there.[168] Beyond its central position in the drug war, "Mexico's economic and geopolitical importance to the U.S. exceeds that of any other drug trafficking/producing country," a State Department memorandum explained in 1991.[169] Responding to these interests, a myriad of U.S. agencies, ranging from the CIA to the FBI to the AID, have worked on antidrug projects in Mexico. The two countries have worked on eradication and interdiction programs in Mexico's airspace, in its territorial waters, and on its soil. The United States has bolstered its own southern border with military and National Guard forces working with federal, state, and local law-enforcement agencies. Each of these initiatives has produced concern and even resentment in Mexico, where many see such moves as a threat to national sovereignty.

Drawing the greatest fire, however, has been the U.S. Drug Enforcement Administration. With more than forty agents assigned to Mexico, the DEA's largest foreign operation is conducted on Mexican soil.[170] These agents—who are stationed throughout the country—collect intelligence, share information with Mexican authorities, conduct investigations, and perform other law-enforcement tasks shy of arrests. But the presence of the DEA on Mexican territory irritates nationalists both in and out of government. As a consequence, the agents are not allowed to carry firearms. An unwritten agreement from the 1920s permits U.S. drug agents to carry their own personal handguns, but if they are stopped by Mexican police and have such weapons in their possession, they can be arrested. In addition, until recently DEA agents were not issued diplomatic credentials. This fact was particularly grating to the agents, who raged in the mid-1980s that even U.S. government personnel working to wipe out the screwworm, a parasite that infests cattle in northern Mexico and Texas, carried the black diplomatic passports.[171]

Clearly the combination of U.S. hegemony and Mexican sovereignty concerns is a combustible mixture. Periodic explosions in the press and at the diplomatic and agency levels reveal underlying tensions that persist below the surface even during times of cooperation. As noted by Richard Craig, such explosions tend to follow "incidents," such as the murder of Enrique Camarena and the 1990 revelation that a CIA satellite had taken unauthorized surveillance photos of Mexican territory to survey marijuana production.[172] Incidents such as these aggravate relations among Mexican and U.S. diplomats and agency personnel trying to conduct bilateral programs.

A few examples illustrate the pattern. Camarena's death unleashed a torrent of public criticism from U.S. agencies usually given to behind-the-scenes maneuvering. As it became clear that Mexican government, police, and military officials were involved in obstructing the murder investigation and perhaps in the agent's death, the DEA, normally known for its pursed lips, hit the papers and the talk shows. The U.S. Customs Service virtually closed down the border by stepping up inspections, a move that Customs Commissioner William von Raab took without consulting superiors in the Treasury Department or at the White House. Congress went haywire with special hearings aimed at disclosing Mexican corruption, economic mismanagement, and culpability in the drug trade. The Mexican government was assailed as undemocratic at best, totalitarian at worst.[173] Mexico bashing was elevated to a national sport.

On the Mexican side, Washington's public tirade and border shutdown was greeted with nationalist outrage. The media and political leaders rebuked the United States for ignoring Mexico's substantial contributions to the fight against drugs, which included the deaths of scores of Mexican law-enforcement agents and soldiers. Washington was accused of putting the death of one agent, who had died in the line of duty, ahead of the larger priority of cooperative relations.

As is typical of U.S.-Mexico relations, the rhetoric cooled, and binational drug control efforts continued. After the election of Salinas the relationship became downright friendly. But then a series of unilateral actions by the United States severely violated Mexican sovereignty and upset the surface calm: The DEA put bounties on the heads of individuals involved in Camarena's murder and put out the word in the right circles that it wanted the perpetrators brought to the United States to stand trial. Between 1986 and 1992 five kidnappings resulted from the DEA offer, setting off burst after burst of Mexican anger and demonstrating the "cowboy" approach to international relations for which the United States is so often criticized.[174]

Those outbursts, too, were followed by calm, but not by a reassessment of U.S. policy. Then in 1992 the U.S. Supreme Court ruled that U.S. extradition agreements with Mexico did not rule out the right of the United States to try Humberto Alvarez Machain, one of the suspects in the Camarena case, even though he had been abducted and brought to the United States without Mexico's authorization.[175] In one of its strongest moves ever, Mexico reacted by suspending the activities of the DEA on its soil and putting on hold the extradition treaty with the United States. Within days, however, the Salinas government had quietly retracted the decisions and returned to negotiations with the United States over extradition policies, moves that underlined the asymmetry of the relationship and U.S. dominance within it.

## Failed Policies

With all these joint efforts and with Mexico's own vastly increased antidrug activities, the drug trade continues to flourish. Record-breaking seizures of cocaine and record numbers of marijuana and poppy plots destroyed since 1990 have not diminished the supply of drugs on the U.S. market. Drugs are readily available on the streets, and, according to the National Narcotics Intelligence Consumers Committee 1991 report, they are still cheap enough and pure enough to satisfy the market. In fact, in the case of cocaine—the drug that most frightens the United States and Mexico—the street price was less in 1991 than it was in 1990, and its potency was increasing, although it was nowhere near as potent as it was in 1988, a reflection of successful interdiction efforts.

At the same time the social factors that feed the trade are still in place. Poverty and unemployment limit economic options and encourage citizens in both countries to turn to the drug trade as a survival strategy. Low salaries for most law-enforcement officers are a fact of life on both sides of the border, leading to corruption. In Mexico the Salinas government has cracked down on this problem, at some risk to its own popularity among certain circles. But at the state and local levels some of the forces that have facilitated the drug trade for years are still in place. Many Mexican Federal Judicial Police who were fired for corruption, for example, were simply rehired at the state level.[176]

In the United States, as well, although the problem has been less studied and less reported, corruption is common. And for good reason. It is in the United States that ninety cents out of every dollar spent on the drug trade is generated. That provides an awful lot of cash to use to buy the services—or the temporary blindness—of law-enforcement officers making civil service salaries.

Huge profits and persistent demand also provide momentum to the drug trade that a few years of intensified drug-control programs cannot combat. Although U.S. drug use is down slightly on the whole and down measurably among certain populations, the size of the market is still more than large enough to fuel the multibillion-dollar enterprise that drug trafficking has become.

Other factors also tend to encourage the drug trade. They are the unintended side effects of U.S.-Mexico trade policies and Mexico's economic reforms since the mid-1980s. The privatization of government-held businesses carried out under Salinas, for example, provided a flood of reasonably priced enterprises for purchase by legitimate investors and drug dealers alike. According to the State Department's Elizabeth Carroll, some of these businesses are being snapped up by traffickers in order to launder and invest the profits from their drug operations.

Ironically the sweeping antinarcotics efforts of the United States and Mexico will be contradicted at least in part by trade-liberalization measures that the governments have worked hard to conclude. With NAFTA, for instance, the border is expected to boom with development. New entry stations will open, and on each side, *colonias* and tiny sister cities like Santa Teresa and San Jerónimo on the New Mexico–Chihuahua border are expected to swell with people wanting employment from the trade boom. Roads will be widened, airports constructed, and bridges erected or expanded to handle the hoped-for jump in U.S.-Mexico commercial traffic. If all goes as planned, new businesses will move in, with their eyes trained on markets and business partners that lie across the border. In large population areas that already bustle with transboundary movements, each of these trends will be magnified.

This buildup of urban areas will provide nourishing environments for traffickers. Economic growth on each side of the border will spawn a proliferation of bonded warehouses and other industrial sites that can serve as fronts for drug smuggling because customs inspectors are less likely to scrutinize shipments from bonded enterprises. Vast amounts of drugs are already spirited into the country in commercial vehicles, hidden in containerized shipments, in false panels beneath crates of oranges and raisins, in boxcars, hidden compartments, and fuel tanks. Customs inspectors—even when they are aided by teams of National Guard troops and sniffer dogs—can inspect only a few of these shipments each day at current traffic loads. Most vehicles are waved through as it is. With the trade increases anticipated over the next few years, the border is likely to be swamped with drugs.

Efforts are already under way to respond to these concerns. Surveillance systems are being upgraded and are becoming more high-tech. Mobile X-ray vans, fiber optics, and portable contraband detectors are being added to the arsenals of customs inspectors at some border crossings. Truckers hauling Mexican produce or tourists returning from a sunny stay on the beaches at Guaymas may one day pass their vehicles through border X-ray sensors like those at airports. Dope-sniffing dogs already wind their way through lines of waiting vehicles in U.S. customs lines. National Guard troops hunting for drugs pick through lettuce bins and scour suspicious vehicles for signs of hidden compartments, lending a helping hand to overworked customs agents.

But cracking down too heavily on cross-border traffic in order to stop drugs causes other problems. The affront to Mexican sensibilities is a sharply negative consequence of stepped-up border enforcement, especially because U.S. traffic into Mexico is subject to virtually no inspection whatsoever. Filtering Mexican entrants to the United States through a sieve of surveillance mechanisms sends a bleak message of distrust at the same time that the United States is hoping to improve relations with its southern neighbor.

The slow pace of U.S. customs inspections already draws a lot of criticism anyway. Besides the aggravation of delays, produce in unrefrigerated trucks runs the danger of spoilage in the hot sun, and incoming cars and trucks backed up with their engines idling increase air pollution in cities like El Paso and San Diego. In addition, using National Guard troops and canine teams to enhance inspections adds to the appearance—and reality—of border militarization.

For all these reasons, greatly intensified searches at border checkpoints are not likely to be a serious option. Instead, most U.S. and Mexican antidrug activities will probably still focus on eradicating supply within Mexico, interdicting traffickers before they get to the United States, and disrupting trafficking organizations through intelligence and law-enforcement operations.

But persisting with this supply-sided law-enforcement orientation has its drawbacks. For one thing, large-scale, expensive law-enforcement actions tend to rid the playing field of small, weak trafficking organizations but do little to dent the power of the big families and cartels. Such organizations are strong enough and big enough to adjust to enforcement pressures and even to profit from them. They have the funds needed for hefty bribes, the connections in high places needed to facilitate secure operations, and the sophisticated skills and equipment required to outmaneuver antidrug initiatives. When law-enforcement agents clear the field of their competitors, these big organizations are often able to increase their own holdings and the scope of their operations.[177]

Moreover, funneling support to military and police forces in Mexico is a questionable remedy to the drug trade, especially in view of the persistence of corruption and human rights abuses in these institutions. Given the extent of producing areas and the reliance of many poor and unemployed people on the drug trade for their livelihoods, law-enforcement and eradication activities are only partial and inadequate solutions that bolster the power of agencies often known for resorting to the heavy hand. In the United States as well, the danger to civil liberties and human rights from drug-control efforts is growing. From random urine testing to strip searches, personal privacy is increasingly threatened. Antidrug agents along the border have even more freedom than most national and state laws allow police agencies. Because many of these agents have been cross-deputized by the DEA and U.S. Customs Service, these forces—whether from customs, police, or immigration agencies—are entitled to do searches without warrant in border communities and inland areas vulnerable to smuggling.

Effective remedies to the drug trade will require more than punitive measures. Pulverizing organized crime interests is one thing; pouring scarce national resources—whether U.S. or Mexico—into an ineffective war against drugs that violates human rights is another. By not considering options beyond militarization and law enforcement, not facing squarely the importance of U.S. demand and its social causes, and not grappling with the poverty that drives many people to join the drug trade, U.S. and Mexican antinarcotics initiatives are themselves doomed to failure.

# Calling in

# the Troops

National Guard troops searching trucks entering from Mexico, marine observation posts in the desert, aerial reconnaissance, and joint patrols by the Border Patrol and army troops all are signs of a military buildup along the U.S.-Mexico border. Unlike many other international borders, this militarization is the result not of conflictual binational relations but of heightened U.S. concern that south-north migratory and narcotics traffic is endangering its national security. This one-sided response to these international problems underlines the asymmetry of U.S.-Mexico relations while raising new concerns that the increasing military presence will aggravate existing cross-border tensions and lead to new civil rights violations.

Considering that the U.S.-Mexico border was largely the creation of the land-grabbing Mexican-American War, the international boundary has been largely free of direct military conflicts between the two countries, especially since the 1920s. The infamous raid on Columbus, New Mexico, in 1916 by Pancho Villa marked the beginning of the only serious cross-border military encounter with Mexican forces in the borderlands during this century. General "Blackjack" Pershing's "punitive expeditionary force" of twenty thousand men spent more than a year in northern Mexico, unsuccessfully hunting down the revolutionary bandit. On the U.S. side of the border some hundred thousand federalized National Guard troops kept order from Yuma to Brownsville. By 1919 U.S. control over the region was clearly established. With the creation of the Border Patrol in 1924, the United States had the beginnings of a permanent civilian enforcement presence on the border.

With few exceptions, border control operations over the next decades had more of a civilian law-enforcement nature than a military one. But Operation Wetback, a 1950s action carried out by the Border Patrol and

73

other elements of the Immigration and Naturalization Service, took a distinctly military approach. The INS was headed at the time by an ex-general who had participated in Pershing's expeditionary force, and he recruited other former officers to help with the operation. Using military tactics, the INS carried out the biggest mass roundup and deportation of undocumented Mexicans in U.S. history. Ground units and aircraft herded groups of Mexicans to the border, where the Mexican government helped out by shuttling the deportees into the Mexican interior by train.[178]

Recent efforts to beef up control over the border started under President Carter. Heightened concern over undocumented migration and drug trafficking prompted the buildup. At that point the military itself was not involved in the border-control operations, but Carter did appoint another ex-general to head the INS, and the administration moved to upgrade Border Patrol equipment and to construct new lengths of chain-link fence in high-traffic crossing areas.

By the early 1980s the momentum toward an increased military presence in the borderlands was unmistakable. Dictated by the concerns of conservative Reagan and Bush administrations, tighter immigration border controls came also in response to mounting fears about the spread of narcotics and new anxieties about job loss to "hordes" of immigrants from Central America and Mexico.

As a result, the United States has steadily expanded the role of military and law-enforcement agencies in the borderlands. Increasingly these agencies have a common mission that draws on military means to carry out law-enforcement tasks. Using sophisticated communications and surveillance technology, civilian and military forces from federal, state, and local levels have tried to squeeze off the flow of illegal drugs and undocumented immigrants into the United States. Although only partially successful, the scope of this new military presence sounded alarm bells for concerned observers worried about the impact of "militarization" on human and civil rights in the borderlands.

Militarization refers to an approach to law enforcement and border control that relies on military expertise, technology, equipment, facilities, and strategies, as well as personnel.[179] It represents the integration of military and law-enforcement functions and approaches, with members of the armed forces taking on domestic police functions and law-enforcement agents taking on the tactics and technologies of the military. As Timothy Dunn, a close observer of the process in the borderlands, described it, "It's when cops act like the military and the military act like cops."[180]

At large ports of entry like San Diego this militarization is most conspicuous. Customs officers with their canine partners zigzag through lines of pedestrians and vehicles passing through the customs station. The dogs sniff out drugs and undocumented immigrants stashed in trunks of cars and other hiding places. National Guard troops inspect cargo for contraband. Mobile X-ray vans and other high-tech detection devices are becoming more commonplace, while just down the way from official entry stations, tall steel barrier walls, chain-link fences, and floodlight systems block the illegal traffic by more prosaic means.

Along the many miles of open border, this militarized approach is also evident, although usually less obvious because of the remote nature of the terrain. But bumping into today's border-control operations in the back-country can be shocking, and even frightening. Many Border Patrol agents carry military-issue M-16s, responding to the increased firepower of drug traffickers. The agents are also authorized to carry personally owned semiautomatic pistols.[181] Marines on reconnaissance exercises, radar balloons hovering overhead, and the whir of helicopters fitted with searchlights and infrared radar systems give the air of a war zone. Infrared body sensors and magnetic footfall detectors, having once been used in Southeast Asia, are now placed along desolate stretches of border, forming a technological front line of defense for the Border Patrol.

Critical to this new military presence on the border have been presidential and congressional initiatives to loosen the restrictions on the involvement of the armed forces in domestic law enforcement. In 1981 the U.S. Congress reformed the law that previously had strictly circumscribed the military's role in domestic activities. It also wrote new legislation on drug and immigration control that included a role for the armed forces in enforcement efforts. Although still restricted from pursuit, interdiction, search, seizure, or arrest, the military was authorized to help detect and monitor suspicious activities along the border, in partnership with law-enforcement agencies.[182]

Congressional appropriations were even more explicit, funding various types of programs designed to integrate military and civilian forces in border law-enforcement activities. Other legal changes throughout the decade progressively loosened restrictions on military involvement in domestic affairs and broadened the role of the military in law-enforcement functions concerning drug and immigration control. A 1986 presidential declaration that the narcotics trade constituted a threat to national security helped Congress justify the legal changes and push border militarization forward.[183] Congress authorized the military to provide "expert advice" to civilian agencies on tactical and technological matters such as surveillance and intelligence gathering. In an attempt to forge an effective interagency network devoted to cutting off the flow of illegal drugs, the Department of Defense also assumed charge of integrating the command, control, communications, and intelligence assets of the United States.

By 1991 the armed forces could pick from a menu of ways they could help out with antinarcotics activities, many of which overlap with immigration-control efforts. Besides providing training and advice to civilian agencies, the military can conduct aerial and ground reconnaissance operations in the borderlands to gather intelligence and monitor suspicious movements. Indeed, Congress mandated that the military conduct training exercises "to the maximum extent possible" in high-traffic areas like the borderlands. The looser guidelines on military involvement allow the armed forces to carry out drug eradication campaigns and other operations that support law-enforcement programs.

With new legal freedoms like these plus extra funding and the emphasis on border control under the Reagan and Bush administrations, military and law-enforcement functions became increasingly intertwined in the borderlands. The 1986 launching of Operation Alliance—a multiagency law-enforcement initiative targeting the border area—and the subsequent designation of the U.S.-Mexico border as a "High Intensity Drug Trafficking Area" in 1990 pushed these efforts forward. Operation Alliance's mandate is "to foster interagency cooperation and to interdict the flow of drugs, weapons, aliens, currency, and other contraband across the Southwest border."[184] It represents the largest, most ambitious interagency action of its kind ever attempted by the U.S. government.

To plan and coordinate military support to Operation Alliance, the Pentagon created Joint Task Force 6 (JTF-6) in 1989 and stationed the new unit at Fort Bliss in El Paso. Representatives from various branches of the military serve on the task force, which fields requests for support from the civilian agencies and arranges for military participation in their law-enforcement efforts. The National Guard, marines, and army have been especially active in these operations, as have special forces, like the Army Rangers, Green Berets, and paratroopers. Among other things, they offer transportation assistance, deploy and monitor ground radar and seismic sensors, conduct trainings, carry out surveillance and reconnaissance missions, clear brush, build and improve roads, construct and repair fences, provide intelligence, and inspect cargo at border crossings.[185]

One operation coordinated by JTF-6 was a reconnaissance training exercise carried out near Naco, Arizona, in August 1992. Around two hundred marines from Camp Lejeune, North Carolina, set up observation posts and marched in foot patrols fully armed with M-16s. Wearing green greasepaint and camouflage, the troops crept through the tall grass along the border or bounced over rugged terrain in Humvees, the four-wheel-drive vehicles used for conducting motorized patrols. Their task was to practice surveillance, reconnaissance, and all the other skills necessary for a "wartime mission," according to the commander of the battalion.[186] But they also helped Border Patrol agents stationed in Naco and Douglas by keeping an eye out for suspicious activities that might indicate drug trafficking or immigrants trying to enter the United States illegally.[187]

Prohibited from actually stopping, searching, or arresting subjects themselves, military troops, like the marines stationed outside Naco, stay in radio contact with civilian enforcement agencies. If the troops run into someone doing something they suspect is illegal, they summon the Border Patrol. In addition, Border Patrol agents and other law-enforcement officers often accompany the troops in the field to supervise the operations, make arrests, and receive or provide training. When a small force of marines patrolling the Arizona border near Nogales in 1989 came on a group of drug smugglers, for instance, there was a Border Patrol agent with them who authorized the troops to exchange fire with the traffickers.[188]

Operations like these are becoming more common along the border. In fact, military spokespersons acknowledge that ten such operations probably take place at any given time. A spokesperson for JTF-6 told a reporter investigating the maneuvers around Naco in August 1992 that there were sixty-two joint military-civilian exercises occurring at the time.[189] Cooperative exercises aimed at border control have occurred simultaneously along the border in all four border states.[190]

The campaign to integrate and coordinate activities, resources, and strategies among military and civilian agencies has been far-reaching but not always successful.[191] Illegal immigration and narcotrafficking continue at high levels, and many border residents express concern that the borderlands have become a virtual war zone. In fact, that is exactly what Border Patrol agents and military troops often call the most highly trafficked sections of the boundary.

Joint operations between the border police and the military have steadily become more sophisticated technologically. At five sites along the border immense aerostat radar balloons patrol the airspace. Although there are many difficulties with them—they have to be taken down in bad weather, they cannot "see" over hills or in canyons, and they require frequent maintenance—they contribute to the image of a militarized border. For Operation Alliance, the Department of Defense contributed Blackhawk helicopters, high-speed interceptor planes, and radar planes, including an AWACS. Military troops have flown intrusion detection missions designed to monitor air traffic into the United States that may be involved with drug running. From the Department of Defense the INS obtained A-Star 350 helicopters outfitted with powerful Nite Sun searchlights and infrared radar to track smugglers and undocumented immigrants entering the United States at night.

In one case the marines deployed a drone (a small, remotely piloted aircraft) equipped with high-tech observational equipment. It flew along the Texas-Mexico border for a couple of weeks, transmitting its observations to U.S. marine monitors. They passed along the information to the Border Patrol, which used the tips to locate and seize several large marijuana shipments and to pick up double the number of undocumented immigrants usually captured during the same time period.

The National Guard tends to provide most of the labor and muscle for these operations, inspecting cargo at border crossings, building roads, cleaning ditches, and repairing fences, for instance. But it, too, increasingly relies on various types of high-tech equipment. Forward-looking infrared radar, side-looking airborne radar, and secure voice radio communications support National Guard troops who carry out photoreconnaissance missions or other technical border-control activities. Likewise, the Border Patrol has enhanced its arsenal of detection devices. On the ground, its agents and their military colleagues use sensitive detection devices that use seismic vibrations or infrared to pick up movement that may mean undocumented immigrants or traffickers are trying to cross the border. Outfitted with night scopes, night-vision goggles, tripod- and vehicle-mounted scopes, they monitor high-traffic areas. They even monitor some stretches of the border with low-light closed-circuit television systems.

Critics of these types of programs fear the erosion of human and civil rights in the borderlands. Because military troops are trained to kill, not to make careful legal distinctions, they are dangerous additions to law-enforcement efforts. Along with efforts during the 1980s to devise "contingency plans" for border civil control and roundup of unwanted populations, these operations at their worst could provide the framework for police-state intervention like that seen during the Los Angeles riots in 1992.[192] During those riots Border Patrol agents were dispatched to Latino immigrant communities, where they picked up one thousand undocumented people and dispatched them to the INS for deportation.[193]

Even without going that far, the effect on the human and civil rights of people who look "foreign" has already been negative. Civilian law-enforcement agencies like the Border Patrol, Drug Enforcement Administration, customs, and state and local police forces are increasingly cross-designating (deputizing) personnel from other agencies, giving such agents broad authority over a range of jurisdictions. Through cross-designations, such agencies take on the role of a national police force. If "deputized" by customs, for example, agents can conduct warrantless searches if they suspect that someone is entering the United States illegally or with contraband.

Because civil rights violations like these are becoming more common and because the use of force—even deadly force—is occurring more frequently, a law professor at the University of Arizona described the borderlands as a "deconstitutionalized zone."[194] Roberto Martínez, director of the American Friends Service Committee's San Diego office, told a congressional subcommittee: "As long as a segment of this society and government continues to lump together undocumented immigrants, drugs, crime, and terrorism to justify increased enforcement and militarization, attitudes toward immigrants will not only not change but will continue translating into open hostility and violence."[195]

# Manufacturing

# on the Margin

Border business has long been regarded as a fringe economy, one that has little to do with the overall binational economic relations between Mexico and the United States.[196] Because of changing patterns of trade and investment and the rise of the Sun Belt, the perception of the marginal character of the border economy needs some updating.

Increasingly business along the international boundary line represents the shape of things to come throughout the United States and Mexico. Goods that were once available only in border stores are now available in supermarkets far outside the borderlands. Investment once restricted to Mexico's northern border is penetrating the interior. Like the border communities, the rest of the United States is waking to challenges of global production sharing. Instead of hosting entire industries, the goal now is to hold on to supply businesses and the high-skill end of production. The informal service sector of Mexican maids and child care providers is emerging in cities far removed from the international border. Free trade—and investment—are nothing new to the borderlands but are now coming as a shock to the rest of Mexico and the United States. "It's a new phenomenon for Washington and Mexico, but not for us," observed Elsa Saxod, San Diego's binational affairs director. "The industrial world and the developing world are coming together here on the border."[197]

When the line was drawn between Mexico and the United States in the mid-1800s, it gave rise to a new economy that fed on the differences between the two countries. In many cases, contraband dealings originally gave life to the border towns, in both Mexico and the United States. Although the vice business still exists, it has devolved into a minor sideline of the greater border economy. Trade liberalization has reduced the incentives for the trade in contraband consumer goods, with the exception

80

of narcotrafficking, which has assumed a central, although clandestine, place in many border towns.

Investment and trade along the border have carved their own distinctive patterns. Especially for the Mexican border region, but also for the United States, these economic relations have pulled the two border economies closer together. The Mexican government has launched numerous programs designed to draw the borderlands closer to the national center, while the U.S. government has until recently mostly ignored the special economic problems of its southern border.

For Mexico, the northern border region has long been regulated by radically different economic policies from the rest of the country. The government's export-oriented development policies for the northern borderlands have been the prominent exception to Mexico's long history of import-substituting industrialization, protectionism, and nationalistic investment regulations. Since the late 1850s border states have at various times established free zones along the border to increase the ability of Mexican retailers to compete with their U.S. competitors. In 1965 the Mexican government opened its northern border to export-processing U.S. investment through its Border Industrialization Program, an initiative that stood in stark contrast to the domestic focus of its national economic policy. On the one hand, the Mexican government encouraged U.S. companies to move to the borderlands and set up *maquiladoras*, while on the other, it discouraged foreign investment in the country's interior with its "Mexicanization" policies.

The Border Industrialization Program was Mexico's first major departure from its stragegy of restricting foreign investment and reducing dependence on the international economy. This program waived a number of foreign investment restrictions and import rules for export-oriented assembly plants. With few exceptions, plants set up under this program, called *maquiladoras*, could be 100 percent foreign-owned.[198] Initially they had to be located within 12.5 miles of the border, but in 1972 the Echeverría administration eliminated this restriction, prohibiting *maquilas* only in Mexico's three largest cities: the capital, Guadalajara, and Monterrey.[199]

Originally seen as a gimmick to provide employment to returning braceros, the *maquila* program had by the mid-1980s become a "priority sector" for Mexico, according to President de la Madrid.[200] By the early 1990s export-oriented industrialization and the production-sharing model of the *maquilas* were central to the Salinas administration's development strategy for Mexico as a whole.

The *maquila* program works this way: The XYZ Corporation leases land in Tijuana, let's say, and sets up a wholly owned subsidiary called XYZ de México. XYZ and its U.S. suppliers send leather, electric motors, rubber wheels, and a variety of other parts to the Tijuana *maquila*. In addition, suppliers in Singapore ship computer chips to the plant. XYZ de México employees assemble the parts into self-propelled golf carts, package them in Mexican-made foam and cardboard, and send them to an XYZ Corporation warehouse in Chula Vista, where they are stamped "Made in America." XYZ de México pays no Mexican duties on any of the imported parts, and the XYZ Corporation pays U.S. duties only on the value of the Singaporean computer chips, the Mexican packaging, and the value of the Mexican labor.[201]

The Border Industrialization Program represented the first step toward the integration of Mexico into the U.S. manufacturing base. But regional integration was hardly what Mexico had in mind in establishing the program. Until the mid-1980s the country's economic planners viewed it largely as an employment program. Although employee training is an additional potential benefit, most jobs are unskilled, and many positions in engineering and management (with the exception of personnel administration) are held by foreigners.

Along with allowing full foreign ownership, the most attractive aspect of the Border Industrialization Program for foreign manufacturers was the exemption from duties of all imported inputs—materials, components, machinery, and tools. To qualify for these exemptions, a firm was required to ship all waste and scrap by-products out of the country along with the finished product and had to post a bond for the value of the duties that were waived. This latter requirement led to the phrase *in-bound assembly operations*, which is used interchangeably with *maquiladoras* and *maquilas*.

By any name the program has changed the face of Mexico's northern border region. Industrial parks have sprouted up from Tijuana to Matamoros, and around them *maquila* workers and other impoverished border residents have constructed shantytowns of makeshift huts. *Maquila* operations span a very wide range of activities, from the assembly of plastic toys and polyester lingerie to the highly complex management of a modern lumber mill. At eight *maquiladoras* owned by the A. C. Nielsen Company, workers sort millions of coupons for U.S. manufacturers and retailers. Catalina Offshore Products sends U.S. sea urchins to its *maquiladora* in Ensenada for processing into sushi. At the Allen Coach Works plant in Nuevo Laredo, workers saw Cadillacs and Lincoln Continentals in half and then refashion the luxury cars into limousines.

Despite the shift from a regional to a national development program, the *maquila* sector remains concentrated on the northern border. It is here where foreign investors find the combination of cheap labor, proximity to U.S. markets and suppliers, and infrastructure that best enhances their competitive advantage. About 80 percent of the assembly plants are still found along Mexico's northern border, mostly in the major cities of Juárez, Tijuana, Nogales, Mexicali, Matamoros, Reynosa, and Nuevo Laredo.[202] In search of still-cheaper labor, some firms have established plants as far away from the border as the Yucatán and Oaxaca, while others looking for an untapped skilled-labor market have set up *maquilas* in such places as Chihuahua, Hermosillo, and the outskirts of Guadalajara. But proximity to U.S. suppliers and the U.S. market ensures that the border is likely to remain the premier location for export-processing industries, even after a U.S.-Mexico free trade accord.

## From Screwdrivers to Robots

*Maquila* trade—imported inputs to Mexico and exported assembled goods to the United States—constitutes one-third of the two-way trade between the two nations. Economic changes and aggressive promotion have prompted rapid growth in the *maquiladora* program. The number of assembly plants jumped from 585 in 1982 to 1,125 in 1987 and passed 2,000 in 1992. The number of employees grew even faster, because of the increasing size of the average plant's workforce (see Table 1).

Not only have the numbers of factories and workers increased since the 1960s, but the types of industries setting up *maquiladoras* have also dramatically changed. No longer do low-tech or so-called screwdriver industries dominate the *maquila* sector. Instead electronics and auto-parts plants that increasingly feature high-tech production systems are the leading industries, together accounting for about half the *maquila* workforce and value-added production (see Table 2). Automatic insertion machines and surface-mount technology have been added to circuit board assembly lines, clean rooms to the semiconductor industry, and robots to metal machining processes. Value added per employee—one indication of the technological level of a process—increased from $5,780 in 1983 to $7,794 in 1989.[203] As Ford's engine plant in Chihuahua and dozens of other state-of-the-art Mexican facilities demonstrate, Mexican workers are quite capable of turning out high-quality, high-technology products.

## Table 1

Maquila industry by plants, employees, and value added, 1967–92 (value added in millions of U.S. dollars)

| Year | Number of Plants | Employees | Value Added |
|---|---|---|---|
| 1967[1] | 72 | 4,000 | 77.08 |
| 1968 | 112 | 10,927 | 81.25 |
| 1969 | 149 | 15,900 | 81.08 |
| 1970 | 160 | 20,327 | 86.25 |
| 1971 | 205 | 28,483 | 102.25 |
| 1972 | 339 | 48,060 | 151.66 |
| 1973 | 400 | 64,330 | 201.25 |
| 1974 | 455 | 75,977 | 217.50 |
| 1975[2] | 454 | 67,214 | 321.20 |
| 1976 | 448 | 74,496 | 352.27 |
| 1977 | 443 | 78,433 | 314.95 |
| 1978 | 457 | 90,704 | 438.59 |
| 1979 | 540 | 111,365 | 637.85 |
| 1980 | 620 | 119,546 | 770.82 |
| 1981 | 605 | 130,973 | 973.86 |
| 1982 | 585 | 127,048 | 811.63 |
| 1983 | 600 | 150,867 | 824.53 |
| 1984 | 672 | 199,684 | 1160.64 |
| 1985 | 760 | 211,968 | 1265.56 |
| 1986 | 890 | 249,833 | 1295.41 |
| 1987[3] | 1125 | 305,523 | 1635.00 |
| 1988 | 1396 | 369,489 | 2339.00 |
| 1989 | 1655 | 429,725 | 3057.00 |
| 1990 | 1930 | 460,293 | 3362.00 |
| 1991[4] | 1954 | 489,000 | 4100.00 |
| 1992 (May)[5] | 2129 | 511,000 | 4300.00 |

[1]Data for 1967 to 1974 are from Leslie Sklair, Assembling for Development, 54.

[2]Data for 1975 to 1986 are from Instituto Nacional de Estadística, Geografía, e Informática, Estadística de la Industria Maquiladora de Exportación (Mexico, D.F., 1988).

[3]Data for 1987–90 from INEGI cited in SourceMex 4/17/91.

[4]1991 estimate provided by Asesoría Económica Especializada (Mexico, D.F.), cited by SourceMex (Latin America Data Base: Albuquerque, New Mexico).

[5]INEGI data cited by SourceMex (Latin America Data Base: Albuquerque, New Mexico, August 25, 1993).

## Table 2

Employment in *maquiladoras* by industry, 1979 and 1991

| Industry | 1979 | 1991 |
|---|---|---|
| Food processing | 1481 | 7791 |
| Apparel/textiles | 17631 | 45726 |
| Leather | 1655 | 7269 |
| Furniture | 3515 | 26,528 |
| Chemical | * | 7,560 |
| Transportation equipment | 5,035 | 111,956 |
| Electrical machinery & electronics | 63,661 | 101,432 |
| Other manufacturing | 7,775 | 64,120 |

*There were so few chemical plants in 1979 that the Mexican government did not reveal the employment total so as not to reveal company-specific data.

Sources: For 1979 data, Sklair, *Assembling for Development*, 70. For 1991 data, American Chamber of Commerce in Mexico, *Review of Trade and Industry* including Maquiladora Newsletter, second quarter, 1992, 13.

Border towns such as Juárez and Mexicali have become high-tech centers for leading defense and aeronautical corporations such as Hughes Aircraft, TRW, Rockwell, McDonnell Douglas, and Bell and Howell. Auditors and quality-control agents from the Defense Contract Administration Services regularly cross the border to monitor the military-related manufacturing in the *maquila* plants.

### Jobs, Jobs, Jobs

On a certain level the success of the Border Industrialization Program is beyond dispute. The economic boom of Mexico's northern cities is largely attributable to the *maquiladoras*, and the U.S. border cities have benefited from an associated service industry and a healthy commercial sector fueled by the *maquila* boom and population growth. Although it is not hard to find critics of the pay levels and the environmental repercussions of the *maquila* industry, most borderlanders, or *fronterizos*, support the presence of the industry. Especially in Mexico, they recognize it as a major source of jobs.

As an employment-generating strategy, the Border Industrialization Program has certainly worked. Unemployment in most Mexican border cities is minimal, especially when compared with elsewhere in Mexico. From around 20,000 employees in 1970, *maquila* employment grew to nearly 130,000 in 1980 and to more than 500,000 by the end of 1992. A recent survey in Nogales, Sonora, found that 45 percent of the workforce in that Mexican city was directly or indirectly tied to the *maquila* industry.[204]

Mexico's net income from the program, the vast majority of which corresponds to workers' wages, replaced tourism as the country's second-largest source of foreign exchange in the late 1980s. In 1992 nearly five billion dollars flowed to Mexico's central bank as *maquila* owners traded dollars for pesos to pay their workers and other costs in Mexico.[205] Only oil exports, worth almost eight billion dollars in 1992, earned more foreign currency. Direct investment in *maquiladora* plants and equipment brings in another few hundred million dollars in an average year.[206]

The *maquiladoras* have incorporated more sophisticated technology and higher value-added activity into their assembly systems, but wages are still extremely low (about sixty dollars per forty-five-hour week) despite increasing productivity.[207] The low wage rates caused by the devaluation of the Mexican peso sparked the *maquila* boom of the 1980s. These wages—lower than those paid in other leading export-processing centers and lower than those paid by Mexican manufacturers—are not nearly enough to provide for a family, and they keep *maquila* workers living in makeshift homes in squatter colonies that often lack water and sewerage.[208]

Rather than attempt to reduce high turnover rates and to increase worker productivity by offering higher wages, the *maquiladora* managers entice workers with such perks as free lunches, beauty contests, company transportation, showers at work, and company-sponsored sports. Rather than raise wages, an article in *Twin Plant News* advised *maquila* managers: "There are some things you can do to help, such as setting up a clothing exchange in the plant. . . . Buy some bulk food items such as flour, beans, potatoes, etc., and distribute these among your employees."[209]

*Maquila* associations in every important city share information about their members' wage structure. The wage reports serve as guidelines and help ensure that companies do not enter a bidding war for the available labor force. Although the associations deny that their intention is to hold down wages, numerous investigators have found that *maquila* managers feel great pressure from their peers to maintain wages within a certain range.[210] The government aids employers in this endeavor, according to managers of two U.S.-owned auto plants. "We even get help from the government making sure that we don't settle too high" in negotiations with the union, said one. "The labor ministry takes an active part in negotiations, especially in companies our size. And they steer the level of increases," confirmed another.[211]

Extremely low wages produce high employee turnover in the *maquiladoras* as workers jump at any opportunity to earn more money. It is common for plants to lose one-tenth of their entire workforces in some months and to see more employees quit in one year than are employed at any given time.

Although some employers complain that such turnover costs them a significant amount of money—because of the constant need to retrain new workers—for most *maquiladoras* turnover is at worst a minor annoyance and sometimes even helpful. Only a handful of *maquiladoras* provide more than a day or two of training for their assembly-line positions—where pay is lowest and turnover highest—and for many training lasts only a few hours.[212] In those plants that do provide greater training, it is generally provided only to workers with a minimum level of seniority—usually at least three months. Since most turnover occurs before this cutoff point, few workers with significant amounts of training actually leave their jobs.

Many *maquiladoras* produce consumer goods the demand for which in the United States varies seasonally. The size of the workforce in these plants can drop by more than one-fourth from December to January. In these cases high turnover relieves management of the need to meet legal requirements for laying off workers.[213]

Managers are clearly aware that raising wages would reduce turnover, yet the problem is not grave enough to have provoked wage hikes. According to a manager at one plant with 100 percent turnover in 1990, workers quit because "the pay is poor, the work is heavy, and the company always asks for more."[214] High turnover rates create a false feeling that unemployment is low along the border. Official statistics indicate that unemployment hovers around 3 percent in border towns. This figure is meaningless since the government counts as employed anyone who worked at least one hour during the previous week, including through "self-employment" like washing the windows of cars stopped at street-lights. The fact is that earnings in the informal sector often surpass those paid by *maquiladoras*, leading many to opt for underemployment.[215]

## Enclave Industrialization

Much as it had during the dictatorship of General Porfirio Díaz (1876–1911), foreign investment in the *maquiladoras* has created an enclave economy. It is an economy geographically located within Mexico but largely dependent on decisions made by corporate executives, consumers, and policymakers in the United States, and it generates few benefits for that part of society outside the enclave.

A major failure of the Border Industrialization Program has been its inability to spur the creation of linkages with the rest of the Mexican economy. This means that few Mexican industries, either along the border or elsewhere in Mexico, supply the *maquiladoras*. Neither do many Mexican businesses buy *maquila*-manufactured goods that are then used as part of their own production process. Consequently, the beneficial impact in northern Mexico of the *maquila* sector is largely limited to job creation and the economic activity generated by worker spending.[216]

The logic of the *maquiladora* program, which relies on minimal government interference in corporate decisions to encourage foreign investment, has stifled efforts to extend its benefits beyond the creation of jobs. Mexican attempts to build linkages between the *maquiladoras* and the rest of the economy—through supply contracts or technology transfer, for example—have failed. Throughout the program the proportion of the value of production in *maquiladoras* that comes from Mexican-owned businesses has been under 2 percent.[217]

Because of its lack of linkages with the domestic economy and its export orientation, the *maquila* industry can be fairly described as a foreign-owned enclave economy. But the *maquilas* do not operate independently of the government and local capitalists. From the beginning of the Border Industrialization Program, a close partnership has developed among the Mexican state bureaucracy, the domestic economic elite, and the transnational corporations that operate the *maquilas*.[218] Not only has the government financed construction of numerous industrial parks, but it has also supported the *maquilas* by providing land, roads, and public utilities—and by leaving them virtually untaxed and unregulated.

By keeping a tight lid on independent union activity and by having government-affiliated labor confederations work closely with the *maquila* management, the Mexican government has also sided with the interests of the *maquila* sector to the detriment of Mexican workers.[219] In the mid-1970s, when labor organizing was threatening to drive wages up, the government and the *maquila* industry even entered into an "Alliance for Production."[220] Shortly thereafter the CTM, the official labor confederation, regained control of the plants, independent organizing was suppressed, and the peso was devalued, all of which made Mexico once again a desirable offshore location for production-sharing industries. So compatible are the industry and official unions that many corporations actually favor having a union to reduce the turnover rate and increase productivity.[221]

Like the government, Mexican capitalists and professionals play an important role in making the *maquila* sector work smoothly. Their most important role is facilitating *maquila* operations by managing industrial parks, providing legal and accounting services, arranging transportation, and serving as customs brokers.[222] In each of the main border cities, a local bourgeoisie feeds off of the *maquila* sector.[223] According to one estimate, the Mexican companies that run the industrial parks can clear as much as fifty cents an hour per *maquila* employee.[224] The most powerful of these firms is Grupo Bermúdez of Juárez, founded by Antonio Bermúdez, the same man who ran the government's nationalist PRONAF (national border program) campaign in the early 1960s.[225]

Whereas the Mexican government has gone to great lengths to assist the *maquila* industry and shelter it from labor and environmental regulations, it has largely ignored the basic needs of its workforce. The small amount of revenue collected from the *maquiladoras* goes not to local governments but to the national treasury, leaving Mexican border towns no funds to cope with immense public health and housing problems.

Although central to the economy of the Mexican borderlands, *maquila*-based development has accentuated the planning and infrastructural problems faced by Mexican cities. Most obvious are the housing crisis and the lack of waste disposal and wastewater treatment facilities. Electricity, water, and roads were extended to the *maquiladoras*, but little thought was given to the social and environmental costs of the *maquila* boom. So grave are some of these problems that Juárez at one point even began to discourage new *maquila* growth. At a time when growing environmental consciousness, high labor turnover, and urban congestion are making the border region less desirable, some companies are discovering the advantages of establishing *maquiladoras* deeper in Mexico. New communications and transportation networks will make nonborder locations increasingly attractive, especially considering the still-lower labor costs of most nonborder sites.

The Border Industrialization Program has accomplished its chief objectives of generating employment for the border region and increasing the inflow of foreign exchange. But it has failed to build a foundation for the broad-based economic development of northern Mexico. After more than twenty-five years the *maquila* sector remains an assembly-manufacturing enclave controlled by transnational corporations. The Mexican government now hopes that the *maquilas* can serve as a model for export-oriented industrialization along the lines experienced by Taiwan, South Korea, Singapore, and Hong Kong. Unlike the Asian tigers, however, Mexico has failed to use the *maquila* sector as a stepping-stone to full-fledged industrialization.[226]

Recent trade and investment liberalization initiatives on the part of the Mexican government show no sign of sparking more integral development. Thus far there is nothing to indicate that Mexico will be able to foster more meaningful technology transfer or increase the economic linkages outside the foreign-owned enclave.[227] What few inputs come from the borderlands region are generally supplied not by Mexican companies but by firms on the U.S. side, especially in Texas and Southern California.[228] In the absence of foreign-investment regulations that require more linkages with the national economy if willing and able suppliers are available, it makes more sense for companies to look to U.S. suppliers for the inputs they need. At this point companies have little incentive to seek out local suppliers in the Mexican interior unless quality can be guaranteed and there exist real price advantages.

The most fervent proponents of export-processing industrialization assert that Mexico is poised for an economic takeoff similar to that experienced by the Asian tigers more than two decades ago. But a visit to any one of the *maquila* zones that hug the border gives one a more sobering picture of Mexico's prospects for using *maquila* production as a base for broader economic development. Hundreds of workers in Nogales, Sonora, produce automatic garage door openers for Sears at a massive warehouse-style factory, and many live in hovels of their own making just outside the high barbed-wire fence surrounding the plant. Like many other *maquila* workers, their homes are worth less than the products they assemble every day. Can economic growth and prosperity be the product of such misery?

Economic growth, meaning the expansion of the gross domestic product (GDP), can result from minimum-wage manufacturing. But making export-processing zones into development zones is a challenge that Mexico has not met after more than a quarter century of hosting *maquilas*. No matter how many *maquilas* come to the border, or anywhere else in Mexico, it appears likely that development will not follow unless the Mexican government aggressively promotes more linkages with domestic producers, genuine technology transfer, and better wages and conditions for the *maquila* workforce. In addition, as is becoming increasingly obvious, economic growth—whether through *maquila* manufacturing or domestic industrialization—will actually subvert development unless it is environmentally sustainable and its costs and benefits are fairly distributed.

The problems of environmental destruction, inadequate social infrastructure, and the exploitation of the country's workforce are, of course, not attributable solely to the *maquilas* or the government's export-oriented development strategy. Rather they are symptoms of Mexico's failure to shape economic policies that ensure that the benefits of economic development are broadly shared.

The expectation in the Mexican borderlands is that expanded economic integration—as represented most dramatically by the prospects of free trade—will mean more investment and jobs for the region. Furthermore, many predict that the advance of production sharing and flexible production strategies will result in the increased flow of high-tech industry to the northern border states. However, to ensure that this projected flow of investment, technology, and jobs nurtures broad-based and sustained development, the Mexican government will need to assume more control over the nature and direction of export-oriented manufacturing—a challenge that will be increasingly difficult within the context of a free trade agreement.

The danger, as industry spokespeople are fond of repeating, is that government regulation, such as increased minimum wages or mandatory local-supply requirements, will "kill the goose that lays the golden eggs." This is the same implied threat, of course, that industries are using against the U.S. government and U.S. workers. Throughout the Mexican borderlands there exists a deep awareness about how dependent the regional economy is on the *maquila* industry. Although few borderlanders outside the *maquila* business sector would describe the eggs laid by the *maquilas* as golden, a future without these assembly plants looks even more grim than the present borderland reality.

As many *maquila* workers are well aware, their wages are low—but not as low as those being paid in places such as Haiti and Malaysia or, for that matter, by the *maquila* sector farther south in their own country. Although companies publicly talk of relocation to lower-wage locations mainly as an idle threat to keep wages low and the government cooperative, some *maquilas* have indeed closed down and moved to Southeast Asia.[229] Increasingly the structure and the mobility of global production limit the development choices open to Mexico and its borderlands.

## The Runaway Phenomenon

The flip side of the enclave nature of the *maquiladoras* within Mexico is their function viewed from the United States as an appendage of the U.S. economy. The finished products and the profits from the operation generally go to the United States, but the production is exempt from U.S. laws and enforcement. In effect, a corporation with *maquila* production is importing Mexican labor to the United States but employing the workers according to Mexican laws.[230] The Mexican government recognizes this aspect of the *maquila* production process. Mexican trade statistics ignore the in-bond import of components for assembly and the export of the finished products or subassemblies. Instead the government's trade department counts the value of wages paid to *maquiladora* employees as an export of a service, called the service of transformation, to the United States.[231]

Whether this is a service the United States should import is the central question in a debate that has raged since the mid-1960s. A primary focus of the debate is the offshore assembly provision (OAP) of U.S. tariff law. Existing in various forms since 1930, this provision allows firms to import goods without paying duties on any U.S.-made components or materials that were used to produce those goods.[232] The provision thus makes it cheaper for U.S.-based manufacturers to take advantage of in-bond programs like Mexico's Border Industrialization Program. Proponents of the tariff exemption argue that it preserves U.S. jobs by encouraging manufacturers to use U.S.-made components and materials in their foreign assembly operations. Opponents argue that it destroys U.S. jobs by encouraging manufacturers to set up foreign assembly operations in the first place.

The American Federation of Labor and Congress of Industrial Organizations (AFL-CIO) used this latter argument in 1967, when it first went on record opposing these tariff breaks.[233] At that time Mexico was but one host country among many, and the U.S. industrial base did not seem nearly as weak as it now appears to be. Hundreds of corporations sent their labor-intensive and easily transportable work to duty-free "export-processing zones" in East Asia or the Caribbean. Although transportation costs to those locations were often higher than they were to Mexico, political and regulatory factors—including a receptive attitude toward foreign investors and control over organized labor—were often more important in siting decisions.

In 1968, 112 Mexican *maquiladoras* assembled or processed approximately $40 million worth of U.S. inputs for duty-free reexport to the United States.[234] This represented less than 15 percent of the total value of goods the United States imported duty-free under the offshore assembly provision that year.[235] By 1977 Mexico had eaten into the market share of export-processing zones in East Asia and the Caribbean. That year there were 443 *maquiladoras*, and the duty-free portion of their exports to the United States totaled $631.1 million—32 percent of the global total (see Table 3). Another nine years later, in 1986, the number of *maquiladoras* had doubled to 890 and the value of U.S. components they imported, processed, and exported had more than quintupled to $3.4 billion. By 1986 Mexico was processing more U.S. inputs for duty-free export to the United States than all other countries combined, and that continues to be the case today.

Considering the large and growing volume of goods entering the United States duty-free under the offshore assembly provision, it is not surprising that the OAP is controversial. From 1968 through the 1980s the AFL-CIO tried numerous times to scuttle the provision: twice in 1969, once each in 1971 and 1974, with twenty-two separate bills in 1976, and on four occasions in the early and mid-1980s. But viewed in isolation, the effects of the OAP are not great.[236] On the one hand, the offshore assembly provision adds somewhat to the demand for U.S. inputs by creating what is in effect a 5 to 10 percent price advantage over equivalent foreign materials. These inputs help support manufacturing jobs in the United States. On the other hand, the provision increases U.S. demand for products assembled abroad. This is because in most industries the tariff exemption lowers the cost of imported products that use duty-free U.S. components. If there were no exemption, domestic assemblers using

**Table 3**

Imports under the Offshore Assembly Provision (all figures in millions of U.S. dollars)*

|  | 1975 | 1983 | 1991 |
|---|---|---|---|
| Total OAP imports from all sources | 5,162.4 | 21,575.9 | 57,527 |
| OAP imports from Mexico | 1,019.8 | 3,714.9 | 14,335.8 |
| Duty-free portion of imports from all sources | 1,265.9 | 5,386.6 | 14,517.2 |
| Duty-free portion of imports from Mexico | 552.4 | 1,968.7 | 7,254.9 |

*Known as TSUS 806.30 and 807.00 until 1990 and as HTS 9802.00.60 and 9802.00.80 from 1990 to the present.

Source: Official statistics of the U.S. Department of Commerce, Bureau of the Census.

93

domestic components would have a small cost advantage over assemblers located abroad. In this way the offshore assembly provision tends to decrease U.S. employment.

When seen in the light of the broader debate over economic strategy, the offshore assembly provision—and the U.S. economy's relationship to *maquiladoras* in general—take on much greater significance. The arguments against encouraging U.S. investment in the *maquiladoras* are often the same ones heard in opposition to NAFTA. Indeed, the open trade and investment rules characterizing the *maquila* program and the OAP have provided a preview of the most controversial part of NAFTA: the ability of U.S. companies freely to relocate operations to Mexico and export their products and services back to the U.S. market unimpeded. Hundreds of manufacturers and service providers have done just that since the 1960s, leaving behind tens, maybe hundreds of thousands of U.S. workers and their communities.

This movement is known as the runaway plant phenomenon. Although companies have "run away" to a multitude of low-wage export-processing zones across the globe, nowhere is the phenomenon more visible than right across the border in Mexico (see Table 4). One of the first companies to shift work to Mexico was Fairchild Electronics, which opened a *maquiladora* in Tijuana in 1966 to take over component assembly previously performed in California. Sears, Roebuck & Company gave a boost to the program by pushing its suppliers to shift some or all of their work to Mexico. Sears wanted to trim suppliers' costs but keep the "Made in America" label on its products.[237] Dozens of apparel and appliance manufacturers took the huge retailer's advice. Other Fortune 500 companies followed slowly but surely, along with hundreds of smaller firms, many of which went belly up after a few years of operation.

By no means were all new *maquiladoras* runaways. In a few cases old product lines using proven technology were sent to Mexico, to be replaced in this country by newer, top-of-the-line goods. In some others, *maquiladoras* replaced facilities elsewhere, usually in East Asia. But in hundreds and hundreds of cases the new Mexican assembly plants were tied to corporate decisions to replace higher-wage U.S. production, either directly or through contract bidding in which low-cost *maquiladoras* won out over their U.S. competitors.

Near the beginning of the *maquiladora* program Mexico was sensitive to the charge that it was stealing jobs from U.S. workers. In 1968 the Mexican government claimed that no existing *maquiladoras* were runaways and pledged to reject any firm that planned to lay off U.S. workers as part of its move to Mexico.[238] Mexico backed off somewhat from this patently absurd claim in 1970. But it continued to maintain that the *maquiladoras* were not significantly harming U.S. workers and that the government was "carefully reviewing applications" to ensure that no runaways set up shop in the country.[239]

There is no evidence that Mexico believed its own claims. The Ministry of Commerce and Industrial Development was not even able to keep track of those *maquiladoras* operating in the country at any one time. In any case the pretense was dropped later, when it became apparent that labor's allies in the U.S. Congress were unable to cancel the offshore assembly provision. Increasingly entrepreneurs were promoting the *maquiladora* concept to healthy corporations as well as those suffering from low-cost competitive challenges. By the mid-1970s such U.S. giants as Zenith, General Motors, General Electric, Westinghouse, Parker-Hannifin, Du Pont, ITT, Quaker Oats, Honeywell, Burroughs, and Motorola had joined RCA and Fairchild in establishing *maquiladoras*.

The U.S. tariff exemption for offshore assembly of U.S. components encouraged the growing exodus of manufacturing to Mexico, and it is likely that Mexico's weak and laxly enforced environmental and labor standards also played a role.[240] But by far the most important factor in the choice of Mexico as an export-processing site was—and is—the low wages paid to Mexican workers. This was made clear by the rapid expansion of *maquiladoras* after Mexico's minimum wage fell from a high of $1.53 per hour in 1982 to $.68 per hour in 1983, and then to a range around $.50 per hour from 1986 through 1990.[241] Whereas in 1981 Mexican workers were paid more in dollar terms than workers in South Korea, Taiwan, Hong Kong, and Singapore, by 1983 their wage and benefits package had moved into last place among the five countries.[242]

Armed with wage figures such as these and with increasing evidence of high-quality production in Mexico, *maquiladora* promoters found their jobs easier and easier. In brochures, videos, seminars, and personal visits, companies like Assemble in Mexico, Cal Pacifico, IMEC, and Inter-American Holdings claimed they could save the right kind of firm between ten and twenty-two thousand dollars per year for every job transferred to Mexico. The U.S. government even got into the act. In 1986 the Department of Commerce cosponsored Expo-Maquila '86, a business conference held in Acapulco at which investors were told of the savings they could enjoy by moving some or all of their production from the United States to Mexico. When the U.S. Congress found out that taxpayer money was being used to encourage runaway plants, it required that the

# Table 4

| Company | Location | Product | Jobs Lost | Time Span |
|---|---|---|---|---|
| Allied-Signal | Greensville, AL, & Knoxville, TN | Seat belts | 1,700 | 1986–1990 |
| A.O. Smith | IL, KY, & OH | Electric motors & water heaters | 2,860 | 1988 |
| AT&T | AR, VA, & LA | Telephones & answering machines | 470 | 1989 |
| Chrysler | AZ, WI, & IN | Electrical automotive parts | 1,675 | 1988–1990 |
| Emerson Electric | AZ, FL, MO, PA, & WI | Electric motors | 270 | 1986–87 |
| Fisher-Price | Holland, NY | Toys | 425 | 1990 |
| Ford Motor | IN, MI, & NY | Auto parts | 1,700 | 1981–1993 |
| General Electric | CA, IN, MA, MI, NY, OH, & TN | Motors, lights, & parts | 2,150 | 1983–1992 |
| General Motors | IN, MA, NY, OH, & WI | Cars, engines, radios & parts | 10,075 | 1974–1993 |
| Haggar Apparel | OK & TX | Men's clothes | 1,356 | 1986 & 1990 |
| Honeywell | Gardena, CA, & Plymouth, MN | Heating & A/C thermostats | 600 | 1988–1991 |
| Levi Strauss | TN, TX, & VA | Men's denim jeans & Dockers | 835 | 1988 |
| Leviton Manufacturing | Warwick, RI | Wiring devices | 800 | 1988–91 |
| Mattel | Covina & Paramount, CA | Toys | 1,050 | 1986–1990 |
| Maytag/Hoover | North Canton, OH | Vacuum cleaners & laundry equipment | 300 | 1985 |

| Company | Location | Product | Jobs Lost | Time Span |
| --- | --- | --- | --- | --- |
| Motorola | Phoenix, AZ | Semiconductors | 900 | 1985 |
| Philips Industries | CA, IL, PA, TN, VA, & WV | Lights, televisions, & components | 3,000 | 1991 |
| Pillsbury/Green Giant | Watsonville, CA | Broccoli & cauliflower processing | 670 | 1983 & 1991 |
| Proctor-Silex | Aberdeen & Southern Pines, NC | Irons, coffeemakers, popcorn poppers | 852 | 1991 |
| RCA | Bloomington & Indianapolis, IN | Televisions & parts | 2,355 | 1980–1993 |
| R.G. Barry | NC, OH, & TN | Women's slippers | 672 | 1984–1991 |
| Sanyo Manufacturing | Forrest City, AR | 13" & 20" TVs & microwaves | 1,400 | 1986–87 |
| Schlage Lock | Rocky Mount, NC | Locks | 700 | 1988 |
| Smith Corona | Cortland, NY | Typewriters | 800 | 1992–93 |
| Sunbeam-Oster | Dayton, TN, & Milwaukee, WI | Blenders & small appliances | 400 | 1987–88 |
| Tonka | Mound, MN | Toys | 400 | 1983–84 |
| Trico Products | Buffalo, NY | Windshield wipers | 1,200 | 1987–1990 |
| Volkswagen | New Stanton, PA | Rabbits, Jettas | 2,500 | 1988 |
| Westinghouse | Bellefontaine, OH, & Beaver, PA | Electric motors & switches | 930 | 1980s |
| Zenith Electronics | IL, IN, IA, & MO | Televisions & TV equipment | 7,600 | 1978–1992 |

practice be halted, but of course, the expositions have continued without U.S. government assistance.[243] During the Salinas administration the Mexican government helped establish two development funds, called Amerimex and Ventana, to assist Mexicans who want either to purchase U.S.-based companies and move them to Mexico or to form a joint venture with a U.S. firm for that purpose.

Runaway plants added to the epidemic of plant closings that wreaked havoc in cities and towns across the United States during the 1980s. A network of community- and labor-based activists formed in response to this epidemic. These activists usually focused on immediate issues such as dissuading local companies from shutting down and pushing for a national requirement that companies give their workers advance notice of plans to close down a facility.

Toward the end of the decade the movement to halt plant closings focused increasingly on the issue of manufacturing relocation to low-wage areas around the world, especially to Mexico. In doing so, these activists hooked up with a grassroots network largely made up of church-based groups and progressive political organizations. Concerned with issues of corporate responsibility, this second group of activists had enjoyed comparative success in drawing attention to U.S. corporate support for the apartheid South African regime and in attaching a stigma to foreign investment in that country.

Hoping to accomplish similar objectives in Mexico, the two networks joined forces with national labor unions, including the AFL-CIO, and two grassroots Mexican organizations. In early 1991 they announced the formation of the Coalition for Justice in the Maquiladoras. The coalition vowed to push for minimum standards of corporate behavior in Mexico's *maquiladora* industry, including observance of U.S. environmental and occupational health standards, and fair employment practices.[244] The coalition's guiding principle—that corporations should act just as responsibly in poor countries as they are expected to in wealthy ones—became a centerpiece of later efforts to establish minimum environmental and labor standards as part of any North American free trade agreement.

### Whither the *Maquiladoras* Under Free Trade?

Talk of free trade raised questions about the future of the *maquila* sector. At the very least Mexico would have to revamp the legal framework of the Border Industrialization Program. Since the ability to import parts duty-free into Mexico from the United States would no longer remain unique to *maquiladoras*, there would be no need for in-bond treatment of those imports. In addition, requiring certain manufacturers to export their production would become meaningless when those exports could reenter Mexico duty-free.[245]

The NAFTA text signed in late 1992 required Mexico to phase out the *maquiladora* program over the course of seven years. But few, if any, of the *maquiladoras* themselves would be forced out of business by the pact. Many *maquila* managers had feared that their reliance on Asian components would disqualify their products for duty-free status under NAFTA. The amounts in question are not small. Roughly 45 percent of all *maquila* inputs have traditionally originated outside the United States and Mexico. In the end, though, negotiators adopted a loose rule of origin, as it is called, for most industries. To qualify for duty-free status, a product that came into North America under one tariff heading had only to be transformed sufficiently within the continent to be classified under a different tariff heading. Even if no tariff classification change occurred, up to 40 percent of the value of a product was allowed to originate outside the North American region without invalidating that product's duty-free status. These rules posed little threat to most *maquiladoras*.

Of greater importance to *maquila* operators were the special restrictions tacked on to a number of the sector's most prominent products: auto parts, televisions, computers, and textiles. As a result of strong lobbying efforts by politically powerful U.S. industries, producers of these goods will either have to meet higher regional content requirements or incorporate specific regionally produced components to gain duty-free status.[246]

Although these special restrictions demonstrate that NAFTA—like all regional free trade agreements—is as much about managing trade as freeing it, they are unlikely to cause many *maquiladoras* to close up shop. Most producers who do not currently meet the regional-content rules will be able to shift sources of supply relatively quickly. After analyzing NAFTA's provisions, one major economics forecasting firm predicted the *maquiladora* industry would grow by an average annual rate of 8.5 percent from 1993 to 1997.[247]

Having paved the way for U.S.-Mexico integration and having set the tone for Mexico's economic development strategy, the labor-intensive assembly plants are here to stay even if the *maquiladora* program is phased out. But the residents of the borderlands are ambivalent about free trade and further economic integration. The prospect of new manufacturing investment, higher levels of trade, and increased cross-border retailing has raised hopes in the region. But the failed promises of the past and the likely costs of economic growth cast some doubt on claims that the benefits of any rise in cross-border trade and investments will be widespread.

# Dual Development: The

# Never-ending Promise

In its early days the Border Industrialization Program was promoted on the U.S. side as the Twin Plant Program. The idea was that for every *maquiladora* on the Mexican side there would be another plant on the U.S. side of the border in charge of supply and final assembly. But this promise was never realized. Companies did open offices and warehouses on the U.S. side, but only rarely were actual manufacturing operations established in the U.S. twin city. Customs regulations requiring that assembled manufactures crossing the border be "finished" in the United States have been largely ignored. As one U.S. customs agent revealed, sticking a "Made in the U.S.A." sticker on the *maquila* products or warehousing them on the U.S. side are often the only "finishing" operations done in the United States.

What has emerged along the U.S. border are service industries to support the Mexican factories with transportation, communications, financing, warehousing, and some intermediate supplies (mainly packaging). The owners of these service and supply industries quickly became the strongest backers of the *maquila*-centered model of economic growth on the U.S. side of the border. Despite the inaccuracy of the term, it is still used by groups like the Twin Plant Wives Association and the *Twin Plant News* to propagate the idea that *maquiladoras* foster substantial economic growth in the U.S. borderlands.

In 1990 the mayor of El Paso proclaimed the city the "*Maquila* Capital of the World," kicking off a week of events promoting the *maquila* industry that was organized by members of the local Twin Plant Wives Association. There are no *maquiladoras* in El Paso and only a few of what could be described as twin plants. Nonetheless, El Paso considers itself the *maquila* capital because Juárez is the twin city with the largest *maquila* workforce.

For most U.S. border towns, the economic development strategies of town leaders have been closely linked to attracting businesses from the Rust Belt to the Sun Belt. The sunnier climate of the borderlands—including the possibility of "playing golf year-round," as most development brochures point out—is always part of the sales pitch. But knowing that corporations do not make siting decisions on the sunshine factor alone, the industrial development organizations get quickly to the main sales pitch: "the abundant labor at low, low cost" of the borderlands.

The border towns are, of course, not the only communities that have based their economic development on the attraction of corporations with guarantees of low wages, no unions, government subsidies, and tax incentives. For the past three decades this type of strategy has been common throughout the South and the Southwest. Seeing their industries run away to the South, towns in the Midwest and Northeast in the 1980s also frantically began to match the kinds of incentives advertised by the southern states while workers offered voluntarily to reduce wages and benefits if companies would stay in town.

What has made the industrial development strategy of the U.S. border communities so distinctive is that they search out companies to move not to their own hometowns but to their twin cities in Mexico. The low wages of El Paso do contrast sharply with industrial wage rates farther north, but the city's economic planners rightly recognize that El Paso's main attraction is its proximity to Mexico. The benefit to El Paso—and other border cities, such as Brownsville, that rely on similar development strategies—is not a large increase in the employment base. Instead the payoff is more service business (banking, warehousing, transportation, etc.) and to a lesser extent the retail trade (as *maquila* workers spend their paychecks) generated by the new *maquiladoras*.

In pursuit of this *maquila*-based development, the El Paso Industrial Development Corporation has sent its representatives out to the Rust Belt in search of runaway industries. While wining and dining prospectives, they try to lure them south with tales of ten-dollar-a-day workers, no unions, and golf in December. For the most part, however, the border cities rely on business-magazine advertising. "We Introduce the Movers to the Shakers" is the come-on used by an advertisement placed by the El Paso Industrial Development Corporation in the *Twin Plant News*. In the early 1990s the group began trying to shake some of the defense industries loose from California and persuade them to move to El Paso or to Juárez, the Mexican city that is already the location of several firms producing for military contracts, including Westinghouse and General Electric.[248]

## Maquiladora Colleges

Joining the city managers and business establishment, the postsecondary institutions of the borderlands are also playing a part in fostering the expansion and development of the *maquila* sector.[249] In the belief that what is good for the *maquila* sector is good for U.S. border communities, area colleges are training both U.S. and Mexican students to meet the employment needs of the *maquilas*. Recognizing the rising demand for high-tech services, some of these institutions also serve the *maquilas* by facilitating the incorporation of high-tech operations into their local assembly process.

Community colleges along the border—from Texas Southmost College in Brownsville to Southwestern Community College in Chula Vista, California—have introduced courses specifically designed to train *maquila* technicians, direct-line supervisors, and managers. An article in *Twin Plant News* aptly called the community colleges along the border the "*Maquiladora* Colleges."[250] At its International Trade Center, Southwestern Community College offers courses that instruct students in the legal aspects and labor-management problems of the *maquila* industry. Texas Southmost College, like many of the region's community colleges, offers courses in customized manufacturing processes tailored to specific plants in Mexico.

The federally supported Advanced Technology Center (ATC) at the El Paso Community College goes a step further, directly contracting with the *maquiladoras* to offer technology transfer and training courses to the management and workforce—all done in Spanish and at the company's plant in Mexico. The ATC's director Mike Roark explained that the center was founded to "meet the expanding *maquila* industry's need for specialized skills" but noted that it provides customized training only for 100 percent U.S.-owned *maquilas*, not for joint ventures with Mexicans or foreign-owned *maquilas*.[251] When ATC promotional brochures state that its mission is to "promote economic development" and respond to the needs of "local industry," by *local* they mean not only El Paso but also Juárez.

Besides offering customized training in plastics injection techniques and other technologies to meet the needs of companies like Delco-Remy, the El Paso Community College also works closely with Mexico's National College of Professional Technical Education (CONALEP) in a plastics injection training project sponsored by the Grupo Bermúdez *maquila* promoters. "We're training them to train their own people," said Roark.[252]

103

Working closely with the Maquila Association in Juárez, CONALEP is expanding its support role to the *maquilas*, including the construction of a new facility built in a Juárez industrial park that will train people in plastics injection molding, computer technology, and other skills needed by the *maquiladoras*.[253] The ATC also trains operators for the sizable plastics injection industry in El Paso, but one wonders how long this and other high-tech service industries will remain on the U.S. side.

This partnership between academia and industry is still more pronounced at the University of Texas. In Brownsville the Pan American campus has a Center for Entrepreneurship and Economic Development, which provides technical assistance to firms starting or expanding *maquila* operations. The University of Texas at El Paso (UTEP) is continuing its long history as an industry school (it was founded in 1914 as the School of Mines and Metallurgy). The difference is that the industry it is now serving is found increasingly in Mexico.

The university is a top player in turning the *maquila* sector into a high-tech industry. With the help of university staff, the *maquiladoras* are incorporating such technologies as robotics, computer vision, and real-time process control into the assembly process. The center of support services for the *maquila* industry at UTEP is the Institute for Manufacturing and Materials Management ($IM^3$), which depends on federal and state funds as well as private contracts. Asked about the propriety of using government and university funds to assist *maquila* production, $IM^3$'s Erin Ross replied, "I feel we are subsidizing the American economy and the American companies, which make American profits and pay American taxes."[254]

Founded by and closely associated with $IM^3$ is the Machine Vision Applications Laboratory (MVAL), which serves such firms as Ford, General Motors, and Honeywell in Juárez to help them apply advanced technologies and techniques to their manufacturing processes. Partnership between academia and business is built into the MVAL. Kenneth Chapman helped establish the machine-vision technology application program, which provides automated quality-control processes, while on leave from Intelledex, a leading machine-vision equipment manufacturing company. At Ford's Coclisa air-conditioning assembly plant, MVAL installed a machine-vision computer system to inspect the quality of the finished parts after they concluded that "operator fatigue" was the main reason for faulty assembly.

Any remaining illusion that the *maquila* sector relies solely on low-technology production is quickly dispelled at such institutions as $IM^3$, ATC, or MVAL, all of which promote the idea that the *maquilas* should use "World-Class Manufacturing" techniques. As MVAL's Chapman advises, "These new technologies such as machine vision and robotics, coupled with quality-control techniques, such as statistical process control (SPC), kan-ban, just-in-time (JIT), and Poke-a-yoke, provide a path for continuous improvement and increased ability to compete effectively."[255] While this may well be true, critics of the economic development strategy embraced by most border cities believe that U.S. citizens are losing out when tax dollars are used to underwrite technology transfer programs that aid such companies as Delco-Remy, Honeywell, and Ford that closed down plants in the United States to open up their Juárez *maquilas*.[256] The promotion of high-tech production in Mexico belies the claims of free marketers that U.S.-Mexico production sharing merely transfers undesirable low-tech operations to a low-wage country. But the real question facing border planners is to what extent industrial development in Mexico—either the low- or high-tech variety—contributes to economic growth and prosperity on the U.S. side.

## The Vision of Dr. Michie

Besides directly serving the *maquila* industry, IM³ is one of the borderlands' leading promoters of the *maquila*-centered strategy of economic development. Donald Michie, often described as IM³'s "mastermind," has probably been the region's leading spokesperson for the concept that the future of the borderlands is linked to *maquila* growth.

Before founding IM³, Michie served on the faculty of UTEP's business school and worked closely with the *maquila* industry and industrial promotional groups to prove that *maquilas* directly benefit U.S. border communities. In the mid-1980s the El Paso Foreign Trade Association, an organization of those servicing and promoting the *maquila* sector, of which Michie was a board member, together with the El Paso Industrial Development Council and Juárez Economic Development commissioned a Project Link study by a researcher at UTEP's business school to demonstrate the links between *maquilas* and job creation in El Paso. The Project Link report concluded that one of every five new jobs in El Paso was linked to *maquila* growth in Juárez between 1976 and 1985.[257]

Although the study has been discredited because of its faulty methodology—not including job losses caused by *maquilas*, for example—Project Link's findings have been widely used by Michie and other *maquila* promoters, such as the Border Trade Alliance, to demonstrate that *maquilas* are good not only for Mexico but also for the U.S. border region.[258] Project Link continued the border tradition of having business-sponsored research support contentions by the *maquila* sector and its U.S. facilitators that *maquilas* boosted the U.S. economy and employment. Much of the early self-promotional research was sponsored by Grupo Bermúdez, the Juárez firm that is the region's largest operator of industrial parks.

In the early 1970s Grupo Bermúdez hired ex–U.S. army officer William Mitchell to search out U.S. corporations and persuade them to move to Mexico. Besides being enormously successful in this effort, Mitchell compiled "economic surveys" that purported to show how many U.S. jobs depended on *maquila* operations. This type of unabashed promotion of the *maquila* sector was continued in the 1980s by UTEP's Michie. Besides his association with Project Link, Michie worked closely with the El Paso Foreign Trade Association and the Border Trade Alliance in producing its *Maquiladora Impact Survey* in 1987. Extrapolating from the survey results, Michie and the Border Trade Alliance have made highly exaggerated claims about the number of companies and jobs the *maquila* industry supports. Like earlier "studies," the survey made no attempt to balance job losses against job creation. Moreover, Michie and the Border Trade Alliance used the survey to show that many companies—and all their employees—have been sustained simply because a *maquila* may have purchased a part or two from them. Michie went so far as to imply that the survey indicated that three million U.S. jobs depended on border maquilas.[259]

The promotional research by UTEP's Michie has continued into the 1990s. As the head of IM[3] Michie remains a chief proponent of border development strategies linked to the production-sharing operations of the *maquila* sector. Heavily backed by government and the private sector, this approach has come to dominate economic development planning in the region. Among the principal functions of IM[3] are community outreach to support development and the supply of borderlands economic data and analysis to the region's association of governors.[260] With the advent of free trade with Mexico and rising government attention to the borderlands, IM[3] has benefited from large infusions of government research and technology transfer grants.

A 1991 report by IM[3] persisted in claims about the "dramatic economic impact" of the *maquila* industry on the El Paso area. Although figures showing the high job creation effect of the *maquilas* are still presented as valid estimations, Michie and IM³ have begun to stress the role of the U.S. borderlands in integrating "higher technology processes into production-sharing industries."

According to IM³, "The ability of materials management to combine technology with a relatively inexpensive labor force lies at the heart of our region's competitive advantage in the global economy." Furthermore, "U.S.-owned companies operating in Mexico play an increasingly important role in maintaining this competitive advantage."[261] IM³ believes that the El Paso area's future development lies in supplying materials, services, and technology to the *maquila* sector. In many ways, this is exactly the same line of reasoning used by the leading promoters of NAFTA and other global trade accords. When assembly operations leave for Mexico or other third world nations, they argue, the U.S. economy benefits not only by keeping its corporations competitive but also by supplying the capital goods and supplies needed by the *maquiladoras*. By virtue of its border location, El Paso stands first in line to provide those services, say groups like IM³: "The U.S.-Mexico border has become the front door, not the back door, to U.S.-Mexico and global commerce."[262]

Although this development strategy has certainly worked for many *maquila* facilitators and such institutions as the Advanced Technology Center and IM³—which have been swimming in government grants and private contracts—its benefits to the entire population have been less clear. The propaganda bandied about by Michie, IM³, and the Border Trade Alliance that the borderlands have benefited from a *maquila*-based development strategy based on the presence of twin plants and *maquila* supply and service firms does not square with the dismal economic state of U.S. border cities. In 1975 El Paso's per capita income was 22 percent below the statewide average for Texas. It then dropped to about 35 percent under the average by 1990 even though the *maquila* sector in Juárez exploded in the 1980s. On the other side of the border the manufacturing sector has boomed, but the sad state of the infrastructure and the desperate living conditions of *maquila* workers challenge claims that *maquila* manufacturing is promoting economic development.

The updated high-skill services vision of border development is also problematic. Like the earlier version, it predicates U.S. border prosperity on the flourishing of low-wage industry in Mexico. But the plan to convert the U.S. borderlands into a center of higher technology and technology transfer may be based on an optimistic view of the globalization process. It is true that there may be an expanded role for a small sector of technology transfer consultants and those U.S. high-tech industries still reluctant for whatever reason to leave U.S. soil. But most firms are finding that there is no need to depend on U.S.-based suppliers of capital goods and high-tech services. As the forces of globalization build momentum, U.S. firms are no longer simply relegating their labor-intensive and low-technology production to Mexico. They are also relocating high-technology and capital goods manufacturing south of the border. Furthermore, the high-tech systems such as plastics injection molding that border cities like El Paso hoped to corner are now slipping over to Mexico-based firms. Indeed, taxpayer-supported centers like ATC and IM$^3$ are among the ones facilitating the technology transfer process.

Promoting economic development in the borderlands is no easy task. Proximity to the abundant, low-wage labor supply in Mexico exerts downward pressure on wage rates on the U.S. side while a steady influx of immigrants keeps unemployment high. Strategies to attract low-wage, low-tech assembly industries to the U.S. borderlands have met with some success, but numerous manufacturers have later decided to move all or part of their operations over to the Mexican side. Since 1986 El Paso has lost at least 2,750 manufacturing jobs as firms such as Farah, Billy the Kid, and Dale Electronics have relocated to Juárez and other Mexican border towns.[263] The city's economic development specialists have lately attempted to promote El Paso as a sourcing center for high-tech supplies and services. Although they have met with some success, particularly in the field of plastics-injection molding, this new twist of the earlier version of *maquila*-tied development has not supplied the quantity and quality of jobs that El Paso needs if it is to lower its unemployment rate and raise wage levels. There is also the latent threat that as the economic infrastructure and skill levels in Juárez and other border cities improve, these high-tech industries may also find it more economical to do business entirely in Mexico.

But officials of El Paso's development agencies are not worried. They feel that as the Mexican economy improves and industrialization expands, the benefits will boomerang back to El Paso in the form of increased retail trade and supply sourcing. But the question about whether the foundation for prosperity in the U.S. borderlands can be constructed from low-wage industrialization in Mexico remains. Border planners are also faced with the challenge of raising educational levels, productivity, and wage rates while lowering unemployment at the same time they offer tax abatements to industry, discourage unionization, and promote the region as a low-cost center.

## Free Trading and Cross Shopping

With the Border Industrialization Program and the rise of the *maquila* economy, the international border became increasingly meaningless as a barrier to U.S. investment and production sharing. But long before the borderlands turned into an export-processing zone for foreign investors, cross-border shopping had made economic integration a daily reality.

In the mid-1800s a boundary line was drawn between the freewheeling capitalism of the U.S. frontier and the highly protectionist and highly taxed Mexican society.[264] Distance and the northern deserts isolated the Mexican interior from the lures and advances of U.S. traders, but the population of *el norte* was more vulnerable. In fact, it had little choice—given the expense, lack of variety, and poor quality of goods shipped from central Mexico—but to do its shopping on the U.S. side. In response to surveys showing that as much as two-thirds of border spending was going to U.S. retailers and wholesalers, in 1971 the federal government introduced the Artículos Ganchos or "hook items" program whereby Mexican consumers could buy certain U.S. manufactured goods from Mexican stores at the same prices available on the U.S. side. The main focus was to boost the sagging sales of Mexican retailers, but like other such free trade initiatives, the program seemed only to spur more smuggling.

Cross-border shopping is the lifeblood of many U.S. border communities.[265] The downtown stores commonly rely on Mexican shoppers for 90 percent of their business, while 25 to 70 percent of the entire retail trade business of the border towns comes from Mexican buyers.[266] Although border merchants have depended on Mexican consumers, they have generally not provided them with any special services. Retailers reach out to Mexicans with electronic and newspaper advertising. Border newspapers, like the *El Paso Times*, have Spanish-language sections aimed at Mexican readers. Consumers from Juárez can be seen carrying the ad-packed *Vecinos (Neighbors)* along on shopping trips to El Paso. Advertising for U.S. brand-name jeans, athletic shoes, and other hot items attracts many Mexican consumers. But advertising hype explains only a small portion of the cross-border retail trade. Because of trade barriers, the lack of domestic production, and the absence of a large concentrated market, many manufactured goods are cheaper in the United States and often of superior quality. In fact, many assume that anything made in the United States is superior to the counterpart Mexican product.

Before the 1976 and 1982 devaluations of the peso, it was commonly estimated that *maquila* employees were spending well over half their disposable income across the border. That percentage declined sharply immediately after the 1982 devaluation, although it later rose as the peso stabilized and inflationary pressures in Mexico intensified. Estimates of what percentage of *maquila* wages is spent in the United States still vary widely, but most agree that *maquila* workers now spend a considerably smaller portion of their wages across the border than they did before 1982. Earning about sixty-five dollars weekly, *maquila* workers live on a tight budget and have little money for cross-border shopping trips. A recent study of Juárez *maquila* line workers found that half spent nothing in El Paso and the rest spent less than ten dollars a week.[267] A similar survey in Nogales reported that *maquila* line workers were spending about a quarter of their wages on the U.S. side, although technicians and managers were spending considerably more.[268]

Most of the direct leakage from the *maquila* sector seems not to be coming from the *maquila* production workers but from salaried professionals whose numbers have been steadily increasing, especially in high-tech sites like Juárez and Mexicali.[269] Generally, Mexican white-collar workers have cars and prefer shopping at the malls, department stores, and flea markets on the U.S. side, while blue-collar workers with little income and no personal transportation do considerably less cross-border shopping.[270] Of the money that *maquila* workers do spend in the United States, more than 70 percent goes to such basic items as clothes and food.[271]

*Maquilas* are only one factor supporting the border retail trade. The U.S. border cities attract consumers from throughout northern Mexico, especially from such large cities as Chihuahua and Monterrey that are within easy driving distance of the border.

As merchants discovered in the 1976 and 1982 peso devaluations, their dependence on these Mexican consumers for such a large portion of their sales implies certain risks, because when the value of the peso drops in relation to the dollar, it means that U.S. goods are suddenly out of reach for most Mexican families. The downtown business districts, which capture most of the pedestrian traffic, are hardest hit, but the effect of a peso devaluation reverberates throughout the entire border economy.

For local government, it means less revenue from bridge and sales taxes. Real estate markets slump, bank deposits drop, and hotel rooms remain empty. Just as poor Mexicans are no longer able to buy their food and clothes on the U.S. side, so wealthy Mexicans can no longer afford a condominium on South Padre Island (offshore of Brownsville). Cities without their own industrial bases, such as Brownsville and Laredo, suffer more than the diversified economies of El Paso and San Diego. Following the 1982 devaluation, employment dropped by 11 percent in Brownsville and by nearly 20 percent in Laredo because of reduced retail trade.[272]

By the mid-1980s the peso had stabilized and U.S. border towns began perking up again. Once again the streets of downtown El Paso and the malls of Laredo were filled with Mexican shoppers. In fact, retail chains such as Sam's reported having a higher retail value of sales per square meter of floor space than stores in much larger cities like New York or Dallas. At one shopping mall in Laredo, sales were double the national average for the twenty other malls owned by the company.[273] By 1990 Mexicans were spending as much money in the United States as they had in the boom year of 1979 before Mexico slid into *la crisis*.[274]

Retail sales picked up in all border towns, but the new boom was probably most evident in Nogales, Arizona. Border fences and customs checks keep Ambos Nogales physically divided, but family and shopping bring the two border communities together socially and economically. Those that do not have the proper permits slip through one of the many person-size holes cut in the border fence. On a typical Saturday morning hundreds of *nogalenses* without border-crossing cards become illegal aliens for a day as they scurry across the boundary to do their weekly shopping at Safeway and the department stores on the U.S. side. The Border Patrol usually does not bother these illegal shoppers, and certainly not when they are making their return trip to Mexico carting bags of U.S. goods.

Downtown Nogales has become a retail battle zone. Local realtors say that retail space on the two blocks of Morley Avenue is more expensive than on Central Avenue in Phoenix. Safeway is doing three times the business it was built to handle, and the Payless shoe store in Nogales outsells all but a few of the three thousand other branch outlets around the nation. As in other border cities, there is a distinct Asian-American flavor to this retail frenzy. Seizing the opportunity, Korean-American and Chinese-American entrepreneurs in the 1980s began opening up stores in the downtown districts of Nogales, El Paso, and other border cities. Lumping all Asians together, Nogales locals call one shopping strip—which hosts Seoul II, Tienda De Lee, and Su's Kitchen—the Ho Chi Minh Trail.[275] Unlike the past, when the typical border merchant gouged Mexican consumers with high prices, the new wave of merchandisers wages war with one another to offer the lowest prices. Not only is the downtown district booming, but the whole town of Nogales is riding the crest of soaring retail and home sales.

Although most border business and government officials lined up behind NAFTA, the merchandising sector regards free trade with some trepidation. Even before the signing of the accord, retailing giants such as Price Club and Wal-Mart began moving across the border. As Mexico's program of trade and investment liberalization advances, U.S. wholesalers have begun to sell directly to large Mexican department stores such as Aurrera and Gigante while the larger U.S. retailing chains are deciding to open their own stores in Mexico. As more and more U.S. goods are available in stores on their own side, fewer Mexican consumers will see the need to cross the line to do their shopping. Mexicans will still be buying U.S. goods—and probably more of them—but their money will not be entering the economies of the border towns.

In anticipation of free trade, some border retailers are planning to relocate to Mexico while others will probably shut down. Overall the drop in border retail trade may be as high as 50 percent. The other great fear is that in the event of another large peso devaluation Mexican consumers would once again stay at home and set off another wave of bankruptcies and layoffs across the U.S. borderlands. However, with the increase of U.S. goods moving into Mexico, well-positioned border businesses may find themselves ideally situated to act as distributors for merchandise headed south.

Transboundary retail trade is not a one-way street. Although lopsided, this business also benefits the Mexican side, mostly through tourism. This has been especially true for the so-called Gold Coast strip between Tijuana and Ensenada, which has become a prime vacation and retirement destination for Californians. To boost this tourism trade, the Baja California state government is promoting a quality rating system for the hotels and restaurants located on this strip. Increased cross-border trade has translated into boom times for the red-light district in Nuevo Laredo, known alternately as Boys' Town or the Zona de Tolerancia, where some three thousand prostitutes serve mainly U.S. clients.[276]

U.S. residents also go to Mexico border towns for their health. Crossing the border bridges into Mexico, one sees publicity for the ophthalmologists, dentists, and plastic surgeons who have set up offices along the border to serve U.S. consumers. Whether you want a nose job, a new pair of eyeglasses, or a root canal operation, it is cheaper in Mexico. Although the quality of these services might not be as high as in the United States, most clients agree that it is steadily improving. For many the less expensive health and dental services in Mexico offer a way to beat the prohibitive costs of the same care in the United States. Many also travel to Mexico to get medication restricted or prohibited north of the border. Pharmacists commonly sell over the counter drugs and medicine that are available only with a doctor's prescription in the United States. Even when pharmacies do require prescriptions for antibiotics and other drugs, many doctors will gladly write desired prescriptions for a small fee. Although this can benefit border residents who cannot afford a visit to a doctor's office in the United States, self-medication on both sides of the border commonly results in drug-related illnesses and medical problems.[277]

Throughout the borderlands the benefits of free trade are obvious. For the region's residents, customs duties and prohibitions make little sense and serve only as annoying obstacles to the free flow of trade and services. Economic integration is not a plan or a prospect; it is a foundation of border life. At the same time, however, there also exists a deep sense of caution about plans to broaden the economic relations between the two countries. In Mexico entrepreneurs worry about the invasion of U.S. retailers and U.S. merchandise. Others agree that more jobs may be coming, but they are concerned about the environmental impact of more U.S. investment. In the United States there is also deepening apprehension about the likely environmental repercussions of increased trade and investment, and many fear that open economic borders will facilitate narcotrafficking and quicken the pace of illegal immigration. On both sides the most immediate concern, however, seems to be that the border cities do not have the social and economic infrastructure to handle increased growth.

## Everybody's Talking Infrastructure

City officials, *colonia* activists, *maquila* promoters, and just about everybody else along the border have infrastructure on their minds. Aside from free trade, *infrastructure* is the term probably most commonly used by those discussing public policy and economic development in the border region. Long before presidential candidate Clinton raised the issue of insufficient public-sector investment in infrastructure, borderlanders had recognized that the lack of adequate social and economic infrastructure lay at the heart of their region's development problems.

On both sides of the border, local governments have found themselves unable to respond adequately to the infrastructure shortfalls created by rapid population and industrial growth in the 1970s and 1980s. Throughout the region there is widespread agreement that the border zone is sadly lacking the underlying foundation of social and economic facilities (adequate housing, roads, bridges, wastewater treatment plants, etc.) necessary for continued growth.[278] In public forums, industrial development promoters now echo the calls by environmentalists for better sewage systems, and factory owners nod their heads approvingly when *colonia* residents demand that governments provide improved housing, water facilities, and transportation. Few disagree that a tremendous infrastructure gap faces the region, and most concur that without immediate remedies this critical situation only stands to worsen in the near future, threatening not only the health and welfare of the region's inhabitants but also the ability of corporations to do business profitably.

The infrastructure crisis on the border points to the failure of the kind of economic policies that have guided development on both sides of the border. According to free traders and *maquila* proponents, economic growth should provide the revenues to cover the infrastructure costs of this development. At least on the border this has not occurred. Trade and investment have boomed, but the host communities are suffering from severe infrastructure deficiencies because governments have not used tax and regulatory powers to direct some of the region's profits back into community development.

Further complicating the infrastructure crisis is the confusion about who is responsible for solving the problems. In the United States, border communities that have long promoted *maquila*-style development and their advantages as gateways to Mexico charge that it is largely a federal issue. For its part the federal government has been willing to assume a certain level of responsibility for border infrastructure, although far below what is needed and what local communities demand. Washington has been still more reluctant to consider the desperate socioeconomic conditions that characterize much of U.S. borderlands as primarily a federal responsibility.

During the 1980s rapid *maquila* expansion strained the physical infrastructure of border communities. Increased truck traffic, cross-border communications, and daily border crossings underlined the need for more international bridges, customs facilities, and roads.[279] All along the border citizens and businesspeople began griping about backed-up lines at the border, inadequate customs staffing, downtown streets clogged with trucks, and deteriorating connecting roads and bridges. Laredo already prides itself as the country's largest inland port of entry, with fourteen hundred eighteen-wheelers rumbling through its city streets each day. On the downside, though, inhabitants of this Texas border town tell stories about being caught in their cars for hours behind long lines of trucks waiting to enter customs. For northbound traffic at major border cities, waits of an hour to cross through U.S. customs are common.

But that frustration is now often mixed with an excitement about the prospects of free trade. Despite infrastructure nightmares, support for more liberalized trading relations along the border is widespread. Expanded binational trade and investment are predicted to bring more money and jobs for the border communities—a prospect that many along the border find exhilarating.

Free trade also means more competition among the U.S. border cities as they jockey for the lead in the race to attract new cross-border business and trade. San Diego is planning a new binational airport, Brownsville is expanding port facilities and bridges, Laredo is expanding its airport, and McAllen is opening a third international bridge. On the south side of the border, highway upgrades are the priority, including a new toll superhighway connecting the border and the industrial center of Monterrey. Just as the major cities of the border states, such as Monterrey, Chihuahua, and Hermosillo, expect to benefit from expanded binational trade, so, too, do the principal cities of the U.S. Sun Belt. Although they do not sit directly on the border, such cities as San Antonio, Houston, Dallas, Los Angeles, and San Diego are vying to become the distribution, communications, and financial capitals of the new trading bloc. All this means that adequate connecting highways, telecommunications networks, international airports, and border crossings must be in place.

Recognizing their new identities as key players in expanding regional trade, border towns are also demanding that their respective state and federal governments respond to the urgent need for expanded sewerage and waste treatment facilities. In the heat of free trade talks, both Washington and Mexico have promised to finance public sanitation infrastructure as part of their mutual commitment to improve border conditions.[280] The concerns expressed by local governments and environmental activists about the public health crisis along the border have spurred the *maquila* industry and groups like the Border Trade Alliance to join the chorus calling for new wastewater treatment facilities and sewage systems.

Both government and business duly recognize that the crisis arises from the lack of both economic and social infrastructure. Yet the urgent need to upgrade housing, schools, neighborhood water systems, community services, and public health care has generally not received the same level of attention as other infrastructure projects.[281] Carlos Villarreal, Laredo's director of community planning, complained, "There are so many needs here—for housing, development, streets, basic services—and what does Washington build for us? An inspection station. They think of the border only in one way, when they think of it at all."[282]

All agree that more infrastructure is urgently needed along the long-neglected border. But what are the priorities—social or economic projects? And who is going to pay—business or citizens, Mexico or the United States, local or federal governments? Also to consider is the fact that the drive to improve the region's roads, bridges, and public utilities might further whittle away at the fragile resource base of the borderlands. Some large infrastructure projects, especially wastewater treatment plants and sewage systems, will help the border environment and improve border health, but more border crossings, more border bridges, and more and wider roads will impact negatively by increasing the traffic flow through the borderlands. In addressing such matters, the borderlands population will be tackling some of the tougher issues facing both nations in regard to the costs and benefits of closer economic ties.

In all areas of infrastructure, rhetoric and promises have far outstripped real financial commitments. This has been especially true on the U.S. side, where initial promises by the federal government in 1991 to fund $379 million over two years in environmental infrastructure projects turned out to be simply the repackaging of already existing projects.[283] At the same time the Mexican government committed $460 million for environmental and community infrastructure projects over a three-year span. The needs far outstrip promised revenues. The International Boundary and Water Commission (IBWC) estimated that wastewater collection and treatment alone will require an investment of nearly $3 billion through 2005. The Border Trade Alliance estimated that nearly $6 billion is needed to pay for all the infrastructure needs in the U.S. borderlands, while a study by the Northern Border College (COLEF) in Mexico estimated that a $15 billion deficit in needed infrastructure investment had developed in the 1980s.[284] But nobody is saying where all this money will come from.

Yet another concern is that the infrastructure projects being planned are catch-up projects to satisfy existing needs rather than forward-looking planning that anticipates future growth. Although reluctant to criticize free trade, many community planners and health officials along the border are concerned about the dimensions of the region's expanding infrastructure crisis. Considering that infrastructure financing is already failing to keep pace with present needs, they ask just how bad the infrastructure crunch will be if free trade delivers the promised boost in cross-border trade.

Local governments on either side of the border look primarily to the respective federal governments to solve their infrastructure problems. Secondarily they charge the state governments with this responsibility. Both U.S. and Mexican border communities argue that most of their problems are not local but international in origin. Why, they ask, should the burden of facilitating cross-border business fall disproportionately on them?

On the U.S. side, border communities are already experiencing budget woes even before undertaking new infrastructure projects. Being poor, the border towns do not have the tax base to pay for both social and economic infrastructure improvements. The border states, particularly Texas and California, are among the largest exporters to Mexico, but the income generated by these sales flows mostly to bigger, nonborder cities such as Los Angeles, San Antonio, and Houston. Furthermore, the steady flow of Mexicans crossing into their towns severely impacts the local educational, health, and police systems. Given the badly deteriorated condition of local health and education systems, many border residents, including government bureaucrats in charge of social services, are angry that economic infrastructure projects are being given top priority by the local, state, and federal governments.

The financial shortfall is still more pronounced on the Mexican side, where border towns rely almost exclusively on federal revenues. In the past, through programs such as PRONAF, the Mexican government has attempted to direct more revenues to the border region to attract tourism, retain a larger portion of transboundary retail trade, and keep the *maquila* sector content by supplying it with water, electricity, transportation, and other infrastructure needs. Low-cost public utilities, especially electricity, have constituted a de facto government subsidy of industrial development, especially before the public utility price hikes in recent years.

In Mexico the creation of infrastructure is entirely dependent on the federal government since every major tax and spending program—with the exception of property taxes—is channeled through Mexico City. The federal government collects sales, income, and corporate taxes but returns only about 20 percent of the federal budget to the states. The states, in turn, depend on federal revenues for about 80 percent of their annual budgets, with less than one-fourth of these budgets being distributed to the municipalities.[285] The problem here is twofold: the absence of an adequate tax structure in Mexico and the centralism that makes local governments politically and economically dependent on Mexico City. The governor of Baja California, Ernesto Ruffo, complained, "Look, for

117

every $1.00 in tax revenues that the state sends to Mexico City, we get only 30 cents in return to pay for all public services and infrastructure. It's not fair."[286]

Even if the northern border cities do attempt to plan their communities to ensure that the proper social and economic infrastructure is in place, they have no control over the allocation of funds to finance their projects. As a result, city planning is virtually nonexistent. Tax revenues from border economic activity do flow to Mexico City, but only a small portion of these funds are returned to the border. Yet even if all the revenues were returned, they would still be far less than needed to meet the needs of these booming border towns.

Mexico's public-sector investment has dropped sharply since the 1982 debt crisis, decreasing from about 13 percent of the GDP in 1981 to just 4 percent in 1991. The rapid population and job growth of the borderlands is making the infrastructure gap particularly acute in this region. According to one estimate, infrastructure investment in the northern states is lagging behind job growth by ten years.[287] Despite promises to improve the border infrastructure, Mexico's financial ability to undertake massive new public-sector investment is highly questionable.

The northern border cities are facing the consequences of more than a quarter century of *maquila*-based growth. Neither the infrastructure directly used by the *maquilas* (roads, industrial parks, and public utilities) nor the infrastructure needed by the half-million-member *maquila* workforce (housing, transportation, public utilities, and social services) is paid for by the skimpy tax revenues created by the industry.

For the Mexican government, the in-bond program means forfeiting customs revenue. It also means giving up most tax revenue; because the *maquiladoras* are set up to earn little or no profit, there is nothing to tax. (Workers' earnings also suffer, since the lack of profit renders meaningless the legal requirement that employers distribute 10 percent of their profits to employees.) Virtually all *maquiladoras* conduct their in-bond trade among affiliates of the same corporation. The firm has great leeway in setting the prices it likes on the export and import of parts and materials from one affiliate to another, and generally elects to balance them. In this case the in-bond plant's only net revenue on the exchange is the value of the labor employed in Mexico and some overhead expenses. Since this revenue is just enough to cover wages, benefits, and items such as utility costs, the *maquiladora* shows zero net earnings. The only government income, then, comes from payroll taxes and purchases of electricity, water, waste disposal, and other such services.[288]

To redress this problem partially, the Mexican government imposes a 2 percent Company Asset Tax on foreign-owned and domestic business assets—whether a firm shows net income or not. But the *maquiladoras* and their lobbyists in Mexico City have succeeded in gaining year-to-year exemptions from this tax since it took effect. The government has also tried to tax foreign citizens working temporarily in Mexico, with an eye on the U.S. engineers and managers who commute or travel occasionally to work in the *maquiladora* industry. In late 1991 the legislature passed a law taxing nonresident workers on the income they earn from work in Mexico. Again, heavy pressure from the industry forced the government to back off and severely weaken the new tax.[289]

A 1990 study of eighty *maquilas* in Nuevo Laredo found that together these companies paid only $279,000 in payroll taxes that year—hardly enough to pay for the social services needed by their workers let alone sufficient to cover the costs of infrastructure construction. The industry, however, is quick to complain that the 5 percent payroll tax it pays to subsidize government housing programs has generally not come back to the border.[290] "Tithing to INFONAVIT [the federal housing agency] is like dumping money down a rat hole," complained one *maquila* manager.[291] Under NAFTA even the import duties that the *maquilas* pay will be eliminated.

Business groups like the Border Trade Alliance and the various *maquila* associations readily acknowledge that weak border infrastructure acts as a constraint on further growth. Infrastructure deficits increase the cost and risk of doing business. Rising public concern about the environmental repercussions of the *maquiladoras* has pushed the industry to improve its own environmental controls while leading to discussions about establishing privately financed infrastructure to supply services and treat *maquila* wastes. Responding to social infrastructure problems faced by their workers, some companies sponsor company housing, child care centers, medical services, and busing. Although generally appreciated by the workers, such initiatives are undertaken less in the spirit of charity than in the hope that they will reduce employee absenteeism and improve job performance.

For both ideological and financial reasons the Mexican government has encouraged the private sector to get into the business of infrastructure projects that would otherwise be the responsibility of the state. For example, the government has given concessions to the private sector for the building and management of new toll highways throughout the country. The U.S. government is also inviting the private sector to play a more prominent role in planning and providing infrastructure.[292]

At a binational conference on the border environment sponsored by the U.S. Environmental Protection Agency and Mexico's SEDESOL in June 1992, *maquila* representatives spoke about the possibility of directly financing new utility districts in Mexico. A spokesman for General Electric told the conference that his company was pitching in by providing computers, phones, and other office equipment for SEDESOL. Some industry promoters are also advancing the idea of having the industrial parks and *maquiladoras* establish housing for the workers alongside the assembly plants.[293] Inter-American Holdings is pushing forward a plan to create a private binational association that would plan, develop, and manage a new border crossing and twin city a short distance from Mexicali/Calexico.

Although appealing to financially strapped local governments, the concept of having the private sector, particularly the foreign-owned *maquila* industry, private infrastructure is a dangerous one on either side of the border. These plans would reinforce the enclave nature of the *maquila* industry while raising new questions about the role of government, national sovereignty, and the dominant role of business. They would also raise questions about the wisdom of creating "company towns" and the responsibility for upkeep and repair of facilities should the business benefactors decide to close up shop or withdraw support for infrastructure improvements. Privately financed and managed infrastructure, especially in the face of municipalities with little financial clout, runs the risk of handing de facto planning power over to business. Gabriel Székely, a Mexican scholar at the Center for U.S.-Mexican Studies, has warned that private-sector initiatives may be particularly counterproductive: "In the long term, these are not in the public interest. They are not building this infrastructure in an orderly fashion."[294]

Certainly government needs to bring the private sector into the planning process, and there is no question that business should be paying its fair share for infrastructure improvements. But the private sector cannot be considered the solution to the major infrastructure problems that face the border. Better local and transboundary planning by governments is necessary. Border communities, especially in Mexico, need increased fiscal authority to collect revenues to cover planning and construction costs. On both sides the national governments must recognize that the border infrastructure crisis is as much an international problem as a local one.

In line with the "polluter pays" principle, some members of the U.S. Congress and a number of environmental organizations have suggested that a targeted cross-border tax be imposed on *maquila* operations to help pay for the cost of border infrastructure or to help Mexico create a better environmental control infrastructure. Others have proposed taxes on all those who profit from free trade to consign a portion of their earnings to cover public health and environmental programs. But free traders have generally criticized such proposals on the ideological grounds that such taxes run counter to the concept of free trade. That may be. But one way or the other, money will have to be found to pay for the social and economic infrastructure needed to ensure that communities teetering on the fulcrum of cross-border business are not its first victims.

# Notes

1. For an extensive history of the border, see Leon C. Metz, *Border: The U.S.-Mexico Line* (El Paso: Mangan Books, 1989). Also see Oscar J. Martínez, *Troublesome Border* (Tucson: University of Arizona Press, 1988).
2. This was the Chamizal dispute, which began in the 1850s and 1860s, when a series of floods and torrential rainfalls caused the channel of the Rio Grande to move south. Assuming that the border had also moved south, the United States assumed jurisdiction of the tract of land. It was not until 1963 that the dispute was finally settled when a concrete channel for the Rio Grande was constructed through El Paso-Juárez and 630 acres were returned to Mexico and another 193 acres came into U.S. possession. Although the settlement was amicable, it came only after a century of binational tensions over the Chamizal tract.
3. There are several human interest books about the borderlands society that describe the cross-border life in all or most of these twin cities, the best of which is Alan Weisman, *La Frontera: The United States Border with Mexico* (San Diego: Harcourt Brace Jovanovich, 1986).
4. In Baja California, all of which is a free trade zone, there are no customs checks for ground traffic. These border *municipios* are, from east to west, Matamoros, Río Bravo, Reynosa, G. Díaz Ordaz, Camargo, Miguel Alemán, Miér, Guerrero, Nuevo Laredo, Anáhuac, Hidalgo, Guerrero, Piedras Negras, Jiménez, Ciudad Acuña, Ocampo, Ojinaga, P. G. Guerrero, Guadalupe Bravo, Juárez, Ascensión, Janos, Agua Prieta, Naco, Cananea, Santa Cruz, Nogales, Saríc, Altar, Caborca, Puerto Peñasco, San Luis R.C., Mexicali, Tecate, and Tijuana. Because of the close interaction between these *municipios* with the border economy and society, the Northern Border Development Program in 1985 also included the *municipios* of Ensenada (Baja California), Manuel Benavides (Chihuahua), and Valle Hermoso (Tamaulipas), which do not actually touch the border.
5. Some argue, however, that Nuevo León is not really a border state since it only touches the border for several miles and only 1 percent of its population is found near the border. This compares to 85 percent for Baja California, 42 percent for Tamaulipas, and 31 percent for Chihuahua.
6. From east to west these are Cameron, Hidalgo, Starr, Zapata, Webb, Dimmit, Maverick, Kinney, Val Verde, Terrel, Brewster, Presidio, Jeff Davis, Culberson, Hudspeth, El Paso, Doña Ana, Luna, Hidalgo, Cochise, Santa Cruz, Pima, Yuma, Imperial, and San Diego.

7. Jorge Bustamante, "A Conceptual and Operative Vision of the Population Problems on the Border," *Demographic Dynamics of the U.S.-Mexico Border*, (El Paso: Texas Western Press, 1992), v.

8. Rene M. Zenteno Quintero and Rodolfo Cruz Piñero, "A Geodemographic Definition of the Mexican Northern Border," Ibid., 19.

9. Ideas of a changing cultural landscape along the border drawn from a talk delivered by Lawrence Herzog at the University of New Mexico's Latin American Institute, 1 October 1992.

10. Lawrence A. Herzog, "Transboundary Ecosystem Management in the San Diego–Tijuana Region," in Oscar J. Martínez, ed., *Across Boundaries: Transborder Interaction in Comparative Perspective* (El Paso: Texas Western Press, 1986), 97–115.

11. Lawrence A. Herzog, *Where North Meets South: Cities, Space, and Politics on the United States–Mexico Border* (Austin: University of Texas Press, 1990).

12. These are Tijuana, Baja California/San Ysidro–San Diego; Mexicali, Baja California/Calexico, California; San Luis Rio Colorado, Sonora/Yuma, Arizona; Nogales, Sonora/Nogales, Arizona; Agua Prieta, Sonora/Douglas, Arizona; Naco, Sonora/Naco, Arizona; Las Palomas, Chihuahua/Columbus, New Mexico; Ciudad Juárez, Chihuahua/El Paso, Texas; Ojinaga, Chihuahua/Presidio, Texas; Ciudad Acuña, Coahuila/Del Rio, Texas; Piedras Negras, Coahuila/Eagle Pass, Texas; Nuevo Laredo, Tamaulipas/Laredo, Texas; Reynosa, Tamaulipas/McAllen, Texas; and Matamoros, Tamaulipas/Brownsville, Texas. Six main twin cities account for 96 percent of the urban population on the U.S. side and 84 percent on the Mexican side. These are Brownsville/Matamoros, McAllen/Reynosa, Laredo/Nuevo Laredo, El Paso/Ciudad Juárez, Mexicali/Calexico, and San Diego/Tijuana.

13. Weeks and Ham-Chande, *Demographic Dynamics*, 19.

14. This concept of the changing function of the border is drawn from the works of Lawrence A. Herzog, especially Lawrence A. Herzog, ed., *Changing Boundaries in the Americas: New Perspectives on the U.S.-Mexican, Central American, and South American Borders* (San Diego: Center for U.S.-Mexican Studies, 1992), 3–12.

15. The poverty line is defined as a "minimum needs threshold" of $13,359 per year for a family of four in 1990.

16. According to Harry King of the University of Texas at El Paso, cited in *The San Diego Tribune*, 7 October 1991.

17. Hispanic Policy Development Project, Inc., *A More Perfect Union: Achieving Hispanic Parity by the Year 2000, A Report from the 1989 and 1990 Aspen Institute Conferences* (Aspen, CO: Aspen Institute, 1991).

18. Mercedes Pedrero Nieto, "The Economically Active Population in the Northern Region of Mexico," in Weeks and Ham-Chande, *Demographic Dynamics*, 214.

19. James Pick and Edgar Butler, "Socioeconomic Inequality in the U.S./Mexico Borderlands: Modernization and Buffering," *Frontera Norte* 2, no. 3 (January–June 1990).

20. Linda S. Peterson and Eduardo E. Arriaga, "Comparative Sociodemographic Indicators at the U.S.-Mexico Border," in Weeks and Ham-Chande, *Demographic Dynamics*, 69.

21. Leopoldo Núñez Fernández, "Estimates of Infant Mortality for the Northern Border of Mexico," ibid., 152.

22. Minimum wage is set by the federal government to match the cost of living in different regions. The minimum wage along the border is the same as in Mexico City.

23. "Cheap Labor Festers in Mexico's Hong Kong," *Arizona Republic*, 16 April 1989.

24. *Rural Development: Problems and Progress of Colonia Subdivisions near the Mexican Border* (Washington: General Accounting Office, November 1990).

25. Jane Grandolfo, "Border Crisis: Prosperity Plan a Bust in Poverty-Ridden Juárez," *The Houston Post*, 2 July 1989.

26. For a good description of northern Mexico's history, see Martínez, *Troublesome Border*, 106–23.

27. Interview with Víctor Clark Alfaro, 24 April 1991. For more information on this "economy of discards" that exists in the northern borderlands, see Joan Anderson and Martin de la Rosa, "Economic Strategies of Poor Families on the Mexican Border," *Journal of Borderlands Studies* 6, no. 1 (Spring 1991).

28. Carlos Monsiváis, "Los Angeles: Heart of the Mexican Dream," *New Perspectives Quarterly* (Winter 1991).

29. The number of Latinos is probably underestimated given the low counts of undocumented residents and those Latinos living in major urban areas.

30. Statistical information from Jeffrey S. Passel, "Demographic Profile," *Report on the Americas* 26, no. 2 (September 1992).

31. Figures from U.S. Bureau of the Census, as cited in Marta Lopez-Garza, "Los Angeles: Ascendant Chicano Power," *Report on the Americas*, Sept. 1992, 34.

32. Cited in David Rieff, *Los Angeles: Capital of the Third World* (New York: Simon and Schuster, 1991), 155.

33. For a provocative discussion of the impact of the Voting Rights Act on Latino politics, see: Peter Skerry, *Mexican Americans: The Ambivalent Minority* (New York: The Free Press, 1993).

34. Raúl Hinojosa-Ojeda, Sherman Robinson, and Goetz Wolff, *The Impact of a North American Free Trade Agreement on California: A Summary of Key Research Findings* (Los Angeles: UCLA Lewis Center for Regional Policy Studies, September 1992), 5.

35. Workforce figures from Saskia Sassen, "Why Immigration?," *Report on the Americas* 26, no. 1 (July 1992), 19.

36. For a provocative discussion of standardized terminology, see Martha E. Gimenez, "Latino/Hispanic—Who Needs a Name? The Case Against a Standardized Terminology," *International Journal of Health Services* 19, no. 3 (1989). She argues that the Hispanic label imputes to Latin Americans a contrived Hispanic ethnicity while classifying as minorities many people who historically have never been oppressed as such in the United States. Instead she advocates the broader use of theoretical and descriptive categories of analysis related to social class, minority groups, national origin, and socioeconomic status.

37. U.S. Department of Commerce, Census Bureau, Ethnic and Hispanic Branch, 1990 Census Special Tabulations. The corresponding figures for the two other border states were 57 percent in New Mexico and 17 percent in Arizona. In New Mexico the relatively low Mexico-origin figure is accounted for by the high percentage in the category of "other Hispanic origin."

38. According to U.S. Decennial Census 1990, the top states by Latino percentage of state population and percentage of U.S. Latinos (respectively) are as follows: California, 25.8, 24.4; Texas, 25.5, 19.4; New York, 12.3, 9.9; Florida, 12.2, 7.0; Illinois, 7.9, 4.0; New Jersey, 9.6, 3.3; Arizona, 18.8, 3.1; New Mexico, 38.2, 2.6; Colorado, 12.9, 1.9.

39. David Hayes-Bautista, Werner Schink, and Jorge Chapa, "The Young Latino Population in an Aging American Society," in *U.S.-Mexican Relations: Labor Market Interdependence*, eds. Jorge Bustamante, Clark Reynolds, and Raúl Hinojosa (Stanford: Stanford University Press, 1992), 27.

40. Martínez, *Troublesome Border*, 95.

41. Ibid., 95–96.

42. One explanation of the term *Chicano* is that it comes from *mechicano*, the Nahuatl (or Aztec) pronunciation of the Spanish word describing people living in Mexico. F. Chris Garcia and Rudolph O. de la Garza, *The Chicano Political Experience: Three Perspectives* (North Scituate, MA: Duxbury Press, 1977), 14–16.

43. Martínez, *Troublesome Border*, 96.

44. Aztlán was the legendary place of origin of the Aztecs, the site of seven caves where the Aztec Empire was born.

45. Vasconcelos, who served as the rector of the national university and as one of revolutionary Mexico's first education ministers, popularized this concept in his book *La Tesis de la Raza Cósmica*. He wrote that "we will succeed in the Americas [not including in his concept the United States or Canada], before anywhere else in the globe has come near, in creating a new race, fashioned out of the treasures of all the other races: The final race, the cosmic race."

46. U.S. Census Bureau, *The Hispanic Population of the United States*, March 1990; *Current Population Reports*, no. 449 (March 1991), table 4.

47. Hispanic Policy Development Project, *A More Perfect Union*.

48. Hinojosa-Ojeda et al., *Impact of a North American Free Trade Agreement*. Also affected by international immigration, global restructuring, and free trade are African Americans, who have seen manufacturing jobs leave their cities and the low-wage job market cornered by immigrants. An alarmist but nonetheless important view of immigration's impact on Los Angeles blacks is Jack Miles, "Blacks vs. Browns," *Atlantic Monthly* (October 1992). "The almost total absence of black gardeners, busboys, chambermaids, nannies, janitors, and construction workers in a city with a notoriously large pool of unemployed, unskilled black people leaps to the eye," writes Miles.

49. Quoted in Diana Solis, "Trade Pact Puts Mexican Americans in a Dilemma over Jobs in Border Area," *The Wall Street Journal*, 7 August 1992.

50. Bureau of the Census, *Voting and Registration in the Election of November 1992* (Washington: 1993).

51. More than 90 percent of Latino elected officials are Democratic, but the Republican Party has since the 1980 election made strong inroads into the Latino community. Forty-four percent of Latino voters supported Ronald Reagan in 1984 and 35 percent supported George Bush in 1988.

52. Annette Fuente, "New York: Elusive Unity in La Gran Manzana," *Report on the Americas* 26, no. 2 (Sept. 1992), 27–33.

53. On the differences within the Latino community see Earl Shorris, "Latinos: The

Complexity of Identity," *Report on the Americas* 26, no. 2 (September 1992), 19–26.

54. De la Garza et al., *Latino Voices*, 14. The authors suggest that a common Hispanic political agenda could perhaps be developed around a liberal domestic agenda since most survey respondents did indicate support for increased government involvement in solving social problems.

55. Many of these arguments were presented in Governor Richard D. Lamm and Gary Imoff, *The Immigration Time Bomb: The Fragmenting of America* (New York: E. P. Dutton, 1985). The main national conservative immigration-reform organization is the Federation for American Immigration Reform (FAIR).

56. See George J. Borjas, *Friends or Strangers: The Impact of Immigrants on the U.S. Economy* (New York: Basic Books, 1990) and Julian L. Simon, *The Economic Consequences of Immigration* (Cambridge, Mass.: Basil Blackwell, 1989).

57. See Jeffrey S. Passel, "Undocumented Migration," *Annals of the American Academy of Political Social Science*, no. 487 (Sept. 1986), 181–200, and Gregory de Freitas, "The Effects of Recent Immigrants on American Workers," *Migration World* 16, no. 1 (1986), 7–15.

58. Whether undocumented immigrants use more in public services than they contribute in taxes is an extremely difficult question to answer. Local, state, and federal services and tax revenues are variously affected, and data collection is hampered by the informal nature of many jobs held by undocumented workers. One estimate that argues that the overall economic benefit of undocumented workers "probably outweigh[s] the economic costs of fiscal deficits" is given by Thomas J. Espenshade and Tracy Ann Goodis, *Economic Consequences of Immigration*, testimony presented to the Subcommittee on Economic Resources, Competitiveness, and Security Economics of the Joint Economic Committee (22 May 1986). For a case study of the perception of crime caused by undocumented immigrants, see Daniel Wolf, *Undocumented Aliens and Crime: The Case of San Diego County* (San Diego: Center for U.S.-Mexican Studies, 1988).

59. One of the best overviews of the place of Mexican immigrant workers in U.S. society and economy is James Cockcroft, *Outlaws in the Promised Land: Mexican Immigrant Workers and America's Future* (New York: Grove Press, 1986).

60. Deportation campaigns occurred in the early 1920s, the early 1930s, the mid-1950s, and the mid-1970s. The most important immigration reforms have been:
   • The 1924 Immigration Act, establishing an immigration quota system based on nationality, but exempting Western Hemisphere countries, including Mexico. It required all immigrants to have valid visas, placing the first legal restriction on casual migration from Mexico to the United States. The act also established the U.S. Border Patrol.
   • The 1942 bracero program, providing U.S. employers with legally contracted Mexican workers.
   • The cancellation of the bracero program in 1964.
   • The Immigration and Nationality Act amendments of 1965, which established a quota for immigration from Western Hemisphere countries. Immediate relatives of U.S. citizens—spouses, unmarried children under twenty-one years of age, and parents of adult citizens—and certain skilled workers

were exempted from the quotas. The amendments also required the U.S. secretary of labor to find that a prospective immigrant would not adversely affect the jobs of U.S. workers before a visa could be issued.
- The 1976 establishment of a quota of 20,000 visas for Mexican immigrants. The exemptions established in 1965 continued to apply.
- The 1986 Immigration Reform and Control Act (IRCA), establishing sanctions for employers of undocumented foreigners and providing legal status for foreigners residing in the United States continuously since January 1982. Also provided legal status to agricultural workers who had worked a minimum number of days in the previous three years.
- The Immigration Act of 1990, which expanded the quota for total legal immigration from 270,000 per year to 340,000 per year. "Independent" visas—those granted for job-related or investment reasons—were separated from "family preference" visas so that applicants in the two categories would not compete with each other. Nearly all the quota increase was allocated to independent visas, but within the family preference category, the quota for immediate relatives of permanent residents was doubled. This change was a direct response to the increased numbers of legal permanent residents resulting from IRCA's legalization provisions. Immediate relatives of U.S. citizens continued to be exempted from any quota.

61. The classic account of the Mexican experience in the United States during this period is Carey McWilliams, *North from Mexico* (New York: Greenwood Press, 1968).

62. This point is explored in detail in Cockcroft, *Outlaws in the Promised Land.*

63. From 1948 to 1951 no formal agreement was in effect, but the program continued on an informal basis with employers directly recruiting workers. In 1951 Congress enacted PL-78, which eliminated the Mexican government's role and downgraded that of the U.S. government from labor contractor to program regulator.

64. U.S. Immigration and Naturalization Service, *Statistical Yearbook of the Immigration and Naturalization Service, 1990* (Washington, D.C.: Government Printing Office, 1991).

65. The changing composition of Mexican immigrant workers is described in Wayne A. Cornelius, "Los migrantes de la crisis: el nuevo perfil de la migración de mano de obra mexicana a California en los años ochenta," in *Población y trabajo en contextos regionales,* ed. Gail Mummert (Zamora, Michoacán: El Colegio de Michoacán, 1990).

66. Fernando Lozano Ascencio, *Bringing It Back Home: Remittances to Mexico from Migrant Workers in the United States* (San Diego: Center for U.S.-Mexican Studies, forthcoming).

67. A great number of studies on this topic have been carried out. The conclusions of nineteen such studies are summarized in Jorge Durand and Douglas S. Massey, "Mexican Migration to the United States," *Latin American Research Review* 27, no. 2 (1992). Durand and Massey note that a minority of studies have found significant productive investment resulting from remittances. The contradictory findings probably reflect the varying conditions of the towns and cities to which the remittances are sent.

68. This concept is developed in Eric Wolf, *Europe and the People Without History* (Berkeley: University of California Press, 1982).

69. Sassen, "Why Migration?", 14. Also see two excellent studies by Sassen of the impact of global restructuring: *The Mobility of Labor and Capital: A Study in International Investment and Labor Flow* (Cambridge: Cambridge University Press, 1988) and *The Global City* (Princeton, N.J.: Princeton University Press, 1992).

70. Sassen, "Why Migration?," 15.

71. For analysis about capital-labor collaboration, see Beth Sims, *Workers of the World Undermined: American Labor's Role in U.S. Foreign Policy* (Boston: South End Press, 1992) and Daniel Cantor and Juliet Schor, *Tunnel Vision: Labor, the World Economy, and Central America* (Boston: South End Press, 1987).

72. See, for example, Wayne Cornelius, "One Way Travel to the U.S. on the Rise," *Hemisfile* 2, no. 2 (March 1991).

73. Richard Mines, Beatriz Boccalandro, and Susan Gabbard, "The Latinization of U.S. Farm Labor," *Report on the Americas* 26, no. 1 (July 1992), 43. Two out of five U.S. farmworkers are migrants, meaning they travel seventy-five miles or more for their work.

74. Peter Francese, "Aging America Needs Foreign Blood," *The Wall Street Journal*, 27 March 1990.

75. Douglas S. Massey, "The Settlement Process Among Mexican Migrants to the U.S.," *American Sociology Review* 51 (October 1986), 670–84.

76. Georges Vernez and David Ronfeldt, "The Current Situation in Mexican Immigration," *Science* (8 March 1991), 1189. Also see Durand and Massey, "Mexican Migration."

77. In 1975 INS chief Leonard Chapman warned that the United States faced a "vast and silent invasion of illegal aliens."

78. Quoted in *Newsweek* (25 January 1984).

79. The Centro Binacional de Derechos Humanos in Tijuana has documented the widespread extortion and human rights abuses of migrants. See Víctor Clark Alfaro, *Los aspirantes a indocumentados: Una fuente segura de ingresos (el caso de Tijuana)* (Tijuana: Centro Binacional de Derechos Humanos, 1988).

80. Survey conducted by Colegio de la Frontera Norte in Nogales, cited in Francisco Lara Valencia, "Programa Paisano: Problemas y Retos en Sonora," *La Voz del Norte* 11 (June 1990).

81. Understandably, the Mexican government is reluctant to cooperate with the INS in halting the flow of its own citizenry. But Mexican immigration authorities have been encouraged and assisted by the INS in a campaign to obstruct the stream of migrants from Central America. Mexico's Interior Ministry joined the INS, DEA, and the CIA in Operation Hold the Line, which among other things employed undercover agents to infiltrate the clandestine network that helps migrants enter the United States. In large part because of this cooperative relationship with the INS along Mexico's southern border, which includes INS training and intelligence sharing, the number of Central Americans that Mexico stops on the Guatemala border has steadily increased. In 1990 Mexico deported more than 110,000 Central Americans. See Bill Frelick, "Update on Interdiction of Central Americans in Mexico" (Washington: U.S. Committee on Refugees,

16 July 1991); *Running the Gauntlet: The Central American Journey to Mexico* (Washington: U.S. Committee for Refugees, January 1991); Leo Chavez, Estevan Flores, and Maria López-Graza, "Migrants and Settlers: Comparison of Undocumented Mexicans and Central Americans in the United States," *Frontera Norte* 1, no. 1 (Tijuana, January–June 1989). Chavez et al. make the point that most Central Americans leave their countries with the intention of returning someday, whereas Mexicans increasingly are interested in settling permanently in the United States.

82. *Sealing Our Borders: The Human Toll* (Philadelphia: American Friends Service Committee, February 1992), 6.

83. Interview with Rubén García, director of Annunciation House, 29 November 1991.

84. Americas Watch, *Brutality Unchecked: Human Rights Abuses Along the U.S. Border with Mexico* (New York, May 1992).

85. *Sealing Our Borders*, 10.

86. Figures compiled by the U.S.-Mexico Border Program of the AFSC in San Diego.

87. *Immigration Control: Immigration Policies Affect INS Detention Efforts* (Washington: General Accounting Office, June 1992). Criminal aliens are defined as those charged with breaking other than immigration laws. The two other main INS categories are deportable aliens and excludable aliens.

88. San Diego Association of Governments, "The Impact of Undocumented Aliens on the Criminal Justice System" (San Diego, October 1986), 5.

89. Wolf, *Undocumented Aliens and Crime*, 23.

90. Ibid., vii.

91. Wayne Kirkpatrick, U.S. Border Patrol, quoted ibid., 40.

92. IRCA granted "amnesty" to 1.8 million undocumented residents, 1.2 million of whom were Mexican citizens. The act also legalized the status of 1.3 million migrants claiming to be temporary agricultural workers. Of these, 1 million were Mexican.

93. Prior to IRCA, immigration law referred only to illegal entry and/or presence, not to employment. Undocumented workers enjoyed the same rights as nonimmigrant workers. For detailed discussions of undocumented immigrants' post-IRCA legal rights, see Linda S. Bosniak, "Exclusion and Membership: The Dual Identity of the Undocumented Worker Under United States Law," *Wisconsin Law Review* (1988), 955–1042, and Robin Alexander, "Labor Rights Protections after IRCA," *Immigration Newsletter* 17, no. 1. Examples of IRCA's effect on labor rights are given in María Blanco and Pauline Kim, *How Employer Sanctions Undermine the Enforcement of Federal Labor Laws* (San Francisco: Equal Rights Advocates, n.d.). All three of these resources are cited in Cathi Tactaquin, "What Rights for the Undocumented?" *Report on the Americas* 26, no. 1 (July 1992).

94. Peter A. Schey, "North American Economic Integration: A Multilateral Approach to Migration and the Human Rights of Migrant Workers," paper presented at the 16th Annual Conference on Immigration and Naturalization at the University of Texas at Austin School of Law, San Antonio, Texas, 17–18 September 1992.

95. For a classic example of this reasoning, see the Council of Economic Advisers,

*Economic Report of the President, Transmitted to Congress, February 1986* (Washington, D.C.: Government Printing Office, 1986), especially ch. 7, "The Economic Effects of Immigration." See also Bureau of International Labor Affairs, U.S. Department of Labor, *The Effects of Immigration on the U.S. Economy and Labor Market* (Washington, D.C.: Government Printing Office, 1989). For a survey of the role of Mexican labor in nine varied sectors of the U.S. economy, see Wayne A. Cornelius, ed., *The Changing Role of Mexican Labor in the U.S. Economy* (San Diego: Center for U.S.-Mexican Studies, forthcoming). A review of twenty-five methodologically varied studies of the labor market impact of undocumented workers is given in Frank D. Bean, Edward E. Telles, and B. Lindsay Lowell, "Undocumented Migration to the United States: Perceptions and Evidence," *Population and Development Review* 13 (December 1987).

96. See James E. Pearce and Jeffrey W. Gunther, "Illegal Immigration from Mexico: Effects on the Texas Economy," *Southwest Journal of Business and Economics* 6 (Winter–Spring 1989) and David Hensley, "The Impacts of Immigration Reform on the California Economy," *Labor Law Journal* (August 1989).

97. Personal communication from Philip Martin, a farm labor economist at the University of California, Davis.

98. For an insightful article on the social effects of this tension, see Miles, "Blacks vs. Browns," 41–68.

99. *Immigration Reform: Employer Sanctions and the Question of Discrimination* (Washington, D.C.: General Accounting Office, 1990). The GAO found that employer discrimination based on national origin constitutes "a serious pattern of discrimination." Of employers surveyed by the GAO, 10 percent reported that they began to discriminate on the basis of a person's foreign appearance or accent, and 9 percent indicated they began to discriminate on the basis of a person's citizenship status. These numbers are low-end estimates since many employers may not have wanted to disclose that they discriminated in their hiring practices.

100. See Philip Martin, *Harvest of Confusion: Migrant Workers in U.S. Agriculture* (Boulder, Colo.: Westview Press, 1988), 131–35.

101. The Census Bureau does not collect information about the legal status of U.S. inhabitants. The most common method of estimating undocumented immigrants is to subtract the INS's number of legal foreign-born residents from the Census Bureau's number of total foreign-born residents, after attempting to correct for misreporting during the census. Robert Warren and Jeffrey S. Passel describe this procedure and their results using 1980 census figures in "A Count of the Uncountable: Estimates of Undocumented Aliens Counted in the 1980 United States Census," *Demography* 24, no. 3 (August 1987). Data from the 1980 Mexican census—in which respondents who reside or have resided in the United States have no reason to lie about their legal status—led Jeffrey Passel (in 1985) to estimate that 1.9 million undocumented Mexicans resided in the United States.

102. Quoted in Benjamin Shore, "Low-Key Attitude Shift Favors Getting Tough on Immigration," *San Diego Union-Tribune*, 26 September 1992.

103. An econometric study by University of California researchers indicates that 610,000 people are likely to migrate from Mexico to the United States if Mexican

corn subsidies are removed and U.S.-Mexican agricultural trade is opened. See Sherman Robinson et al., *Agricultural Policies and Migration in a U.S.-Mexico Free Trade Area: A Computable General Equilibrium Analysis*, Working Paper no. 617 (Berkeley: Department of Agriculture and Resource Economics, 1991). Luis Téllez, Mexico's undersecretary of agriculture, estimated that as many as fourteen million people will migrate from rural areas to urban areas between 1990 and 2010. Tim Golden, "The Dream of Land Dies Hard in Mexico," *The New York Times*, 27 November 1991, sec. A, p. 1.

104. See David Clark Scott, "Free Trade and Mexican Migrants," *The Christian Science Monitor*, 15 June 1992.

105. Cited in William Branigan, "Violence, Tensions Increasing Along the U.S.-Mexican Border," *The New York Times*, 25 June 1990.

106. Proposals for an international agreement protecting the rights of immigrant workers have been put forth. See, for example, Schey, "North American Economic Integration."

107. Weisman, *La Frontera*, 25. In the mid-1980s Starr County received national attention and notoriety as the extent of local involvement in the drug trade came to light. From top to bottom, the county's elected officials and government agencies participated in the drug trade in one way or another. Before the system was broken up through law-enforcement efforts, even the county road crews received payoffs for leveling airstrips needed by drug smugglers. Interview with Mike Gallagher, *Albuquerque Journal*, 4 September 1992.

108. Most of the discussion of early contraband traffic on the border is drawn from Terrence E. Poppa, *Drug Lord: The Life and Death of a Mexican Kingpin* (New York: Pharos Books, 1990).

109. See Weisman, *La Frontera*, for a discussion of these trading relationships. Weisman's interviews along the U.S.-Mexican border during the mid-1980s showed that even Mexican government agencies took advantage of the quicker pace of import transactions that were concluded outside authorized Mexican customs channels.

110. See Douglas Clark Kinder, "Nativism, Cultural Conflict, Drug Control: United States and Latin American Antinarcotics Diplomacy through 1965," in *The Latin American Narcotics Trade and U.S. National Security*, ed. Donald J. Mabry (New York: Greenwood Press, 1989), 13.

111. William O. Walker III, *Drug Control in the Americas* (Albuquerque: University of New Mexico Press, 1981), 58.

112. Report of the Bilateral Commission on the Future of United States–Mexican Relations, *The Challenge of Interdependence: Mexico and the United States* (Lanham, Md.: University Press of America, 1989), 123. For a less sanguine view of white America's perceptions of the Hispanic community and marijuana consumption, see Kinder, "Nativism, Cultural Conflict, Drug Control," 15–16.

113. On Mexico's concerns about traffic in and domestic use of opiates during the early twentieth century, see Walker, *Drug Control in the Americas*, 22, 37, 58.

114. Report of the Bilateral Commission, *The Challenge of Interdependence*, 125.

115. Ibid., 12.

116. The figures are from the U.S. government–sponsored National Narcotics Intelligence Consumers Committee. Cited ibid., 124–26.

117. Although Mexico contributes nearly two-thirds of the marijuana imported to the U.S. market, it is not the major source of pot smoked in the United States. That achievement is claimed by domestic producers in the United States, where marijuana is grown nearly nationwide. The National Narcotics Intelligence Consumers Committee (NNICC, pronounced "nick") is an interagency effort of the U.S. government. Members include federal agencies responsible for policy development, intelligence gathering, research, and law enforcement. The annual NNICC report estimates global drug production and reports eradication and interdiction figures. The figures are from National Narcotics Intelligence Consumers Committee, *The NNICC Report 1991: The Supply of Illicit Drugs to the United States* (Washington, D.C.: Drug Enforcement Administration, July 1992), 46.

118. The percentage given is based on qualitative analysis of six hundred samples of heroin seized during interdiction operations in 1991. According to Bob Rae, coordinator of the NNICC, this figure—as well as all estimates of illegal drug availability—must be taken only as a general indicator of a given drug's availability and source. Regional variations will reflect different totals, depending on which countries tend to supply given areas, and the limited sample size—in which large and small samples are rated equally—may distort real national totals. Interview with Bob Rae, Office of Intelligence, Drug Enforcement Administration, 9 September 1992. For more information on the methodology used by the NNICC to estimate Mexican heroin's share of the U.S. market, see ibid., 23–24.

119. U.S. Department of State, Bureau of International Narcotics Matters, *International Narcotics Control Strategy Report* (Washington, D.C.: U.S. Department of State, June 1991).

120. *Department of State Bulletin*, October 1989.

121. President's Commission on Organized Crime, Report to the President and the Attorney General, *America's Habit: Drug Abuse, Drug Trafficking, and Organized Crime* (Washington, D.C.: Government Printing Office, 1986).

122. Samuel I. del Villar, "The Illicit U.S.-Mexico Drug Market: Failure of Policy and an Alternative," in *Mexico and the United States: Managing the Relationship*, ed. Riordan Roett (Boulder, Colo.: Westview Press, 1988), 192.

123. "Drugs in Mexico," *Latin America Weekly Report*, 12 December 1991.

124. Peter Reuter, *Eternal Hope: America's International Narcotics Effort* (Santa Monica, Calif.: Rand Corporation, 1987), cited in Samuel I. del Villar, "Rethinking Hemispheric Antinarcotics Strategy and Security," in *The Latin American Narcotics Trade*, 106.

125. Quoted in *Drug Control: U.S.-Mexico Opium Poppy and Marijuana Aerial Eradication Program* (Washington, D.C.: General Accounting Office, January 1988), 19–20. Campesinos who worked as field labor for El Búfalo, a marijuana-growing, storage, and processing complex in Chihuahua, earned about six dollars for a day's work in 1984. The complex, which handled marijuana grown throughout Mexico for Guadalajara kingpin Rafael Caro Quintero and a syndicate of his associates, utilized state-of-the-art agribusiness techniques. Elaine Shannon, *Desperados: Latin Drug Lords, U.S. Lawmen, and the War America Can't Win* (New York: Viking, 1988), 195.

126. The figures cited are from the mid-1970s. Peter A. Lupsha, "Drug Trafficking:

Mexico and Colombia in Comparative Perspective," *Journal of International Affairs* (1981), 97.

127. National Narcotics Intelligence Consumers Committee, *The NNICC Report 1991*, 46.

128. U.S. Department of State, Bureau of International Narcotics Matters, *International Narcotics Control Strategy Report* (Washington, D.C.: U.S. Department of State, March 1991), 162.

129. Weisman, *La Frontera*, 28.

130. Quoted in Shannon, *Desperados*, 346. This sort of patronage has bought loyalty and admiration from some in Mexico. In the highlands of Sinaloa, there is even a shrine to Jesús Malverde, a bandit hanged in 1909. Revered as something of a Robin Hood, Malverde is now considered the patron saint of traffickers and exploited peasants alike. Larry Rohter, "In a Most Unsaintly City, a Bandit Wears a Halo," *The New York Times*, 11 May 1989.

131. Interview with Dick Kamp, Border Ecology Project, 4 February 1991.

132. Steven Strasser, "The Southwest Drug Connection," *Newsweek* (23 November 1987).

133. Cited in Mark T. Sullivan, "Drug Money Fills Vacuum in Strapped Border Towns," *San Diego Union-Tribune*, 30 November 1990. The effect of drug money can be seen in the interiors of Mexico and the United States as well. José Leonardo Contreras Subias, a top Mexican trafficker wanted in connection with the murder of DEA Agent Enrique Camarena, moved into Atoka, Oklahoma, in the mid-1980s. He bought land at generous prices to help ranchers who were facing bankruptcy after the crash in land prices. He hired ranch hands and paid them well, purchased vehicles and farm equipment, and otherwise used his money to buy loyalty—or at least blindness to his activities. When he was finally arrested, police discovered that he had been laundering money by buying real estate in Texas, Oklahoma, and Salt Lake City. Kevin Kelly, "The Oklahoma Town That Drug Money Bought," *Business Week* (23 May 1988).

134. Interview with Mike Gallagher, 4 September 1992.

135. Report of the Bilateral Commission, *The Challenge of Interdependence*, 126.

136. Statement of Thomas A. McDermott, senior agent in charge, U.S. Customs Service, Arizona, in a hearing before the U.S. Senate Committee on Appropriations, *The Frontline of the U.S. War on Drugs: The Southwest Border*, 101st Cong., 1st sess., 1990, 32.

137. Craig Pyes, "The War of the Flowers," *Oui* (10 October 1977).

138. Shannon, *Desperados*, 343.

139. McDermott before hearing, *The Frontline of the U.S. War on Drugs*.

140. Poppa's *Drug Lord* describes the day-to-day reality of life in Ojinaga under Pablo Acosta and a series of his trafficking predecessors. For a view of the same systems of violence and intimidation in Guadalajara, see Shannon, *Desperados*.

141. On the potential for such an outcome in Mexico, see Richard B. Craig, "Mexican Narcotics Traffic: Binational Security Implications," in Mabry, *The Latin American Narcotics Trade*, 29–32. For the Mexican government's concerns, see the interview with Enrique Alvarez del Castillo in "From Beyond the Border," *New Perspectives Quarterly* 6, no. 2 (Summer 1989).

142. Alan Riding, *Distant Neighbors* (New York: Vintage Books, 1986), 164–65.

143. See, for example, Peter A. Lupsha, "Drug Lords and Narco-Corruption: The Players Change but the Game Continues," in *War on Drugs: Studies in the Failure of U.S. Narcotics Policy,* eds. Alfred W. McCoy and Alan A. Block (Boulder, CO: Westview Press, 1992).

144. On the shoot-out, see: Edward Cody, "Drug Bust Goes Awry in Mexico," *Washington Post,* 29 Nov. 1991; Tim Golden, "Mexican Panel Faults Army in Death of Drug Agents," *New York Times International,* 7 Dec. 1991; and ibid. As another example, news reports in November 1992 indicated that Manuel Bartlett Díaz—a former education minister who was elected governor of Puebla state in 1992—may have been linked to the killings of a Mexican journalist and U.S. drug enforcement agent Enrique Camarena. Both the journalist and Camarena were reportedly investigating Bartlett's ties to the drug trade. A Drug Enforcement Administration report linking Bartlett to the murders was obtained by a reporter at the *Mexico City News* who intended to run a story on the charges prior to the gubernatorial elections in which Bartlett was a candidate. According to press reports, executives at the newspaper—including a close friend of Bartlett—ordered the reporter to kill the story. "A Governor's Free Ride?" *Newsweek* (23 November 1992).

145. See: Lupsha, "Drug Lords and Narco-Corruption;" and Candice Hughes, "Slaying of Drug Agents Touchy Issue in Mexico," *Albuquerque Journal* (28 November 1991).

146. The family of Jaime ("Don Jaime") Herrera-Nevarez is the economic and political power structure in Durango, and it has not been seriously weakened by U.S. or Mexican law-enforcement efforts that have put members of the family in jail on occasion over the years. Originally enriched by traffic in heroin, the Herrera family expanded into cocaine trafficking in response to market demands in the United States. The family is now linked to Colombian traffickers, through both business ties and marriage. With a network of several thousand relatives and operatives linked in a cartel of related family groups, the Herrera operations stretch from Durango to Chicago, New York, Philadelphia, Boston, Detroit, and Louisville. Interview with Mike Gallagher, 2 September 1992; Howard Abadinsky, *Organized Crime* (Chicago: Nelson-Hall, 1990), 230–31. Other important trafficking families are the Talavera organization in Juárez–El Paso and the Juan Garcia Abrego family in Brownsville-Matamoros.

147. Richard Craig, "*La Campaña Permanente:* Mexico's Antidrug Campaign," *Journal of Inter-American Studies and World Affairs* (May 1978), 107–33.

148. As noted by Elaine Shannon, Nixon had domestic political reasons not related to the drug trade for getting tough on trafficking. Nixon campaigned in 1968 on a law-and-order ticket, vowing to rein in the "permissiveness" of U.S. society and clean up street crime. Once in office, however, he found himself constrained by the requirements of the federal system, in which decisions about most aspects of crime and punishment are reserved to state and local governments. The administration seized on drug trafficking for its get-tough policies because antinarcotics efforts fell within the responsibilities of the executive branch and had an impact on U.S. street crime. Shannon, *Desperados,* 47. On Operation Intercept, see Richard B. Craig, "Operation Intercept: The International Politics of Pressure," *Review of Politics* 42, no. 4 (October 1980).

149. According to Samuel I. del Villar, Nixon's Operation Intercept was designed in part to force Mexico to use chemicals to destroy marijuana and poppy crops. Nixon aide G. Gordon Liddy, one of those involved in implementing the plan and a culprit in the Watergate scandal, was straightforward about the coercive intentions of the operation: "It was an exercise in international extortion, pure and simple and effective, designed to bend Mexico to our will. We figured Mexico could hold out for a month; in fact, they caved in after two weeks, and we got what we wanted." Quoted in del Villar, "The Illicit U.S.-Mexico Drug Market," 200.

150. Richard Craig, "Operation Condor: Mexico's Antidrug Campaign Enters a New Era," *Journal of Inter-American Studies and World Affairs* (1980), 345, 360.

151. See the summary of these programs in *Drug Control: U.S.-Mexico Opium Poppy and Marijuana Aerial Eradication Program* (Washington, D.C.: General Accounting Office, January 1988). Also see ibid.

152. Craig, "Operation Condor."

153. For good descriptions of the extent of corruption during the mid-1980s, see Shannon, *Desperados*.

154. Agency for International Development, *U.S. Overseas Loans and Grants and Assistance from International Organizations* (Washington, D.C.: Government Printing Office, various years).

155. Interviews with Elizabeth Carroll, State Department, Bureau of International Narcotics Matters, 3 September 1992 and 29 July 1993.

156. Interview with Fred Schellenberg, CIA analyst at the El Paso Intelligence Center, 29 July 1992.

157. Tim Golden, "Mexico Says It Won't Accept Drug Aid from U.S.," *The New York Times*, 26 July 1992.

158. U.S. Department of State, "Memorandum of Justification for Presidential Determination Regarding the Drawdown of Defense Articles and Services for Mexico," 8 November 1991; and Presidential Determination No. 92–17, "Drawdown from Department of Defense Stocks for Counternarcotics Assistance for Mexico," 26 February 1992.

159. Agency for International Development, *Mexico: Project Assistance (Projects Active as of March 1991)* (Washington, D.C.: Government Printing Office, May 1991).

160. Interview with Elizabeth Carroll, 3 September 1992.

161. Robert L. Wilhelm, "The Transnational Relations of United States Law-Enforcement Agencies with Mexico," *Proceedings of the Pacific Coast Council on Latin American Studies* 14, no. 2 (1987), 161.

162. Cable from the U.S. Embassy, Mexico, D.F., to Secretary of State, No. 250128, 23 October 1989.

163. Cable from the U.S. Secretary of Defense to Army Headquarters in Washington, D.C., No. 221825Z, January 1991; and Cable from the U.S. Secretary of Defense to Army Headquarters in Washington, D.C., No. 141130Z, October 1990.

164. Cable from the U.S. Embassy, No. 250128.

165. Craig, "Mexican Narcotics Traffic," 38.

166. See the assessments of the U.S.-Mexico drug policy relationship ibid. and in del Villar, "The Illicit U.S.-Mexico Drug Market"; del Villar, "Rethinking Hemi-

spheric Antinarcotics Strategy and Security"; and Richard Craig, "U.S. Narcotics Policy Toward Mexico: Consequences for the Bilateral Relationship," in *The Drug Connection in U.S.-Mexican Relations*, eds. Guadalupe González and Marta Tienda (San Diego: Center for U.S.-Mexican Studies, 1989).

167. Each of these initiatives was known as Operation Intercept. The first was designed to pressure Mexico into stepping up its eradication and interdiction activities. The second was intended to push Mexico into pursuing and prosecuting the murderers of Enrique Camarena.

168. Office of National Drug Control Policy, *National Drug Control Strategy* (Washington, D.C.: Government Printing Office, February 1991), 82.

169. U.S. Department of State, "Memorandum of Justification."

170. As of 1990, thirty-nine DEA special agents and three DEA intelligence analysts were stationed in Mexico. DEA offices are located in Mexico City, Guadalajara, Hermosillo, Mazatlán, Merida, and Monterrey. Drug Enforcement Administration, *Mexico: A Country Profile* (Washington, D.C., December 1991).

171. Shannon, *Desperados*, 123.

172. Douglas Jehl and Doyle McManus, "Mexico Assails U.S. Figures on Producing Pot," *Los Angeles Times*, 1 March 1990, and "Mexico Angry at U.S. over Use of Satellite," *The New York Times*, 17 March 1990.

173. The available sources on these topics are manifold. For a detailed look at the Camarena case and DEA in Mexico during the early and mid-1980s, see Shannon, *Desperados*. A good example of Mexico bashing is recorded in the so-called Helms hearings, a set of hearings held in 1986 before the U.S. Senate Subcommittee on Western Hemisphere Affairs. The subcommittee is chaired by Senator Jesse Helms, a sharp critic of the Mexican government. Hearings before the U.S. Senate Subcommittee on Western Hemisphere Affairs of the Committee on Foreign Relations, *Situation in Mexico*, 99th Cong., 2nd sess., 13 May, 17 and 26 June 1986. Also see hearing before the U.S. House of Representatives Select Committee on Narcotics Abuse and Control, *U.S. Narcotics Control Efforts in Mexico and on the Southwest Border*, 99th Cong., 2nd sess., 22 July 1986.

174. Not just a set of cowboy actions, the abductions of the Camarena conspirators also sprang from real human frustration. DEA agents investigating Camarena's disappearance and his subsequent murder found their legitimate efforts repeatedly blocked by Mexican officials. From the DEA perspective, Camarena had not just been killed in the line of duty, as Mexican critics insisted. The brutality of the murder went beyond what was necessary just to get the agent out of the way. Camarena was tortured for some thirty hours. He was beaten with pipes and fists, kicked, and he was sodomized with objects. His murderers finished him off by driving a tire iron through his skull. Collecting evidence, DEA agents listened repeatedly to tapes made by the traffickers of Camarena's last hours. Intended to document the interrogation so that the conspirators could determine how much was known of their operations and protectors in Mexico, the tapes also recorded the bitterly slow death of the agent. Worse, informants told DEA that Camarena was kept alive longer than naturally possible by Humberto Alvarez Machain, a Guadalajara physician. The informants said that Alvarez injected Camarena with the stimulant lidocaine to keep his heart from failing

until the traffickers had all their questions answered. The failure of the Mexican government to pursue a timely and thorough investigation of the murder—one that would look into the full reach of the conspiracy—reinforced DEA inclinations to act unilaterally. Although this explanation does not justify the violation of Mexican territory, the justice and human rights concerns raised by the murder and its aftermath demonstrate the complicated nature of the DEA abductions. But the fact that the United States could get away with these actions, Mexican opposition notwithstanding, clearly illustrates the asymmetry between the two countries.

Adding another twist to this grim account, when Alvarez was brought to trial in the United States, a district judge acquitted him after the prosecution had rested its case. The judge found that the prosecution had produced insufficient evidence to convict Alvarez and dismissed the case before the decision was even turned over to the jury. Linda Deutsch, "Judge Clears Mexican Doctor in Camarena Slaying," *Albuquerque Journal*, 15 December 1992. Later newspaper reports indicated that the DEA had been told by an informant two months before the trial that *another* doctor had administered drugs to Camarena to keep him alive. The DEA did not even tell the prosecution about this information until well into the trial, and the information was not given to the judge until immediately before his decision to clear Alvarez. Linda Deutsch, "Informant Blames Other Doctor in Camarena Death," *Albuquerque Journal*, 17 December 1992.

175. Alvarez Machain was the physician who allegedly prolonged Camarena's life with drugs so that his torturers could finish their interrogation. Mexico had made no effort to indict him for his participation in the crime.

176. Interview with Mike Gallagher, 4 September 1992.

177. For a brief but informative overview of the pitfalls of a drug control strategy that relies primarily on enforcement and interdiction, see Peter Reuter, *Can the Borders Be Sealed?* (Santa Monica, Calif.: Rand Corporation, August 1988).

178. Juan Garcia, *Operation Wetback* (Tucson: University of Arizona Press, 1980), 175.

179. The best overview of border militarization under the Carter, Reagan, and Bush administrations is Timothy J. Dunn, *The Militarization of the U.S.-Mexico Border, 1978–1992: Low Intensity Conflict Doctrine Comes Home* (Austin, Texas: Center for Mexican-American Studies, forthcoming). Much of the discussion in this section draws on Dunn's excellent work.

180. Interview with Timothy Dunn, 11 November 1992.

181. According to James Olech, the Border Patrol's chief of management support, 10 percent to 50 percent of the agents carry semiautomatic pistols. Cited in Americas Watch, *Human Rights in Mexico: A Policy of Impunity* (New York, June 1990), 86.

182. For example, Congress amended the Posse Comitatus Act, a law dating from 1878 that restricts military involvement in domestic law-enforcement activities. The 1981 revisions clarified and expanded the ways the military could contribute to civilian law-enforcement operations. The amended law permitted the armed forces to share information, equipment, and facilities with civilian law-enforcement agencies and to provide them with training and the personnel to operate and maintain equipment lent to them by the military.

183. The 1986 Omnibus Drug Control Act required the military to become more active in interdiction efforts, and the 1989 Defense Authorization Act designated the Department of Defense the lead agency for detecting and monitoring aerial and maritime transport of illegal drugs.

184. Statement of James E. Bowen, senior tactical coordinator of Operation Alliance, in a hearing before the U.S. Senate Committee on Appropriations, *Federal, State, and Local Drug Enforcement and Interdiction Efforts Along the Southwest Border*, 100th Cong., 2nd sess., 1989.

185. See the extensive coverage of these services and their importance to U.S. border control in Dunn, *Militarization of the U.S.-Mexico Border*.

186. Lieutenant Colonel John Kiser, quoted in Ruben Hernandez, "Marines Aid Border Agents," *Tucson Citizen*, 31 August 1992.

187. Ibid.

188. During the confrontation the marines launched an illumination flare into the night sky. When the flare fell to earth, it ignited a fire that burned three hundred acres of national forest land. Moreover, it turned out that local law-enforcement officials had not been informed that marines were patrolling in their jurisdiction. Miriam Davidson, "Militarizing the Mexican Border," *Nation* (1 April 1991). So far this has been the only incident in which military forces have engaged in a shoot-out while on these operations, but when they are in the field, they operate on rules of engagement that authorize them to shoot to kill if they or their civilian companions are endangered.

189. Hernandez, "Marines Aid Border Agents."

190. Interview with Ruben Hernandez, *Tucson Citizen*, 12 November 1992.

191. Many of these efforts, in fact, have been strongly criticized for being disorganized, badly coordinated, understaffed, inefficient, and ineffective. See, for instance, Committee on Government Operations, *Operation Alliance: Drug Interdiction on the Southwest Border* (Washington, D.C.: Government Printing Office, 1988), and *Drug Interdiction: Operation Harvest: A National Guard–Customs Anti-Smuggling Effort* (Washington, D.C.: General Accounting Office, June 1988).

192. On the Alien Border Control Committee and other border emergency contingency plans, see Dunn, *Militarization of the U.S.-Mexico Border*, 67–71.

193. Ibid., 198.

194. Davidson, "Militarizing the Mexican Border."

195. Statement before Subcommittee on Human Rights, June 18, 1990.

196. For a valuable, although dated, book-length overview of the border economy, see Niles Hansen, *The Border Economy: Regional Development in the Southwest* (Austin, Texas: University of Texas Press, 1981).

197. Quoted in Bruce Stokes, "Boom at the Border," *National Journal*, 29 July 1989. Saxod has since become director of the Border Progress Foundation.

198. *Maquiladoras* in the textile industry must be 51 percent Mexican-owned. The textile industry is subject to export quotas under the Multilateral Fiber Agreement, to which both the United States and Mexico are parties.

199. Despite the constitutional prohibition against foreign ownership of any land within a hundred kilometers of the border, foreign businesses gain the ownership rights they want through *fideicomisos*, which are thirty-year trusts that make

Mexican banks the legal owner of land but grant foreign businesses primary use of the property. If a new foreign investment law President Salinas planned to submit to Congress in 1993 passes, any company incorporated in Mexico will reportedly be able to purchase land in Mexico's forbidden border zone. If true, *maquilas* would no longer need *fideicomisos*.

200. Quoted in *Business Mexico* (February 1986).

201. Vast literature exists on the *maquiladoras*. Probably the best source of data, analysis, and historic detail is Leslie Sklair, *Assembling for Development: The Maquila Industry in Mexico and the United States* (Winchester, Mass.: Unwin Hyman, 1989). Other valuable sources include Joseph Grunwald and Kenneth Flamm, eds., *The Global Factory: Foreign Assembly in International Trade* (Washington, D.C.: Brookings, 1985); and *The Use and Economic Impact of TSUS Items 806.30 and 807.00* (Washington, D.C.: U.S. International Trade Commission, 1988).

202. Of the 2,042 *maquiladoras* operating in 1992, 12 percent are not located in the six Mexican border states and another 9 percent are located a little more than twelve miles (twenty kilometers) from the border within the border states. American Chamber of Commerce, *Maquiladora Newsletter*, third quarter (1992). According to Sklair, the main differences between border and nonborder *maquilas* are lower wages, less infrastructure, and the greater propensity of some nonborder *maquilas* to make local purchases. Sklair, *Assembling for Development*.

203. Data from Mexico's National Institute of Statistics, Geography, and Information, (INEGI) and the Ministry of Programming and Budget (SPP), cited in Business International Corporation, *Succeeding in the New Mexico: Corporate Strategy, Globalization and the Free Trade Agreement* (New York, 1991), 198. Making the increase in value added per employee even more impressive is the fact that real wages were lower in 1989 than in 1983. The wage rate is relevant because wages make up a large portion of value added in the *maquiladoras*.

204. Francisco Lara Valencia, "La fuerza de trabajo en la industria maquiladora de la región fronteriza de Sonora: Caracteristicas socioeconomicas y transición ocupacional," paper prepared for the XV Simposio de Historia y Antropología de Sonora, Hermosillo, Sonora (21–24 February 1990), 6.

205. Data from SECOFI cited in *La Jornada*, 14 December 1992.

206. Fixed direct investment in the *maquiladoras* has been estimated at five billion dollars. Leslie Sklair, *The Maquiladoras: Present Status, Future Potential*, study submitted to the U.S. Office of Technology Assessment (December 1991). This amount implies average annual investment of more than six hundred million dollars if standard depreciation rates are assumed. It is impossible to know how much of the direct investment is recorded in Mexico since a great deal of the equipment used in *maquilas* is leased from U.S.-based parent companies. In such cases the investment dollars stay in the United States.

207. Patricia A. Wilson, "The New Maquiladoras: Flexible Production in Low-Wage Regions," in *Maquiladoras: Economic Problem or Solution?*, ed. Khostrow Fatemi, (New York: Praeger, 1990). For the increasing productivity of *maquila* workers, see Bernardo González-Aréchiga and José Carlos Ramiréz, "Productividad sin distribución: Cambio tecnológico en la industria maquiladora mexicana (1980–86)," *Frontera Norte* 1, no. 1 (January–June 1989).

208. See, for example, Roberto A. Sánchez, "Condiciones de vida de los trabajadores de la maquiladora en Tijuana y Nogales," *Frontera Norte* 4, no. 2 (July–December 1990). The average total compensation cost per worker-hour in Mexican manufacturing as a whole was $2.17 in 1991. For the *maquiladora* sector by itself the figure was $1.55. These amounts reflect direct wages, such benefits as annual bonuses, vacations, and subsidized meals, and payroll taxes. From U.S. Department of Labor, Bureau of Labor Statistics, "International Comparisons of Hourly Compensation Costs for Production Workers in Manufacturing, 1991," Report 825 (June 1992), and from unpublished data compiled by the Bureau of Labor Statistics.

209. *Twin Plant News*, January 1987.

210. See, for example, U.S. Congress, Office of Technology Assessment, *U.S.-Mexico Trade: Pulling Together or Pulling Apart?* ITE-545 (Washington, D.C.: Government Printing Office, October 1992), 81; G. W. Lucker, "The Hidden Costs of Worker Turnover: A Case Study in the *Maquiladora* Industry," *Journal of Borderlands Studies* 2 (1987); and Sklair, *Assembling for Development*, 179.

211. Quoted in Harley Shaiken, "The Auto and Electronics Sectors in U.S.-Mexico Trade and Investment," study submitted to the U.S. Office of Technology Assessment (May 1992), 44–45.

212. Beginning in the late 1980s, some researchers argued that the composition of *maquiladoras* was shifting toward increasingly high-technology industries and that *maquiladoras* were adopting new forms of work organization and greater training. See Jorge Carrillo, "Transformaciones en la industria maquiladora de exportación," in *Las Maquiladoras: ajuste estructural y desarrollo regional*, eds. Bernardo González-Aréchiga and Rocío Barajas Escamilla (Tijuana: COLEF and Fundación Friedrich Ebert, 1989); and Leonard Mertens and Laura Palomares, "El Surgimiento de un Nuevo Tipo de Trabajador en la Industria de Alta Tecnología: El Caso Electrónico," in *Testimonios de la Crisis I*, ed. Estela Gutiérrez (Mexico, D.F.: Siglo XXI, 1988).

Many of these studies confused high-technology sectors, like electronics, with high-technology production processes. Furthermore, even where high-technology production processes were used, training requirements for line workers were still minimal, with training focused on plant technicians. One report that asserts that "training occupies a central place within the managerial strategies in the *maquiladora* plants" found nevertheless that only 25 percent of the plants surveyed offered technical training programs in the three years prior to the study. Jorge Carrillo, *Mercados de trabajo en la industria maquiladora de exportación* (Mexico: COLEF and STPS, 1991). For further exploration of these issues, see Wilson, "The New *Maquiladoras*," in Fatemi, *Maquiladoras*; Harley Shaiken and Harry Browne, "Japanese Work Organization in Mexico," in *Manufacturing Across Borders and Oceans: Japan, the United States, and Mexico*, ed. Gabriel Székely (San Diego: Center for U.S.-Mexico Studies, 1991); and Cathryn L. Thorup, ed., *The United States and Mexico: Face to Face with New Technology* (New Brunswick, Maine: Transaction Books, 1987).

213. Many *maquiladoras* dispense with the need to meet legal requirements for severance pay by renewing "temporary" twenty-eight-day work contracts until a

worker is no longer needed. Since these temporary workers do not build up seniority, they can be dismissed at little cost.

214. Office of Technology Assessment, *U.S.-Mexico Trade*, 84.

215. See Andrew Paxman, "Mexican Workers Give Trade Pact Mixed Review," *The Christian Science Monitor*, 14 August 1992.

216. There are many factors explaining this low level of domestic supply, including the failure of the government to mandate a local supply percentage, the low quality and inefficiency of many Mexican producers, and the unwillingness of Mexican industries to retool to meet the needs of firms that may withdraw their investment at any time. On the border, isolation from the Mexican interior and close commercial relations with the U.S. side (including a history of free trade) have discouraged the development of local industry.

217. Numerous studies have addressed Mexico's failure to establish linkages between its *maquila* sector and its domestic economy. One important look at this question is Joseph Grunwald, "Opportunity Missed: Mexico and *Maquiladoras*," *Brookings Review* (Winter 1990–91).

218. For more on the "triple alliance," see Leslie Sklair, "The *Maquila* Industry and the Creation of a Transnational Capitalist Class in the United States–Mexico Border Region," in Herzog, *Changing Boundaries*, 69–88.

219. What little serious labor organizing there is in the *maquilas* has occurred in the Rio Grande Valley, mainly in Matamoros. See Edward J. Williams, "Attitudes and Strategies Inhibiting the Unionization of the *Maquiladora* Industry: Government, Industry, Unions, and Workers," *Journal of Borderland Studies* VI, no. 2, and Edward J. Williams and John T. Passé-Smith, *The Unionization of the Maquiladora Industry: The Tamaulipan Case in National Context* (San Diego: Institute for Regional Studies of the Californias, San Diego State University, 1992).

220. Peter Baird and Ed McCaughn, "Hit and Run: U.S. Runaway Shops on the Mexican Border," *Report on the Americas* (July–August 1975).

221. Talli Nauman, "Maquiladoras Thrive Despite Doubts," *El Financiero International*, 9 (November 1992); Brad Stratton, "Learning English Is Not Enough," *Quality Progress* (January 1989).

222. In 1988, 44 percent of the *maquilas* and 75 percent of the jobs were found in specialized industrial parks for the *maquila* sector. Thomas P. Lee, ed., *In-Bond Industry/Industria Maquiladora* (Mexico, D.F.: Administración y Servicios Internacionales, 1988).

223. Mexican capitalists and professionals also play an important role in the *maquila* sector mainly by setting up industrial parks, providing services, and acting as subcontractors. See Alejandra Salas-Porras, "Maquiladoras y burguesía regional," *El Cotidiano*, Edición Especial, 1987.

224. Sklair, *Assembling for Development*, 235.

225. The Programa Nacional Fronterizo (PRONAF) was established by President López Mateos in 1961 to promote social and economic development and make the border a "window on Mexico." The program was short-lived and not well funded, but it did result in the construction of the PRONAF tourist centers in Juárez and Tijuana.

226. This point is made well by Sklair, who observes, "The great hopes on which the

*maquila* strategy rests, namely that Mexico could supply substantial quantities of material inputs to the *maquila* industry, backward linkages, and that it could derive massive, virtually free technology spinoffs and genuine technology transfers, have not been realized." This was based on a faulty understanding of the ideology and practice of production sharing, according to Sklair, *Assembling for Development*, 227. Also see Joseph Grunwald, "U.S.-Mexican Production Sharing in World Perspective," in *The Maquiladora Program in Trinational Perspective: Mexico, Japan, and the United States*, ed. Paul Ganster (San Diego: Institute for Regional Studies of the Californias, San Diego State University, 1987).

227. For analysis of why Mexico has failed to increase domestic linkages and use the *maquila* sector to spur broader industrialization, see Patricia A. Wilson, "The Global Assembly Industry: *Maquiladoras* in International Perspective," Community and Regional Working Paper Series, no. 10 (Austin: University of Texas, July 1989), and Grunwald, "Opportunity Missed."

228. See Sklair, *The Maquiladoras*, 16.

229. One such company was Ansell International of Columbus, Ohio, a surgical glove manufacturer. *The Wall Street Journal*, 14 January 1991.

230. In an imaginative effort to drive this point home, U.S. Representative James A. Traficant, Jr. (D-Ohio), introduced a bill in 1992 that would improve the competitive position of Ohio businesses by exempting them from otherwise applicable health, safety, and wage standards.

231. Although this statistical treatment is logical, neither the United States nor such multilateral institutions as the International Monetary Fund, GATT, OECD, and the World Bank use this method. For the sake of consistency the trade figures we use in this book include the value of in-bond imports and exports unless otherwise noted.

232. U.S. duty benefits extend beyond the reimport of U.S. components in some cases. By warehousing the *maquila*-assembled goods in U.S.-designated free-trade zones (FTZs), the importer can delay paying duties until the goods are sold or processed further. "In the case of the major automobile manufacturers with *maquiladoras*, the warehouses and transfer points in the border cities and the assembly plants in other regions of the United States, such as the upper Midwest, all are designated as FTZs. Consequently, the duties on the *maquiladora* products do not become due until the automobile is shipped from the plant to a dealer." James E. Groff and John P. McCray, "*Maquiladoras*: The Mexico Option Can Reduce Your Manufacturing Cost," *Management Accounting* (January 1991).

233. Cited in José A. Méndez, Tracy Murray, and Donald J. Rousslang, "U.S.-Mexico Employment Effects of Repealing the U.S. Offshore Assembly Provision," *Applied Economics* 23 (1991), 553–66.

234. Customs officials record OAP-qualified imports in two tariff lines now called HTS 9802.00.60 and 9802.00.80. These lines correspond to the pre-1990 tariff lines called TSUS 806.30 and 807.00. The total value of U.S. imports from Mexico under 806.30 and 807.00 in 1968 was seventy-three million dollars. Since the proportion of nondutiable U.S.-made components and materials in *maquila* exports to the United States has held fairly constant at just over 50 percent over the years, we have estimated roughly forty million dollars in duty-free exports in 1968. See Sklair, *Assembling for Development*, 12.

235. Note that Mexico's portion of the duty-free total of imports under TSUS 806.30 and 807.00 varies greatly from its portion of total imports under these codes. This is because Mexican *maquiladoras* use a much higher proportion of U.S.-made components in their assembly processes than do assemblers in such developed countries as Japan. As an illustration, in 1986 Mexico accounted for 18 percent of total imports under the offshore assembly provision, but 54 percent of the duty-free portion of these imports.

236. A recent attempt to provide what the authors call "reasonable upper-bound estimates" for the employment effects of the tariff breaks led to the conclusion that repealing the offshore assembly provision would have small, negative effects in both Mexico and the United States. See Méndez et al., "U.S.-Mexico Employment." For a survey of several earlier estimation efforts, see Gregory Schoepfle and Jorge Perez-Lopez, *U.S. Employment Impact of TSUS 806.30 and 807.00 Provisions and Mexican Maquiladoras: A Survey of Issues and Estimates*, Economic Discussion Paper 29, Bureau of International Labor Affairs, U.S. Department of Labor (Washington, D.C., 1988).

237. One of the first of these was Form-O-Uth, which manufactured brassieres for Sears in California and Texas. The company closed its California plant in 1969, when its *maquiladora* came on-line in Reynosa, Tamaulipas. (The Texas plants were later closed when the company began operations in El Salvador.) In 1970 another Sears supplier, Warwick Electronics (owned by Whirlpool), opened a *maquiladora* in Tijuana. Sklair, *Assembling for Development*, describes Sears's campaign on 50–52 and 131. Sklair cites James Worthy, *Shaping an American Institution: Robert E. Wood and Sears, Roebuck* (Chicago: University of Chicago Press, 1984).

238. Sklair, *Assembling for Development*, 48, citing a Department of State "Airgram."

239. Ibid., 48, citing Anna-Stina Ericson, "An Analysis of Mexico's Border Industrialization Program," *Monthly Labor Review* 12 (May 1970), 33–40.

240. Until Mexico adopted its General law on Ecological Equilibrium and Environmental Protection in 1988, the country's environmental policies were inadequate to deal with the pressures of industrialization and were largely unenforced. See Stephen P. Mumme, C. Richard Bath, and Valerie J. Assetto, "Political Development and Environmental Policy in Mexico," *Latin American Research Review* 23, no. 1 (1988). Despite the improved legal framework resulting from the 1988 law, inadequate regulations and enforcement remain significant obstacles to environmental protection. Mexico has not consistently enforced its strong labor standards since 1940.

241. "History of Cost per Hour in Dollars," *Twin Plant News* (August 1989), 56.

242. Business International Corporation, *Succeeding in the New Mexico*, 187.

243. After Congress raised its objections in October 1986, the Department of Commerce backed out of Expo-Maquila '86, turning responsibility over to a private public relations firm. According to the General Accounting Office, the exposition would have generated income for the government through fees paid by participants and exhibitors and thus did not represent a net cost to taxpayers. According to congressional opponents, the GAO's calculations failed to take into account all the overhead expenses—salaries, office space, etc.—attributable to the expo. See testimony of Allan Mendelowitz to the Subcommittee on Com-

merce, Transportation, and Tourism of the House Committee on Energy and Commerce, 10 December 1986.

244. In its first two years the coalition has launched campaigns to change the practices of more than a dozen U.S.-owned corporations, including Du Pont, Ford, General Motors, Stepan Chemical, and Zenith. Coalition for Justice in the Maquiladoras, "Summary Update on Focus Companies," 13 May 1992.

245. NAFTA requires Mexico to phase out the heart of the Border Industrialization Program—its duty-free provisions—by 1 January 2001. "NAFTA to End *Maquila* Program," *El Financiero International*, 7 September 1992.

246. Auto parts are subject to the general 60 percent regional-content rule under NAFTA, but they are affected indirectly by the rule of origin governing automobiles. In calculating the local content of autos, NAFTA requires that the foreign-origin portion of auto parts be considered as foreign content in the finished car, even when the parts themselves pass the regional-content test. In all other industries such foreign content in components may be "rolled up" and considered as local content if the component meets the applicable rule of origin. Medium-size and large televisions must contain North American–made picture tubes in addition to the standard regional content to qualify for duty-free status, and computers must contain a regionally produced motherboard. The restrictions on textiles and apparel are probably the most onerous of all. Local content must be at least 80 percent, and not only the fabric used to make the apparel but even the yarn used to make the fabric must be sourced from the United States, Mexico, or Canada. See James Bovard, "NAFTA's Protectionist Bent," *The Wall Street Journal*, 31 July 1992; Douglas Karmin, "Rules of Origin and the North American Free Trade Agreement," *CRS Report for Congress*, 21 August 1992; and *Rules of Origin Issues Related to NAFTA and the North American Automotive Industry*, USITC Publication 2460 (Washington, D.C.: U.S. International Trade Commission, November 1991).

247. "Wharton Econometrics Projects High Growth for *Maquiladora* Industry, 1993–1997," *La Jornada*, 3 December 1992.

248. Interview with Sam Drake, El Paso Industrial Development Corporation, 23 July 1992.

249. A study of forty-three education centers along the border found that more than half had *maquila*-related courses and many of the teachers were *maquila* staff. Carrillo, *Mercados de Trabajo*, cited in Sklair, *The Maquiladoras*, 21.

250. John F. Garmon, "The *Maquiladora* Colleges," *Twin Plant News* (August 1990). Garmon is dean of Occupational Technical Education at Texas Southmost College.

251. Interview with Mike Roark, 28 October 1992.

252. "Back to School: Community Colleges Offer Specialized *Maquila* Education," *Maquila Magazine* (September 1990).

253. Brad Cooper, "Becoming Part of the Solution," *Maquila Magazine* (October 1991).

254. Interview with Erin Ross, IM[3]'s director of communications, 30 October 1992.

255. Kenneth W. Chapman, "UTEP Transfers Technology," *Twin Plant News* (May 1992).

256. One of the most prominent critics of this partnership between academia and

144

*maquilas* has been the AFL-CIO's Victor Muñoz, former chair of the El Paso Central Labor Council. One of the first published accounts of this partnership is Jim Dougherty, *McBorderland USA: The Maquiladora Industry and the Selling of El Paso, Texas and Ciudad Juárez, Mexico,* working paper series (Buffalo, N.Y.: University of Buffalo, Baldy Center for Law and Social Policy, 1992). Among the Juárez-based *maquilas* directly assisted by IM$^3$ and MVAL that moved to Mexico after closing down operations in the United States are Johnson & Johnson, Thompson Consumer Electronics, Advance Transformer, Baxter Health Care, Delco Products (a division of GM), Honeywell, and Ford Motor Company.
257. Dr. Richard Sprinkle, "An Investigation of the Employment Linkage between Cd. Juárez and El Paso" (El Paso: University of Texas–El Paso, 1986).
258. See Sklair, *Assembling for Development,* 109–10, 182–83. Sklair notes that "the direct causal connection between Juárez *maquilas* and El Paso jobs must remain a statistical artifact within the Link methodology." It is interesting to note that the Border Trade Alliance was established in 1987 as an outgrowth of a partnership of industry, border governments, and academics to promote the concept of *maquila*-based development. Initially, the campaign was a response to charges by the AFL-CIO and some members of Congress that the Department of Commerce was directly facilitating the growth of the *maquila* sector and hence the number of runaway plants. The position papers prepared in the late 1980s by Michie and others purporting to demonstrate the benefits of the *maquila* sector to the U.S. borderlands were part of a major lobbying effort in Washington by the Border Trade Alliance.
259. Interview with Donald Michie in *San Francisco Chronicle,* 29 February 1988. See Sklair, *Assembling for Development,* 185–86, for further analysis of the suspect nature of Michie's data. Even forgetting about jobs lost to competition from *maquiladoras,* using the Department of Commerce statistic that 20,000 jobs result from every one billion dollars of exports indicates that the *maquila* industry supported no more than 80,000 jobs in the United States in 1987. This figure includes blue- and white-collar employees in export-related industries and assumes that two jobs are indirectly created by each job directly involved in export production.
260. Interview with Donald Michie, 10 November 1992.
261. *Paso del Norte Regional Economy: Socioeconomic Profile* (El Paso: Institute for Manufacturing and Materials Management, August 1991), iv.
262. Ibid., 3.
263. Harry Browne and Beth Sims, *Runaway America: U.S. Jobs and Factories on the Move* (Albuquerque: Resource Center Press, 1993).
264. See Raúl Fernández, *The United States–Mexico Border* (Notre Dame, Ind.: Notre Dame Press, 1977).
265. Border cities are not alone in their dependence on Mexican trade and visitors. Texas, for example, does more business with Mexico than does any other state: 30 percent of its exports go to Mexico. It used to be that petroleum equipment formed the overwhelming bulk of these exports, but Mexico is now importing a much broader variety of goods, including chemical, paper, and metal products as well as an increasing quantity of foodstuffs. *Business Mexico* (September 1990).

266. See *Increased United States–Mexico Trade*. There are no region-wide studies of the percentage impact of purchases by Mexican nationals, but most researchers and observers reported a dramatic decline after the 1982 devaluation, much of which has subsequently been recouped.

267. Study by E. George, "Impact of the *Maquilas* on Manpower Development and Economic Growth on the U.S./Mexico Border" (El Paso: University of Texas–El Paso, 1986), cited in Sklair, *The Maquiladoras*, 19.

268. See Francisco Lara Valencia, "La Fuerza de Trabajo en la Industria Maquiladora de la Región Fronteriza de Sonora," paper prepared for the XV Simposio de Historia y Antropoligía de Sonora, Universidad de Sonora (21–24 February 1990). According to Lara, *maquila* production workers in Nogales spend sixty-seven dollars of their wages in the United States on food and clothing each month.

269. Sklair, *The Maquiladoras*, 19.

270. Interview with Henry King, associate director of Center for Enterprise Development Advancement Research and Support, 4 November 1992.

271. Yazmin Venegas Peralta, "Retorno a la Economía de Estados Unidos," *El Financiero*, 4 December 1990.

272. *Increased United States–Mexico Trade*, 17–20. In December 1984 Laredo and McAllen had the highest and second highest unemployment rates in the United States.

273. J. Williams, "Mexicans Shopping in Texas Add to Profits of Border Malls," *The Washington Post*, 7 January 1990.

274. According to estimates by the Banco Nacional de México, cited in *The Washington Post*, 7 January 1990.

275. For an entertaining account of the new Nogales, see Jim Henderson, "Border Boom Town," *American Way* (1 November 1990).

276. "Brothels Bloom in Nuevo Laredo," *Herald Post*, 16 October 1990.

277. P. R. Casner and L. G. Guerra, "Purchasing Prescription Medication in Mexico," *Western Journal of Medicine* (1 May 1992).

278. Jan Gilbreath, "Financing Environmental and Infrastructure Needs on the Texas-Mexico Border: Will the Mexican-U.S. Integrated Border Plan Help?" *Journal of Environment and Development* 1, no. 1 (Summer 1992).

279. Between 1987 and 1990 northbound border truck traffic increased more than 40 percent, but customs services have not been able to keep up with this new pace. During the same period the Customs Service increased the number of inspectors by just 12 percent. *U.S.-Mexico Trade: Concerns About the Adequacy of Border Infrastructure* (Washington, D.C.: General Accounting Office, May 1991), 13.

280. See *Integrated Environmental Plan for the Mexican-U.S. Border Area* (Washington, D.C.: EPA and SEDUE, 1992).

281. The GAO's report *U.S.-Mexico Trade*, for example, addresses only the need for better customs and transportation infrastructure, saying nothing about social services.

282. Cited in David Maraniss, "On Both Sides of the Border, Laredo's Alienation Runs Deep," *The Washington Post*, 29 June 1986.

283. See Gilbreath, "Financing Environmental and Infrastructure Needs," 166–67, and Gilbreath, *Planning the Border's Future*, U.S.-Mexican Occasional Paper No. 1. Lyndon B. Johnson School of Public Affairs, Austin, March 1992, 31.

284. Eduardo Zepeda Miramontes, "La Infraestructura en la Frontera Norte y El Proceso de Liberalización Comercial," (Tijuana: COLEF, 1992).
285. A good overview of Mexico's centralized tax system is Ted Bardacke, "Reforms Aside, Hacienda Still Controls the Purse Strings," *El Financiero International*, 14 December 1992.
286. Quoted in George Baker, "Who's Afraid of the FTA?" in *The Mexican-U.S. Border Region and the Free Trade Agreement*, eds. Paul Ganster and Eugenio O. Valenciano (San Diego: Institute for Regional Studies of the Californias, San Diego State University, 1992), 17.
287. George Baker, "Mexican Labor Is Not Cheap," *Rio Bravo: A Journal of Research and Opinion* 1, no. 1 (October 1991).
288. Some *maquiladora* operators declare minimal net income in Mexico to avoid the slight chance of an audit by the Ministry of Finance. Two experts on *maquila* accounting issues recommend that "transfer prices should be established which will result in Mexican taxable income equal to about 1 percent or 2 percent of sales." Cheryl D. Hein and Neal R. VanZante, "Maquiladoras: Should U.S. Companies Run for the Border?," *CPA Journal* (October 1991).
289. The tax—30 percent of total wages prorated for work-time spent in Mexico—was to apply to anyone working 15 days or more in the country during a given year. After revision to accommodate *maquiladora* protests, the tax rate remained the same but was applied only to persons working more than 183 days in the country. Diane Lindquist, "*Maquiladora* Operators Gain Break on New Tax," *San Diego Union-Tribune*, 7 May 1992, sec. C, p. 1, and American Chamber of Commerce/Mexico, "Mexico Adjusts its Taxation—Non-Residents Now Included," *Review of Trade and Industry*, second quarter (1992), 4–8.
290. Some firms have, however, benefited from INFONAVIT funds used by official unions to create housing for *maquila* workers.
291. Quoted in David Clark Scott, "Mexico's Border Industry Faces Housing Crisis," *The Christian Science Monitor*, 28 June 1991.
292. This was the leading theme of the widely touted Border Environmental Infrastructure Colloquy, sponsored by the U.S Environmental Protection Agency and Mexico's SEDESOL, in Santa Fe, New Mexico, 26 June 1992. Also see Cooper, "Becoming Part of the Solution."
293. One of the leading advocates is border promoter Charlie Crowder, who told one reporter, "If we want to be the problem, we can be. All we've got to do is build some factories. And we can take an impossible paralysis of social infrastructure and human misery, and contribute to it. But it is not good business." Sandy Tolan, "The Border Boom: Hope and Heartbreak," *The New York Times Magazine*, 1 July 1990.
294. Quoted in Stokes, "Boom at the Border."

# Part II

# Environmental Showdown

# The Lesson of

# the Cobalt Man

Vicente Sotelo Alardín sits in a Juárez prison, accused of a theft that triggered one of the border's worst environmental catastrophes. More than four thousand people were exposed to high levels of radioactive cobalt 60 from a cancer therapy machine taken in 1983 from the Medical Center for Specialities in Ciudad Juárez.[1] Like many other border incidents, the causes and the repercussions of the cancer therapy machine "theft" were not isolated to one side of the international border. Described as the worst radiation disaster in North America, the cobalt 60 incident in Juárez was truly an international affair.[2]

While working as a hospital custodian/electrician, Sotelo claims he was told by his supervisor to dispose of some unused equipment that was languishing in a hospital warehouse. One of the pieces of junk he carried away to the Yonke Fénix junkyard was a twenty-year-old radiotherapy machine that the hospital had purchased secondhand in the United States but had never used.

Loaded with the cobalt 60 isotope, in the form of some six thousand pellets each the size of a pinhead, the machine was used by the Methodist Hospital in Lubbock, Texas, to burn away cancers. Although the use and transfer of such nuclear devices are strictly regulated in the United States, international sales are not monitored. In this case U.S. brokers were not required to notify the nuclear authorities of the Mexican government, nor did the deal require a check on the competence or the licensing of the purchaser. In selling the cancer therapy machine to a doctor at a Juárez hospital, X-Ray Equipment Company of Fort Worth violated no U.S. rules, even though a similar sale to an unlicensed purchaser would have meant a fine or a jail sentence in the United States.[3]

After collecting dust in the hospital storeroom for six years, the device was hauled away to a Juárez junkyard that later sold the machine along

151

with other scrap metal to two steel foundries for recycling, one of which is a subsidiary of a St. Louis company. Mixed in with other metal, the pellets contaminated thousands of steel rebars (used to reinforce concrete) and furniture parts that were subsequently manufactured with recycled metal. Because the device was partially dismantled before arriving at the junkyard, an unknown quantity of the metal pellets spilled out of Sotelo's truck, contaminating various sections of Juárez.

Five weeks after Sotelo dropped off the machine at Yonke Fénix the same cobalt 60 isotopes set off alarms at the Los Alamos National Laboratories near Santa Fe, New Mexico. A driver for the Smith Pipe & Steel Company of Albuquerque made a wrong turn when making a delivery at the nuclear weapons research center. The contaminated steel rebars triggered the center's radiation detector, thus beginning an international effort to track down and retrieve all the deadly steel. Radioactive rods and metal furniture were eventually recalled from twenty-three states and four other countries including Mexico.

Mexican officials calculated that close exposure to the leaking cobalt 60 would be equivalent to absorbing thirty-five thousand chest X rays. Already one junkyard worker has died from a rare bone cancer, and others have suffered from sterility and skin discoloration. Apparently feeling that someone had to take the blame for the catastrophe, Mexican authorities eventually decided to arrest Sotelo for theft. By mid-1992 Sotelo had been waiting a year and a half for his case to come before a judge. The hapless Sotelo, whom prison guards call El Cobalto (the Cobalt Man), charges that the Mexican government is using him as a scapegoat.

Sotelo's story mixes personal tragedy, startling coincidence, and social injustice. But perhaps more than anything it highlights the many noneconomic implications of unregulated cross-border trade. The fate of the Cobalt Man underlines the close links that exist between the public health and environmental future of the two neighboring nations.

In this part of the book we focus largely on the environmental and health repercussions of U.S.-Mexico relations along the border. The disposal of industrial wastes, air and water pollution, threats to occupational and public health, loss of flora and fauna, and ineffective environmental regulation along the border serve as a vivid regional portrait of the ecological and health problems resulting from increasing economic integration.

But these and other similar problems extend far beyond the borderlands. The increasingly close economic relations between the United States and Mexico raise new questions about the compatibility of development and the environment. Mexico, like most countries, has long favored economic development at the expense of environmental quality. Beginning in the late 1980s, environmental initiatives by the Mexican government indicated a new ecological sensibility, at least in terms of public discourse. At the same time, however, the government's drive to deregulate the economy and the urgency with which it has sought to attract foreign investment raise concern that environmental protection will continue to take a backseat to economic stimulation. Underlining this concern was a 1992 World Bank report that stated that "Mexico suffers from grave environmental problems exacerbated by several decades of industrialization without assessment of, or attention to, environmental costs."[4]

Although the industrial development of the Mexican borderlands serves to illustrate many of the environmental repercussions of liberalized trade and investment, questions about the environmental sustainability of development are not peculiar to the border. For the most part, both nations still fail to account for the environmental and health repercussions of growth when calculating the effects of increased trade and investment no matter where they occur.

For its part, the United States has since the early 1980s been pushing Mexico to adopt a more open economy and give a freer rein to foreign investment with little regard to the environmental consequences. Although the United States has advocated that Mexico adopt U.S.-style environmental regulations, it has largely ignored the fact that Mexico has neither the funds nor the political will to enforce such rules.

Certainly the Mexican government, business community, and citizenry bear primary responsibility for the environmental degradation caused by its past and present development policies. But in this epoch of economic integration, responsibility must also be shared by the United States, which stands in a better position to guide the forces of global integration. Unfortunately U.S. economic policies tend to aggravate Mexico's environmental crisis. Left out of binational negotiations are such matters as the environmental effects of increased oil exports to the United States and the restructuring of Mexico's food system, both of which Washington has been advocating. Also explicitly omitted have been any controls on natural resources harvesting, such as guidelines for mining, forestry, water exports, and the use of agricultural land.

The lack of environmentally conscious economic planning is perhaps most apparent in the ongoing reform of the agricultural sector. As Mexico opens its domestic market to U.S. grain imports and seeks to increase its share of the U.S. market for fruits and vegetables, it has failed to consider the health and environmental costs of this integration of regional agricultural markets.

Since the 1950s Mexico has promoted horticultural exports to the United States, using subsidized water and energy to underwrite the agroexport industry. Trade liberalization and changes in Mexico's agrarian reform have increased the incentives for U.S. agribusiness to transfer production and packing operations south of the border. But like the western United States, Mexico will soon have to confront the environmental costs—contamination caused by pesticide and fertilizer runoff, drying up of underground aquifers, erosion, and salination of irrigated lands—brought on by modern agribusiness. Whether Mexico can afford to continue subsidizing basic energy and water costs of these large export operations, which in many cases are controlled by such transnational corporations as Del Monte and Unilever, is another question that has not yet been answered.

Mexico's gradual switch to a trade-based food policy—depending on cheaper food imports to substitute for beans and corn produced by the peasantry—also has untold environmental consequences. As imported basic grains and the elimination of state protection undermine traditional peasant agriculture, rural-urban migration will increase, compounding the environmental crisis facing an increasingly urban Mexico. Economic crisis in the countryside will at the same time probably escalate the levels of soil erosion and deforestation as desperate peasants seek to eke out livings on marginal lands. In this way, the specter of poverty-induced ecocide in rural Mexico looms ever larger.[5]

With or without a formal free trade accord, economic integration also means rising threats to Mexico's environment in other sectors as the country opens up to foreign investment and pushes export production. After a decade of declining investment in the petroleum industry, increased onshore drilling threatens the Lacondon tropical forest in southeastern Mexico and stepped-up offshore drilling in the Bay of Campeche further endangers the fisheries and the marine environment. Symptomatic of the fundamental lack of environmental consciousness on the part of both the U.S. and Mexican trade officials was the section on petroleum and energy of the proposed NAFTA accord in which the term *environment* was not mentioned once. New foreign investment in the country's mineral reserves represents another potentially adverse environmental repercussion of Mexico's trade and investment liberalization.

Achieving sustainable development is becoming the most important challenge for industrialized and underdeveloped nations alike. Considering the increasing fragility of transborder ecosystems and the toll that unregulated economic growth takes on public health and welfare, the environmental and social costs of development can no longer be ignored.

In this era of global communication, financial, and production systems, crossing international borders comes easily to modern investors and traders. Yet just as national political boundaries do not make economic sense to the proponents of free trade, neither do borders have much meaning for environmentalists interested in conserving and rehabilitating ecosystems. Measures to protect one nation's environment do little good if companies can simply cross borders to avoid those regulations.

The chapters in this part of the book point to the wisdom of environmentalists, who have long insisted that ecosystems and environmental contamination extend across international boundaries. Together the following chapters on ecological deterioration, air and water pollution, hazardous dumping, and pesticide poisoning paint a grim picture of ecological devastation. But there is a positive side, too. A new international environmental consciousness is developing as community leaders, government bureaucrats, and social justice activists from Mexico and the United States come together to work out common solutions. No longer isolated on the radical fringe of the environmental movement, the concept of sustainable development has moved into the center of the debate over the future of regional economic integration.

# The Nature of

# the Borderlands

The lack of water defines the border's natural environment. From east to west along the boundary, the aridity of the surrounding region is its most striking feature.[6] The semiarid grassland steppes of the Rio Grande Valley along the Texas border give way to the unforgiving Sonoran desert of the Arizona and California border. Rising above the hot and arid lowlands are the "mountain islands" that are the southern extensions of the Rocky Mountains, offering cooler temperatures and high forest vegetation. The summer heat is intense but is relieved in most parts by "monsoons" that sweep across the desert skies in August.

Availability of water was the most pressing issue facing the Southwest's earliest developers. Theirs was not an environmental concern about how best to conserve scarce resources. Rather, they rushed to divvy up the water among the most powerful private and public players. Not until the last couple of decades has the use of nonrecharging groundwater reserves become a contentious development issue. With wells drying up or becoming contaminated, the residents of the borderlands are waking up to the fact that finite groundwater resources also impose severe limits on future growth.

Quantity, of either surface water or groundwater, is just one part of the region's water crisis. Also critical is declining water quality. Above and below the ground, water has become dangerously contaminated with human, agricultural, and industrial wastes.

## Desert Rivers

Two main river systems unite—and divide—the United States and Mexico. These are the Rio Grande and the Colorado River. Descending from the eastern slopes of the Continental Divide in southeastern Colorado, the Rio Grande slices through New Mexico before reaching the Mexican border at El Paso. For 1,264 miles the river or the riverbed defines the border. The flow of the Rio Grande disappears in the desert sand at Fort Hancock and does not appear again for 50 more miles until receiving the waters of the northbound Río Conchos. Finally the Rio Grande trickles into the Gulf of Mexico. Early explorers, approaching the river from different directions, believed the 1,800-mile river—the fifth longest in North America—was actually several different waterways. Seen from the Gulf, it was labeled the Río de las Palmas (river of palms), and from the south it was christened the Río Bravo del Norte (fierce river of the north), the name of honor it still holds in Mexico.[7]

The Colorado River, which springs to life in the fourteen-thousand-foot peaks of Wyoming and Colorado, forces its way through the most arid expanses of North America, plunging 2.5 miles on its 1,450-mile path to the Gulf of California. The only major source of water between the Rocky Mountains and the Sierra Nevada, the Colorado River marks the entire Arizona-California line but defines the international boundary for only 24 sandy miles. This mighty river, which carved the Grand Canyon and turns the turbines of more than thirty hydroelectric plants, crosses into Mexico a defeated, lifeless stream. During its trip to Mexico the Colorado is tripped up by ten major dams and straitjacketed to serve the manifold demands of rural and urban communities in the otherwise waterless expanses of the Southwest.

The Colorado and the Rio Grande share common lifelines. One on the east side of the Continental Divide and the other on the west, the two rivers are conceived on snow-capped peaks in the Rockies. They are mighty rivers, pushing their way past formidable natural barriers and giving life where there is no other. But their power has been sapped and their beauty scarred by the ranchers, farmers, miners, and urban developers who have claimed the rivers as their own. Despite their magnificent beginnings, the Rio Grande and Colorado River come to tragic ends. So depleted is the Rio Grande by the time it reaches Brownsville-Matamoros that the salty waters of the Gulf of Mexico now wash into its shallow channel. More shameful still is the fate of the Colorado, whose waters in most years do not even reach the Sea of Cortez. Instead its briny remains simply disappear into the burning sands of Sonora. And the Cucapá Indians—the "river people"—who once depended on its flow into the gulf no longer have a river to fish in or call their own.[8]

The two rivers have long been central elements in U.S.-Mexico relations. As might be expected, sharing the rivers in these scorched borderlands has not always been easy or equitable. To a large extent, the law of the strongest has prevailed. Mexico's relative lack of technical expertise and economic resources has historically placed it at a disadvantage in claiming its water rights.[9] The asymmetry in U.S.-Mexico relations has in the case of water rights been aggravated by the different geographic positions of the two nations as upstream and downstream riparians. Nonetheless, international water agreements that have proved to be models of bilateral resource management have been hammered out. The joint International Boundary and Water Commission (IBWC), which has been managing boundary and surface water disputes along the border since 1889, has succeeded in resolving most disputes in an amicable fashion, leaving both sides generally satisfied.[10] But the challenges over water use and quality now facing the two nations are daunting.

Disputes over the international sharing of the Colorado River and Rio Grande date back at least to the 1870s.[11] Tensions have also arisen over the use and abuse of the waters of lesser waterways, such as the San Pedro River, which flows north from the mountains surrounding the Cananea mining district; the Santa Cruz River, which waters the twin cities of Nogales; the New River, which flows north from Mexicali; and the Tía Juana (or Tijuana) River, which laces into Southern California.

Faced with the rapid development of the Southwest, the United States took the lead in shaping the course and distribution of the Colorado River. In 1922 the states bordering the river signed the first interstate compact regulating the Colorado. The agreement specified that the flow of the river would be divided equally between the upper and lower basins, with the midpoint being Lees Ferry in northern Arizona.[12] Recognizing that Mexico had some claim on the Colorado, the Interstate Compact of 1922 specified that Mexico would receive the surplus over the 16.9 million acre-feet (maf) that was tentatively allocated between the upper and lower basins. (One acre-foot is the quantity of water needed to cover an acre with one foot of water.) But the river's average flow was grossly inflated, having been based on an extremely wet period, with the mean average flow probably some 2 maf less than the original optimistic calculation.[13] Furthermore, if no surplus was available, the compact provided that the burden of supplying water to Mexico would be equally shared by both basins.

More than two decades later an international treaty stipulated just how much water Mexico was entitled to.[14] It was agreed that Mexico would annually receive at least 1.5 maf—about 10 percent of the Colorado River's flow—except in years of extreme drought, and that the IBWC would be the implementing agency. At least for a couple decades the treaty eased tensions between the two countries over water allocation. But the treaty was silent on the issues of water quality and on the pumping of transboundary groundwater aquifers—the very issues that later emerged as the most prominent concerns on both sides of the border.

Most early tensions over water in the borderlands were over the sharing of surface water, not over its quality. But because of the increasing salinity of the Colorado River water delivered to Mexico, the quality of surface water became a major international issue in the 1960s.[15] The Colorado is naturally a highly saline river, and as it descends toward Mexico, its salinity increases dramatically. Before all the major economic development in the southwestern states, the river's salinity would rise from 50 parts per million (ppm) in Wyoming to about 400 ppm at the border. As the water became increasingly used and reused on its journey toward Mexico, the salinity levels doubled to 800 ppm or more. Rising salinity became a new irritant in border relations.

In 1961 the salinity of the water moving into the Mexicali Valley became so extreme that the Colorado River water delivered to Mexico proved disastrous to the valley's agricultural production.[16] The sudden increase in salinity that year, caused by the release of highly saline groundwaters into the international stream by the U.S. Bureau of Reclamation's Wellton-Mohawk Irrigation Project east of Yuma, eventually forced Washington to intervene. After twelve years of debate and minor adjustments a definitive solution was reached in 1973 in which it was agreed that the water delivered to Mexico must be of approximately the same quality as U.S. users receive.[17] The agreement was the result of Mexico's formal protest to the U.S. government, its threat to take the matter to the World Court, and President Echeverría's announcement that the salinity crisis was his country's leading bilateral priority. Instead of closing down the responsible irrigation project, Washington sought an alternative solution. The Nixon administration turned to the Bureau of Reclamation—the government agency dubbed the Bureau of Wrecklamation by many environmentalists for its habit of damming and channeling rivers.

In its continuing effort to keep western farmers and ranchers happy while not egregiously violating agreements with Mexico, the Bureau of Reclamation constructed a large desalination plant near Yuma, Arizona. Rather than restrict use of the Colorado's waters so as to comply with the 1944 and 1973 accords with Mexico, the U.S. government spent some $260 million for a plant to treat the highly saline water from the Wellton-

Mohawk Irrigation Project. But after a dozen years under construction, the finally completed Yuma desalination plant is now regarded more as a white elephant than as a credible solution to the Colorado's salinity. Politics, not practicality, dictated the creation of the plant, which will cost $38 million annually to operate and was not finished until 1992. Once regarded as the state of the art in reverse osmosis desalination, the Yuma plant was technologically obsolete even before it came on-line in 1992.[18] This technological solution to the problems created by the Wellton-Mohawk Irrigation Project is just one in a long line of federal projects that have dipped into U.S. tax revenues to subsidize the wasteful and exorbitantly expensive irrigation of the desert lands of Southern California.[19] It would have been much less expensive for the government simply to buy out the water rights of the Wellton-Mohawk than to build the desalination plant. But the powerful agricultural lobbies and their attacks on anyone challenging the prevailing system of federal subsidies of western agriculture kept other solutions to the water crisis from being seriously considered.[20]

Notwithstanding the contribution of the Yuma desalination plant, high salinity continues to exacerbate cross-border tensions. As the end of the pipeline, Mexico suffers disproportionately from the thickening salinity of borderland waters. In a classic case of trying to solve one problem only to create another, the brine from the Yuma desalination plant flows to the Santa Clara Slough and upper gulf waters in Mexico, damaging a natural habitat for many birds, fish, and dolphins.[21] Salinity, however, is a major concern along both sides of the border. The Bureau of Reclamation estimates that the nine million tons of salt flowing down the Colorado River have caused $311 million in annual damage in the lower basin because of increased treatment costs, crop loss, and corrosion of water-handling facilities.[22] As historians can attest, salinity can have calamitous consequences not just for farmers but for entire societies. Largely because of accumulated salt buildups in the soil, for example, the Sumerian civilization of ancient Mesopotamia collapsed.[23] The economic boom of the borderlands does not yet show signs of decline, but the region seems to be reaching the limits of development, as established by available water resources and the decreasing quality of what little water there is. If current salinization trends continue, the salinity of the Colorado will reach 1,150 ppm by the year 2010, spelling the death of agriculture in the Mexicali and perhaps even the Imperial Valley.[24] Because of the burst of population growth and the increased energy development in the region, it is becoming ever more difficult to control salinity. Despite an array of engineering and

160

conservation measures implemented by the IBWC and affected local governments, the salinity crisis persists. In fact, the Texas Water Commission warned the Environmental Protection Agency that unless salinity levels dropped along the Rio Grande not only will crops face ruin but saline water will threaten the *maquila* industry, which also depends on good-quality water.[25]

The case that may best illustrate the complexity and inherent tensions of transboundary water sharing is that of the All-American Canal, which transfers Colorado River water into the Imperial and Coachella valleys of California. The canal, and its history, also represent the asymmetry and lack of parity between the two international neighbors. The All-American Canal was preceded by another canal with a similarly pretentious name, the Imperial Canal. Early developers of the Imperial Valley decided that it would be much easier to move the water they needed through a dry riverbed in Mexico than to attempt to construct a channel through the Yuma Sand Hills, which separated the river from the valley.

In typical fashion the developers found a Mexican willing to lend his name to the project, thereby giving it legal standing in Mexico. It also helped that this *prestanombre* (name lender), Guillermo Andrade, was a relative of the dictator at the time, Porfirio Díaz. The Imperial Canal was a great success in that it not only provided irrigation waters to California but also opened up the Mexicali Valley for agricultural development. It was not, however, Mexicans who benefited, but rather U.S. investors, such as Harry Chandler of the *Los Angeles Times*, who together with other investors in the Colorado River Land Company bought up eight hundred thousand acres of the Colorado River delta land in Mexico.[26]

Accumulated silt deposits and poor river management laid waste to the Imperial Canal in 1906, when a flood changed the course of the river, resulting in extensive crop and home damage on both sides of the border. It was then that the U.S. government came to the rescue with a commitment to construct a new canal completely on U.S. territory. Hailed as one of the engineering marvels of the epoch, the All-American Canal has been providing some seven hundred farmers in the Imperial and Coachella valleys with all the water they want since the early 1930s. Rising urban demand for water has turned the heads of city planners in San Diego and Los Angeles toward the Imperial Valley, where much water is lost through wasteful irrigation practices and through immense seepage from the All-American Canal. It has been estimated that some 106,000 acre-feet of water would be saved per year if the canal were completely lined in concrete, thereby preventing seepage.

But what seems an ideal solution—and one that adheres to conservationist principles—has touched off new cross-border tensions over water-resource sharing. On the Mexican side, groundwater users are protesting that the proposed, and congressionally approved, canal-lining project will mean economic ruin. The water that seeps through the sands below the All-American Canal is not lost but instead serves to recharge the aquifer. It is then pumped to the surface again through hundreds of wells located on the Mexican side.

So who really owns this water? The answer to that question will not come easily because there are good legal arguments proffered by both sides and because little is known about sources, quantity, and cross-border flow of aquifers.[27] But more than the complexity of water rights in this individual and unusual case, the controversy over the All-American Canal may finally force Mexico and the United States to address the pressing issue of shaping an international treaty that provides for the equitable and sustainable mining of transboundary aquifers. As it is, both sides are busily pumping as fast as they can to quench the demands of area farmers, industries, and cities.[28]

This pumping frenzy would be all right if the reserves, called *bolsones* in some areas, were being recharged as fast as they were being mined. But they represent the accumulation of millions of years of rainfall and surface seepage. With an average annual rainfall of three inches in Mexicali-Calexico or even eight inches in El Paso–Juárez, combined with the extreme exploitation of surface waters in the borderlands, the recharge rate is extremely slow. The discharge of treated wastewaters into the groundwater basins can help build up groundwater reserves, but this does not come close to resolving the escalating crisis of falling groundwater supplies.

In the El Paso area, for every twenty gallons of water extracted each year from the Hueco Bolson only one gallon is restored. As a result, this reserve, which serves as the sole water source for Juárez and provides about two-thirds of El Paso's water, probably will be sucked dry of potable water in thirty years.[29] Since 1900, groundwater levels have dropped seventy-three feet in El Paso and eighty-five feet in Juárez—a rate of decline that has sped up in recent years.[30]

An interesting twist on the Hueco Bolson drawdown saga is that both El Paso and Juárez, recognizing the dangerous implication of their mutual dependence on this one reserve, have cast their eyes west to the nearby Mesilla Bolson, another transboundary aquifer that lies almost exclusively under New Mexico. In negotiations and court cases with New Mexico, El Paso has failed to gain access to the Mesilla, although it did reach an out-of-court settlement with New Mexico that calls for water to be shipped from the Elephant Butte Reservoir (created by a dam on the Rio Grande) by canal for El Paso's use. No U.S. court, however, can stop Juárez from pumping water out of the same contested aquifer, small amounts of which are now being appropriated to meet the water needs of Mexico border residents.

An international groundwater treaty is clearly in order.[31] More than twenty groundwater basins lie beneath the border. In most cases the groundwater reserves exploited on one side of the border come from the same basins that the other side is also depleting. But what makes good sense makes bad politics. The four U.S. states contiguous to Mexico are the country's largest groundwater users and vehemently reject proposals to share their reserves with other states, let alone Mexico. All four states have different and conflicting laws regulating groundwater appropriation. In Texas the laws of the Wild West prevail, allowing the person with the bigger and faster pump to use as much water as is deemed needed, the result being disastrous drops in groundwater levels throughout the state.[32] Finally waking up to the fact that diminishing groundwater reserves are undermining the state's future economic and environmental stability, the Texas Water Commission in 1992 took the unusual step of declaring one aquifer that reaches into the borderlands an underground river; underground rivers, like surface waters, are subject to state control. New Mexico, where the strict rule of prior appropriation is regulated by the state, has the most enlightened and most tightly controlled groundwater pumping.[33] Although the rule of prior appropriation is more equitable than the right to capture principle that applies in Texas, it is not a doctrine that encourages water conservation or the use of water-saving technology, but rather encourages the user to exploit as much groundwater as possible.[34] In Mexico the federal government regulates water rights in its determination of what constitutes the public good, but in practice water rights are a free-for-all in which the most powerful interests usually win, often with the direct support of the government.

For its part, the IBWC has generally stayed clear of groundwater issues. Except for some regulation of groundwater pumping in the Yuma–San Luis area, the binational commission has little authority over groundwater conflicts, except by way of offering technical consultation. In 1973 the groundwater issue was mentioned in one of the commission's amendments (or minutes). Minute 242 provided that "each nation shall consult prior to undertaking any new development of surface or groundwater in its own territory in the border area that might adversely affect the other country." In the same minute the IBWC excused itself from any major role in groundwater conflicts "pending the conclusion by the governments of the United States and Mexico of a comprehensive agreement on groundwater in the border areas."[35] Although groundwater issues are discussed confidentially by the IBWC and its counterpart in Mexico, it has been unwilling to play a lead role in promoting the importance of apportioning groundwater resources along the border.

In fact, such a groundwater accord has not even been seriously discussed by the two nations. But the conflict over the rights of seepage from the All-American Canal may be what is needed to push such a treaty forward. As both nations wake up to the fact that the future of the borderlands is endangered by dramatic drops in the groundwater tables, support for a groundwater treaty may expand even among the U.S. border states. Meanwhile, the prevailing rule seems to be "We'll race you to the bottom of the aquifer." This lack of regulation and institutional controls fosters overdevelopment of the borderlands, paving the way for social and economic crisis while aggravating border tensions.[36]

Although most binational water conflicts have focused on the distribution and quality of Colorado River waters, the sharing of the Rio Grande has also been problematic.[37] Because of the tremendous population growth along the Rio Grande, the future of agricultural development in the lower Rio Grande Valley and other areas is threatened. Water-deficient cities like El Paso are buying water from water users in rural areas, converting irrigation water into drinking water. In the lower Rio Grande Valley—a region that depends on the river for 98 percent of its water needs—farmers use about 90 percent of the water. They could use more, too, since the valley has another five hundred thousand acres that could be farmed if irrigation water were available for a reasonable price.

But with the region's 4.3 percent annual rate of population growth driving up the cost of water, the agricultural economy is beginning to suffer. Water quality is also quickly deteriorating. Like the Colorado River, increasing salinity is making the water more difficult to treat and hazardous for crops. Farmers also contaminate the Rio Grande through the extensive runoff of pesticides, fertilizer, and herbicides that converts the Rio Grande into a chemical stew. The biggest culprit in the contamination of the Rio Grande, however, is probably the wastewater that is discharged into the river from both sides.

It is in the hundreds of *colonias* lining the Rio Grande that one can best appreciate the magnitude of population growth—and the accompanying water problems—along the Texas-Mexico border. Scattered behind the bluffs and mesas of high Chihuahuan desert around El Paso are dozens of makeshift communities that lack water and sanitation facilities. Although historically El Paso has resisted popular pressure to extend city water to the *colonias*, it has not hesitated to resort to artful gerrymandering to annex undeveloped land slated for affluent suburbs. Responding to the complaints of *colonia* residents and their advocates, in 1987 El Paso's former water district director offered this advice: "All they have to do is boil it, or put a few drops of bleach in it or toss in some pills like we did in Europe during the war."[38] Since then the city has adopted a more enlightened attitude and has worked with citizens' groups and the Texas Water Development Board to bring water to the *colonias*.

The water conflicts arising along the border—from the controversy over the lining of the All-American Canal to the demands of *colonia* residents for water services—are typical of a rapidly developing region with diminishing natural resources. Both sides of the border are water-short, and on both sides the competition for scarce water between rural and urban users is intensifying.

In the U.S. Southwest this conflict between agricultural and city users is aggravated by two additional factors: the increasing demands of upper basin states for their share of the surface water and the mounting demands of the Indian tribes seeking to secure their treaty and prior appropriation water rights. Because the upper basin states never fully appropriated their stipulated share of Colorado River water, the lower basin states, mainly California, have grown accustomed to using more water than was apportioned to them. But with the expanding water demands of the upper basin states and the coming on-line of the Central Arizona Project (meeting the needs of Tucson and Phoenix), the water supply future of Southern California looks increasingly grim.[39] San Diego, which imports 90 percent of its water, depends on the Colorado River for 70 percent of its total water needs. To meet the water demands of San Diego and Los Angeles, city and state planners will increasingly be looking at the cheap water enjoyed by agribusiness, which soaks up about 80 percent of California's water. Large and inefficient water users, such as the rice and livestock industries, will have a particularly difficult time justifying their appropriation of subsidized water in the desert environment of Southern California.

As the dimensions of the water crisis become clearer, the urgency for water conservation will become more apparent. Already cities across the borderlands, from El Paso to San Diego, are limiting lawn watering and car washing to certain times of day and days of the week. Especially in times of drought, lush green golf courses and swimming pools in desert hot spots like Palm Springs may be luxuries that California will no longer be able to afford. As they get the message that water is not an unlimited resource and that it stands to become increasingly costly, farmers and ranchers are waking to the idea of conservation, installing more efficient drip irrigation systems to replace wasteful spraying.

The same scarcity and conservation issues face the Mexican side. Desert cities such as Juárez, Nogales, Mexicali, and Tijuana are exploding with hundreds of thousands of new residents demanding municipal water. These cities have fallen far behind in meeting these demands, but to expand their water services puts them in direct competition with the farm sector, which in Baja California uses more than 90 percent of the available water. With the growing demand for produce in the Mexican border cities and in the United States, agriculture could expand further, if only there were more water.

Not only are many of the water concerns on either side of the border similar, but they are also closely linked in most cases. Take, for example, the case of the widespread lack of water and wastewater treatment facilities in Mexico, which is causing a public health crisis on both sides of the border. As a result, U.S. border cities are calling on the federal government to help solve the wastewater treatment problems of the Mexican border cities. One El Paso study predicted that without financial assistance "the area will become an example of everything that is wrong with free trade between countries that do not have equal economic status."[40] Clearly, there is also the urgent need for joint planning efforts. In the case of El Paso–Juárez, until 1991 there had not been any direct formal contact between the respective water utilities despite their using the same water and facing the nightmarish scenario of the wells' running dry.[41] Mushrooming development throughout the borderlands threatens environmental disaster but also may contribute to border tensions. At least one high ranking Mexican official who has closely followed U.S.-Mexico water issues predicts that by the year 2000 the United States will be unable to meet its commitments under the 1944 treaty.[42]

## Badlands Biosphere

Concerns about diminishing water supplies point to a broader crisis threatening to turn the fragile border environment into a wasteland. Ironically, that is exactly how many outside the region have customarily viewed the borderlands—as wastelands without beauty or life. But many who have lived along the border see instead a land of enchanting panoramas, glorious sunsets, and endless diversity.

Until the late 1800s the borderlands were regarded as badlands or *malpaís*—the realm of rattlesnakes, *bandidos*, and desert rats. But when eastern doctors began prescribing the Southwest climate for treating pulmonary ailments, the environment in places such as Tucson, Phoenix, and Albuquerque came to be regarded as less hostile and more healthful. More recently the U.S. southern border became one of the homing spots for the millions of elderly snowbirds seeking warmer and cheaper climes in which to spend their retirement years. In contrast, Mexico's northern border region was never valued for its therapeutic properties. Nor is it a place where Mexico City residents dream of living their last years. Rather, it has been the lure of border trade and services—and eventually *maquila* manufacturing—that has always shifted Mexican attention northward.

With the border's aridity comes an environmental fragility that is increasingly evident. The wide-open spaces of desert grama grass and sagebrush were turned over to cattle, both north and south of the border, and the result has been severe overgrazing and associated erosion. Over time stirrup-high grasslands became mesquite deserts, and arroyos cut their way deeper through the barren plains following heavy summer rains. Studies of the state of Sonora have pointed out that more than 70 percent of the land shows signs of severe erosion.[43] The process of desertification continues to turn some beautiful borderlands into what are truly badlands.

Despite its despoliation and rapid urbanization, the borderlands remain an enchanting and visually spectacular place.[44] In fact, the term *desertification* tends to underscore the common perception that deserts are unnatural and unappealing. "But a true desert can't be created," said Caroline Wilson, interpretive specialist for Organ Pipe Cactus National Monument in Arizona. "Deserts are no more manmade than are rain forests or prairies."[45]

Although the danger signals about the unsustainability of present development trends are already flashing, for the time being the region seems slated for more growth. Cities keep expanding, and the wells just get deeper. This uncontrolled and undirected growth is taking an increasing toll on the borderlands biosphere. Yuccas and cacti are being yanked out of the desert and transplanted to the front yards of water-conscious homeowners in El Paso, San Diego, and Tucson. One analyst at the College of Sonora in Hermosillo claimed that the Sonoran desert is being turned into a barren strip as a result of all the desert trees and plants being smuggled into the United States. Mexican researchers have revealed that many fish species in the Rio Grande have been lost or severely threatened because of increasing salinity and that unregulated pumping has substantially decreased spring flow in the border states of Coahuila and Nuevo León.[46]

Water pollution is having a devastating impact on marine life at either end of the border. Clams and sand dollars, once abundant in the South Bay area below San Diego, are now rare. The dumping of sewage into the ocean has taken its toll in disappearing shellfish, crabs, and game fish. Environmentalists in Mexico warn that the Gulf of California is rapidly losing its ecological stability, as evidenced by the plummeting shrimp catches and the gradual disappearance of such endangered species as the vaquita porpoise and the totoaba fish, which tastes like white sea bass and often grows to six feet in length. Just as harmful as pollution to this rich marine ecology are the loosely regulated fishing industry and the sports fishermen from Southern California.[47]

In the Gulf of Mexico some 95 percent of the commercial fish and shellfish rely on coastal estuaries (wetlands and adjacent sea grass habitats in open water) during at least part of their life cycles. Oil production and coastal urbanization in both the United States and Mexico have resulted in a serious water pollution crisis, which has led to the permanent or conditional closure of 57 percent of the shellfish-growing areas along the U.S. Gulf Coast. Up to three thousand square miles of bottom waters off the Louisiana and southeastern Texas coasts are known as dead zones, where nothing lives because pollutants have depleted the oxygen. Other water pollution issues in the Gulf of Mexico include the escalating marine debris that poses a special threat to sea birds and marine mammals.[48] Texas Water Commissioner Gary Mauro testified at the EPA's 1992 hearings on its border environmental plan that the plan ignored the Gulf of Mexico, which he called the "most important border" between the two nations and the area that represents "our greatest risk of bilateral environmental calamity."[49]

Rose Farmer of the National Audubon Society in Brownsville pointed out that the lower Rio Grande Valley is really a delta region; this means that all the liquid wastes in this expansive area eventually make their way to the Gulf of Mexico. Once characterized by extensive palm and bush forests, the region is now a mix of plowed farmland, trailer parks, and orchards, where most of the native animal species are threatened or endangered. Environmentalists charge that the deformed birds and fish found in the Rio Grande and the Laguna Madre estuary on the Gulf of Mexico are the products of uncontrolled population and industrial growth in the region.[50] According to the Texas Land Commission, more than a third of the Gulf shellfish beds are contaminated, and a three-thousand-square-mile oxygen-deficient dead zone exists off the Texas and Louisiana coasts—at least partly created by increased U.S. and Mexican offshore petroleum development.[51]

## Exotic Goods

As an international crossroads the U.S.-Mexico border serves as a center of commerce in exotic species, especially birds. The U.S. Fish and Wildlife Service estimates that wildlife species with a retail value of ten to fifty million dollars are smuggled into the United States each year from Mexico.[52] Like most smuggling businesses, the illegal trade in tropical birds and animals involves a broad range of operatives—from the big entrepreneur to the small-time contraband artist. Bill Myers, one of only four U.S. Fish and Wildlife Service inspectors along the border, said that illegal birds often come in with undocumented immigrants. "It's as constant as drugs," observed Myers.[53]

In Brownsville it is common to see Mexicans selling birds out of paper bags at the flea market. At shops near the Tijuana market you can buy green and yellow parrots prepared for a quiet border crossing, their beaks and wings taped and wrapped inside a paper bag small enough to stuff inside your jacket. Although Mexico prohibits the export of birds, roughly 150,000 exotic birds are smuggled into the United States each year, most of them through Mexico from Central and South America.[54] It is a high-profit, low-risk business, one that is fueled, like the narcotics trade, by the large U.S. demand. In many cases the trade is transacted in back rooms, much like the stolen art business, but smugglers also sell exotic species openly to pet stores or through bird magazines with no questions asked.

The World Wildlife Fund, Defenders of Wildlife, and other conservation groups warn that the increased U.S.-Mexico trade that will result from a free-trade accord will create opportunities for expanded trafficking in wildlife from the tropics.[55] The United States stations four U.S. Fish and Wildlife Service inspectors along the border but plans no increase in agents despite projected rises in trade. In 1991 Mexico signed the Convention on International Trade in Endangered Species (CITES), which prohibits commercial trade in endangered species, but enforcement is minimal. The country serves as an international trading center and pipeline for protected animals from all over the world, but particularly from Latin America. Mexican conservationists claim that the traffic in pelts of such endangered feline species as jaguars, ocelots, and pumas is contributing to the disappearance of these wildlife in Mexico.[56] The fondness of many U.S. tourists and consumers for boots and other leather goods fashioned from the skins of turtles, lizards, and caribou is also eliminating Mexican wildlife. Despite their complete protection under Mexican law, many endangered species, such as sea turtles and crocodiles, continue to be threatened by illegal trade with the United States. Wildlife trade, along with the continuing clearing of forest for timber, agriculture, and pasture, has resulted in the complete loss of 50 percent of the country's forests and means that only 25 percent of the remaining forests are biologically fully intact.[57]

Another dimension of illegal wildlife trade has been the movement northward of such desert and tropical plants as cacti and orchids. Generally these plants are not cultivated commercially in Mexico but are part of an unsustainable harvest and trade in wild specimens in Mexico. One such problem is the contraband trade in mesquite from the high deserts of northern Mexico. Enterprising importers are scouring the high deserts of northern Mexico to meet the rising U.S. demand for steaks flavored by mesquite charcoal. Urban development, ranching, and the recent surge of fuel-wood cutting are stripping arid areas that suffer among the world's slowest rates of vegetation recovery. As the shrubs, trees, and cacti disappear, the ambient temperatures in some areas have increased by several degrees. According to Ciprés Villarreal, president of the Mexican Ecology Movement, the Sonoran desert is turning into a Saharalike inferno because of rapid loss of vegetation.[58]

Perhaps it is because this arid land seems so endless that it is treated so carelessly by many of its inhabitants and visitors. But the natural environment of the U.S.-Mexico border region—its water, plants, animals, birds, and even insects—is seriously endangered. Biologists warn that hundreds of plants, including dozens with known benefits to humans, merit special conservation efforts.[59] Obviously, conserving the borderlands bioresources cannot be a one-sided initiative but will depend on binational efforts, including joint environmental regulation programs and the creation of an international park system along the border.

# The "Other America"

Environmental crisis along the U.S.-Mexico border is nothing new to most border residents. Over the past three decades they have seen their streams and rivers die, their air become clogged with pollution, and the natural habitats for wildlife disappear. Closely related to these assaults on shared ecosystems is a public health crisis characterized by high incidences of such infectious diseases as hepatitis and tuberculosis. Frightening new reports of birth deformities, possibly a result of parental exposure to toxic chemicals, have given the public health crisis a doomsday quality.

For many years Dr. Laurance Nickey, director of the El Paso City-County Health and Environment District, has been sounding the alarm. Born in El Paso, Nickey went swimming in the Rio Grande as a boy but now is afraid to go near the river for fear of all the disease and toxicity it channels. "The U.S.-Mexico border is burning, and the flames need to be extinguished before they consume us," warned Nickey. In his view, border communities like El Paso are "the other America, the forgotten America."[60]

Not all those living along the border feel as strongly about environmental health issues as Dr. Nickey, but in places such as El Paso, Matamoros, Nogales, and San Diego there is rapidly spreading concern about the degradation of the natural and human environments. San Diegans are most upset about the pollution of their beaches by untreated waste from booming Tijuana, while those living along the Rio Grande complain that the border river has turned into a sewage ditch. On the Mexican side, concern is growing about the health effects of all the toxic wastes being dumped in its backyards by border industries.

It was not until the 1980s that environmental issues on the U.S.-Mexico border were given major diplomatic attention. Although concerns about water quality and sanitation had been raised as early as the 1940s, they were localized, low-level issues. However, it was the salinity crisis in the

Colorado Basin, not water contamination, that resulted in the first serious diplomatic tensions between the two countries over water quality in the borderlands.[61] Gradually complaints about the transboundary flows of sewage and air pollution pushed the two governments to address border sanitation problems.[62] But not until the 1990 announcement of a proposed free-trade agreement did the border environmental crisis become a full-blown foreign policy issue. Free trade suddenly pushed the "other America"—the one where Mexico and the United States meet—into the national spotlight.

Not all border residents are optimistic about the benefits of free trade—at least not from an environmental perspective. With the increase of overland trade, cities such as Laredo and El Paso will have more trucks rumbling through their streets. But as one border city official remarked, economic development should mean more than becoming the nation's largest truck stop. For Jesús Reynoso, El Paso's air-quality supervisor, "Free trade will be an environmental disaster. More vehicles and more people mean more pollution."[63]

Environmentalists, citizen watchdog groups, and the labor movement focused public and congressional attention on the borderlands in their attempt to forge a trade agreement that would adequately address health, safety, and environmental concerns. The border economy and society, while illustrative of the many benefits of close U.S.-Mexico relations, also reflect many of the problems resulting from U.S. trade and investment in Mexico. For opponents of a business-dominated free trade agreement, the borderlands present an excellent case study of the devastating health and environmental consequences of unregulated and undirected economic development.

Recognizing that environmental issues might become a sticking point in the effort to push a free trade accord through the U.S. Congress, the Bush and Salinas administrations quickly attempted to demonstrate their concern for the environmental and infrastructural crisis at the border. Previously the Mexican environmental agency SEDUE (later merged into SEDESOL) had concentrated what little regulatory capacity it had on the heavily polluted Mexico City metropolitan region. With the free trade debate stirring and U.S. concern about border pollution escalating, the Salinas administration opened new SEDUE/SEDESOL offices along the border and promised to deploy dozens of new agents. The flagship of this binational environmental campaign was the Integrated Border Environmental Plan (IBEP) coauthored by SEDUE and EPA. Critics of the fast-track approach to free trade regarded the IBEP and other official environmental initiatives more as part of a lobbying blitz than a demonstration of sincere concern and commitment. According to Mary Kelly, director of the Texas Center for Policy Studies, "In the rush to sign a free trade agreement, both the U.S. and Mexican governments are on the verge of relegating the border environmental issues to a high-profile sideshow, long on promises, but very short on meaningful changes and enforceable commitments to action." As Kelly noted, the IBEP did not even examine the potential environmental impacts of a free trade agreement on the border region.[64]

The new focus on the border, however, actually highlighted the fallacy of the free traders' standard argument that economic growth and a clean environment go hand in hand. Along the border, at least, that had certainly not been the case. The Border Industrialization Program of 1965 sparked a boom in population and economic growth, but in its wake came ecological catastrophe. Foreign investment and trade rose to unprecedented heights during the 1980s, but it was not until the free trade talks opened that the Mexican government demonstrated any serious concern for maintaining a clean border environment. On the U.S. side, communities watched as scores of Fortune 500 companies set up modern assembly plants in Mexico, but the borderlands seemed to look more like the third world all the time.

Attention to the border region has stirred up a heated debate about where financial responsibility lies. Who is to blame for the despoiled environment and for the public health crisis, and who should pay? For U.S. citizens living along the border, the answers come easily. Border communities—with the exception of San Diego—are among the poorest in the nation. Their tax bases do not even cover the cost of local public services, let alone extend to resolve international problems. Although many of the region's environmental problems, such as inadequate waste treatment facilities, come from the south side of the border, local government officials in the United States hesitate to blame Mexicans. Being from generally poor and crisis-ridden communities themselves, they are often sympathetic to the plight of Mexican border communities that do not have the financial resources to pay for needed environmental infrastructure projects. Nor is criticism of the *maquila* industry widespread on either side of the border, especially in official and business circles. The *maquiladoras* do boost the border economy—although not to the degree many would like—and there is a fear that too many regulations and taxes will drive away these footloose industries.

Instead U.S. border communities look to Washington for assistance to solve what they believe are essentially international problems. But congressional representatives from the northern states ask why they should pay to treat sewage from Nuevo Laredo, to provide water services to the *colonias*, or to increase the public health budget of El Paso. These are essentially foreign aid projects, some members of Congress have contended, pointing out that the traditional manufacturing centers of the Northeast and Midwest are also suffering from economic hard times and deteriorating infrastructure.

This search by U.S. border communities for funds to solve environmental and public health crises is also laced with irony: Many of these same cities have for years been trying to sell themselves as havens from high taxes and wages. Cities like El Paso are still actively trying to entice businesses from other states to open *maquiladoras* in neighboring Juárez. Border communities are clearly right that they face problems of an international nature. Yet why should federal funds underwrite the solutions to environmental problems that have in part been created by U.S. companies that ran away to Mexico to escape higher wage rates and perhaps even environmental regulations at home?

In Mexico, while the government has agreed that it should pay for the pollution created on its side, it has other priorities. Referring to the concern in San Diego that beaches have been closed because of inadequate or no sewage treatment in Tijuana, one government official commented, "You talk about the problems of surfers on Imperial Beach. Go to the neighborhoods in Tijuana where they have no pavement, no water or sewage system, and tell them about the big problem of the surfers."[65]

## Black Waters

At the historic La Fonda Inn in Santa Fe, conference participants made their way past demonstrators to attend the First Annual U.S.-Mexico Border Environmental Assembly in June 1992. It was a conference sponsored by the Border Progress Foundation, a private, nonprofit organization founded with a seed grant from the U.S. Environmental Protection Agency. But demonstrators from the Coalition for Justice in the Maquiladoras and even a few skeptics attending the assembly considered the gathering a sham. Instead of an honest effort to resolve border environmental problems, they saw the affair as part of a well-orchestrated public relations effort to push through a free trade agreement.

The protestors thought that the conference participants, mostly government and industry officials, were due for a reality check. Wearing rubber gloves, one of the protestors presented the conferees with a jar of dark, fetid water drawn from one of the sewage canals that run behind the *maquiladoras* in Matamoros. Many of the local government officials from the borderlands also thought that the conference sponsors needed some shock treatment. "I've got some news for those from Washington, Mexico City, or Austin for that matter," offered the county health supervisor, Dr. Laurance Nickey. "Santa Fe may be a very nice place, but it is not a border town. Next time they want to talk about the border they should have their conference in a real border city like El Paso so they can really see the problems we face."[66]

Even a short visit to El Paso or Ciudad Juárez, or any of the other border twins, reveals the immensity of the region's environmental crisis. It quickly becomes apparent that the international boundary is no barrier to pollution. Rising 828 feet next to the Rio Grande in El Paso is the smokestack of the ASARCO smelter, a company long considered one of the nation's worst polluters. Yet its closest neighbors, the ones who probably have been affected most by its lead and arsenic emissions, are not El Paso residents but the poor squatters who live across the river in Juárez *colonias*. Recent pollution-control and cleanup measures have significantly reduced arsenic and lead emissions from the ASARCO smelter pollution, but the air and water pollution from the smelter and El Paso's large refineries continue to present a cross-border pollution concern. In the mornings, the Mexican *colonia* residents on the banks of the Rio Grande claim they can taste metal in the air.

It is the same story throughout the borderlands. Environmental problems of one side sooner or later also become the problems of the opposite side. Clouds of white dust rising from Agua Prieta's unpaved roads settle over Douglas, Arizona. Knowing that untreated wastes from Tijuana and its 530 *maquilas* flush into the Pacific Ocean keeps many San Diegans from chancing a dip into their coastal waters. A steel fence erected to guard the U.S. border runs between Mexicali and Calexico, but its effectiveness is limited. The New River, reputed to be one of North America's most contaminated rivers, flows north past Mexicali's *maquiladoras* and sewerless *colonias*, under the border fence, and into the Imperial Valley.

The transboundary dimensions of contamination reach beyond air and water pollution to concerns for food quality. Fruits and vegetables sold on the streets of U.S. border cities are cultivated using wastewaters for irrigation, and the produce is then often carried by hand across waterways like the Rio Grande that are highly contaminated with raw sewage. Both the Mexican vendors and their contraband produce carry strains of such infectious diseases as hepatitis, dysentery, and even cholera—just one reason why the disease statistics of many U.S. border towns remind one of third world health profiles.

The border area, according to the American Medical Association, is "a virtual cesspool and breeding ground for infectious disease."[67] The main vehicle for disease transmission is what is called *aguas negras* (black water) throughout Latin America. *Aguas negras* is a generic term that describes most wastewater—the murky liquid that flows out of homes, neighborhoods, and industries in areas without sewers and wastewater treatment plants. As border cities expand so do the massive quantities of sewage. In the absence of industrial waste treatment facilities, mixed in with fecal matter are the chemical wastes from industrial manufacturers, mostly *maquiladoras*. Historically most Mexican towns have treated their *aquas negras* just as most individual families have: letting it flow off out of sight and out of mind. Finding more sanitary alternatives has usually not been a priority for either the poor Mexican family or the financially strapped municipal government. Nor have border industries in Mexico made proper waste disposal a priority. Extending electricity and water lines are the first development priorities. Although many Mexican border cities do now have drainage systems in place, effective wastewater treatment is still a rarity.

Along the border the *aguas negras* have become so voluminous that they can no longer be ignored. Running eighteen miles along the edge of Juárez and only a couple of hundred yards from the international border with El Paso is a large ditch (the *acequia madre*) that *juarenses* also call *el Agua Negra*. Every day this city of 1.2 million people produces some thirty million to sixty million gallons of wastewater. The black water is pumped out of the city and into outlying agricultural areas or into the Rio Grande.

The absence of a waste treatment facility in Juárez is not the exception. Instead it reflects the state of sewage disposal along the length of the U.S.-Mexico border. Juárez and other border cities have begun building waste treatment plants. The heart of the problem, however, is the tremendous and virtually unplanned population and industrial growth of the region. This growth, when combined with the generalized poverty of the borderlands and the lack of public financial resources, has made it difficult for government officials, particularly on the Mexican side, to maintain adequate sanitation and treatment facilities. In Mexico the absence of sewage systems is widespread and extensive—from the largest to the smallest population centers.

The problem is not confined to south of the border. Hugging the border on the U.S. side are the hundreds of uncharted subdivisions called *colonias*, that lack both water and sanitation systems, adding to the black water problem. Even when sewage treatment structures are in place in U.S. border cities, they often fail to meet federal standards and resort to the dubious practice of dumping treated water into nearby rivers and oceans. Both El Paso and Las Cruces, New Mexico, have been cited by state and federal authorities for dumping untreated sewage into the Rio Grande.[68]

Concern about the declining quality of the water on the border has exploded in recent years to become one of the main sources of cross-border tensions. But almost a half century ago, when the two nations established the binational International Boundary and Water Commission, water pollution was not even a topic of discussion. The 1944 treaty that established the commission set up the legal context for the integrated management of all U.S.-Mexico water conflicts. Focusing mainly on the sharing of surface water, the IBWC paid relatively little attention to the crisis of water pollution until the late 1970s, when public outcry made it a hot international issue. In 1979 the IBWC specifically acknowledged its responsibility in resolving waste treatment problems with the promulgation of its Resolution of Sanitation Problems.[69] Even so, the commission has been slow to act, and environmentalists have frequently criticized it for narrowly construing the phrase *border sanitation problems* and limiting its concern to projects such as sewage disposal works.[70] So bad is the reputation of the IBWC among many border activists that they are convinced that the commission's mandate should not be explicitly extended to all water quality issues because it would do an unacceptable job. Instead they call for a new binational border organization with a clear environmental mandate.[71]

Most transboundary water-quality surveys indicating industrial pollution along the border have been undertaken by private groups, such as the Border Ecology Project or the National Toxic Waste Campaign, not by the IBWC—or the EPA or its Mexican counterpart, SEDESOL. For its part, the IBWC has collected hydrological data on transboundary groundwater, but it has been unwilling to stick its neck out on this issue by releasing the results of its studies or proposing solutions to this developing crisis. Such inactivity and irresponsibility have led many to call for a radical revamping of the IBWC or for the creation of a more environmentally conscious binational commission.[72] For many environmentalists and local government authorities on the border, hope that the two federal governments would begin to devote more serious attention and financial resources to resolving the water-quality crisis was dashed in 1992 with the publication of the widely criticized Integrated Border Environmental Plan. The plan met with sharp public criticism because of its vague promises, absence of funding mechanisms, and narrow scope.

The fouling of surface and groundwater occurs on both sides of the border and generally results from untreated or inadequately treated human and industrial wastes as well as from the increased salinity arising from the overuse of scarce water supplies. Along the U.S.-Mexico border twin cities face increasingly severe water pollution. The ditches and rivers have a different odor, color, and character depending on their location. In some places the "water" is unusually bubbly, apparently because of rapid organic waste decomposition. Near industrial sites a rock thrown in a ditch will release ominous vapors from the darkness below. At other sites the odor of fecal matter is especially nauseating, while sometimes the smell has a more chemical bite. Usually the *aguas negras* are decked with a brownish froth, and you can often see the glint of unnatural colors. After dark the Tijuana River frequently turns a metallic red as the night lights mix with some unknown toxic. Squatter settlements are often found by the sides of these waterways, but evidence of other life is rare. In the few cases where water has been tested, fecal coliform counts are frightfully high. Mosquitoes also seem to thrive, and looking down into the New River in Mexicali, you can occasionally see a few fish—probably a mutant breed—cavorting in the waste stream.

At the border's western end the Tijuana River crosses the international line on its course toward the Pacific Ocean. Like most rivers and streams along the borderlands, it has turned into a sewage canal. Its putrid waters gurgle from decomposing waste, alarming area residents, who have formed a protest group called Citizens Revolting Against Pollution. The sewage coursing through the Tijuana River has threatened some of the most beautiful beaches in Southern California. Joggers still run along the beaches, and a few foolhardy surfers ignore the posted warnings: CONTAMINATED WITH SEWAGE. KEEP OUT. AVOID ALL CONTACT. A survey of its San Diego members by the Surfrider Foundation detected such health problems as ear infections, hepatitis, and giardiasis and other gastrointestinal problems.[73]

Unlike some other Mexican border cities, Tijuana has waste treatment facilities. But these overloaded and inefficient plants do not have the capacity to process all the sewage and industrial wastes produced by this 1.7-million-person metropolis. At least a third of the city's liquid waste goes untreated, and much of that flows northward into San Diego County through the Tijuana River and assorted gullies and gulches. Various solutions have been proposed. But many people are skeptical that the problem will ever be solved, and there is also much disagreement about who should pay to treat Tijuana's wastes.

One answer has been simply to pipe the wastewaters back to Mexico in what is known as a "return to sender" solution. But it has been an exercise in futility, since Tijuana does not have the facilities to treat this waste. Furthermore, the wastes that are piped into waste treatment plants are inadequately treated and then flow back up along the coastline to sully San Diego beaches and coastal waters. Lately San Diego has been treating the ten million to thirteen million gallons of waste that flows through the Tijuana River at its own Point Loma Wastewater Treatment Plant.

All is not well on the U.S. side either. The EPA has a four-year-old lawsuit against San Diego, accusing the city of endangering the environment and human health by inadequately treating its sewage. The Point Loma facility is overloaded, and its 2.2-mile drainpipe into the Pacific recently ruptured, spilling wastes onto city beaches. The best solution seems to be a four-hundred-million-dollar treatment plant to be financed by a combination of city, state, and federal agencies along with a fifty-million-dollar commitment from the Mexican government. But the unwillingness of many U.S. congressional representatives to fund border projects and of most border residents to pay for projects they consider a federal responsibility threatens the completion of this and other environmental cleanup projects in the borderlands.

Even if the proposed wastewater treatment plant in the Tijuana River valley went forward, few would predict that the sewage problem in Tijuana–San Diego or any other twin city area would soon be solved. There would remain the problem of renegade waste that never enters the city's sewers because half the inhabitants are not hooked up to the municipal system. "One way or another, Mexico keeps growing and their sewage keeps coming over here," remarked David Gomez of Citizens Revolting Against Pollution.[74] Gomez and his group want San Diego to assume more responsibility for resolving the environmental health problems along the border. "If your moats are full of sewage," Gomez said, "it doesn't matter if you live in a castle."[75]

The U.S. border is so contaminated by untreated wastes from Tijuana that California health authorities have prohibited the sale of produce from the truck farms in the San Ysidro area. Along the entire length of the border prospective immigrants often wrap plastic bags around their feet and shins before crossing the rivers and waterways that mark the border. But keeping themselves dry is only one reason that they don the plastic wraps. At a place nicknamed Smugglers' Gulch on the Tijuana–San Diego border, one veteran immigrant explained that even with plastic coverings the sewage he had to wade through was so toxic that he often ended up with an itchy rash on his lower legs.[76]

For the immigrants, crossing the border into the United States often means wading across a border line of filthy water. And for health officials in San Diego and other border cities, that means exposing themselves and U.S. citizens to salmonella, shigella, cholera, and hepatitis. An increasing concern is that these *aguas negras* are laden with mosquito larvae, which are increasing the risk of outbreaks of even more exotic health threats, such as malaria and encephalitis.

East of Tijuana lies Mexicali, the capital of Baja California, which does have an elementary waste treatment facility, but it is unable to process all the city's wastes. Consequently, some of the city's raw sewage and industrial waste flows directly into the New River, which flows through Calexico, California, emptying eventually into the Salton Sea, which lies southeast of Palm Springs. More than ninety toxic chemical compounds have been found in the New River, including carcinogens such as PCBs, trichloroethylene, acetone, and vinyl chloride. As in the San Diego area, residents of the Imperial Valley resent receiving Mexicali sewage. Some farmers complain that they are required to have their wastes treated before dumping them into the New River even though the river is already badly polluted with untreated sewage from Mexico.[77]

Since the late 1950s the Nogales border cities have had an international agreement whereby a waste treatment plant on the U.S. side would process the wastes from its twin city. The capacity of the treatment plant soon became overloaded by the wastes from the mushrooming population on the Mexican side. Another problem, one that is common up and down the border, is that the sewer system in Nogales, Sonora, does not serve the majority of the city's residents. Instead the liquid wastes accumulate in pungent pools and eventually trickle down the city's barren hills into arroyos often flowing across the border. As a result of all this raw sewage accumulating in its streets, storm canals, and rivers, the hepatitis rate of Nogales, Arizona, is about twenty times the national average.

The Nogales Wash, which flows north from Mexico, regularly contains such toxic chemicals as mercury, nitrates, lead, and cyanide. So contaminated is this waterway that in 1991 it exploded and set on fire a city block in Nogales, Sonora. But the chemical pollution is not limited to surface transboundary flows. Water testing has revealed the existence of a ten-mile underground plume of chemical contamination flowing north into Arizona.[78]

*Piperos* are the salvation of hundreds of thousands of *colonia* residents on both sides of the border. These are the men who fill up tanker trucks with water for delivery to the dusty parts of town where water lines do not reach. Residents wait as the *piperos* pump a week's supply of water into fifty-five-gallon metal drums that once held industrial chemicals, the toxicity of which is often clearly (but in English) described on attached labels. But on the border one outrage always seems overshadowed by another. Such is the case in Nogales, Sonora, where the water the *piperos* deliver to water-starved communities and to *maquilas* is badly contaminated by toxic chemicals. Although an alternative well exists, the city permits the *piperos* to continue to draw their water from a municipal well that was recently found to be polluted with industrial solvents. The Nogales Wash, which runs through town and near the polluted well, has been posted with DANGER, KEEP OUT, POLLUTED WATER signs on the U.S. side.[79]

Farther east, such cities as Nuevo Laredo that have no treatment facilities simply pump their wastes into the Rio Grande. As the river flows through downtown Nuevo Laredo, it has a fecal contamination level exceeding two hundred thousand coliform bacteria per milliliter—a thousand times the limit in Texas, which closes public recreation lakes if they have more than two hundred bacteria per milliliter.[80] "It's like living in Calcutta," remarked Adolph Kahn of Laredo, who is spearheading an effort to cleanse the Rio Grande.[81] Cities on the U.S. side such as Laredo and Brownsville also dump their wastewater in the river but only after a dual treatment and disinfection process.

Urbanization is the most obvious cause of the current water pollution crisis in the borderlands. Closely related to the uncontrolled population growth has been the industrial explosion over the past three decades, but particularly since the early 1980s. Just as the *juarenses* or the *tijuanenses* have no waste facilities, neither do most *maquiladoras*. Their liquid wastes, like those of the squatter colonies surrounding the factories, flow into ponds and ditches that eventually contaminate the rivers and groundwater. Toxic chemicals such as methylene chloride and toluene mix with human feces in the *aguas negras* of the U.S.-Mexico border. Yet another largely unaddressed sanitation problem along the border—and throughout Mexico—is the use of untreated wastewater to irrigate crops on the outskirts of urban areas. This practice represents a health threat not only to Mexican consumers but also to U.S. shoppers who buy fruits, vegetables, and meat produced in Mexico.

## Darkened Skies

The uncontrolled flow of black waters may be the most serious environmental danger in the borderlands, but the darkening of the borderlands skies is probably the best evidence that borders do nothing to obstruct the free flow of pollution.

Many border towns have become large cities with freeways and skyscrapers, but the gritty dust of the border is still part of the picture. In fact, the skies that hang over the borderlands are browner and dustier than ever. But what you see, breathe, and smell in the air is not all dust. The winds now also carry alarming quantities of such pollutants as ozone, carbon monoxide, sulfur dioxide, and lead as well as particulate matter. Like the black waters of the border region, the brown pallor of these southwestern skies has become a major health hazard.

The full extent of air pollution along the border is not known. In major U.S. border cities, air-monitoring stations do measure local pollution for violations of the U.S. National Ambient Air Quality Standards. Less is known about more remote locations on the U.S. side. But until recently there was no attempt to monitor air standards on the Mexican side. The Mexican government has promised to begin air pollution sampling, but as yet the full scope of the problem can only be guessed.

Vehicle emissions, dust from unpaved roads, and industrial pollutants are the major culprits. Carbon monoxide and ozone contamination is most serious in El Paso and San Diego because of their large size and the temperature inversions that afflict those areas. Increasingly many observers are pointing the finger of blame at U.S. customs and immigrations officials whose slow border inspections keep incoming traffic backed up with engines running. So lethal are the resulting fumes that the customs officials are rotated every half hour at some border crossings to give the agents some relief.

Lax vehicle emissions regulations in Mexico also contribute to high ozone and carbon monoxide levels across the border. It was not until 1991 that Mexico mandated that all new cars produced for the domestic market must have pollution control devices. Because of the difficulty of finding unleaded gasoline in Mexico, there is a booming business among mechanics to remove the catalytic converters from cars imported from the United

States. Border cities have recently begun enforcing emissions levels on newly registered cars. While applauding these new controls, health officials in El Paso point out that the maximum levels permitted in Juárez are 3.5 times higher than those enforced on the U.S. side. Another problem is the relative ages of cars on either side of the border. El Paso has more vehicles than Juárez, but the average age of those on the Mexican side of the border is almost twice that found on the U.S. side. In Juárez the average age of vehicles is twelve years.[82] As a result, the Mexican vehicles are far more likely to lack pollution control devices and to be poorly tuned.[83] Not only are Mexican vehicles generally older and poorly maintained, but they also use low-quality gasoline. On the U.S. side, regular gasoline has 0.1 grams of lead per gallon and unleaded contains just 0.05 grams, but in Mexico regular Pemex gas is loaded with 1 to 2 grams of lead, and unleaded gas also has a higher lead content. In Juárez an estimated 90 percent of the gas sold is leaded—in contrast with 15 percent across the border.[84]

A closely related problem is the flow of Mexican traffic into the United States. According to San Diego County Supervisor Brian Bilbray, vehicles coming from Mexico account for less than 1 percent of the city's traffic but produce 13 percent of the vehicle-generated pollution.[85] One solution would be to require Mexican vehicles to meet local standards if traveling in the United States. But as with other attempts to control pollution along the border, proposals to enforce strict emissions standards mean additional economic hardships for a poverty-stricken population. As an environmental consultant observed, "To buy a set of points and plugs is a week's wage in Mexico. You can't expect them to spend a week's wages to meet our standards."[86]

In an attempt to meet federal air quality standards, El Paso has recently begun to pave most of its dirt alleys and roads. But one has only to look across the Rio Grande at the dusty *colonias* on the Juárez hillsides to see that the high particulate concentrations in the city's air are not likely to improve appreciably even though some Mexican border towns have begun paving more of their roads.

The scene is repeated along the entire length of the border. The central portions of the Mexican border towns generally have paved streets, but outside the downtown areas extends an uncharted maze of dusty roads. Barren hillsides are covered with concrete and plywood shacks, and ankle-deep dust covers many of the streets during the dry seasons.

Actually, the longest-running concern about air pollution in the borderlands has not been about either carbon monoxide or particulate matter but rather about smelter pollution. Following a groundswell of citizen protests, the Mexican and U.S. governments undertook cooperative efforts to lower sulfur dioxide emissions from the copper smelting operations on both side of the Sonora-Arizona line involving smelters in Cananea, Nacozari, and Douglas (which was later shut down). Although greatly reduced, the emission of sulfur dioxide and trace minerals remains an environmental concern along this part of the border. Recent privatizations of Mexican mines followed by the 1992 overhaul of the Cananea smelter raise new concerns that the specific provisions of the 1983 binational agreement regarding smelter emissions from the Nacozari and Cananea smelters may not be respected.[87] Farther east in El Paso, the ASARCO copper smelter and the city's petroleum refineries also present a cross-border pollution problem.[88]

Whereas the smoke belching out of ASARCO's smelter has diminished in recent years as the result of new pollution controls mandated by the government, citizen concern on both sides of the border has increasingly focused on other border industries, particularly the chemical factories and *maquiladoras* scattered along the Mexican side from Matamoros to Mexicali. In the Matamoros-Reynosa area alone, there have been seven major industrial accidents since the late 1980s that have sent more than 350 people to hospitals and forced thousands to flee their homes to avoid massive discharges of toxic fumes from chemical plants.

The most striking air pollution problem along the border is neither vehicle nor industrial emissions but the open fires on the Mexican side. Looking down on Juárez from the hills of El Paso, you can see wisps of gray smoke from household heating fires rising everywhere during the winter months. Darkening the skyline are the black plumes that result from the open burning of garbage at the city dump. A steady stream of smoke also rises from the part of town where brickmakers use old tires and sawdust to fire their kilns.

In Juárez, as in many Mexican towns, small industries and individual families generate heat during the cold winter months by making their own fires because they have no electricity or heaters. They burn wood, old tires, cardboard, and just about any kind of trash to fuel those fires, and the resultant smoke darkens the skies and clogs lungs on both sides of the border.

Considering the widespread poverty in Mexican border towns, it would be difficult for Mexican authorities to prohibit household fires that provide the only source of heat for many families. But the open burning of wastes in municipal dumps and the brickmakers' practice of burning old tires are problems that may more easily be controlled, as seen in Juárez where all brickyards are being converted to gas-fired kilns. Still, the pervasive poverty in Mexico—not only of individual families but also of government institutions—stands as a major obstacle in the battle against pollution and for improved environmental health. As Jesús Reynoso, El Paso's air quality supervisor, pointed out, "I don't even think Juárez owns a street sweeper."[89] Although generally an urban problem, air pollution is also a product of the rural borderlands. Tilled fields on both sides of the line and the common practice of burning ditch banks and fields further degrade the air.

Although primarily an environmental health issue, air pollution is also an aesthetic concern. The once deep blue skies of the borderlands are losing their clarity. No longer an isolated and largely untouched region, the borderlands now share the environmental problems of other industrial and population centers.

Worsening air and water pollution add up to an alarming state of environmental health along the border. Texans living near the Rio Grande are three to five times more likely than other Texas residents to suffer from intestinal illnesses. In the border community of San Elizario, near El Paso, 90 percent of all adults contract hepatitis by age thirty-five, and there are more cases of tuberculosis in El Paso County than are found in nineteen states.[90] The incidence of most communicable diseases, including syphilis, is significantly higher in U.S. border communities than in the rest of the country.[91] In the poor *colonias* strung along the U.S. border, residents suffer third world rates of dysentery.

Disease, like air and water pollution, does not respect national boundaries. "We can't keep chicken pox north of the border, and measles south," said one border health official.[92] To protect the health of their own citizens, U.S. border health authorities recognize the urgent need for increased cooperation with the Mexican government and nongovernmental organizations in matters of public health. This was brought home to many on the U.S. side by the spread of cholera in Mexico and then in April 1992 by the appearance of a case of cholera in Brownsville, Texas.

Although environmental health conditions are severe on both sides of the border, the problems are much worse on the Mexican side. Ironically, however, the health status along Mexico's northern border compares favorably with the nation as a whole. Although many of the environmental risk factors, such as poor water and air quality, are similar and health facilities are also inadequate, Mexican border residents are better off with respect to disease and mortality rates. This reduced health risk level is apparently due to the relatively higher standard of living found in the northern borderlands.[93]

Border health officials in the United States feel overwhelmed by the spreading public health crisis throughout the borderlands. Cutbacks in federal and state health programs are largely responsible, but also worrisome has been the mushrooming of *colonias* on the U.S. side of the international line. The Mexican-American families who live in these isolated *colonias* usually dig their own wells, and they are often sunk fewer than ten yards from the outdoor privies they have constructed. In light of conditions such as these, the high incidence of communicable diseases—particularly gastrointestinal ailments—does not surprise public health officials in places like El Paso or Brownsville.

The public health crisis is magnified across the border, where rather than the exception the lack of adequate water and sanitation services is the rule. Also in stark contrast are the public health infrastructures in Mexico and the United States. The disparities here are immense and expanding. The El Paso City/County Health and Environmental District, serving more than 600,000 people, operates on an annual budget of $11.3 million, while the 1.5 million population of Juárez is served by a health department with an estimated annual budget of just $500,000.

For residents of the borderlands, the public health crisis is not news. But as free trade talks heated up, horror stories about living and working in the border area made U.S. national headlines for the first time. City, county, and state officials in the United States took advantage of the rising national interest in the U.S.-Mexico border to alert the U.S. public and Congress to the third world conditions that existed along long stretches of the border—and to ask for increased federal assistance. At the same time, activists questioning the advisability of a free trade treaty with Mexico and journalists examining U.S. trade and investment in Mexico highlighted the environmental and occupational health hazards associated with the *maquila* industry.

*Maquiladoras* suddenly found themselves under scrutiny not only for waste disposal practices but also for their treatment of their low-paid workforce. Environmentalists in the United States, thrust into the free trade debate, began to express concern not only about natural resource issues but also about broader environmental health issues, such as the chemical pollution inside the *maquiladoras* and the unhealthy living conditions of *maquila* workers. For more than a quarter of a century the *maquiladoras* operated in relative obscurity. The Mexican government left the industry alone, imposing virtually no environmental regulations and giving the plants nearly free rein in their treatment of the workforce.

Especially when compared with most local industries, the *maquilas* seem modern and attractive. Inside, many of these assembly plants have a high-tech ambience and are generally cool, clean, and bright—not your typical sweatshop. Although the *maquiladoras* may in fact have better and safer working environments than many Mexican-owned manufacturing plants, they have fallen far short of being responsible corporate citizens. Since 1965, when the *maquiladora* program was instituted, the *maquilas* have taken full advantage of Mexico's lax regulatory climate and the lack of unions. Assembly operations were transferred from the United States but not U.S. environmental and occupational health standards. The results of this quarter century of neglect are predictable: low occupational safety standards, contaminated water near the industrial parks, widespread illegal dumping, and little monitoring of the use and disposal of hazardous chemicals.[94] The foul-smelling liquid that the Coalition for Justice in the Maquiladoras presented to EPA officials in Santa Fe was offered as a symbol of all these abuses.

"The land will never be the same. It's lost," said Ernestina Sánchez, whose home sits next to the holding pond of Retzloff Chemical, a pesticides manufacturer in Matamoros. Her father established this neighborhood a half a century ago, and her family used to be able to drink the well water here until the U.S. factories moved in.[95] Now the neighborhood smells as if it has just been sprayed with pesticides, and the groundwater is tainted with unknown substances.

Dipped into a chemical bath, the borderlands and its residents are learning just how hazardous some of the toxic chemicals that border industries use really are. One of the most shocking cases is that of the Mallory children, the daughters and sons of women who worked at the Mallory Capacitors plant in Matamoros during the 1970s. Doctors have identified at least fifty-four profoundly handicapped or deformed children—known in Matamoros as *los niños de Mallory*—born of mothers who worked at the plant. As part of their job, the Mallory workers washed capacitors in a chemical wash that they called *Electrolito* 95, apparently containing polychlorinated biphenyls (PCBs). The chemical covered their hands and arms and sometimes splashed into their faces. The former *maquiladora* workers also say they suffered from rashes, headaches, nausea, and fainting while employed at Mallory.[96]

The women are suing the company. But they have difficulty in proving the link between their jobs and the fate of their children because tests have found no PCBs in either the mothers' or the children's blood. Another obstacle is getting the corporate father of the Mallory children to admit responsibility for the sins of a past owner. Ownership of the company has changed hands several times, passing from Mallory to Kraft to North American Capacitor Company to Black & Decker.

In 1991 the Brownsville area was hit by another disturbingly high cluster of deformed children. Doctors found thirty-one babies with neural tube defects in a twenty-five-month period—significantly higher than U.S. national or statewide rates for these birth deformities known as anencephaly. Since 1986 there have been more than eighty incidents of anencephalic babies in the lower Rio Grande Valley. Most were born within a couple of miles of the Rio Grande, and there was widespread speculation that the prevailing winds carried toxic chemicals discharged from Matamoros *maquiladoras* across the river into Brownsville. Others suspect that pesticides sprayed on nearby farms may be the culprit. A yearlong study by the Centers for Disease Control and the Texas Department of Health was unable, however, to point to an environmental explanation for this abnormally high incidence of anencephalic babies. It did mention the environment, along with genetics, poor prenatal care, and malnutrition as possible contributing factors. Mexico has one of the highest rates of anencephaly in the world—six times the U.S. rate and three times the rate for South America.[97]

The Coalition for Justice in the Maquiladoras blames the *maquila* industry, pointing to studies linking the use of two industrial solvents— xylene and toluene—to neural stem defects.[98] According to this activist group, at the time the anencephalic babies were conceived the Stepan Chemical Company and General Motors were dumping xylene and other hazardous chemicals into open canals behind their plants at levels that exceeded U.S. standards by six thousand to fifty-three thousand times. No firm link, however, has yet been established between the hazardous chemicals released by the *maquiladoras* and the large anencephaly cluster in this border city. One doctor in Brownsville speculated that this frightening deformity may actually be the "tip of the iceberg" of toxic chemical problems in the area.[99] In reaction to the controversy, the Mexican government's secretary of health in Juárez issued a "Protocol for the Study of Anencephaly," which had the bad taste to advise that "with NAFTA imminent, it's imperative that we clear up all doubts about the country's sanitation infrastructure as well as about our control of hazardous wastes."[100]

Traveling along the border, one soon discovers that assigning blame for the environmental crisis is an exercise in futility. Who is the culprit? The Mexican government for not enforcing strict environmental controls or the U.S.-owned *maquiladoras* that set lower environmental and occupational health standards than at plants based in the United States? Or is it really a cultural issue, or perhaps a problem rooted in the different levels of economic development found on either side of the border?

Even when responsibility can be fairly assigned, finger-pointing does not help solve what usually have become common problems. Instead border communities and their government representatives increasingly realize that the time has come to search for common solutions to the mounting ecological catastrophe. Archie Close, El Paso regional director of the Texas Air Quality Board, expressed the common sentiment of border officials that "the problems are obvious, and so it serves no purpose to find fault with the other side because we need their cooperation to accomplish anything."[101]

Local authorities in the United States complain that federal officials fail to recognize the international causes of air quality violations, and that regional offices of EPA are ill equipped to deal with binational issues.[102] Rather than wait around for the federal governments to act, many border cities have initiated joint programs. El Paso, for example, regularly sprays the sewage canal in Juárez to keep the mosquito population down, and Douglas, Arizona, has offered to provide Agua Prieta with the pitch and slag to pave its dusty roads. The international border, however, places a severe limit on locally arranged solutions. Expressing this frustration, one San Diego official remarked, "We share the same air basin and the same sources of water for most things in Tijuana, but we sometimes have to wait for Washington to take the circuitous route to talk with Mexico City."[103] The fragmentation between various local, state, and federal agencies in the United States continues to obstruct solutions to the border's environmental crisis.

Yet even with better and quicker cross-border communications on both a local and national level, the problem of money remains. SEDUE's former director and current director of SEDESOL's National Ecology Institute (INE) Sergio Reyes Lujan observed, "Everyone knows how to stop pollution in the river, you construct a treatment plant for the sewage. The technological solution is simple, but for economic reasons, many cities are not able to apply the solution."[104] But money is only part of the solution. Also lacking in Mexico are representative governments and legal systems in which local citizens can exert pressure on their government officials. In the United States the mechanisms for citizen participation do exist, but the voices of border residents are often ignored. Some also question the technology fix proposed by SEDESOL and EPA, pointing out that more front-end solutions are needed to prevent hazardous wastes from entering the waste stream in the first place and to encourage more appropriate and natural solutions that contribute to sustainable development.

Local officials in U.S. border cities have applauded the promise of the Mexican government to increase SEDESOL's presence along the border but are waiting to see if it is more than a rhetorical commitment. Despite pronouncements that enforcement of environmental regulations would be dramatically increased, SEDESOL appears to be falling short on its promises. At the same time, border officials complain about the EPA's lack of presence along the border, despite all the rhetoric from Washington about its concern for border environmental problems. "The United States spends millions to help faraway countries. Why can't we help the people who live next to us?" asked Dr. Nickey. "By helping them, we help ourselves." Patrick Zurick, Nickey's counterpart in Nogales, Arizona, noted that the environmental and public health crisis along the border is not a local but an international crisis. He complained, "It's as if we're supposed to be waiting for a body count before we get action."[105]

# The Poison Trail

International commerce and investment involve more than the cross-border flow of materials and money. Increasingly poisons also flow back and forth across borders. Because of stricter dumping laws in the United States and other developed nations, many firms are shipping their toxic wastes—legally or illegally—to third world countries, where the regulatory climate is much looser.

Some corporations go a step further. Frustrated by environmental health and occupational safety regulations, they pack up their plants—or at least the most hazardous operations—and move overseas, or south of the border. They run away to what some economists call pollution havens. In these less regulated locations they can dump toxic chemicals and ignore occupational safety standards without any government agency looking over their shoulders.

In a global economy it is hard to have toxic chemicals and substances stay put. They sometimes boomerang back across borders. This is especially true with contaminated food products, which may be sprayed with pesticides banned in the United States or irrigated with untreated wastewater, but end up in the food baskets of U.S. consumers. Similarly, pharmaceuticals and various consumer products that have been either banned or restricted or are unregistered in their countries of origin often are exported to third world countries. This practice has been called the "corporate crime of the century."[106]

Neither do ecosystems respect international borders. Wildlife, such as birds found in the estuaries of the Gulf of Mexico and Southern California, have, for example, been found to have high levels of DDT in their tissues. Banned in the United States, DDT is used by the government for pest control in Mexico. In the 1980s two environmental concerns—stratospheric ozone depletion and climate change caused by the accumulation

191

of "greenhouse gases"—gave environmentalism a new global context. Public concern and new scientific findings have combined to create a deepening sense of global interconnection. Not only are nations interconnected as contamination—in the form of acid precipitation, air pollution, marine and water pollution, and transboundary waste shipments—crosses national boundaries, but government officials and activists alike are finding that economic and environmental issues are also linked. No longer can such matters as trade, debt, or even personal lifestyle choices be separated from the environment.[107]

## Circle of Poison Becomes Two-Way Street

Free trade talk has renewed the circle of poison issue in the United States.[108] Environmentalists and consumer advocates are now warning that food safety regulations protecting consumers against pesticide-tainted produce may be weakened as trade barriers break down. The fear is that pesticide residue standards will be harmonized downward so as not to act as a barrier to international trade. Another concern is that the threat of plant closures and relocation abroad will be used by industry to keep local and federal governments from imposing stricter environmental and safety standards for products and production.

In 1962 Rachel Carson's book *Silent Spring* alerted U.S. consumers to the frightening repercussions of uncontrolled agrochemical use on the natural and human environment. Gradually, stiffer food safety regulations were set by the Environmental Protection Agency. Numerous pesticides, particularly the long-lasting organochlorines like DDT, were banned or heavily restricted in the early 1970s because they persist in the environment and accumulate in animal and plant tissues. Companies producing those and other chemicals began exporting them to countries like Mexico, where regulations were more lax or nonexistent.[109]

At the same time, the United States began importing more of its food, especially fruits and vegetables, from foreign countries. This set off fears about a circle of poison in which U.S. consumers were eating tomatoes, bananas, strawberries, and bell peppers contaminated with pesticides outlawed by the U.S. government but produced by U.S. companies and shipped abroad. To protect consumers and to allay concerns about this circle of poison, the Food and Drug Administration (FDA) placed agents along the border to inspect incoming produce.

With about three billion pounds of produce annually crossing the border from Mexico, finding pesticides on a strawberry or a head of lettuce can be a daunting task. A stream of refrigerated truckloads passes through customs from Mexico, supplying about half of the vegetables and fruits consumed in the United States during the winter months. Nationally, about 1 percent of imports are checked for illegal pesticide residues.[110] In contrast with the occasional character of food safety testing, most produce coming from Mexico is checked to guarantee that it is up to the cosmetic quality demanded by the U.S. market and to ensure that it does not carry insects that could menace U.S. growers.

Jack Grady, one of two FDA agents stationed at the El Paso border crossing, acknowledged that contaminated produce is not being stopped at the boundary. For one thing, he said, the FDA office is only open during weekdays, while some truckers pass through customs on weekends or after 5:00 P.M. Moreover, the U.S. Department of Agriculture, which has to stamp all food shipments but does not check for pesticides, commonly does not even notify the FDA that produce is at the dock. When Grady does take a sample, he ships it by bus to Dallas for a multiresidue laboratory test, and if the laboratory does not report back to him by 5:00 P.M. the next day, the produce is free to enter the United States. FDA records in El Paso showed that some produce is being stopped at the border, as were recent shipments of lettuce, papaya, and squash, some of which were tainted with DDT.[111]

Of those Mexican vegetables and fruits that are tested, some tests have shown that pesticide residues are generally twice the levels commonly found on domestically grown produce, although only a small percentage is so high that the EPA considers it a threat to health.[112] About 5 percent of the tests reveal unacceptable residues—approximately double the rate for domestic samplings—but most of this contaminated produce is already purchased and consumed by the time the test results are available.[113] Of additional concern to those persnickety eaters who worry about the carcinogenic and gene-damaging properties of pesticides is the inadequacy of the FDA tests, which are capable of detecting fewer than one-half of the estimated six hundred pesticides on the market. According to Jay Feldman of the National Coalition Against the Misuse of Pesticides, "The basic information that EPA needs to make food-safety decisions does not exist for many widely used pesticides."[114]

As the U.S. border opens up to increased agricultural trade, the circle of poison issue has gained new attention. Like other environmental concerns, questions of pesticide use and abuse have suddenly become subjects of the international trade debate. Not just environmentalists and consumer advocates are grumbling about lax pesticide controls in Mexico. Agribusiness representatives like William Ramsey of the Western Growers Association have gone to Congress to complain that Mexican farmers enjoy an unfair advantage since "U.S. producers are unable to use some chemical tools that their counterparts in Mexico can utilize."[115]

As with other environmental issues, the problem in Mexico is not so much the absence of laws regulating pesticide use as the lack of enforcement. Pesticides that the government prohibits or restricts are commonly used, especially for the domestic market. Another concern is the lack of education about chemical inputs in agriculture. With the cutbacks resulting from structural adjustment measures in recent years, the secretary of agriculture's extension department has all but disappeared. Mexican consumers are unprotected from high pesticide residues on produce, more and more of which is imported as trade barriers break down with the United States and Central America.

With an increasing percentage of the produce consumed in the United States coming from Mexico, there is obvious reason for concern—in terms of both food safety and economic competition. Five of the dozen agricultural chemicals labeled the "Dirty Dozen" by the Pesticide Action Network International are registered for restricted use in Mexico. These are chlordane, aldicarb, lindane, paraquat, and pentachlorophenol. Mexican growers also use thirty-six chemicals that are prohibited in many industrial countries or are found among the UN's list of extremely hazardous agrochemicals.

In Mexico there is extensive use of pesticides that are either banned or heavily restricted by the EPA. For example, the herbicide Haloxifop and the insecticide Protiophos are not registered in the United States because of their dangerous properties but are exported to Mexico. In fact, the Mexican government through its Fertimex state enterprise has long been the chief manufacturer of several of the organochlorine poisons, including DDT.[116] In 1992 the Fertimex division producing pesticides was privatized. It is now owned by an affiliate of Velsicol USA, which plans to continue production of DDT, BHC, parathion, and other dangerous pesticides.

It is also true that U.S. firms, prohibited from selling certain chemicals at home, either sell them to Mexico or have affiliates in Mexico processing and distributing the EPA-restricted agrochemicals. Among the transnational corporations manufacturing pesticides in Mexico are such companies as Ciba-Geigy, Bayer, Du Pont, Dow Chemical, ICI, and Monsanto. About 30 percent of the pesticide compounds for which the EPA has not set residue standards (mostly because these chemicals are not registered as the result of their hazardous qualities) are registered for use in Mexico.[117] Pesticide companies in the United States export not only hazardous chemicals but also production technologies and facilities (which are often obsolete) to Mexico and other third world nations.[118]

To focus on the circle of poison issue, however, overlooks the other hazards of increased pesticide use. In Mexico pesticide use more than doubled in the 1980s, and the pesticides of choice have been mostly ones with EPA-established residue levels. As in the United States and other industrial countries, growers in Mexico—particularly vegetable and fruit producers—have largely desisted from using the persistent organochlorides and have adopted the less persistent organophosphates, which were discovered by scientists in their search to develop nerve gas.

But even though organophosphates are less persistent in the environment and in foods, they are far more toxic than the pesticides they have replaced. Parathion, for example, which is now commonly used in Mexico, is twenty to fifty times as toxic as DDT if taken orally or absorbed through the skin. The great advantage is that the organophosphates break down rapidly so that residues are minimal by the time the treated produce reaches the market or the laboratories for testing. According to one close observer of pesticide practices in Mexico, Angus Wright of California State University in Sacramento, it has become increasingly rare for Mexican agroexporters to use chemicals banned or heavily restricted in the United States. However, because of the acute toxicity of the organophosphates and other chemicals, such as the herbicide paraquat, that are now used, "the shift to EPA-approved chemicals has substantially increased the immediate public-health danger."[119]

The circle of poison is still a concern, but the more critical health and safety issue in the vegetable and fruit industry is the welfare of the farmworkers who are directly exposed to these highly toxic agrochemicals. The tomatoes and strawberries that U.S. consumers now eat come largely from estates in the northwestern states of Baja California, Sinaloa, and Sonora, where Mixtec and Zapotec Indians work in a chemical fog. What U.S. consumers do not see or think about as they eat their blemish-free fruits and vegetables are the thousands of farmworkers poisoned each year by this intensive spraying.

Noting that area growers place little value on the lives of their destitute workforce, a doctor in Hermosillo, Sonora, reported a dramatic rise in pesticide poisoning, "Farmworkers are expendable—and when they die it is just another dead Indian." He told of a case only a few days before our visit in which a young farmworker, Juan Zavala, died from poisoning by a synthetic fertilizer that is banned in the United States. On the same day at the same clinic where the farmworker died, three other farmworkers, ages fourteen, sixteen, and eighteen, were treated for chemical burns, wounds, and inflammations caused by farm chemicals.[120] Each of the four Social Security clinics in the Culiacán Valley in Sinaloa reports from eight to ten cases of organophosphate poisoning a day during the winter months.[121]

Agribusiness throughout northwestern Mexico produces cosmetic fruits and vegetables for U.S. tables through a combination of chemical wizardry, heavy irrigation, and careful hand picking by low-paid workers. Women and men laborers are paid less than five dollars for a ten-hour day, with the more ambitious or foolhardy—usually young men—getting a dollar or two more for pesticide duty. In the San Quintín Valley, south of Ensenada in Baja California, Mixtec Indian boys and men apply the chemicals to the strawberries, tomatoes, and cucumbers destined for the U.S. market. As they loaded up their backpack applicators before heading out to the fields on a recent summer morning, they explained that they got used to the bitter chemical smell of the pesticides even as they gasped for breath. Some complained of headaches and dizziness but generally thought that their youth, macho confidence, and the kerchiefs worn as masks would protect them from permanent physical damage. In any case they needed the extra pesos. As they walked down the rows of tomato plants with their backpack sprayers, wearing no protective gear at all, they inadvertently sprayed each other as they passed on either side. Some had leaky spraying rigs that dripped the chemicals down their backs. Elsewhere *banderilleros* stand in the fields, waving their flags to direct the oncoming bush planes with the chemical mist descending upon them time and again.

The land and the companies these farmhands work for are usually Mexican, but as much as 90 percent of the financing comes from U.S. banks, and many of the producers are really just *prestanombres* or national stand-ins for U.S. growers and packers.[122] Others are subcontractors for California agribusiness firms or for such multinationals as Campbell's or Castle & Cooke.

Most of these Mixtec Indians are the second or third generation of migrants from the southern state of Oaxaca who fled their overpopulated and eroded homelands for farmworker jobs in the north.[123] Lucio Rojas left his mountain village in Oaxaca, Mexico's poorest state, fifteen years ago with his father and seven brothers. After leaving the economic desperation of their Oaxacan home, they worked for two years in Sinaloa, the state that produces more than half the country's vegetable exports to the United States. Then they made their way to the San Quintín Valley, which was just beginning to experience its agricultural boom. There they formed the backbone of a farmworker organizing effort that helped raise wages for the Mixtec laborers—at least half of whom are women—while at the same time forcing the government and growers to grant the farmworker community land and sanitation services. Today the Rojas family lives in a largely Mixtec settlement named after Lucio Rojas's brother, a leader of the farmworker union who was killed by vigilantes in the fight to secure land for the Indian farmworkers.

Like others, Lucio Rojas has not stopped seeking opportunity. Although conditions have been much improved by the organizing work of the Independent Central of Farm Workers and Peasants (CIOAC), better wages and working conditions are still found north of the border. Returning home to San Quintín on the weekends, Lucio Rojas works during the week as a field foreman for an agricultural concern in San Diego's North County area.

One weekend when he was at home with his family in San Quintín, Rojas revisited the estates where he used to work and the squalid housing where he and his family formerly lived. Posing as an evangelical leader, he gained easy access to the strawberry farms and the corresponding labor camps.

Here was the dark underside of the international agricultural production system. Hundreds of men, women, and children were picking strawberries and packing them into boxes marked with the labels of California agribusinesses. After working all day in the adjoining fields, the workers retired to the converted poultry sheds where they live. Drift from pesticide-spraying routinely blows over the sheds, where in their desperation families use discarded pesticide drums for water storage.

Open borders for international trade—especially when pesticide controls are also loosened—increases the threat of a circle of poison. But to concentrate only on pesticide residues on the $2.5 billion in agricultural produce (about half of which are fruits and vegetables) shipped north annually to the U.S. market misses other more serious environmental hazards associated with transborder and global economic production. In the San Quintín Valley, as throughout northern Mexico, foreign and Mexican companies are producing cheap fruits and vegetables by paying farm laborers starvation wages and carelessly exposing them to acutely and chronically toxic chemicals.

More than a circle of poison, it seems like a two-way street, with dead ends on each side. From the south comes a steady stream of immigrants, crossing the border with hopes for better wages and a better working environment. At the same time, more companies are heading south with their capital, seeking cheaper production costs and a less restrictive regulatory climate. But north of the border there are fewer jobs and rents are prohibitively expensive, forcing many migrants to live under plastic tarps in the hills and canyons of Southern California. To the south, the repercussions of nonsustainable agricultural practices and the overreliance on agrochemicals place new limits on growth. Both in San Quintín and on the other side of the Sea of Cortez in the Hermosillo area, the end of the agricultural boom is already in sight as underground water supplies dry up and the seawater seeps in, killing the crops. As was the case earlier with the demise of cotton production in many parts of northern Mexico, the pests are becoming resistant even to the most toxic chemical cocktails that are being thrown at them, thereby threatening the continued viability of monocultural vegetable and fruit production in some areas.[124]

Increasingly pesticides are becoming a subject of international dispute. No longer is it automatically accepted that chemical saturation is essential for modern agricultural development. In the United States the market for chemical-free food is booming at the same time that the aftertaste of pesticide dependence is being increasingly recognized. In California the EPA has found that one-fifth of the wells are contaminated with pesticides, and United Farm Worker (UFW) leader Cesar Chavez protested the immediate and long-term health effects of working with acutely poisonous chemicals. Meanwhile, the evidence is mounting in favor of the economic viability of organic farming and integrated pest management practices that rely on natural predators and other less toxic methods to combat insect plagues.[125] Consumer concern has given rise to a small but expanding organic farming industry in Mexico to supply natural-foods stores and restaurants in the United States.[126]

As border trade barriers break down, the expanding community of environmentalists is demanding that global pesticide regulations be strengthened, not harmonized downward. "The notion that 'harmonized' maximum levels of protection should be enshrined in GATT regulations is inappropriate at a time when farmers and governments are acknowledging that alternative farming methods can vastly reduce the use of chemical inputs," observed Monica Moore of the Pesticide Action Network.[127] In keeping with expanding consciousness of common responsibility for global ecological health, support is building in Congress for a measure that would ban the export of all chemicals prohibited for use in the United States and for requiring importers to tell customs officials what pesticides were used on produce destined for the U.S. market. Most advocates of free trade denounce such proposals as creating new obstacles to the free flow of goods across international borders, and Jay Vroom, president of the Agricultural Chemicals Association, has called it "environmental imperialism."[128]

In Mexico, too, pesticides have become a matter of public debate. As in the United States, agrochemicals initially signaled the opening of the door to a brave new world of agricultural modernization characterized by cheaper and more abundant food. This new age started with the agricultural research sponsored by the Rockefeller Foundation in the early 1940s. But the promise held out by the Green Revolution for greater food self-sufficiency and for a more developed rural economy was only partially realized. Instead the Green Revolution heralded an increasing emphasis on an export-oriented and capitalist-controlled agricultural system that depended on new seed varieties requiring plenty of water, fertilizer, and chemical pesticides. By the 1960s traditional peasant agriculture was being pushed aside by what one author called "strawberry imperialism."[129] In places like El Bajío and the Culiacán Valley food crops such as corn and beans, and the small producers of those crops, were pushed out of the way in the drive to increase agroexports to the United States. Vegetable and fruit production for export depends heavily on chemical inputs, which are commonly applied twenty or more times a season to guarantee the cosmetic quality of the produce.

Even as the pressure to increase exports to the United States intensifies, the alarm is sounding in Mexico about the resulting environmental havoc and occupational hazards.[130] At universities throughout the country investigators are cataloging the consequences of this chemical dependency. At the College of Sonora one investigator reports cancer clusters in communities repeatedly exposed to aerial spraying.[131] Another researcher estimates that 90 percent of the food in Mexico, where there is no enforcement of food safety regulations, is contaminated.[132]

At his office in downtown Mexicali professor Jesús Román Calleros of the Colegio de la Frontera Norte commented on the acrid smell in the air of the city. Calleros, an international water specialist, remarked that "with the summer wind from the south [Mexicali Valley agricultural area] and the winter wind from the north [Imperial Valley of California], Mexicali is continually covered with pesticides, and as a result, we all seem to be suffering from allergies."[133]

Pesticide spray is a major problem in Mexicali, but not all the chemical threat comes from the surrounding agricultural valley. As an industrial center, the border city is also the site of several chemical companies, including at least one pesticide manufacturer. In January 1992 a fifty-thousand-liter tank at the Química Orgánica pesticide-manufacturing plant (owned by the Mexican conglomerate CYDSA) ruptured, sending thirty-seven neighbors to the hospital from the noxious fumes and forcing the evacuation of nearby *colonias*. The incident came on the heels of fire at a pesticide plant in Córdoba, Veracruz, that provoked a catastrophic release of pesticide fumes. Contrary to an international agreement signed in 1983 by the United States and Mexico requiring notification of border environmental incidents, the Mexican environmental agency SEDUE did not alert the EPA. Instead the responsibility for cross-border environmental communication fell to two activist nongovernmental organizations, the Civil Committee for Ecological Disclosure in Mexicali and the Border Ecology Project in Naco, Arizona. As a result of strong citizen protests, the plant was closed.

Shutting down Química Orgánica has not solved the allergy epidemic in Mexicali or cleared away the chemical mist, but it is a sign that questions about pesticide production and use are becoming public policy issues. More than simply a matter of agricultural modernization and cosmetic quality, the trade in pesticides and contaminated produce raises larger questions about the human rights of farmworkers, sustainable agricultural practices, ecological diversity, and cross-border environmental responsibility.

## The Border as a Wasteland

Along with questions of food safety and the pesticide trade, the transboundary flow of hazardous wastes is also becoming a prominent public concern on both sides of the border. The focus has been on two problems of increasing magnitude: the dumping of U.S. wastes in Mexico and the disposal of the wastes created by the *maquila* industry.

There is no inventory of illegal hazardous waste dumps throughout Mexico.[134] Nor is there an informed estimate of the amount of chemicals exported from the United States for clandestine disposal. But there are plenty of indications that the practice of shipping hazardous wastes to Mexico is widespread, even though Mexico does not license dumps to handle foreign-produced wastes.[135]

In 1981 Mexican officials indicted a U.S. citizen for illegally dumping 160 drums of chemical waste, including 42 drums of PCBs, at a clandestine site in the state of Zacatecas. In the border community of Tecate, Mexican authorities found ten thousand gallons of heavy hydrocarbons and other toxic wastes that had been turned over to an unlicensed Mexican recycling company by several U.S. firms. Apparently on their way to a clandestine site in Chihuahua, four trucks carrying 175 barrels of PCBs were found parked two blocks from the border by El Paso authorities in 1989.

For companies facing disposal costs of three hundred to a thousand dollars a barrel for toxic wastes in the United States, the possibility of paying forty dollars for dumping or "recycling" in Mexico is attractive indeed. Soaring disposal costs in the United States and the shrinking number of landfills have encouraged some firms to choose clandestine dumping south of the border. The ease with which vehicles can enter Mexico makes illegal dumping of U.S. wastes a low-risk gamble. On the U.S. side the chances of being detected are remote since U.S. Customs normally does not check the cargo but only the accompanying paperwork, which is easily doctored.[136] In the view of William Carter, a Los Angeles deputy district attorney specializing in environmental crimes, unscrupulous firms and waste haulers consider Mexico "a big trash can."[137] Carter estimated that tens of thousands of gallons of toxins flow south from California to Mexico each month. The rising costs of disposing wastes in the United States have increased clandestine cross-border dumping in Mexico. "The bottom line is greed and money," said an environmental crimes investigator in California.[138]

To discourage illegal toxic dumping either in California or in Mexico, the California Highway Patrol has a squad of "green cops." In one celebrated case, the green cops caught a California "wastelord" red-handed in a 1988 scheme to smuggle fifty-five-gallon drums of toxic chemicals across the border. Ray's Industrial Waste contracted with an aluminum corporation in the town of Torrance to dispose of fifty-seven barrels of hazardous wastes for a twelve-thousand-dollar fee. But instead of legally disposing of the load, the owner paid a Mexican accomplice thirty dollars a barrel to store the wastes in a dilapidated warehouse in Tijuana. When Mexican and U.S. officials searched the site, which is only yards from an elementary school, they found that it was filled with leaking barrels of toxic trash, including some marked "highly flammable." Reflecting on his job, green cop Gary Hanson said, "I think of these cases as investigating homicides. Only we're trying to break them 20 or 30 years in advance."[139]

It has been estimated that each North American citizen generates one ton of toxic waste every year.[140] Ironically the expanding clout of environmentalists in the United States and other industrialized countries has contributed to the export of hazardous wastes to third world countries, both legally and illegally.[141] To counter this trend, environmental organizations like Greenpeace have mounted new educational and organizing campaigns aimed at stopping the north-south flow of toxics. But as Jim Vallette, the waste trade coordinator for Greenpeace, pointed out, "The only real solution to the toxic waste problem is to reduce the waste at its source—to stop it from ever being produced."[142]

Cross-border dumping of hazardous wastes is only a minor part of the hazardous waste menace facing Mexico. Industrialization has been Mexico's chosen model of development for more than a half century, but little attention has been given until recently to ensuring that industrial wastes are disposed of properly. When Mexico opened its northern border in 1965 to U.S. assembly plants, virtually no safeguards were put in place to protect the environment and the population from the toxic substances that the firms brought with them. The government did provide the companies with water and electricity, but waste disposal facilities apparently were not a priority—for either the government or the *maquiladoras*.

At first, hazardous wastes were not a serious problem since many of the early *maquiladoras* were garment industries. But the diversification into electronics, electrical components, chemicals, automotive, and other high-tech industries has resulted in the predominance of those sectors most likely to use hazardous substances.[143] In recent years the fastest-growing segments of the *maquila* sector have been the chemical, furniture, automotive, and electronics industries.

More than a quarter of a century after the *maquila* program was launched there is widespread concern in the borderlands that uncontrolled dumping may be converting the region into another Love Canal. In 1990 spot sampling of wastewater discharges at twenty-three *maquiladora* sites by the Boston-based National Toxic Campaign Fund confirmed these fears. Laboratory tests revealed that 75 percent of the sites tested were contaminated with highly toxic wastes. A water sample taken near one GM-owned plant showed a concentration of xylene that was sixty-three hundred times higher than the standard for U.S. drinking water. An employee told one of the scientists that the company routinely flushes untreated solvents down the drain.[144] Explaining just how contaminated the region's water is, Marco Kaltofen of the National Toxic Campaign Fund said that if one were to try to duplicate the sampling, you would have to "drain a couple of cups from the bottom of your hot water tank where it gets lots of iron, add four or five tablespoons of used motor oil, spray in every aerosol can from your house, and add a little Drāno for taste."

The U.S. Commerce Department keeps excellent statistics on U.S. exports and imports, but no government agency—in either the United States or Mexico—has been keeping track of the transboundary flow of hazardous substances. Although hundreds of thousands of tons of toxics travel to Mexico each year, neither country has a record of them. After the chemicals are used in the production process, they are disposed of in a variety of ways. For the most part, it seems, they simply drain out of the plants into the ditches, arroyos, and streams that run past the plants.

Since there have been no requirements that companies pretreat their industrial wastes, many companies drain their wastes into city sewer systems or into open ditches. Even in Mexican cities, such as Matamoros, that do have wastewater treatment systems, the facilities are designed to treat human wastes, not toxic substances. As a result, toxic pollutants pass directly through these systems into the ecosystem. Moreover, the toxins knock out the biological treatment balance of the sewage treatment plants by killing the microorganisms that neutralize fecal contamination.[145]

A 1983 U.S.-Mexico accord requires that the *maquiladoras* return their wastes to the country of origin or have them recycled in Mexico. Few U.S.-owned *maquiladoras* have returned their wastes to the United States. According to EPA records, fewer than 1 percent of the *maquiladoras* reported sending their hazardous wastes back to the United States in 1988.[146] Instead of returning the wastes to the United States, most have either left the barrels of chemicals in back lots or handed them over to local recycling industries. Because of increased public and official concern, U.S. firms have begun returning substantially more of their hazardous wastes to the United States since 1990.

Unlike the United States, Mexico has no maximum ninety-day storage rule, and it is common to see stacks of rusting, and often leaking, barrels piling up behind plants. Many of the "recyclers" or *materialistas* contracted by the *maquiladoras* are of questionable integrity. Instead of taking the wastes to an authorized dump or processing facility, the *materialistas* load up their pickups and take barrels to some clandestine desert spot for illegal disposal.[147] Reacting to stricter enforcement by the Mexican authorities, some *maquiladoras* are buying all their chemicals in Mexico or are paying duties on imported chemicals, thereby avoiding the reexportation requirement.[148]

Mexico is working to create a stronger waste management program, but it has a long way to go. The government does not yet know the number of *maquiladoras* that generate hazardous wastes, the amount of waste generated, or the final disposition of that waste.[149] In 1990 SEDUE estimated that about half of the approximately two thousand *maquiladoras* generate toxic wastes, but only some three hundred had provided the agency with the required waste manifests.[150] But the manifests are exceedingly vague in that they often do not even specify the exact toxic substance being imported. In 1990 SEDUE estimated that only 30 percent of *maquila* reports on waste generation in Baja California provided enough information to be of any value.[151]

This reflects the fierce resistance on the part of the *maquila* industry to share information about the quantity and nature of the chemical substances they use. The lack of right to know provisions for communities and workers in Mexico helps keep this information from becoming public knowledge. Mexicans are not the only ones being kept in the dark about the transboundary flow of hazardous wastes. Although more regulations are on the books in the United States, the EPA does not have the capacity to monitor the disposal of *maquila* toxins. The nearest EPA office to the western border is in San Francisco, where the team tracking the hazardous wastes of the entire *maquila* industry consists of just one person.[152]

Finding itself in the international spotlight, the *maquila* industry has begun to improve its waste disposal practices. After media publicity about its illegal dumping and lack of the most elementary waste treatment facilities, General Motors decided in 1991 to install water treatment facilities at its thirty-five plants in Mexico. Increasingly, *maquila* trade associations are prodding their members to comply with government environmental regulations.

Mexico is sadly lacking in hazardous waste sites. It was not until 1981 that the country's first toxic dumps were opened, but these do not meet U.S. standards, and their capacity is not even adequate to meet the needs of domestic industries. Although the government is attempting to expand its waste management capacity, there are only a few commercial hazardous waste dumps in the entire country and only one full-service disposal facility. Fewer than a dozen companies are authorized to handle toxic wastes.[153] In Hermosillo, the location of a major Ford manufacturing plant, the industrial waste dump is located less than a half mile uphill from the city's drinking water supply. Recently, especially since the beginning of the free trade negotiations, the Mexican government has begun to clamp down on clandestine dumping. But as Tijuana's chief of sanitation said, "The creation of clandestine dumps is uncontrollable, since one or more new ones appear every day."[154] One company, Precision Microelectronics, shut down in 1989, leaving 142 employees without pay and some eight hundred gallons of toxics behind. The barrels were marked with the warning in English "Inhalation of Concentrated Vapors Can Be Fatal" and were stored only yards away from a Juárez neighborhood.

The EPA and SEDESOL have promised to install a computer database and tracking system to ensure that the toxic chemicals used by the *maquila* industry are properly disposed of. But data entry does not seem like much of a step forward to communities directly affected by hazardous wastes from border industries. They already know what the plants do with their wastes. In many cases they are dumping the wastes in their front yards. For the past ten years the people of Chilancingo, a Tijuana *colonia* of twenty-five thousand—mostly *maquila* workers—have seen a forty-eight-inch drain pipe spew chemical-laced water down on their homes. It is not a daily occurrence, only when rains flood the waste ponds of the companies that sit above Chilancingo on Otay Mesa. But when the water does come shooting over the mesa, it spills wastes containing lead, copper, chrome, zinc, and cadmium onto the rutted streets in which their children play.[155]

Some worry about the potential of a Bhopal-like accident along the border. In Matamoros that fear is focused on the multinational Química Flúor, a hydrogen fluoride factory partly owned by Du Pont that was previously given government permission to locate in an existing residential neighborhood. Concerned that an accident might endanger the neighborhoods surrounding the plant, President Salinas in 1991 created an "Intermediate Safeguard Zone" around the plant. The decree halts additional settlements within a 1.25-mile radius of the chemical plant's central smokestack.[156] Thousands of poor Mexicans already live within the danger belt, and many have demanded that the plant be moved to a more deserted location. Joining the debate, U.S. environmental groups have charged that the imposition of a safety zone around the plant and the forced relocation of area residents rather than the plant itself are other indicators that all is not well with Mexico's regulatory system.[157]

Closely related to the threat to public health created by the irresponsible chemical dumping practices of the *maquiladoras* are the health and safety hazards faced by the *maquila* workforce. Government and industry on both sides of the border have proved more willing to address public concerns about environmental deterioration than to negotiate occupational health standards. Roberto Sánchez of the Colegio de la Frontera Norte in Tijuana speculates that proposals to improve worker health constitute more of a threat to industrial production than do environmental protection measures. Problems of worker health have also received less media attention and are therefore not seen as a major obstacle to liberalized trade and investment.[158]

A study by the National Safe Workplace Institute concluded that many U.S. companies in Mexico do not enforce the occupational and environmental standards normal to U.S.-based operations. "We found that workers are seldom given training, that machinery is not safeguarded, and that instructions on chemical hazards are nearly always written in English. Work-related injuries and illnesses are typically ignored and workers who complain are typically discharged." The institute also found that the work pace is more accelerated and the hours longer than in the United States.[159]

Workplace accidents are more common in Mexico than in the United States. In 1989 there were twenty-six incidents of partial amputations at factories in Nogales. Altogether there were two thousand accidents in Nogales *maquiladoras*, about three times the rate experienced at comparable factories in the United States.[160] Whereas Mexico is moving fast to develop emissions and other environmental standards, there has been little progress on regulating air concentration levels and improving occupational health standards in Mexican factories.[161]

For roughly a dollar an hour, *maquila* workers become the human factor in fast-paced assembly processes that commonly result in back pain, eye strain, conjunctivitis, carpal tunnel syndrome, and mind-numbing boredom. From contact with hazardous substances, workers also complain of skin rashes, nausea, and other physical reactions to the chemicals used on their jobs.[162] A lack of protective clothing and of access to information about workplace hazards is also common. In one factory women work with lead solder forty-eight hours every week, but few of them can read the labels warning that lead can cause birth defects and advising workers to wash their hands before eating or smoking. Workers experiencing unusual or persistent health problems such as breathing difficulty, stomach problems, or sudden emotional changes are sometimes told by company doctors that their problems are psychological.[163]

Occupational health problems are by no means limited to factories south of the border, but Mexican workers are even less protected than their U.S. counterparts and do not have the same avenues to seek redress through the legal system. An interesting case in this respect is that of GTE Lenkurt in Albuquerque, New Mexico, where a group of workers and their attorneys were awarded two million to three million dollars in 1987 for health problems, including cancer, neurological damage, and numerous hysterectomies, resulting from their exposure to chemical compounds in the electronics factory. In 1982, after experiencing years of worker protests and complaints of unsafe working conditions, GTE Lenkurt decided to transfer the bulk of the most hazardous jobs to its plant in Juárez. Although the peso devaluation in Mexico was probably the main factor in the relocation, worker discontent also figured in the decision.[164]

It would be wrong to conclude, however, that the *maquiladoras* treat their workers worse than do domestic industries in Mexico. The assembly plants, despite all their problems, may be among the safest and cleanest places to work in Mexico's manufacturing sector. Although complaints about few rest periods, exposure to toxins, excessive noise levels, repetitive assembly work, and insufficient training seem to indicate a careless attitude about workplace safety on the part of *maquila* management, many workers credit the *maquiladoras* for providing meals, educational and sports programs, and some medical services.

According to one study, *maquila* workers reported backaches, headaches, and dizziness, but not any more than did employees in service industries in Tijuana.[165] Such surveys do not, however, reveal the possible long-term health problems, such as cancer and birth defects, resulting from regular and relatively uncontrolled exposure to hazardous chemical compounds used by many of the *maquila* industries. As it is, there is not enough epidemiological evidence to form any overall conclusions about the severity of the occupational health climate inside the *maquiladoras*. The industry has fiercely resisted most studies of worker health and safety by denying researchers access to the factories and company records.[166]

Among the proponents and advocates of free trade, a debate rages about the significance of environmental and occupational health factors in influencing plant relocation. On the face of it, logic would seem to be with those who argue that the higher environmental and worker safety regulations enforced in the United States play a major role in driving companies out of the country to "pollution havens," such as Mexico. Already the amount that U.S. firms spend on controlling pollution is one of the highest in the world, and loose enforcement of environmental regulations in Mexico makes such high expenditures unnecessary.

A recent study by a New Mexico State University professor found that the rates of growth of nine *maquiladora* industries over the 1982–90 period were highly correlated with those industries' pollution abatement costs in the United States.[167] And according to a survey by the Colegio de la Frontera Norte in Tijuana, about 10 percent of the *maquiladoras* surveyed cited environmental regulations as a primary factor in their decision to leave the United States. Another 17 percent considered environmental regulations an important factor.[168]

These findings are controversial, however. The office of the U.S. trade representative claims that the pollution haven argument advanced by environmentalists and labor unions in their opposition to more liberalized global trading is spurious.[169] Backing its claim that environmental compliance costs are not a deciding factor in plant relocation decisions, the office of the U.S. trade representative cites numerous academic studies and its own data.[170] According to most academic studies, it does appear that environmental and occupational health compliance costs are usually not the deciding factor in investment relocation for most large corporations. Only in the case of major polluters and smaller firms are these considerations an important reason for relocation.[171] There is some evidence that the largest transnational corporations seek to standardize their operations throughout the world, with the result that their foreign branches may abide by higher environmental and worker safety standards than domestically owned companies.[172] When these large corporations make capital investments, they may anticipate rising standards and find the old, highly polluting equipment and technology unprofitable when compared with modern, clean technology that conserves materials and energy.[173] Other studies have demonstrated no widespread pollution-driven relocation of U.S. industries except in a few highly toxic industries, such as asbestos manufacture, or those producing such metals as copper, zinc, and lead.[174]

This is not to say that other firms do not consider the advantages of less government regulation in their relocation decisions but only that in many cases these may not be as critical as nonenvironmental factors, such as labor costs, production strategy, and global marketing plans. In the case of agricultural companies, longer growing seasons and the lack of freezes are also major siting considerations.

Even if most companies do not intentionally seek pollution havens, it does not mean that they maintain the same environmental and worker safety standards once they have located abroad. In fact, a double standard between U.S.-based firms and their foreign branches is common worldwide. This has certainly been the case in Mexico, where *maquiladoras* have ignored the most basic environmental and occupational health standards. Even if companies have standardized occupational safety and environmental guidelines, such regulations are often ignored by local managers for cost-saving purposes. A study sponsored by the International Labor Organization (ILO) found that the home-based operations of transnational corporations generally had better health and safety performance than those of their foreign branches and subsidiaries, particularly those in less developed countries such as Mexico.[175]

Although most U.S.-based transnational corporations are not relocating to Mexico to avoid pollution abatement costs, these costs may be an important consideration for some major companies. Eastman Kodak, two of whose plants were named among the top twenty emitters of air toxics in the United States, is setting up new plants in Mexico along with other high-tech chemical and electronics manufacturers.[176] The fact that at least five Firestone workers had contracted leukemia and that unsafe exposure to benzene was suspected as the cause may have been the reason why the company moved a tire plant from Salinas, California, to Mexico. As mentioned earlier, the fastest-growing industries in the *maquila* sector are ones where contamination, hazardous wastes, and occupational safety are major concerns. Liberalized foreign investment rules, particularly in the petroleum and petrochemical industries, are likely to attract an increasing number of U.S. chemical companies to Mexico.

Dozens of furniture companies in Southern California are clearly seeking a pollution haven on the other side of the border. Reacting to new controls in the South Coast region restricting the use of solvent-based paints and requiring the installation of spray chambers to contain fumes, at least forty furniture firms in the Los Angeles area have moved or are planning to move to Baja California. This flight southward by the furniture industry endangers a $1.3 billion industry and sixty-three thousand workers in Southern California. Three percent of the hydrocarbon pollution in Los Angeles has been attributed to the paints, stains, and lacquers currently favored by woodworking companies.

Stricter air control regulations are not the only reasons companies like Fine Good Furniture are relocating. High workers' compensation bills in California and the cheaper labor costs across the border—about 13 percent of U.S. pay—have also pushed and pulled furniture firms toward Mexico.[177] In Mexico there is virtually no workers' compensation. And such companies as Muebles Fino Buenos (a translation of "Fine Good Furniture") no longer must deal with the constant intrusions of air quality inspectors, emissions monitors, and lawyers for aggrieved workers and neighbors of the polluting factory. In Los Angeles the factory owner paid tens of thousands of dollars in fines and penalties, but the company's reincarnation in Tijuana is easily meeting local environmental standards. Neighbors of Muebles Fino Buenos complain of dizziness, sore throats, nausea, and the smell of solvents all day long. The fine dust of lacquer settles over nearby homes and vehicles.[178]

209

Despite a dramatic improvement in Mexico's environmental regulations since 1988, Mexico has no established air quality standard to regulate paint and solvent emissions. This lack of environmental and worker safety regulations helps explain the boom in the furniture industry along Mexico's northern border. As one factory owner acknowledged, "I can find lots of Mexican workers in the United States. What I can't find here in Tijuana is the government looking over my shoulder."[179] The number of furniture *maquiladoras* increased from 59 in 1980 to 274 in 1990, with employment rising from 3,200 to 25,700 workers.[180] These runaway plants may only be postponing the day of reckoning if SEDESOL follows through with promises to bring its standards up to U.S. levels.[181] But relocating companies are betting that any upward harmonization of air quality regulations to the strict standards of Southern California will be a long time coming.

The case of the furniture industry demonstrates that fears that Mexico serves as a pollution haven cannot be dismissed. When strict standards for asbestos manufacture took effect in the 1970s, companies set up new plants in Juárez and Agua Prieta. Dick Kamp of the Border Ecology Project, who lives in the Arizona border town of Naco, points to the Sonocal lime plant across the border as a case of what he wryly calls "low-grade technology transfer." In 1976, after the EPA shut down the then U.S.-owned facility for particulate noncompliance, it was purchased by Sonocal, which then packed up the plant and reassembled it on the other side of the border with no pollution controls.[182] Mexico serves as a pollution haven for the U.S. firm, but the fine lime dust blows across the international border. Kamp, a leading advocate for the incorporation of strong environmental and occupational health standards into international trading agreements, is concerned that the lime dust is damaging the health of his children and other area residents.[183]

# Governments Face

# the Environment

The environment was largely ignored in official U.S.-Mexican relations until relatively recently. Toward the end of the 1970s, however, the environmental repercussions of being neighbors and the consequences of increased development along the border became more pressing concerns. As pollution levels climbed, border communities, environmentalists, and public health workers demanded government action. Moving into the 1990s, concerned citizens in each country also began urging their elected representatives to broaden the focus of joint efforts to include the Mexican interior. Much of the interior has already suffered from rapid, unplanned development, and although many areas are likely to experience increased pressure as U.S.-Mexican economic integration goes forward, these have mostly been ignored in joint environmental initiatives.

The U.S. and Mexican governments responded to the public outcry by concluding several agreements that address environmental problems. They also committed their environmental agencies to stepped-up efforts to combat deteriorating environmental conditions. The effectiveness of these government responses to environmental contamination depends on political will, the resources available, and the quality of the institutions and agreements set up to coordinate joint action.

Unfortunately, policy and performance have remained out of step with government promises. With their attentions focused on economic objectives, the two governments have had other priorities besides solving environmental problems. Their development strategies have emphasized growth over sustainability—the careful stewardship of natural resources to ensure that future generations will be able to meet their own needs. More concerned about promoting economic growth than about regulating or taxing businesses to protect the environment, the two governments generally put off finding remedies to environmental problems caused by industrial development until pushed to do so by public pressure. Even then, they have balked at hiking taxes to make business pay for environmental programs.

Problems of political will and development strategy aside, resolving international environmental concerns is a complicated task with both technical and diplomatic features. Solving the problems requires comprehensive, binational planning and overcoming differences between U.S. and Mexican social, economic, political, and administrative systems. When soot from family fire pits in Juárez drifts across the river to El Paso, for example, solutions must deal realistically with the economic roots of the contamination and the political and social consequences of cleanup. The stark differences in wealth and other resources between the United States and Mexico are also evident in the limited financial and technical resources available to Mexico for attacking environmental problems.

In addition, the problems affect so many different communities, activist organizations, business groups, and government agencies that finding solutions is a tricky combination of confrontation and compromise. A multitude of local, state, and federal government agencies from both countries are responsible for monitoring environmental problems, devising solutions, and implementing them. At the federal level the U.S. Environmental Protection Agency (EPA), Mexico's Secretariat of Social Development (SEDESOL), and the binational International Boundary and Water Commission (IBWC) have primary authority for working on joint environmental problems. Their efforts are multiplied by state and local agencies, community groups, private organizations, businesses, and environmental organizations whose priorities and agendas frequently compete with those of the federal governments. In fact, these frontline institutions often find themselves at odds with their own federal agencies over the pace, scope, and financing of environmental projects, while working more closely with counterparts across the border.

Also bogging down the search for solutions to shared environmental woes are questions about who is to blame for the problems and who will pay to fix them. Because much of the pollution along the border emanates from the Mexican side, U.S. policymakers and taxpayers have often fought against paying big bills for cleanup or infrastructure development. And taxpayers rightfully question why they should foot the bill for pollution caused by U.S. businesses that have moved to Mexico and profited from lax environmental standards and concessionary tax and tariff policies.

Increasingly, however, communities and government officials in both countries appear to be realizing that finger-pointing is a waste of time and that common solutions to the mounting catastrophe are needed. But coming to an agreement about how many of the costs are to be paid by the United States or Mexico, by local, state, or federal revenues, and by businesses or private citizens is a ticklish political challenge.

Border communities in both countries are typically too strapped financially to generate the funds required for large environmental and infrastructure projects. They depend on support from state and federal governments that is often inadequate and slow in coming. In the United States, for instance, decisions about national appropriations are made in the U.S. Congress. States located away from the border area are reluctant to chip in for environmental protection programs that do not benefit their own citizens. In Mexico funds for border projects generally have come from the federal government, which has had only limited resources for environmental programs. Until public pressure in the United States mounted because of the NAFTA negotiations, the Mexican government prioritized cleanup in Mexico City and paid scant attention to border problems.

But the reality of U.S.-Mexico integration means that for practical and ethical reasons, costs must be divided among sectors in both countries. The problems along the border are a direct result of industrial integration between the two countries, and environmental protection will benefit communities on both sides of the line.[184] Governments—whether local, state, or federal—and private actors in both Mexico and the United States have promoted the development strategies whose effects are endangering the environment. With development have come strains on the infrastructure and natural resources that are the responsibilities of public and private parties in both countries.

Free trade will add a new complexity to U.S.-Mexico environmental relations. While the border was a logical focus of common concern before NAFTA, a free trade agreement would sharply expand the territory in Mexico that is affected by U.S.-Mexico economic integration and that is subject to rapid development. Energy and resource consumption, pesticide use, hazardous waste production, and vehicle and industrial emissions are expected to increase in the Mexican interior. Rapid urbanization and heightened infrastructure pressures are also expected, as government policies squeeze small farmers out of rural areas and people rush to the cities hopeful of employment. Until all these problems are confronted adequately, the future economic and environmental vitality of the entire region will be threatened.

## Building the Joint Environmental Framework

Water sanitation problems along the border were the first environmental issues to draw joint attention from the U.S. and Mexican governments. Efforts to deal with these problems—primarily through monitoring water quality and constructing wastewater treatment facilities—go back to the 1940s. The vehicle for resolving these problems was the U.S.-Mexico International Boundary and Water Commission (IBWC). Composed of a U.S. section and its Mexican counterpart, the Comisión Internacional de Límites y Aguas (CILA), the IBWC is one of the few institutions created by the two countries that is binational in structure and not just in rhetoric.[185]

The IBWC grew out of the first truly binational U.S.-Mexico institution. The International Boundary Commission was set up by treaty in 1889 to resolve disputes over the location of the boundary between the two countries. Over the years the organization's authority expanded to include boundary water problems. The Water Treaty of 1944 renamed the body and added water supply and quality issues to the commission's mandate. It was not until the late 1970s, however, that mounting public criticism of water quality in the borderlands prodded the IBWC to broaden its responsibility over a wide range of water pollution issues.[186]

As was the case with water pollution, cooperation between the United States and Mexico on other environmental issues moved forward in the 1970s. These first efforts were halting and incomplete, however, in part because the Mexican government had decreed some general environmental principles but had not set standards for enforcement. At the same time, formal responsibility for protecting the Mexican environment was assigned to a low level in the Ministry of Health.

But increasing environmental awareness and concern in Mexico helped push the government to step up its own programs, and growing demands from border communities spurred the United States and Mexico to expand joint programs. In 1978 the EPA and Mexico's environmental subsecretariat signed a memorandum of understanding committing the two agencies to work together on environmental problems. Although the agreement was flawed in various ways, it was a milestone because it was the first comprehensive attempt to approach environmental problems on a joint basis.[187] Targeting pollution control and abatement and promising information exchanges, annual meetings, consultations, policy coordination, and the establishment of parallel projects, the memorandum anticipated the framework of later agreements.[188] Beginning in the early 1980s, the United States and Mexico intensified their joint approach to environmental problems, producing a flurry of agreements over the next ten years.[189] The effectiveness of U.S.-Mexico environmental programs has depended in part on the quality of the institutions set up to carry them out. Although the EPA has never had the funding or authority it has needed to carry out a full-scale program of environmental protection, Mexico's institutions have been even weaker and more politicized. When President de la Madrid established the Secretariat of Urban Development and Ecology (SEDUE) in 1982, the move seemed to signal a strengthening of Mexican environmental policies.

With SEDUE's creation, responsibility for environmental protection no longer rested in a low-level agency attached to the Health Ministry. Instead, SEDUE was a cabinet-level ministry with all the authority of its predecessor as well as new responsibilities over housing, public works, and agricultural and water policy.[190] Authority over many environmental programs was centralized in the new secretariat, which, in becoming the country's lead agency for environmental issues, assumed an oversight and coordinating role over the other environmental activities of agencies—at least on paper.

Thus strengthened, SEDUE signed a broad-ranging environmental accord with the EPA in 1983. Where the 1978 memorandum had represented a handshake between two lower-level agencies in each country, the 1983 framework agreement, commonly called the La Paz agreement, was a presidential-level accord that resulted from a summit meeting between presidents Ronald Reagan and Miguel de la Madrid.

Designed as a broad framework within which the United States and Mexico could confront shared environmental problems on the border, the La Paz agreement was purposely written in general terms. It named the EPA and SEDUE as the lead agencies in handling joint environmental issues but reaffirmed the IBWC's jurisdiction over water pollution along the border. Follow-up agreements, known as annexes, committed the two countries to working on specific problems, such as sewerage needs in Tijuana. Between 1983 and 1992 the EPA and SEDUE appointed binational working groups on water, air, hazardous waste, emergency response, enforcement, and pollution prevention, as authorized by the annexes. These groups were authorized to investigate problems under their jurisdiction and devise joint solutions.

The La Paz agreement represented a big step forward for U.S.-Mexico environmental protection efforts. It helped clear up questions about

215

which agencies were responsible for which problems by specifying the jurisdictions of the IBWC, EPA, and SEDUE. Flexible and inclusive, it provided a mechanism for the two governments to reach agreement on whichever environmental questions they chose to take up. More than under any previous arrangement, federal agencies were encouraged to cooperate with local, state and nongovernmental actors on transboundary environmental problems. Finally, in designating the border area as a strip of land that extended a hundred kilometers (about sixty-two miles) on either side of the actual U.S.-Mexico boundary, the agreement recognized the integrated reality of the border region.

But like the 1978 memorandum, the La Paz agreement has a number of serious weaknesses.[191] Because it is an executive agreement, not a treaty, implementation is left up to the discretion of the two governments. The agreement is neither binding nor enforceable. Although it provides a framework for cooperation and coordination, its nontreaty status means that the governments are not obligated to use it or to follow through on decisions made subsequent to it. Its success therefore depends heavily on the political commitments of the incumbent administrations in each country. Perhaps reflecting the halfhearted zeal of the two governments, the programs resulting from the La Paz agreement have not received adequate funding. This crucial shortcoming means that the responsible agencies have never been funded to carry out a thorough program of needs assessment or enforcement, much less border cleanup, pollution prevention, and resource conservation.

## Winning NAFTA with Environmental Promises

Economics and politics, not the environment, have prompted the burst of joint environmental initiatives undertaken after 1990. As the two governments moved a free trade agreement to the tops of their priority lists in the late 1980s, public concerns about potential environmental impacts threatened to derail the accord. The governments responded with a series of high-profile initiatives that built on the La Paz agreement and other earlier efforts at environmental protection and binational cooperation. While those attempts had looked good on paper, they had been poorly implemented, a fact that the two governments said they were going to correct with the new initiatives.

Until the NAFTA negotiations got under way, SEDUE was known as a politicized operation that was lax about enforcing the country's environmental regulations. Beset by corruption and patronage, the troubled agency had few trained personnel and never received the full support of the government.[192]

This picture began to change when Mexico and the United States began barreling toward the free trade agreement. SEDUE's budget increased significantly after 1989, expanding by some 613 percent by 1991. Whereas in 1989 Mexico was spending about eight cents per person on environmental activities, by 1991 that figure had increased to forty-eight cents. Even so, SEDUE's budget was still inadequate—only thirty-nine million dollars in 1991—and funding was sought from outside sources, including the World Bank, Japan, and the United States, to help invigorate its programs.[193]

Bolstered by new funds and motivated by the need to convince U.S. policymakers that NAFTA would not further threaten the border environment, SEDUE enhanced its enforcement efforts. New inspectors were added, and sanctions—even plant shutdowns—were leveled against some environmental offenders, especially in Mexico City and along the border.[194]

There were two other major outcomes of the governments' efforts to win the early support of legislators, environmentalists, and border communities for NAFTA. The Integrated Border Environmental Plan (IBEP) and the Environmental Review (ER) were released on the same day in February 1992. The border plan laid out a laundry list of current border problems, especially those afflicting the largest sister cities. The ER was supposed to examine the effect of the proposed NAFTA on environmental conditions in Mexico, whether along the border or elsewhere. In reality, however, the ER also focused primarily on the border, with the exception of discussing a few other issues, like air pollution in Mexico City.

Formulated by the EPA and SEDUE, the border plan committed the United States and Mexico to cooperate on a variety of border environmental problems. As a subsidiary to the La Paz agreement, the plan inventoried many of the problems of the border region but left detailed programs for resolving the issues to be developed in subsequent agreements, similar to the minutes of the IBWC or the annexes of the La Paz accord. Topics covered included hazardous waste, emergency response, water supply and quality, air quality, housing and infrastructure, habitat protection, and municipal solid waste.

If the intent of the planners was to silence opposition to NAFTA, their hopes went unmet. Activists, community residents, scholars, public health workers, and state and local government leaders blasted the IBEP for a string of shortcomings ranging from its vagueness to funding inadequacies to its avoidance of crucial issues.[195] They also criticized the plan for its reliance on the IBWC and for neglecting to look at the likely impacts of free trade on the border environment.[196] When, in the fall of 1991, communities all along the U.S.-Mexico border turned out to comment on the draft IBEP, the meeting rooms buzzed with anger from San Diego to Brownsville. "We knew we'd get creamed," said Sylvia Correa, the EPA's manager of Latin American programs. "But we wanted to hear what the people had to say."[197]

Response to the Environmental Review was even more critical.[198] As Lynn Fischer of the Natural Resources Defense Council put it, "The Environmental Review was a farce." Despite its mandate, Fischer said, the ER "didn't really look at the environmental impacts of free trade."[199] The review fell far short of safeguarding the environment by failing to outline enforcement mechanisms or recommend provisions to protect state and local standards from assault as barriers to free trade.

The joint environmental activities of the United States and Mexico reflect the limitations of these agreements. They emphasize education and information sharing as opposed to enforcement and are generally parallel instead of truly binational. In addition, funding inadequacies plague the programs, especially those involving infrastructure development at the local level.

Still, the two countries are cooperating on a range of activities, the need for which is undeniable. In recognition of the limited technical resources available in the country, training and technical assistance dominate the EPA's assistance to Mexico.[200] These include things like inspector trainings and technical presentations to help Mexico design vehicle inspection and auto emissions programs. The United States also funded an Environmental Technology Clearinghouse, known as Envirotech, a computerized data system that indexes more than five hundred databases on pollution control and energy conservation technology available in the United States. According to the Environmental Review, the EPA will help Mexicans develop environmental regulations and will work with Mexico on other issues, such as comparing pesticides and their usages and tolerances in Mexico to U.S. standards in order to resolve differences between the two countries.[201]

Under the authority of binational environmental agreements and the minutes of the IBWC, Mexico and the United States cooperate on informational programs, such as data collection, trainings, technology transfers, and needs assessments. Pollution-monitoring programs are also being set up. Although moving sluggishly, the two countries are working to provide wastewater treatment plants and sewage systems that are lacking up and down the border. They also plan to devise a system for tracking shipments of hazardous materials from the United States into Mexico and for collecting data about how the waste by-products are disposed of. This kind of information is not available at present and is greatly needed if enforcement efforts are to be enhanced.

But the example of the Inland Joint Response Team (JRT) highlights the fact that despite advances, the governments have not gone far enough with their cooperative initiatives. In 1988 the JRT was authorized to coordinate joint emergency response plans in case of natural disasters or accidental toxic releases along the border. Participating sister cities are supposed to create their own emergency response teams. Known as Local Emergency Planning Committees (LEPC) in the United States, and Local Committees on Mutual Assistance (CLAM) in Mexico, these teams are to devise joint plans and interact together during emergencies. The need for such bodies is clear, but most have existed only on paper and have never received adequate funding. Those that do exist tend to function parallel to one another instead of in tight coordination. Their effectiveness is further limited by lack of training, little or no information about toxic substances in their communities, and inadequate border infrastructure such as bridges and water delivery systems.

## Changing the Playing Field in Mexico

The restructuring of the Mexican government carried out under Salinas swept up the country's environmental protection agency in May 1992. At that time Salinas created a new superministry known as the Secretariat of Social Development (SEDESOL) and announced that many environmental functions would be decentralized and privatized. The restructuring of Mexico's environmental apparatus will surely affect the quality of joint U.S.-Mexico activities, although it is too soon to evaluate their effect.

But the way the new ministry has been structured raises many questions about just how effectively it will be able to safeguard the environment. At a symbolic level, protection of the environment has been visibly downgraded from SEDUE's cabinet-level ministry to the status of an agency within SEDESOL. Even SEDUE's former director, Patricio Chirinos, said the move would transform the environmental protection agency into a "second-floor institution."[202]

Among other tasks, SEDESOL was charged with formulating environmental policy and enforcing Mexico's laws regarding the environment.[203] Two new bodies—the National Ecology Institute and the Attorney General's Office for the Protection of the Environment—were created within the new secretariat to handle analysis, policy development, and enforcement. Although some of SEDUE's environmental functions were passed on to different ministries—contributing to bureaucratic fragmentation—SEDESOL retained control over the issues that had caused most public outcry in U.S. and Mexican constituencies with influence over the future of NAFTA. These functions included control over toxins and pollution problems in urban areas and on the border. SEDESOL also received authority over conservation programs and implementation of the border plan.[204]

Concerned observers fear that in SEDESOL one highly politicized and patronage-plagued institution—SEDUE—has been replaced by another that is even more highly politicized. SEDESOL's first director, Luis Donaldo Colosio, was a former head of the PRI and a major contender for the position of PRI presidential candidate for 1994.[205] His appointment suggests that the new ministry fills a political need for the ruling party. In addition to environmental programs, SEDESOL oversees another intensely politicized initiative, the National Solidarity Program (Pronasol), a public works program that funnels development projects and material assistance to the poor. The fact that environmental programs are subsumed under the same agency as Pronasol raises fears that environmentalism will be treated only as a political tool.

Along with SEDUE's dissolution, authority over environmental programs is being decentralized and privatized. Funded in part by a four-year World Bank loan, the process of "modernization" of Mexico's environmental regime and transfer of much authority to the states is to be complete by 1994. Mario Aguilar, SEDESOL's attaché to Washington, explained that under the changes, Mexican state and local governments will take on "concurrent authority" with the federal government over environmental problems.[206] They are authorized to write legislation and enact standards that can be "more, not less stringent" than federal legislation, Aguilar said, and they will be responsible for enforcing compliance with environmental regulations.

The sources of funding for the state and local programs were not identified in the restructuring plans, making it likely that Mexico's state and local governments will be unable to pursue their new programs. Even if the states and local governments write tough technical standards, their programs will lack real power unless their enforcement provisions are equally strict, which is not guaranteed under current plans. What is more, as long as Mexico's budgetary, administrative, and political systems remain centralized and dominated by the PRI, federal influence over environmental policies will remain intact.

Mexico is also privatizing many environmental functions. Under the new system, similar in many ways to that of the United States, private consultants and contractors will take over functions that once were handled by the government. These tasks include designing standards, monitoring pollution and compliance, licensing, and inspection.

Although privatization could improve efficiency, it increases the danger of corruption and conflict of interest. For example, a consultant to industry can legally act both as an approved plant inspector and as a consultant to a given firm.[207] Patronage in Mexico is commonly dispensed at the state and local levels, increasing the chances of corruption as these functions are privatized. In addition, the state and municipal governments do not have the expertise to supervise private contractors adequately. And in the short term at least, Mexico's environmental inspectors were being cut from the payroll, with some 48 percent of the inspector staff slated for elimination despite government promises to deploy new inspectors.[208]

## Conflicting Viewpoints and Agendas

Resolving shared environmental problems is further complicated by the number of organizations and agencies that are affected and by their different needs and priorities. When the EPA San Diego–Tijuana Border Task Force meets to discuss water treatment initiatives, for example, some thirty representatives of agencies ranging from the U.S. Fish and Wildlife Service to the local health departments attend the gathering.

The involvement of all these different agencies complicates environmental planning. In the United States—and soon in Mexico if the decentralization goes as planned—much enforcement power is left to the states. States often devise their own regulations and standards on things like air pollution and pesticides or other toxins. Variations from state to state *within* the country can be extreme; the problem of coordination is even more severe with cross-border questions.

Tensions result, too, from the different agendas and needs of local areas and states versus the national perspectives of the federal governments. Despite whatever local presence they may achieve—which has been

221

completely insufficient in most areas—the EPA and SEDESOL represent federal viewpoints and must uphold strategies decided on in the capital cities. The contradictions between the federal agendas and the needs of people living in the crisis zones and trying to respond to the problems there cause tensions among local, state, and national bodies. Both the EPA and SEDESOL, for example, were strong promoters of NAFTA during the negotiations, even though many border communities and local and state governments fought for stiffer environmental protections in the accord.

The welter of agencies involved in environmental issues has helped the federal governments pass off responsibility for implementation, enforcement, and funding onto state and local governments. But state and local agencies in both countries find it hard to stretch their revenues to pay for needed improvements in infrastructure and environmental protection. This problem was compounded during the 1980s as federal dollars to states and municipalities dwindled with the recession in the United States and the economic crisis in Mexico. Washington's high-profile advocacy of expensive improvements in border environmental infrastructure has irritated border communities strapped for the funds such improvements would require.

In addition to problems like these, the initiatives being worked out at the federal level do not explicitly protect local and state environmental standards that might be stiffer than national or international norms. The Bush administration in particular pushed for consistency with the principles being worked out in the ongoing round of negotiations of the General Agreement on Tariffs and Trade (GATT). If those principles are accepted, tough local and state standards will likely be preempted by international norms that reflect the lowest common denominator of protective standards agreed to by the many nations involved in the negotiations.

## Policy-Performance Gap

The current level of U.S.-Mexico cooperation on environmental problems is unprecedented. Indeed, the two countries exchanged environmental attachés in the early 1990s, reflecting the importance and cordiality of the relationship. But even with all the joint programs, plans, and meetings, environmental problems and their negative health effects continue to accumulate.

One big problem is lax enforcement of environmental regulations. The problem has been especially severe in Mexico, which has usually tried to work out voluntary agreements with industry, rather than identify and levy penalties against violators. In many cases the country's environmental agencies simply lack the technical and financial resources to enforce monitoring and compliance requirements.

For whatever reasons, noncompliance with environmental regulations is widespread in the country, even though most of Mexico's laws and regulations are advanced. For example, the U.S. General Accounting Office found that in a sample of 6 of the 116 new U.S.-majority-owned *maquiladoras* that began operations in 1990 and 1991, none had prepared environmental impact assessments (EIAs) before starting up. This was true even though Mexican law requires new companies to submit EIAs before receiving operating permits. Even more telling, the Mexican agency that issues operating licenses allowed 4 of the 6 companies to start up before receiving applicable permits for air emissions, water discharges, and hazardous waste management. According to SEDESOL, noncompliance with EIA requirements is extensive throughout the country, not just in the *maquiladoras*.[209]

Cooperative agreements between the two countries compound these problems by relying on voluntary compliance. Carefully guarding sovereignty concerns, the agreements leave enforcement to the discretion of each country. Even the new working group on enforcement established under the La Paz agreement will primarily facilitate data collection, information exchanges, and occasional joint site visits "by invitation."

Because neither government is doing its part to enforce environmental regulations and safeguards, activist groups are picking up the slack. Instead of the governments doing their job of water and air monitoring and keeping track of hazardous wastes, these tasks have fallen to small citizens' groups and environmental organizations like the Border Ecology Project in Naco, Arizona, and the Border Project for Environmental Education in Tijuana.[210] But the effectiveness of these groups is limited, at least in Mexico, because the country does not have right-to-know legislation to make sure that information about toxic materials and other potential environmental hazards is available to the public. Likewise, Mexico has virtually no guarantees of public access to the courts to enforce administrative action against violators.

Another fundamental problem is the persistent failure of the two governments to provide adequate funding to resolve the massive environmental problems caused by rapid development and U.S.-Mexico economic integration. Because insufficient funds have been a major factor in

Mexico's uneven progress on environmental concerns, this oversight is especially glaring. To make a good-faith attempt to carry out the programs outlined in the IBEP, for example, the U.S. and Mexican environmental agencies would surely have to expand their staffs, equip new offices, purchase and set up computer systems, modernize laboratories, and pay transportation expenses. But the plan did not even attempt to estimate the costs of its new programs, much less outline strategies for raising such funds.

The environmental initiatives of the United States and Mexico are also limited by their narrow focus, mostly on the border regions. But expected trade and investment increases will affect areas deep in the Mexican interior. Environmental devastation is already common throughout Mexico, where deforestation, pollution, resource depletion, and biosphere degradation are by-products of poverty and development strategies. As the World Bank explained in 1992, Mexico suffers from "grave" environmental problems "exacerbated by several decades of industrialization without assessment of, or attention to, environmental costs."[211]

All these environmental pressures would likely worsen under a free trade accord, especially without a shift in development policies. The United States has provided some economic aid to Mexico for environmental and conservation programs in the interior—for monitoring air pollution in Mexico City, for instance—but little direct attention has been paid to these needs.

Government officials claimed that an agreement that would remedy these oversights as well as promote private sector involvement in pollution control would be signed. An EPA administrator said that such an agreement would address such issues as hazardous waste management and enforcement throughout the two countries, not just along the border. But the promised agreement was never signed. Without such a commitment to deal with the array of Mexico's environmental problems, some environmental groups warned that Mexico may divert scarce resources from serious and growing problems in the interior to pump up programs on the border that are more visible to U.S. policy makers and activists.

## Co-opting the Critics

When the governments of Mexico and the United States announced in 1990 their common intention to seek a free trade agreement, they knew that citizen concern about runaway plants seeking cheap Mexican labor

224

was a major issue in the United States. But they probably were not expecting that approval of their free trade proposals would be threatened by such matters as black water, clandestine waste dumps, and lime dust. The poison trail running back and forth between the two nations suddenly became a major obstacle to free trade on the fast track.

Border communities, the labor movement, environmental organizations, and consumer groups in the United States joined together in demanding that their environmental concerns be addressed before any trade accord with Mexico was approved. Although not opposed to free trade, border communities quickly seized the opportunity of the trade negotiations with Mexico to focus attention on the festering infrastructure, environmental, and public health problems in the borderlands. But more than sympathy, the border communities wanted an injection of federal dollars for public-sector infrastructure projects such as wastewater treatment plants, water and sewage projects, and new roads and bridges. As the chairperson of the Border Trade Alliance, a business organization devoted to economic development of the borderlands, explained, "We who breathe the air and drink the water along the border are the first to say we support free trade and that we also want a long-term plan for the environment."[212]

Whereas the border communities were for the most part enthusiastic about the economic prospects raised by further trade and investment liberalization in Mexico, a loose coalition of environmental, labor, and consumer groups was generally skeptical about the benefits of free trade. For these groups the border, with its immense environmental and public health problems, represented a worst case scenario of what a free trade agreement without adequate controls could mean for all of North America. After all, they rightly pointed out, the *maquila* sector has enjoyed liberalized trade and investment regulations for more than a quarter of a century and look what havoc it has wreaked. Looking at the past record, many environmental organizations viewed the proposed free trade agreement with great skepticism. The environmental nightmare already seen on the border would be repeated throughout Mexico, they asserted, if proper guarantees were not inserted into the NAFTA treaty.

A couple of years before the NAFTA proposal was announced, national environmental groups such as the Environmental Defense Fund and the Sierra Club began to realize that international trade and investment were environmental issues. Environmental organizations had long been sponsoring conservation efforts abroad, such as the creation of nature reserves. Not until the late 1980s, however, did it become obvious that if the global environment was to be protected, they must jump into the fray over the direction of global economics.

Free trade suddenly became a defining issue for the environmental movement. Washington's assurances that environmental issues would be adequately addressed in free trade negotiations with Mexico persuaded several organizations, including the Natural Resources Defense Council and World Wildlife Fund, to lend their support to congressional approval of a "fast track" for the trade negotiations. The inclusion of environmental provisions in the proposed accord signed in October 1992 was hailed as a victory by the Environmental Defense Fund, although other groups such as the Sierra Club and Friends of the Earth were skeptical. More regionally based environmental organizations, such as the Border Ecology Project, Texas Center for Policy Studies, and Arizona Toxics Information, based their challenges to Washington's free trade proposals on their own experience with cross-border environmental problems.

The labor movement, consumer groups like Citizen Watch, and the left-of-center political sector also raised the environmental banner as part of their overall campaign to turn free trade into "fair trade." Although no firm political coalition was established, this rallying around the common denominator of the environment did help break down the narrow focus of the different special-interest groups. The labor movement moved beyond its strict economic focus to consider the interface between environmental protection and occupational health. Through their association with unionists and progressive consumer organizations some environmentalists broadened their definition of *sustainable development* to include more class-oriented issues, such as worker safety and the basic right to a decent wage and affordable housing. Just as important, U.S. groups began to work and strategize with Mexican activists, broadening the point of view on each side of the border.

The U.S. government responded to this surge of activism in several ways, working with Mexico on the border plan, drafting the Environmental Review, and negotiating a side agreement to NAFTA to deal with environmental concerns, for instance. But it also moved to co-opt critics of NAFTA by creating a set of advisory bodies to channel public participation and siphon off opposition to the accord.[213] Invited to participate on these bodies were representatives of sectors like organized labor and the environmental movement. Keeping these groups on board or at least appearing to give their views careful consideration was critical to government strategies to obtain smooth acceptance of the trade agreement.

But the way these bodies were structured diluted the input of critics and beefed up the position of government and industry free traders. When NAFTA was being negotiated, for example, the Office of the U.S. Trade Representative (USTR) set up a number of policy advisory committees that were supposed to channel recommendations from selected private-sector representatives to NAFTA negotiators. Big business held the largest number of positions on these committees, outnumbering environmentalists by about thirty to one on the few committees that included representatives of environmental interest groups. Organized labor was similarly outnumbered, while groups seeking tough mandatory labor and environmental protections were not represented at all.

Participation was restricted in other ways as well. Although environmentalists won token positions on the services, agriculture, industry, and investment committees, the Bush administration refused to add an environmental committee to advise the USTR on the trade agreement. Nor did the administration appoint environmentalists to committees advising on other areas with environmental impacts such as energy or the auto sector.

As NAFTA steamed ahead, the U.S. and Mexican governments also created Public Advisory Committees (PACs) to keep border activists and environmentalists hooked into the IBEP and on board with the trade agreement. They are parallel bodies, one set up along the border in Mexico and one in the United States, to advise the EPA and SEDESOL and to funnel information to local communities.[214] In general terms, the appointed committees could play a useful role in helping to keep important border environmental issues on the table at the EPA and SEDESOL. But the Mexican government never appointed members to its PAC. In the United States the committees have no actual authority, but they permit some needed public input into government border initiatives.

Winning hearts and minds along the border seems to be the major aim of the Border Progress Foundation, a new binational grant-making organization launched with fifty thousand dollars' seed money from the EPA.[215] Known in Mexico as the Fundación Progreso Fronterizo, the foundation was established to act as a matchmaker between community organizations that need resources and corporations, charitable groups, and government agencies with money to spend. It is intended to supplement the IBEP by pumping up self-help and volunteer efforts in health, environment, and social programs. By providing an easy way for businesses to chip into border improvement efforts—without being required to do so through increased taxes or similar mechanisms—the foundation may help popularize free trade, pacify activists and do a public relations favor for area businesses at one and the same time.

While activists from San Diego to Matamoros were trashing the draft IBEP, Richard Kiy, then EPA's border coordinator, and Timothy Atkeson, director of its international affairs office, hatched the idea for the foundation. Kiy has strong border business ties himself. He worked closely with the *maquiladoras* before he joined the EPA and served as program director for the Border Trade Alliance.[216]

Governed by a binational board of trustees, with top executive positions and staff split between the United States and Mexico, the foundation appears to be a true U.S.-Mexico initiative. Despite its binational structure, however, the Mexican component exists primarily on paper, and the U.S. government is the primary spigot for donations to the foundation. The EPA will provide funds for both administration and grants. But SEDESOL, the agency in Mexico responsible for environmental affairs, has not yet said if it will contribute to the organization, and money from corporations has only begun to flow.

Most border groups are adopting a wait-and-see attitude toward the foundation. Along with many representatives of business interests, respected environmentalists and public health workers sit on the board, and a well-managed grant program could inject deserving border organizations with critically needed resources. But the foundation's government ties raise concerns that its creation was no more than a cynical political move to throw a few bones to environmental and community activists.

These government attempts to enlist activist and community organizations as allies on border programs reflect some gains for those concerned about environmental degradation. At least their views are being considered to some extent. But neither the United States nor Mexico has opened up the planning process to include the full participation of environmental and public health experts. And where they have been included—on the PACs, for instance—their perspectives are diluted by the views of others who wish to push full steam ahead on economic programs that are likely to exacerbate environmental conditions.

Moreover, the three NAFTA partners—the United States, Mexico, and Canada—announced in August 1993 the creation of a trilateral commission to resolve environmental disputes related to free trade. But the three governments do not plan to include citizen representatives on this important body. Instead, the Commission on Environmental Cooperation will consist of government representatives, assisted by a panel of "experts" on trade and the environment but without defined avenues for citizen input. The provision for creating the commission was included in the Agreement on Environmental Cooperation, constructed as a supplemental agreement to NAFTA. Establishing such a body is a step forward in terms of international environmental protection in North America because it provides a forum to discuss problems, resolve disputes, and apply sanctions. But the commission's mandate will be restricted to problems of pollution prevention and wildlife preservation and will not extend to such issues as production processes, occupational health, or natural resource management. Along with few options for the participation of concerned citizens, these restrictions on the commission's scope of authority limit the usefulness of the body.

In response, environmental activists critical of the pact called for the creation of a binational commission to focus not only on environmental concerns but also on health and labor issues generated by increasing integration between the United States and Mexico. They urged that representatives of nongovernmental organizations and local government agencies with no vested interest in trade sit on the commission, along with representatives selected by the federal governments. And they called for this proposed body to have the right to raise funds and allocate them for projects selected by the participants that will advance health and environment concerns and assure sustainable development as U.S.-Mexico economic integration goes forward.[217]

## Sustainable Development

*Sustainable development* has become a key term in the debate over economic integration and the joint future of Mexico and the United States. Although the term has been appropriated by free trade proponents as part of their attempt to persuade the public that international agreements such as the GATT and NAFTA will actually benefit the environment, sustainable development is a more radical concept when used by many environmental activists. Simply defined, it signifies a type of economic development that attempts to meet the needs of the present generation without compromising the needs of future generations.[218] Recognizing the finite quantity of natural resources, sustainable development implies an environmental stewardship of the planet and accepts the natural limits of economic growth. Put in economic terms, sustainability means living off nature's "income" while not dissipating its "capital"— that is, limiting our consumption to the amount that can be sustained indefinitely without degrading the environmental resources that constitute our capital stocks.[219]

This environmentally based concept of development contrasts sharply with those wedded to the trickle-down theory of economic and human progress. This approach casts economic growth in entirely positive terms. As the argument goes, only through economic growth will communities have the resources to devote to environmental protection. As stated by the rightist Heritage Foundation, "growth is more conducive to a clean environment than stagnation."[220] In this view, there is little room in either the free market or free trade to consider such "externalities" as the social and environmental costs of economic growth. Rather, as the economy grows, so will its capacity—and the willingness of the society—to resolve these resultant problems. Rephrasing this philosophy, Michael Gregory of Arizona Toxics Information remarked, "The pro-trade argument that developing nations will be able to clean up and protect the environment when they get rich from free trade might be more accurately stated as: *if* they get rich from free trade they *may* try to clean up the pollution caused by getting rich."[221]

In their efforts to include environmental provisions in such trade agreements as the GATT and NAFTA, environmental organizations clearly want to distinguish themselves from the nationalists and protectionists who also oppose unregulated free trade. Most environmentalists have no argument with removing tariff and nontariff barriers erected solely for the protection of different economic sectors. But there is a belief that individual nations should retain the ability to block trade and investment that contravenes sustainable development principles. The three main concerns in this regard are that international accords will preempt local environmental regulations, will tend to harmonize environmental standards in a downward direction, and will prohibit restrictions on resource exploitation, such as the right of a country to restrict the rate of timber or oil extraction. Closely related to this last concern is the issue of whether a country has the right to prohibit the import of certain goods for strictly environmental reasons, such as outlawing the purchase of tropical timber as a way to protect the world's rapidly diminishing rain forests.

Environmentalists committed to sustainable development principles are concerned that free trade will limit the ability of nations to use tariff and nontariff barriers as part of development strategies that protect open space and family farms. And they object to narrow environmental standards based on cost-benefit analysis, particularly if the costs are being analyzed by those who have no commitment to resource conservation and sustainable development. In such an analysis, they ask, how will such intangible costs as losing a wilderness, undermining the quality of life, or the extinction of another species be measured? Moreover, they argue that the standards and safeguards set in place by local communities, states, or national governments regarding health, safety, and environment should not be open to challenge through free trade accords—even if these measures are open to scientific debate or are not based on strict cost-benefit analysis.

Yet more than a movement of naysayers, the environmentalists who have raised objections to free trade have also proposed reforms that they contend would reduce the environmental repercussions of free trade and economic development. In contrast with the secrecy cherished by trade diplomats, they want trade negotiations to be open to public participation, and they demand that right-to-know principles for workers and affected communities be a condition for all transborder investment. Concerns about runaway plants would diminish, they contend, if corporations were prevented from using double standards for labor and the environment at home and abroad. Some of the suggested measures, such as imposing countervailing tariffs on polluting industries, run directly against the principles of free trade. Other suggestions, such as allowing foreigners to sue U.S. corporations in U.S. courts or insisting that trading partners abide by U.S. environmental standards, would allow more public control of transnational corporations but raise other nationalist concerns about extraterritorial sovereignty.[222]

At the same time that environmental organizations have been fighting to see that more "green language" be inserted into international trade accords, many of them have also been mobilizing citizen environmental activism across international boundaries. They recognize that the most effective way to prevent pollution havens and to protect international ecosystems is to work more closely with local groups in Mexico. These groups can then put direct pressure on their own governments and on corporations in their communities to ensure that appropriate environmental and health safeguards are respected. Such organizations as Pesticide Action Network and Health Action International have demonstrated the effectiveness of coordinated international campaigns in raising consumer and official awareness about the global marketing of harmful substances. Especially along the border, U.S.-Mexico coalitions of environmental and community groups are also slowly emerging. In Mexico such new organizations as the Committee for Ecological Disclosure in Mexicali and Frontera Verde in Tijuana serve as models for new citizen activism around environmental and health concerns.

In Mexico, as in the United States, environmentalism is gaining new political and economic dimensions. Demands for corporate responsibility, environmental and occupational health guarantees, and public disclosure about hazardous wastes raise questions about the lack of democracy and the inequitable development patterns in Mexico. Similarly, environmentalists in the United States have found that demands for the inclusion of environmental protection measures in trade agreements cannot be rightly made without also considering such related issues as occupational safety and the living conditions of Mexican workers at U.S.-owned plants. In both countries the call for sustainable development practices has highlighted the deficiencies associated with current economic policy-making while pointing out the need for national development strategies that both protect the environment and meet basic human needs.

# Notes

1. Some two hundred Mexicans, including Sotelo, received among the largest doses of radiation on record for the public, according to Susan West, "Hot," *Science* (December 1984).
2. In terms of the numbers of exposed people, the Juárez incident falls between the Chernobyl and Three Mile Island catastrophes, according to sources cited in Paul Salopek's excellent investigative report, "Global Trade in Used Technology Imperils the Unwary," *El Paso Times*, 28 July 1991. The following description relies largely on this report and Katherine Silberger, "¡Desastre!", *Village Voice* (16 June 1992) and West, "Hot." Also see Eliot Marshall, "Juárez: An Unprecedented Radiation Accident," *Science* (16 March 1984), 1152–54, and U.S. Nuclear Regulatory Commission, *Contaminated Mexican Steel Incident* (Washington, D.C.: 1985).
3. The importation of the radiotherapy machine by the Juárez doctor did, however, violate Mexican government regulations. By law, importers of such equipment are required to notify the National Commission on Nuclear Safety and Safeguards (CONSENUSA), which has the authority to regulate the import, export, transport, operation, and maintenance of nuclear devices.
4. *World Bank Staff Appraisal*, 1000-5 ME, 19 March 1992.
5. For more on the environmental implications of a trade-based food policy in Mexico, see Steven E. Sanderson, "Mexico's Environmental Future," *Current History* 92, no. 571 (February 1993).
6. Alvar W. Carlson, "Geography and Environment," in *Borderlands Sourcebook: A Guide to the Literature on Northern Mexico and the American Southwest*, eds. Ellwyn R. Stoddard, Richard L. Nostrand, and Jonathan P. West (Norman: University of Oklahoma Press, 1983), 75–80.
7. Leon C. Metz, *Border: The U.S.-Mexico Line* (El Paso: Mangan Books, 1990), 293.
8. Jim Carrier, "The Colorado: A River Drained Dry," *National Geographic* (June 1991), 4.
9. For more on this viewpoint see Francisco A. Malagamba, "Troublesome Equity in the Distribution of Shared Water Resources: The U.S.-Mexico Border," in *Environmental Hazards and Bioresource Management in the United States–Mexico Borderlands*, eds. Paul Ganster and Harmut Walter (Los Angeles: UCLA Latin American Center Publications, 1990), 13–21.

233

10. The IBWC was established in 1932 as the merger of two binational agencies, the International Boundary Commission (created in 1889 to manage disputes along the international boundary) and the International Water Commission, a less important agency, established in the 1920s. An overview of the functioning of the IBWC and an examination of how the U.S. and Mexican counterparts differ is found in Stephen P. Mumme, "Engineering Diplomacy: The Evolving Role of the International Boundary and Water Commission in U.S.-Mexico Water Management," *Journal of Borderlands Studies* 1, no. 1 (Spring 1986), 74–108.

11. A drought in the 1870s resulted in water shortages along the Rio Grande, and Mexico accused Colorado and New Mexico of stealing water. It charged that increased water use by those states was causing Mexicans to suffer water shortages. In 1895 U.S. Attorney General Judson Harmon disputed Mexico's claim, asserting that the United States enjoyed "absolute sovereignty" over the Rio Grande. According to Francisco A. Malagamba, "Mexican agricultural producers have consistently maintained their disagreement with regard to their international rights to the waters of the Rio Bravo" since the turn of the century. For more on Mexico's view of water use along the border, see Malagamba, "Troublesome Equity in the Distribution of Shared Water," in Ganster and Walter, *Environmental Hazards and Bioresource Management*, 13–21.

12. The upper basin states are Utah, Wyoming, Colorado, New Mexico, and northern Arizona, while the lower basin states are California, Nevada, and southern Arizona.

13. Anne M. Morgan, "Transboundary Liability Goes with the Flow? Gasser v. United States: The Use and Misuse of a Treaty," *Transboundary Resources Report* 5, no. 2 (Summer 1991), 1. Furthermore, in a time of extreme drought the river flow may drop as low as 6 maf, and conversely in an extremely wet period rise to 25 maf.

14. The 1944 Treaty Relating to the Utilization of Waters of the Colorado and Tijuana Rivers and of the Rio Grande established the framework to apportion the waters of all ephemeral and nonephemeral streams and rivers crossing the land boundary, not just the Rio Grande and the Colorado River. The rights of the two countries with respect to this other surface water have never been fully defined, however. The standard source on international negotiations regarding the distribution of these two rivers is Norris Hundley, Jr., *Dividing the Waters: A Century of Controversy between the United States and Mexico* (Berkeley: University of California Press, 1966).

15. Albert E. Utton, "Transboundary Water Quality: Institutional Alternatives," in Ganster and Walter, *Environmental Hazards and Bioresource management*, 49.

16. See Francisco Oyarzabel-Tamargo, *Economic Impact of Saline Irrigation Water: Mexicali Valley, Mexico* (Ann Arbor: University of Michigan Press, 1976).

17. It was agreed that the salinity of the water passed on to Mexico must be within 145 ppm of that found at Imperial Dam.

18. Jennifer Warren, "Yuma Desalination Plant Comes of Age—Too Late," *Los Angeles Times*, 8 March 1992.

19. For a revealing look at the uneconomic character of the Yuma plant, see Allen Kneese, "Environmental Stress and Political Conflicts: Salinity in the Colorado River," *Transboundary Resources Report* 4, no. 2 (Summer 1990).

20. The power of western agribusiness, its dependence on government subsidies, and the generally wasteful use of limited water in the West is clearly demonstrated by Marc Reisner, *Cadillac Desert: The American West and Its Disappearing Water* (New York: Viking, 1986).
21. Gail Sevrens, *Environment, Health, and Housing Needs and Nonprofit Groups in the U.S.-Mexico Border Area* (Arlington, Va.: World Environment Center, 1992), 55. This is a valuable overview of environmental health problems and issues as well as a comprehensive directory of nongovernmental organizations concerned with these issues.
22. Salinity over 700 ppm begins to cause crop damage, while 500 ppm is the upper limit for potable water. See Kneese, "Environmental Stress," 1.
23. Warren, "Yuma Desalination Plant."
24. Interview with Jesús Román Calleros, Colegio de la Frontera Norte, Mexicali, 2 May 1991.
25. Testimony by John Hall, chair of the Texas Water Commission, to the Environmental Protection Agency, 20 September 1991.
26. Raul Fernandez, "The Economic Evolution of the Imperial (U.S.A.) and Mexicali (Mexico) Valleys," *Journal of Borderlands Studies* 6, no. 2 (Fall 1991), 10, 11.
27. Mexico claims that lining the canal violates Minute 242 of the 1973 agreement that provides for mutual consultation before the undertaking of new developments affecting either ground or surface waters or of any substantial modifications of present facilities. But the United States responds that the minute requires only consultation, not consent. Furthermore, it asserts that Mexico is regularly receiving its 1.5 maf of Colorado River water and has no claim on additional water. But Mexico contends that the United States never objected to its capturing of All-American Canal seepage—which it has been doing since the 1950s—and that the United States cannot now try to capture conserved waters (meaning waters gained by human initiatives such as dams or vegetation removal projects), a position amply supported by U.S. water rights law. Possible solutions to this problem include pumping a portion of the conserved waters to Mexico or providing Tijuana with treated wastewaters from a planned treatment plant south of San Diego. In her examination of the conflict, Crane observed that the case pits future users of water (California cities buying the water from the Imperial Irrigation District) against the present agricultural, industrial, and domestic users in Baja California. She concluded that "the needs of future users need to be considered certainly, but it would seem less equitable to ruin a vibrant economy in one region than to prevent development in another." Melissa Crane, "Diminishing Water Resources and International Law: U.S.-Mexico, A Case Study," *Cornell International Law Journal* 24 (1991), 318–19. Also see Douglas Hayes, "The All-American Canal Lining Project: A Catalyst for Rational and Comprehensive Groundwater Management on the United States-Mexico Border"; J. Román Calleros, "The Impact on Mexico of the Lining of the All-American Canal," *Natural Resources Journal* 31 (Fall 1991); and Albert E. Utton, "A Tale of Six Cities and the All-American Canal," *Transboundary Resources Report* 4, no. 2 (Summer 1990).
28. See Stephen P. Mumme, *Apportioning Groundwater Beneath the U.S.-Mexico Border* (San Diego: Center for U.S.-Mexican Studies, 1988).

29. See College of Engineering, University of Texas at El Paso, and Public Service Board, *Development and Water in El Paso/Juárez: Limited Resources for Growing Needs* (El Paso, April 1991).

30. John C. Day, "International Aquifer Management: The Hueco Bolson on the Rio Grande River," *Natural Resources Journal* 18 (January 1978), 173.

31. There are, however, few international models for a groundwater treaty, as explained in Crane, "Diminishing Water Resources," 299–323. Not only is international law on groundwater nearly nonexistent, but any attempt to formulate a U.S.-Mexico treaty would have to confront the scientific uncertainty regarding the nature of groundwater, such as its sources and its quantity.

32. Crane, "Diminishing Water Resources," 319.

33. The principle of prior appropriation, which is applied throughout the West except in Texas, stipulates that water is allocated on the basis of first use and that subsequent users will be apportioned amounts less than the first user.

34. C. Richard Bath and Dilmus D. James, "Transborder Flows of Technical Information: Cases of the Commercialization of Guayule and Groundwater Utilization," working paper, U.S.-Mexico Project Series, no. 10 (Washington, D.C.: Overseas Development Council, July 1982), 13.

35. Albert Utton sees Texas as the primary obstacle to an international groundwater treaty, observing, "The political opposition in Texas is so strongly against regulation that the IBWC, which depends on the Texas congressional delegation for its support, has been unable to take a strong role." Cited in Jan Gilbreath Rich, "Bordering on Trouble," *The Environmental Forum* (May–June 1991), 32.

36. See Utton, "Anticipating Transboundary Resource Needs and Issues in the U.S.-Mexico Border Region," 17.

37. The two Rio Grande basins are governed by separate international agreements. The upper Rio Grande Basin, which carries the water south to Fort Quitman, Texas (east of El Paso), is regulated internationally by the U.S.-Mexico Treaty of 1906, which allocates sixty thousand acre-feet to Mexico per year. The lower Rio Grande Basin, extending from El Paso to the Gulf of Mexico, is governed by the 1944 Treaty Relating to the Utilization of Waters of the Colorado and Tijuana Rivers and of the Rio Grande, which roughly divides the flow of the Rio Grande equally between Texas and Mexico. For a brief overview of U.S.-Mexico water history and current issues, see Albert E. Utton, "The Importance of United States–Mexico Water Relations," in *Water and the Future of the Southwest*, ed. Zachary A. Smith (Albuquerque: University of New Mexico Press, 1989), 71–88.

38. Cited in *Life* (November 1987).

39. According to the California Governor's Water Policy Task Force Report (1992), current overuse of groundwater reserves, combined with reduced water availability from the Colorado River as Arizona takes its full legal entitlements, will contribute to a yearly reduction of up to 2.5 million acre-feet of water from current levels. This is equivalent to the amount of water used each year by ten million families of four.

40. College of Engineering et al., *Development and Water*, 3.

41. The Center for Environmental Resource Management (CERM) at the University of Texas at El Paso has guided the creation of the Binational Water Policy

Institute. There are similar proposals for the creation of binational commissions to address the magnitude of environmental and public health problems along the border. Through the offices of the IBWC and the Pan American Health Organization (PAHO) there have long been indirect channels of communication between border cities.

42. Mary E. Kelly et al., "U.S.-Mexico Free Trade Negotiations and the Environment," *Columbia Journal of World Business* (Summer 1991), 51, citing Alberto Székely, legal adviser to the Mexican Foreign Ministry.

43. For an overview of the environmental crisis in Sonora, see José Luis Moreno, "El deterioro del medio ambiente," *Revista de El Colegio de Sonora* 2 (January 1991).

44. For a loving description of the region by a naturalist who has traveled its extent, see Frederick Gehlbach, *Mountain Islands and Desert Streams: A Natural History of the U.S.-Mexican Borderlands* (College Station: Texas A&M Press, 1981).

45. Gary Paul Nabhan, "Desert Rescuers," *World Monitor* 36 (July 1992).

46. Salvador Contreras, *Peces en peligro de extinción: Agua y perspectivas de desarrollo en zonas aridas de México* (Austin: Texas Center for Policy Studies, 1991).

47. Steve LaRue, "Many Gulf of California Species 'in Agony,'" *San Diego Union-Tribune*, 25 July 1992.

48. Larry B. Stammer, "The Gulf of Mexico Besieged," *Los Angeles Times*, 15 June 1990. For a brief overview of environmental degradation of the Gulf of Mexico, also see *Integrated Environmental Plan for the Mexican-U.S. Border Area*, iii, 10–11. In response to increased contamination of the Gulf, the EPA has established a multiagency Gulf of Mexico Program, whose director was cited by the *Los Angeles Times* as saying that the Gulf is quickly approaching the time when it may cross a critical point of irreversible environmental impacts.

49. *Valley Morning Star*, 17 September 1991.

50. Interview with Rose Farmer, 19 August 1992.

51. Testimony by Gary Mauro to the EPA on 16 September 1991 at McAllen, Texas.

52. William Branigin, "Mexico's Other Contraband—Wildlife," *The Washington Post*, 24 June 1989, citing FWS chief of law enforcement Jerome S. Smith.

53. Cited in Steve LaRue, "Profits Keep Bird Smugglers Coming North," *San Diego Union-Tribune*, 16 September 1991.

54. Interview with Kris Sarri, Defenders of Wildlife, 16 July 1992.

55. For an excellent examination of these issues, see Debra A. Rose, *A North American Free Trade Agreement: The Impacts on Wildlife Trade* (Washington, D.C.: World Wildlife Fund, 1991).

56. Branigin, "Mexico's Other Contraband—Wildlife."

57. World Bank Staff Appraisal, 19 March 1992.

58. *Ecología Sonora*, no. 1 (Hermosillo: Movimiento Ecologista de Sonora, 1991).

59. Hartmut Walter, "Borderlands Bioresources: A Unique Scientific and Political Challenge," in Ganster and Walter, *Environmental Hazards and Bioresource Management*, 261–70.

60. Interview with Dr. Laurance Nickey, 30 July 1992.

61. This crisis emerged in 1961 as a result of the U.S. water substitution from the Wellton-Mohawk Irrigation District outside Yuma, Arizona.

62. For a good overview of U.S.-Mexico environmental concerns in the 1980s, see C. Richard Bath, "Environmental Issues in the United States–Mexico Border-

lands," in *Regional Impacts of U.S.-Mexican Relations*, ed. Ina Rosenthal-Urey (San Diego: Center for U.S.-Mexican Studies, 1986), 50–72.

63. Interview with Jesús Reynoso, 23 July 1992.

64. Mary Kelly, *Facing Reality: The Need for Fundamental Changes in Protecting the Environment along the U.S.-Mexico Border* (Austin: Texas Center for Policy Studies, October 1991), 2.

65. Cited in Marjorie Miller, "S.D. Plan for Sewage Plant a Dead Issue," *Los Angeles Times*, 10 March 1984.

66. Interview with Dr. Laurance Nickey, 30 July 1992.

67. "A Permanent U.S.-Mexico Border Environmental Health Commission," a report by the Council on Scientific Affairs, *Journal of the American Medical Association* 263, no. 24 (27 June 1990), 3320.

68. C. Richard Bath, "Environmental Issues in the U.S.-Mexico Borderlands," *Journal of Borderlands Studies* 1, no. 1 (Spring 1986), 57.

69. Minute 261 concerning border sanitation problems was the immediate result of a joint declaration by presidents Carter and López Portillo calling upon the IBWC "to make immediate recommendations for faster progress toward a permanent solution to the sanitation of waters along the border." The key clause of the resolution provides that the two governments recognize as a "border sanitation problem each case in which, in the judgment of the Commission, the waters that cross the border, including coastal water, or flow in the limitrophe reaches of the Rio Grande and the Colorado River, have sanitary conditions that present a hazard to the health and well-being of the inhabitants of either side of the border or impair the beneficial uses of these waters." This language is broad enough to offer the opportunity for the commission to expand its efforts beyond traditional sewage disposal works to cover the range of problems from salinity to toxic industrial and deleterious agricultural practices. See Utton, "Transboundary Water Quality," 55.

70. Stephen Mumme, "The Background and Significance of Minute 261 of the International Boundary and Water Commission," *California Western Law Journal* II (1981), 223, 226. Mumme suggested that the commission "has interpreted its powers conservatively in such a manner as to preclude the possibility of any serious controversy over the propriety of its jurisdiction."

71. For a good discussion of organization reforms recommended by environmentalists, see Stephen P. Mumme, "New Directions in United States–Mexican Transboundary Environmental Management: A Critique of Current Proposals," *Natural Resources Journal*, Summer 1992. Instead of downsizing or eliminating the IBWC and tossing out the La Paz accord in favor of a binational environmental treaty, Mumme argues that a "functional enhancement" (as opposed to a "functional reduction") or reformist approach would be a more realistic and achievable strategy to address such concerns as the lack of planning and enforcement.

72. See, for example, Kelly, *Facing Reality*, 3. The environmental policy center at which Kelly works recommended the "removal of IBWC's lead jurisdiction on water quality problems in border area rivers and underground water and the transfer of that jurisdiction to a new binational agency that is open to public participation and accountable to border area governments."

73. Sevrens, *Environmental, Health, and Housing Needs*, 12.

74. Cited in Greg Moran, "Tijuana Break Again Sends Sewage to U.S.," *San Diego Union-Tribune*, 8 August 1992.
75. Cited in Kathryn Balint, "City Pressed on Border Sewage Pipe," *San Diego Union-Tribune*, 26 July 1992.
76. Seth Mydans, "U.S. and Mexico Agree on Border Sewage Plant," *The New York Times*, 22 August 1990.
77. José Luis Calderón, "Policies and Strategies for the Control of Contamination of Water on the Northern Mexican Border," in Ganster and Walter, *Environmental Hazards and Bioresource Management*, 38.
78. Sevrens, *Environmental, Health, and Housing Needs*, 67.
79. Edward Cody, "Expanding Waste Line Along Mexico's Border," *The Washington Post*, 17 February 1992.
80. James E. García, "Border River Laden with Wastes," *Austin American-Statesman*, 29 September 1991.
81. Cited in Nancy Cleeland, "A Border Boom Has Its Ugly Side, Too," *San Diego Union-Tribune*, 16 February 1992.
82. Interview with Jesús Reynoso, El Paso City/County air quality official, 23 July 1992.
83. Bath, "Environmental Issues," *Journal of Borderlands Studies*, 60
84. Interview with Jesús Reynoso, 23 July 1992.
85. Cited in Sharon Spivik, "Tougher Smog Checks Urged for Commuters from Mexico," *San Diego Union-Tribune*, 29 April 1992.
86. Cited in Michael J. Kennedy, "On Texas Border: Outlook for Air Quality Is Murky," *Los Angeles Times*, 20 November 1991.
87. The Border Ecology Project and the Northeast Sonora/Cochise County Health Council have charged that the Compañia Mexicana de Cananea (majority ownership held by Mexican copper magnate Jorge Larrea with 22 percent ownership held by the U.S.-owned ASARCO) has expanded without meeting control standards specified under Annex 4 of the 1983 La Paz Agreement.
88. Ken Backe, "ASARCO Ranked in Nation's Worst Chemical Polluters," *El Paso Herald-Post*, 16 May 1990.
89. Cited in Kennedy, "On Texas Border."
90. Statement of Dr. Laurance N. Nickey, joint hearing before the Committee on Environment and Public Works, 23 April 1991, 26.
91. *Health Care: Availability in the Texas-Border Area* (Washington, D.C.: General Accounting Office, October 1988), 2.
92. Interview with Dr. Laurance Nickey, 30 July 1992.
93. Ricardo Loewe Reiss, "Considerations on the Health Status along Mexico's Northern Border," in *Views Across the Border: The United States and Mexico*, ed. Stanley R. Ross (Albuquerque: University of New Mexico Press, 1978), 251.
94. Numerous works document the environmental and occupational health problems associated with the *maquiladora* industry. One of the most recent is "Overview of Environmental Issues Associated with Maquiladora Development along the Texas-Mexico Border" (Austin: Texas Center for Policy Studies, October 1990).
95. Cited in James E. García, "Trade Casts Light on Environment," *Austin American Statesman*, 30 September 1991.

96. Jane Juffer, "The Case of the Mallory Children," *Progressive* (October 1988), 27.
97. This is according to statistics for the 1980–88 period published by the International Register of Congenital Deformities. According to Rick Finell, a geneticist at Texas A&M University, Latinos are one of various populations, including the Welsh, Irish, and Chinese, that have shown susceptibility to the disorder. Cited in Ana Arana, "The Wasteland," *San Francisco Chronicle,* 30 August 1991.
98. Coalition for Justice in the Maquiladoras, press release, 1 July 1992.
99. Cited in Gaynell Terrell, "Tragic Puzzle Grips Families on the Border," *The Houston Post,* 19 May 1992.
100. Secretaría de Salud, Jurisdicción Sanitaria No. 2, "Protocolo de Investigación de Anencefalia 1989–92 (Ciudad Juárez, 1992). Translation by authors.
101. Cited in Roberto Suro, "Pollution Tests Two Neighbors: El Paso and Juárez," *The New York Times,* 23 December 1991.
102. C. Richard Bath, "U.S.-Mexico Experience in Managing Transboundary Air Resources: Problems, Prospects, and Recommendations for the Future," in *The U.S.-Mexico Border Region: Anticipating Resource Needs and Issues to the Year 2000,* eds. César Sepulveda and Albert Utton (El Paso: Texas Western Press, 1982), 426.
103. Cited in Mydans, "U.S. and Mexico Agree."
104. *Transboundary Resources Report* 4, no. 2 (Summer 1990), 4.
105. Cited in Paul Salopek, "Crowded Border Imports High Rates of Disease," *El Paso Times,* 14 May 1991.
106. Mark Dowie, "The Corporate Crime of the Century," *Mother Jones* (November 1979), 23–49; Thomas N. Gladwin, "Environment, Development, and Multinational Enterprise," in *Multinational Corporations, Environment, and the Third World,* ed. Charles S. Pearson (Durham: Duke University Press, 1987), 16.
107. See Susan Fletcher, "International Environmental Issues: Overview," *CRS Issue Brief* (Washington, D.C.: Congressional Research Service, 27 July 1992).
108. The term *circle of poison* was popularized with the publication of David Weir and Mark Shapiro, *The Circle of Poison* (San Francisco: Institute for Food and Development Policy, 1981).
109. According to a study by the Foundation for Advancements in Science and Education, every hour U.S. companies export more than four tons of pesticides that are banned, canceled, withdrawn, or restricted from the U.S. market. About a quarter of exported pesticides are not registered by the EPA for use in the United States. Foundation for Advancements in Science and Education, "Special Report: Exporting Banned and Hazardous Pesticides" (Los Angeles, 1991). According to the EPA, about half of Latin American pesticide imports come from the United States. *Food Safety and Quality: Five Countries' Efforts to Meet U.S. Requirements on Imported Produce* (Washington, D.C.: General Accounting Office, March 1990). Also see *Pesticides: Export of Unregistered Pesticides Is Not Adequately Monitored by EPA* (Washington, D.C.: General Accounting Office, April 1989).
110. *Pesticides: Better Sampling and Enforcement Needed on Imported Food* (Washington, D.C.: General Accounting Office, September 1986), 3.
111. Interview with Jack Grady, El Paso, 24 July 1992.
112. Angus Wright, *The Death of Ramón González: The Modern Agricultural Dilemma*

(Austin: University of Texas Press, 1990), 196, citing U.S. government surveys. This excellent book not only offers a compelling personal portrait of the occupational hazards of farmworkers in Mexico but is a persuasive argument for a radical reform of the agricultural economy in Mexico.

113. Ibid.; "Imported Produce," *Los Angeles Times*, 9 April 1989.

114. Cited in Michael Weisskopf, "Pesticide Safety Tests: Can They Be Trusted?" *The Washington Post*, 13 March 1991.

115. Statement of William Ramsey of the Western Growers Association before the U.S. House of Representatives Committee on Agriculture, 24 April 1991.

116. DDT is "restricted" in Mexico and legally used only for the control of malaria and dengue vectors, although the organochlorine continues to be used clandestinely, especially in the more remote parts of the country.

117. *Food Safety and Quality*, Appendix V.

118. Angus Wright, "Third World Pesticide Production," *Global Pesticide Campaigner* 1, no. 3 (June 1991).

119. Angus Wright, "Rethinking the Circle of Poison: The Politics of Pesticide Poisoning Among Mexican Farm Workers," *Latin American Perspectives* 13, no. 4 (Fall 1986), 30.

120. Marco Luis Patiño, "Agroquímico quema a jornaleros," *El Imparcial*, 7 February 1991.

121. Wright, *The Death of Ramón González*, 41.

122. Ibid., 12, citing a 1987 interview with a representative of Mexico's National Union of Vegetable Growers.

123. For the place of Mixtec labor in agricultural production, see Michael Kearney, "Integration of the Mixteca and the Western U.S.–Mexico Region via Migratory Wage Labor," in Rosenthal-Urey, *Regional Impacts*, 71–102.

124. Researchers at the Agricultural Research Station of the Northwest (CIANO) have, among others, predicted this scenario. Ibid., 37.

125. Sources on the economic viability of alternative and traditional farming methods include Jennifer Curtis, *Harvest of Hope: The Potential of Alternative Agriculture to Reduce Pesticide Use* (Washington, D.C.: Natural Resources Defense Council, May 1991), and Miguel Altieri, *Agroecology: The Scientific Basis of Alternative Agriculture* (Boulder, Colo.: Westview Press, 1987).

126. See, for example, Candace Siegle, "Organic Farming Grows Profits," *Business Mexico* (December 1990). The recent creation of the Mexican Association of Ecological Farmers also points to the expanded market for organic produce in Mexico.

127. Monica Moore, "GATT, Pesticides, and Democracy," *Global Pesticide Campaigner* 1, no. 1 (October 1990), 13.

128. Testimony introduced by Senator Patrick Leahy (D-Vt.), Senator Albert Gore (D-Tenn.), and Representative Mike Synar (D-Okla.) before the U.S. Senate Agricultural Committee on the Pesticide Export Reform Act, 28 March 1990.

129. Ernst Feder, *El imperialismo fresa: Una investigación sobre los mecanismos de la dependencia en la agricultura mexicana* (Mexico, D.F.: Ediciones Campesino, 1976).

130. See Iván Restrepo, *Naturaleza muerta: Los plaguicidas en México* (Mexico, D.F.: Centro de Ecodesarrollo, 1988) and the *Boletín de la Red de Acción Sobre*

*Plaguicidas y Alternativas en México*, ed. Fernando Bejarano (Mexico, D.F. 1992).

131. Interview with Catalina Denman, 6 February 1991.

132. Luis Marco del Pont, "Contaminación en alimentos y consequencias," in *Envenamiento*, ed. Marcos López Torres (Ciudad Juárez: Escuela Superior de Agricultura, 1991), 99.

133. Interview with Jesús Román Calleros, 2 May 1991.

134. Such an inventory has, however, been compiled in 1991 for at least one state, Baja California. Hazardous wastes generally refer to those that are corrosive, reactive, flammable, or toxic (determined by various types of tests). Acids, bases, liquids and solids containing heavy metals, metal-plating wastes, organic and inorganic solvents, and cyanide wastes are examples of commonly generated hazardous wastes. For an excellent overview see the Texas Center for Policy Studies' *Overview of Environmental Issues*.

135. Whereas Mexico bans hazardous waste imports for dumping or incineration, it does allow imported wastes to be recycled or otherwise reused. The EPA registered nineteen hazardous waste shipments to Mexico in 1991.

136. Center for Investigative Reporting and Bill Moyers, *Global Dumping Ground: The International Traffic in Hazardous Waste* (Washington, D.C.: Seven Locks Press), 52.

137. Ibid., citing William Carter of the Los Angeles District Attorney's Office.

138. Sergeant Lance Erickson cited in *Los Angeles Times*, 9 May 1990.

139. Cited in Sarah Henry, "The Poison Trail," *Los Angeles Times*, 23 September 1990.

140. Ron Chepesiuk, "From Ash to Cash: The International Trade in Toxic Waste," *E Magazine* (July 1991).

141. For an overview of the problem and international and national efforts to control it, see Mary Tieman, "Waste Exports: U.S. and International Efforts to Control Transboundary Movement," *CRS Issue Brief* (Washington, D.C.: Congressional Research Service, 20 August 1992).

142. Chepesiuk, "From Ash to Cash."

143. See Diane Perry et al., "Binational Management of Hazardous Waste: The Maquiladora Industry at the U.S.-Mexico Border," *Environmental Management* 14, no. 4, 441.

144. Sanford J. Lewis, Marco Kaltofen, and Mary Waygan, *Border Trouble: Rivers in Peril* (Boston: National Toxic Campaign Fund, May 1991).

145. *Improved Monitoring and Enforcement Needed for Toxic Pollutants Entering Sewers* (Washington, D.C.: General Accounting Office, April 1989).

146. EPA, International Activities Office, *Notices of Intent to Import Hazardous Waste* (Washington, D.C.: 1989).

147. Bruce Tomaso and Richard Alm, "Economy vs. Ecology: Toxic Wastes from Border Plants Poorly Monitored," *Transboundary Resources Report* (Spring 1990).

148. Gregory Gross, "Accountability Trail Ends, but Toxic Stream Rolls On," *San Diego Union*, 16 June 1991.

149. *Hazardous Waste: Management of Maquiladora's Waste Hampered by Lack of Information* (Washington, D.C.: General Accounting Office, February 1992), 3.

150. Ibid.

151. Gross, "Accountability Trail Ends."
152. Ibid.
153. For a description of the hazardous waste problem in Mexico, particularly as it relates to the *maquiladoras*, see Roberto A. Sánchez, "Health and Environmental Risks of the Maquiladora in Mexicali," *Natural Resources Journal* 30 (Winter 1990), 163–86.
154. *San Diego Union-Tribune*, March 14, 1992.
155. Cody, "Expanding Waste Line."
156. Patrick J. McDonnell, "Mexicans Fear Plant Could Cause 'Next Bhopal,'" *Los Angeles Times*, 20 November 1991.
157. Mary E. Kelly, *A Response to the Bush Administration's Environmental Action Plan for Free Trade Negotiations with Mexico* (Austin: Texas Center for Policy Studies, May 1991), 12.
158. Roberto A. Sánchez, "Environment: Mexican Perspective," in *U.S.-Mexican Industrial Integration: The Road to Free Trade*, ed. Sidney Weintraub (Boulder, Colo.: Westview Press, 1991), 311.
159. Statement of the National Safe Workplace Institute, United States Free Trade Hearings, 6 and 20 February 1991, 374–75. Also see Rafael Moure-Eraso et al., *Back to the Future: Sweatshop Conditions of the Mexico-U.S. Border* (University of Lowell Work Environment Program, 21 May 1991).
160. Joseph LaDou, "Deadly Migration," *Technology Review* 94, no. 5 (July 1991), 50.
161. Mexican laws—Ley Federal del Trabajo and the Ley General de Salud—have established measures to protect workers, but as Sánchez has observed, in practice these laws are largely unenforced. Sánchez, "Environment: Mexican Perspective," in Weintraub, *U.S.-Mexican Industrial Integration*, 308.
162. See the studies of Catalina A. Denman, professor at El Colegio de Sonora, including "Tiempos Modernos: Trabajar y Morir," paper presented at a round-table sponsored by the Friedrich Ebert Foundation, 6 and 7 November 1989, Hermosillo, Sonora, and her master's thesis, "Repercusiones de la industria maquiladora de exportación en la salud: El peso al nacer de hijos de obreras en Nogales," Colegio de Sonora, 1988.
163. Leslie Kochan, *The Maquiladoras and Toxics: The Hidden Costs of Production South of the Border* (Washington, D.C.: AFL-CIO, February 1989), 11.
164. See Steve Fox, *Toxic Work* (Philadelphia: Temple University Press, 1991).
165. "The Impact on Women's Health of the Maquiladoras: The Tijuana Case," *CarnegieQuarterly* 36 (Fall 1991), 14. According to the director of the study, Sylvia Guendelman, "The results suggest that, when compared with other risks in the community closely related to a poor lifestyle, the adverse effects of *maquiladoras*, previously reported in the literature, seem to have been exaggerated."
166. Sánchez, "Environment: Mexican Perspective," in Weintraub, *U.S.-Mexican Industrial Integration*, 308.
167. David J. Molina, "A Comment on Whether Maquiladoras Are in Mexico for Low Wages or to Avoid Pollution Abatement Costs," *Journal of Environment and Development* 2, no. 1 (Winter 1993).
168. Alejandro Mercado, José Negrete, and Roberto Sánchez, *Capital internacional y relocalización industrial en la Frontera Norte de México* (Tijuana: COLEF, 1989).
169. "Although relocation of investment to avoid stricter environmental restrictions

may be a plausible outcome of differences in environmental standards and enforcement, and such movement has taken place in some instances, the phenomenon does not appear to be widespread, nor is it likely to characterize the formation of a NAFTA. This is because relatively few firms meet all of the conditions required for profitable pollution haven investment—high environmental compliance costs, a big change in locational incentives as a result of removal of trade barriers, low costs associated with new investment, and actual differences in environmental costs." The study concluded that looser pollution enforcement in Mexico would not encourage a systematic transfer of investment because pollution control equipment is such a small share of production costs (averaging 1.1 percent) and that for the industries with the highest pollution control costs, like the chemical industry, Mexican tariffs are low already and these industries are capital-intensive, making relocation costs extremely high. *Review of U.S.-Mexico Environmental Issues*, report prepared by an interagency task force coordinated by the Office of the U.S. Trade Representative (Washington, D.C., February 1992), 171. For a supporting position, see Christopher Duerksen, *Environmental Regulation of Industrial Plant Siting: How to Make it Work Better* (Washington, D.C.: Conservation Foundation, 1983). It should be noted, however, that although *relocation* costs are prohibitive for highly capital-intensive industries, such as chemical production, the decision of where to locate *new* investment is much more easily affected by the expected costs of pollution control and occupational safety measures.

170. A survey by the Colegio de la Frontera Norte in Tijuana did, however, show that environmental factors were significant. About 10 percent of the *maquiladoras* surveyed cited environmental regulations as a primary factor in the decision to leave the United States, and 17 percent considered environmental regulations an important factor. Mercado et al., *Capital internacional.*

171. See Barry Castleman, "How We Export Dangerous Industries," *Business and Society Review* (Fall 1978), 7–14, and Stephen P. Mumme, "Complex Interdependence and Hazardous Waste Management along the U.S.-Mexico Border," in *Dimensions of Hazardous Waste Politics and Policy*, eds. Charles E. Davis and James P. Lester (New York: Greenwood Press, 1988), 227. Mumme observes that export-oriented firms employing toxics in the production process, including several asbestos manufacturers and industries using carcinogenic substances like lindane, chlordane, polychlorinated biphenyls, trichlorethylene, and hydrochloric acid, have taken advantage of lax regulation in Mexico.

172. See, for example, Michael G. Royston, "Control by Multinational Corporations: The Environmental Case for Scenario 4," *Ambio* 4, no. 2–3 (1979), 84–89. An interesting twist is that given their accumulated experience and access to technology, large foreign corporations probably have an advantage over many domestic firms in meeting environmental regulations. See Charles S. Pearson, "Environmental Standards, Industrial Relocation, and Pollution Havens," in Pearson, *Multinational Corporations*, 120. Pearson even suggests that "the combination of in-house technology, expertise, and prior experience—all intangible assets that form the basis of the monopolistic advantage theory—suggest that the introduction of environmental regulations in developing countries will promote foreign investment, not block it."

173. Pearson, *Multinational Corporations*, 123, and Gabriele Knodgen, "Environment and Industrial Siting: Results of an Empirical Survey of Investment by West German Industry in Developing Countries," *Zeitschrift für Umweltpolitik*, no. 2 (1979).

174. See Gene M. Grossman and Alan B. Krueger, "Environmental Impacts of a North American Free Trade Agreement," discussion paper no. 158 (Princeton, N.J.: Woodrow Wilson School, Princeton University, February 1992); Mumme, "Complex Interdependence," in Davis and Lester, *Hazardous Waste Politics and Policy*; Christopher Duerksen and H. Jeffrey Leonard, "Environmental Regulations and the Location of Industries: An International Perspective," *Columbia Journal of World Business* (Summer 1982); and Castleman, "How We Export Dangerous Industries." Also see H. Jeffrey Leonard, *Are Environmental Regulations Driving U.S. Industry Overseas?* (Washington, D.C.: The Conservation Foundation, 1984), in which he concludes that although there has been some migration to Mexico of hazardous industries (especially asbestos and building supplies manufacturing) and nonferrous metal smelting and refining, factors unrelated to workplace health and safety and to pollution control costs were largely responsible for the new investment in Mexico.

175. International Labor Office, *Safety and Health Practices of Multinational Enterprises* (Geneva, 1984), 58–59. At the same time, however, Mexican authorities viewed the health and safety performance of the transnational corporations as being superior to those of domestically owned operations.

176. Gerald V. Poje and Daniel M. Horowitz, *Phantom Reductions: Tracking Toxic Trends* (Washington, D.C.: National Wildlife Federation, 1990).

177. See *U.S.-Mexico Trade: Some U.S. Wood Furniture Firms Relocated from Los Angeles Area to Mexico* (Washington, D.C.: General Accounting Office, April 1991). The report notes that not all industry flight from the Los Angeles area has been to Mexico. Seeking to escape the emissions regulations of the South Coast region, companies have also moved to Northern California and to southern states, such as Georgia, where environmental compliance costs are low.

178. Judy Pasternak, "Firms Find a Haven from U.S. Environmental Rules," *Los Angeles Times*, 19 November 1991.

179. Cited in LaDou, "Deadly Migration," 50.

180. *Comercio Exterior* 41, no. 9 (September 1991), 863. The furniture industry ranks fourth in the number of plants and sixth in the number of employees.

181. Robert Reinhold, "Mexico Proclaims an End to Sanctuary for Polluters," *The New York Times*, 18 April 1991.

182. During the 1976–90 period, the lime plant had no U.S. ownership, but in 1991 Sonocal was purchased by the Texas-based Chemstar.

183. Dick Kamp, "Lime Dust in My Children's Lungs," testimony before the EPA, 26 September 1991, Nogales, Arizona.

184. See Jan Gilbreath, "Financing Environmental and Infrastructure Needs on the Texas-Mexico Border: Will the Mexican-U.S. Integrated Border Plan Help?," *Journal of Environment and Development* 1, no. 1 (Summer 1992), 151–75, for a discussion of these ideas.

185. For an interesting examination of the U.S. section of the IBWC and its special status among U.S. government agencies, see Stephen P. Mumme, "Regional

Power in National Diplomacy: The Case of the U.S. Section of the International Boundary and Water Commission," *Journal of Federalism* 14, no. 4 (Fall 1984). Also see Mumme, "Engineering Diplomacy."

186. The IBWC is responsible for a wide range of administrative and operational duties relating to boundary questions and water resources along the border. These include: resolving boundary disputes; maintaining stable river boundaries; maintaining bridges and other structures that cross the boundary; distributing the waters of the Rio Grande/Rio Bravo and the Colorado River between the two countries; joint operation of international dams; sponsoring joint flood control operations; monitoring water quality; designing and constructing water and wastewater treatment plants; resolving water quality problems, including excessive salinity resulting from U.S. agricultural irrigation; and maintaining surface water reservoirs.

187. This memorandum of understanding committed the EPA and Mexico's Subsecretaría de Mejoramiento del Ambiente and its head agency, the Secretaría de Salud y Asistencia, to a "cooperative effort to resolve environmental protection matters of mutual concern in border areas as well as any environmental protection matters through exchanges of information and personnel, and the establishment of parallel projects which the two parties consider appropriate to adopt." Quoted in Stephen P. Mumme and Joseph Nalven, "National Perspectives on Managing Transboundary Environmental Hazards: The U.S.-Mexico Border Region," *Journal of Borderlands Studies* 3, no. 1 (Spring 1988).

188. A 1980 Joint Marine Pollution Contingency Plan built on the 1978 memorandum and committed the two countries to cooperate on offshore pollution problems such as oil spills. Several other agreements were concluded in the following years.

189. Eight agreements were signed between 1983 and early 1992: Framework Agreement on Cooperation for Protection and Improvement of the Environment (Annexes I, II, III, IV, and V) (1983); Bilateral Agreement for Protection of the Environment along the Border (1983); Agreement for the Conservation of Wildlife (1983); Memorandum of Understanding between Mexico and the United States for the Creation of a Joint Committee on Wild Plant and Animal Life (1988); Memorandum of Understanding for the Creation of the Committee on Protected Areas in Mexico and the United States (1988); Cooperation Agreement for Environmental Protection and Improvement in the Mexico City Metropolitan Area (1989); Agreement to Improve the Quality of Air in Mexico City and its Metropolitan Area (1990); and the Integrated Environmental Plan for the Mexican-U.S. Border Area (First Stage, 1992–1994) (1992).

190. For a description of SEDUE's administrative structure and functional responsibilities, see Stephen P. Mumme, C. Richard Bath, and Valerie Assetto, "Political Development and Environmental Policy in Mexico," *Latin American Review*, vol. 23, no. 1 (1988).

191. There are a number of excellent reports by experts on environmental degradation and environmental policy that examine the flaws summarized here. These reports include: Kelly, *Facing Reality*; Jan Gilbreath Rich, *Planning the Border's Future: The Mexican-U.S. Integrated Border Environmental Plan*, U.S.-Mexican Occasional Paper No. 1, (Austin: Lyndon B. Johnson School of Public Affairs, University of Texas at Austin, March 1992); Michael Gregory, "Environment,

Sustainable Development, Public Participation and the NAFTA: A Retrospective," *Journal of Environmental Law and Litigation* 7 (August 1992, prepublication draft).

192. The economic crisis strangled funding for SEDUE. According to Javelly Girard, its secretary from 1983 to 1985, "The selective credit policy of the [central] Bank of Mexico has not directed revenues to ecology, and for that reason we lack the instruments necessary to fight pollution." Quoted in Francisco Garfias, "Faltan Recursos Financieros para Combatir la Contaminación: Javelly," *Excélsior*, 16 November 1984, A4.

193. In comparison, the United States spends about twenty-four dollars per person on environmental programs.

194. Even before NAFTA negotiations opened, the Salinas government enhanced environmental protection activities because of public pressure and the need to win back voter support for PRI after the 1988 elections. These enforcement actions were described by one U.S. critic as "demonstration projects" designed to "preempt" independent efforts at reform. Stephen P. Mumme, "System Maintenance and Environmental Reform in Mexico: Salinas's Preemptive Strategy," *Latin American Perspectives* 19, no. 1 (Winter 1992), 18.

195. See, for example, "A Response to the EPA/SEDUE Integrated Border Environment Plan" (Austin: Texas Center for Policy Studies, 1 March 1992); Gregory, "Environment, Sustainable Development, Public Participation and the NAFTA"; Kelly, "Facing Reality"; and Rich, "Planning the Border's Future."

196. Environmental activists roundly criticized the IBWC's continuing authority over border water pollution even though the body's treaty status gives its agreements extra weight compared with accords reached through other agencies. Despite its mandate, the commission has moved slowly to resolve sewage and pollution questions along the border. It is reluctant to use its access to the courts to enforce its agreements, relying upon the U.S. and Mexican governments to enforce their own standards for water quality and pollution cleanup. Activists believe that the IBWC neglects to consult with local organizations and communities about their concerns and the impacts of IBWC public works on local environments. Analysts have faulted the agency for operating behind closed doors and for being an unrepresentative, appointed body. See, for instance, Gregory, "Environment, Sustainable Development, Public Participation and the NAFTA," 75–76, and Rich, "Bordering on Trouble," 32.

197. Quoted in Patrick McDonnell, "Environmental Fears Voiced on Free-Trade Plan," *Los Angeles Times*, 24 September 1991, sec. B, p. 2

198. See Gregory, "Environment, Sustainable Development, Public Participation and the NAFTA"; Stewart Hudson, *Comments on the Draft Review of the U.S.-Mexico Environmental Issues* (Washington, D.C.: National Wildlife Federation, n.d.); Justin Ward and Lynn Fischer, *Comments on the Draft Review of U.S.-Mexico Environmental Issues* (Washington, D.C.: Copublished by the Natural Resources Defense Council, Grupo de los Cien, and Instituto Autonomo de Investigaciones Ecologicas, December 1991); and Michael McCloskey and John Audley, *Concerns Arising out of the Environmental Review on NAFTA* (Washington, D.C.: Sierra Club, 29 November 1991).

199. Interview with Lynn Fischer, 3 August 1992.

200. Much of the following discussion is drawn from a paper by Anne L. Alonzo, *Mexico* (Mexico, D.F.: U.S. Embassy, February 1992). Alonzo is the EPA's environmental attaché in Mexico City.

201. The latter task fulfills more than environmental purposes. It also will facilitate increased trade in pesticides between the two countries.

202. Quoted in letter from Dick Kamp, Border Ecology Project, to Charles Ries, deputy trade representative of the USTR, 11 December 1991, 3. For more on the restructuring of Mexico's environmental protection agency, see "Privatizará SEDUE Política Ambiental," *El Imparcial*, 19 November 1991.

203. SEDESOL took over environmental policy formulation and enforcement, urban planning, and administration of the National Solidarity Program (Pronasol). It also included the National Indigenous Institute. *Mexico Environmental Issues: Fact Sheets* (Washington, D.C.: Mexican Embassy, n.d.) and Edward M. Ranger, Jr., and Anne Alonzo, "SEDUE Re-emerges under SEDESOL," *Business Mexico* (September 1992).

204. *Mexico Environmental Issues*, 13–14.

205. David Clark Scott, "Mexico Shake-up Rattles Environmentalists," *The Christian Science Monitor*, 4 May 1992, 6.

206. Interview with Mario Aguilar, 27 July 1992.

207. Dick Kamp, letter to Charles Ries regarding the Draft Environmental Review of NAFTA, 11 December 1991.

208. Rosa Ma. Chavarria Diaz, "Elimina SEDUE al 48% de los Inspectores que Verificaban Empresas Contaminantes," *El Nacional*, 11 November 1991.

209. *U.S.-Mexico Trade: Assessment of Mexico's Environmental Controls for New Companies* (Washington, D.C.: General Accounting Office, Aug. 1992).

210. Noting the need for enhanced monitoring efforts, these two organizations issued a draft report summarizing environmental problems reported in news articles and other documents. Proyecto Fronteriza de Educación Ambiental and Border Ecology Project, *The North American Free Trade Agreement: Environmental and Health Issues in the Interior of Mexico and Options for Environmental Safeguards*, working draft (Naco, Arizona, 8 October 1992). Other groups monitoring border environmental and health conditions and devising programs to respond to them are the Ambos Nogales Project and the Northeast Sonora-Cochise County Health Council. Both are binational working groups with grass-roots origins composed of representatives from local health agencies, nongovernmental organizations, community groups, and government agencies.

211. World Bank Staff Appraisal 10005-ME, 19 March 1992.

212. William F. Joffrey, cited in Roberto Suro, "Border Boom's Dirty Residue Imperils U.S.-Mexico Trade," *The New York Times*, 31 March 1991.

213. Co-optive tactics, often complemented by more repressive measures for intractable critics, have long been practiced by the PRI. Title V of Mexico's 1988 General Law on the environment includes provisions for "social participation," in the form of consultations with sectors such as labor, business, peasants, academics, and nongovernmental organizations. Another section of the law provides that citizens can denounce violations of environmental laws to Mexican authorities and requires an official investigative report and action brief within thirty days of the complaint. These provisions sound good on paper, but in

practice participation has been open primarily to groups that favor the PRI and its environmental policies. In other cases environmental militants from groups like the Pacto de Ecologistas have been solicited into the government and their criticisms thereby quieted. Those groups who have remained sharply critical of the government's policies have complained of being excluded from government-sponsored forums on environmental issues. Others, such as the prominent Grupo de Cien, have accused the Salinas government of more actively quashing dissent with methods such as censorship and harassment. See Mumme, "System Maintenance," 123–43.

214. "United States Environmental Protection Agency Advisory Committee Charter: EPA Border Environmental Plan Public Advisory Committee" (Washington, D.C.: EPA, n.d.).

215. Interview with Gail Sevrens, Border Progress Foundation, 23 July 1992.

216. Sal Drum, "The Final Plan: A Blueprint for Border Environmental Improvement," *Maquila Magazine* (April 1992).

217. See, for example, Proyecto Fronteriza de Educación Ambiental and Border Ecology Project, *The North American Free Trade Agreement*, and Gregory, "Environment, Sustainable Development, Public Participation and the NAFTA."

218. This definition is drawn from the 1987 report of the World Commission on Environment and Development, *Our Common Future* (Brundtland Commission).

219. This definition is taken from Michael Gregory, "Sustainable Development vs. Economic Growth: Environmental Protection as an Investment in the Future," statement before the International Trade Commission, *Hearing on the Probable Economic Effect of a Free Trade Agreement Between the United States and Mexico*, 8 April 1991.

220. For a summary of this viewpoint, see Wesley R. Smith, "Protecting the Environment in North America with Free Trade," *The Heritage Foundation Backgrounder*, 2 April 1992.

221. Gregory, "Environment, Sustainable Development, Public Participation and the NAFTA."

222. For such a proposal, see Alan Neff, "Not in Their Backyards Either: A Proposal for a Foreign Environmental Practices Act," *Ecology Law Quarterly*, no. 471 (1990). Neff, of the Chicago Corporation Commission, proposed the establishment of a U.S. Foreign Environmental Practices Act, modeled after the Foreign Corrupt Practices Act, that could be attached to the Securities Exchange Act of 1934. Under this proposal U.S. corporations and citizens would be subject to both criminal and civil prosecution in U.S. courts for violating applicable U.S. environmental laws and regulations overseas.

# Part III

# The Economic Connection

# Economic Globalization

# Sets the Stage

Money and business are integrating North America. Economic forces—even more than transboundary migration, drug trafficking, or borderless ecosystems—are pulling Mexico and the United States together. In the process the economic future of both countries is being shaped. On a broader scale U.S.-Mexico integration illustrates the dramatic changes taking place in the world economy, as the economic structures of advanced and developing countries alike are being restructured to meet the needs of global traders and investors.

Not a textbook theory, economic globalization is a readily observable movement of people and goods. It can be seen, for example, in the city of Chihuahua in northern Mexico. Every weekday morning a couple of dozen company buses turn off the main avenue leading out of the city and into the parking lot of a Ford Motor Company engine plant. As the 540 first-shift employees report to work in the modern concrete-and-glass facility, hundreds of cars fill an employee parking lot outside a much older Ford engine plant in Lima, Ohio, some fifteen hundred miles to the northeast. Separated by an international border, language, and an average age difference of thirty years, the two groups of workers are nevertheless part of the same corporate web. They produce for the same market with largely the same technology, answer to the same executives, and generate dividends for the same shareholders.

Thousands of similar corporate webs, ranging from very small local operations to the world's largest transnational corporations, link hundreds of thousands of workers in Mexico and the United States, as well as millions of consumers and shareholders. Although the movement of workers between Mexico and the United States remains heavily restricted, the countries have moved much closer together in the areas of trade and investment since the early 1980s.

Economic integration involves a reduction in the importance of national boundaries in the decisions of consumers, workers, and investors. This does not mean that national characteristics such as labor markets, infrastructure, and climate matter less. On the contrary, such characteristics become *more* important with integration because people and corporations are freer to cross borders to take advantage of them.

A profound shift in the organization of manufacturing is to a large degree behind this integration. Advances in telecommunications and transportation technology have made it possible to coordinate extremely complex manufacturing processes—from product design and investment financing to inventory management and marketing—in several countries simultaneously. Managers have "rationalized" their operations and reduced costs by splitting up portions of their production chains and relocating the various links to countries with lower labor costs, more competitive suppliers, cheaper natural resources, or more favorable government policies.

The production of television sets by the Japanese electronics giant Hitachi illustrates the process of globalization.[1] First, Hitachi marketers in the United States estimate how many of which models their distributors will need in six weeks. On the basis of this information, orders go out to a Singaporean subcontractor, who manufactures the specified transistors and ships them to a Malaysian circuit board assembler. From Malaysia the circuit boards travel to Taiwan, where workers assemble controller chassis, again following Hitachi's product mix instructions. With two weeks to go other components are ordered from Hitachi affiliates in Japan. A week later the chassis and other parts arrive in Tijuana, where they are joined by picture tubes and deflection yokes made by a Dutch company in the United States. Mexican workers assemble wood and plastic panels shipped from the United States, attach the electronic innards, and run the televisions through a battery of quality control tests. Workers then package the TVs and ship them to the United States with two or three days to spare.

The replacement of traditional, locally based manufacturing with international assembly lines like Hitachi's is commonly termed the globalization of production. Technological advances and transnational production networks alone do not explain globalization. Although corporations in search of markets and workers are the main actors in the process of integration, governments play a critical role in establishing the rules under which corporations act. A legal framework conducive to foreign investment, low barriers to trade, an efficient international financial system, and a stable, probusiness political atmosphere are also crucial elements. Throughout the post–World War II era the United States has worked to put these elements into place, largely by pushing other countries to adopt open trade and investment policies.

The North American Free Trade Agreement among Canada, Mexico, and the United States was an attempt to shape economic integration on a regional rather than worldwide basis. But regional integration has global implications. The economic relationship taking shape across the Rio Grande bridges an enormous gap in economic development and living standards and represents a prototype for the rapidly changing roles played by the postindustrial north and south in the global economy.[2] North America is a crucible in which advanced technology, subsistence farming, global finance capital, massive underemployment, and contrasting legal and political systems are being mixed for the first time. How policy makers and social forces shape the process of integration and what the results of integration are will help define the development strategies of poor countries, the competitive strategies of wealthier ones, and the ability of all nations and citizens to influence their own destinies.

The United States and Mexico appeared to cement the process of economic integration in the early 1990s with the signing of NAFTA. But mounting evidence in both countries pointed to problems with their governments' economic strategies. Many observers in both countries questioned the management of North American integration and advocated new responses to the challenges of globalization.

## The United States in the Global Economy

The United States pushed the international economy to open up after World War II, making GATT one of the centerpieces of its effort. As the dominant force in the capitalist world the United States was largely able to get its way. Negotiations under GATT resulted in a steady lowering of trade barriers, and U.S. manufacturers saw a widening global market for their goods.

In the 1960s the more visionary corporate managers saw that freer trade flows meant access not just to consumer markets but also to vast labor markets. Led by the electronics and apparel industries, these managers set up labor-intensive facilities in Asia, the Caribbean, and Mexico. In most cases the shift to new, globally oriented plants enabled corporations to weaken the grip of labor unions, cut wage costs, and increase managerial control over the organization of work. As globalization progressed, both workers and governments found themselves in more direct international competition for a limited pool of capital and technology.

Few policy makers noticed these effects as long as the U.S. economy was growing steadily. But the recessions of the 1970s began to draw attention to the fact that U.S. corporations were sending jobs abroad at the same time that employment opportunities at home were becoming scarcer. And the huge trade deficit that the United States racked up in the 1980s spotlighted trade policies as a possible source of declining economic security.

By the late 1980s millions of workers who had formed the backbone of the middle class had been thrown out of work by plant shutdowns. Government studies indicated that more than one-half of all "displaced" workers were still unemployed six months after being laid off. Even among workers who succeeded in regaining employment, more had moved down the pay scale in taking their new positions than had moved up. On average displaced workers suffered real earnings losses of 10 to 15 percent.[3]

Laid-off workers were not the only ones seeing their salaries drop. New entrants to the workforce competed with those experienced workers whose jobs had been eliminated. And although the economy was generating new jobs, few of these paid a family wage. From 1979 to 1987, 21.2 million more jobs were created than had been lost. But more than half the new positions paid less than the poverty line for a family of four—$13,400 per year—and only 7.6 percent paid more than the median annual salary of $26,800.[4] Millions of workers were able to keep their jobs only by agreeing to employers' demands for wage and benefit cuts or, in nonunion settings, by implicitly accepting them. These trends have meant more work and less pay for the average worker, a widening income gap between the top 20 percent of households and everyone else, and fewer opportunities for anyone without postsecondary education.[5]

Two strains of thought developed in the United States about how to respond to these economic trends. In one camp are neoliberals, who believe that the fall in workers' wages, the widening income gap, and the growing trade deficit are the natural results of a globalizing international economy. Tinkering with market forces will only make things worse, they argue, and in the long term the trade deficit will shrink and employment and wages will grow again. Neoliberals point to the massive inflow of foreign capital in the 1980s as evidence of the soundness of the U.S. economy.[6] Investors would be unlikely to buy assets in dollars, they reason, if the country were headed downhill. From this perspective the best policy option is to continue to open the U.S. economy and to encourage other countries to follow the U.S. lead.[7]

A second strain of policy thought, which could be called *Realeconomik*, began to challenge the neoliberal position during the 1980s. According to this view, the United States' reliance on the free market places it at a competitive disadvantage vis-à-vis its trading partners, who play by different rules. In East Asia and Western Europe national governments have developed industrial policies that target strategic economic sectors ranging from steel production and shipbuilding to the semiconductor and aerospace industries. They have also coordinated and subsidized large-scale worker training programs. With government support, businesses in targeted industries are able to win market share from U.S.-based firms, both overseas and in the United States. The trade deficit is exhibit number one for this position. And the inflow of foreign capital, far from being a good sign, represents a huge mortgage taken out by U.S. consumers for which future generations will pay dearly.[8]

Academics and policy makers in the *Realeconomik* camp pushed the United States to adopt an industrial policy to improve the country's international position. Many of them admitted that this was a second-best solution to the United States' international economic problems: Ideally other countries would change their systems by reducing their governments' economic role and by dropping barriers to foreign trade and investment. But attempting to convince them to do so by example and through gentle persuasion was ineffective, especially since industrial policies had served their business interests well over the previous decades. Instead, they concluded, the United States should play by their rules, raise barriers to some imports, and target specific industries for government support. In addition, most proponents of an industrial policy include some form of national worker-training program in their proposals.

The idea of enhancing U.S. competitiveness raises far more questions than it answers. What does competitiveness mean? Is it profits, jobs, quality of life, a trade surplus, or something else? Where does it come from? What factors lead an investor to choose one site over another? Should there be rules to the ways countries seek competitive advantages, such as a ban on slave labor or a cap on government subsidies? If so, how should they be determined and enforced?

For neoliberals, U.S.-Mexican economic relations provided an important part of the answer to these questions. The United States will stay competitive if its companies stay competitive, and its companies can do that by transferring certain jobs to Mexico. The government should facilitate production sharing by removing obstacles to trade and investment. But to those in the industrial policy camp, this strategy sounds like keeping the ship and crew afloat by ordering passengers to jump overboard. Instead of making it easier for companies to move offshore, they argue, the government should adopt a national economic strategy, help businesses upgrade their technology and worker-training programs, fight back against unfair competition, and work to create international social standards.

Although neoliberals and industrial policy advocates disagree on the proper economic role for government, both focus on enhancing the international competitiveness of U.S.-based corporations.[9] A third strain of thought gained strength during the debate over NAFTA in the early 1990s but posed little challenge to the two dominant perspectives. Unlike the neoliberal and *Realeconomik* perspectives, this view rejects unfettered capitalism as the primary basis for domestic or international policy. Advocates of this position are concerned that an industrial policy would tilt the already skewed balance of economic and political power even farther toward the corporate elite and away from workers, small businesses, and grassroots activists. These progressives argue that international economic agreements should cover much more than trade and investment issues. Environmental standards, labor rights, consumer protection, and the ability of nations to regulate capital all are affected by institutions like GATT. Such societal interests, they say, need to be included alongside business interests in negotiations, and their observance enforced by democratically accountable bodies.

Until the election of Bill Clinton in 1992 the neoliberal position held sway in Washington. The treatment prescribed by the Reagan and Bush administrations for the nation's economic malaise was in effect "Take more of the same." Domestically the government refused to consider an industrial policy and in fact moved in the other direction by rescinding the investment tax credit, deregulating a number of industries, and defanging enforcement agencies like the Occupational Safety and Health Administration and the Environmental Protection Agency. Internationally the *Realeconomik* camp had slightly more success, winning official recognition—first by Congress and then by the Office of the U.S. Trade Representative—that the international economic "playing field" was uneven and often sloped against U.S. corporations.

But with the exception of some subsidy and export promotion programs, the Reagan and Bush administrations rejected the "If you can't persuade 'em, fight 'em on their own terms" advice of industrial policy advocates. Instead they pursued a grand vision of global economic policy convergence based on neoliberalism. Ronald Reagan proposed the first element in this strategy—a free trade zone "from the Yukon to the Yucatán"—as a presidential candidate in 1980. But with no immediate takers, he had to settle for a much more modest program: the Caribbean Basin Initiative (CBI). Proposed in 1981 and in place by 1983, CBI consisted of a combination of aid and trade incentives aimed at the politically sensitive and economically troubled regions of Central America and the Caribbean. To participate in CBI, countries had to adopt laws protecting the rights of foreign investors. The initiative was designed to increase economic ties between the United States and CBI participants and to encourage the latter to follow a development path well within the bounds of international capitalism. Although CBI itself did not oblige participating countries to open their domestic markets to imports, the Reagan administration pursued this objective by conditioning much of its economic assistance on import liberalization by recipient countries. The United States applied added pressure for lower trade barriers in the third world through its central role in renegotiating developing countries' international debts and its influence in the International Monetary Fund and the World Bank.

To move toward the broader global vision, Reagan pushed for a broadening and deepening of GATT, proposing an eighth round of talks in 1982. Four years later, following considerable U.S. efforts, talks began in Uruguay. United States negotiators set an ambitious goal for what is called the Uruguay Round: the inclusion of services and agricultural products under GATT's umbrella. Both sectors were excluded from the original GATT mandate because virtually all nations—the United States included—sought to protect their domestic financial and food systems. But the U.S. position shifted as the country's manufacturing industries lost their competitive advantage and as U.S. agribusinesses and financial institutions grew stronger. Trade officials expected that opening up European, Asian, and Latin American markets to U.S. farmers, insurance companies, and banks would go a long way toward correcting the country's huge trade deficit.

With such an ambitious agenda, the Uruguay Round dragged on for years. While GATT remained the top priority for U.S. negotiators, the slow going prompted three regional efforts at trade and investment accords: the U.S.-Canada Free Trade Agreement, signed in 1988; the Enterprise for the Americas Initiative, launched by President Bush in 1990; and NAFTA. The Reagan and Bush administrations advanced these regional proposals with several economic objectives in mind.[10]

The first such objective was to increase the rate of U.S. economic growth, even if only slightly, through free trade and broader investment options. Free traders saw opportunities looking both north and south. Canada is the country's leading trade partner, forms a crucial part of the U.S. automobile-manufacturing base, and has resources—mainly oil and water—of great potential interest to the United States. Mexico ranks third as a trade partner, but with high import barriers in key areas, an agreement with Mexico could boost U.S. exports significantly. At least as important in Mexico's case was the liberalization of investment restrictions in a number of sectors previously off limits to foreigners.

The second objective behind the regional proposals was the Bush administration's hope that North American free trade would speed the GATT process by setting precedents for trade and investment provisions. The U.S.-Canada accord and NAFTA both dealt with the unglamorous but very important subject of intellectual property rights—the protection of trademarks, copyrights, and patents—as well as liberalization of the financial services and agricultural sectors. All these areas were central to the Uruguay Round.

The United States also looked to regional agreements to strengthen its negotiating position within GATT. NAFTA and the proposed Enterprise for the Americas Initiative—George Bush's plan to unite the hemisphere in a series of bilateral and multilateral free trade agreements—improved the United States' "fallback" position. That is, they reduced the cost to the United States of failing to sign a GATT agreement by laying the foundation for a smaller but still significant liberalized trade and investment region.[11] By 1992 the United States had signed sixteen "framework" agreements—a preliminary step to trade negotiations—involving thirty-one countries in the hemisphere. This lent credibility to U.S. statements that it would pull out of the Uruguay Round if its bottom-line offer were not accepted.

With a Democrat taking over the White House for the first time in twelve years, it is unclear to what extent the United States will continue to insist on trade agreements that reflect the neoliberal ideology. During his presidential campaign Bill Clinton placed himself squarely in the *Realeconomik* camp, stating that he supported free trade in principle, but cautioning that "if they won't play by our rules, we'll play by theirs."[12]

## Mexico in the Global Economy

As the globalization of production hollowed out the manufacturing base of many economically advanced countries, it was also transforming many less developed countries. In a handful of Asian and Latin American nations, including Mexico, the foreign investment binge that was a central part of globalization gave birth to modern, export-oriented industrial sectors.

The East Asian countries—in particular Taiwan, South Korea, and Singapore—linked their economies to international markets and leveraged foreign investment into economic growth, trade surpluses, and slowly rising wages. In these cases strong central governments repressed organized labor, adopted stable probusiness foreign investment policies, provided low-cost but well-trained workforces, and carved out distinct economic niches for themselves through national development strategies.[13] Neither Mexico nor other Latin American newly industrializing countries (NICs) like Brazil, Colombia, and Argentina were able to stimulate growth through foreign investment as had South Korea, Taiwan, and Singapore. Governments in both sets of NICs intervened heavily in their national economies, but whereas the East Asian countries shifted to an export-oriented strategy in the 1960s, their Latin American counterparts followed more inward-looking policies until the 1980s.[14]

The experiences of the East Asian tigers provided evidence that participation in the international economy could promote capitalist development, given appropriate government policies. This evidence ran counter to the prevalent view of underdevelopment in Latin America and elsewhere, called dependency theory. Dependency theory held that developing countries could not hope to catch up to the north through trade and foreign investment. Once linked economically, development in the south would depend on and be secondary to the consumer needs and investment patterns of the north. Dependency theorists also argued that the value of advanced northern products would constantly increase relative to the value of southern goods and that foreign investment would only lead to capital outflow through profit repatriation and other means. By undermining a central premise of dependency theory, East Asia's experience with globalization had an indirect political impact that was felt throughout the developing world.[15]

For reasons of history and internal political structures, nearly all Latin American countries—even those in which foreign investment had built export-oriented manufacturing sectors—resisted globalization's pull to join the world economy until the 1980s. Instead they pursued an inward-looking development strategy called import-substituting industrialization (ISI). As its name suggests, the goal of ISI was to develop a strong industrial base by encouraging the domestic production of previously imported goods. Rooted in the region's disastrous experience with international markets in the Great Depression of the 1930s, ISI was also intended to minimize dependence on international trade and foreign investment.[16]

Mexico was one of the most vigorous and successful exponents of ISI. Starting in the 1920s and accelerating after World War II, Mexico raised tariffs and imposed other barriers to imports, assigning the highest duties to those goods that economic planners felt would be easiest to produce domestically, such as apparel, footwear, and bottled beverages.

In some areas domestic capitalists did not have the know-how to replace imports, so the government looked to transnational corporations (TNCs) for help. Foreign corporations were attracted to Mexico because its protected market offered high prices and little competition, and it gave them a chance to milk additional profit out of the technology they had already developed. Mexico hoped that TNCs would transfer their advanced technology and managerial techniques to Mexican workers and managers and that they would spark the development of local supplier industries.

But Mexican decision makers were also deeply distrustful of foreign corporations. Multinational firms could not be counted on to set production targets and marketing strategies that would best serve Mexico's development goals. And they could end up siphoning large amounts of foreign exchange out of the country through profit remittances and royalty payments to their parent firms. To reduce reliance on TNCs over the long term, the country's strategy called for the "Mexicanization" of foreign firms. According to this plan, when domestic industrialists had learned enough and were ready to take over, the government would force TNCs to sell them at least a majority interest in their operations.

Mexico's distrust of foreign corporations—which echoed throughout the third world—stemmed in large part from the country's experience with foreign investors in a previous period: the thirty-five-year rule of General Porfirio Díaz from 1876 to 1910. The economy during the *porfiriato* provides a textbook case of dependent development. Díaz relied on foreign capitalists to improve the country's physical and financial infrastructure. Railroads, mines, oil wells, banks, and large-scale agriculture flourished during the *porfiriato*, but they were thoroughly dominated by foreign firms, mostly from the United States.[17] Díaz and his bureaucrats benefited richly from the gratitude of foreign companies, but the rest of the country was left out of the game. Most of the railroads, for example, served only to transport foreign-owned ores or crops to foreign-controlled ports for shipment abroad.

Frustrated with foreign economic domination and the regime's corruption and aided by the discontent of peasants and workers, a collection of military, business, and middle-class leaders forced Díaz into exile in 1911 and took control of the government. The constitution they adopted in 1917 launched the country on a very different development path. Mexico became a leader among developing countries in advocating a strong economic role for the state, favoring domestic capitalists over foreign, and seeking maximum autonomy from the world economy.

A number of provisions of the new constitution—notably Article 27—gave the state authority to limit severely the control foreign firms could exercise in the Mexican economy. The constitution prohibited foreigners from owning land or obtaining concessions to exploit the land unless they agreed to be treated as Mexican citizens and renounced the protection of their home governments. In addition, the new constitution granted the state ownership of all lands and waters and the right to transfer property title to the private sector under any conditions it chose.

If the revolutionary leaders and their successors did not trust foreign investors, neither were they confident in the abilities of domestic capitalists. By itself, the new policy makers thought, Mexico's private sector was too weak to lead the nation on a development path that would place the country among the advanced economies and protect the interests of workers and peasants. Rejecting both market capitalism and state socialism, the constitution established a central economic role for the state within a capitalist context. Article 27 charged the state with ensuring that private property, private contracts, and natural resources were used in "the public interest [and] for social benefit." The state came to be called the *rector* of the economy.

But the Mexican constitution is more a guide to the state's purposes and goals than a set of hard-and-fast laws. Fulfilling the constitutional goal of subordinating foreign investors to national interests therefore required a series of executive or legislative measures that were variously enforced. The most dramatic decree came in 1938, when President Lázaro Cárdenas announced the expropriation of all foreign oil firms.[18] By the time Cárdenas left office in 1940, foreign capital contributed only 15 percent of total investment in Mexico's economy, down from 66 percent in the first decade of the 1900s.

Subsequent administrations continued to work toward the Mexicanization of the economy, though none challenged foreign firms as directly as had Cárdenas. The government restricted foreign investors to minority ownership of new business ventures. In key economic sectors like mining and electric utilities, regulators used none-too-subtle means to pressure existing foreign investors to sell their majority interests.

The policy of Mexicanization, combined with booming domestic investment, greatly reduced Mexico's overall reliance on TNCs. In the 1950s foreign capital averaged around 10 percent of total investment, in the 1960s it was around 5 percent, and in the 1970s less than 3 percent of total investment each year came from abroad. But in several of the fastest-growing industries—automobiles, pharmaceuticals, and later computers—multinational corporations maintained an overwhelmingly dominant position.

Import-substituting industrialization also succeeded in its initial goals of reducing imports and promoting domestic manufacturing. Domestic firms rushed to meet the demand for basic consumer goods like clothing, footwear, furniture, and household appliances. The government encouraged the creation of huge domestic conglomerates that would have the resources necessary to extend ISI into the capital goods industries. These business groups invested in the heavy industry needed to supply consumer goods manufacturers—often their own divisions—with steel, textiles, glass, plastics, and other basic inputs.

Both foreign- and Mexican-owned firms rapidly expanded their production and profits under Mexico's inward-looking development policies. From 1939 to 1969 imports fell rapidly as a proportion of total Mexican demand and the economy grew at the very impressive average rate of 6 percent per year from 1940 to 1975.[19] Mexico was a model for other countries that employed the ISI strategy.

In the 1970s, however, what had come to be known as the Mexican miracle began to peter out. Although imports had fallen relative to the size of the country's economy, they were growing in absolute terms. Mexico still depended on imports to supply the capital goods, special materials, and technologies demanded by industry. And it had failed to develop more than a few industries (cement, glass, and steel) capable of penetrating export markets. Mexico's inability to feed itself exacerbated the problem. In 1970 Mexico exported 3.5 times as much food as it imported, but by 1980 food imports were exceeding exports by 74 percent.

With imports growing faster than exports, Mexico entered a period of economic instability beginning in the mid-1970s in which it became increasingly dependent on oil revenue and foreign loans. In 1982 Mexico got hit by a double whammy: Oil prices sank and interest rates skyrocketed. The incoming administration of President Miguel de la Madrid had two basic choices: unilaterally alter the terms of debt repayment—risking economic isolation—or accept the limited relief and economic prescriptions offered by the United States, Japan, and the International Monetary Fund. Although neither option was pleasant, the latter appeared to policy makers to offer greater chances of recovery. De la Madrid and others in Mexico's government understood that the world economy was moving toward integration, and they knew that economic modernization would require foreign capital and know-how.[20]

Far from renouncing the debt, de la Madrid fashioned a strategy to become Latin America's "model debtor." His administration kept interest payments current and even pressured other debtor nations to come to terms with their creditors rather than declaring debt moratoriums. The president reasoned that staking out this position would put Mexico first in line for a debt relief package, while quickly enhancing the country's image in the eyes of foreign investors.[21]

At the same time, Mexico did a U-turn in economic policy, dropping ISI and Mexicanization and adopting a neoliberal strategy. Neoliberalism holds that reducing the size of the government and removing all barriers to free market activities will produce economic growth that will eventually benefit everyone. Intent on attracting foreign investment and promoting exports, de la Madrid slashed government spending and rapidly devalued the peso, giving investors more for their dollars and making exports cheaper. To alter the structure of the domestic economy, he began to sell off some of the more than two thousand government-owned businesses. These policy shifts responded to the wishes of the IMF and the United States, but they also reflected the economic orientation of de la Madrid and most of his advisers.

Mexico demonstrated the depth of its changes in 1986, when it signed on to the General Agreement on Tariffs and Trade. De la Madrid cut tariffs far faster than the schedule GATT required, winning considerable acclaim from conservative foreign economists. The strategy wreaked havoc on the country's formerly protected manufacturers, however, since they had neither the resources nor the time to adjust to powerful international competitors.

It took seven years of economic stagnation and a devastating decline in the living standards of the large majority of Mexicans for the new approach to achieve its objective of regaining creditworthiness. In 1989, under the new administration of President Carlos Salinas, Mexico signed a debt reduction deal with representatives of private international lenders. The country was again able to float bonds on international markets, and that same year Salinas opened up Mexico's stock market to foreign participation.

The debt deal, the commitment of Mexico's leaders to liberalization, and the potential for unlimited access to the U.S. market ignited euphoria in international business circles. Supporters of the neoliberal program hailed Salinas as a hero and pointed to Mexico's renewed economic growth even as the global economy slipped into recession.

But even if neoliberalism leads to sustained economic growth—and the verdict is out on that question—it is apparent that a very large portion of Mexico's population will be left out of these gains. Privatization, cuts in government programs, wage repression, and currency devaluations widened the already large gap between rich and poor in Mexican society. Real wages dropped by as much as 40 percent in the last decade, and the ranks of the un- or underemployed expanded rapidly. Workers' share of aggregate personal income declined from 36 percent in the mid-1970s to 25 percent in 1988 and 23 percent in 1992.[22] The vast gulf between the wealthiest 10 percent of Mexicans and the nearly 50 percent who live below the poverty line grew vaster during the 1980s.[23] With the government cutting social programs for urban and rural populations alike, there is little reason to foresee the income gap's closing.

Private-sector economic control also grew increasingly concentrated from 1982 on. The privatization process launched in 1985 and rapidly accelerated by President Salinas served mainly to pass businesses from government hands to the control of Mexico's wealthy elite, although on occasion foreign partners were included. The country's opening to imports also contributed to this trend. Low-cost and high-quality foreign goods forced a great number of small and mid-size Mexican firms to declare bankruptcy or to drop production activities and focus on distributing imported products. As a result, the already high levels of market concentration in the most important Mexican industries have intensified. In steel, iron, aluminum, copper, cement, glass, paper, communications, television broadcasting, tobacco, and some portions of the food industry, between one and four huge firms control all or virtually all domestic production. Many of Mexico's largest companies are controlled by individuals. In 1991, just thirty-seven people controlled firms responsible for 22 percent of the country's gross domestic product.[24] This sort of economic concentration does not bode well for Mexican consumers or for the nation's political stability.

Other Latin American leaders take great interest in the social effects of Mexico's policy shift. Although also influenced by East Asia's development path, Mexico's history and society make its experience more relevant to the Americas. The country's neoliberal experiment has become the continent's experiment as other nations struggle to come to terms with the changing global economy. Many of the region's countries began to liberalize trade and investment laws and to privatize state-owned enterprises in the 1980s, pressured by the debt crunch and constrained by the lack of successful alternatives to market-led development.[25] Chile and Bolivia both adopted strict neoliberal policies prior to Mexico, but Mexico held special importance: Not only was it Latin America's second-largest economy, but it had also been a leading practitioner of inward-looking development.

To Latin American leaders, Mexico's economic growth was good but hardly awe-inspiring: Its per capita gross domestic product grew by 1.3 percent in 1989, 2.4 percent in 1990, 1.5 percent in 1991, and .4 percent in 1992.[26] These figures did not seem to justify the threat to domestic capitalists of extensive trade liberalization, or the loss of national economic control entailed in dropping foreign investment restrictions and cutting back on government subsidies and other programs.

Furthermore, it is unlikely that other Latin American nations could repeat even Mexico's mediocre growth figures simply by following its strategy. In many ways Mexico reaped the benefits of being a model economic "reformer." A desire to reward Mexico has meant that in each year since Salinas took office Mexico has placed first in the world in total nonpoverty lending by the World Bank. In 1992 Mexico became the World Bank's largest recipient, with more than twelve billion dollars in outstanding loans. Nearly 40 percent of all World Bank loans to Latin American nations went to Mexico from 1989 to 1991.[27] The United States Export-Import Bank has also supported Mexico's economic program, making more than half of its Latin American loans to that country.[28]

Political factors provide another reason to hesitate to go farther down the neoliberal path. Apart from the negative impact of foreign competition on a large part of the politically influential business sector, Latin American leaders fear that holding down wages, devaluing currencies, cutting government subsidies, and allowing foreign corporations to operate with few restrictions could spark popular unrest. It is not necessarily that these leaders have the interests of the poor at heart—their history indicates otherwise—but they do have an interest in maintaining social peace. This is especially true for the many governments that are attempting to consolidate fragile electoral democracies after years of harsh military rule. Few nations in the region have the efficient mechanisms of state social control that Mexico has and that Chile had during its shift to neoliberalism.

Mexico's neighbors to the southeast are watching the country closely not just to pick up clues for their own economic policy-making but also because Mexico represents a competitive threat to their economies. Many of its exports compete directly with those of Caribbean and Central and South American countries. These include such agricultural products as coffee, sugar, cattle, fruits, and vegetables and manufactures like apparel and steel. Just as important, all developing nations are in competition for international investment capital, especially as they start to look to exports as an engine of growth. When Mexico makes it easier for multinational corporations to operate there, other countries are pressured to respond in kind. The stock markets of Argentina, Brazil, Chile, and Venezuela have either put in place or announced policies similar to Mexico's opening to foreign stock investors.

It was largely to enhance Mexico's competitive position in both these areas—exporting and attracting investment—that Salinas announced in 1990 that he would seek a free trade agreement with the United States. A successful accord would ensure Mexican products access to the hemisphere's dominant market. This assured access would increase the country's attractiveness to foreign investors who wanted to export to the United States. An accord would also encourage investors by increasing the likelihood that future Mexican administrations would adhere to free market policies. Successor presidents would have the option of backing out of an agreement, but the political costs—a loss of international credibility and investor confidence—would be much higher than if such policies were not part of an international agreement.

The free trade agreement that Mexico and the United States signed in 1992 represents an acceptance and reinforcement of the existing international economic system. Neither administration took an interest in exploring the possibilities for regulating the flows of goods and capital in ways that might benefit those workers, peasants, and others who were already losing out under neoliberalism (although both accepted the "need" to restrict the flow of human beings). Nor did they consider ways to slow or reverse the shift of economic power from workers, citizens, and governments to corporations.

But other social sectors, prompted by the spreading human and social costs of globalization and restructuring, have taken a great interest in just these questions. From labor unions representing blue- and pink-collar workers and low-income community-organizing projects to environmental and consumer groups supported largely by wealthier professionals, nongovernmental organizations are exploring the possible effects of integration and searching for and promoting alternatives.

The globalization of production is pushing free trade in North America, but it is more than a case of regional economic integration; the evolving free trade relationship between the United States and Mexico illustrates the direction of north-south relations. This process of integration of the U.S. and Mexican economies is one of joining countries with vastly different standards of living and highly disparate economic bases. It is just such north-south integration that is the wave of the future, and shaping it for maximum social benefit is the challenge facing all parties involved. What comes out of North American integration will set a critical precedent—not just for this hemisphere but for the entire world.

# Ties That Bind

Even before Mexico and the United States began the NAFTA negotiations, the economic ties that bind the two neighbors were tightening. Mexico's drive to liberalize its economy together with global market pressures and Washington's own drive to open up the hemisphere to U.S. trade and investment have led to a sharp expansion of economic relations between the two nations since the early 1980s. Total binational trade nearly tripled between 1983 and 1992, and the value of authorized U.S. direct investment in Mexico grew even faster.[29]

Automobiles and auto parts led the trade boom, followed by electrical equipment and machinery, telecommunications equipment, and computers. All told, manufactured goods constitute more than 80 percent of U.S. exports to and about 70 percent of U.S. imports from Mexico. *Maquiladoras* account for roughly one-third of the trade in manufactures. Mineral fuels—chiefly petroleum—and agricultural products are also significant elements of U.S.-Mexico commerce, contributing 9 percent and 7 percent, respectively, to total trade.[30]

Both countries have greeted the expanding trade and investment connections enthusiastically. But the larger size of the U.S. economy, the globe-trotting character of U.S. corporations, and the greater demand for U.S. goods mean that binational business is hardly a relationship between equals. For the most part U.S.-Mexico trade and investment are characterized by asymmetry. Although both countries are eager to strengthen economic ties, Mexico is much more dependent on the binational commercial relationship for its economic and political stability.

The United States accounts for more than 70 percent of Mexico's exports and imports and provides some 63 percent of the country's foreign investment. In contrast, Mexico accounts for only 7 percent of total U.S. trade and a minuscule amount of foreign direct investment in the United

States.[31] Mexican exports to the United States add around 13 percent to its gross domestic product; U.S. exports to Mexico barely register above the noise of statistical error at one-half of 1 percent of the U.S. GDP. Only in the binational trade balance have the two countries achieved a degree of parity. During most of the 1980s Mexico enjoyed commercial surpluses with the United States. In 1991, however, Mexico started importing from the United States more than it was exporting there, and by 1992 Mexico's trade deficit with the United States had reached $4.7 billion. Whether such deficits persist depends largely on Mexico's exchange-rate policy and the level of foreign investment in the country.

The economic asymmetry of the U.S.-Mexico relationship is also seen on other fronts. Mexico's large external debt has given Washington and U.S. bankers leverage over its economic policies, and the preponderant influence of the United States in such international financial institutions as the World Bank and the International Monetary Fund also skews the economic relations between the two nations. Also a factor is the array of U.S. agencies—from the promotional and informational services of the Commerce Department and the U.S. Foreign Agricultural Service to the financial services offered by U.S. Eximbank—that support the aggressive expansion of U.S. trade and investment in Mexico.

The more powerful position of the United States along with Mexico's more pressing need to maintain good relations with its northern neighbor place Mexico in a weak and vulnerable position in trade negotiations. Washington has repeatedly taken advantage of the asymmetric partnership to gain Mexican cooperation with U.S. priorities. Because of Mexico's almost desperate need to expand exports to the United States, it has quickly caved in to most U.S. trade demands. Such was the case in 1990, when U.S. Trade Representative Carla Hills placed Mexico on the Priority Watch List of trading partners whose policies the USTR considers unfairly biased against U.S. companies. Washington's threat of withdrawing preferential tariff treatment affecting $220 million of Mexican chemical industry exports persuaded Mexico to rewrite drastically its laws on intellectual property rights—the protection of trademarks, patents, and copyrights—even before NAFTA was negotiated.

The United States has also bullied Mexico with its antidumping and countervailing duties laws. From leather apparel and ceramic tile in 1980 to cement and steel in the early 1990s, the ability of Mexican exporters to reach the U.S. market has been subject to the determinations of the U.S. Treasury Department and International Trade Commission. These agencies have often slapped Mexican exporters with duties intended to compensate for—or "countervail"—alleged advantages gained by selling products below "fair market value" or by receiving "unfair" government subsidies. But in many cases the duties have been politically motivated, intended to satisfy key domestic interest groups or to send messages to the Mexican government.[32]

Even with a free trade agreement in place, such power politics in international trade is likely to continue Mexico's deepening dependence on U.S. trade and investment and its fear of endangering smooth commercial relations with the United States. Such is the nature of business between unequal partners.

## The Changing Face of Mexico

Accelerating U.S.-Mexico trade and investment flows alter more than the figures on international balance sheets. Sparked by Mexico's dramatic economic restructuring and liberalization, the expanded relationship with U.S. traders and investors is the most prominent sign of how the whole character of Mexico is changing. As U.S. investment and goods increase their penetration of Mexico, urban and rural residents are adopting new spending and work patterns. Accentuating the impact of the broadened commercial ties is the steady advancement of U.S. culture.

The two- or three-hour lunch break is rapidly losing ground to the quick-bite-to-eat approach, especially for urban professionals. McDonald's, Kentucky Fried Chicken, Pizza Hut, and a multitude of other U.S.-owned fast-food outlets—even Taco Bell—are sprouting up all over Mexico to meet the demand caused by changing eating habits. Hundreds of foreign franchises are slicing deeply into family-owned food businesses, in effect replacing small entrepreneurs with hourly workers.

The shopping mall, invented and perfected in the United States, is fast becoming a part of Mexican cultural life—at least for the one-third or so of the population able to buy more than bare necessities. The malls seek to create a first world look—one even features an ice-skating rink—making U.S. retailers like Sears, J. C. Penney, and Dillard's increasingly attractive to developers of commercial property. Seeking U.S. marketing experience and inventory technology, established Mexican retailers are eagerly pursuing joint ventures with U.S. chains, including Wal-Mart and Price Club. Although these huge, relatively low-margin operations please their upscale customers, they pose a tremendous challenge to small, locally owned retailers.

Advertising, especially on television, is a primary force in the mixing of U.S. values with Mexican culture. The new U.S. owners or co-owners of Mexican firms use marketing techniques familiar to any U.S. consumer in their promotional campaigns and often use the same ad agencies in Mexico and the United States. Eight of the top ten advertising firms in Mexico are foreign-owned.

No economic sector remains untouched by the penetration of U.S. goods and investment. Most evident has been the wide range of U.S. manufactures and processed foods now offered by Mexico's retail sector. Even before high-powered U.S. retailers began to move into the Mexican market, U.S.-made goods were putting Mexican manufacturers on the defensive—or, in many cases, out of business. Since Mexico began lowering its trade barriers after joining GATT in 1986, the quantity and variety of U.S.-made goods available to the Mexican consumer have mushroomed. Consumer goods accounted for only 7 percent of all Mexican imports from 1983 to 1987, but by 1990 they had grown to represent 17 percent of all imports.[33] Manufacturers of shoes, textiles, toys, and consumer electronics lead the long list of Mexican industries that formerly operated behind strong trade barriers and are now facing ruin.

Residents of rural areas have as yet seen little of the expanding foreign presence because they lack the buying power to attract multinational retailers or franchisees. But in this case out of sight is not out of mind. For the peasant population the winds of competition feel more like a hurricane. Millions of small farmers face the loss of what little cash income they derive from growing corn and beans to cheaper imports. Having suffered decades of neglect and political manipulation by the ruling party, they are incapable of competing with the world's most efficient farmers just to their north. Farmers in the United States and Canada not only use sophisticated growing and harvesting techniques but also receive a variety of subsidies from their governments that serve to reduce costs and risks.

In the export-oriented manufacturing sector only a few Mexican industries operate at the levels of scale and efficiency required to compete in the U.S. market. Thanks to the protectionist, state-directed policies that Mexican economic planners now reject, several private conglomerates that have the financial resources to withstand the challenge of transnational corporations did emerge in the 1960s and 1970s. In such areas as cement, beer, and glass, these business groups are even putting U.S. and European firms on the defensive with their marketing and investment strategies.

For the most part, however, nonpetroleum export-oriented manufacturing is controlled by foreign, mainly U.S., corporations. This U.S. presence is especially prominent in the *maquila* assembly sector, the automotive industry, and other high-tech industries such as computer manufacture. As a sector based on low wages and oriented almost exclusively to the U.S. market, *maquiladoras* represent a preview of the kind of manufacturing partnership that continental free trade may bring. But also important as an indicator of the new economic relationship developing between the United States and Mexico is the automotive sector. In the 1970s U.S. car manufacturers began shifting aspects of their operations—particularly labor-intensive parts assembly—to *maquiladoras* in Mexico. Although *maquila* assembly remains an important part of the Mexico-based automotive industry, since the early 1980s all five car manufacturers in Mexico have also established major manufacturing facilities that produce engines and in some cases entire vehicles, using the most advanced technology and production systems. As U.S. car companies find that they can achieve equal or higher levels of efficiency and quality in Mexico at much lower labor costs, more of their operations are being shut down in the United States and reestablished in places like Hermosillo and Chihuahua.

The automotive industry is not alone in finding that Mexico is suitable not only for low-skill, labor intensive manufacturing but also for more skilled production processes involving robotics, laser technology, and other advanced manufacturing systems. Kodak film, IBM computers, and Whirlpool appliances are among the many products being manufactured, not just assembled, in Guadalajara, Monterrey, and other Mexican cities.

Although U.S. corporations form the backbone of Mexico's export-oriented manufacturing, the level of new U.S. investment in productive industries in recent years has fallen below the expectations of the Mexican government. Investment from the United States and other industrial countries has increased, but most new investors have been attracted to service sectors such as tourism, which absorbed fully 40 percent of foreign direct investment in 1991, and retailing.

Financial service firms have also flocked to Mexico after Salinas took office, banking on his promised "modernization" campaign to open up the country's financial industry and expecting that Mexico would return to international capital markets for the first time since the 1982 debt crisis. Led by Goldman Sachs, Citibank, and J. P. Morgan, U.S. firms dominated the competition to underwrite Mexico's international bond offerings, which totaled more than eight billion dollars in 1991. Mergers and acquisitions work proved just as lucrative, driven by joint ventures between foreign and Mexican companies and by the government's privatization drive.[34] Many of these companies hope to open banking operations eventually, as Mexican restrictions on majority foreign ownership of banks are liberalized either through a free trade agreement or through unilateral changes.

Although important in stabilizing the country's balance of payments, investment in services does not have as broad an impact on the economy as manufacturing investment, which generally creates more jobs, produces backward and forward linkages with other economic sectors, and boosts exports. Whereas nearly 80 percent of new direct investment in 1980 was in manufacturing and just 8.5 percent in services, in 1990 more than 60 percent of new foreign direct investment went to service industries and less than one-third flowed into the manufacturing sector.[35]

To supplement the flow of foreign direct investment and to help tie the larger Mexican companies into international financial markets, President Salinas opened the stock exchange to foreign participation in 1989. In the two years following the opening, more than seven billion dollars in portfolio or indirect foreign investment entered Mexico—approximately the same amount as new direct foreign investment during that period.[36] By mid-1992 foreigners, the vast majority from the United States, held nearly 30 percent of the market's total value.

This portfolio investment represents an important source of foreign exchange and demonstrates a new degree of foreign interest and confidence in the Mexican economy. But the buying spree in the Bolsa Mexicana de Valores is not entirely positive, considering the volatile character of this type of speculative investment. The ever-present danger is that the dollars that flow into Mexico via the stock market can just as easily and quickly flow out of Mexico. This concern was heightened during the summer of 1992, when foreign investors took billions of dollars out of the market, and possibly out of the country.[37] Portfolio investment—unlike direct investment in plant and equipment—makes a weak foundation for national economic stability and development.

## Investing in Mexico's Land and Resources

One of the main legacies of the Mexican Revolution was the prohibition of foreign control over the country's natural resources and land. These restrictions were a direct response to the policies of Porfirio Díaz, who opened the door wide to foreign investors. During the thirty-five year *porfiriato* foreign investment was largely found in extractive or primary industries (oil, mining, and agriculture). After the revolution, however, and until the late 1980s, the government discouraged such investment. Neoliberal restructuring facilitated by changes in the Mexican constitution opened up agriculture, mining, and petroleum-related industries to increased foreign involvement.

Since the 1938 nationalization of British and U.S. oil operations and the creation of Pemex (Petróleos Mexicanos) by President Lázaro Cárdenas, the nation's control over the petroleum industry has represented its resistance to Yankee imperialism. As one of the world's largest oil companies Pemex has served as a symbol of national pride, and the 1938 nationalization is still officially celebrated with a "Day of National Dignity."[38] But the corruption, inefficiency, and environmental record of Pemex have more recently been a source of national embarrassment.

After the major oil discoveries of the 1970s the government touted the petroleum industry as Mexico's pass card into the industrialized world. The country's vast oil reserves gave it the confidence to assert itself as the voice of the underdeveloped south while also placing Mexico in a better bargaining position with the United States. Indeed, the United States took new interest in Mexico, seeing its reserves as a hedge against disruptions in the supply of imported oil from the Middle East.[39]

In the early 1980s Mexico suddenly found that its most strategic asset was also a major liability. The oil industry had absorbed much of the foreign loans that flooded into Mexico during the 1970s, but its production costs, efficiency levels, and exploration and refining capacities compared badly with those of the world's major oil corporations. Compounding Pemex's problems were the low oil prices and the debt crisis of the early 1980s. The government began to drain Pemex of its own capital, forcing severe cutbacks in exploration and drilling and the deferral of maintenance of existing pumping and refining facilities.[40] In the 1980s petroleum-rich Mexico began importing rising amounts of natural gas and petrochemicals. By 1991 aging refineries and the closure of a major facility on the outskirts of Mexico City had obliged Mexico to import 10 percent of its gasoline from the United States. In a dramatic departure from past policies, Mexico began in 1991 to tap U.S. exploration and drilling firms for help.

Mexico's lack of capital—in either the public or private sectors—and its increasing dependence on foreign supplies and technology forced the government to revamp its nationalist development strategy in regard to the petroleum industry. The problem was not the absence of sufficient quantities of petroleum but the industry's lack of adequate financing to develop its untapped reserves and to bring Pemex up to world production standards.

Although it has not gone as far as opening up its reserves to direct foreign ownership, the government has restructured the industry to encourage greater foreign participation. Its first step was to privatize most of the petrochemical industry. The de la Madrid and Salinas administrations reduced from seventy to eight the number of petrochemicals classified as "basic"—and therefore reserved to state-owned operations.[41] The number defined as "secondary"—in which direct foreign ownership is limited to 40 percent—fell from more than seven hundred to sixty-six.[42]

The Salinas administration also split Pemex into four divisions, isolating the ownership and production of petroleum from refining, marketing, and distribution. The reorganization facilitated increased foreign investment in the downstream operations while allowing Mexico to retain ownership over reserves. The changes allowed such transnational corporations as Du Pont, Monsanto, Union Carbide, and Allied Chemical to increase their stakes in the production of petroleum-based chemicals.

But the foreign capital invested in the oil industry by early 1993 fell well short of the eight billion dollars in outside financing that the Mexican government calculated it needed to maintain export levels and to ensure that domestic energy demands were met. Serious doubts about the volume of oil reserves claimed by Pemex and uncertainty about the extent of the Mexican government's commitment to restructure Pemex have undermined the state oil company's efforts to sell securities in foreign markets.

Without substantial injections of foreign capital for exploration and production, some Mexican officials predicted that Mexico would be a net oil importer by the turn of the century. But despite this concern and strong pressure from the major transnational oil companies, Mexico has thus far resisted giving foreign firms "risk contracts" for oil exploration, which would grant the drilling companies ownership rights to part of the oil they found. Instead it has issued service contracts for drilling, paying firms a negotiated fee for each well. In addition, it has given the go-ahead for "performance contracts," which would award bonuses for discoveries but would not give the contracted firms any proprietary rights over the oil. Practical as well as political considerations have guided the decision not to enter into risk contracts with foreign drilling companies. Since oil officials believe they know the general location of Mexico's nonproducing reserves, companies hired by Pemex for exploratory drilling face little actual risk.

Facing the threat of declining production and reserves, government planners are increasingly recognizing that the traditional goals of using the petroleum industry as a springboard for national development and a major source of revenue have to be scaled back. If the restructuring of Pemex and the regulatory changes already implemented continue to fail to attract desperately needed foreign capital, it is likely that all phases of the industry will be opened to foreign participation in the short or medium term despite government declarations to the contrary.

Like the petroleum industry, Mexico's mining sector has also opened to direct foreign investment. Reversing decades of nationalist and statist policies, the Salinas administration in a series of regulatory and legal changes opened almost the entire mining industry to 100 percent private ownership. At the same time the government permited foreign firms to hold majority interest through trust fund schemes, and it is expected that other changes in the foreign investment laws will soon allow direct foreign ownership of mining firms.

Previously, foreign participation was limited to less than 50 percent, and state corporations controlled the mining of "strategic" minerals such as sulfur, potassium, phosphorous rock, iron, and coal. By the end of 1992 the Salinas administration had sold the government's interest in all but a handful of mining firms and released four-fifths of the national mining reserves—almost eleven million acres of land on which minerals had been discovered but private-sector investment had been prohibited since the 1930s.

The changes have renewed foreign interest in Mexican mining. Having been pushed out of the country by the Mexicanization policies of the past, dozens of foreign firms are registering for exploration and development permits. In the gold-rich state of Sonora, at least twenty foreign firms set up Mexican offices within months of the announcement of the 1992 revisions in the mining law. But it remains to be seen if this liberalization of mining investment will translate into the two billion dollars in foreign investment that the government is projecting.

Mexico is an important source of such minerals as silver, zinc, lead, strontium, graphite, and fluorspar for the United States.[43] With increased investment in exploration and mining technology, Mexico's mineral production could rise substantially. Three-fourths of Mexican territory exhibits geological characteristics indicating possible mineral reserves, but less than 20 percent of that area has been carefully surveyed.

As the United States and other industrialized countries exhaust their large ore deposits, the relatively unexplored and untapped mineral map of Mexico looks attractive to transnational mining companies. The attraction is all the stronger considering what one industry executive decried as "the trend of labor costs, the 'greening' of America, and increasing government regulation of the work place" in the United States.[44]

The Mexican government's drive to attract foreign capital to boost production in the mining, petroleum, agriculture, and manufacturing sectors may clash with its expressed commitment to improve environmental regulations, wages, and working conditions. This contradiction between increased production and conservation is particularly evident in mining, a highly polluting industry that faces rising environmental compliance costs in the United States and Canada. Frustrated with long delays and court battles, U.S. and Canadian firms are eager to operate in a less restrictive setting. The editor of a U.S. mining magazine recently observed that "gold and copper investors will be drawn [to Mexico] by less regulation than in the states and lower wages."[45]

### *Et Tu, Agricultura?*

In Torreón, Coahuila, Tyson Foods employees debone chicken legs from Arkansas, pack them, and send them to Japan for sale as frozen yakitori. In Irapuato, Guanajuato, Basic Vegetable Products imports onion seeds, supervises their planting, harvesting, and processing, and exports dried onion flakes and powder back to the United States. Amway International has begun to grow acerola cherries in Mexico that will be processed for their vitamin content in California. Cattle may soon cross the border three times before reaching consumers, as calves born in Mexico are shipped for feeding to the United States, returned to Mexico for slaughter and packing, and then sent back to the United States for distribution.

Transnational agribusinesses are following their manufacturing counterparts in adopting global production, processing, and marketing strategies. These strategies are based on breaking up the production chain and siting individual activities where local conditions are most advantageous. Mexico's climate and low-wage workforce have made it a logical location for a growing number of U.S.-based and other foreign food packers and processors who seek to lower the cost of the goods they sell in the United States, Japan, and Europe. Authorized foreign direct investment in agriculture vaulted from $8.4 million in 1980 to roughly $140 million by mid-1992.[46]

Booming foreign investment has paralleled—and contributed to—an equally impressive hike in the volume of Mexican exports. Mexican food, beverage, and tobacco exports to the United States have more than doubled since 1980. The United States purchases more than 90 percent of all Mexican agricultural exports, with tomatoes, coffee, and livestock heading the list. And the United States supplies Mexico with roughly 80 percent of its food imports, led by grains—especially corn and sorghum—live animals, meat, and oilseeds. About 20 percent of the coffee consumed in the United States is Mexican, as are roughly 40 percent of the frozen broccoli and 20 percent of the fresh tomatoes.[47]

Agri-*maquilas* are the most recent trend in U.S. agricultural investment in Mexico. Like manufacturing *maquilas*, agri-*maquilas* import part of their inputs from the United States and then export most, if not all, of their finished food products. The new foreign companies also join a sizable contingent of more traditional foreign agribusinesses already in Mexico. PepsiCo, Ralston Purina, Campbell, Nestlé, Kraft General Foods, Del Monte, Gerber, Kellogg, and other transnationals generally process foods for the domestic market or grow tropical products like bananas, melons, and pineapples for export. Most of these companies came to Mexico in the late 1950s and the 1960s, when Mexican agricultural policy began to encourage foreign investment as a way to modernize the country's food sector.

Despite the presence of dozens of foreign agribusinesses in Mexico, total foreign investment in the agricultural sector is tiny, representing less than one-half of 1 percent of total authorized foreign direct investment as of December 1991.[48] Nevertheless, they exert great influence because of their buying power, technology, and marketing skills. By the late 1970s transnational corporations were present in twenty-seven of the forty agricultural subsectors and were responsible for more than half of Mexico's production in eleven of them.[49] In crops ranging from oilseeds and sorghum to broccoli and mangos, transnationals direct seed selection, soil preparation, the timing of the harvest, the marketing of the product, and all steps in between.

Until 1992 foreign firms were prevented by law from purchasing large plots of land. This did not discourage many agribusinesses, however, since even where large-scale landownership is legal—in the United States, for example—they generally prefer to contract with a large number of growers rather than engage in direct production.[50] Foreign firms have followed this pattern in Mexico, entering into production contracts or rental agreements with local peasants and better-off landholders.[51] In general these contracts obligate the processors to purchase that part of the harvest that meets specified quality standards and to provide seeds, financing, and technical advice.[52] In exchange the processors gain direct control over the entire production process.

U.S. influence over Mexican agricultural decisions extends beyond the power of transnational corporations in Mexico to that of the tightly knit distribution networks that move food from the Mexican border to retailers throughout the United States and Canada. Some 80 to 90 percent of Mexico's winter vegetable exports enter the United States through Nogales, Arizona.[53] At that point the fifty U.S. distributors that belong to the West Mexico Vegetable Distributors Association take over, deciding what quantities of which products to send where on the basis of existing contracts and closely monitored market conditions that change from hour to hour.

These packers and shippers help organize the production of fruits and vegetables in northwestern Mexico through annual contracts that set out crops, quantities, quality, and timing. In most cases the contracts do not specify a price for the produce. Instead deliveries are taken on consignment, insulating the distributors from the risk of low market prices. As do the food processing giants in Mexico, U.S. distributors provide most of the financing and seeds for Mexican growers.[54] Nevertheless, the influence of U.S. buyers is considerably less than that of the huge food processors in Mexico. In part this is because the northern growers with whom they negotiate contracts are larger and have more options than the captive growers of central Mexico.

High-technology leveling, fertilizing, and irrigation techniques together with the use of hybrid seeds and synthetic pesticides have brought yields for most vegetables in Mexico up to U.S. levels.[55] They have also created a dependence on U.S. chemicals, genetic inputs, and farm equipment. As yields have increased, the agricultural workforce has steadily declined in Mexico. A study of the Bajío region of Mexico—the country's breadbasket located north and west of the capital—found that after twenty years of foreign domination of agriculture, yields per acre had generally doubled or tripled, but total farm employment had dropped nearly 30 percent.[56]

To the matters of inappropriate technology and crop selection, those agribusinesses geared to exports add a third problem: the highly seasonal nature of their production and processing needs. The Birds Eye broccoli and cauliflower plant in Irapuato employs nineteen hundred workers at the peak of its cycle, and only three hundred during the off-season. Adding in the temporary employees of growers under contract to Birds Eye puts the seasonal fluctuation at around forty thousand to fifty thousand people.[57] This pattern is repeated dozens of times over by other foreign firms like Green Giant, Campbell, Del Monte, United Brands, and Chiquita Tropical Products. Hundreds of thousands of Mexicans work as migrant laborers for these firms and their growers, competing with local peasants and their children who rely on seasonal employment to augment their meager incomes. This pattern of production has left 80 percent of the rural population in Mexico without steady work. Employers rarely meet the minimum wage, which is lower for farm laborers than for industrial workers, or allow workers the required rest periods, much less pay overtime or provide other benefits required under Mexico's labor laws.[58]

The seasonal nature of employment in Mexico's modern agricultural sector stems less from nature—since the land in this sector is irrigated and climatic conditions are relatively steady—than from U.S. production patterns. From spring to fall, growers of many fruits and vegetables in the United States enjoy competitive advantages over those in Mexico as the result of technology, infrastructure, and transportation costs. For some producers threatened by Mexican competition, the U.S. government provides some protection during the growing season. Tariffs protect U.S. growers from Mexican competitors during most of the year, falling only when U.S. production declines during the winter. Tomato importers, for example, pay a duty of less than 7 percent from November 15 through February, but the rate increases to 11.5 percent for most of the rest of the year. Cucumber rates vary from 9.4 percent to 37.6 percent, and lettuce from 1.8 percent to 6.5 percent.[59]

The combination of competitive advantages and government protection places Mexico in the role of complementary producer, satisfying the winter vegetable and fruit appetites of U.S. consumers. From December to May, Mexican tomatoes supply 35 percent of the U.S. demand, with most of the rest met by producers in Florida. Mexican cucumbers, peppers, melons, and strawberries also help satisfy U.S. consumers' winter appetites.[60]

But the U.S.-Mexico food relationship is anything but complementary for most Mexicans. Much of Mexico's most productive land now produces sorghum, soybeans, and alfalfa for animal feed; oranges for frozen concentrate; potatoes for potato chips; and strawberries, broccoli, asparagus, and a host of other fruits and vegetables largely exported to the wealthier nations of the world. These foods were either not known or rarely found in the Mexican diet before 1950, and in most cases they are still inaccessible to the large majority of Mexicans, who cannot afford such luxuries.

The expansion of production linked to foreign markets and the domestic elite has contributed to a decrease in the availability of domestically produced corn and beans—the staples of the traditional diet. The introduction of genetically improved sorghum in the mid-1960s and the growth of "factory-raised" poultry and swine operations relying on the grain for feed displaced corn on a huge scale. By the mid-1970s sorghum occupied up to one-fourth of Mexico's prime corn-growing land.[61] Less acreage was devoted to corn in 1990 than in 1965, despite the doubling of the country's population over the same period.[62] Although per capita corn consumption grew by one-fourth from 1965 to 1980, in the 1980s these gains were erased, leaving consumption at only 72 percent of its 1965 level in 1990. Bean consumption reflects a similar pattern, and by 1990 the amount of beans in the average Mexican diet had dropped more than one-third from its 1965 level.[63]

The replacement of basic food production for domestic consumption with nontraditional crops dependent on foreign demand is the direct result of what one expert in Mexican agriculture called the "distorted development" strategy of the Mexican government, meaning policies that focused on the creation of modern, productive, and profitable industrial and agricultural sectors while ignoring the development needs of the impoverished and increasingly dispossessed majority sector of peasants and laborers.[64]

Under President Salinas the government's modernization effort has shed all that remained of the revolution's populist traditions. The Salinas administration halted the distribution of land to peasants, slashed subsidies to traditional crop producers, and liberalized foreign investment laws. Foreign and domestic firms were allowed for the first time since the revolution legally to establish landowning corporations with no effective limit to the size of their holdings, giving them access to enormous tracts of land and paving the way for major new investments in the farm sector.[65] Demonstrating again the tremendous power of the Mexican presidency, Salinas pushed through a radical change in the national constitution, effectively demolishing the legal basis for communally owned plots of land known as *ejidos*.[66] The change makes it likely that the large landowning *terratenientes* of prerevolutionary times will return.

Private investors and *ejidos* responded rapidly to the legal changes. Within fifteen months 120 joint ventures had been launched, according to Mexico's agriculture secretary.[67] These included a 20,000-acre eucalyptus tree project in San Luís Potosí, a plan to harvest "fine wood" on 125,000 acres in Campeche, and a 125,000-acre vegetable export operation in Sonora. Tropicana Foods is joining forces with an *ejido* to produce oranges and orange juice, and PepsiCo is involved in a joint venture with an *ejido* to produce wheat for its snack-food products in Mexico.[68]

The modernization effort has so far exacerbated Mexico's uneven distribution of wealth and income, one of the world's most skewed. At the same time the country has lost its agricultural trade surplus. Exports are up, but imports have gone up more. Even if the country succeeds in regaining a surplus, however, its neoliberal policies mean that the beneficiaries of this success will be Mexican and foreign agribusinesses, not the rural poor. The farmers who have lost their livelihood as the result of the failure of government to support small-scale agriculture have no access to the dollars brought in by export crops. As subsidies for corn and bean production—the last symbols of Mexico's strictly symbolic revolutionary commitment to a strong peasant sector—fall to make way for North American free trade, the ranks of displaced peasants forced into urban underemployment, migratory labor, or the poverty of genuine subsistence farming will swell by the millions.

The Salinas administration acknowledged as much in unveiling its Program for the Productive Conversion of the Ministry of Agriculture in 1992. According to this program, 72 percent of all corn farmers—representing two million families—are uncompetitive and "will have to search for alternatives in other crops, reorganize their land holdings, . . . associate with private capitalists, or become wage laborers in rural or urban areas."[69] Mexico's undersecretary for agriculture sees up to thirteen million peasants forced to abandon the countryside by the year 2010.[70]

## The Investment-Trade Connection

Foreign investment and international trade are intimately tied to each other in third world countries like Mexico. When Miguel de la Madrid responded to the debt crisis by shifting Mexico from an import-substituting strategy to one centered on exports, an essential part of the plan was encouraging foreign investment. And when Carlos Salinas de Gortari sought to attract huge inflows of private investment capital, he placed free trade with the United States—to guarantee trading access to that market—on top of his list of priorities.

Transnational corporations are central to Mexico's export goals. By the end of the 1980s affiliates of foreign-owned corporations accounted for 60 percent of all Mexican-manufactured exports.[71] Transnational corporations not only have the know-how and the capital to establish internationally competitive facilities but also enjoy a close relationship with distributors in their home countries and usually in third countries as well. In many cases they are their own "customers," exporting from a plant in one country to a warehouse or plant in another. This arrangement opens the door for corporate "transfer pricing" practices that hide the real value of local production.

Measuring the extent to which a country's trade is conducted among divisions of the same parent company provides one indicator of the trade-investment connection. Such "intrafirm" trade accounts for a very high proportion of U.S.-Mexico trade. According to the U.S. Commerce Department, nearly 40 percent of the total bilateral trade in manufactured goods is between U.S. firms and their affiliates in Mexico, while the U.S. International Trade Commission estimated that more than half of U.S. imports from Mexico are from intracompany or related-party sales.[72]

The globalization of production is responsible for the increasing proportion of worldwide trade that is conducted among corporate affiliates. As companies distribute pieces of their production processes to several countries the flow of parts and materials between facilities is counted as exports and imports. As a result, countries increasingly import and export products in the same industries, such as electronics or auto parts. The new "intraindustry" trade raises important questions about the relevance of traditional trade theory, which was based on the theory of comparative advantage and competition between nations. Rather than a relationship between nations, international trade is increasingly a relationship that occurs within corporations.

Long considered an unreliable partner whose power had to be restricted and channeled by the government, international capital now has virtual carte blanche in Mexico. In half a decade limits on foreign ownership of productive assets have been reduced or eliminated in industry after industry. The state has stopped intervening in technology transfer and franchising contracts, and the protection of intellectual property rights—copyrights, patents, and trademarks—has been greatly strengthened.

Even before signing a free trade agreement with the United States, Mexico had cast its lot with the proponents of unrestricted international trade and investment. Like the United States, Mexico has decided that adherence to the demands of global trade and production represents its only viable economic development option. If successful, it has much to gain in the way of expanded access to capital and technology, new jobs, and increased productivity. But given the shocking asymmetry between the two nations, Mexico faces the danger of further restricting its development alternatives by making its trade, labor, and productive core more subject to the state and direction of the U.S. economy.

# Free Trade:

# The Ifs, Ands

# & Buts

In 1990 the term *free trade* slipped out of the economics textbooks and into the everyday conversation of Mexicans and Americans when presidents Salinas and Bush agreed to initiate negotiations leading to a regional free trade agreement. Canada joined the talks in 1991, and after more than a year of intense negotiations, the leaders of the three countries signed the North American Free Trade Agreement in December 1992. At the insistence of newly elected U.S. president Bill Clinton, in 1993 the parties added two "side agreements" concerning the enforcement of environmental and labor laws. By November of that year the national legislatures of the three countries had approved the accord, and NAFTA was set to take effect on January 1, 1994.

Under the agreement all tariffs and import quotas will be eliminated within fifteen years.[73] Nontariff barriers to free trade, such as product safety standards, will be subject to a trinational panel of judges. By lowering trade barriers NAFTA will facilitate the flow of goods and services within the region. But more than a trade agreement, NAFTA will encourage increased cross-border investment by requiring that foreign investors be given the same rights and opportunities as domestic investors, except in a few economic sectors such as the media and the petroleum industry.

Actually NAFTA spelled out no major changes in U.S. or Canadian policies toward trade and investment. Although the agreement required more changes in Mexican policies, there were only a few changes that the country had not already made or was not planning to make with or without it. In all three countries, NAFTA represented just another step down the road toward global economic integration. For the most part, this economic liberalization had been occurring within the context of the multilateral General Agreement on Tariffs and Trade. But the free trade bandwagon had also been pushed forward by bilateral "framework agree-

287

ments" on trade that Washington had been promoting since the early 1980s.

Free trade with Canada had been a sleeper issue with the general U.S. public. But free trade with Mexico ignited large-scale public debate. More than a discussion of the specific provisions of NAFTA, the debate revolved around broader economic and social questions. Would freer trade generate prosperity as promised or lead to further economic decline? Would further trade and investment liberalization limit the ability of nations to adopt their own industrial policies and development strategies? Was free trade nothing more than a corporate bill of rights that ignored the basic needs and social values of citizens? And finally, what alternatives are there to the agenda represented by NAFTA and GATT in a world increasingly shaped by the forces of global integration of finance and production?

## The Ideal and Reality of Free Trade

Free trade is a powerful ideal that has guided many economists and policy makers since the 1700s. It conjures a vision of a harmonious international system in which goods flow as freely among nations as they do among the states of the United States of America. With no tariff barriers, no quotas, and no customs inspections to impede products or services as they cross national boundaries, market forces are able to allocate resources among all nations in a way that eventually maximizes everyone's income. Free trade would allow consumers in each country to benefit from the skills and resources of others, businesspeople to earn top dollar on their investments, and workers to enjoy the fruits of their ever more productive labor.

Undergirding this vision of trade-induced prosperity is classic free market economic theory, which postulates that economies grow most rapidly when markets are unfettered by artificial barriers, such as government regulations. Taken to its logical extreme, free trade ties national economies so closely together that they operate as a single global economy. But where trade barriers divide national markets, it is the theory of comparative advantage that supports the assertion that lowering the barriers creates greater wealth for all parties. Introducing the theory in 1817, British economist David Ricardo demonstrated that if England could produce textiles more efficiently than it could produce wine, and if Portugal could produce wine more efficiently than it could cloth, both countries would benefit from trading textiles for wine. In more general terms, Ricardo's models showed that global welfare would increase if all nations specialized in making those goods that they could produce most efficiently and then traded freely among themselves.

The free trade vision of Ricardo and his latter-day followers is beautiful in its simplicity and breathtaking in its scope and implications. But like the free market economic model of which it is an extension, free trade works far better on paper than as a realistic guide to economic policy.[74] Indeed, free trade theory suffers from some of the same problems that afflict free market theory, such as the tendency for markets to become dominated by a handful of huge firms, rather than remain truly competitive.

Many of the problems with the free trade ideal have to do with the assumptions that form its foundation. Free trade theory is based on the lack of government interference in international markets. It assumes that the governments of trading partners are much the same in that they serve the general welfare of their citizens and adhere to the principles of free and competitive markets.

But such assumptions clash with the real world. Rather than being neutral overseers, governments generally respond to the interests of a domestic elite and work to enhance national power. They use export subsidies to help domestic firms penetrate foreign markets, currency devaluations to lower the cost of exports and raise the cost of imports, public money to fund private research, government procurement to promote critical industries, and mercantilist policies to build large trade surpluses. According to free market theory, each of these policies reduces economic efficiency and thus the overall welfare of the countries that pursue them. Yet governments adopt them both to gain advantages over other nations and to satisfy important domestic constituencies.

Furthermore, not all societies have the same understanding of social welfare. And much of what goes into the concept is difficult or impossible to include in economic calculations. Nations create laws and institutions that distort markets to accomplish differing social goals, such as national security, a healthy population, a clean environment, equitable income sharing, and cultural preservation.

Were government barriers to trade suddenly to be removed from the real economy, rather than from mathematical models, the differences in national goals and values would translate into serious trade conflicts. Countries with economically inefficient but socially valuable policies would find themselves disadvantaged relative to others that made economic efficiency their first priority. Governments that followed a laissez-faire strategy would find their nation's firms suffering at the hands of governments that provided subsidies or other assistance to their corporations. To minimize the conflicts likely to arise from such a trading system, governments must negotiate the rules under which economic integration will occur.

But the very fact that free trade must be negotiated makes achieving the free trade ideal unlikely in the real world. Negotiators come to the table with vastly different resources and needs. Those with greater resources and fewer needs have the power to bend the terms of a trade agreement in their favor, resulting in an uneven playing field.

These real-world obstacles to implementing free trade have been around for centuries. The last three decades have seen another, more fundamental problem arise that renders the basis of free trade theory obsolete. When Ricardo developed the theory of comparative advantage, a country's capital and technology were nearly as fixed as its land. But both now cross national borders at will, and modern corporations can establish operations in most parts of the world. No longer can a country rely on its capital base and technological lead to give it a trade advantage.

Despite its appeal to mainstream economic theoreticians, until World War II almost all nations rejected the idea of lowering their own tariff walls and other trade barriers, believing that free trade would give an unfair advantage to the trading partner with the most advanced industrial base. As the dominant industrial power until the early 1900s, Britain stood alone in its push for free trade. Britain's trading partners, including the United States, rejected its overtures, preferring to help their industries develop behind protective trade walls.

While largely refusing to lower their own tariffs on imports from competing countries, the world's imperial powers often used the banner of free trade to justify military campaigns to open up the markets and natural resources of the world's less developed nations. The colonial trading blocs that resulted led to conflicts between the major industrial powers over access to markets and raw materials. Escalating protectionism and disputes over discriminatory trade practices were major causes of the two world wars in the twentieth century.

Without its own colonial system to serve as an outlet for goods and a source of supplies, the United States has historically been a leading proponent of open global markets. The country appealed to this principle to justify going to war in 1898 with Spain, claiming that Spanish mercantilism was obstructing the free flow of trade and colonial institutions were retarding the development of democracy. World War II and the disastrous experience of the United States' own protectionist measures in the 1930s reinforced the free trade position.

World War II placed the United States in a position of uncontested economic dominance, from which it was able to push its European allies to open their markets gradually. With its capitalist allies in tow, the United States sought to establish a new conflict-free trading regime that would lower tariff barriers and regulate trade by establishing rules of fair play. In 1944 they created the International Monetary Fund (IMF) to stabilize currency markets and monitor domestic economic policies. In 1947, overruling a European proposal for a more managed system of world trade, the United States convinced its allies to approve the General Agreement on Tariffs and Trade. The IMF and especially GATT would not only facilitate larger trade flows in the short term but also ensure that economic liberalization remained high on the global agenda for decades.

GATT and the IMF were designed by the industrialized market economies to serve their own interests, and they ignored the needs of developing countries until the mid-1960s. Beginning in the 1970s and accelerating in the 1980s, both institutions came to play a central role in the capitalist north's effort to steer developing countries away from state-directed development strategies such as import-substituting industrialization and toward closer integration into the international market economy. Assisted by the globalization of production and finance and the growing domination of transnational corporations, free trade advocates began to press developing countries to sign on to GATT and to limit governmental interference with markets.

Espousing the principles of economic liberalism of the 1700s, neoliberals today argue that developing countries need to embrace free trade because the gains from trade between poor and wealthy countries could be far greater than those from trade among the industrialized nations. This is because the products of wealthy economies generally incorporate similar resources—capital, technology, and skilled labor—so that what one country exports often could as easily be made in the importing industrial country. But poor countries' exports are likely to embody different resources—unskilled labor and raw materials—that will complement those of wealthy countries and create gains from specialization and trade, according to the theory of comparative advantage.

In the case of North America, Mexico's relatively high ratio of workers to good farmland is said to give it a comparative advantage in "labor-intensive" agricultural goods—those that involve much manual labor, such as vegetables and fruits. Mexico also has a relatively high ratio of low-skilled workers to capital, giving it a comparative advantage in low-technology, labor-intensive manufacturing.

As Mexico opens trade with a capital-abundant country like the United States, the theory holds that Mexico will be able to sell more of the labor-intensive products it makes to the United States and will buy more of the capital-intensive products that U.S. firms produce. Under free trade Mexican workers will benefit from the increased demand for their labor, as will skilled workers producing high-technology goods and services in the United States. Capitalists in the United States will also gain from the wider range of investment opportunities and increased demand in Mexico for their capital, and consumers in both countries will in theory have more options and lower prices.

## The Goals of Regional Free Trade

Embracing the ideals of free trade, the concept of a North American free trade region won the backing of all three of the area's governments by early 1991. What was so striking was not that Canada and the United States—two developed nations of the north—should join in a free trade agreement but that the less developed Mexico would be included as an equal partner in such an accord. A shared commitment to neoliberal free market principles united the three countries, but their vast economic and political disparities meant that each country approached NAFTA with different goals.

Mexico looked to a free trade agreement with the United States primarily to attract foreign investment. An injection of dollars and technology would fuel economic growth, pull the country out of the stagnation of the "lost decade" of the 1980s, and help modernize crucial elements of its infrastructure. Mexico needed foreign capital because the nation's debt and its neoliberal economic strategy precluded a large infusion of public investment. Furthermore, Mexican capitalists were unlikely to provide the necessary investment. In some cases, Mexican investors lacked confidence in the staying power of the new probusiness government outlook. More important, they saw a flat domestic market, and with a few exceptions they lacked the technology and distribution networks to penetrate foreign markets. Attracting significant foreign investment to Mexico through free trade would not only help solve these problems but also provide immediate balance of payments relief.

Considering the country's reputation for sudden policy shifts and the unpredictable nature of presidential succession, increasing investor confidence in the stability of Mexico's economic policy was a crucial part of attracting investment. A formal trade agreement would send a powerful signal to both domestic and foreign investors that Mexico had made a clean break with its history of governmental economic leadership.

A free trade agreement would also serve to enhance Mexico's position as an export platform to the United States, one of the country's major attractions to foreign investors. Rising protectionist sentiment in the United States—although directed mainly against the persistent surpluses of East Asian trading partners—threatened Mexico's access to the U.S. market as well. Already, potentially attractive investment opportunities in several industries—apparel, steel, and some agricultural products—were subject to bilateral or multilateral marketing arrangements that effectively set quotas on U.S. imports. If a free trade agreement exempted Mexico from such restrictions and guaranteed long-term access to U.S. consumers, the country would have a clear leg up in the international competition for export-oriented investment.

Opening Mexico's markets to one of the world's most efficient economies carries significant dangers for domestic businesses. In most sectors those companies least prepared for international competition had already gone bankrupt during the market liberalizations preceeding NAFTA. But protection remained in place for a number of industries, topped by the production of basic agricultural goods, such as corn, soybeans, sorghum, and beans. Along with agricultural producers, U.S. providers of services from banking and insurance to engineering represented great threats to their Mexican counterparts, and to a lesser extent so did industries such as rubber, plastics, and scientific instruments.

For Washington, too, the free trade proposal offered the opportunity to achieve multiple objectives. In strictly economic terms it presented the chance to open the door to Mexico's long-protected market even wider than it had been opened by the country's drive to liberalize trade and to give U.S. products an edge over those produced in Japan or Europe. Although Mexican consumers do not have the buying power to make a significant contribution to the U.S. economy, a decade of rapid economic growth sparked by free trade might change the picture, and an agreement would give U.S.-based producers a head start in meeting that growing demand.[75]

Furthermore, a boom in industrial investment and production would result in greater demand for U.S. products, especially in critical industries like machine tools and information processing, since Mexican industry purchases the large majority of its capital and intermediate goods from U.S. firms. In addition, opening new sectors of Mexico's economy—such as financial services and automobiles—to U.S. exports and investment could boost specific troubled industries in the United States. The gains to many industries exporting to Mexico and to those that would increase their investment in the country—such as financial and telecommunications firms—would more than compensate for losses that could be expected in many protected areas of the U.S. economy, free trade advocates claimed.[76]

Beyond its own economic reasons, the United States had long sought to ensure that its southern neighbor remained politically stable, even when Mexican leaders attacked the United States rhetorically. A free trade accord could accomplish this, U.S. strategists reasoned, both by aiding a friendly administration and by supporting Mexico's neoliberal economic strategy. Economic growth would also reduce the flow of Mexican migrants seeking a better life north of the border, according to reports by numerous commissions over the years.[77]

Washington also saw an opportunity to use free trade with Mexico as a springboard for its hemispheric free trade aspirations. NAFTA could serve as a model for multilateral trade agreements with other countries of the Americas, establishing precedents viewed as crucial by Washington, such as equal treatment of foreign and domestic investors and strong protection of intellectual property rights. Some observers suggested that NAFTA could even serve as the mechanism by which the free trade component of George Bush's Enterprise for the Americas Initiative would be implemented. Provisions in NAFTA allow additional countries to "accede" to the pact by negotiating with the Free Trade Commission it establishes.[78]

Canada had little choice but to join the talks. Having already opened its markets to U.S. corporations with the U.S.-Canada Free Trade Agreement in 1988, it faced having to share the preferential access to the U.S. market it had gained in exchange. Automobiles and petroleum give Canada its fourteen-billion-dollar trade surplus with the United States, and both are top Mexican exports to the United States as well. Furthermore, Canadian corporations in capital goods and other high-technology industries feared ceding the potentially important Mexican market to their U.S. competitors if Canada stayed out of NAFTA. To defend its interests as best it could, Canada asked to join the negotiations in February 1991.[79]

NAFTA represents an attempt to shape economic integration along neoliberal lines, using trade as a lever to limit government's ability to interfere with business priorities. Lowering barriers to trade and investment necessarily involves raising barriers to governments' ability to regulate those flows. The North American trading partners of the United States sought precisely this effect in signing on to free trade. According to former Canadian trade negotiator Michael Hart, a key goal for Canada in NAFTA is "to further lock in the market orientation of the Canadian economy."[80] President Salinas and his top aides made clear on several occasions that a free trade agreement would attract foreign investment to Mexico by increasing the likelihood that his successors will continue his probusiness policies.

In accordance with free trade theory, proponents of NAFTA believe that leaving as much decision-making power as possible to markets and the private sector will result in an efficient regional economy and rapid growth, especially in less developed Mexico. Furthermore, economic growth will then create the wealth and political stability needed to enhance the enforcement of environmental and labor laws.

## No Longer a Theoretical Debate

The debate over NAFTA that emerged in the United States and Canada was essentially the same one building about the direction of free trade initiatives within GATT. On the one hand, labor organizations and certain business sectors are concerned that unregulated trade and investment flows, especially between such unequal partners as the United States and Mexico, will mean that jobs and industries will be lost and there will be a downward pressure on wages. On the other hand, environmentalists and consumer advocates believed that the health, safety, and conservation standards they worked hard to achieve would be endangered by free trade agreements that emphasized business over people and environment. In both cases, opponents called for their governments to protect living standards and social values from what they feared would be the "downward harmonization" caused by the leveling force of free trade.

In Mexico objections to the free trade deal were not as widespread, although public opinion surveys showed that opposition to NAFTA was significant and growing.[81] Many businesses feared they would be overrun by U.S. goods and investment. The PRI's influence over the media and the national congress greatly restricted the breadth of the debate over free trade in Mexico.[82] But a genuine desire on the part of Mexicans for drastic economic change also explained the lack of a strong popular opposition. Many Mexicans appeared to have chosen the promise of new jobs and economic growth resulting from closer links with the world's largest economy over traditional nationalistic concerns about the Colossus of the North.

Most opposition in Mexico focused on issues of sovereignty and self-determination and on the lack of democratic process. Historian Lorenzo Meyer declared that "our way of life is at stake." Similarly, a columnist normally supportive of Salinas observed that an agreement would result not in integration but in the "annexation" of Mexico.[83] Such statements express the deep concern that by adopting free trade and hitching its future to the U.S. star, Mexico will be losing the opportunity to determine its own economic and political future. Will Mexico become just another Puerto Rico, totally dependent on the whims of U.S. investors and forever denied the potential of embracing a development model different from one dictated by the needs of the U.S. economy?

In all three countries opponents argued that NAFTA should be linked to social and environmental issues and pointed to the rules devised by the European Community as a model. Starting as they did from a more regulated capitalism, the member nations of the EC understood that the effects of integration reach well beyond strict economics and accepted the need for a significant government role in managing that integration for the greater good. They therefore included rules covering migration and environmental and labor standards, a managed agricultural policy, and a European Parliament in the process.[84] NAFTA, on the other hand, focused almost exclusively on business issues. Although it allows countries to impose minimum standards on the safety and cleanliness of imports, NAFTA ignores labor rights, work standards, and pollution abatement goals.

Despite negotiators' efforts to present NAFTA as a business-only pact, free trade agreements are inherently about more than economics. What to include to ensure that all parties benefit in the long term, what restrictions to place on government policy-making, and what institutions to establish to carry the integrative process forward through the decades are fundamentally political questions. That is, the answers to those questions help determine who has what power within society.

NAFTA opponents argued that the agreement had been designed to give a great deal of power to corporations, and they feared that if it were approved, it would lock in a probusiness bent to all three countries' domestic policies. The pact could not accomplish these objectives merely by stipulating what governments can and cannot do since future leaders could abrogate the agreement—albeit at some political cost. The staying power of an agreement like NAFTA stems from the fact that the economies of the three countries will gradually be restructured to reflect the integrated continental market. Firms will make their production and investment decisions based on unrestricted access to consumers, workers, investors, and other resources of the three countries. After a decade of such private-sector decisions, pulling out of the agreement would impose large costs on corporations and a country's trade flows. This economic cost, combined with the political fallout caused by angering the corporate elite, would make unilateral changes to or withdrawals from NAFTA highly improbable if and when the agreement was fully implemented.

NAFTA threatened to tie policy makers to a probusiness agenda in a second, subtler way. Without safeguards along the lines of those included in the European Community's plan for integration, competitiveness becomes the bottom-line consideration for all national and international policies. The deregulatory drive of the Reagan and Bush administrations provided a preview of the competitiveness effect. Citing concern for the international competitiveness of U.S. firms, the two presidents launched an all-out attack on regulations intended to protect workers, consumers, and the environment. In 1990 Bush empowered his Council on Competitiveness—headed by Vice President Dan Quayle—to review all new and existing regulations for their "anticompetitive" impact. The council forced changes in EPA regulations, pressed the heads of the U.S. Department of Agriculture and the Food and Drug Administration to reconsider consumer safety rules, and sought to overhaul the nation's civil justice system to reduce the threat of lawsuits against businesses. In each of these cases the council claimed the regulations cost U.S. businesses money, putting them at a disadvantage vis-à-vis foreign competitors while costing U.S. workers their jobs.[85]

The same deregulatory juggernaut swept through Canada in the wake of its free trade agreement with the United States. The country moved away from its strict standard for pesticide safety toward the weaker U.S. version.[86] Social programs were cut back or attacked, as were unemployment insurance and the minimum wage, both of which were more generous than in the United States.[87] The Canadian Chamber of Commerce challenged its federal and provincial governments to adopt the standard applied by Quayle's council, demanding that "all Canadian governments must test all their policies to determine whether or not they reinforce or impede competitiveness. If a policy is anti-competitive, dump it."[88]

Canadian and U.S. corporations not only pressed their governments for more favorable policies but also used the free trade agreement to attack environmental and other programs through the bilateral commission set up to rule on trade disputes. U.S. firms sued to overturn Canada's efforts to reduce acid rain through subsidized pollution control equipment, claiming the subsidies constituted unfair government assistance. Likewise, Canadian companies attacked the U.S. ban on asbestos, arguing that it illegally blocked their exports to this country.[89]

Such examples illustrated the argument made by many opponents of NAFTA and other free trade initiatives that inattention to social policies leaves open the possibility of competition based on the abuse of workers or the environment. Standards are needed to protect against a downward spiral of deregulation intended to attract industry and give domestic firms cost advantages on the international market, much as the rules of GATT and the IMF were set up to prevent destructive competition based on export subsidies or predatory exchange rate policies. From this perspective the problem with NAFTA and the broader free trade agenda is not the fact that it would set global rules but rather who is setting them—and for whose benefit.

Proponents of a broader trinational agreement point to Europe as evidence that free trade need not take an antiregulatory course. They argue that the United States and its trading partners could adopt the strictest rather than the loosest regulation in any given area, phasing in changes over a decade or so and providing financing for technology transfer and enhanced enforcement. This would level the playing field for businesses, eliminate socially destructive competition, and force companies to compete on the basis of productive factors such as quality, efficiency, and innovation.[90]

The conflict between those who approached NAFTA from a purely business perspective and those who preferred these broader approaches to a trade accord encompassed many issues. Two areas that stimulated the most vigorous controversy, however, concerned the trade agreement's potential effects on wages and employment, on the one hand, and the environment, on the other. Aside from drawing the most fire, these issues also exemplified the difficulties of establishing a free trade relationship between such markedly unequal partners as the United States and Mexico. For example, questions over which jobs will be lost or gained, how well basic needs will be met by wages and benefits, and how many resources are available for environmental protection illustrate the effects of asymmetry on the relationship as well as the macroeconomic realities faced by each country individually. In addition, these crucial areas highlighted the role played by the U.S. and Mexican governments in shaping the accord to satisfy particular constituencies and to achieve their own political and economic goals.

## The Wage and Employment Debate

The Bush, Salinas, and Mulroney administrations campaigned vigorously to convince their publics that North American free trade would create jobs and raise living standards in all three countries as did the Clinton administration after it entered office.[91] With the three North American administrations all touting the economic benefits of continental free trade, the debate over NAFTA's effect on workers in the three countries took center stage. In the face of the conventional free market arguments advanced by their national leaders and other free trade supporters, U.S. and Canadian opponents of NAFTA contended that the pact would accelerate the deindustrialization of their countries by encouraging firms to move production to Mexico. Investment in the two wealthier countries would slow as capital flowed south, and this would limit the growth of productivity.

In hearings, at rallies, and on television documentaries, blue-collar workers across the United States and Canada expressed fear for their jobs. If their corporate employers did not lay them off in search of higher profits from a cheaper labor force, workers worried, they might do so out of necessity in the face of competition from other companies that did move to Mexico. NAFTA opponents also argued that removing the last barriers to competition with workers in Mexico would dramatically increase the downward pressure on wages, labor rights, and working conditions that U.S. and Canadian workers had been facing since the 1970s.

Canadian workers had already experienced the free trade slide. In the years following the U.S.-Canada Free Trade Agreement, many Canadian manufacturing facilities moved south—to the United States, where wages and labor laws were generally much more favorable to employers than in Canada. According to the Canadian Labour Congress, nearly 250,000 jobs were lost because of the agreement in its first two years.[92] Statistics Canada reports that a total of 461,000 manufacturing jobs vanished between June 1989 and October 1991, representing nearly one-fourth of manufacturing employment.[93] It is difficult to determine how many of these jobs were lost as a direct result of liberalizing trade and investment flows with the United States in light of the global recession that hit at the same time, but anecdotal evidence and the fact that manufacturing suffered far more in Canada than in the United States indicated that the free trade agreement at least exacerbated the downturn.[94]

Not only do Mexican workers receive far lower wages than their counterparts to the north, but the laws that protect their health and safety as well as those that set maximum work hours and a minimum age limit are commonly ignored. As with other areas of Mexican social standards, the laws are strong—in some cases stronger than those of the United States—but enforcement is spotty. Both in the *maquiladoras*, the focus of numerous investigations, and in the rest of the economy, which has received far less attention, abuses of occupational safety, overtime, and child labor laws are commonplace.[95]

To minimize the competitive advantage to be gained by abusing these laws, labor activists, children's advocates, and others campaigned to gain assurances within NAFTA that standards in all three countries would be strengthened by the pact. But the three North American administrations refused to include the subject in negotiations. To demonstrate their concern for the issue, however, presidents Bush and Salinas directed their secretaries of labor to negotiate an agreement as NAFTA was being hammered out. The result was a series of studies and seminars emphasizing technical assistance and cooperation but explicitly rejecting the notion of tying labor laws or their enforcement to trading privileges.[96]

Even after President Clinton campaigned to include protections for workers in a side agreement to NAFTA, guarantees of such labor rights as collective bargaining, freedom of association, and information about occupational hazards remained off the table. The side agreement on labor that was signed in September 1993 allowed enforcement through fines or trade sanctions only for violations of individual nations' laws covering minimum wages and maximum work hours. No mechanism was included for raising these or other standards, and the commission that was called for to hear cases was to be composed of government appointees only. Labor unionists and other worker activists vigorously condemned the side agreements as failing to address their concerns with NAFTA.

Labor was not the only group predicting that U.S. industry would pick up stakes and move to Mexico if NAFTA passed. In a *Wall Street Journal* poll of 505 senior executives of U.S. manufacturing companies, 40 percent said it was at least likely that their firms would shift some production to Mexico in the few years following a free trade pact. Not all the new investment would cost jobs in the United States—some firms would shift their Asian operations to Mexico—and some of the movement would occur without NAFTA, but the overall effect was made clear by a follow-up question. Thirty-nine percent of respondents said NAFTA would have a "mostly unfavorable" or "very unfavorable" impact on U.S. workers.[97] Independent presidential candidate H. Ross Perot opposed NAFTA steadfastly, in part on the basis of his informal survey of fifteen executives of top U.S. corporations. All of them, he reported, would locate their next facility in Mexico if NAFTA passed.

Lastly, NAFTA was unlikely to help Mexican workers, according to opponents of the agreement, because it contained no mechanisms that would allow them to resist their government's repressive, low-wage strategy. That strategy had already produced hundreds of thousands of jobs in foreign-owned assembly plants in Mexico. Despite the added employment and the increasing productivity of Mexican workers, their real wages fell by between 20 and 40 percent from 1982 to 1991. Nor did the trade agreement include provisions for any financing to help Mexico pay off its debt and invest in education, infrastructure, or other projects needed to foster long-term growth.

To help it evaluate the competing claims, the U.S. Congress asked the U.S. International Trade Commission (ITC) to conduct a study of the likely economic effects of a free trade agreement with Mexico. The ITC found that the nation as a whole would benefit slightly but that unskilled workers "would suffer a slight decline in real income."[98] When pressed to spell out what it meant by "unskilled workers," the ITC revealed that the category included nearly three-quarters of the U.S. workforce. A few months later the ITC made a few "minor adjustments" in the data it had used to reach its conclusions and issued a revised report finding that both skilled and unskilled workers would benefit from NAFTA.[99]

Whether or not the ITC's data switch was based on political considerations, the ability of a minor change to alter significantly the results of an economic model demonstrates the importance of examining the assumptions that economic forecasters make. The economic models cited by NAFTA proponents are virtually all based on sophisticated versions of Ricardo's theory of comparative advantage. As did Ricardo, the models assume that wage and price levels are set by the free play of supply and demand in smoothly functioning markets. Although economists know better, they use these models because they do not have the tools to analyze the real economy, and they believe that making a few simplifying assumptions will at least enable them to predict general trends, if not specific outcomes. But if a model starts by assuming full employment and the equations it uses are based on maintaining full employment, it should hardly be a surprise that its results show continued full employment.

301

Under these conditions, jobs merely shift from one area of the economy to another.

It could be very difficult to figure out how these job shifts will take place, so economists assume perfect markets. When demand for a company's products increases thanks to greater exports, it will hire more workers to boost production. In a perfect market the company must offer a wage higher than that paid elsewhere to attract new workers. By doing so, it raises the cost of labor for all other companies, forcing less productive firms to lay off workers or even go bankrupt. According to free market theory, firms will continue to hire workers until the wages they pay equal the value of the increased production contributed by each additional worker. That means that wages will end up closely tied to productivity.

Free trade skeptics offered North America's experience during the 1980s as exhibit one against these assumptions. Real manufacturing wages in the United States declined 5 to 10 percent even as labor productivity increased.[100] Although the number of jobs in the economy increased by over twenty million during the decade and the unemployment rate fell, workers' incomes barely improved. Manufacturing workers who lost jobs during the decade often could find no new work, and when work was available, it paid an average of 10 to 15 percent less than their previous wage.[101]

In view of the oft-voiced concern that NAFTA would spark a flow of capital from Canada and the United States to Mexico, the most glaring flaw in the economic models supporting the pact was their assumption that U.S. capital stock would be unaffected even as Mexico attracted billions of dollars in new investments. As one economist noted, "That's equivalent to assuming that Mexicans will wake up one morning to find an extra $25 billion in the middle of Main Street."[102]

When one economic model was adapted to take into account an increase in U.S. foreign investment in Mexico, the results it produced changed dramatically, from a finding of a likely small positive effect on U.S. employment to one of a shift of 550,000 U.S. jobs from high-wage to low-wage industries.[103] A study by four economists who used very different assumptions found that NAFTA would cause the loss of between 290,000 and 490,000 U.S. jobs over a decade.[104]

Despite such evidence, the mainstream models designed to predict the effects of NAFTA are based on the theory of comparative advantage and make the assumptions of full employment and perfect markets. Inevitably the results they spit out "confirm" the theory. A 1991 study by KPMG Peat Marwick found that NAFTA would create 29,800 new jobs in some sectors of the U.S. economy, would cause the loss of 29,800 jobs in others, and would increase real wages by 0.02 to 0.03 percent. A University of Michigan study the same year estimated U.S. job gains in some sectors to be 99,993 as a result of NAFTA, job losses in others to be 99,993, and real wages to increase by 0.2 percent. Such forced symmetry reflects the unreality of the underlying assumptions: Neither study shows a net gain or loss of jobs since at full employment neither is possible.

Released in 1991 were at least six other studies using this methodology, known as computable general equilibrium modeling.[105] Most declined to put specific numbers on job shifts, but all agreed that the United States would gain in capital-intensive areas and Mexico would gain in labor-intensive areas. And they agreed that the jobs gained would be more productive and therefore better paying than the jobs lost.[106]

Labor advocates questioned whether new jobs would be created in capital-intensive, high-productivity sectors in the United States and Canada. For one thing, they pointed out, the vast majority of new jobs created in the 1980s—when two million manufacturing jobs disappeared—were in low-paying, service-sector positions. In addition, there was little guarantee that the capital-intensive, high-technology industries that free traders were banking on would not join their less advanced brethren in moving to Mexico.

By the time Salinas proposed free trade to Bush, there was plentiful evidence that it was not just low-wage, low-skill jobs that were likely to move to Mexico. Workers in the United States began to face competition from low-paid workers in increasingly high-skill industries, challenging a tenet of the theory of comparative advantage. Often the competition facing U.S. workers was from overseas subsidiaries of their own firms. In 1983 the Ford Motor Company set up a state-of-the-art engine plant in Chihuahua, Mexico, that directly competed with a Ford plant in the United States. With wages less than one-tenth of those in the northern plants, the only question was whether inexperienced Mexican workers could operate the robots efficiently and achieve high quality standards. Within thirty months the Mexican plant had proved that it was comparable in both respects to the U.S. plant.[107]

Examples of high-quality, high-tech production by low-paid workers on the U.S.-Mexican border have multiplied. From superclean rooms and surface-mount technology in advanced electronics production to flexible manufacturing systems for automobiles, corporations have found that it pays to set up shop in Mexico. That firms are sending advanced production to Mexico defies conventional economic wisdom, which holds that market forces will allocate labor-intensive, low-productivity work to a low-wage, underskilled country like Mexico. It also belies the sanguine pronouncements of free market economists that plant shutdowns, including runaways, were a sign of a healthy U.S. economy shedding undesirable activities to make room for new, more valuable ones. Clearly, NAFTA threatened not just low-wage "undesirable" jobs but the more advanced high-technology jobs the Bush and Clinton administrations were counting on. More and more U.S. workers find themselves wondering what will prevent *their* jobs from moving to Mexico. This worry is echoed by members of the communities that depend on those workers' wages.

Evidence that advanced production can be shifted to Mexico gives employers a big stick in contract negotiations with workers. The threat of relocation and the loss of jobs when plants do move away drive wages down. Fully one-quarter of the executives surveyed by *The Wall Street Journal* acknowledged that they would be likely or somewhat likely to use NAFTA as a bargaining lever to hold down wages.[108] According to an economist at the University of California, Los Angeles, increased competition from Mexican workers will depress the wages of unskilled workers in the United States by an estimated one thousand dollars per year.[109]

In the mid-1980s General Motors' Packard Electric Division told its union local in Cleveland, Ohio, that workers would have to accept a 62 percent pay cut for new hires or their jobs would go to Mexico. Packard had no trouble backing up the threat, since GM already employed tens of thousands of workers in Mexico at a dollar per hour and less. When negotiations ended, the union had a small victory: The pay cut was only 43 percent. In Centralia, Ontario, Fleck Manufacturing carried out the threat: Only hours after its workforce went on strike the plant closed down and moved to Ciudad Juárez, Mexico.

Under free trade, wages have a long way yet to fall. Acknowledging the effect of global integration, a Goodyear executive vice president said that "until we get real wage levels down much closer to those of the Brazils and Koreas, we cannot pass along productivity gains to wages and still be competitive."[110]

## Free Trade, the Environment, and the Consumer

Efforts to protect health and environment have in recent years clashed with the free trade agenda. On a global level these conflicts have increasingly occurred within GATT and have come under consideration for the first time by the Organization for Economic Cooperation and Development (OECD), and the United Nations Conference on Environment and Development (UNCED). On a regional level the tension between free trade principles and regulations safeguarding the environment and consumers has surfaced within the European Community and as part of the NAFTA negotiating process.

Environmentalists and consumer advocates have been pushing since the 1970s for international agreements and standards on such matters as endangered species protection, deforestation, and ozone control.[111] But it was not until 1990 that these groups made strong demands that the links between international trade and environmental and consumer issues be directly addressed as part of global and regional trade negotiations.

For too long environmental and safety concerns have been considered merely obstacles to the free flow of goods, services, and investment. At the heart of the environment and trade debate are national or local regulations that protect the environment or consumer safety but also function as nontariff trade barriers. Issues of sovereignty and extraterritoriality also arise in the intensifying debate about the place of environmental and consumer issues in free trade negotiations. Unregulated free trade would restrict a nation's ability to manage and conserve its own resources. Nations that adopt measures to preserve the family farm or to control the sale of timber, for example, could be faulted for resorting to unfair trade practices. Free trade agreements could also be used to block trade from nations with production processes that are harmful either to the environment or workers, such as drift-net fishing or the widespread use of child labor. In this sense, a lack of environmental regulations or insufficient enforcement of such regulations by exporting countries could be considered hidden trade subsidies.

Another contentious issue that must be resolved in free trade talks is the role of international standards for consumer products and the environment. It might seem that international standards set by the United Nations or some other global forum would be the ideal solution to resolve differences between trading nations. But although such international standards may represent an upward harmonization for less developed nations, they frequently represent a downward harmonization for industrialized countries with more advanced consumer and environmental regulations.

During 1990, as the Uruguay Round of the GATT entered what was expected to be its final year, these and other environmental/consumer concerns were raised for the first time.[112] In 1971 GATT had established a Group on Environmental Measures and International Trade, but it was not until 1991 that the rules committee was convened.[113] When the United States entered into free trade negotiations with Canada in 1986, the major U.S. environmental and consumer organizers showed little interest. The NAFTA negotiations, however, awakened great concern that regional integration under the banner of free trade was directly threatening the viability of U.S. environmental and health standards.

For many within the environmental community, alarm bells began ringing in early 1991, when a GATT dispute panel ruled in favor of a Mexican complaint that the United States could not fairly ban the importation of Mexican tuna. The United States, acting on the provisions of the Marine Mammal Protection Act, had prohibited the purchase of Mexican tuna on the grounds that Mexican tuna-fishing methods were killing substantial numbers of dolphins.[114] Environmentalists also became alarmed by new reports about environmental degradation along the U.S.-Mexico border. The fact that industries had begun using the 1988 U.S.-Canada Free Trade Agreement to challenge environmental standards and programs in both countries also increased environmental and consumer interest in international trade negotiations.

Recognizing that free trade talks represented the largest and most immediate threat to national and global efforts to protect the environment and citizen welfare, such groups as the Natural Resources Defense Council, Sierra Club, and Public Citizen dramatically increased their attention to international trade issues. Fair trade suddenly became the rallying call not only for labor and leftists who had long been questioning the direction of economic globalization but also for environmentalists and consumer advocates.

Environmentalist pressure did succeed in forcing GATT to consider the trade and environment connection for the first time, but it never became an integral issue within the Uruguay Round. With NAFTA the environmental community was more successful. Trade's impact on the environment and to a lesser degree on consumer health and safety became a prominent issue in the NAFTA debate. The relegation of environment to a "parallel track" in the negotiations frustrated environmentalists.[115] But because of their continuing pressure, the final NAFTA draft proved to be an improvement over the 1991 draft of the Uruguay Round (known as the Dunkel Draft), which had come under sharp criticism from environmental and consumer organizations.

The trade treaty signed in December 1992 was, in the words of EPA director William Reilly, "the greenest trade treaty ever."[116] Most critics of the free trade proposal acknowledged the truth of that assessment but noted that previous trade agreements had virtually ignored environmental concerns. In response to concerns raised by environmental and consumer organizations, NAFTA contains provisions that reduce the threat that domestic health and environmental standards will be challenged as constituting nontariff barriers. Standards set by local, state, or national governments may be challenged only if they were designed primarily to block trade.

Rather than define consumer and environmental regulations as trade barriers, the agreement specified that such regulations would not be considered unnecessary barriers to trade if they have a legitimate objective and do not discriminate against particular countries. Among the legitimate objectives specified in NAFTA are measures to promote the interests of safety; human, animal, and plant life and health; environment; consumers; and sustainable development. However, the pact limits each party's protection of human, animal, and plant life to that within its own boundaries. A Canadian law intended to conserve Mexico's biodiversity would thus appear to be illegitimate under NAFTA.

Without requiring upward harmonization of standards, as many environmentalists and citizen groups had been advocating, the agreement stated that free trade should occur without reducing environmental and consumer safeguards even if they were stricter in one country than another. In an important departure from GATT, where the burden of proof in disputes over nontariff barriers lies with the defending nation, NAFTA states that the party challenging an environmental or consumer measure must prove that the defending country's regulation is inconsistent with the agreement.

Two other areas where the final draft shows improvement over earlier drafts concerns scientific justification and risk assessment of environmental and consumer measures. Although still ambiguous, the agreement appears only to require that some scientific basis exist to support the formulation of these measures. Rather than insisting on risk/benefit analysis to justify environmental and consumer trade restrictions, the agreement instead states that these measures be based on risk assessment and merely specifies that each party "should take into account the objective of minimizing negative trade effects" in establishing food safety levels. Risk assessment is defined simply as an evaluation of potential adverse effects rather than a judgment that would also consider the economic costs and benefits of these measures. Measures specifying "zero tolerance" for carcinogens would probably meet the obligation for risk assessment but might not be considered valid when employing risk/benefit analysis.[117]

In late 1993 the trinational Agreement on Environmental Cooperation, signed as a supplemental accord to NAFTA, brought many of the major U.S. environmental organizations on board in favor of NAFTA. These included the National Wildlife Federation, Conservation International, Natural Resources Defense Council, World Wildlife Fund, National Audubon Society, and Environmental Defense Fund. These environmental groups supported NAFTA not only because of new governmental commitments to pollution prevention, but also because they believed that NAFTA would open new channels of communication with Mexico over natural resources conservation and environmental protection. In her public endorsement of NAFTA, Kathryn Fuller, president of the World Wildlife Fund, noted that Mexico has more biological resources than almost any other country and that by acquiring greater economic opportunity through the trade agreement, Mexico would have more money available to protect the environment.[118]

Although gratified that their lobbying and organizing had some success, many environmentalists remained critical of NAFTA as a model for international trade. One objection focused on the accord's failure to promote sustainable development, a concept whose goals include natural resource conservation, biological and cultural diversity, and equity. Although NAFTA lists the promotion of sustainable development as one of its objectives and defines it as a legitimate purpose for environmental regulations, it does not explicitly link trade and the environment. Addressing this link is crucial to achieving sustainable development, these environmentalists argue. An increasingly influential sector of the environmental movement also questions what free trade advocates assume—namely, that economic growth is necessarily positive. It instead points to the environmentally destructive, exploitative, and inequitable character of what is commonly considered economic progress.

The continuing skepticism about global free trade proposals shared by many environmental and consumer organizations—and their opposition to NAFTA—were based on more nuts-and-bolts considerations as well. These include the lack of funding and oversight to ensure that environmental regulations are enforced, the absence of public participation, the lack of rules governing production processes, sovereignty issues, and the lack of clear language defending the rights of communities and nations to set nondiscriminatory health, safety, and environmental regulations.

A common complaint among critics of NAFTA and GATT is that international trade regulations override democratic processes. Not only do the negotiations themselves take place behind closed doors with little opportunity for participation by citizens and nongovernmental organizations, but the dispute process for settling conflicts between trading parties is completely closed to citizen involvement and review. NAFTA allows only the executive branch of each party to bring a complaint to the Free Trade Commission created to resolve disputes. Individuals, unions, environmental groups, and local and state governments must persuade their country's executive branch to make their case for them under NAFTA. All arguments and documents presented to the commission will remain secret until fifteen days after the commission makes its decision, and if the parties agree not to publish a final report of a given decision, the evidence and reasoning behind that decision will remain under wraps.[119]

Compounding this problem of the lack of citizen scrutiny and participation is the undue influence exercised by major corporate interests in the negotiating process. Not only are corporate representatives asked to participate in government working committees on international trade, but these same interests are also generally the ones who help write international standards for pesticide use, food safety, and consumer products.[120]

For both environmental and consumer groups, right-to-know provisions should also be incorporated into free trade agreements. International product-labeling requirements would give consumers information about the substances and technologies used in making imported goods, while workers would have access to similar information under right-to-know principles.

Closed dispute procedures, ambiguous language, and the lack of strong guarantees in NAFTA leave open the possibility that environmental and consumer protection regulations would not be insulated from trade-motivated challenges. Environmental and consumer groups want better guarantees that local, state, and national standards will be respected. In this regard, they say that regulations that protect consumers and the environment should not be open to challenge simply because they are higher than the international standard. Similarly, they argue that international standards should be considered mainly a regulation floor rather than a ceiling. Simply because a product is acceptable by the international standard does not mean that the affected government should not follow its own review and approval procedures for new products.

One of the key trade issues for environmentalists and consumer advocates is the need to apply standards to production processes as well as to products themselves. Such standards would protect the regional environment and cut down on destructive competition by ensuring that imports are not produced in a manner that would violate environmental or health laws in the importing country. NAFTA fails to distinguish itself from GATT in this regard, a fact that worries environmentalists. They looked, for example, for NAFTA expressly to reject GATT's interpretation of the rules regarding the tuna and dolphin dispute, thus making room for unilateral environmental measures that have an extraterritorial effect.

Environmentalists share labor activists' fear that even if free trade agreements protect local regulations, higher standards will be undermined as investment and jobs flow to countries with lower standards. Free trade agreements, they argue, must go further to facilitate the upward harmonization of health and environmental regulations to ensure that pollution haven investment does not result. In this regard, funding mechanisms are essential to guarantee that countries like Mexico have the capacity to enforce their environmental laws. Furthermore, they say, lack of enforcement of such laws should constitute an unfair trade practice.

The fear that U.S. investment will seek pollution havens in Mexico stems from the basic disparities in environmental laws and enforcement between the United States and Mexico. But free traders argue that more integrated regional and global markets will promote economic growth. With this growth will come expanded environmental consciousness among a growing Mexican middle class and increased revenues to support strong environmental programs. Most environmentalist organizations reject such reasoning, charging instead that economic growth inevitably means increased resource depletion and pollution without necessarily leading to tougher environmental regulation. In the best of circumstances, free trade without proper safeguards, funding, and guidelines may generate short-term economic gain for both trading partners but will not result in long-term or sustainable growth, according to environmental critics.[121]

## Sovereignty, Internationalism, and Protectionism

Sovereignty and internationalism are two concepts that environmentalists and consumer advocates are struggling to reconcile. It is commonly agreed that the sovereign right of nations to protect their citizenry, conserve their environments, and uphold social values must be recognized in free trade agreements. But at the same time certain international rules and norms are clearly needed to protect the global environment and to regulate the increasingly global economy. To make such global standards meaningful, nations must cede some of their sovereignty.

Generally the more industrialized nations would benefit from an upward harmonization of environmental and health standards. As all standards improved, less developed countries would be less able to use lower standards as a type of indirect subsidy to their exporting industries, and corporations from the more developed nations would have less incentive to relocate. But countries like Mexico could rightly charge that their sovereignty would be undermined if they were forced to abide by the regulations established by more developed and wealthier nations. Reacting to demands by environmentalists and consumer advocates for phased-in upward harmonization, a spokesperson for the Bush State Department accused U.S. environmentalists of being "latter-day colonialists" and said that such proposals were simply a "new justification for keeping the Latins down."[122]

Sovereignty also becomes an issue with recent proposals to regulate the foreign operations of U.S. corporations and to create increased access to foreign citizens with complaints against U.S. investors or products. One such proposal is for a U.S. Foreign Environmental Practices Act modeled after the Foreign Corrupt Practices Act, which would make U.S. citizens and corporations subject to both criminal and civil prosecution in U.S. courts for violating applicable U.S. environmental law. Such a law would probably go a long way toward persuading U.S. corporations investing in Mexico to improve their environmental practices. Its supporters say that it would  also increase corporate accountability by making firms more responsible to consumers, workers, and the communities in which they invest. Given the fact that Mexican courts will not consider suits against corporations for violating environmental laws, this proposal has gained support among many Mexican as well as U.S. environmentalists. But for other Mexicans such proposals revive fears of Yankee domination. Mexican problems should be resolved by Mexicans, they say.[123]

In relation to free trade, the sovereignty debate also extends to such issues as saving the family farm, protecting small businesses, restricting the exploitation of natural resources, and fostering certain industries as part of a national development policy. Questions of sovereignty also come into play when we consider if free trade agreements should contain clauses requiring respect for basic human, labor, and political rights.

If free trade is to be more than a corporate bill of rights, such issues need to be considered in establishing rules for global and regional integration. Strong and enforceable norms for basic human rights are essential to guarantee that countries do not achieve unfair trade advantages because their workers are repressed and exploited. Such standards already exist in the UN's International Labor Organization and in the UN's Universal Declaration of Human Rights.[124]

Linking free trade agreements to this kind of internationalism would help ensure a "level playing field" for trade. Arguments about national sovereignty represent the worst kind of protectionism when they defend a country's failure to meet international standards for human rights, labor organizing, and political freedom. But a new world order cannot and should not mean one in which communities and nations no longer have the right to protect their own social or cultural values or to set their own development policies.

The ideal of free trade and global integration must make room for such protections if economies are to grow and societies are to prosper. Even if some economic inefficiencies and trade barriers are involved, free trade agreements should allow for measures that save family farms, sustain local cultures, or protect other important social values of trade partners. Similarly, community and national economic development goals—such as food security, agrarian reform programs, or industrial development policies—cannot be ignored simply to make it easier for transnational investors and traders to conduct their business.

Some of the harshest criticism of NAFTA and U.S. free trade initiatives has come from Ralph Nader's consumer watchdog group Public Citizen. Nader has accused GATT of "imposing a mega-corporate view of the world." Staff attorney Lori Wallach charged that the revisions reflected in the final NAFTA draft were merely cosmetic and that the two side agreements reached in 1993 did not do nearly enough to outweigh the overall negative impact of the proposed agreement. According to Wallach, "The United States and other nations are at a crossroads. The rapidly expanding global marketplace threatens to overwhelm citizens' ability to exercise democratic sovereignty by legislating rules that will govern their societies. Multinational corporations want global commerce but without corresponding global law to hold them accountable."[125]

## Shaping the Alternatives

Free trade by itself will not solve Mexico's development problems, reinvigorate the U.S. economy, or make the Western Hemisphere more competitive in the global market. Developing needed infrastructure and paying social costs like educating the young, retraining displaced workers, preventing and remediating environmental degradation, and safeguard-

312

ing the public health are tasks that can be accomplished only by managing the integration process to promote equity and sustainable development.

Neoliberal trade and investment agreements like NAFTA, however, rely on market forces to pay these costs. Deregulation, unfettered foreign investment, privatization, liberalized trade, and public-sector austerity are supposed to lead to economic growth. The benefits of growth, in turn, are to trickle down to workers and other participants in the emerging economic order. But after a decade of liberalization and deregulation in the United States and Mexico, falling real incomes, sharply increased poverty rates, rising long-term unemployment, widening gaps between rich and poor, infrastructure decay, and environmental deterioration shot holes through these market-based approaches to development. Corporate and national competitive strategies based on low wages and feeble protections for workers eroded living standards and undermined unions and other representatives of working people. Of even greater concern, mechanisms like the accession clause to NAFTA, programs like the Enterprise for the Americas Initiative, and global frameworks like GATT threaten to spread these economic strategies and their deficiencies throughout the hemisphere and around the world.

Economic problems like these, with their potentially negative effects on political stability, are not the inevitable outcomes of increased trade and investment flows. Economic integration and expanding trade can be made to serve a broader agenda embracing social values. The goal is to construct a framework for integration that protects human beings, their communities, and the environment, not just the trade and investment decisions of transnational corporations. Constructing agreements that explicitly aim to defend labor rights and working conditions, build and rebuild livable communities, safeguard the environment, and protect the public health requires mechanisms that guide market forces to compensate for problems generated by unrestricted development.[126] These mechanisms fall into four related categories: democratization of the decision-making process, compensatory financing, legal and normative frameworks, and institutional innovations.

## Out of the Back Rooms

Transparency, accountability, and public participation are prerequisites for a fully functioning economic and political system based on equity and sustainability. Because of the weighty decisions being made and their wide-ranging impacts, the process of integration and the formulation of agreements like NAFTA make it crucial that those who have traditionally been left out of the decision-making process advance their own agendas, projects, and alternatives in policy forums. "Perhaps the most important question dodged by NAFTA enthusiasts," noted a team of concerned observers, "is who should be making the vital decisions about the shape of the increasingly intertwined future of the three North American nations."[127] As traditionally structured, most of those decisions are made by free traders in government and corporate leaders with a vested interest in minimizing constraints on their international activities.

In addition to the negotiating process itself, international economic frameworks such as GATT and agreements like NAFTA undermine democracy by taking important decision-making powers out of the hands of local, state, and national elected leaders and vesting them in unelected, unrepresentative, and unaccountable institutions.[128] For example, the Free Trade Commission mandated by NAFTA and the two commissions set up under parallel accords include only government officials, excluding independent representatives from sectors like labor, consumers, and community groups who would often be better able to evaluate the effects of policy on their constituents. Negotiations held in secret and disputes settled behind closed doors do little to ensure that the needs and concerns of affected communities and interest groups are taken into account, much less protected. By allowing international trade agreements to preempt local and national regulations in areas such as product safety, democracy is further weakened. In many cases these standards and regulations are the product of years of work by activists who used the legislatures and the courts to devise safeguards for the environment and for public health. Undermining their efforts not only does not advance democracy but sets it back.

More is required than just pulling back the curtain on decision-making sessions held by others. Transparency and disclosure are not enough, although they are fundamental if affected members of the U.S. and Mexican publics are going to make informed choices about their options and strategies as integration progresses. From community right-to-know legislation to electoral reform and human rights protections to representation on commissions with the power to oversee integration and implement policies, the democratization process must allow wide-ranging participation. As a consequence, democratic structures are a necessary component of all the other institutions and legal and normative frameworks that might complement trade and investment accords.

## Compensatory Financing

Democratic openness and participation help equalize the political influence of government and business elites vis-à-vis other affected parties, such as labor, community groups, and environmentalists. But adjustments also have to be made for persistent north-south differences and for the economic disparities between those who are likely to benefit from integration and those who—at least in the short term—are likely to suffer. In addition, knotty problems such as transboundary pollution and resource depletion that are bound to be worsened by unrestrained development present funding dilemmas for both governments. Each of these difficulties raises obstacles to integration and diminishes its appeal to groups that are negatively affected, yet each can be ameliorated if solutions to them are pursued with the vigor that has been devoted to free trade.

Compensatory financing mechanisms are needed to help Mexico—the more disadvantaged economy—make the costly changes required by integration.[129] The costs of integrating Mexico's economy with regional and global markets will sharply expand the country's need for capital, both foreign and domestic. But the capital flows likely to enter the country during the years when most critical adjustments are being made are not likely to be enough to meet the need, especially considering the global slowdown that has squeezed the international economy in recent years. Without some sort of compensatory mechanism, the Mexican government will be encouraged to solve its adjustment problems, reduce debt and unemployment, and resolve other economic issues by competing for capital based on low wages and lax regulations. To help avoid such strategies and to pay for aspects of integration like developing infrastructure and installing new norms and standards, compensatory financing is essential. As opposition leader Cuauhtémoc Cárdenas explained, "Making the fundamental disparity of the three economies the cornerstone of the [free trade] agreement means making compensatory financing its centerpiece."[130]

Mexico, however, will not be the only party that suffers at least temporary dislocation and increased financial pressures from integration. Workers in the United States and Canada who lose jobs to runaways, family farmers and the rural poor in all three countries, and communities buffeted by plant closures and other symptoms of economic transformation will require assistance if sustainable and equitable integration is to go forward.

Providing financing for these and other needs might be the task of a

315

new institution like the North American Development Bank and Adjustment Fund (NADBAF) proposed by three economists.[131] Capitalized by contributions from participating countries and modest taxes on international transactions, the bank could help protect communities and workers from unremediated dislocation and the environment from unrestrained degradation. Modeled on initiatives like the European Regional Development Fund and the European Social Fund, created to facilitate integration of poorer members into the European Community, the bank could finance both long-term development projects and short-term adjustment strategies. Among the many possible uses of NADBAF financing are worker training and retraining, retooling and other conversion investments, job creation in rural areas, health and safety programs, and the development and upward harmonization of norms, standards, and regulations. Support for such projects is critical in order to keep a safety net under those at risk and to accelerate rises in wages, working conditions, and social standards in the North American economy as a whole.

## Legal and Normative Frameworks

Another important way to help shape integration is to position trade and investment agreements within a larger structure of international legal and normative frameworks. These frameworks, like the United Nations conventions on civil, political, economic, and cultural rights, indicate priorities and aspirations and enforce propeople and proenvironment provisions. There are many options for such frameworks, ranging from those with rather specific objectives—like devising a code of conduct for transnational corporations—to those with very broad-ranging agendas like a North American social and environmental charter.[132]

International frameworks like these help compensate for the declining ability of national governments and their citizens to oversee and restrain the international activities of TNCs and other transnational actors. They also bind the signatory governments themselves to pursue policies and paths of development consistent with the goals outlined in the agreements. If constructed with adequate enforcement mechanisms, such as an international court and trade sanctions, these international frameworks may provide avenues for nations, nongovernmental organizations, communities, and even individuals to pursue legal judgments outside domestic court systems when provisions of the agreements are violated. Finally, when devised so that trade and investment policies are linked to social issues, they can help make sure that the effects of one upon the other are considered in tandem and not artificially separated.

International agreements on labor, migration, and human rights, for instance, would be logical components of a broad package of initiatives designed to commit governments to protecting and upgrading living conditions in the hemisphere.[133] With economic integration will come increased levels of social, cultural, and political integration, requiring commitments to manage the process and remedy ill effects. Trade and investment relations will spill over into these other areas, by spurring at least temporary increases in migration, for example, or by threatening labor rights as governments and corporations pursue low-wage and union-repressive competitive strategies. From ratification of the American Convention for Human Rights to totally new agreements on issues like migration, these instruments would obligate the U.S. and Mexican governments to deal with these social by-products of integration. Specialized bodies that allowed substantive access by all affected parties—a North American Human Rights Commission and a North American Human Rights Court, for instance—could be given jurisdiction over disputes and litigation arising from the pacts.[134]

The most extensive proposal to come out of considerations like these has been for a social charter modeled on the one passed by the European Community as part of its integration process.[135] A North American social and environmental charter, for example, would commit the signatory governments gradually to standardize norms relating to issues like labor rights, migration, and the environment. Linked to NAFTA or some similar trade agreement, the charter would be designed to ensure that the conditions under which people live and work in the North American countries would be harmonized in an upward direction and not allowed to fall as part of the bidding war for capital.

It is not that such a charter could overcome the vast gaps in living conditions that separate the United States or Canada from Mexico. Instead, by recognizing that people in each country have congruent and effective rights to collective bargaining, community right-to-know, occupational health and safety, and other such protections, the charter would provide a trilateral, enforceable set of "threshold protections" for workers, their communities, and the environment.[136] By including provisions for democratic participation and accountability in the institutions set up to enforce the charter, such a document would advance not only the economic and social rights of the region's citizens but their political rights and influence as well.

## Institutional Innovations

Carrying out a successful, equitable, and sustainable form of economic integration requires representative and accountable institutions, many of which must be created anew. In addition to the institutions described above, bi- and trilateral commissions and similar bodies are needed to guide integration and manage its challenges. The number and mandates of these new institutions should be broad enough to encompass all aspects of integration and to account for the full social costs that will accompany the integration process. From health care and labor standards to housing, education, taxation, and debt, there are manifold tasks for such community-based institutions to accomplish.

Along the U.S.-Mexico border, for example, a binational commission with fund-raising and enforcement authority could monitor and find solutions to health, environmental, and labor issues.[137] In a similar vein, a Sustainable Development Commission composed of representatives from public interest, business, and governmental organizations could assess and, if necessary, overrule provisions of trade accords like NAFTA or attempts to implement them because of their impacts on the environment.[138] Commissions for labor and social welfare, international work councils linking unionists employed by the same transnational employers, and a commission on political democracy could also be established to advance people-based agendas and direct investments to meeting social needs.

The proceedings of these institutions should be public, and documents, decisions, hearing dates, and the like will need to be readily available to all interested parties in order to achieve the goal of transparency. In addition, in most cases at least, participants and decision makers who sit on the bodies should be elected, not appointed. If they are appointed, the process must be carefully structured in order to maximize public input. For instance, participants might be chosen from a slate of candidates nominated by organizations that are recognized leaders among such sectors as labor, environmentalists, community activists, health care providers, business associations, and consumer groups. To preserve accountability, some community recall provision must also be included so that participants on these bodies can be removed if their constituents do not think that their interests are being served. To guarantee independence, the institutions must have fund-raising mechanisms built into their structure, whether derived from user fees, taxation, or dedicated funding from government or community funds.

## Uphill Battle

Creating a welter of new institutions, laws, regulations, and bureaucracies is not the objective of these suggested strategies. Shaping the emerging economic order in a way that preserves a livable and fruitful environment for future generations and provides healthy, safe, and satisfying living conditions for the hemisphere's people are the goals of such endeavors. In order to accomplish these difficult but reasonable objectives, the policy-making terrain must be reclaimed from those who are shielded from the fallout of their decisions inside the bunker of ideology, wealth, and power. Because of the way NAFTA was structured by the Bush and Salinas administrations, however, enhancing citizen participation in the decision-making process is an uphill battle. This structure was not altered by the parallel agreements tacked on by the Clinton administration.

NAFTA offers few options for challenge by communities or interest groups. The dispute resolution mechanism, for instance, is so secret that relevant documents are not available to interested parties who are not directly involved in the dispute. Nor are members of the public—environmentalists, labor, and consumer groups, for example—eligible to bring cases up for resolution or to be present at hearings. Because NAFTA was not submitted to the U.S. Congress as a treaty, it is open to court challenges when and if it preempts local standards. As a last resort, opponents can push their legislatures to abrogate the pact, but that would likely be a lengthy process during which time potentially damaging structural changes in the economies of the United States and Mexico would go forward.

As a consequence of this grim forecast, when NAFTA was signed by Bush and Salinas in late 1992, those who sought trade-linked protections for labor, consumers, and the environment redoubled their efforts either to kill the trade pact or to get it renegotiated. The 1992 national elections in the United States boosted their chances slightly. Not only was the neoliberal government of George Bush removed from office, but an exceptionally large number of new representatives were elected to Congress, most on platforms calling for an end to "business as usual" in Washington.

President Clinton attempted to juggle competing constituencies—corporations, organized labor, environmentalists, ethnic minorities, and the poor—by endorsing NAFTA on the condition that parallel agreements with Canada and Mexico, along with domestic legislation, protect the environment and the rights of workers. But the two additional agreements reached by the NAFTA partners in 1993 satisfied few of the pact's critics and left the Democratic Party badly split on the issue.

Although NAFTA eventually gained approval, the fair trade campaign offered a crucial opportunity to begin building international coalitions and generating a broad-based vision of democracy and economic development. The trade agreement itself raised so many issues of importance in so many areas that criticisms of the pact were almost always interlaced with propeople and proenvironment agendas. With careful attention to devising not only arguments but alternatives, those agendas can help form the foundation for future efforts to shape integration so that development does not take place at the expense of communities and the world in which we live.

# Labor Solidarity

# Faces the Test

The proposal for North American free trade sounded a wake-up call for organized labor in the United States and forced a long-overdue effort to strengthen relations between unionists in each country. But NAFTA also highlighted the different interests of U.S. and Mexican labor as far as free trade was concerned. In the United States workers feared that NAFTA would intensify the runaway plant phenomenon and the loss of production and jobs to foreign imports. In Mexico, however, workers hoped that free trade would bring them jobs and a brighter economic future. Added to a history of uneasy relations between organized labor in the two countries, these differences in perceptions about the value of NAFTA have made cross-border organizing a difficult task.

These differences aside, NAFTA also presents some common challenges to U.S. and Mexican labor. In the current atmosphere workers on either side of the border are in effect competing for investment capital. Although trade liberalization may provide more jobs for Mexican workers, this competition threatens to increase the downward pressure on wages and benefits that has characterized the global economy since the 1970s. NAFTA makes it much harder to safeguard against this pressure. The need to respond to these dilemmas is stimulating new levels of communication and cooperation between labor organizations in both the United States and Mexico.

The free trade proposal and its challenges to U.S.-Mexican labor solidarity came at a time of weakness and demoralization in the U.S. labor movement. Since the mid-1960s workers had been plagued by runaway manufacturing and cheap imports from low-wage countries. At first the industries most affected involved relatively low-paying, labor-intensive work often performed by women: sewing apparel, making shoes and boots, and assembling toys or consumer electronics. But increasingly during the

321

1970s imports challenged higher-wage, traditionally male occupations: steel, autos, semiconductors, and sophisticated electronic components.

As plants closed and firms laid off workers, union membership dropped sharply. Efforts to reverse the declining position of U.S. workers were mostly unsuccessful. The labor movement's "Buy American" strategy of voluntary and legislated protectionism, for example, alienated large segments of the general public while failing to produce long-term solutions.[139] And the strategy of wage concessions and cooperative labor relations adopted by many unions during the 1980s collided with the $1.50-per-hour reality of low-wage competition under NAFTA, raising the question of just how low workers would have to go to retain their jobs.

In addition to tactics like protectionism and concession bargaining, U.S. labor tried to shore up its position by seeking legislation to reduce plant closings, protect specific industries, fund worker retraining, and condition access to the U.S. market on respect for international labor rights. Despite at least partial victories in each of these areas, political forces during the 1980s were as damaging to unions as economic changes were. Under Ronald Reagan the National Labor Relations Board accelerated its rightward shift and companies felt increasingly free to replace strikers permanently and to harass and fire union activists among their employees. Legal defeats and the increasing dominance of largely nonunion service industries in the U.S. economy also cut into the ranks of organized labor. The proportion of U.S. nonfarm employees holding union cards fell from 31 percent in 1970 to roughly 16 percent in 1991.[140]

Pressured on all sides, U.S. labor was in no condition to take on the powerful business interests arrayed in support of free trade when the United States and Mexico initiated negotiations in mid-1990. So while they vigorously pushed their friends in Congress to "just say no" to NAFTA, union leaders also sought to join forces with other NAFTA opponents. Unions took a small step toward adopting a broader social agenda—a direction that progressive activists had long been advocating—by finding allies among environmental activists and consumer advocates. These two groups enjoyed strong support in many western states and among upper-middle-class citizens, nicely complementing labor's working-class base of support in the Midwest and Northeast.

To varying degrees U.S. unions and the main U.S. labor federation, the AFL-CIO, began to reshape their international strategies as well as their domestic political work. A number of people within U.S. labor recognized that building an international coalition of unions and other activist organizations spanning the vast gulf between poor and rich nations should be an essential part of labor's response to NAFTA and to economic globalization. The AFL-CIO, several individual unions, and a number of small labor-based groups have taken the first steps in this direction. After years of neglect they are seeking out Mexican counterparts to develop joint strategies and cooperative projects and to improve communication and understanding.

Because of its large budget and its traditional leadership role in setting U.S. labor's foreign policy, the AFL-CIO is the most important labor organization involved in the search for a new international approach. The federation represents the majority of U.S. unions and has by far the greatest resources both for lobbying and for international activities. But some individual unions—both AFL-CIO affiliates and independents—are pushing farther and faster, especially in the area of building cross-border links.

## Organized Labor in Mexico

The effort to forge international alliances faces serious obstacles. For one thing, Mexican unions are somewhat skeptical of the new cross-border initiatives. From their perspective, U.S. labor has been at times arrogant, ignorant, and racist in its relations with their unions and workers. According to a close observer of the process, a Mexican union leader recently asked his U.S. counterpart, "Why, all of a sudden, are you calling us 'brothers'? Is it because today you realize you need us, because you are about to lose your jobs—even perhaps your unions—and because you think we stand to gain from your loss? Where have you been for the past forty years, when many times we were in need of you?"[141]

The fact that a gain for Mexican workers might indeed be a loss for U.S. workers also hinders better U.S.-Mexican union relations. Mexican unions largely supported NAFTA, agreeing with their country's president that a free trade pact is likely to attract foreign investors to Mexico and therefore to increase employment. It is difficult, however, to judge the sincerity of Mexican unions' support for free trade because of the dependence of labor leaders on the ruling party.[142] In fact, most unions are formally affiliated with the ruling Institutional Revolutionary Party (PRI), which has a corporatist structure that links the "official" labor unions, peasant associations, and other important sectoral groups directly to the decision-making centers of the government.[143]

The PRI allocates a portion of its congressional seats and an occasional governorship to leaders of the official unions and uses their workplaces and community networks to get out the vote in support of the party at election time. Until 1991 the collective bargaining agreements of official unions required union members to join the PRI. This forced mass affiliation of workers has ended on paper, but local union leaders still put great pressure on their members to sign up with the PRI. Local union leaders who fail to deliver votes are unlikely to climb the promotional ladder.[144]

Even more important to the system than getting out the vote is the role of official unions in ensuring labor's cooperation with the government's economic programs. During the five years of economic crisis from 1982 to 1987, for instance, Mexico's labor leaders opposed the government's severe austerity programs in their speeches but failed to mobilize workers to protest the policies. The workers suffered accordingly: The real minimum wage was cut roughly in half during this period.

Mexico's official unions also have a part to play in setting and implementing economic policies. As in other corporatist systems, such as in Germany, all workers are covered by broad national accords negotiated among representatives of the government, business groups, and labor. These accords set guidelines for wage hikes, for example, or targets for productivity increases. Official union leaders dominate the representation of labor at these negotiations and take primary responsibility for enforcing the limits that are set.

Since 1987 the government has signed a series of tripartite "economic pacts" with labor and business representatives.[145] The pacts spell out the government's policies regarding peso devaluation, subsidies, and prices for state services and products. Business representatives pledge to respect price hike limits, and labor leaders agree to a cap on wage hikes. In every pact the negotiated increase in the minimum wage has lagged behind inflation.

The largest and most powerful official union organization is the Confederation of Mexican Workers (CTM).[146] The CTM claims to represent 5 million workers in fourteen thousand unions, but the real number is probably between 1.5 million and 2 million. For forty years the CTM has been headed by Fidel Velázquez, who has personified the close relationship between the PRI and the official unions. In 1992 Velázquez was elected to another six-year term as general secretary of the CTM. He will be ninety-eight years old when the term expires, unless he defies the conventional wisdom that he is immortal. A strong believer in organizational and personal discipline, Velázquez has argued against probusiness policies in public but has dutifully enforced the decisions of the president. Since the mid-1980s Velázquez has agreed to real wage cuts as part of the government's economic policies, and he has repressed activists opposing these policies.

Leaders who turn against the party risk a serious fate. President Salinas made this very clear soon after he took office by sending the army to arrest and jail Joaquín Hernández Galicia on questionable charges of murder and gunrunning.[147] Hernández, better known in Mexico as La Quina, had been the powerful head of the Mexican Petroleum Workers Union but made the mistake of verbally attacking President Salinas during the 1988 presidential race and of expressing support for Salinas's political foe, Cuauhtémoc Cárdenas, even while formally backing the PRI.[148]

There is no doubt that La Quina had grossly enriched himself and his coterie of union officials through corruption. This was also true of many other union leaders, though none rivaled La Quina's creativity, conspicuous wealth, or power. His replacement, handpicked by the Salinas administration, had long been a part of La Quina's circle of corrupt officials. Far from heralding a change in direction for the union, La Quina's imprisonment served a number of other purposes, including establishing Salinas as firmly in control of the state, publicizing Salinas's limited anticorruption campaign, and signaling organized labor that its relationship with the state was under review. But the action's primary purpose was to warn others not to challenge the party structure.

There is a much smaller but growing group of unions that are not formally affiliated with the PRI but that support the economic modernization program begun under Salinas. Often tagged modernizing unions for this reason, the group is headed by the Mexican Telephone Workers Union and the Mexican Electricians Union. These two unions stand at the center of a new labor group, the Federation of Goods and Services Unions, which claims more than two hundred thousand members. Numerous observers have accused FESEBES, as the federation is known, of serving as merely another tool of the government, more suited to the long-term goal of reducing the state's economic role than are the older official unions.[149]

Francisco Hernández Juárez heads both FESEBES and the telephone workers' union. He was at one time an aggressive, independent leader, ousting the corrupt hierarchy of the phone union in 1976 and leading five strike efforts. But government repression—combined with the enticement of political prominence by working within the system—convinced Hernández to join the PRI in 1987. He has since defended the economic pacts much as has Fidel Velázquez, insisting that controlling inflation is top priority and that wage hikes must be tied to productivity improvement.[150]

The crucial question facing Hernández and other union leaders in areas where technology is rapidly advancing is not whether their industries should modernize but how. Should employees be downgraded to mere monitors of the automated equipment they operate, or should they receive the training necessary to suggest improvements in the efficiency and quality of their work, helping to shape the way technology is implemented and the purposes for which it is designed? Hernández has opted to push for small advances in the participation of the union within management, but after winning 4.4 percent ownership in the newly privatized telephone company for his union, he has been marginalized from managerial decision making. In addition, he has largely ignored shop floor issues of everyday importance to workers: work rules, the physical layout of work stations, the monitoring of operators' performance, and the pace of work. Instead Hernández has remained within the traditional concerns of official Mexican unions: wage and benefit issues and protecting existing workers' jobs.

Although the modernizing unions are formally independent of the government, there is another group of labor organizations that has earned classification as independent unions. They not only got their start outside the official labor movement but have maintained their independence over time. Although they are small in number, the independent unions play an important role in Mexico by challenging government labor policy and the official unions. Various factors work against the success of these unions, however. Except for a brief period in the 1970s, for instance, federal labor authorities have denied almost all independent union petitions for registration. In recent years, privatization, closures and layoffs at national industries, and government repression have also undermined them.

The most important independent labor organization is the Authentic Labor Front (FAT), which claims forty thousand members. FAT's membership includes farmworkers, urban activists, members of cooperatives, and approximately ten thousand industrial workers. Since its founding in 1962, FAT has never requested government recognition as a labor union or federation, so it cannot itself represent workers. Instead FAT helps its affiliated unions or preunion organizing efforts with strategic, legal, and organizational advice, as well as with financial support. Often it is FAT itself that launches an organizing effort by encouraging workers to form their own organizing committee.

Many of the legally recognized independent unions sprouted in the 1970s, when President Luis Echeverría temporarily opened up the process. Since then federal and state labor authorities have denied almost all independent union petitions for registration. Prevented from forming new unions, democratic union activists have created rank-and-file movements within official unions. The most important of these is the National Coordinating Committee of Education Workers (CNTE), created in 1979 within the National Education Workers Union (SNTE)—Latin America's largest union. The CNTE led one of the few successful efforts to hold a national leader of an official union accountable to union members.[151] In 1989 it organized a national strike that convinced Salinas to remove the SNTE's corrupt and violent leader, Carlos Jonguitud.

Another kind of union in Mexico is the *sindicato blanco* (white union). Such unions are unions in name only, the fictional creations of managers, lawyers, and corrupt union officials. Workers seldom know of the existence of white unions, much less who their union "representative" is. They find out quickly, however, if they try to organize their own union. When workers file a request for a union election, the existing white union blocks the action, arguing that it already holds the collective bargaining contract for that work site. With probusiness state and federal labor bureaucracies and court systems, the task of decertifying the white union to pave the way for genuine representation can take many years and is often impossible.

White unions are very common among the *maquiladoras*. A study by one expert on *maquila* labor issues indicates that they may represent roughly 15 percent of all *maquila* workers, about the same number as are represented by official unions.[152] White unions also permeate the non-*maquila* sectors of Mexico's economy. According to one estimate, white unions account for fully two-thirds of all unionized workers in the state of Nuevo León, which includes the industrial powerhouse of Monterrey.[153] In the wake of the 1985 Mexico City earthquake, workers digging through the rubble of their former work sites found documents confirming that the practice was widespread there also.

## A Tight Grip on Mexican Labor

Mexico's state and labor relationship is a very effective system of social control, a fact that works against transboundary organizing and U.S.-Mexican labor solidarity. The foundation of this system is the government's authority to disapprove union applications for legal recognition, to declare strikes illegal, and to resolve intraunion disputes, including overseeing union elections. When two unions compete to represent one workplace, the government can tilt the balance toward the union it favors.

In some cases the government has encouraged cooperative unions to challenge more assertive ones to force the existing union to change its strategy or to replace the union altogether.[154] Where dissident unionists challenge docile leaders, the state can stack the deck heavily in favor of the leaders.

The government prefers not to intervene in labor disputes too often. It therefore allows union bosses to maintain nearly authoritarian control over their organizations—as long as they continue to support the PRI and the government's policies. The "elected" leaders of union locals have nearly unlimited power to revoke the union memberships of individual workers. This is a powerful lever of control over local dissidents since an employer is usually required to fire any worker who loses his or her union membership. (Corporate managers often find it easier to pay off a corrupt union head to revoke the membership of a troublemaking worker than to fire the worker directly.) Unless the government desires to "get" a given union by scrutinizing its practices, anything goes in elections for local union leaders, including voting by nonmembers, explicit threats that a wrong vote will cost a worker his or her job, the requirement that workers sign their ballots, and violence committed by hired thugs.

The state-dominated labor system benefits corporations at the expense of workers. It also encourages the kind of worker repression that NAFTA opponents fear will increase under the free trade accord. But those who profit from the system express few concerns about issues like these. Nicholas Scheele, for example, director of the Ford Motor Company's Mexican operations, commended the Mexican labor system. "It's very easy to look at this in simplistic terms and say this is wrong," he said, referring to official union corruption. "But is there any other country in the world where the working class . . . took a hit in their purchasing power of in excess of 50 percent over an eight-year period and you didn't have social revolution?"[155]

Scheele participated in one of the most flagrant and best-known abuses of worker rights in recent decades. The case so clearly exemplifies the way the Mexican system can undermine labor and international solidarity that it is worth a close look. In 1987 Ford decided that the wages it was paying at its plant in Cuautitlán, just north of Mexico City, were too high. With the acquiescence of both the government and the CTM—with which the Ford workers' union was affiliated—Ford "closed" the facility for several months and paid the legally required severance pay to its workers. When it "reopened," it hired back most of the previous employees, but at half their former wages. The employees lost all seniority, benefits were cut drastically, and work rules were revamped to give management much greater flexibility.

Angered at the betrayal by their union, dissidents won control of the Cuautitlán local and threatened the union's national leadership. The company soon fired the local's executive committee, however, sparking months of protests and occasional work stoppages. In January 1990 thugs hired by the union hierarchy fired on workers, wounding nine and killing one.

To end a subsequent series of strikes, Ford announced it was firing twenty-three hundred employees. Federal Secretary of Labor Arsenio Farrell stepped in to "mediate" and called a meeting with Scheele and representatives of both the CTM and the local dissidents. Scheele reportedly informed the dissidents that they would agree to Ford's terms or be fired. When Farrell refused to object to this violation of the workers' rights, they signed on.

In an unusual combination of Supreme Court and Labor Board victories, the dissidents succeeded in forcing an election to change union affiliation. The election was marred by blatant fraud and high-pressure threats from the CTM leadership.[156] In a subsequent strike settlement, Ford agreed not to fire the workers who voted against the CTM, but only after each signed a statement of repentance, reaffirming loyalty to the CTM.

Demonstrating the potential power of international coalitions, Ford also demanded that the Ford Democratic Workers Movement, which had spearheaded the dissident movement, put a stop to its successful efforts to gain international publicity and to build ties with U.S. and Canadian Ford workers. The government seconded this condition, noting during the negotiations that "this conflict has hurt the government's image outside the country."[157] The workers agreed not to request a sympathy strike or a boycott but maintained the contacts they had developed.

Tactics such as these are an important component of government efforts to attract foreign investment by keeping wages low and worker activism under control. The government's privatization efforts have also slashed union ranks. In numerous cases the government has declared a state-owned enterprise "bankrupt," allowing it to cancel its union contract and increasing its attractiveness to private investors. The company opens up again after it has been sold off, but either without a union or with a much more favorable union contract.

As a result of political repression and the country's economic ills, Mexican labor organizations are in crisis. In the early 1990s between 16 and 20 percent of the workforce was unionized, far below the level of the 1960s. Pressure from above to enforce wage cuts and to stifle militancy and union leaders' obedience to government and corporate demands have eroded much of what credibility these leaders enjoyed in the eyes of their members. Labor's political role within the PRI has been considerably reduced as well, leaving it little to show for its loyalty.

## Flaws in the International Strategies of U.S. Labor

The Mexican labor system is not the only impediment to effective organizing for a trade agreement that protects U.S. and Mexican workers. The overseas activities of organized U.S. labor have often worked against international solidarity and union militancy. From the end of World War II to the mid-1960s most U.S. unions, led by the AFL and, after 1955 the AFL-CIO,[158] strongly supported U.S. efforts to build an open trading system with minimal government obstacles. Labor backed the U.S. government's proposal for GATT, intended to lower tariffs and limit other trade restrictions progressively. Labor continued to support tariff reductions through the Kennedy Round of trade negotiations in the early 1960s.

The pro–free trade strategy was based on the belief of labor leaders that expanding trade opportunities meant more and better jobs for U.S. workers. The country's vast lead in technology and infrastructure allowed U.S. firms to export advanced products embodying high-wage labor in exchange for cheap, entry-level goods. At the time the imports posed little challenge to a relatively privileged U.S. workforce. Given the utter dominance of U.S. industry after the war, the biggest obstacle facing exporters in this country was preventing the recovering European economies from returning to pre–World War II protectionist policies or joining the Communist bloc.

The AFL-CIO and most individual U.S. unions accepted the corporate agenda, calculating that the international expansion of their U.S. employers best served their own interests. The U.S. labor federation actively encouraged the development of procapitalist unions in Europe and across the third world, receiving millions of dollars—covertly and overtly—from the U.S. government in exchange.[159] This gave organized labor the appearance of a split personality. As unions duked it out with businesses at home over labor law, workplace rules, and contract provisions, the AFL-CIO helped undermine some of the most independent and militant foreign labor unions because of concerns over communism.[160]

The AFL-CIO's tactics in pushing open markets and U.S. corporate expansion are understandable in economic terms, but they were strategically shortsighted. For two decades an expanding near-full-employment economy allowed U.S. workers to share in the gains from increasing productivity. But in the mid-1960s the first flaws in labor's strategy became evident. Foreign governments may have gone along with the U.S. vision of open trade, but they would not continue to accept second-class positions as exporters of low-end goods in exchange for expensive U.S. products. Barred by GATT from raising tariffs to protect domestic firms, Western Europe and Japan turned to what proved to be a more effective strategy: direct government support for strategic industries such as steel, electronics, chemicals, and aerospace. A relatively open U.S. market meant that European and Japanese exporters competed directly with U.S. producers.

Another flaw in labor's strategy was the belief that the large corporations that gave the United States its lead in technology and investment capital would continue to behave like national firms rather than transnationals. But U.S. corporations rapidly increased their overseas investments, first displacing U.S. exports to regional markets, then displacing U.S. production for the domestic market. With evidence building that foreign workers could manufacture goods as well as their U.S. counterparts, corporate threats to shift production overseas gained credibility. This threw unions on the defensive, as they battled downward pressure on wages and benefits stemming from a labor market that increasingly included low-wage workers around the world in competition for U.S. jobs.

Ironically, the AFL-CIO's foreign policy fed the process of runaway jobs and downward wage pressure by undermining independent labor movements abroad, many of which opposed U.S. economic imperialism. By supporting the expansionist, probusiness foreign policy of the U.S. government rather than building international labor institutions that could take on multinational corporations, the AFL-CIO helped lay the foundation for labor's helplessness in the face of the globalization of production.

## U.S.-Mexican Labor Relations

In Mexico, as elsewhere, the AFL's promotion of "business unionism"[161] and its support for conservative workers' movements predate World War II. Samuel Gompers, the federation's flamboyant leader, supported the overthrow of Porfirio Díaz in Mexico, but he also sought to prevent Mexico's revolution from challenging corporate power. In 1915 Gompers pushed successfully for U.S. recognition of the most conservative of the revolutionary leaders, Venustiano Carranza. He also convinced President Wilson covertly to fund the Pan-American Federation of Labor in 1918 by presenting it as an instrument for enforcing the Monroe Doctrine. Gompers immediately turned the new Latin American federation into an arm of the AFL.[162] In the early 1920s Washington worried that Mexico's new president, Álvaro Obregón, might challenge foreign investors' property rights. Gompers conveyed this concern to Obregón and obtained his commitment to refrain from placing new restrictions on existing foreign-owned corporations. With this in hand, Gompers campaigned successfully for recognition of the Obregón government.

Following Gompers, successive AFL leaders continued to use Latin American labor organizations to extend U.S. influence. The Interamerican Confederation of Workers, founded in 1948, and its more successful offspring, the Interamerican Regional Organization of Workers (known by its Spanish acronym, ORIT), founded in 1951, were clearly within this tradition. The AFL, working with a consultant paid by the U.S. State Department, established ORIT as a counterweight to the Confederation of Latin American Workers and other nationalist Latin American organizations.[163] After the United States had blackballed Argentina's labor federation from joining ORIT, the head of the Confederation of Mexican Workers (CTM), Fidel Velázquez, withdrew his organization. ORIT "has no Latin American head or feet," Velázquez said. "It is merely the instrument of the United States State Department, to be manipulated by the big three United States labor organizations and their Cuban satellites."[164]

Pressure from the Mexican government forced Velázquez to rejoin ORIT in 1952, but his perception of U.S. dominance remained accurate, and the organization continued to function as an anti-Communist mouthpiece, especially after the Cuban Revolution in 1959.[165] Over time these objections seemed to matter less to Velázquez, however. By 1955 he felt "an affinity of ideals and a community of interests" between the CTM and the AFL-CIO. But the CTM was still unwilling to throw its full support behind ORIT's anti-Communist line, noting that U.S.-backed dictators in the region posed more of a threat to labor than did Moscow.

The CTM began to move to the right in the late 1950s, after leftists in the federation had mounted a strong challenge to Velázquez. The government stepped in to crush the dissident movement, arresting several hundred people. Coming on the heels of the Cuban Revolution, in which leftist forces threw out the leaders of the Confederation of Cuban Workers, the revolt prodded Velázquez and the CTM to move more fully in line with ORIT's ideology. In the following decades the CTM played an increasingly central role in ORIT and maintained closer relations with the AFL-CIO.

Organized U.S. labor's domineering attitude toward Latin American labor organizations and Mexican unions inspired distrust and worked against cooperative relations, especially among more independent factions of the Mexican labor movement. Mexican workers and union leaders also resented the racism they saw in the U.S. labor movement. Between the world wars some U.S. labor leaders organized anti-Mexican drives that were carried out by public officials and even vigilante groups. These drives involved the Ku Klux Klan–style intimidation of immigrants and the illegal deportation of tens of thousands of Mexicans. For much of the century many U.S. unions or union locals refused to admit Mexicans or Mexican Americans as members. And the AFL-CIO and others have frequently blamed Mexican immigrants—and, more recently, workers in the Mexican *maquiladora* industry—for causing unemployment in the United States.[166]

Nor did the U.S. federation's position on Mexican-U.S. immigration issues enhance cross-border goodwill. In 1925 the AFL met with the Regional Confederation of Mexican Workers (CROM), then enjoying a position of influence with Mexico's government, to discuss immigration. Where the CROM spoke of international solidarity and suggested international union cards and cross-border organizing efforts, the AFL focused on convincing Mexico to restrict emigration to the United States. In a compromise both parties promised to explore all ideas, but neither side followed through.[167]

In the 1950s the AFL-CIO and its Mexican counterpart were again at odds over immigration. The AFL-CIO pushed for immigration controls, for sanctions against employers of undocumented workers, and eventually for repeal of the bracero temporary farm labor program.[168] The CTM (which had taken over CROM's role as the main government-supported labor organization in Mexico) suggested that it organize all braceros before they were hired by U.S. growers and that U.S. farm labor unions accept the CTM card. This idea met with no more success than it had in the 1920s. The AFL-CIO continued to stress immigration reduction over the protection of immigrants' labor rights and was unable to force its affiliates to accept a Mexican union card.[169]

As late as 1986 mainstream labor organizations in the United States were rejecting calls to address undocumented immigration through increased organizing efforts among immigrants, cross-border union cooperation, and redoubled efforts to enforce labor rights. Instead the AFL-CIO and most large unions backed the 1986 Immigration Reform and Control Act (IRCA), which imposed sanctions on businesses that knowingly employed undocumented workers. Employer sanctions had been vigorously opposed by immigrant rights and Latino activists, who argued that the law's requirement of legal documentation would give employers yet another tool for controlling their undocumented workers. These activists pointed out that undocumented workers who made trouble or refused to accept employer abuses could be weeded out by selective scrutiny of their documents, while the phony papers of cooperative workers would be accepted with a wink. A few progressive unions such as the United Electrical Workers (UEW) opposed sanctions, but labor's overall support for IRCA irritated Mexican union leaders.

For decades AFL-CIO policies fueled alienation and suspicion among Mexican unionists, especially among the independent factions that would be needed as allies in the fight against the ill effects of globalization. But in the late 1980s, especially after the free trade proposal, the federation began to pay for its neglect. The AFL-CIO's central role in organizing and funding the Coalition for Justice in the Maquiladoras made some Mexican organizations wary of the coalition's purposes. In at least one case a U.S. group turned down the coalition's invitation to join for fear of damaging its working relations with Mexican counterparts. And U.S. labor's new efforts to work with Mexican unions are provoking responses like that quoted earlier: "Where have you been for the past forty years, when many times we were in need of you?"

## By Fits and Starts

The first signs of changing attitudes and strategies within the labor movement appeared at the grassroots level. In the late 1970s a number of union locals and district offices of the AFL-CIO scrapped efforts to prevent immigrants from entering the United States, focusing instead on organizing new workers and improving the observance of their labor rights. Not surprisingly the first to do so were mostly in the Southwest. In California's Los Angeles and Orange counties the AFL-CIO launched an organizing drive in 1977 targeted at undocumented workers and followed this several years later with a similar drive in El Paso. Numerous Los Angeles union locals followed suit, signing up undocumented workers and helping defend them against deportation when necessary. These efforts blossomed after the 1986 passage of IRCA, with a number of local or regional union offices supporting and participating in community-based efforts to help immigrants apply for the law's amnesty provisions.[170]

In a context of increasing economic integration the theoretical jump from organizing immigrant Mexican workers and improving their working conditions here to working with Mexican unions toward the same ends in Mexico is a small one. In both cases empowering workers with the lowest wages and the worst working conditions is not only morally commendable but also helps protect the standards of better-off workers. However, the practical jump from working with Mexicans in the United States to seeking cross-border partners, developing joint strategies, and devoting limited resources to international solidarity is daunting. For the most part organized labor failed to recognize the growing interdependence of the United States and Mexico or failed to respond to the process. As a result, cross-border work remained limited to isolated efforts by relatively small unions (or by a few individuals within larger unions) until the late 1980s.

Farm labor unions, many of whose members are Mexican immigrants, led the way in transboundary work with Mexican organizations. Beginning in 1979, the Arizona Farm Workers union won clauses in many of its labor contracts requiring employers to contribute ten (and later twenty) cents per worker-hour to a development fund. The fund paid for agricultural and community projects in the workers' hometowns in Mexico.

In 1987 the Ohio-based Farm Labor Organizing Committee (FLOC) sought help from the National Union of Farm Workers (SNTOAC) in Mexico. A year earlier, during FLOC's negotiations with Campbell Soup, the company threatened to move tomato paste production to Mexico, where it already operated a cannery. Backed by a national boycott of Campbell's products, FLOC overcame this threat and won a unique three-way agreement among the union, Campbell, and family farmers who grew crops under contract with Campbell.

Anticipating Campbell's use of Mexico as a bargaining tool in future negotiations, FLOC leader Baldemar Velasquez asked the AFL-CIO to arrange a meeting with Fidel Velázquez of the CTM. The CTM chief in turn introduced Velasquez to SNTOAC leader Diego Aguilar, who represents workers at Campbell's tomato paste factory in Sinaloa. The two unions reached an agreement, and Velasquez returned to Mexico the next year to watch the harvest and visit Campbell's operations.

FLOC and SNTOAC launched the U.S.-Mexico Exchange Program at that time. They have continued to exchange information and develop bargaining strategies to work for "wage vs. living cost parity," full employment, protection of "guest workers" in the United States, and the development of "strong and democratic" unions in both countries. In 1989 FLOC's solidarity and the mobilization of its support network helped SNTOAC win a wage increase some 15 percent higher than the government's legal cap for that year. In FLOC's own negotiations with Campbell that same year, "not once did we hear any mention of Mexico," according to Velasquez.

Until 1990 none of the industrial unions came close to forging similarly close ties with Mexican counterparts. This failure occurred despite the fact that U.S. corporations frequently threatened to ship work to Mexico during contract negotiations and despite the ties that the AFL-CIO has maintained with the CTM. Until recently, for instance, the AFL-CIO posted a full-time staff person to CTM headquarters in Mexico City. The AFL-CIO also provides training in the United States for up to twenty CTM staff members each year, in a program funded by the U.S. Agency for International Development.

But the U.S. labor federation has been unable to parlay its relationship with the CTM into an effective organizing drive among export-oriented assembly plants, the part of the Mexican economy of greatest importance to U.S. workers. CTM officials have repeatedly promised to make organizing these plants—especially the *maquiladoras*—a priority and just as repeatedly have committed themselves to encouraging the growth of the industry by ensuring labor peace. In 1966, the year Mexico's Border Industrialization Program took effect, Velázquez pledged that "the CTM would not pressure without cause the industrialists who come to [the border]. . . . On the contrary, in every occasion, it would support those investments, avoiding unjustified labor-management conflicts."[171]

Velázquez and most of his regional deputies appear to have upheld this pledge. In the mid-1970s the official unions collaborated with the government and *maquila* employers to crush a series of strikes and the independent labor groups that organized them. In 1983 Velázquez himself intervened to break a strike at Zenith's Reynosa plant—then the largest *maquiladora* in the country—twice nullifying elections for local CTM officials and cooperating with Zenith's forced resignation of ten local activists.[172] In 1989, after the CTM had won an interunion battle for representation at a number of plants in Reynosa, Velázquez reportedly promised visiting U.S. members of Congress that there would be no further labor problems.[173]

There is not necessarily a contradiction between Velázquez's commitments to organize the *maquiladoras* and to promote the industry. The *maquiladora* program competes directly with low-wage export-processing zones around the globe, and one of the principal arenas of competition is the stability of the workforce. Attracting investors means controlling worker activism, and the most direct way the CTM and other official unions can do that is to organize workers under their own banners. Accounts abound of the efficiency with which official unions perform this function. The Jalisco Maquila Association, for example, has advised new members to accept the CTM, "especially since unions in Guadalajara tend to facilitate rather than impede internal plant relations."

The founder of Mexico's first industrial park, located in Ciudad Juárez, had nothing but praise for the city's labor chief in 1981: "Luis Vidal has always been understanding. He has been a big help to us, and I think it's been to our advantage to have a labor leader like Vidal—very, very advantageous."[174] The general manager of an assembly plant in Reynosa was even more explicit: "We had some labor problems, so along with a dozen other plants we went to Mexico City to make a special arrangement with the CTM. It was time-consuming and expensive, but we arranged to have a special union leader that our companies can deal with. . . . If you have any disruptions in the plant, they are very helpful with that, too."[175]

The CTM's reluctance to stray from government economic policy and its repression of independent labor activists who might take a more militant stand have not persuaded the AFL-CIO to support other unions or independent organizing efforts. Until recently the federation failed even to expand its contacts outside official union circles. The reason most frequently cited for this commitment to the CTM is the weakness of the independent union movements; it makes more sense, in this view, to work with an imperfect partner that can get something done than with a partner that agrees on all the issues but is powerless. But the AFL-CIO's overseas history suggests that another reason for its past failure to support democratic union movements in Mexico may be its interest in political stability, which includes preventing the emergence of leftist labor movements. Yet another likely reason is that established unions and labor federations in all countries are reluctant to deal with dissident movements abroad for fear of setting a precedent. As one academic observer of international labor relations noted, many union leaders believe that "as soon as you start dealing with nonofficial labor unions in other countries, you open it up to their dealing with nonofficial bodies in this country."[176]

Like the federation itself, most AFL-CIO affiliates either worked with the CTM or had little involvement with Mexican unions until the late

1980s. In some cases U.S. union leaders even rejected the approaches of independent Mexican labor groups. The September 19 National Garment Workers Union—named for the date of Mexico City's devastating 1985 earthquake—provides a case in point. Seeking international support for its fledgling organizing effort among the seamstresses of Mexico City's sweatshops, September 19 union representatives traveled to New York and then across the country to Los Angeles, visiting the headquarters and a number of locals of the two largest U.S. garment workers' unions. The Mexicans were largely ignored by the hierarchy of the International Ladies Garment Workers Union (ILGWU) and the Amalgamated Clothing and Textile Workers Union (ACTWU). What is more, both headquarters sent instructions to their locals "warning them not to receive the visitors since they weren't part of the CTM," according to a U.S. labor activist working with the visiting group. This attitude was especially surprising in the case of ACTWU, which was an outspoken opponent of the AFL-CIO's policies in Central America at the time.

"The [U.S.] unions were uninterested" in the visit, according to a former ACTWU staff member. "Mexico just didn't exist in the minds of the trade union hierarchy at the time. All they talked about was the Caribbean Basin Initiative."[177] But the farther the Mexican workers got from New York, the more receptive U.S. unionists were. In Los Angeles local leaders organized a Labor Solidarity Network to support the new union's efforts. They were forced to do so informally, however, without official union backing.

NAFTA ended labor's inaction. A number of union officials recognized that political activity within the United States was only half the response that NAFTA required. The anti-NAFTA coalitions of labor, environmental, consumer, and other groups represented exciting new possibilities, but as the political director of the United Electrical Workers said, "much of the work in those coalitions is ultimately legislative. We don't think that's enough. . . . In the last ten years, [the UE] has lost 10,000 jobs to Mexico alone. The answer that too often gets ignored by the labor movement is solidarity across borders."[178]

## Forging Cross-Border Links

What ties workers in different countries together is not an abstract concept of worker solidarity, but the concrete phenomenon of the internationalization of capital. The internationalization of organized labor—in a variety of forms—has to be part of the solution. A new international outlook for U.S. labor would of course have to extend beyond this hemisphere.[179] But North America is the first testing ground, and whether optimism or pessimism is warranted will be determined by the evolution of nascent U.S.-Mexico-Canada labor ties. Activists see two paths that must be blazed: one that leads to coordinated bargaining strategies among employees of individual transnational corporations and another that leads to the adoption by all three countries of enforceable minimum labor standards.

Given the history of cross-border relations, however, both Mexican and U.S. unions have proceeded cautiously. In many cases a lack of knowledge about complex labor and political issues in each country hinders effective cross-border cooperation. Worker to worker exchanges, conferences, and other opportunities to meet and discuss problems and solutions are helping overcome these barriers and establish links between counterparts. Such exchanges play a crucial role in enhancing rank-and-file understanding of the process of globalization and add a human significance to calls for international solidarity.

Cross-border worker to worker exchanges have grown exponentially in number after a group called Mujer a Mujer (Woman to Woman) began sponsoring visits by Mexican unionists to the United States in 1985. Likewise, a small New York–based group called Mexico-U.S. Diálogos has sponsored a series of bi- and trinational exchanges that started in 1988. Bringing together North American counterparts from different social sectors, these events provide a forum for activists to share perspectives and explore goals and strategies.

Other U.S. unions have made contacts through efforts to link NAFTA opponents across North America.[180] At an October 1991 trinational anti-NAFTA meeting in Zacatecas, Mexico, for example, UE representatives met officials of the Authentic Labor Front. The two groups have since embarked on the most concrete example of labor solidarity to date, agreeing to cooperate in organizing *maquiladora* workers. The effort is focusing on runaway plants that started up in Mexico after shutting down UE-represented shops in the United States.

ACTWU has actively promoted worker to worker exchanges and has begun to share information about specific companies with several Mexican labor organizations, including some independent groups. "We're talking with anybody we can talk with" in Mexico, said ACTWU research director Ron Blackwell. In some cases the talking includes programmatic work, potentially involving joint campaigns targeting specific companies.

Several locals of the Service Employees International Union have traveled to Mexico to meet with counterparts. Representatives of Local 790 in San Francisco were impressed with opposition party leader Cuauhtémoc Cárdenas—an ally of FAT—and sent observers to monitor state-level elections in Michoacán in 1992.

In another example of nascent cross-border cooperation the Communications Workers of America (CWA) and the Communications and Electrical Workers of Canada signed a "strategic alliance" in early 1992 with the Mexican Telephone Workers Union—a modernizing union that strongly supported NAFTA.[181] The agreement is more of a confidence-building measure that could lead to greater future involvement than a specific commitment to joint action. The three signatories committed themselves to "the permanent exchange of trade union information" and, "when necessary and possible," to "support joint mobilization."[182]

As these examples show, once the networks of labor unions in each country have been established, coordinated bargaining strategies and joint actions become more feasible. There are many obstacles to building strong international worker alliances, however. These include the dependence of the workers on their companies for jobs and the reluctance of top labor leaders to push too hard against corporate management.

In the case of the Ford Democratic Workers Movement in Mexico, for instance, solidarity responses in Canada and the United States helped advance the cause of the Mexican dissidents at first but were cut short because of company pressure and foot-dragging by the union leadership. After the murder of a Mexican Ford worker in January 1990 several dissident Ford workers traveled to the United States and Canada, seeking support from the United Auto Workers (UAW) and the Canadian Auto Workers (CAW). The Canadians and a couple of UAW locals—in St. Paul, Minnesota, and Kansas City, Missouri—launched publicity campaigns and encouraged their members to write Ford's corporate headquarters and the Mexican government. Delegations of U.S. and Canadian auto workers traveled to Cuautitlán to meet with the dissidents and to pass out leaflets at the plant's gates. Officials of the St. Paul local publicly challenged several Ford executives, including the chief executive officer, Harold Poling, to explain the company's apparent violation of basic labor rights in Mexico. The activists caused enough trouble for Ford in the United States that the company demanded that Mexican unionists cut their ties to U.S. groups before they would receive their severance pay.

If the UAW as a whole had picked up on these members' efforts, activists argue, Ford would think twice before abusing its Mexican workers' rights again. But the UAW hierarchy has been reluctant to follow the activists' lead and has refrained from organizing a symbolic union-wide action, much less sponsoring trips to Mexico or providing financial support to the Ford Democratic Workers Movement. The dissident New Directions movement within the UAW has made pursuing closer ties with Mexican workers one of its campaign issues in trying to unseat established officials. According to a New Directions supporter, "the international union has stood in our way" in developing North American solidarity. "They want nothing to do with the connections we have made, with our efforts toward international solidarity. Their support for the 'become more competitive' concept puts them at cross-purposes with solidarity.

"We posed to the International the funding of the strike [in Cuautitlán] by collecting a dime a month from every U.S. Ford worker on a voluntary basis, to point up the disparity in wages and to point out the idea that ten cents a month can really accomplish something. They weren't interested. We said, 'Well, if we don't support people like this, then what's the long-term answer from the international union about protecting our work?' If you can't do this on a moral basis or a solidarity basis, then it would make sense in our own self-interest to do it."[183]

According to UAW international economist Steve Beckman, efforts such as these are ineffective. "In terms of fundamentally affecting the labor situation, they have a limited impact. In terms of educating people, it's fine. . . . But if it's presented as a solution to the problem, I disagree." Beckman also points to a very real difficulty. "The UAW doesn't want to tell other unions how to run their affairs," he noted.[184] When is the participation of U.S. unions in disputes such as that at Ford's Cuautitlán plant justified, and when does it merely constitute interventionism? The answer to this question must be based on the democratic structures of the unions involved since it is only through such structures that workers in each country can evaluate the interests of their cross-border counterparts.

Several observers noted that the politicization of the Mexican Ford Workers' struggle within the UAW contributed to the refusal of the union's leadership to become more involved with the Mexican dissidents. "There was a dire need for a unified message from the UAW, not an infight," said one. But support for the Mexican strikers "became a bitter issue that was used to stoke the fire between New Directions and Solidarity House [UAW's national office], rather than to force a statement of the International as a whole."[185]

In addition to building direct contacts and forging joint strategies with cross-border counterparts, a second international labor strategy involves the establishment of enforceable minimum labor standards. Enforcing existing laws is a first step in this process. In the United States this means using the provisions of the 1984 Trade and Tariff Act that require countries to meet internationally recognized minimum labor standards in order to gain duty-free access to the U.S. market for their goods.

In 1991 a group of U.S. activists filed a petition with the Office of the United States Trade Representative requesting that Mexican exports be denied eligibility for duty-free treatment, on the basis of violation of workers' rights at the Ford plant in Cuautitlán, among other items. The USTR rejected the petition out of hand, illegally failing to detail its reasons. "How do you overlook the fact that Mexican workers are routinely fired, beaten, disappeared, shot, and even killed for exercising their right to democratic trade unionism?" asked petitioner and Ford worker Tom Laney in a "reminder letter" to USTR Carla Hills. "The only reason for their rejection I can think of is that it would mess up their negotiations of NAFTA," he said.[186]

The trade office's rejection of the petition highlighted the difficulty of relying on individual nations to enforce international labor rights. The process as it is now structured is hostage to the political priorities of the executive branch. But labor rights activists argue that only by bringing cases, filing suits, and demonstrating the system's ineffectiveness will they be able to force the issue onto the national agenda. And only by working closely with labor organizations around the globe will activists be able to build trust, incorporate concerns, and create an international movement to include labor rights in international trade and investment agreements.

This is an area ripe for U.S.-Mexican labor cooperation. Such issues as occupational health and safety, the rights to bargain collectively and to strike without being fired, and the enforcement of child labor laws are issues on which both sides should be able to agree. The debate over NAFTA provides a platform for raising labor standards in policy circles, even if NAFTA itself appears unlikely to be modified. "We're meeting . . . with people from Mexico and Canada to discuss parallel talks, where we'll develop counterproposals to put before Congress," according to AC-TWU's Ron Blackwell.

Much trickier, however, and more important in the long run is the question of how to guarantee that workers are free to join the union of their choice and to elect their leaders democratically. Working toward these goals may well mean that U.S. labor will have to weaken or sever its ties with official Mexican unions. It almost certainly means providing moral and material support to independent unions in Mexico and applying strong political pressure in the United States.

But U.S. unions must also strengthen their own positions through grassroots organizing, democratize their own internal structures, and learn to think on a consistently global plane. "Corporations already make plans and build alliances as though national borders were not even there," notes Joe Fahey, president of Teamsters Local 912, which lost hundreds of jobs when its Green Giant plant ran away to cheaper pastures in Mexico. "Labor has a long way to go to catch up."[187]

# Notes

1. The description of this process comes from interviews with Shigemasa Ito and Gilberto Ibarra, executives of Hitachi Consumer Products de México, S.A. de C.V.
2. The "industrializing" south refers largely to middle-income countries, including most of Latin America. Few of the world's poorest nations will find that Mexico's strategy is relevant to them.
3. U.S. Department of Labor, *Economic Adjustment and Worker Dislocation in a Competitive Society: Report of the Secretary of Labor's Task Force on Economic Adjustment and Worker Dislocation* (Washington, D.C., December 1986) and U.S. Congress, Office of Technology Assessment, *Technology and Structural Unemployment: Reemploying Displaced Adults*, OTA-ITE-250 (Washington, D.C., February 1986). The Bureau of Labor Statistics defines "displaced" workers as those who permanently lost their jobs after at least three years in their positions.
4. Lisa Oppenheim, "Introduction," *Labor Research Review* 19 (Chicago: Midwest Center for Labor Research, 1992).
5. Comprehensive descriptions of the changing U.S. economy can be found in Donald Barlett and James Steele, *America: What Went Wrong?* (Kansas City, Mo.: Andrews and McMeel, 1992); Bennett Harrison and Barry Bluestone, *The Great U-Turn: Corporate Restructuring and the Polarizing of America* (New York: Basic Books, 1988); and Juliet Schor, *The Overworked American: The Unexpected Decline of Leisure* (New York: Basic Books, 1991). See also the Economic Policy Institute's voluminous collection of employment and wage data for the decade in Lawrence Mishel and Jared Bernstein, "Declining Wages for High School and College Graduates: Pay and Benefits Trends by Education, Gender, Occupation, and State, 1979–1991" (Washington, D.C.: Economic Policy Institute, 1992).
6. The accumulated value of foreign direct investment in the United States rose from $83 billion in 1980 to $403 billion in 1990 (measured in current dollars). Department of Commerce, *Survey of Current Business*, August 1991. See also Norman J. Glickman and Douglas P. Woodward, *The New Competitors: How Foreign Investors Are Changing the U.S. Economy* (New York: Basic Books, 1989).
7. Leading advocates of neoliberal policy during the 1980s were Treasury Secretary Donald Regan and Office of Management and Budget directors David Stockman and Richard Darman. An important think tank supporting continued efforts to

use GATT to open international trade is the Institute for International Economics in Washington, D.C. See, for example, William Cline, ed., *Trade Policy in the 1980s* (Washington, D.C.: Institute for International Economics, 1983).

8. One of the most visible proponents of the *Realeconomik* strategy is Clyde V. Prestowitz, a former U.S. trade negotiator. See his book *Trading Places: How We Allowed Japan to Take the Lead* (New York: Basic Books, 1988).

9. One prominent industrial policy advocate argues that it is not the competitive position of U.S.-*based* corporations that matters but rather the competitiveness of corporations *operating* in the United States, whether foreign- or domestic-owned. Even more important, he argues, are the specific functions that corporations decide to locate in the country—engineering or assembly, for example. See Robert Reich, *The Work of Nations: Preparing Ourselves for 21st-Century Capitalism* (New York: Alfred A. Knopf, 1991).

10. For a discussion of the addition of a regional strategy to the United States' traditional multilateral approach, see Sidney Weintraub, "Regionalism and the GATT: The North American Initiative," *SAIS Review* (Winter-Spring 1991). Note that in addition to the trade-related reasons discussed here, the Bush administration was motivated by a desire to support Salinas politically and to reward his economic reforms.

11. According to Treasury Secretary James Baker, the U.S.-Canada Free Trade Agreement "is also a lever to achieve more open trade. Other nations are forced to recognize that the United States will devise ways to expand trade—with or without them. If they choose not to open markets, they will not reap the benefits." *The International Economy* (January/February 1988), 41, cited in Peter Morici, *Trade Talks with Mexico: A Time for Realism* (Washington, D.C.: National Planning Association, 1991), 113.

12. Clinton detailed his position on trade policy in a speech at North Carolina State University on 4 October 1992. "Without a national economic strategy," he said, "this country has been allowed to drift. Meanwhile, our competitors have organized themselves around clear national goals to save, promote, and enhance high-wage, high-growth jobs. . . . We have to have an overall trade policy that says to our trading partners, particularly our wealthy ones, if you want access to our market, you've got to give us access to yours."

13. Two valuable studies of development in South Korea, Taiwan, and Singapore are Walden Bello and Stephanie Rosenfeld, *Dragons in Distress: Asia's Miracle Economies in Crisis* (San Francisco: Institute for Food and Development Policy, 1990), and Frederic C. Deyo, ed., *The Political Economy of the New Asian Industrialism* (Ithaca, N.Y.: Cornell University Press, 1987).

14. The failure of the Latin American NICs to turn investment into broad-based development was not due to a lack of foreign investment: Multinational corporations produced between 31 and 44 percent of these countries' industrial output, compared with 16 percent in Taiwan and 19 percent in South Korea. See Rhys Jenkins, "Learning from the Gang: Are There Lessons for Latin America from East Asia?," *Bulletin of Latin American Research* 10, no. 1 (1991).

15. An outstanding survey of dependency theory and an application of one version to Mexico is Gary Gereffi and Peter Evans, "Transnational Corporations, Dependent Development, and State Policy in the Semiperiphery: A Comparison

of Brazil and Mexico," *Latin American Research Review* 16, no. 3 (1981). For a review of dependency theory in the light of evidence that third world governments can promote development, see Peter Evans, "After Dependency: Recent Studies of Class, State, and Industrialization," *Latin American Research Review* 20, no. 2 (1985).

16. Although ISI was already under way in practice in the 1930s, its theoretical underpinnings developed in the immediate post–World War II period. Leading the work was Raúl Prébisch, the first head of the United Nations' Economic Commission for Latin America and the Caribbean. For an examination of how ISI worked in Mexico, see James Cypher, *State and Capital in Mexico: Development Policy Since 1940* (Boulder, Colo.: Westview Press, 1990).

17. Mexico's petroleum industry, the second-largest in the world after that of the United States, was almost entirely owned by seventeen British and U.S. firms. Agribusinesses in the United States owned millions of acres of rich land that they used to grow such export crops as cotton and sugar. One-quarter of Mexico's entire territory was in foreign hands by 1910. Foreign capitalists dominated the railroads, the mining industry, and the banking sector. The United States was the largest source of foreign investment, with almost 40 percent of the total. The role of foreign investment in Mexico during the *porfiriato* is described in Harry K. Wright, *Foreign Enterprise in Mexico: Laws and Policies* (Chapel Hill, N.C.: University of North Carolina Press, 1971); Roger D. Hansen, *The Politics of Mexican Development* (Baltimore: Johns Hopkins University Press, 1971); Mira Wilkins, *The Emergence of Multinational Enterprise: American Business Abroad from the Colonial Era to 1914* (Cambridge, Mass.: Harvard University Press, 1970); and Clark A. Reynolds, *The Mexican Economy: Twentieth-Century Structure and Growth* (New Haven, Conn.: Yale University Press, 1970).

18. By far the two most important oil companies were Standard Oil of New Jersey and Royal Dutch Shell, which together controlled more than 70 percent of total Mexican production in 1938. An exhaustive account of the oil expropriation is contained in Lorenzo Meyer, *Mexico and the United States in the Oil Controversy, 1917–1942* (Austin: University of Texas Press, 1977).

19. In nondurable consumer goods imports fell from 22 percent of total demand in 1939 to 5 percent in 1969; in intermediate goods the decline was from 56 to 22 percent over the same period, and in capital and durable consumer goods the figures were 91 percent for 1939 and 51 percent for 1969. René Villarreal, *El desequilibrio externo, en la industrialización de México (1929–1975)* (Mexico, D.F.: FCE, 1979).

20. The decision not to challenge the rules of the international financial system was consistent with Mexico's conservative financial policies from the 1940s on. See Sylvia Maxfield, *Governing Capital: International Finance and Mexican Politics* (Ithaca, N.Y.: Cornell University Press, 1990), and Judith A. Teichman, *Policymaking in Mexico: From Boom to Crisis* (Boulder, Colo.: Westview Press, 1988).

21. One analysis of Mexico's shift to the position of model debtor is found in George Grayson, *Oil and Mexican Foreign Policy* (Pittsburgh: University of Pittsburgh Press, 1988), 47–51.

22. David Barkin, from the introduction to the Japanese edition of *Distorted Development* (Albuquerque: Latin America Data Base, 12 and 19 August 1992).

23. Between 1984 and 1989 the proportion of national income received by the poorest tenth of Mexicans declined by 8.8 percent to roughly 1 percent of total national income. In the same period the wealthiest 10 percent increased its share of national income by 16 percent. Enrique Quintana, "Hombre Rico, Hombre Pobre," *El Financiero International*, 28 May 1992. In 1990 the government reported that forty-one million Mexicans fell below the poverty line, with seventeen million living in conditions of extreme poverty. Consejo Consultivo del Pronasol, "El combate a la pobreza: Lineamientos programáticos," cited in *La Jornada*, 1 September 1990.

24. Gustavo Lomelin, "Reprivatization of Mexican Banks: A 'Sweet Deal' Expected to Consolidate & Enhance Inequality" (Albuquerque: Latin America Data Base, 1 May 1991). See also William Schomberg and Ted Bardacke, "Doing Business with the Big Boys," *El Financiero International*, 19 October 1992, 14; Noe Cruz Serrano, "Privatization Enhances Monopoly & Oligopoly in Mexican Market" (Albuquerque: Latin America Data Base, 15 May 1991); and Noe Cruz Serrano, "Tan Sólo 5 Emporios Compraron 30 Paraestatales de 148 Vendidas," *El Financiero International*, 19 June 1990.

25. For a discussion of the varied extent to which Latin American governments are shifting economic decision-making power to the private sector, see "Latin America in the 1980s," *International Economic Insight* (November–December 1990).

26. *Economic and Social Progress in Latin America: 1992 Report*, Table B-2 (Washington D.C.: Inter-American Development Bank, 1992), and "Two Private Studies Say Government's Targeted Three Percent G.D.P. Growth Rate for 1993 Is Unrealistic," (Albuquerque, NM: Latin America Data Base, 10 February 1993). Several estimates made in mid-1993 estimated per capita GDP growth rates between –.1 percent and .4 percent.

27. Agency for International Development, *U.S. Overseas Loans and Grants and Assistance from International Organizations* (Washington, D.C.: Government Printing Office, n.d.) and the U.S. Council of the Mexico-U.S. Business Committee, "Report on Mexico: Recent Economic Developments" Second Quarterly Report, 19 June 1992. For a brief description of the cozy relationship between the World Bank and Mexican economic planners, see Damian Fraser, "Like Minds Underpin Mexico-Bank Intimacy," *Financial Times*, 3 March 1992.

28. American Chamber of Commerce in Mexico, "The Role of Development Banks in U.S.-Mexico Trade," *Review of Trade and Industry* (Second Quarter, 1992).

29. In 1983 total binational trade stood at $25.9 billion, it rose to an estimated $71 billion in 1992. *Total trade* means both U.S. exports to and imports from Mexico. These figures include the full value of *maquiladora* trade. M. Angeles Villarreal, "Mexico-U.S. Merchandise Trade," *CRS Report for Congress* (Washington, D.C.: Congressional Research Service, 26 August 1992). The most readily available and oft-cited data for FDI in Mexico is compiled by two agencies within Mexico's Ministry of Trade and Industrial Development (SECOFI). These data record not the actual investment amounts but the amount that a firm has requested permission to invest. These figures therefore probably overstate the actual levels of FDI since firms are likely to request amounts greater than that which they expect to invest, so as to avoid going through the investment approval process again in case of a cost overrun. In addition, investment financed through

domestic borrowing is counted by SECOFI as FDI, but it does not represent actual inflows of foreign exchange.

30. Data from Villarreal, "Mexico-U.S. Merchandise Trade." At $4.3 billion in 1991, oil represents over 15 percent of U.S. imports from Mexico. More than half of Mexico's petroleum exports go to the United States. In 1990 Mexico was the third most important supplier of oil to the U.S. market, behind Saudi Arabia and Nigeria. Mexico is the third-largest export market (after the Soviet Union and Japan) for U.S. agricultural commodities, and it is the second-largest supplier of U.S. agricultural imports. The leading U.S. agricultural exports to Mexico are corn, sorghum, soybeans, dairy products, seeds, and animal fats, while the United States imports tropical products and specialty crops, including coffee, vegetables, fruits and nuts, and cattle.

31. In 1990 Mexican direct foreign investment in the United States was $554 million out of nearly $404 billion in total direct foreign investment. U.S. Department of Commerce, *Survey of Current Business*, August 1991.

32. See Andrew James Samet and Gary Clyde Hufbauer, *"Unfair" Trade Practices: A Mexican-American Drama*, U.S.-Mexico Project Series Working Paper No. 1 (Washington, D.C.: Overseas Development Council, 1982) and Steven E. Sanderson, *The Transformation of Mexican Agriculture: International Structure and the Politics of Rural Change* (Princeton, N.J.: Princeton University Press, 1986), especially ch. 2.

33. *Mexico: Country Profile 1991–92* (London: Economist Intelligence Unit, 1992).

34. The top seven firms in terms of Mexican debt and capital offerings abroad were based in the United States, as were eight of the top ten. Rossana Fuentes Berain and Ignacio Rodríguez, "Brokers Prosper in Mexican Miracle," *El Financiero International*, 20 April 1992.

35. "Investment: Inflow Is Heading for a New Record," *Latin American Weekly Report* (1 August 1991).

36. The Mexican government considers foreign investment in the stock market foreign direct investment, but by most definitions "direct investment" and "portfolio investment" (meaning the purchase of stocks, bonds, and other securities) are distinct items. According to Mexican law, the stock shares owned by foreigners are nonvoting, meaning that they carry no managerial control but do represent a claim on assets and are entitled to the same dividends as Mexican-owned shares.

37. Foreign investment in the stock market dropped by 28.53 percent, from $27 billion on 31 May to $19.4 billion as of 24 July. Much of this is due to the declining value of their shares, but foreign investors withdrew $5.339 billion (U.S.) from the stock market between May and August in 1992, according to the central bank and the *Bolsa*. *SourceMex* (Albuquerque: Latin America Data Base, 6 August 1992 and 23 September 1992). Also see Matt Moffett, "Mexican Market Sees Foreigners Streaming Out," *The Wall Street Journal*, 18 June 1992, sec. C, p. 1, and "Pressure for Devaluation Builds," *The Mexico Report* (7 July 1992), 1. Analysts blamed the exodus on a number of factors, including presidential possible Ross Perot's statements opposing a free trade agreement. That such external politicking should be magnified so greatly on the Mexican market worried observers, prompting some to call for greater government regulation.

38. The world's five largest oil companies are: (1) Aramco, (2) Royal/Dutch Shell, (3) Exxon, (4) Pemex, and (5) Petróleos de Venezuela.

39. See Grayson, *Oil and Mexican Foreign Policy.*

40. Investment fell from a peak of $9.5 billion in 1981 to a low of $2 billion in 1989. *Mexican Oil: Issues Affecting Potential U.S. Trade and Investment* (Washington, D.C.: General Accounting Office, March 1992), 16.

41. "Mexico Is Easing Rules on Making Petrochemicals," *The Wall Street Journal,* 18 August 1992. The government maintains exclusive control of the production of ethanol, propane, butanes, pentanes, hexane, heptane, and raw materials used in processing selected oils and lubricants according to a *Notimex* news service report on 18 August 1992 (Albuquerque: Latin America Data Base).

42. A further regulatory change allowed up to 100 percent foreign ownership of secondary petrochemicals through the use of a trust fund held by a Mexican bank.

43. Mexico possesses reserves of eighteen strategic minerals, seventeen of which are considered "vital" by the U.S. Department of Defense. Virtually all strontium used in the United States comes from Mexico, as well as half the graphite and more than two-fifths of the fluorspar. Mexican mines and mills also supply significant proportions of the U.S. demand for silver, zinc, and lead.

44. Allen Born, "Mining in the 21st Century: What Will It Mean for Mexico?," speech delivered before the XVIIIth National Mining Convention, Acapulco, Mexico, 18–21 October 1989, reprinted in *Vital Speeches of the Day,* 246–49.

45. Gary Dillard, editor of *Paydirt,* cited in Dick Kamp, "Mexico's Mines: Source of Wealth or Woe?," *Business Mexico* 3, no. 1 (Special Edition, 1993).

46. SECOFI, "La inversión extranjera directa en el primer trimestre," *Comercio Exterior* 42, no. 6 (June 1992), 542.

47. These agricultural trade data come largely from "Agricultural Trade—Big Business for U.S. & Mexico," *Agricultural Outlook* (March 1992) and "U.S.-Mexico Agricultural Trade Under a NAFTA," *Agricultural Outlook* (June 1992). The figure for broccoli is from Western Growers Association, "The Effects on the U.S. Agricultural Sector of a Free Trade Agreement with Mexico," testimony submitted to the U.S. House Committee on Agriculture. "Proposed United States–Mexico Free-Trade Agreement and Fast-Track Authority," hearing before the U.S. House of Representatives Committee on Agriculture, 102nd Cong., 1st Sess., 24 April 1991, 323.

48. SECOFI, "La inversión extranjera."

49. Rosa Elena Montes de Oca, "Las empresas trasnacionales en la industria alimentaria mexicana," in *Transnacionales, agricultura y alimentación,* ed. Rodolfo Echeverría Zuno (Mexico, D.F.: Colegio Nacional de Economistas and Editorial Nueva Imagen, 1982).

50. Although the huge food processors and distributors now in Mexico are unlikely to expand their land holdings dramatically, the radical changes in Mexico's agrarian laws are very likely to lead to a concentration of land ownership in the hands of large-scale growers and ranchers, both domestic and foreign.

51. The illegality of the rental contracts is sidestepped by the use of Mexican front men *(prestanombres)* and flexible legal interpretations by a government that wishes to encourage foreign efforts to increase Mexican agricultural productivity.

See Jean Etiene Dasso and Tomás Bustamante Álvarez, "Capital extranjero e industrialización de la agricultura mexicana: el caso de las multinacionales meloneras en el valle del Río Balsas (estado de Guerrero)," *Cuadernos Agrarios*, no. 2 (1991), 71–78.

52. Ibid. and Martha Stamatis M., "Hortalizas para U.S.A.," *Ciudades* 5 (January–March 1990), 19–25. In addition to the sources cited in the notes to this subsection, the information and analysis presented owe much to Steven Sanderson's thorough treatment of the issues in *The Transformation of Mexican Agriculture*.

53. Sanderson, *The Transformation of Mexican Agriculture*, 85, and testimony of Héctor Miguel González, president of the Confederation of Fruit and Vegetable Growers Association in Mexico, in a hearing before the U.S. House of Representatives Subcommittee on Domestic Marketing, Consumer Relations, and Nutrition, "Changing Structure of the U.S. Fruit and Vegetable Industry," 100th Cong., 2nd Sess., 10 May 1988, 111.

54. Philip L. Martin, "U.S. Agribusiness under NAFTA: Mexico-Sourcing or Direct Investment?," *Enfoque* 1, no. 1 (San Diego: Center for U.S.-Mexican Studies, Fall 1992).

55. According to Laura Carlsen in "Reaping Winter's Harvest," *Business Mexico* (May 1991), "There is a general consensus among researchers and industry alike that vegetable yields per acre in Mexico and California are now nearly equal." Data submitted by the Mexican National Union of Vegetable and Fruit Producers to the U.S. House Committee on Agriculture indicate that Sinaloan yields of cucumbers and squash are higher than those in Florida. Florida's farms produce more tomatoes, bell peppers, and eggplant per acre than Sinaloa's, however. "Changing Structure of the U.S. Fruit and Vegetable Industry," loc cit., 373–85.

56. Linda Wilcox Young, "Economic Development and Employment: Agroindustrialization in Mexico's *El Bajío*," *Journal of Economic Issues* 22, no. 2 (June 1988). The study's results were based on data from 1960 and 1982–83.

57. Carlsen, "Reaping Winter's Harvest."

58. Amado Ramírez Leyva, Marcos Portillo Vásquez, and Cecilia Sánchez Solano, "Mexican Agriculture: The Potential for Export Production and Employment Generation in Rural Areas," Paper No. 49 (Washington, D.C.: Commission for the Study of International Migration and Cooperative Economic Development, July 1990); Martine Vanackere, "Conditions of Agricultural Day Laborers in Mexico," *International Labor Review* 127, no. 1 (1988), 91–110; and Sanderson, *The Transformation of Mexican Agriculture*, 80 and 82.

59. *U.S.-Mexico Trade: Extent to Which Mexican Horticultural Exports Complement U.S. Production* (Washington, D.C.: General Accounting Office, March 1991), 10. Products protected year-round by significant tariffs include onions (9.1 percent of value), bell peppers (14.1 percent), and green beans (9.4 percent).

60. General Accounting Office, *U.S.-Mexico Trade*.

61. David Barkin, "The New Shape of the Countryside: Agrarian Counter-reform in Mexico," carried on PeaceNet (San Francisco: Institute for Global Communications, 22 November 1992).

62. Ursula Oswald Spring, "El campesinado ante el Tratado de Libre Comercio," *Cuadernos Agrarios* 2, no. 4 (January–April 1992), 56.

63. From Raúl Salinas de Gortari, "El campo mexicano ante el reto de la modern-ización," *Comercio Exterior* 40, no. 9 (September 1990), 823; and ibid., 55. All of the decrease in per capita corn consumption occurred in the 1980s, when stagnant production and import controls cut the supply of corn almost in half.

64. David Barkin, *Distorted Development: Mexico in the World Economy* (Boulder, Colo.: Westview Press, 1990).

65. Although the law limits foreigners to a 49 percent share in landowning opera-tions, a company's landholdings may be divided from its other assets, and special "T" shares corresponding to the land may be issued. A foreign firm could therefore own virtually all of a domestic company's assets, as long as Mexicans owned 51 percent of the "T" shares. Gray Newman, "Mexico's New Agrarian Law Opens Fresh Frontier for Agribusiness Firms," *Business Latin America* (6 April 1992), 106–07.

66. Before the legal change, *ejidos* accounted for roughly 43 percent of Mexico's farmland and 60 percent of Mexican farmers, yet they produced only 10 percent of the country's agricultural output. Although they are generally poorly suited for agriculture, *ejidos* do include some potentially very productive areas. For decades capitalists and neoliberal economists considered the *ejidos* a significant impediment to modernization. In February 1992 that impediment was mostly eliminated. Individual *ejido* members may now sell their portions of *ejido* lands, and the *ejido* communities may now enter into long-term leasing contracts with individuals or corporations. But ten months after the legal change few *ejidatarios* had gained title to their plots of land.

67. Alva Senzek, "Industrializing Zempoalxochitl," *El Financiero International*, 20 April 1992, 12.

68. Gray Newman, "Mexico's New Agrarian Law"; Wesley R. Smith, "Salinas Pre-pares Mexican Agriculture for Free Trade," *Heritage Foundation Backgrounder*, no. 914 (1 October 1992); and Christine MacDonald, "Planting Privatization," *Business Mexico* 7, no. 3 (September 1990).

69. From a report on the program in *La Jornada*, 1 October 1992, 28, cited in Barkin, "The New Shape of the Countryside."

70. Golden, "The Dream of Land Dies Hard in Mexico."

71. Kurt Unger, "Mexican Manufactured Exports and U.S. Transnational Corpora-tions: Industrial Structuring Strategies, Intrafirm Trade and New Elements of Comparative Advantage," in *Unauthorized Migration: Addressing the Root Causes*, research addendum sponsored by the Commission for the Study of International Migration and Cooperative Economic Development, 1987–1990, vol. 2. To accompany the final report of the commission: *Unauthorized Migra-tion: An Economic Development Response.*

72. *Business America*, 18 June 1990; *Background Study of the Economies and Inter-national Trade Patterns of the Countries of North America, Central America, and the Caribbean* (Washington, D.C.: U.S. International Trade Commission, 1981), 163.

73. NAFTA intends to phase out 99 percent of all tariffs over ten years and eliminate remaining tariffs on politically sensitive products such as corn and beans over fifteen years.

74. Recent theoretical work on free market economies has spawned a growing school

of thought that argues that even on paper free market models do not necessarily produce optimal outcomes. This work focuses on the role of technological innovation as the driving force for economic growth. The new models have fundamental implications for free trade theory as well and imply that free trade and investment flows between countries with similar endowments of capital and skilled labor are likely to produce greater long-term economic growth than free trade between countries with different levels of those factors. This surprising result stems from the fundamental difference between the production of goods and services and the "production" of technological innovations. In the former case, each additional unit of production "uses up" some of the finite supply of labor and, on a macroeconomic scale, capital. In the latter case, reproduction of a given technology is essentially cost-free, implying great efficiency gains from its widespread application. Joining relatively advanced countries in free trade allows for wider dissemination of technological innovations and for specialization in research and development activities. See Gene Grossman and Elhanan Helpman, "Comparative Advantage and Long Run Growth," *American Economic Review* (September 1990), 796–815; Paul A. Krugman, *Rethinking International Trade* (Cambridge, Mass.: MIT Press, 1990); Luis A. Rivera-Batiz and Paul M. Romer, "Economic Integration and Endogenous Growth," *Quarterly Journal of Economics* 106, no. 2 (May 1991), 531–55; and Paul M. Romer, "Are Nonconvexities Important for Understanding Growth?," *American Economic Review* 80, no. 2 (May 1990), 97–103.

75. A calculation by William Spriggs of the Economic Policy Institute found that even if NAFTA added two percentage points to Mexico's growth rate—a very generous estimate—the increase in U.S. exports to that country would represent only one-sixth of 1 percent of the U.S. gross domestic product.

76. Industries that stood to suffer if Mexican competitors gained equal access to their U.S. customers included textiles, apparel, footwear, leather goods, steel, glass products, automobiles, and consumer electronics. Some agricultural products, especially citrus fruits and winter vegetables, were also threatened by the prospect of free trade. This list is taken from Peter Morici, *Trade Talks with Mexico*, 60–62.

77. The belief that economic development in Mexico will stem the flow of emigrants to the United States has attained the status of conventional wisdom in Washington. A number of migration experts have cast doubt on this analysis, arguing that per capita income growth actually spurs emigration among those who formerly did not have the resources to make the trek. Furthermore, tightening economic relations between the United States and Mexico both strengthens the social networks that facilitate migration and lowers the cultural barrier to migration by making the United States seem less foreign. See Scott, "Free Trade and Mexican Migrants"; Sassen, *The Mobility of Labor and Capital*; and Sassen, "Why Migration?"

78. Working step by step through bilateral and multilateral free trade agreements with eligible countries, the Enterprise for the Americas Initiative aims eventually to have the entire Western Hemisphere joined under the same economic regime. The EAI offers access to the U.S. market, financial and technical resources, and some help with debt reduction to countries that liberalize their trade and

investment policies, cut back government spending, and generally adhere to neoliberal economic prescriptions. President Bush announced the initiative in late June 1990, just weeks after announcing the planned free trade talks with Mexico. For more on the EAI, see Betsy A. Cody and Raymond J. Ahearn, *The Enterprise for the Americas Initiative: Issues for Congress* (Washington, D.C.: Congressional Research Service, 30 October 1992); Peter Hakim, "The Enterprise for the Americas Initiative: What Washington Wants," *Brookings Review* (Fall 1992); and "Enterprise for the Americas Initiative," interview with Xabier Gorostiaga, *Free or Fair Trade?*, no. 1 (Bogotá, July 1992).

79. The United States and Mexico agreed, but with the explicit understanding that if Canadian objections significantly slowed the process, the two countries would return to a bilateral arrangement. This stance effectively eliminated Canada's bargaining power.

80. Quoted in Bruce Campbell, "Beggar Thy Neighbor," *NACLA Report on the Americas* 24, no. 6 (May 1991), 23.

81. "U.S., Canada & Mexico Still Unable to Resolve Differences over Environment & Labor Accords for NAFTA," *SourceMex* (Albuquerque: Latin America Data Base, 4 August 1993).

82. Television news media, which reach twenty times more Mexicans than all print media combined, are rarely critical of the government. All but a handful of magazines and newspapers are heavily influenced in their coverage of important issues by direct government payoffs to reporters and editors and by their dependence on the government for roughly half their advertising budgets. For several recent accounts along these lines, see Marjorie Miller, "Mexico Press Is Still Far from Free," *Los Angeles Times*, 22 October 1991; David Clark Scott, "Mexico's Press Guards Its Freedom," *The Christian Science Monitor*, 26 September 1991; and Andres Oppenheimer, "Mexican Government Pays Media for Good Press," *Albuquerque Journal*, 2 August 1992. On presidential control of the PRI and the Congress, see Andrew Reding and Christopher Whalen, *Fragile Stability: Reform and Repression in Mexico under Carlos Salinas* (New York: World Policy Institute, 1992) and Wayne A. Cornelius, Judith Gentleman, and Peter H. Smith, eds., *Mexico's Alternative Political Futures* (San Diego: Center for U.S.-Mexican Studies, 1989).

83. Larry Rohter, "Free-Trade Talks with U.S. Set Off Debate in Mexico," *The New York Times*, 19 March 1990, sec. A, p. 1.

84. Although the European process of integration has a much stronger social component than does NAFTA, it is a model only in that it points the way to greater possibilities. Many advocates of broadening NAFTA and many European activists believe that the European Community's standards were watered down out of concern for the international competitiveness of the Continent's businesses. See Matthew Sanger, "Free Trade and Workers' Rights: The European Social Charter," *Briarpatch* 20, no. 7 (Saskatchewan, September 1991).

85. The council was abolished in the early days of the Clinton administration, indicating that the neoliberal principles of the two previous administrations were being modified by a government that understood the need to respond to a constituency larger than the corporate sector.

86. In the wake of the U.S.-Canada Free Trade Agreement, Canada agreed to lower

its pesticide standards to reach "equivalence" with U.S. regulations. See Steven Shrybman, "Trading Away the Environment," *World Policy Journal* (Winter 1991–92).

87. Soon after the U.S.-Canada FTA was approved, the Canadian Manufacturers Association, the Chamber of Commerce, and the powerful Business Council on National Issues called on the government to cut spending on unemployment insurance (UI). The conservative government was responsive to these demands, eliminating its two-billion-dollar annual contribution to UI from its April 1989 budget and making several other changes that brought Canada's UI system in line with lower U.S. standards. Ecumenical Coalition for Economic Justice, *Economic Justice Report* 2, no. 3 (October 1991), 12.

88. Quoted in Canadian Labor Congress, *Free Trade Briefing Document*, no. 7 (January 1991), 13.

89. See Shrybman, "Trading Away the Environment," and "Selling Canada's Environment Short: An Environmental Assessment of the First Two Years of Free Trade between Canada and the U.S." (Toronto: Canadian Environmental Law Association, 1991).

90. A free trade agreement could include a clause restricting trade with nations that failed to respect accepted standards to discourage firms from relocating outside North America to avoid regulations. There is a precedent for requiring countries to enforce minimum labor standards in order to export goods to the United States duty-free. The U.S. Trade Act of 1974 established a Generalized System of Preferences under which the president decides which developing countries will have duty-free access to the U.S. market, and for which products. In 1984 Congress prohibited the president from naming a country as a beneficiary "if such country has not taken or is not taking steps to afford internationally recognized worker rights to workers in the country." These measures include the right to organize and bargain collectively, standards for minimum working age, maximum hours of work, occupational safety and health, and an "acceptable" minimum wage.

91. The Bush administration, for instance, cited economic studies based on the theory of comparative advantage showing that NAFTA would produce more jobs than it would destroy—135,000 more, to be precise. Although this number represented one-ninth of 1 percent of the U.S. workforce, the new jobs would be in the export sector and therefore likely to pay above-average wages, officials said. Secretary of Labor Lynn Martin, citing a study by the Institute for International Economics, gave this number in response to congressional questioning. Administration officials used the figure in public presentations throughout 1992. See Gary Clyde Hufbauer and Jeffrey J. Schott, *North American Free Trade: Issues and Recommendations* (Washington, D.C.: Institute for International Economics, 1992).

92. Canadian Labour Congress, *Free Trade Briefing Document*, no. 7 (January 1991). Half the 250,000 jobs lost were directly attributed to free trade–induced closings or layoffs, and the other half to indirect losses in supplier industries and the service sector. The report notes that if job creation had remained at its average level of the previous five years, the Canadian economy would have gained 582,000 more jobs than it did. And the Ontario provincial government found

that more than 55 percent of all layoffs in 1989 were caused by plant closings, as opposed to 22 percent of layoffs in 1982.

93. Cited by Jeff Faux and Thea Lee, "The Effect of George Bush's NAFTA on American Workers: Ladder Up or Ladder Down?," Briefing Paper prepared for the Economic Policy Institute (Washington, D.C.: 1992). Manufacturing employment in Canada dropped by 1 percent from 1981 to 1988.

94. For a more optimistic view of Canada's prospects under free trade with the United States, see Peter Morici, "Making the Transition to Free Trade," *Current History* (December 1991). Morici argues that Canada's tight monetary policy, hard-nosed union negotiators, and overly progressive provincial governments have encouraged the exodus of manufacturing jobs.

95. See Dan La Botz, *Mask of Democracy: Labor Suppression in Mexico Today* (Boston: South End Press, 1992); Matt Moffett, "Underage Laborers Fill Mexican Factories, Stir U.S. Trade Debate," *The Wall Street Journal*, 8 April 1991; and the testimony of William Treanor, director of the American Youth Work Center in Washington, before the U.S. Senate Committee on Foreign Relations, Subcommittee on Western Hemisphere and Peace Corps Affairs, 102nd Cong., 1st Sess., 14 and 22 March and 11 April 1991, 123–28.

96. U.S. Secretary of Labor Lynn Martin and Mexican Secretary of Labor Arsenio Farrell signed a Memorandum of Understanding on 1 May 1991, and an Agreement on Labor Cooperation on 14 September 1992. The latter recognized "that the two governments have the sovereign right to apply their laws in accordance with their jurisdiction and competence," a recognition that was not extended in NAFTA to such questions as copyright law and farm policy.

97. George Anders, "Heading South: U.S. Companies Plan Major Moves into Mexico," *The Wall Street Journal*, 24 September 1992, sec. R, p. 1. The figures were more striking when only companies with sales over one billion dollars per year were included. Some 55 percent of the executives of these large corporations said they were likely to shift some production to Mexico in the coming years.

98. *The Likely Impact on the United States of a Free Trade Agreement with Mexico*, USITC Publication 2353 (Washington, D.C.: U.S. International Trade Commission, February 1991), 2–6.

99. Testimony of William E. Spriggs of the Economic Policy Institute, before a hearing of the U.S. House of Representatives Committee on Energy and Commerce, Subcommittee on Commerce, Consumer Protection, and Competitiveness, "Free Trade Agreement," 102nd Cong., 1st Sess., 20 March and 8 and 15 May 1991, 330–31. In the ITC's updated report it found that "unskilled workers" would enjoy a wage increase of 0.011 percent. See also Jeff Faux and Richard Rothstein, "Fast Track, Fast Shuffle," Briefing Paper prepared for the Economic Policy Institute (Washington, D.C., 1991).

100. Edward E. Leamer, "Wage Effects of a U.S.-Mexican Free Trade Agreement," paper presented at the Mexico-U.S. FTA Conference, Brown University, Figure 4, October 1991.

101. U.S. Department of Labor, *Economic Adjustment and Worker Dislocation* and U.S. Congress, Office of Technology Assessment, *Technology and Structural Unemployment: Reemploying Displaced Adults*, OTA-ITE-250 (Washington, D.C., February 1986). The Bureau of Labor Statistics data include only "dis-

placed" workers, defined as those who permanently lost their jobs after at least three years in the position. See also Michael Podgursky, "Estimated Losses due to Job Displacement: Evidence from the Displaced Worker Surveys" (Washington, D.C.: Economic Policy Institute, April 1991).

102. Thea Lee, "Happily Never NAFTA: There's No Such Thing as a Free Trade," *Dollars & Sense*, (January–February 1993). The Congressional Budget Office recently reviewed eleven of the most prominent academic studies of the trade pact's likely effect on the U.S. economy. Ten assumed NAFTA would have no effect on investment in the United States and one used trickle-down logic to conclude that investment here would actually increase, thanks to higher profits from moving operations to Mexico. "Estimating the Effects of NAFTA: An Assessment of the Economic Models and other Empirical Studies," *CBO Papers* (Washington, D.C.: Congressional Budget Office, June 1993).

103. Jeff Faux and William Spriggs, "U.S. Jobs and the Mexico Trade Proposal," Briefing Paper prepared for the Economic Policy Institute (Washington, D.C., 1991).

104. See Timothy Koechlin and Mehrene Larudee, "The High Cost of NAFTA," *Challenge* (September–October 1992).

105. Some studies proceed one step further, to attempt to include the possibility of changes in employment levels. They first estimate an increase in overall wage earnings, based on full employment, just as the first set of studies does. They then reason that some portion of the rise in wages paid is due to increased employment rather than just to changed wage rates. These studies are less honest than their cousins since they acknowledge the existence of unemployment but still use assumptions of full employment and perfect markets in the equations that form their models. See *Economy-wide Modeling of the Economic Implications of a FTA with Mexico and a NAFTA with Canada and Mexico*, USITC Publication 2508 (Washington, D.C.: U.S. International Trade Commission, May 1992).

106. Another set of studies focuses on the expected increase of exports from the United States to Mexico and uses the U.S. government's estimate that roughly twenty thousand jobs are created by every $1 billion in new exports. There are two problems with this approach. First, a large percentage—at least one-quarter—of U.S. exports to Mexico go to manufacturers whose production has replaced U.S. production. In this case exports create no new jobs in suppliers—since the same products previously were shipped to U.S. firms—and in fact indicate that jobs have been lost in the United States. The second problem stems from the fact that the trade-employment connection works both ways. If some exports create jobs, some imports must cost jobs. The studies that found employment increases caused by increased U.S. exports to Mexico often failed to explore how many jobs might be lost by dropping barriers to imports from Mexico.

107. See Louis Uchitelle, "America's Newest Industrial Belt," *The New York Times*, 21 March 1993, and Harley Shaiken and Stephen Herzenberg, *Automation and Global Production: Automobile Engine Production in Mexico, the United States, and Canada* (San Diego: Center for U.S.-Mexican Studies, 1987); and Harley Shaiken, *Myths About Mexican Workers*, Democratic Study Center Report Series (Washington, D.C., 29 June 1993).

108. Anders, "Heading South."
109. Leamer, "Wage Effects."
110. Quoted in Louis Uchitelle, "As Output Gains, Wages Lag," *The New York Times*, 4 June 1987.
111. In addition to new environment and trade issues being raised, trade negotiators are being forced to reconcile trade and environmental issues with respect to such international agreements as the Montreal Protocol on Substances That Deplete the Ozone Layer, the Basel Convention on the Control of the Transboundary Movement of Hazardous Wastes and Their Disposal (still awaiting the consent of the U.S. Senate), and the 1973 Convention on the International Trade in Endangered Species (CITES), which imposes strict trade controls on species that would otherwise become endangered and bans trade in species that are endangered.
112. See two excellent reports published by the Congressional Research Service: *Environment and Trade* (Washington, D.C., 15 November 1992) and *International Environmental Issues: Overview* (Washington, D.C., 27 July 1992). The Uruguay Round had not been concluded as of December 1993.
113. The convening of GATT's environmental committee was the direct result of a request by the European Free Trade Association (EFTA), reflecting rising concerns in Europe about the effect of free trade on national environmental and consumer law.
114. In the wake of unfavorable U.S. reaction, Mexico indicated that it was asking for a postponement of a final GATT ruling, but other tuna-exporting countries still pushed for a final judgment on this precedent-setting trade ruling.
115. In his 1 May 1991 "Action Plan" aimed at swaying environmental and, to a lesser extent, labor critics of the "fast-track" NAFTA negotiations, President Bush said that some environmental concerns would be treated within the agreement itself while also promising that labor and environmental issues would be addressed more thoroughly in initiatives that would run "in parallel with" the actual negotiations. The first examples of this parallel tract were the Integrated Border Environmental Plan and the Environmental Review of U.S.-Mexico Environmental Issues, both released in February 1992. Bush also included representatives of a few environmental organizations on the working groups that advised U.S. NAFTA negotiators but declined to create a working group specifically on the environment.
116. Reilly repeated this statement often. One instance was reported in Keith Schneider, "Trade Pact vs. Environment: Clash at a House Hearing," *The New York Times*, 16 September 1992, p. C1.
117. The Sierra Club and Public Citizen have argued that a zero tolerance regulation could be challenged under NAFTA because of the agreement's requirement that standards be consistent among the three countries.
118. Keith Schneider, "Environmentalists Fight Each Other Over Trade Accord," *The New York Times*, 16 September 1993.
119. See chapter twenty of NAFTA, "Institutional Arrangements and Dispute Settlement Procedures," especially Articles 2001, 2016, and 2017.
120. Lori Wallach, "The NAFTA Does Not Measure Up on the Environment and Consumer Health and Safety" (Washington, D.C.: Public Citizen, 1992).

121. Rather than rely on economic growth to create the needed revenues for environmental protection and enforcement, such national environmental organizations as the Sierra Club, the Natural Resources Defense Council, and the Environmental Defense Fund have proposed a variety of directed revenue-generating measures. Adhering to the "polluter should pay" principle, some propose that corporations investing in Mexico should turn over a percentage of their profits to an environmental protection fund or that a "green tax" be levied on cross-border trade. It has also been suggested that countries should collect pollution control bonds from industrialists and that countervailing duties should be imposed on goods manufactured by using environmentally destructive practices.

122. Robert B. Zoellick of the U.S. State Department, in testimony before the U.S. Senate Committee on Foreign Relations, "North American Free Trade Agreement: Extending Fast Track Negotiating Authority," 102nd Cong., 1st Sess., 11 April 1991. The Salinas administration apparently attempted to bolster this line of attack. A major daily newspaper in Mexico, *Excelsior*, ran a front-page story on 27 December 1992 reporting that a prestigious group of Mexican environmentalists had accused U.S. environmental groups of using "pseudoenvironmentalist arguments" and "tendentious propaganda" to "manipulate" public opinion in opposition to free trade. Had the story been true it would have represented a significant blow to U.S. groups, which count on the support of their Mexican counterparts to overcome right-wing accusations that environmental measures are merely disguised protectionism. The organization quoted by *Excelsior*, however, immediately denied having made any such accusations. Homero Aridjis, head of the environmentalist Group of 100, accused the Mexican government of planting the story in an effort to influence the upcoming meeting of Salinas and U.S. President-elect Clinton, at which NAFTA was topic number one. Ethel Riquelme, "Argumentos Seudoecologistas Manipulan en EU: Los 100," *Excelsior*, 27 December 1992, 1, and interview with Geoffrey Land, Border Ecology Project, 21 January 1993.

123. Francisco Lara, director of the Colegio de la Frontera Norte in Nogales, Sonora, quoted in Marc Levinson, "The Green Gangs," *Newsweek* (3 August 1992).

124. See John Cavanagh et al., *Trading Freedom: How Free Trade Affects Our Lives, Work, and Environment* (San Francisco: Institute for Food and Development Policy, 1992).

125. Testimony of Lori Wallach before the U.S. House of Representatives Committee on Foreign Affairs, Subcommittee on International Economic Policy and Trade and the Subcommittee on Western Hemisphere Affairs, 9 December 1991.

126. Inspired by concerns about NAFTA, coalitions of environmentalists, labor organizations, religious groups, and community activists in the United States and Mexico worked to draw the broad outlines of a propeople and proenvironment framework for economic integration. Organizations such as the Alliance for Responsible Trade, Citizen Trade Watch Campaign, Coalition for Justice in the Maquiladoras, Fair Trade Campaign, Action Canada Network, and Mexican Action Network on Free Trade were among the most active. Most of the following discussion about ways to shape integration draws on the very important work of groups like these and the publications of analysts and activists who share their concerns. See, for example, George E. Brown, Jr., J. William Goold, and

John Cavanagh, "Making Trade Fair," *World Policy Journal* (Spring 1992); Gregory, "Environment, Sustainable Development, Public Participation and the NAFTA"; Andrew A. Reding, "Bolstering Democracy in the Americas," *World Policy Journal* (Summer 1992); and Cuauhtémoc Cárdenas, "The Continental Development and Trade Initiative," speech given before the Americas Society, New York, 8 February 1991.

127. Brown et al., "Making Trade Fair," 312–13

128. A number of writers have criticized the economic and trade policy process for its undemocratic nature. For one of the most detailed examinations, see Gregory, "Environment, Sustainable Development, Public Participation and the NAFTA."

129. For a detailed look at these issues and a potential solution, see Albert Fishlow, Sherman Robinson, and Raul Hinojosa-Ojeda, "Proposal for a North American Regional Development Bank and Adjustment Fund," presented at a conference on North American Free Trade sponsored by the Federal Reserve Bank of Dallas, Texas, 14 June 1991.

130. Cárdenas, "The Continental Development and Trade Initiative," 6.

131. Fishlow et al., "Proposal." See also Office of Technology Assessment, *U.S.-Mexico Trade: Pulling Together or Pulling Apart?* The United States and Mexico created a North American Development Bank (NADBank) as part of the legislation each country passed to implement NAFTA. The NADBank bears little resemblance to the NADBAF, however, being almost entirely restricted to funding environmental projects. See "NAFTA—Related Border Funding," *Border Briefing* no. 1 (Albuquerque, NM: Inter-Hemispheric Education Resource Center, November 1993).

132. The basic aspects of an international strategy for labor, including a code of conduct for transnational corporations, are described in Jeremy Brecher and Tim Costello, *Global Village vs. Global Pillage: A One-World Strategy for Labor* (Washington, D.C.: International Labor Rights Education and Research Fund, 1991). In a major setback to efforts to install such a code, an intergovernmental group at the United Nations declared in late 1992 that no consensus was possible on provisions of the code. The group's conclusions marked the end of a thirteen-year process to create and install the code under UN auspices.

133. See Reding, "Bolstering Democracy in the Americas"; Schey, "North American Economic Integration"; and Minnesota Advocates for Human Rights, "No Double Standards in International Law: Linkage of NAFTA with Hemispheric System of Human Rights Enforcement Is Needed" (Minneapolis, 1992).

134. Schey, "North American Economic Integration," 6.

135. Among the many authors or organizations that have explored the idea of a social charter that would parallel or be contained within a free trade agreement are: Office of Technology Assessment, *U.S.-Mexico Trade*, 48–50; Brown et al., "Making Trade Fair"; Seminario Permanente de Estudios Chicanos y de Fronteras, "Proposal for a Tri-National Declaration of Human Rights" (Mexico, D.F., 1992); J. M. Servais, "The Social Clause in Trade Agreements: Wishful Thinking or an Instrument of Social Progress?," *International Labour Review* 128, no. 4 (1989); Gijsbert van Liemt, "Minimum Labour Standards and International Trade: Would a Social Clause Work?," *International Labour Review* 128, no. 4 (1989); and Sanger, "Free Trade and Workers' Rights."

136. Office of Technology Assessment, *U.S.-Mexico Trade*, 48.

137. See the proposals in Proyecto Fronterizo de Educación Ambiental and Border Ecology Project, "The North American Free Trade Agreement" and Gregory, "Environment, Sustainable Development, Public Participation and the NAFTA."

138. This idea was proposed in October 1992 in an electronic forum on NAFTA by Robert W. Benson, a law professor at the Loyola Law School in Los Angeles, California. He described the initiative as part of a "Clean Hands Amendment for NAFTA" that would also include a NAFTA Human Rights Commission to oversee elections and hear complaints about human rights abuses.

139. Although diminished in intensity, the simplistic Buy American campaign continues to be pushed by some unions in the early 1990s. As one observer noted, such campaigns have "done little over the years to encourage U.S. workers to understand more deeply the complex process of globalization." Frances Lee Ansley, "U.S.-Mexico Free Trade from the Bottom: A Postcard from the Border," *Texas Journal of Women and the Law* 1, no. 1 (1992).

140. Ray Marshall, "Labor in a Global Economy," in *Labor in a Global Economy: Perspectives from the U.S. and Canada*, eds. Steve Hecker and Margaret Hallock (Eugene, Ore.: Labor Education and Research Center, 1991), 11. It is interesting to note that the downward trend of union membership in the United States is not part of a broader worldwide pattern. Japan's unionized workforce fell from 35 percent to 28 percent from 1970 to 1987, but almost all other industrialized nations saw their proportions increase or stay stable over the same period. In Germany, another important international competitor, it increased from 37 to 43 percent.

141. Quoted in David Brooks, "The Search for Counterparts," *Labor Research Review* 19 (Chicago: Midwest Center for Labor Research, 1992), 83.

142. The largest labor organization that does *not* rely on government support, the Authentic Labor Front (FAT), has led Mexican opposition to NAFTA.

143. In addition to the party itself, the PRI's corporatist structure includes three major components: labor unions, peasant associations, and the "popular sector." The popular sector is a catchall grouping that includes business, the military, community organizations, professionals, teachers, and government bureaucrats.

144. Two excellent treatments of labor's position in Mexico are La Botz, *Mask of Democracy*, and Kevin J. Middlebrook, ed., *Unions, Workers, and the State in Mexico* (San Diego: Center for U.S.-Mexican Studies, 1991). For a history of Mexican labor through the austerity of the 1980s, see Kevin Middlebrook, "The Sounds of Silence: Organized Labour's Response to Economic Crisis in Mexico," *Journal of Latin American Studies* 21, no. 2 (1989), 195–220, and Dan La Botz, *The Crisis of Mexican Labor* (New York: Praeger, 1988).

145. The most recent economic pact was signed in October 1992 and is slated to expire in December 1993.

146. Other important official labor organizations are the Regional Confederation of Mexican Workers (CROM), the Revolutionary Confederation of Workers and Peasants (CROC), the Federation of State Workers' Unions, the National Education Workers Union, and the Miners and Metalworkers Union.

147. For a summary of La Quina's defense, see George Baker, "Political Trial or Poetic Justice in the Case of La Quina?", *Mexico Policy News*, no. 8 (Fall 1992), 18.

148. The oil workers' union donated nearly two hundred thousand dollars to the PRI campaign in 1988, and La Quina declared himself a "friend" of candidate Salinas. Nevertheless, he berated the PRI for ignoring the plight of workers, let it be known that he thought highly of Cárdenas, and refused to order his union members to vote for Salinas as all PRI-affiliated unions traditionally do. Victoria Novelo O., "Las fuentes de poder de la dirigencia sindical en Pemex," *El Cotidiano* 28 (March–April 1989), 13.

149. Dan La Botz, for example, writes that FESEBES "can be considered nothing but a *papier-mâché* model of the CTM, and yet another attempt by the Mexican government to strangle labor reform by installing a new labor organization from above." La Botz, *Mask of Democracy*, 101–02. See also Matt Witt, "Mexican Labor: The Old, the New and the Democratic," *Multinational Monitor* (January–February 1991), 32.

150. See "Making Mexican Unionism More Responsive," *El Financiero International,* 5 October 1992, 13, and "Making Changes," *Business Mexico* (September 1991), 15–17. See also *SourceMex* (Albuquerque: Latin America Data Base, 28 October 1992), in which Hernández is reported to have said that price hikes for gasoline and electricity—agreed to by labor in the economic pact—will not affect consumers because businesses will absorb the costs. This is highly unlikely in Mexico's oligopolistic economy, and to make such a statement places Hernández in the traditional official union role of government apologist.

151. Backed by a nationwide strike, the coordinating committee succeeded in forcing the resignation of the SNTE's corrupt and violent leader, Carlos Jonguitud. Overwhelmed by the vast resources of the official union, however, the CNTE was unable to win a majority of the SNTE's executive committee in subsequent union elections. The definitive English-language work on the CNTE is Maria Lorena Cook, "Organizing Dissent: The Politics of Opposition in the Mexican Teachers' Union," Ph.D. diss., University of California, Berkeley, 1990.

152. See Edward Williams, "Attitudes and Strategies Inhibiting the Unionization of the Maquiladora Industry: Government, Industry, Unions and Workers," *Journal of Borderlands Studies* 6 (Summer 1991), no. 2, 51. This study did not attempt to quantify the number of workers covered by white unions, so the figure of 15 percent should be considered a very rough estimate.

153. La Botz, *Mask of Democracy*, 42.

154. See Kevin J. Middlebrook, "State Structures and the Politics of Union Registration in Postrevolutionary Mexico," *Comparative Politics* 23, no. 4 (July 91), 459–78.

155. Quoted in Matt Moffett, "Mexico's Union Boss, Ally of Salinas, Is a Stumbling Block in Trade Talks," *The Wall Street Journal*, 5 February 1991.

156. Independent observers of the election found a series of abuses, including:
    • The vote was not by secret ballot. Instead, workers had to vote out loud in front of management and CTM personnel and then sign their names next to their votes.
    • The government allowed the company to decide which workers could vote.
    • The government allowed the company to bring a large number of people to vote who were not eligible.
    • The company and the CTM were permitted to warn workers on their way to vote that if they voted against the CTM, they would be fired.

- The company was allowed to videotape some of the voters as they stated their names and which union they preferred.

This summary, as well as most of the information for this account, is from La Botz, *Mask of Democracy*, 148–59.

Despite the fraud and pressure, the official tally showed 1,112 workers voting to switch to the Revolutionary Workers Federation, versus 1,325 for the CTM. "Keeping the Unions in the Family," *Latin American Weekly Report* (20 June 1991), 8.

157. *Mexico-US-Canada Solidarity Newsletter* (Washington, D.C.: American Labor Education Center, 13 January 1992).

158. The American Federation of Labor, long the dominant force in the U.S. labor movement, merged with the Congress of Industrial Organizations, a fast-growing challenger to the AFL, in 1955. The CIO had a much more progressive track record since its founding in 1936 than did the AFL, but by the early 1950s it had moved considerably to the right.

159. Government funding of AFL-CIO programs and the federation's role in pushing procapitalist unions in Europe, Africa, Asia, and Latin America are described in Jonathan Kwitny, *Endless Enemies: The Making of an Unfriendly World* (New York: Congdon and Weed, 1984); Hobart A. Spalding, Jr., "U.S. Labor Intervention in Latin America: The Case of the American Institute for Free Labor Development," in *Trade Unions and the New Industrialization of the Third World*, ed. Roger Southall (London: Zed Books, 1988); Beth Sims, *Workers of the World Undermined: American Labor's Role in U.S. Foreign Policy* (Boston: South End Press, 1992); and Cantor and Schor, *Tunnel Vision*. See also Tom Barry and Deb Preusch, *AIFLD In Central America* (Albuquerque: Inter-Hemispheric Education Resource Center, 1990) and Paul Garver, "Beyond the Cold War: New Directions for Labor Internationalism," *Labor Research Review* 13 (Chicago: Midwest Center for Labor Research, Fall 1989). For a response to this last article and a defense of the AFL-CIO's Department of International Affairs, see Tom Kahn, "Beyond Mythology: A Reply to Paul Garver," *Labor Research Review* 13 (Chicago: Midwest Center for Labor Research, Fall 1989).

160. Some labor activists question whether U.S. unions were even duking it out with corporations at home. See Kim Moody, *An Injury to All: The Decline of American Unionism* (New York: Verso, 1988).

161. The term *business unionism* refers to a philosophy that sees workers and businesses as potential partners in economic development rather than as inevitable adversaries. Business unionism accepts market capitalism as an economic model while rejecting a free labor market as socially unproductive. In this form of unionism workers fight for the wages and benefits that the market will bear, and organizing takes place at the level of the factory, industrial sector, or confederations among sectors. But business unionism rejects a class analysis that would link workers across sectors and across countries.

162. The roles of Samuel Gompers, the AFL, and other U.S. labor organizations and activists during Mexico's revolution and postrevolutionary period are described in: Gregg Andrews, *Shoulder to Shoulder? The American Federation of Labor, the United States, and the Mexican Revolution, 1910–1924* (Berkeley: University of California Press, 1991); Harvey A. Levenstein, *Labor Organizations in the United*

States and Mexico: A History of Their Relations (Westport, Conn.: Greenwood, 1971); and Philip S. Foner, U.S. Labor Movement and Latin America: A History of Workers' Response to Intervention (South Hadley, Mass.: Bergin & Garvey, 1988).

163. Sims, Workers of the World Undermined, 40, and Levenstein, Labor Organizations in the United States and Mexico, 193–95.

164. Levenstein, Labor Organizations in the United States and Mexico, 196–97. Much of the following discussion of the CTM and ORIT is drawn from Levenstein, especially 216–33.

165. ORIT has taken a more independent stance in recent years. In a 1989 report it argued that class considerations could not be excluded from an analysis of labor conditions in Latin America. Although it still received AFL-CIO funds, ORIT's philosophy moved closer to those of European Social and Christian Democratic unions. See ORIT, Desafío del Cambio: Nuevos Rumbos del Sindicalismo (Caracas, Venezuela: Nueva Sociedad, 1989).

166. For accounts of U.S. labor's racist attitudes toward Mexican immigrants, see Cockroft, Outlaws in the Promised Land; Richard Louv, The Mexican Migration: Southwind (San Diego: The San Diego Union, 1980); and McWilliams, North from Mexico.

167. Levenstein, Labor Organizations in the United States and Mexico, 116–24.

168. Ibid., 202–14. The California AFL-CIO opposed the bracero program nearly from its inception, as did the AFL until 1955. The newly merged AFL-CIO, however, refused to condemn the program until 1962, not wanting to antagonize the CTM, which it regarded as a valuable partner in the fight against communism in Latin America.

169. In any case, the CTM was offering more than it could deliver. In the Mexican political system it is not the CTM that represents the small landholders and communal farmers who took part in the bracero program. This function is allotted to the National Confederation of Peasants, which is more of a political organization than a labor union. Ibid., 208–10.

170. Two sources on unions' changing attitudes are Jeff Stansbury, "L.A. Labor and the New Immigrants," Labor Research Review 13 (Chicago: Midwest Center for Labor Research, Fall 1989), and Glenn Scott, "An Organizer's Guide to Free Trade," Democratic Left 20, no. 5 (September–October 1992).

171. Williams, "Attitudes and Strategies," 61.

172. Sklair, Assembling for Development, 135, and Gene Erb, "Mexicans Fight 'Injustice' of U.S. Firms," Des Moines Register reprint of Made in Mexico: The Migration of Jobs, 1986.

173. Williams, "Attitudes and Strategies," 61, and Sklair, Assembling for Development, 135.

174. Examples from Sklair, Assembling for Development, 152, and Williams, "Attitudes and Strategies," 62. According to a longtime academic observer of labor relations on the border, "Border unions, especially those affiliated with the large national confederations, have as one of their functions that of worker control." Jorge Carrillo and Miguel Ramírez, "Maquiladoras en la Frontera Norte: Opinión sobre los Sindicatos," Frontera Norte IV 2, no. 4 (July–December 1990), 127.

175. "A Plant Manager Admits: 'The Company Chose the Union,'" *American Labor*, no. 37 (Washington, D.C.: American Labor Education Center), 3.
176. Interview with Steven Hecker of the Labor Education and Research Center at the University of Oregon, Dec. 1992.
177. Interview with former ACTWU staff member who wished to remain anonymous, January 1993. Another factor in the lack of interest on the part of union leaders was the composition of the September 19 union, according to this former staff member. "It was not only that they were an independent union but that it was a union made up of all women and with female leadership." Because of a personal interest in the September 19 union's organizing efforts, this staffer convinced a vice president of ACTWU to hold a reception for workers at his own joint board right down the street from the international headquarters.
178. Bob Kingsley, quoted by Laura McClure, "Workers of the World Unite! New Labor Strategies for Confronting the International Economy," *Dollars and Sense* (September 1992), 19.
179. A number of international trade secretariats in which U.S. and Mexican unions participate are working on international codes of corporate conduct. The International Federation of Chemical, Energy and General Workers' Unions (ICEF), for example, is promoting a set of reporting requirements and restrictions to be applied to all new investments. The code would require disclosure of a corporation's investment intentions and its use and disposal of hazardous materials. It could also prohibit child labor, regulate the discharge of pollutants, set minimum standards for plant closing notice and severance pay, and require neutrality in union-organizing efforts.
180. The Canadian Labour Congress and several individual Canadian unions should get credit for starting the process of trinational labor organizing against NAFTA in the summer of 1990.
181. The CWA and the CWC first joined forces several years earlier in the Northern Telecom International Solidarity Coalition. This is an alliance of unions from eight countries in which Canada's Northern Telecom has a presence. Mexico, where Northern Telecom operates two nonunion plants, is not a member of the coalition. See Fred Pomeroy, "Mobilizing Across Borders: Unions and Multinational Corporations," in Hecker and Hallock, *Labor in a Global Economy*.
182. Just when such mobilization might be deemed "necessary" by the Mexican phone workers under Hernández Juárez remains to be seen. Hernández is committed to modernizing the phone company by using foreign investment capital, and he is unlikely to risk scaring off that capital by taking any hard-line stands in support of U.S. or Canadian organizing efforts. Nor has the Mexican union shown interest in cooperating with the CWA on workplace issues, despite the latter's long experience with the opportunities and pitfalls presented by the phone technology now being installed in Mexico.
183. Interview with Mike Connolly in "UAW/Fightback/New Directions," *The Organizer* (May 1992). According to New Directions executive board member Tom Laney, the UAW's vice president in charge of Ford asked, "What will happen the next time somebody else wants a dime?" At that time Ford workers earned an average of seventeen dollars an hour, said Laney. "We said we felt we could probably afford that one too."

184. Interviews with Steve Beckman, April 1992 and November 1992. The UAW feels no such compunction regarding the affairs of its locals, however. In May 1992 the union audited Local 879 in St. Paul, according to the local's recording secretary, Tom Laney. "They've ordered us to stop this [solidarity] work. They say we are duplicating the educational, recreational, and free trade programs that are available from the international union," Laney said in a speech published in *The Organizer* in October 1992.

185. In February 1992 the UAW did make a concrete expression of international solidarity, contributing fifteen thousand dollars to the strike fund of a *maquiladora* union in Matamoros, Mexico. The contribution came in response to the Mexican government's arrest of that union's leader, Agapito González, on charges of tax evasion. The arrest was a blatant and effective effort to give *maquila* operators in Matamoros an advantage in their negotiations with the union. González, a longtime CTM official, was released nine months later. He heads the Industrial Journeymen and Workers Union, which represents workers at numerous plants owned by U.S. automakers. His relatively assertive negotiating tactics achieved wages in the Matamoros *maquiladoras* roughly 25 percent higher than those in other border cities. The charges against González were several years old, but police acted on them only when employers in the city pressured the Mexican government to do something to curb his wage demands. After the union leader's arrest the union agreed to accept a lower wage increase than that it had won just weeks before. See the *Brownsville Herald*, 30 January 1992, 3 February 1992, and 4 February 1992, *La Jornada*, 13 February 1992, and Nauman, "Maquiladoras Thrive Despite Doubts."

186. Rebekah Greenwald, "Uncanny Silence from Crafty Carla," *NAFTA Thoughts* 1, no. 1 (Washington, D.C.: Development GAP, Dec. 1991).

187. Quoted in Matt Witt, "Labor and NAFTA," *Latin American Labor News*, no. 5 (Fall 1992), 7.

# Part IV

# Official Relations

# Conflict and

# Cooperation

Times have changed. As recently as 1989 a leading expert on U.S.-Mexico relations observed that "it is not so much that the two countries do not understand each other—and this is particularly true at the governmental level—but rather that they disagree fundamentally in a number of areas."[1] As of the early 1990s, however, the two governments not only appear to understand each other quite well but have increasingly seen eye to eye on issues ranging from economics to international affairs. They have signed a free trade agreement, set up binational working groups to study shared problems and recommend solutions, and accelerated joint responses to such concerns as drug trafficking and environmental degradation. Great asymmetries in power and wealth still overshadow the relationship, of course, giving greater weight to U.S. wishes and policy demands, and the needs of those people who occupy the grass roots are not at the forefront of policy concerns in either country. But official relations since the late 1980s have been more harmonious than at any time since before the Mexican Revolution, with the brief exception of genial relations during the presidency of Miguel Alemán (1946–52).[2]

The increasingly cordial tone of U.S.-Mexico relations during the 1980s reflected the rise to power of like-minded neoliberal forces in each country. Carlos Salinas and George Bush had an especially warm relationship. Both men were dedicated to deregulation, privatization, government cutbacks, the promotion of large corporate interests, global economic integration, and the free market. Both men gave global economic issues a higher priority than democratization, environmental protection, labor rights, and other items on the sociopolitical agenda. Under the two presidents, economic ties proliferated between the two countries, nationalist tensions subsided, and analysts began speaking of a new era of cooperation and converging interests.

The election of Bill Clinton to the U.S. presidency in 1992 was expected to reduce U.S.-Mexico consensus over some issues, especially regarding worker protections, democratization, and the environment. Analysts predicted that Clinton, who was elected by U.S. voters concerned about domestic economic problems, environmental degradation, and human rights, would emphasize these issues more than his predecessors. Given Clinton's constituency, neglecting these concerns could backfire if he intended to run for president again in 1996.

The long-term threat to Clinton's reelection may well be correct, but as of mid-1993, Clinton's policies toward Mexico have closely adhered to those laid out under Bush. In fact, the amount of continuity between the Bush and Clinton administrations' Mexico policies is "amazing," according to the State Department's desk officer for Mexico, and there have been "no significant changes in the way things are done."[3] For example, Clinton, an advocate of market approaches, trade and investment liberalization, and U.S. economic expansion, has supported the North American Free Trade Agreement as negotiated by the Bush and Salinas governments.[4]

Clinton endorsed NAFTA with the stipulation that the three NAFTA partners also negotiate side agreements to work out protections for the environment and labor, and to offset potential job loss due to import surges. Despite Clinton's stated concerns, the parallel accords still fall short in terms of enforceability and the scope of protections—at least from the point of view of NAFTA critics.[5] Although they represent some improvement to NAFTA as negotiated by the Bush administration, the new accords do not indicate that Clinton will make issues like labor rights an overriding priority in relations with Mexico. Rather, like Bush and Reagan, Clinton will continue the course toward an economically integrated North America—the same goal sought by Mexico's political and economic leaders. Shared markets and shared production are the twin lights seen at the end of a tunnel of economic uncertainty and crisis, for both the United States and Mexico. Although Clinton is likely to be forced by domestic economic needs to cut back on aid programs to Mexico, the emphasis on expanding economic and political relations between the two countries will almost surely remain secure under the Democratic administration.

Official programs carried out by both governments are helping advance the integration that is under way. Although official relations are only one part of a broader socioeconomic process of integration, they are worth highlighting because they shape the framework within which most other interactions—trade and investment, for example—take place.[6] Much of the next two chapters focuses on U.S. government initiatives, not because the United States is more worthy of study but because greater U.S. resources equal more U.S. programs. In addition, as the dominant partner Washington is helping shape the ongoing integration in favor of the United States, while making sure that the PRI stays powerful enough to carry out the required transformations of the Mexican economy.

Looking closely at the U.S. side is also important because the deal worked out with Mexico is intended to have an impact regionally and globally. It is a significant component of Washington's strategy for coalescing a hemisphere-wide economic bloc dominated by the market, business entities, and financial structures of the United States. Washington also hopes to use NAFTA and other features of the U.S.-Mexico integration to influence negotiations on the rules for international trade and investment.

## Converging Policies, Persistent Tensions

The United States and Mexico have had a troubled and uncertain relationship. Years of conflict have alternated with years of cooperation and still other periods of neglect and indifference. But the two countries are forever bound together by proximity and interdependence, if divided by asymmetry, culture, and language. "We have with Mexico a marriage without possibility of divorce," U.S. Ambassador John Gavin observed, catching in one comment the simultaneous ambivalence and necessity of the relationship.[7]

It has been the necessity of the relationship that has drawn the most official attention since the 1980s. Political and economic realities—economic woes at home, the end of the Cold War, international economic integration, and a global recession—forced each government to rethink the terms and objectives of the relationship. It is drawing Gavin's analogy too far to say the U.S. and Mexican governments "renewed their vows," but that they committed themselves to deepening and improving official ties is clear.

The binational relationship is now treated as a potential source of prosperity and growth by both governments. It is also seen as a vehicle for resolving long-term problems like drug trafficking and undocumented migration that have as often caused contention as collaboration. Both government programs and official and nongovernmental linkages have proliferated over the last decade, responding not only to their own logic but also to government-sponsored stimulation.

But focusing too closely—as some do—on the converging interests, even converging destinies, of the United States and Mexico is misleading.[8] North-south tensions still strain the relationship and pull important long-term national interests of the two countries in different directions. Mexico's need for jobs and investment, for instance, makes its view of U.S. runaway plants much more positive than the view taken by U.S. workers or congressional representatives. Likewise, the two countries find themselves on opposite sides as far as undocumented Mexican migration to the United States is concerned.

International politics is not necessarily a zero-sum game in which one wins and the other must lose. But asymmetries of wealth, power, and size do translate into policy effects that are the source of greater wins for the United States, more frequent losses for Mexico. "The United States is bigger, stronger, and richer than Mexico," wrote the Bilateral Commission on the Future of United States–Mexican Relations. "Under these conditions bargaining tends to be unequal."[9] The United States is dominant in more than just bilateral terms. The country is also a key player in global markets, international lending institutions, trade negotiating forums like GATT, and other international arenas important to Mexico's economic success.

Washington's stamp of approval for the Mexican government, its economic aid, trade, loan support, and debt assistance all have come with strings attached. These have been used to encourage and enforce Mexican economic policies that open the door for increased U.S. trade and investment and slash the role of government in the economy. In addition, the Mexican government has had to go along with other U.S. initiatives when its own interests might well have led to different policy choices. It has had to pull out the stops in the war on drugs, for example, not only because of its own interest in eliminating challenges from traffickers but also to win White House certification and congressional approval, which are in turn conditions for aid, trade, and lending packages.

Recent Mexican governments have not just been punching bags for Washington. The collapse of aging economic strategies, conditions attached to international debt and aid packages, political repercussions from the government's inadequate response to the 1985 earthquake, and upheavals like the 1988 elections shook up Mexican political structures. These events boosted the fortunes of Mexican policy makers who shared the economic worldview of counterparts in Washington and who believed strongly that solving Mexico's problems would require close alliances with highly developed countries like the United States. Since the Harvard-educated Carlos Salinas took over as budget and planning minister under President Miguel de la Madrid, Mexican political leaders have often found themselves on common ground with Washington. The new cooperation that analysts observe is actually a partnership between sectors of the U.S. and Mexican economic and political elite that share the same diagnosis of Mexican and global economic problems and the same prescriptions for overcoming them.

## Aims and Interests

The stakes are high for both the United States and Mexico as they work out a new relationship in the rapidly changing global economy. Traditional interests still hold, but the challenges of a globalizing economy and keeping Mexico's economic transformations on track have spawned new interests and objectives, while adding special urgency to satisfying them. Priorities like making sure that Mexico remains stable politically and that both countries are economically healthy occupy the top of the agenda. Most bilateral efforts, as well as unilateral government programs, are designed to serve such interests. Other interests, such as making sure the United States has secure access to strategic minerals like oil and strontium and resolving drug and immigration problems are also important, as are Mexico's recent concerns about cultivating a positive image among the U.S. public.

Ensuring Mexican political stability is an interest that both governments share and that motivates a variety of U.S. government programs. A quiet southern flank is important to Washington, not only in bilateral or regional terms but also because a peaceful border makes it easier for the United States to project its power elsewhere. Washington also wants to make sure that Mexico's economic reforms get fully implemented, a condition that requires compliance from the Mexican public and the continued strength of neoliberal forces in the Mexican government. Moreover, Washington sees Mexico not only as an important neighbor but also as a door to the rest of Latin America. A Mexico that is aligned with the United States both economically and politically serves as a buffer from the poverty and radicalism that have characterized much of Latin America.[10]

Likewise, political stability and maintaining the dominant position of the PRI are two major interests of the Mexican government that are served by current U.S.-Mexico relations. The legitimacy of the PRI government—undermined by widespread allegations of election fraud, corruption, abuse of authority, and economic failures—has been severely tested over the last decade. Developing closer relations with the United States, once off limits because of antigringo sentiments, has been one of Salinas's primary strategies for strengthening the PRI's standing in the country. That strategy has allowed the Mexican government to tap into U.S. programs and assistance packages that have helped Mexico sort its way out of its economic crisis and recoup some lost political support among its population.

These other interests aside, the central, overriding issue in official U.S.-Mexico relations is economics. With the exception of Mexican political stability, everything else takes a backseat. All the other issues on the bilateral agenda have been subordinated to economic concerns. Mexico has put up with U.S. drug agents on its soil and mounted only pro forma protests when Mexican nationals were kidnapped for trial in the United States on drug charges. Its government has grudgingly accepted U.S. unilateral formulations of immigration policy and has plowed ahead with bilateral economic discussions even while being bashed by the U.S. Congress and media for corruption and authoritarianism. For its part, the U.S. government has turned its head from ongoing patterns of election rigging and abuse of authority in Mexico. Likewise, despite opposition from U.S. drug and customs authorities because of violence against U.S. drug agents, the executive branch under the Reagan and Bush administrations concluded trade, investment, and debt management agreements with Mexico that advanced economic integration.

The economic relationship that is emerging between the two countries is the product of many forces. Corporate and financial sectors that stand to gain from exploiting cheap Mexican labor and enhanced trade and investment opportunities have strongly influenced the specific features of NAFTA and other economic agreements. The vast majority of the members of the Advisory Committee on Trade Policy and Negotiations, for example—created to give private citizens an advisory role in trade negotiations—are representatives of Fortune 500 corporations. But the self-interest of some sectors of the U.S. economic elite is only one factor shaping integration. Both countries also have real economic needs that they hope to satisfy, at least in part, through increased economic integration.

Placing its bets on expanding trade and foreign investment in order to finance major portions of the country's "modernization," the Mexican

374

government turned to the United States, its major trading partner. In a speech to the U.S. Congress in 1989 President Salinas explained the government's perspective: "In order for Mexico's modernization to be lasting, we must grow; but growth requires greater and more secure access to the world's largest market, the United States."[11] Ensuring Mexico's access to the U.S. market is not enough. A weak and sluggish U.S. economy will not generate enough demand for Mexican products or create the investment dollars needed to galvanize the country's economy. Given the country's economic dependence on its northern neighbor, Mexico needs the U.S. economy to be stable, robust, and open.

With the changes in the global economic and political system and a stagnant economy at home, the United States is no longer just the "Colossus of the North." It hopes to ensure Mexican economic cooperation partly because of its own need to crank up the domestic economy. In fact, many observers believe the United States—long the hemisphere's hegemonic power and now the world's sole military superpower—is in the throes of national decline.[12] As one expert on its foreign policy explained grimly, "The only light in a dismal economy is the growth of U.S. exports."[13] This very fact means that Washington and the political and economic forces with a stake in the system are moving to shore up U.S. spheres of influence overseas. The improved relationship with Mexico reflects this trend, just as it reflects changes in Mexican attitudes and development strategies that have permitted closer relations with its northern neighbor.

Ever since the end of World War II, when the United States clearly dominated the international economy and had the world's only standing industrial plant, Washington has promoted exports as the main engine of growth in the country. The engine has been sputtering since the 1970s, however, and U.S. policy makers hoped to crank it up by stimulating exports even more. Despite the intensity with which the objective has been pursued, recent U.S. efforts to pump up trade have been stymied by a sluggish international economy plagued by slow growth and recession.[14]

A stagnant global economy means a slowdown in export sales, and given the magnitude of the U.S. need for capital inflows to pay off its debts and refurbish its productive base, the global recession has hit the United States hard. With European integration, German reunification, and increasing economic turmoil in Japan, demand from these traditional trading partners has fallen off. Along with Canada, these regions still purchase the vast majority of U.S. exports, but because their economies are contracting, their consumers and businesses cannot afford to purchase the *quantity* of exports needed to pull the United States out of its economic doldrums. In addition, these important U.S. trading partners are increasingly turning to each other to form regional trading blocs. Staying competitive with the European Community and with the Japanese-dominated East Asian bloc is a major reason that the United States has moved to integrate the Western Hemisphere into a free trade area through mechanisms like NAFTA and the Enterprise for the Americas Initiative.

For the United States to maintain its status as a superpower and satisfy the social and employment needs of its people, it must reinvigorate its economy. With the decline in export potential to its traditional trading partners and staying faithful to an export-driven development strategy, Washington has looked south. That fact has drawn the country closer to Mexico.[15] At the end of the NAFTA negotiations, President Bush summarized the administration's hopes: "The Cold War is over. The principal challenge now facing the United States is to compete in a rapidly changing and expanding marketplace. This agreement [NAFTA] will level the North American playing field, allowing American companies to increase sales from Alaska to the Yucatán."[16] But in a sense, mechanisms like NAFTA reflect a "rediscovered Monroe Doctrine," observes one noted analyst, referring to the policy pronounced by President James Monroe warning European powers to forgo expansionist ambitions in Latin America.[17] Rather than level the playing field, agreements like NAFTA are intended to bias the regional trading game in favor of the United States. By restricting competition from heavyweights like Germany and Japan through the terms of Western Hemisphere free trade agreements, the United States is trying to stake out Latin America as its own economic turf at a time when competition on the world market is increasingly difficult.

In addition to its own economic health, therefore, the United States needs and wants Mexico's economy to be strong and vigorous. Mexico's economic health not only contributes to its own stability but directly benefits the U.S. economy by providing increased trade and investment opportunities. "A growing economy and increased employment in Mexico," according to U.S. Ambassador John Negroponte, "translates into a stronger boost to U.S. exports than virtually anywhere else abroad."[18] Policy makers also expect a healthy, stable, and growing Mexican economy to help slash undocumented immigration to the United States. If Mexico can provide enough decent-paying jobs, they argue, the urge to seek work illegally in the United States will be blunted.[19]

Assuring that Mexico continues to liberalize its economy and that current reforms are locked in are other objectives that Washington and its private-sector allies have pursued in Mexico. The free trade agreement will accelerate integration that is already under way but not change the fundamental process itself. More important, from the perspective of its backers, is the guarantee against backsliding that a signed free trade accord will send to potential investors and traders. NAFTA will assure businesses that future Mexican governments are committed to following the market-oriented policies begun under de la Madrid and Salinas. "Mexico is becoming a showcase" because of its economic reforms, Negroponte maintained. "A NAFTA will help ensure the permanency of these visionary new economic directions."[20]

## From Conquest to Cooperation

Congratulatory words and joint responses to shared problems are relatively new in U.S.-Mexico relations. A history of conquest and intervention strained relations between the two countries for nearly a century. The annexation of Texas, followed by the "war of the North American invasion" that cost Mexico almost half its territory, and subsequent U.S. support for political leaders like Porfirio Díaz who would support U.S. territorial and economic claims soured relations. These interventions, U.S. interference in the Mexican Revolution, and the ham-handed arrogance of U.S. corporations in Mexico left scars on Mexican sovereignty that remained sensitive throughout the society until the late 1980s.[21]

After the Revolution Washington's direct intervention in Mexican politics subsided. The Mexican government's institutional stability and its capacity to keep public order satisfied two of Washington's central interests. Except for occasions when the United States thought Mexico trod too heavily on its business interests—as when Lázaro Cárdenas nationalized the country's oil reserves—the two governments mostly maintained an aloof coexistence. Incoming presidents like Dwight Eisenhower pointed to the necessity of improving relations with Mexico, but the issue generally faded in importance as the United States pursued other international concerns like fighting the Vietnam War and standing off against the Soviet Union. As one observer described it, U.S.-Mexico relations went into a "deep freeze" after the Revolution stabilized, until the tensions of mounting problems and increasing interdependence kicked the relationship into a position of top priority decades later.[22]

Aside from conflicts over oil nationalizations in the 1930s and a few drug war–related blips of increased attention in the 1960s, the Carter administration was the first to act on Mexico's growing importance to the United States. Mexico's discovery of massive oil reserves in the mid-1970s followed close on the heels of a major oil crisis in the United States and preceded another oil shock that hit in 1979. The discovery of new Mexican reserves triggered both hopes and anxieties in Washington. "Mexico," President José López Portillo told Carter in a 1979 meeting, "has suddenly found itself the center of American attention—attention that is a surprising mixture of interest, disdain and fear."[23]

Despite Washington's renewed interest in its southern neighbor, relations were not entirely cordial during Jimmy Carter's term. Administration high-handedness while negotiating the purchase of Mexican natural gas in 1977, for example, irritated the Mexican government, which burned its surplus fuel rather than sell it to Washington. Personal relations between Carter and López Portillo were so rocky that the Mexican president's foreign minister, Jorge Castañeda, remarked candidly, "I discount the possibility of any sudden, newly discovered or rediscovered goodwill, sympathy or moral consideration on the part of the United States that could change its attitude toward Mexico. The past history of U.S. policy, its present-day prepotency, its selfishness and conservative mood will not allow for such a change."[24] But Carter and his staff did begin to see Mexico as a midlevel regional power with potential influence over U.S. well-being. His foreign policy team began a top-level review of U.S.-Mexico relations and decided to bring better focus to U.S. policy by setting up a new office of coordinator for Mexican affairs in the State Department.[25]

The bureaucratic innovations launched under Carter were short-lived. They changed almost immediately under Ronald Reagan, who reintroduced an ad hoc approach to U.S.-Mexico policies. But the objective factors that inspired Carter—growing interdependence and a heightened sense of U.S. vulnerability where Mexico was concerned—colored relations throughout the next decade. For the first year or so after Reagan's election, relations were congenial and optimistic. Flush with oil money and as stable as ever, Mexico seemed like a good bet for protecting U.S. access to oil, stimulating trade, and even smoothing the way with other third world countries.

The collapse of the good times was not long in coming. Mexico's economic crash, bank nationalizations, and friendly relations with Central American revolutionary movements in Nicaragua and El Salvador prodded the already activist Reagan administration into a frenzy of activity designed to get Mexico's house in order. Keeping Mexico afloat economically rocketed to the foremost position on the U.S.-Mexico policy agenda. But the Reagan government used Mexico's need for a bailout to push for its own objectives in political as well as economic spheres, and Mexico's compounded economic and political troubles provided more leeway for direct U.S. intervention than had been available for years. In the words of one expert, "A heightened sense of invincibility and moral superiority on the part of the United States contrasted sharply with a deepening sense of vulnerability and social decay in Mexico."[26]

Even with the sharp edge of asymmetric power so evident during these years, Mexico's concessions to U.S. desires did not come easily. Mexico's prickly independence and the complicated structural origins of many of the problems that most concerned Washington defied both easy solutions and ready compliance with the U.S. agenda. As the problems of drug trafficking, burgeoning Mexican migration, and Mexican authoritarianism were added to the laundry list of Washington's dissatisfactions with Mexico, the relationship spiraled downward. Likewise, Mexico's participation in multilateral third world bodies, like the Contadora group, that were trying to reach a negotiated solution in Central America irked the Reagan administration, which was then supporting military actions in the region.[27] With all these points of contention, the two countries roller-coastered through the mid-1980s.

Behind all the public hubbub, however, financial policy makers in the two countries were hard at work on debt, trade, and other economic issues. Mexico's announcement in August 1982 that it could not meet its international financial obligations sent shock waves throughout U.S. and global financial communities. Rather than let the Mexican ship of state sink—an event that would have towed under U.S. banks and destabilized the global economy—a team of U.S. government officials and private bank leaders organized a bailout that helped Mexico over the worst of the crisis.[28] Other packages worked out in 1986 and 1989 under the so-called Baker and Brady plans (named after the U.S. secretaries of the treasury who proposed them) also helped Mexico manage its debt obligations. These packages provided Mexico with a combination of new money, credits, and lengthier repayment periods on old loans. Under all three plans, Mexico was required to implement free market strategies, such as liberalizing trade, selling off government enterprises, devaluing the peso, and shrinking government spending. The process meant that U.S. and other foreign financial leaders gained more and more influence over Mexico's economic policies, inspiring one critic to blast the "dizzying process of denationalization of the decision-making apparatus for economic policy."[29]

More than Mexico's economic policy was being targeted by the United States during these years. Mexico's financial troubles lifted some spirits in U.S. policy-making circles, hopeful that Mexico's concessions on economic issues would spin off into other policy areas. "With the wind out of its sails, Mexico is likely to be less adventuresome in its foreign policy and less critical of ours," predicted a confidential memorandum of the State Department's Office of Inter-American Affairs in the early 1980s."[30] A secret presidential directive signed in 1984 authorized U.S. officials to pressure the Mexican government to get on board with U.S. initiatives in Central America.[31] By the end of the decade, the early hopes of U.S. policy makers seemed close to realization. After Salinas first called for the negotiation of a free trade pact, the U.S. ambassador to Mexico, John Negroponte, cabled Washington that the agreement would "institutionalize [Mexican] acceptance of a North American orientation to Mexico's foreign relations."[32]

As Mexico plodded into alignment with U.S. foreign policy, it was moving much more rapidly into a partnership on trade and investment that laid the foundation for current U.S.-Mexico relations. A bilateral subsidies code signed in 1985 gave Mexico greater access to the U.S. market in exchange for Mexico's phasing out its export subsidies. Along with other changes Mexico was making in its economy, the agreement helped lay the groundwork for Mexico's entry into GATT the following year. By 1987 the two countries had signed a Bilateral Trade and Investment Framework Understanding that provided the most comprehensive and flexible mechanism up to that time for enhancing trade and investment relations. Opening the doors even further, in 1989 the United States and Mexico signed an agreement on "trade and investment facilitation." In going beyond the voluntary provisions of the 1987 framework understanding to mandate negotiations on bilateral trade and investment, the new agreement was the last major stepping-stone to NAFTA.

By the end of 1989 the two governments were increasingly acting as if they were engaged in a "special relationship" with reconcilable, if not common, objectives.[33] Reaching such a point required profound adjustments in Mexico's usual nationalistic approach to the United States. Whether the relaxation of nationalist rhetoric will hold over the long term—especially as the foreign business and U.S. government presence increase in the country—is unclear. But along with Washington, the Salinas government has been careful to stay focused on what the two governments have defined as their top priority: the rapid integration of their economies. In the process they are underlining the points on which they agree, while minimizing the differences.

## Model for the Hemisphere

As Mexico gradually moved from the back burner to the forefront of U.S. policy concerns, Washington took a new top-level approach to bilateral relations. It was not that Mexico eclipsed other U.S. foreign policy concerns, but rather that its importance as a key player in regional economic integration was recognized by U.S. policy makers and private-sector free traders. Mexico, as a bridge between north and south in the hemisphere, was increasingly seen as a model not only for other potential bilateral trade and investment agreements but for emerging relationships between industrialized countries and midlevel developing countries. Speaking of the proposed U.S.-Mexico free trade agreement, an American trade official observed, "It's possible this could be a prototype arrangement between an industrial and a developing country."[34]

Working out a satisfactory trade and investment regime with Mexico was seen by U.S. policy makers as the first link in a chain of bilateral agreements with other governments in Latin America. The Bush administration intended these bilateral agreements to act as stepping-stones to a hemisphere-wide free trade arrangement and to advance the goals of the Enterprise for the Americas Initiative. Enhancing economic ties with the United States was only one objective of initiatives like these. Washington also expected them to strengthen U.S. positions in international trade negotiations and to help lock in neoliberal economic reforms implemented during the 1980s by governments in the region. With the second-largest economy in Latin America and as the major trading partner of the United States in the region, Mexico served as a significant model of the neoliberal strategy of development. NAFTA, according to Bernard Aronson, assistant secretary of state for inter-American affairs under Bush, gave "momentum to the entire hemisphere's drive to lower trade barriers."[35]

Mexico's status as a model had political roots as well. The country's standing as a critic of U.S. interventionism and its efforts to carve out economic and foreign policies independent of the United States gave its new pro-U.S. tilt added weight in Latin America. Likewise, the government's decision to abandon import-substituting industrialization strategies and inwardly focused development policies in favor of closer links to the United States and the world market had more than just domestic significance. Moves like these implicitly challenged dependency explanations of underdevelopment and state-driven development strategies common in Latin America.

Mexico was not the first Latin American nation to make these changes—Chile under Augusto Pinochet was the pioneer[36]—but when Mexico hitched its wagon to the U.S. star, the decision reverberated throughout Latin America. The country's proximity to the region's largest market threatened the export potential of other Latin American countries that were following export-driven growth strategies. Concerns that Mexico would edge out their products in the U.S. market led other Latin American governments to move toward similarly close ties with the United States. Along with a general neoliberal trend evident in the 1980s, these concerns helped advance the U.S. objective of extending its own economic influence in the region.

In addition to serving as a model for regional and north-south relationships, Mexico and NAFTA play important roles in Washington's global economic strategies. In a cable outlining "Talking Points on NAFTA" for U.S. consulates, John Negroponte, ambassador to Mexico under Bush, explained the tactic: "A vibrant North American partnership for open trade and investment greatly strengthens our leverage in fostering an open global economy to counter the troubling tendencies towards regionalism in Europe and Asia."[37]

## Whose Agenda?

Among the forces urging the kind of global economic integration sought by Washington are U.S. think tanks and U.S. corporations with interests in Mexico. Through their public relations, lobbying, and educational efforts, they have promoted a positive view of the trade pact and of the Mexican government among U.S. policy makers and important interest groups. Some of these organizations have gone well beyond advocating for NAFTA and other policies that affect U.S.-Mexican relations. They have been incorporated into the policy-making process itself, to the near exclusion of groups that seek more rigorous protections for labor and the environment.

The business organizations that were most influential in the push for NAFTA represented some of the largest transnational corporations in the United States. Many of the associations were ad hoc, formed simply to promote the free trade accord. The Emergency Committee for American Trade and the U.S. Alliance for NAFTA, for example, included members from corporate giants like American Express and Eastman Kodak, both with major investments in Mexico that are likely to get even more of a boost with the trade agreement. One megaeffort was conducted by the Coalition for Trade Expansion, a lobbying umbrella that included more than five hundred corporations and lobbyists from five major trade associations. Representing the Business Roundtable, U.S. Chamber of Commerce, Emergency Committee for American Trade, National Association of Manufacturers, and National Foreign Trade Council, the coalition held weekly strategy sessions to determine how best to press its cause with Congress.[38]

The U.S. Council of the Mexico-U.S. Business Committee conducted a major campaign to see to it that a free trade pact agreeable to U.S. business was negotiated.[39] With more than fifty top corporations as members—including American Telephone & Telegraph Company, Bank of America, Citibank, Coca-Cola, and General Motors—the council testified to Congress, held forums on the trade talks, and saw itself as a "resource for the U.S. government and the U.S. business community" as far as bilateral trade negotiations were concerned.[40] It set up committees on areas such as trade and regulation, investment and financial services, and production sharing to devise policy proposals for incorporation into the trade agreement.

The various private-sector committees mandated to advise the U.S. trade negotiating team about their needs and concerns under a free trade accord were heavily stacked in favor of large corporate and financial interests. The Advisory Committee on Trade Policy and Negotiations (ACTPN), for example, represents forty-two major corporations but only two labor organizations, the AFL-CIO and ACTWU.[41] Included in the ACTPN are top corporations like IBM, Hewlett-Packard, and Dow Chemical. Likewise, the special advisory committees that were set up to advise the NAFTA negotiating team on specific issues vastly overrepresented business in comparison with other sectors. On the committees where environmentalists were included, for example, business members outnumbered environmentalists by about thirty to one.

Although they were not as influential as the business committees, conservative think tanks like the Heritage Foundation and the Center for Strategic and International Studies were tireless supporters of NAFTA. The Heritage Foundation, in fact, has been promoting the notion of a U.S.-Mexico free trade area since the early 1980s. But conservative research and advocacy institutes were not alone in supporting NAFTA and other aspects of U.S.-Mexico economic integration. Study groups at liberal and moderate establishments such as the Inter-American Dialogue, Brookings Institution, and Council on Foreign Relations also explored the issue, generally coming down in favor of the idea of free trade. Through their working groups, conferences, panel discussions, and publications, these institutions helped popularize the trade agreement among key sectors and provided forums for dialogue between policy makers and the private sector.

The agenda promoted by these different entities has served the interests of corporations and banks likely to profit from free trade far more than the interests of working people or the poor. In pursuing this agenda, these business advisory groups and think tanks took an approach similar to that of the U.S. and Mexican governments. Neither Salinas nor Bush sought a trade accord that would compensate those already harmed by rapid integration, much less those who might suffer in the future. Although the Clinton administration pushed for somewhat greater protections for labor and the environment, the strict business focus of the agreement as negotiated excludes most socioeconomic considerations.

Under Bush and Salinas, however, the two governments established a package of aid programs that not only advanced economic integration but also threw a temporary safety net under many of the Mexican people who suffered most from the dislocations of restructuring. By siphoning off discontent, these programs allowed the Mexican government to continue liberalizing the economy while helping maintain stability and the political dominance of the PRI. At the same time, they opened Mexican markets to U.S. exports and promoted trade and investment ties among U.S. and Mexican businesses. Programs like these—to be explored in the next two chapters—furthered the probusiness agenda and shielded both the trade agreement and Mexico's economic reforms from much of the political fallout that might have threatened their survival.

# Boosting Business

The integration of the U.S. and Mexican economies is steaming ahead, propelled by many forces. When U.S. tourists head south for sight-seeing and shopping or when Mexican men cross into San Diego to their daily jobs as gardeners, they are helping blend the economies of the two countries together. Peso devaluations over the past decade have savaged local economies on both sides of the border. *Casas de cambio* dotting the streets in U.S. border communities help Mexican shoppers spend their money in the United States by converting their pesos into dollars. On the Mexican side, currency exchanges are not even necessary for many transactions; dollars will do just fine. Economic integration is proceeding steadily and rapidly, energized by the differences in resources, skills, needs, and desires of people in each country.

When we look only at these everyday linkages, it is easy to assume that integration is occurring strictly as a natural process. But the U.S. and Mexican governments are accelerating and shaping the process, both through the trade and investment agreements discussed previously and through specific programs that promote economic ties. The United States has a distinct advantage over Mexico in these programs. Despite its own economic woes, Washington has many resources at its disposal that it can use as leverage to pry open Mexican markets and chip out a place of dominance for U.S. exports. Working closely with private-sector trade associations and national and regional export organizations like the National Peanut Council and the Washington State Apple Commission, U.S. government agencies are making sure that Mexico's liberalization enhances the U.S. economy.

This is not to say that all the efforts to promote economic ties are unilateral. On the contrary, over the past decade the two governments worked more closely together than at any time in recent history to advance

385

commercial relations and investment opportunities. The big changes in the Mexican economy and the Mexican government's decision to shelve anti-U.S. attitudes laid the groundwork for these expanding ties. The Joint Commission on Investment and Trade, for example, and an assortment of binational working groups hammered out many of the details of the changing U.S.-Mexican economic relationship before, during, and after the NAFTA negotiations.[42]

Nor do all economic promotion efforts come solely from the national level. Trade offices run by state governments in the United States are springing up in Mexico. Texas, Illinois, California, Louisiana, Arizona, and New Mexico, for example, have opened offices there, aiming to get more of their state's goods and services sold in Mexico. The value of these ties to state economies can be impressive. California does more trade with Mexico than with the entire European Community. Likewise, Texas conducts nearly eleven billion dollars in trade with Mexico each year.[43]

Washington, however, is the big player in trade and investment promotion. Government agencies offer a full range of export-financing mechanisms and market promotion programs designed to hike U.S. exports to Mexico. Institutions such as the Commodity Credit Corporation (CCC) and the Export-Import Bank (Eximbank) provide lines of credit, loan guarantees, and insurance to take much of the risk out of doing business in Mexico and give U.S. exporters a competitive edge. At the same time, agencies like the Foreign Agricultural Service (FAS) and the Commerce Department provide insight into the Mexican market and play matchmaker between U.S. businesses and Mexican trade representatives. These agencies sponsor trade shows, conduct trade missions, investigate market trends, and implement various other programs that enhance U.S. export opportunities.

## Harvesting Profits

A special target for U.S. export promotion programs is the market for U.S. agricultural products. The restructuring of Mexico's agricultural sector and the government's efforts to cut away trade barriers threw open the door to imports from the United States. As a result, U.S. agricultural exports to Mexico more than doubled after the mid-1980s, climbing to nearly $3 billion in 1991 and to $3.5 billion in 1992.[44] According to Wendell Dennis, an economist at the Foreign Agricultural Service, the growth in U.S. agricultural exports to Mexico is "unprecedented" and the number of new U.S. industry groups looking into doing business in the country is "overwhelming."[45] The trend has not diminished under Clinton. Dennis said that agricultural trade with Mexico has "heated up much more than expected" in the last year, with extimates on trade levels being exceeded in 1992 and the same expected in 1993.[46] Mexico is the third-largest customer for U.S. agricultural goods, and U.S. export promotion programs are designed to boost sales of everything from lunch meat to table eggs to feed grains and beef.[47]

The Export Enhancement Program (EEP) is one such effort. The EEP is the major U.S. agricultural export subsidy program. Funded by the Commodity Credit Corporation, the program awards cash bonuses to U.S. agricultural producers, processors, and exporters so they can offer lower prices on the world's markets for their products. The EEP is one of the more obvious contradictions in the neoliberalism being practiced by conservative U.S. administrations in the 1980s. As a subsidy program it puts the U.S. government squarely on the side of its business beneficiaries, reducing the power of the market to winnow out uncompetitive enterprises.

Rather than a free market approach, the EEP fits more in the *Real-economik* framework of the "if they won't play by our rules, we'll play by theirs" maxim. At least in principle the program is intended to counteract the agricultural subsidies of other governments, especially those of the European Community, whose farm products often compete directly with those of the United States in global markets.[48] As with NAFTA itself, programs like the EEP are used to increase U.S. clout in multilateral trade negotiations. Wendell Dennis explained that the EEP is "our leverage against unfair trade practices," especially by other GATT members. One of the main objectives of the program, according to the Department of Agriculture, is to "encourage other countries exporting agricultural commodities to undertake serious negotiations on agricultural trade problems."[49]

But the EEP provides more mundane benefits as well. Combined with other U.S. government economic promotion programs, it helps U.S. businesses sew up parts of the Mexican market. In Mexico the program is not especially large in dollar terms, but it did help the United States beat out its competitors in the Mexican wheat market. From 1988 to 1990 wheat was the crop most subsidized under the EEP in Mexico, providing a big boost to U.S. producers, especially when other U.S. government supports were factored into the equation.[50] Subsidies from the program, along with U.S. government credit guarantees, allowed the United States to capture a full 95 percent of the Mexican market for wheat in 1989–90.[51]

Other products supported by EEP subsidies include vegetable oil and canned peaches, although barley malt is the major commodity promoted under the program as of this writing.[52] In addition to the EEP, U.S. export subsidy programs focusing on dairy, sunflower seed oil, and cottonseed oil products are active in Mexico.[53] As contradictory as it seems, these subsidies will not be affected by NAFTA. The negotiators wrote into the agreement explicit protection for the programs.[54]

Those who profit from the EEP are not the hard-pressed "family farms" that politicians in the United States embrace in speeches and media appearances. On the contrary, large transnational companies benefit most. During the big wheat push of the late 1980s, for example, huge grain producers and exporters like Cargill, Continental Grain, and ADM took the greatest advantage of the program.[55] Like these heavyweights, the Mexican government has benefited from the program. The government's basic foods distributor, Conasupo, was the largest user of the EEP in Mexico at least until the late 1980s.[56] Because of the country's economic reforms, more private-sector buyers began to participate in the program. But Conasupo's strong participation in this and other U.S. export promotion programs allowed the Mexican government to continue providing inexpensive food even in the face of social service cutbacks and other by-products of restructuring. Through programs like these, U.S. taxpayers in effect help pay for the export operations of transnational agribusiness as well as some of the social costs of Mexico's economic liberalization.

Subsidies like the EEP are only one component of a package of U.S. government export promotion initiatives that include market development programs and credit guarantees. The strategy is simple: Subsidies keep the prices competitive. Market development programs help ensure that there is a receptive market for U.S. businesses to penetrate, and credit guarantees make financing easier to come by.

The Market Promotion Program (MPP) and the Foreign Market Development program (FMD), for example, help U.S. businesses stir up interest in Mexico for products they want to export to the country. These programs use funds from the Commodity Credit Corporation to help pay the costs of U.S. producers and exporters for some of their market development activities in targeted countries.[57] The FMD helps U.S. businesses provide technical assistance and trade services—like training seminars, demonstration farms, and roving marketing representatives who solicit new business and promote new products.[58]

Focusing more on direct advertising of products is the MPP (known until 1990 as the Target Export Assistance [TEA] program). Through the program, U.S. businesses can get support for everything from radio jingles to television commercials to food fairs.[59] On a global basis, programs like these are being cut back, but in Mexico they are expanding. The U.S. government spent $1.2 million on these programs in 1988 and $2.7 million in 1990, a trend that is expected to continue.[60]

"Without the MPP," according to Wendell Dennis of the FAS, "we wouldn't be able to achieve the level of exports we have in the world."[61] Mexico is no exception, although because it is a relatively new market under the MPP, there are little data to show how effective the promotions have been. But Dennis attributes at least some of the sharp increase in U.S. commodity exports to Mexico to the effects of the MPP. If NAFTA is ratified, the program will play an even stronger role because the trade agreement will open up so many new areas to U.S. access. High-value and consumer-ready U.S. exports like breakfast foods, snack items, frozen foods, table eggs, meat, poultry, and microwave foods will be able to enter Mexico more freely. The Market Promotion Program will play a strong role in convincing Mexican consumers that these products are just what they need and in influencing Mexican retailers to stock up on these U.S. products.

Providing the biggest boost for U.S. agricultural exports to Mexico are the GSM (general sales manager) credit guarantees of the U.S. Department of Agriculture. As with other government insurance and guarantee programs, GSM programs reduce the risk to business and the U.S. banking community of operations in Mexico. Through the programs, the U.S. Department of Agriculture underwrites letters of credit issued by Mexican banks to Mexican buyers of imports from the United States. By providing guaranteed repayment in case of default by the Mexican importer or bank, the GSM programs help protect U.S. exporters and the U.S. banks involved in the transactions. Since Mexico's external debt is still large enough to make U.S. banks skittish about lending even more money to Mexican buyers, the program is instrumental in keeping U.S. export sales climbing in Mexico. Both the Mexican government and commercial importers are able to get the cash they need to buy U.S. agricultural products because of the GSM programs. At the same time, U.S. financial institutions are guaranteed repayment at commercial rates of interest—all thanks to the U.S. taxpayer.

Mexico is the world's largest beneficiary of these credit guarantees. The country's use of the GSM programs jumped from $38 million in 1982 to $1.2 billion in 1988, reflecting the country's dramatic opening to U.S. exports, as well as Conasupo's rising purchases of corn.[62] Most of these transactions are covered under GSM-102, whose repayment terms range from six months to three years.[63] In recent years Mexico has used more than one-fifth of the total allocation for GSM-102 credit guarantees worldwide. In fiscal year 1992, for example, some $1.3 billion in GSM-102 credit guarantees were used by Mexico, covering more than twenty commodity lines. Another $1.45 billion in credit guarantees has been allocated for 1993.[64] Most of the GSM-102 guarantees have traditionally covered bulk commodities like corn, coarse grains, oilseeds, and wheat. The recent increased interest in high-value and consumer-ready products, however, has stimulated sales of such products as meats, hides and skins, table eggs, and nonfat dry milk.[65] To give an idea of the magnitude of this assistance, USDA guarantee programs cover $40 million worth of meat exports to Mexico out of a total of $100 million in such exports.[66]

Programs like these represent a boon to U.S. transnationals and banking institutions by allowing Mexican buyers to purchase U.S. agricultural products they might otherwise be unable to afford. Since Mexico needs many of these products—the country no longer produces enough corn to feed its people, for instance—the programs seem like a win-win proposition. But they have a dark side as well. The U.S.-backed shift to export-oriented agricultural production in Mexico has widened the gap between the country's need for foodstuffs like corn and the agricultural sector's ability to meet that need. By filling the gap with low-cost U.S. products subsidized by the U.S. taxpayer, Washington has helped the Mexican government compensate for some of the immediate ill effects of restructuring the agricultural sector.

At the same time, however, these programs help to undercut domestic production of basic foods in Mexico and remove incentives for devising policies to achieve food self-sufficiency. They also increase Mexico's dependence on U.S. sources for food and agricultural inputs like feed for livestock. Moreover, they provide only a temporary safety net that must be held in place by an increase in Mexico's debt obligations to the United States. If Mexico loses out on its gamble that liberal economic reforms will launch a new period of dynamic growth—that is, if enough jobs are not created for displaced workers and if exports cannot provide the foreign exchange to pay for increased dependence on U.S. agribusiness—the safety net will come crashing down amid the notes due to U.S. creditors.

These programs—and the reliance on the United States that they encourage—pose other potential dangers for Mexico. In the case of products that are not normal fare in Mexico—such as high-priced and specialty items like beef and microwaveable foods—U.S. export promotion programs are helping transform the Mexican market so that it comple- ments the needs of U.S. suppliers. Mexico's turning toward the United States for such products enhances the economic prospects of some U.S. agribusinesses and of the Mexican and U.S. retail stores that can capitalize on changing tastes in the country. But over the long haul these policies are likely to make Mexico more economically and culturally dependent on its northern neighbor—especially if consumption is artificially stimu- lated by U.S. credit and market development programs.

Some of these programs are influencing a shift in Mexican production strategies with untold consequences. For example, the U.S. Feed Grains Council, a private-sector trade association that participates in many USDA programs, is using U.S. government funding to promote the use of feedlots in the Mexico beef industry. Aside from helping to pump up sales of U.S. feed grains to Mexico, using feedlots represents a shift from Mexico's traditional range-fed approach to raising livestock. Although the feedlot use could potentially reduce deforestation and degradation of pastures, it also heightens Mexican dependency on U.S. feed grain tech- nology and supplies, which in turn are highly dependent on petroleum- based products and processes during production.

What is most striking about these programs is the fact that they appear to contradict the neoliberal agenda pursued by conservative administra- tions in Washington over the last decade. While these administrations pushed countries like Mexico to remove government supports for local businesses, they made sure that U.S. government programs bolstered and protected large U.S. export-oriented enterprises. Admittedly, programs like the EEP and MPP were promoted in part by the Democratic-con- trolled Congress in response to the competitive problems faced by U.S. agricultural enterprises. But they were also welcomed by many conserva- tive Republican policy makers, not only because their own constituents faced the crunch of global competition but also because these programs— in tandem with NAFTA and the Enterprise for the Americas Initiative— strengthened U.S. negotiating positions in forums like the GATT talks and in bilateral trade disputes.

What these programs did not reflect was a concern for the hungry in the United States. On the contrary, these export promotions reflected the elite agenda being pursued by Washington policy makers. One example is especially glaring. While Washington was helping transnational grain giants like Cargill extend their global reach, the U.S. government under President Bush moved to cut off supplies of flour to domestic programs serving the elderly, Native Americans, soup kitchens, child nutrition programs, and other charities. On a global basis, the USDA spent nearly eight hundred million dollars on export subsidies during the first five months of 1992, with 90 percent of the support going to wheat and flour products. In contrast, the domestic flour donations targeted for elimination were valued at fifty million dollars.[67]

## Financing the Trade Explosion

Far more than just U.S. agricultural products are promoted in Mexico through U.S. programs. The explosion of exports to Mexico in services, retail and capital goods, and high technology was ignited not only by Mexico's economic liberalization but also by Washington's trade promotion programs. Virtually every facet of the Mexican economy is a target for such promotions. From the Commerce Department's matchmaker and research services, to the Trade and Development Program's funding for feasibility studies and consultancies, to the export-financing services of Eximbank, the U.S. government is helping U.S. businesses carve out market shares in sectors as wide-ranging as petrochemicals, insurance, and environmental protection.[68]

Mexico's own developmental objectives influence the kinds of goods and services that receive top promotion. An example is the environmental sector. Mexico's plans to step up environmental protection and clean up the country's air, water, and soil caught the attention—and the promotion budgets—of several government and nongovernmental agencies in the United States. Helping draw that attention were huge loans from the World Bank—still heavily influenced by the U.S. vote—and untied credits from Japan designated for environmental projects.[69] Responding to factors like these, the U.S.-Mexico Joint Committee for Investment and Trade identified Mexico's environmental and pollution control sectors as top priorities in terms of trade and investment opportunities. The Commerce Department's International Trade Administration sponsored trade missions, published articles in business journals, and provided information and other assistance to U.S. exporters hoping to take part in the sales boom. Newly formed institutions like the Environmental Technology Export Council—a partnership of U.S. corporations, national laboratories, and trade associations—set their sights on Mexico as a gold mine of export opportunity in the field.

Helping make sure that export opportunities do not get lost to foreign competitors is the U.S. Export-Import Bank. Eximbank is the principal export financing arm of the U.S. government, and its programs have been instrumental in keeping binational trade thriving. Its services are offered in some 155 countries, but Mexico is by far the favored beneficiary. This position is not surprising, given Mexico's status as the United States' third-largest trading partner. Even with that status, however, the share of Eximbank funding that goes to Mexico is remarkable. As of 1992 more than 25 percent of the bank's portfolio was devoted to backing sales of U.S. goods and services to Mexico although the country accounts for only 7 percent of U.S. trade.[70] The bank supports U.S. exports to Mexico under all its programs: direct loans to foreign buyers, intermediate credits to U.S. lending institutions, loan guarantees, and export credit insurance. Available to both public and private buyers, these services protect U.S. banks and businesses from risk, while offering loans at the lowest rates possible under international agreements.[71]

Protecting U.S. corporations from many of the risks that are normal by-products of doing business overseas is a major reason Eximbank exists. Loan guarantees, for example, mean the U.S. taxpayer will foot the bill if the buyer or Mexican bank defaults. Similarly, Eximbank's insurance programs protect businesses from both political and other noncommercial risks for a reasonable premium. "By neutralizing the effect of export credit subsidies from other governments and by absorbing risks that the private sector will not accept," the bank explains, "Eximbank enables U.S. exporters to compete effectively in overseas markets."[72] That objective has certainly been met in Mexico, where Eximbank has been active since 1946. The amount designated for Mexico expands or contracts depending on the state of the Mexican economy, with Mexico's trade liberalization sparking a whopping increase. From 1946 to 1990, for example, Mexico received more than $3 billion in Eximbank loans and credits.[73] Within two short years, though, Mexico's outstanding loans and credits with the bank had more than doubled, climbing to $7.5 billion by the end of 1992.[74] As of 1993, the total was $8.2 billion.[75]

The bank's services have covered nearly every sector of the Mexican economy, from telecommunications to aviation to construction and power. Working with Nafinsa, for example, the bank developed a guarantee program to support the privatization and modernization of Mexico's agroindustry and electronics sectors.[76] The bank's services are also available to support Mexican purchases of U.S. antidrug defense items. Over the years Eximbank has helped U.S. companies like General Electric, Beech Aircraft Corporation, and the Fuller Company increase their exports to Mexico. Many of these sales—especially of goods like locomotives and railway equipment, aircraft, and inputs for Mexico's cement industries—not only provide short-term profits for U.S. exporters but also strengthen the infrastructure and competitive standing of Mexican companies. Some of the largest conglomerates in the Mexican cement industry, for example, have become so successful that they are now competing in the United States.[77]

The most controversial Eximbank programs among Mexicans are those transactions involving Mexico's petroleum sector.[78] Washington's support for Mexico's oil industry has payoffs in terms of the U.S. need for dependable oil supplies and Mexico's interests in modernizing the industry and developing new oil fields. But U.S. involvement in this sector concerns Mexicans worried about losing control over the country's valuable reserves. More than half its annual petroleum exports are sold to U.S. oil companies, and for several years in the 1980s Mexico was the largest contributor to the U.S. Strategic Petroleum Reserve.[79] Considering the country's proximity to the United States and the size of its reserves, helping Mexico expand exploration and development of its oil supplies is a vital interest that Washington is meeting with programs like these. As of late 1992 the United States seemed well on its way to assuring secure access to Mexican oil. By that time, about 20 percent of Eximbank's Mexican loan portfolio was tied up with loans to Pemex, Mexico's state-owned oil giant.[80]

## Trade, Aid, and Runaways

Just as government export-financing programs foster U.S. exports to Mexico, so do other U.S. programs make it easier for U.S. corporations to do business in Mexico or set up shop in the country. By financing feasibility studies, training, research studies, conferences, and other needs, the development assistance of the U.S. Agency for International Development (AID) may well be encouraging some U.S. businesses to relocate to Mexico. It is not that promoting runaways is an explicit objective of the agency. Rather, the types of services that the AID funds to make *maquiladoras* and other targets of foreign investment more profitable and productive often attract U.S. corporations that may or may not already be considering a southward move.[81] The issue points to a dilemma faced by U.S. aid policies as the economy globalizes: Boosting development in poor countries often means helping foreign exports and low-wage workers compete against U.S. products and workers, a particularly troublesome reality in a declining economy.

The fact that this is so prompts periodic outbursts from Congress and the media. Sensitivities in AID about the issue of stimulating foreign competition with foreign assistance run so hot that when Arthur Danart of the Mexico desk was asked about this aspect of AID's programs, he responded, "I choose not to answer." AID, he noted, had been receiving adverse publicity in the previous weeks about just such concerns, leading Congress to tighten its restrictions. In fact, legislation that prohibited using congressional appropriations to lure U.S. businesses to set up operations outside the United States was first written as early as 1986.[82]

The practice of providing services *useful* to such businesses has continued, however. It is defended by AID officials as a boon to Mexican development and by members of other U.S. commerce and trade agencies as a prudent intervention designed to keep U.S. plants from moving to Asia.[83] If they move to Mexico instead, the argument goes, then more jobs are saved in the United States that would otherwise be shipped offshore to foreign suppliers, transportation companies, services, and other such links in the production process.

Up to two million dollars was allocated by AID in 1992 to promote U.S.-Mexico trade and investment.[84] The money was used to help build infrastructure needed for these activities, as well as to transfer know-how and equipment to get Mexican recipients on a "more equal footing" with their U.S. counterparts.[85] In one program, for example, the agency funded the Techological Institute of Higher Education in Monterrey (ITESM) to show Mexican shrimpers how to construct, install, and use turtle excluder devices (TEDs) in their fleets. Because they were catching too many protected sea turtles in their nets, their shrimp was not allowed access to the U.S. market. By using the TEDs, however, they would be able to sell their catches in the United States.

Likewise, some of the research studies funded by AID are designed to solve problems faced by U.S. businesses in Mexico, especially the *maquiladoras*. Working with business organizations like the American Chamber of Commerce in Mexico and the Mexico-U.S. Business Committee, AID grantees identify problem areas and explore potential solutions. One AID-funded study, conducted by the University of the Americas, investigated the problem of high employee turnover in the plants, looking at issues like unionism, wages, housing, and working conditions.[86] In another case AID financed a survey of industries in Mexico to find out what kinds of technical skills were needed by employees. This information was then used by Mexican technical training schools to design curricula to meet those needs.[87]

Another research project planned by the AID looked at the feasibility of creating *maquiladora* industries in various parts of the Mexican interior.[88] Once again, this study reflects the north-south contradictions that exist between long-term Mexican and U.S. interests. Since most of the *maquilas* are owned by U.S. enterprises, this kind of program is clearly in danger of promoting plants that run away to Mexico. On the other hand, expanding the number of *maquilas* in the Mexican interior might indeed reduce population and environmental pressures on the border and help stimulate the Mexican economy through wages and backward linkages.

Other AID programs besides research studies are intended to help solve the problems of businesses in Mexico—whether owned by Mexicans or by U.S. companies. AID's 1991–92 Action Plan for Mexico noted that "the lack of adequate housing and infrastructure" was a big reason the *maquiladoras* had trouble retaining employees. Although not offering to subsidize housing or "other amenities," the AID proposed to put together a technical assistance and training package to help the construction, business, and banking communities meet the needs of *maquila* communities in terms of housing and infrastructure.

The AID's recent budgets in Mexico included funding for trade promotion and implementation of NAFTA, even before the agreement was ratified. For example, the agency sponsored a three-day business development conference in Austin, Texas, which included business leaders interested in expanding cross-border trade under a free trade agreement.[89] In another case, an AID-funded study looked at regional infrastructure, characteristics of local labor, and commercial and educational facilities so that potential investors would know where the best opportunities lay for investment.[90]

The Agency for International Development also worked to get NAFTA provisions carried out, even before the trade agreement was signed. Gerard Bowers, its representative in Mexico City under Bush, said that "one of AID's roles here [in Mexico] is not only to make sure that NAFTA's passed but also to make sure of its implemented success."[91] These AID programs aim to achieve compatibility between NAFTA and the regulations, standards, and day-to-day operations of Mexican businesses and relevant government agencies. In the case of intellectual property rights, for example, the AID worked with the Mexican Ministry of Trade and Industrial Development (SECOFI) to install new regulations for copyrights and other such protections. It also funded training for Mexican businesses to set up and operate environmental protection devices to meet NAFTA standards.

## Taking Aim at the U.S. Market

Mexico has a few of its own programs designed to expand business ties with the United States. Although these initiatives are part of Mexico's attempt to win a bigger piece of the economic pie for its own industries, they are dwarfed in size and scope by U.S. programs. Given the other disparities in the relationship, Mexico's chances of vastly enlarging its market in the United States are unsure. But many of these programs are also designed to attract U.S. investment to Mexico, one of the country's main objectives as its economy opens up. That objective will more likely be fulfilled—not just because of these efforts, by any means, although they are important for providing information about markets, policies, and trade services. Whether Mexican businesses will be able to stand up against the greater resources of the U.S. competitors attracted to the country with such programs is far less clear.

The country's foreign trade bank, Bancomext, provides funding for infrastructure development and other projects that support Mexican exports and joint ventures with foreign businesses. As with some U.S. government programs, the infrastructure that is developed sometimes crosses the line between the two countries. In one case Bancomext put up a $105 million loan to finance construction of the McAllen Produce Terminal Market in McAllen, Texas. When completed, the market will warehouse Mexican agricultural products for sale in the United States.[92] Similarly, the national finance bank, Nafinsa, set up a special loan fund to help finance joint ventures by companies in Mexico and U.S. businesses owned by Latinos.[93]

Aside from financial support, government programs in Mexico provide other services to stimulate trade and investment relations. In Mexico City the Exports Promotion Commission (Compex) helps small and medium-size would-be exporters get loans from Bancomext and Nafinsa and find market niches in the United States. Compex, launched in early 1992 by the government of Mexico City, focuses mostly on the assembly sector, such as appliances, shoes, and dressmaking, but it also promotes other industries, such as chocolate producers and flower growers. In addition to promoting exports, projects like Compex are intended to offset some of the negative effects of economic restructuring. According to Compex director Gina Dalma, "a lot of the smaller industries were being left out" when the economy began to pick up in the late 1980s. "Compex came about as an attempt to help them participate in the opening up of the economy," Dalma explains. "No company will survive long these days if it isn't an exporter."[94]

On a national scale, the Trade Commission of Mexico provides information and matchmaker services. With offices in major cities across the
United States, the government-sponsored commission helps businesses
in the United States and Mexico find trading or investment partners in
the other country. Ironically, the majority of the services offered by the
commission seem designed to move U.S. enterprises into Mexico, as
opposed to promoting Mexico's own exports. Of the seven major types of
information services provided by the commission, five are specifically
aimed at attracting U.S. investment or exports. Companies can find out
how to set up a *maquila* along the border or how to go about getting
products made or assembled in Mexico. Details about what opportunities
are available in specific regions of the country can also be obtained from
the commission, as can information about market development activities
like trade shows. In fact, these are some of the same types of services
offered by the U.S. Commerce Department. With both the Mexican and
U.S. governments working to expand export and investment options for
U.S. businesses, it is no wonder that trade and investment relations surged
in the past few years and that economic integration has advanced so
quickly.

# Development,

# Democracy, and

# Military Aid

Programs designed to boost trade and investment ties between the United States and Mexico do not stand alone. Other U.S. and Mexican programs are designed to respond to issues such as drug trafficking, political liberalization, and the needs of Mexicans dislocated by economic reforms. These programs have not received as much funding in overall terms as those intended to stimulate economic ties. Nonetheless, they have helped in crucial ways to underpin the economic policies of the Mexican government, while enhancing the image of that government and extending the influence of the United States.

Information and exchange programs have drawn the two countries closer together, providing a common pool of knowledge and skills in fields like trade relations, drug control, and environmental regulation. United States development assistance, food aid, and military assistance have been used to spawn links among counterparts in each country, promote Mexico's development agenda, and protect the Mexican government from the political fallout resulting from restructuring. In addition, U.S. democratization programs, though far more modest in Mexico than in many other developing countries, have helped to spread free-market beliefs and have supported the efforts of some civic groups trying to make the Mexican political system more competitive.

## Wooing the Public

In a democracy, even imperfect democracies like those in Mexico and the United States, generating public support for governmental initiatives is essential. The interest groups and social sectors that the U.S. and Mexican governments woo on behalf of initiatives like NAFTA or the border environmental plan are the same voters who can vote thumbs up or down on election candidates and, in many cases, on their pet projects. Successful passage of a free trade accord, for instance, depended first on U.S. business and mainstream environmental groups signing off on at least the fast-track provisions. Determined pressure from these sectors on congressional representatives could have derailed fast track, meaning that NAFTA would have been scrapped before it even reached a negotiating table.

Washington courts the Mexican public to some extent—mostly through delegations and conferences—but political differences between the two countries make that task less essential than Mexico's courtship of U.S. social and political forces. The Mexican system is far more central-ized and is still subject more to the wishes and aims of the PRI than to any other social force. By making direct appeals to the most powerful decision makers in the party and in its core constituencies, the U.S. government can rather easily make its case.[95]

In contrast, the U.S. political system has thousands of vulnerable points of influence that can make or break a piece of legislation or dramatically change the content of proposed laws, regulations, or international agree-ments. Convince a key congressional committee chair or his or her top staffer to oppose a particular proposal, for instance, and the initiative is well on its way to the trash heap. Hiring former U.S. government officials as consultants means back-door entry to executive branch offices, as well as insight on the best way to run the bureaucratic gauntlet. Similarly, generating a political constituency—say, in business or ethnic communi-ties or in the labor or environmental sectors—means domestic political pressure will be applied to elected U.S. officials.

Needing to assure NAFTA's passage and secure access to the U.S. market, the Mexican government concentrated on countering U.S. back-lash against the trade accord and fears about economic interdependence and job loss. Hoping to improve its image in the United States, the Mexican government moved into a new embassy in Washington, ex-panded its staff, and ordered consulates across the United States to promote the free trade pact and reach out to local Mexican Americans. In a highly sophisticated campaign, Mexico hired public relations firms and lobbyists to sell the U.S. public, media, and political leaders on the importance and benefits of initiatives like NAFTA. At the same time, it drafted high-priced U.S. lawyers and consultants to make sure that the country got the best terms possible out of binational deals.

Mexico had conducted some public relations and advertising campaigns in the United States as far back as 1946 under President Miguel Alemán. Until 1990, however, these efforts mostly focused on promoting tourism or the concerns of certain export industries, like cement.[96] By mid-1990 Mexican principals—including government agencies like SE-COFI—were beginning to step up their lobbying and public relations activities aimed at U.S. audiences. These efforts really took off in 1991, when the government began hiring some of the most prestigious U.S. firms to press its case in the United States.[97]

Reportedly spending more than six million dollars annually on lobbying and public relations (a figure that includes neither government contracts for special studies and other consulting services nor the expenses of the quasi-private Mexican business coalition COECE), Mexico went all out.[98] It hired former officials from the Office of the U.S. Trade Representative to consult on trade policy questions, high-powered lawyers to handle tricky trade negotiations, Republican and Democratic lobbying firms, and top-drawer public relations specialists. The burst of activity launched Mexico to the forefront of foreign governments that maintain lobbying and public relations operations in the United States, edging out Japan in the process.

Feeling the heat from environmental and labor opponents of NAFTA, the Mexican government made countering their arguments a top priority. It hired William Brock, for instance, a former secretary of labor and U.S. trade representative, to consult on the policy and politics of U.S. labor and trade.[99] At the same time, lobbyists like the Republican firms of Gold and Liebengood and Charls E. Walker Associates, as well as the Democratic firms of Public Strategies Washington Inc. and TKC International Inc., pressed Mexico's position in influential congressional committees like the Senate Finance and House Ways and Means committees. TKC, headed by Gabriel Guerra-Mondragon, a former special assistant to the U.S. ambassador to Mexico in the early 1980s, also urged U.S. labor to take another look at the free trade agreement and abandon its opposition to the pact.

Enlisted in the campaign were representatives of large corporate interests bound to profit from the free trade accord. Mexico hired Michael B. Smith, a former deputy trade representative, for legal and policy services.[100] Smith heads SJS Advanced Strategies Inc., a unit of the law firm of Steptoe & Johnson. Until mid-1992 he advised a coalition of large Mexican companies about which types of policy proposals might be successful in Washington. Likewise, the Mexican Business Council on Foreign Trade (COECE), an association of Mexican business interests established at the initiative of the Salinas administration, hired Steptoe & Johnson to provide legal and other services that would help the free trade campaign.[101]

Not left out of these efforts were U.S. Latino organizations and Mexican-American communities. Working through consuls in the United States, past Mexican governments had occasionally responded to pleas by Mexican-American organizations like the League for United Latin American Citizens (LULAC) for assistance in their struggles against discrimination. It was not until the Echeverría administration (1970–76), however, that formal ties were developed between Mexico and Mexican-American leaders. Recognizing the mounting political force of Mexican Americans, President Echeverría initiated a series of meetings with the new Chicano leaders of the Southwest. Besides maintaining regular communications, Echeverría and his successor, López Portillo, sponsored scholarship programs for Mexican Americans to attend Mexican universities.[102]

Mexico had both ideological and strategic reasons for these new initiatives. Both presidents regarded the Mexican-American community as *el Mexico de afuera* (the other Mexico)—part of the third world that Mexico was purporting to represent in the 1970s. Mexico also viewed the Mexican-American community as the basis of a pro-Mexico lobby in the United States that would bolster its own position in binational negotiations about such issues as immigration, foreign lending, and petroleum sales.[103] The debt crisis and Mexico's move away from third worldism to neoliberalism resulted in drastic cuts in the scholarship programs and the relegation of outreach to the Mexican-American leadership to low priority status during the de la Madrid administration. While some cultural exchange programs continued, the political relations that had been previously cultivated were de-emphasized.[104]

The advent of free trade rekindled Mexican interest in courting the rapidly expanding Latino communities in the United States. In 1990 the Mexican government established the Program for Foreign Mexican Communities under the foreign affairs ministry. A wide-ranging program, it includes outreach initiatives in such areas as culture, sports, health, and bilingual education. During its first three years, however, the main thrust of the program has been in the areas of business connections, higher education exchanges and seminars, and political outreach. It has sponsored a Council for Business Promotion with Foreign Mexican Communities and has arranged meetings between Mexican business associations and the local and national Hispanic Chambers of Commerce to promote free trade and U.S. investment in Mexico. Furthermore, the program has renewed scholarship and exchange programs for Mexican-American students and educators as well as cooperated closely with the U.S. Department of Education to meet the "growing education demands of Mexican communities" in the United States. Educational outreach has also included seminars attended by Mexican government officials and Mexican-American leaders and professors.

Under the auspices of this new program the Mexican government has reached out directly to Latino organizations and politicians. Program representatives regularly speak at meetings of the congressional Latino caucus and at the conferences of such groups as the National Council of La Raza, LULAC, Mexican American Legal Defense and Educational Fund (MALDEF), Southwest Voter Education Project, Southwest Voter Research Institute, Mexican American Bar Association, and National Association of Chicano Studies. In addition, the program publishes a tabloid called *La Paloma* from its offices in San Antonio.[105]

Also part of the new initiative to build alliances with the Latino populace are high-level, government-sponsored public relations trips to Mexico City to discuss free trade and other bilateral issues. Mirroring such activities are the top-level visits of Mexican officials to the United States to persuade influential sectors of the value of supporting NAFTA and similar ventures. Salinas himself campaigned extensively throughout the United States on NAFTA's behalf. Meeting with the media, environmentalists, congressional representatives, business representatives, and other interest groups, the Mexican president assured them that his country would uphold labor and environmental standards, especially in the heavily industrialized borderlands. He also sought to reassure U.S. labor's fears that jobs would run away to Mexico along with U.S. investment. Without NAFTA, Salinas warned, immigrants from Mexico would continue to cross the border to find jobs in the United States. With NAFTA, he assured, more decent jobs would be created in Mexico, stemming the tide of migration and expanding U.S. export opportunities.

Another part of the Salinas administration's campaign for NAFTA's approval included the hiring of two prominent Mexican-American politicians—Toney Anaya and Jerry Apodaca, both former governors of New Mexico—as registered lobbyists and foreign agents for the Mexican government. Other hired lobbyists included former Navy Secretary Edward Hidalgo and Abelardo Valdez, who served as President Carter's chief of protocol. In its contract with Anaya, the Mexican government's Office for Free Trade Negotiation obligates the Latino leader to, among other things, promote the NAFTA accord among "hispanoamericanos," secure their support for free trade, and see that they pressure their congressional representatives to approve the proposed agreement. Several Latino communications and public relations firms throughout the country were also apparently targeted for consulting contracts by the Mexican government.

Beginning in 1990, U.S. Latino leaders also became the favored recipients of the Orden Mexicana del Aguila Azteca, the country's highest national honor for foreigners. In the heat of the free trade lobbying campaign, President Salinas awarded the medal to eight Latino leaders for their services to Mexico and humanitarianism. No non-Latino leaders were honored. In the 1990–92 period Salinas presented the decoration to honor Los Angeles County Supervisor Gloria Molina, National Council of La Raza President Raul Yzaguirre, MALDEF President Antonia Hernández, Chicano community leader Blandina Cárdenas, farmworker organizer Cesar Chavez, and university professors Luis Leal, Julian Samora, and Américo Paredes. During the 1992 awards ceremony, recipients Molina and Yzaguirre were both commended for their efforts to support NAFTA in the United States. Henry Cisneros, another NAFTA supporter, was also nominated for the 1992 Aguila Azteca but could not accept it because of his impending appointment to the Clinton administration.

The strongly favorable response of many leading Latino organizations to NAFTA suggested that the Mexican government's initiatives within the Latino community were not wasted. Such organizations as the National Council of La Raza and the Hispanic Chamber of Commerce jumped on the free trade bandwagon, supporting fast-track negotiating authority and later backing the agreement itself. No major Latino organization joined the early citizen opposition to NAFTA, and most Mexican-American politicians lent their strong support to the agreement. The persistent courtship of the Mexican government gave rise to a curious marriage between such Latino groups as MALDEF and the National Council of La Raza, which defend the rights of Mexicans and Mexican Americans in the United States, and the Mexican government. In their support of free trade these Latino groups generally made no mention of the pressing issues of the human rights violations and economic exploitation of Mexicans in Mexico.[106] The largely supportive positions taken by the national Latino organizations also underlined the class differences that continue to exist between these organizations and the Latino majority.

But courtship by the Mexican government was not the only factor in the early involvement of Latino organizations in the free trade debate. Latino leaders wanted to be players in their own right, and many honestly believed that NAFTA would be mainly beneficial to the country's Hispanic communities. The often enthusiastic Latino support for NAFTA arose from the widespread belief that free trade would boost the economies of the border states and open new opportunities for Latino businesspeople and professionals, the sectors that most Latino organizations represented. Economic motives do not, however, fully explain this generally supportive position. Also a factor, especially among Mexican-American leaders, was the perception that the political and economic reforms of the Salinas administration were earning new international respect for Mexico and that this upgraded status would help improve the standing of Latinos in the United States.

As the NAFTA debate evolved, initial Latino support for free trade became more qualified as some Latino leaders came to recognize the possible dangers of economic integration. Business groups such as the Hispanic Chamber of Commerce remained steadfast supporters of the agreement, but other groups began to call for modifications that would address the rising labor, infrastructural, and environmental concerns.

Southwest Voter Research Institute spearheaded a campaign to form a "Latino Consensus on NAFTA." As the congressional debate on the treaty began in late 1993, an informal coalition of Latino groups expressed conditional support for NAFTA. Instead of calling for the renegotiation of the treaty, these groups proposed a set of initiatives and implementing laws that would alleviate the adverse impacts of NAFTA by providing job retraining for displaced workers, increasing funds for border infrastructure, and creating a North American Development Bank.[107]

In the end, the Mexican government's efforts to convene Latino support for what was framed as a foreign policy issue met with only partial success. Like other U.S. social sectors, many within the Latino community became increasingly concerned that NAFTA was not simply a foreign policy and trade issue but an agreement that could threaten U.S. jobs and economic stability. Cuban-American groups threatened to oppose NAFTA because of Mexico's relations with Cuba, and Puerto Rican organizations expressed their fear that free trade with Mexico would endanger the territory's status as an attractive low-wage export-processing zone.

### Informing the Debate

In addition to Mexico's public relations and lobbying campaigns, the U.S. government funds educational, information, and visitor exchange programs targeting Mexico. Offered through a full range of U.S. agencies, including the Commerce Department, AID, Drug Enforcement Administration, Department of Defense, Federal Bureau of Investigation, and U.S. Information Agency (USIA), the programs are designed to create linkages between U.S. and Mexican counterparts, transmit U.S. skills and technology, and promote a positive image of the United States in Mexico. Many of these programs are aimed especially at Mexican leaders in various fields, or at those who, by virtue of education or background, are likely to become leaders in the country.

The USIA is the lead agency for conducting these types of programs. In Mexico the USIA generates support for present and proposed U.S. policies through publications, radio and television broadcasts, visitor exchanges, trainings, seminars, and educational opportunities. Over the past few years its major focuses in Mexico have been NAFTA and drug control, although other areas, such as political studies, cultural interchanges, and environmental issues, are also subjects of its programs.

Working with a large number of private organizations and universities, the information agency sponsors visitor exchanges that reach out to a full complement of potentially influential social sectors. Participants include government officials, journalists, educators, artists, youth leaders, athletic coaches, and more. During the negotiations on NAFTA, the USIA made sure that a positive view of the proposed accord was promoted both in the United States and in Mexico during visitor exchanges in each country that targeted academics, farmers, government officials, labor, business leaders, and financial and banking officials.

The agency also produces a number of publications distributed in Mexico, including the "Wireless File" news service, the quarterly *Dialogue (Facetas)*, and *Problems of Communism (Problemas Internacionales)*, a bimonthly magazine. Through other publications its research office reports findings of overseas opinion polls and research studies. Aside from offering interesting information about the viewpoints of Mexican audiences, these polls help shape U.S. policy initiatives and indicate whether past policies have been successful. Recent polls have focused mostly on the drug war and NAFTA.

Like Mexico's public relations efforts, many of these programs are devoted to boosting bilateral trade and investment and to carrying the flag for NAFTA. In at least one case, in fact, a USIA visitor program may well have supported Mexico's own lobbying and public relations activities aimed at the U.S. Congress and influential interest groups. In that instance the USIA sent Lenore Sek, an analyst and investigator for the Congressional Research Service of the Library of Congress, on a trip to Hermosillo. There she met with a PRI representative who is also a prominent state legislator, head of the PRI's economic think tank, and host of a half-hour news program dealing with economic issues. Sek described the U.S. fast-track procedure to the PRI legislator and outlined which U.S. groups were most likely to support or oppose the free trade accord.[108] From that meeting Sek went on to have similar discussions with the manager of a U.S.-owned *maquiladora* and a Mexican college. Whether or not Sek's visit did help Mexico drum up U.S. support for NAFTA is unclear. That it could have done so, however, by demystifying the fast-track process and indicating which groups were lined up for and against it, is certain.

A new binational commission also promotes educational and cultural ties between the two countries and reflects the growing mutuality of some aspects of the U.S.-Mexico relationship. The U.S.-Mexico Commission for Educational and Cultural Exchange was established following an agreement at the November 1990 summit held by Bush and Salinas in Monterrey. Representing a top-level commitment to these programs, the commission's ten-member board is appointed by the Mexican foreign minister and the U.S. ambassador to Mexico and is evenly divided between Mexican and U.S. members. The commission is funded by the U.S. and Mexican governments as well as by some private organizations, such as the Rockefeller Foundation.

The commission administers a variety of educational and cultural exchange programs for U.S. and Mexican participants. For example, it administers the Fulbright Scholarship program in Mexico, offering grants for faculty development, English language training, a multidisciplinary master's degree program, and postdoctoral research. The commission's Fund for Culture sponsors small grants (under twenty-five thousand dollars) for nonacademic cultural exchanges in fields as diverse as dance, translation, and library management. It also supports nondegree research in cultural scholarship and conferences on cultural themes. With the nonprofit Debt-for-Development Coalition, the commission designed a debt swap program called Debt for Science, Technology, and Human Resources to support research and exchanges between U.S. and Mexican universities.

Despite the commission's binational origins, the United States dominates the educational effort. This is true not only because the United States is the major source of funding but also because the commission took over programs that used to be administered by the USIA. It is still housed in the same building as USIA offices in Mexico City, maintaining direct connections with the USIA but operating as a bilateral program.

More than the public relations, lobbying, and legal efforts of Mexico aimed at U.S. audiences, these U.S.-dominated information and education programs are shaping the face of the ongoing integration. Though these exchanges are two-way, favoring a better understanding between the two countries, they more often transmit a U.S. way of doing things and seeing the world than the reverse. Although the USIA attempts to achieve diversity in the viewpoints of people chosen for these programs, Mexican and U.S. participants must be selected and approved by the USIA and often the U.S. Embassy in Mexico. The result is a blending of the two cultures, but one that is guided in many ways by U.S. government functionaries.

## Development Assistance

Mexico is not the top recipient of U.S. development assistance. It is not even in the top tier. With the emphasis on trade, not aid, and with Mexico's economic restructuring winding to a close, development assistance from the United States is declining.[109] In 1992 direct U.S. economic assistance to Mexico totaled $40.6 million, including about $27 million in food aid. In 1993, however, U.S. aid levels dropped to $21 million, and food aid was phased out.[110]

Although current aid levels are being cut, the timing of U.S. assistance in previous years was critical. The assistance that Mexico received beginning in the early 1980s was crucial to the government's "modernization" efforts. Maintaining Mexican stability, underpinning the country's neoliberal reforms, and implementing NAFTA have been central U.S. government interests in Mexico for years, and Washington's development assistance and food aid programs helped advance those objectives. By creating linkages between Mexican institutions and U.S. counterparts, these programs also helped to promote exports of U.S. goods and services. At the same time, focusing on areas like population control, health services, strengthening the private sector, and global warming, U.S. aid programs responded to concerns shared by the two governments.

Until the 1980s Mexican nationalist sensitivities were as much an obstacle to increased U.S. aid as the fact that U.S. foreign policy priorities lay elsewhere. Other factors—such as Mexico's relative wealth among developing countries, its overall stability, and political differences between the two countries—also kept aid levels low. From start-up in the mid-1940s until the 1960s, the United States provided an assortment of loans, grants, and food aid programs in the country. Despite the variety, these programs were minimal in dollar terms. From 1962 to 1971, for example, loans and grants from the Agency for International Development totaled only seventy million dollars, the lowest on a per capita basis of any country in Latin America.[111]

Most development aid was cut off by mutual agreement in 1966, in part because Mexico refused to sign a provision guaranteeing U.S. private investment but also because the United States considered Mexico too "rich" to participate in programs designed for poor countries.[112] Mexico's economy was growing steadily at the time, and, according to the AID, both governments thought the country would be able to satisfy its technical and financial needs by direct purchase or borrowing.[113] Following the decision, the AID closed its offices in Mexico, leaving only a few projects running until they completed their funding cycles in the early 1970s. Over the next years Washington channeled support for several modest development programs through the government-funded Inter-American Foundation, such international organizations as the United Nations World Food Program, and a few nongovernmental organizations, but official government-to-government aid dried up.

Getting back into the aid business in Mexico was a gradual process. Mexico requested U.S. help on population control programs in 1977, but it took Mexico's economic crisis and subsequent restructuring efforts to revitalize bilateral aid relations. In 1983 significant U.S. assistance began to "fade in again," according to Gerard Bowers, the AID's representative in Mexico City during the Bush administration.[114] The agency moved an office into the U.S. Embassy and started food aid and other development assistance programs to ease the impact of the crisis and of the austerity plans being implemented by de la Madrid.[115]

Because the AID designates Mexico an advanced developing country (ADC), it did not open a full-scale mission despite widespread poverty and uneven development. In contrast with large, visible operations in other developing countries, the AID office in Mexico maintains a low profile and is run by a bare-bones staff. But Washington funnels aid to Mexico through many other avenues as well. According to Samuel Taylor, who headed the AID's Mexico City office in 1989, Mexico has the "largest nonmission program in the world," with "hundreds of projects" being channeled through government agencies ranging from the Commerce Department to the U.S. Forest Service.[116]

Contributing to the agency's low profile in the country is the fact that most assistance is run through U.S. or Mexican nongovernmental organizations. Organizations like the U.S.-based Northwest Medical Teams, the Mexican Foundation for Rural Development, and the Mexican Federation of Private Family Planning Associations (FEMAP) use U.S. funds to carry out their health care and development programs. By offering training, institutional and program support, research grants, and technical assistance in essential fields like community health, child survival, AIDS prevention, sanitation, and microenterprise development, these programs have helped maintain political stability while Mexican government social service cutbacks were pulling the rug out from under vulnerable populations.

United States aid could not have been more timely. On top of the crash of the early 1980s, Salinas's economic restructuring squeezed the middle and lower classes hard. Wage controls and price increases wiped out the purchasing power of Mexican workers and professionals alike, and labor unions were too weak and too tied to the government to guard against further erosion of their members' living standards. By signing on to the government's economic solidarity pacts, Mexico's major unions gave the go-ahead to Salinas's programs, even as their members suffered.

Government cutbacks, private-sector bankruptcies, and slow growth meant too few jobs for the country's workforce, which grows by nearly 1 million new job hunters each year. Unemployment climbed, standing in the early 1990s at about 18 percent. Those who do have work often scrimp together meager livings in the informal sector, pooling their earnings with other household members to get by. According to the United Nations' Economic Commission on Latin America, underemployment in Mexico, such as that found in the informal sector, afflicts 40 percent of the country's workforce. Half the country lives in poverty, lacking adequate housing, health care, and basic services.

Washington's aid programs helped offset some of the effects of the crisis and the restructuring by providing a social safety net and helping create employment alternatives like microenterprises. Given the government's austerity budgets of the 1980s, many of these programs might never have started up and would almost surely have been eliminated had they relied on government sources of support. In the case of family planning services, for example, AID pointed out in 1984 that "Mexico's economic crisis . . . sharply reduced the financial resources needed to maintain public support of social services, including family planning."[117] Lowering birthrates was already a major objective of the Mexican government, which hoped to get the annual population increase down to 1 percent by the year 2000. AID helped Mexico keep from losing ground in its effort to lower birthrates—with all the implications for food production, job creation, health care, education, housing, infrastructure development, and migration. In fact, as an AID strategy plan noted in 1990, "far and away" the largest share of the Washington office's contribution for programs in Mexico went to population programs: some $5.7 million in 1990.[118] Working through voluntary organizations and government institutions, AID not only guaranteed that programs would not be cut back but actually helped Mexico expand its population control services.[119]

Other programs, such as microenterprise development and support for community and national health care, also helped keep a safety net under some of the people at risk from Mexico's economic crisis and its new economic strategies. Organizations like ADMIC (Asesoría Dinámica a Microempresas) and the Murrieta Foundation use AID funds to offer credit, technical assistance, and training in a "free enterprise philosophy" to small businesses in both urban and rural areas. The Mexican Foundation for Rural Development, for example, helped establish apiculture enterprises in Chiapas and Oaxaca and provided training in honey production and business management.[120] The AID also provides training for rural health promoters, pharmacists, physicians, and nurses in maternal and child health care. Likewise, Ministry of Health personnel have been trained in child survival technologies like oral rehydration therapy.

Washington's aid programs do not concentrate solely on these safety net operations. One of the newer initiatives will mean a big boost in conservation and environmental funding. Because Mexico was declared a "key" country in the effort to combat global warming, assistance to conservation projects intended to curb deforestation and air pollution will climb dramatically.[121] Other types of programs, such as training in wildfire suppression and search and rescue, media campaigns to prevent drug abuse, and scientific research grants also receive AID funding.

Even with the cutbacks, programs carried out with U.S. development aid tend to reinforce the asymmetry that already characterizes the relationship. According to AID, its projects are intended to "acquaint potential leaders [in Mexico] with [U.S.] societal and cultural values, develop trade and investment relations between the United States and [the Mexican] private sector, and increase the utilization of U.S. technology."[122] Developing such linkages is a key objective of AID assistance packages in Mexico, as in other advanced developing countries. The idea is to hook up U.S. institutions with Mexican counterparts so that U.S. expertise, goods, and services will flow steadily into the country. As AID explained in 1984, "The proximity and diversity of U.S. technologies in almost all areas corresponding to Mexico's needs make the U.S. a highly attractive source."[123] Using education, strategies, skills, technology, equipment, and management techniques designed mostly in the United States, these programs increase the dependence of Mexican recipients on U.S. counterparts.

Another problem is that while these programs enhance Mexican dependency on the United States and further the integration that is under way between the two countries, they may not always meet Mexico's long-term development needs. For example, Mexico needs to develop backward linkages to multiply the economic benefits of the *maquiladoras*. It needs to foster its own technological and agricultural base so that it will not always have to base its development strategies on cheap labor. And microenterprises, while perhaps providing short-term economic relief to a few employees, may be seriously threatened by collapsing trade barriers and potential competition from outside the country.

## Food Aid

In tandem with Mexican government initiatives like the Solidarity program, U.S. food aid programs helped the Mexican government carry out economic transformations that might otherwise have had to be scrapped because of political fallout. From 1983 through 1992 surplus U.S. food commodities helped compensate for cutbacks in Mexican social programs, providing a safety net for some of the sectors hardest hit by Mexico's restructuring. Over the years commodities such as powdered milk, corn, cheese, rice, wheat flour, and sorghum were distributed to needy populations or sold on the market to raise funds for development activities.

Most of the food aid to Mexico went through the Section 416 program of the Commodity Credit Corporation.[124] The U.S. donations started in 1983, coinciding with the worst years of Mexico's economic crisis. Programs like Section 416 recognized the reality of Mexican poverty and the crucial role government welfare and subsidy programs played in keeping the lid on discontent. As a consequence, even though Mexico was identified as an advanced developing country, it was one of the world's largest recipients of Section 416 donations.[125] In 1989 Mexico was second only to India as a recipient of 416 commodities.

Thanks to 416 donations, the Mexican government's social welfare agency, DIF, was able to expand its feeding programs, even while the

412

government was cutting out ambitious consumer and producer subsidy programs like the Sistema Alimentaria Mexicana (SAM). But such efforts had more than just humanitarian objectives. They resulted in plenty of political currency for the PRI government, which used the food distribution and companion community development activities to extend its outreach and generate goodwill among those most affected by the restructuring. But these programs were less helpful where the chronically poor were concerned, a fact pointed out by an AID assessment in 1990.[126]

Undergirded by U.S. food aid, the Mexican government had more political freedom to maneuver when carrying out its radical reforms of the country's economy. Without such support, pressures for more populist responses to the country's economic dilemma would likely have increased, perhaps to the boiling point in those parts of the country hardest hit by government cutbacks, privatization, agricultural restructuring, and other changes. Aside from offering a possible threat to the country's stability, such opposition might well have endangered the new policies themselves, outcomes thoroughly opposed by both the U.S. and Mexican governments.

## Modernizing the Military

The warming of relations between Washington and Mexico City also strengthened the bonds between the U.S. and Mexican military establishments. Mexico's armed forces are still among the most nationalistic in the hemisphere, but the growing role of the Mexican military in antidrug operations and the government's emphasis on providing the armed forces with updated equipment and training opened the way to increased assistance from the United States.[127] By licensing commercial sales, providing training, leasing equipment, and supporting military sales to Mexico, Washington has backed the modernization of the Mexican armed forces.

Military aid to Mexico reinforces long-term U.S. interests while helping to bolster the Mexican government's control over social sectors like labor and rural populations disrupted by the economic crisis and subsequent restructuring. Ensuring domestic order has been the military's main concern since the 1940s. Under Salinas, however, the military stepped up its police functions, intervening much more frequently when political and labor discontent flared into confrontation.[128] As far as it is possible to tell, Washington's aid to the Mexican armed forces has not been directed specifically at supporting these police functions. Instead it has helped strengthen the military institution by providing access to updated equipment and training, thus making the task of social control more easily accomplished. The Mexican government's wish to keep control over restive sectors of the population dovetails with Washington's interests in a "secure, stable, and friendly" southern neighbor.[129] Aside from guaranteeing a peaceable southern border, though, staying on friendly terms with Mexico and its military forces helps protect U.S. access to strategic raw materials, including petroleum, strontium, fluorspar, and antimony.[130]

But Washington wants more than stability on its southern flank. It wants Mexico to look to Washington for cues and technical support when it comes to international policies, whether military or otherwise. Security assistance to Mexico's military encourages just such a turn toward the United States, as do other U.S. aid programs.[131] As the Department of Defense told Congress, U.S. military programs in Mexico have the goal of "expanding U.S. influence in the [Mexican] military."[132]

Obtaining this influence in Mexico has not been easy compared with doing so in many other Latin American countries. In relative terms, military assistance to Mexico and the size of the U.S. military presence there have been very low, partly because Mexico's own military budget is small. In 1989, for example, Mexico's expenditures on its armed forces amounted to only about 0.6 percent of the GNP, one of the lowest in the hemisphere.[133] Although U.S. security aid to the country climbed during the late 1980s, almost all of it went to the Mexican attorney general's office for antidrug programs.[134]

Despite these caveats, the United States, more than any other country, has maintained a steady influence on the Mexican armed forces, one that is, however, tempered by Mexico's own independent and nationalist approach to the relationship. In one of the few close looks at the subject, Stephen J. Wager explained that "geographic proximity, a common border, and easy access to equipment and training material have contributed to the creation of a special relationship between both countries, a relationship which has by no means enabled U.S. influence to become dominating or pervasive."[135]

The broad outlines of this ambivalent relationship took shape during World War II and the early postwar years.[136] The threat of fascism first drew the two countries together, resulting in a Joint Mexico-U.S. Defense Commission. After the war, however, the commission became inactive, and differences in their approaches to international politics pulled the two countries farther apart. Mexico refused to accede to such U.S. initiatives as the Rio Treaty, a hemisphere-wide mutual defense pact concluded in

1951 and designed to forge links among the U.S. and Latin American militaries. In contrast with the rest of the region, Mexico barely participated in U.S. security assistance programs. It received almost no support under the Military Assistance Program (MAP), a U.S. grant program that finances the purchase of defense articles and services, training, and technical assistance.[137] Likewise, the United States has not had a military assistance advisory group (MAAG) stationed on Mexican territory. Symbolically this fact—that a MAAG has not been deployed in Mexico—underscores the country's fierce independence from Washington when it comes to military ties; other than tiny Caribbean countries, Cuba is the only other Latin American country to share this distinction.

Most of the direct assistance that does occur is in the form of training. The International Military Education and Training Program (IMET) is key to increasing U.S. access to the Mexican armed forces. IMET is a cornerstone of U.S. military programs around the world, providing training for military personnel and their civilian colleagues either in the United States or at overseas facilities. Mexico sends more military personnel to the United States for military training than to any other country.[138] Although in numerical terms the number of annual trainees is relatively small, the program is instrumental in building ties between armed forces in the two countries. As Elliott Abrams, assistant secretary of state for Latin American affairs under President Reagan observed, Mexico is a country "where our access to the military results from and depends to a large degree on IMET."[139]

With the exception of funding for drug control activities, discussed previously, IMET has been the major source of direct U.S. military aid to Mexico during the postwar years. From 1946 to 1992 the United States provided almost $5.8 million for trainings under IMET, with more than one-third of the total allocated during the 1980s.[140] Over the last few years the IMET grants have financed professional military education, maintenance courses, and instruction in how to operate and maintain antidrug equipment. IMET programs in Mexico increased sharply during the 1980s. During the three decades from 1950 to 1978 some 906 Mexicans participated in these training programs. From 1984 to 1992, however, some 575 Mexican military personnel were trained through IMET, with another 150 trainees scheduled in 1993.[141]

The modernization of the Mexican military that began in the early 1980s received important backing from commercial and government military sales supported by Washington. Although it does not receive U.S. funding for the purchases, Mexico buys U.S. equipment, spare parts, and technical assistance through the Foreign Military Sales Financing Program (FMS), a government program designed to support military sales to foreign countries. This has historically been a small program in Mexico, but it was stepped up in the 1980s. From 1946 to 1989 Mexico made more than $45 million in purchases under the FMS, with two-thirds of the transactions occurring after 1987.[142] In fact, between 1982 and 1990 Mexico leased or purchased more military goods and services via the FMS system, commercial sales, or transfers of excess defense articles than it did in the previous three decades. Mexican leases or purchases of U.S. military goods and services totaled $29.5 million from 1950 to 1978. That figure skyrocketed to $500 million from 1982 to 1990.[143]

A top beneficiary of purchases and leases undertaken in the 1980s has been the Mexican Air Force, although the army has also benefited. Through programs like FMS Mexico purchased a squadron of F-5E aircraft, as well as Bell 212 helicopters, C-130 transport planes, and other aircraft.[144] The country leased U.S. UH-1H helicopters and purchased a variety of Jeeps, light trucks, and other vehicles. Communications equipment, weapons, and spare parts also came through U.S. government channels.[145]

Although less vigorous and dynamic than other aspects of the U.S.-Mexico relationship, the growing ties between the militaries of the two countries are important. Training programs, for example, transmit U.S. national and regional security perspectives, along with technical skills and military tactics. Collegial relationships sparked by sharing problems and expertise during these classes can be expected to persist into the future. Just as important, the fact that Mexico is acquiring so much in the way of U.S. defense equipment and services means that the country will need to stay hooked into U.S. supply lines for spare parts and technical assistance.

Whatever the merits of wanting a strong Mexican military to help guarantee stability and, as a consequence, U.S. interests, these military aid programs inspire ethical concerns. As long as the Mexican armed forces continue to act as backup police forces to quell disturbances that result from the PRI's authoritarianism and economic restructuring, U.S. military aid is helping to reinforce strong-arm approaches in the country.[146] Bolstering the repressive arm of the Mexican government may well help ensure that the country's radical economic reforms become fully entrenched. This result is especially likely because the strengthening of the military has been complemented by development aid, public relations campaigns, and economic promotion programs that help siphon off discontent. Given the authoritarianism for which the Mexican government is known, however, the human costs of such programs may be too high.

## Democratization and the Perfect Dictatorship

From the day he took office, Salinas kept the throttle wide open as he steered the country toward an outward-looking market economy, while simultaneously dragging his feet on reforms to the country's authoritarian political system. By emphasizing economic over political reform—wagering that foreign investment, trade, and modernization would stimulate economic growth and goodwill toward the PRI—Salinas hoped to "keep the 'perfect dictatorship' from unraveling."[147] Some reforms did occur— opposition parties won a few governorships, for example, the first ever lost by the PRI—but for the most part Salinas explicitly put off political changes so that the government's centralized power could be used to guarantee that the economic changes would go through.[148] Washington, which has promoted "democratization" as one of the major pillars of its recent foreign aid programs, looked the other way as political repression and electoral fraud continued under Salinas.[149] As shown by the U.S. assistance programs described above, the Reagan and Bush administrations actually bolstered the Salinas government, while not pressuring Mexico to liberalize politics as rapidly as the economy.[150]

Whether this pattern will change under Clinton is still not certain. Some new U.S. government-funded programs have supported civic organizations aligned with the opposition, but as of yet there is little sign that Mexican democracy is as important in Washington as good trade and investment relations.

At a time when Mexico needs the greatest possible popular input into and consensus on the historic changes under way in the country, effective civic participation is stifled by Mexican politics-as-usual. Dissent, opposition organizing, and other forms of independent political activity are certainly common in Mexico. When they get too strong or vocal, however, opponents are co-opted or otherwise silenced by the government. On the electoral front the PRI also holds sway, not only because of its historical claims to legitimacy and its uncanny ability to deliver the goods in terms of economic growth or patronage but also because of structural features of the political system that could be remedied if the political will existed to do so. For example, despite opposition representation, the PRI controls the National Election Commission, which is headed by the minister of the interior, who is in turn subordinate to the country's president. Likewise, a controversial "governability clause" instituted under Salinas virtually guarantees the PRI's dominance in the Chamber of Deputies. From questionable voter rolls to de facto control of the media to the PRI's enormous financial advantage over opposition parties, the governing party holds the upper hand in election contests and thus in decision making about the country's future.[151] Marred by government-sanctioned fraud, postelection violence, and government crackdowns, the elections themselves indicate both Mexico's need for democracy and the PRI's wavering hold on the country's political reins.

Washington, however, has always been more interested in Mexican stability than in its fortunes—ill or fair—in terms of democratic processes. Since the latter half of the nineteenth century the United States has generally accepted whichever government was running the show in Mexico, as long as political stability was maintained. Indifferent to the dictatorial excesses of Porfirio Díaz in the years before the Mexican Revolution and mostly silent about human rights abuses and one-party dominance under the PRI, Washington has offered virtually no assistance for democratization efforts across its southern border.[152] To some extent this nonaction has been justified as deference to Mexican sovereignty concerns. Looking at the big picture, though, one sees that Mexican sovereignty is just a smoke screen: The United States readily ignores such worries when fighting the drug war and when its policy makers condition economic aid and debt management packages on Mexico's carrying out economic liberalization and austerity measures.

For a short period in the mid-1980s Washington was somewhat more active on the democratic front, but even those efforts were primarily confined to rhetoric and admonitions. Moreover, the timing of its interest in the fairness of Mexico's political system was significant. The years of greatest attention coincided with Mexico's economic crisis, the PRI's loss of standing among the electorate, the strengthening of conservative political parties like the National Action Party (PAN), and clashes with the Mexican government over U.S. policies in Central America. Loosening the governing party's grip on power during those years would likely have improved the electoral chances of conservative forces that shared Washington's economic and political views. When in 1988 it appeared as if support for political openings would favor the center-left opposition and not ideological allies in the PRI or the PAN, Washington openly threw its support to the PRI, ignoring the fraud-riddled election that brought Salinas into office.[153]

Some U.S. programs have purported to build democracy in Mexico, although until recently these have mostly aided the conservative opposition or traditional PRI forces. Since 1985, for instance, the National Endowment for Democracy (NED) has funneled U.S. government grants to a few Mexican organizations (see Table 5).[154] Until 1992, most of the grants supported Mexico's economic transformations, in keeping with NED's philosophy that a free market complements, and is a requirement for, political liberalization. In addition, most NED grants in Mexico were funneled through the most conservative of the endowment's core grantees: the Center for International Private Enterprise and the National Republican Institute for International Affairs (now known as the International Republican Institute).[155]

Nearly half of NED's grants to Mexico from 1985 to 1991 went to business organizations promoting free-market economies and advocating economic liberalization.[156] For instance, NED sponsored grants to train journalists in free-market economics and to help them place their economic policy op-ed pieces in Mexican newspapers. NED also funded the "Young Entrepreneur" training program of the Mexican affiliate of Junior Achievement, the Mexican Entrepreneurial Development Program (Desem). Desem later became a recipient of funding from the Agency for International Development. Other NED grants went to associations representing business interests, including Coparmex and Concanaco—Mexico's leading confederation of business organizations. From 1987 to 1988, for example, Coparmex received $173,118 to distribute a program teaching free-market principles in Mexico's technical-vocational schools. Likewise, Concanaco received a major grant to help its member chambers of commerce improve their skills in political advocacy. NED also financed training courses for Mexico's government-backed union and a conference for conservative Latin American political parties. The conference was cosponsored by the PAN and coincided with the party's fiftieth anniversary.

Over the years, the major recipient of NED grants in Mexico has been the Democracy, Solidarity, and Social Peace Association (Demos Paz) and its parent organization, the Superior Institute for Democratic Culture (ISCD). Grants to Demos Paz and the ISCD are channeled through NED's core grantee linked to the U.S. Republican Party, the International Republican Institute (IRI). Of all NED's grants to Mexico, those to Demos Paz have totaled the most in dollar terms and have spanned the greatest number of years. From 1988 to 1992, Demos Paz received $451,000 from NED. Another $120,000 grant was awarded in January 1993.[157]

An organization mostly composed of middle-class social Christians, libertarians, and conservatives, Demos Paz is close to the PAN but not directly affiliated with the party. Demos Paz has only limited influence on the majority of Mexico's population, partly because of its middle-class

**Table 5**

NED's Grant Allocations

| ORGANIZATION NAME | U.S. PASS-THROUGH GRANTEE* | DESCRIPTION OF ORGANIZATION | PURPOSE OF GRANTS | YEARS | FUNDING AMOUNTS |
|---|---|---|---|---|---|
| Confederation of Mexican Workers | FTUI | Mexico's largest official trade union | Education programs and training seminars | 1985 | $100,000 |
| Center for Studies in Economics and Education | CIPE | Nonprofit research institute in Monterrey | Seminars for Mexican journalists on economic policy and theory; support for production and distribution of op-ed pieces | 1986 | 33,000 |
| Coparmex | CIPE | Voluntary business organization representing 34,000 Mexican businesses | To continue its Empresa program, teaching free market economic principles in Mexican technical-vocational schools | 1987–88 | 173,118 |
| Democracy, Solidarity, and Social Peace Association (Demos Paz) | NRIIA/IRI | Nonprofit organization focusing on civic education and training | To conduct opinion polls, sponsor seminars and conferences, produce publications, and hold briefings for the press | 1988–1992 | 451,000 |
| NRIIA | NRIIA/IRI | International arm of the U.S. Republican Party | To convene a July 1989 conference of conservative Latin American political parties cosponsored by the PAN | 1989 | 50,000 |
| Mexican Entrepreneurial Development Program (Desem) | CIPE | Mexican counterpart to Junior Achievement Program | For its "University Impact" program, teaching private enterprise to students at University of Monterrey | 1989 | 40,000 |

**Table 5 (Continued)**

NED's Grant Allocations

| ORGANIZATION NAME | U.S. PASS-THROUGH GRANTEE* | DESCRIPTION OF ORGANIZATION | PURPOSE OF GRANTS | YEARS | FUNDING AMOUNTS |
|---|---|---|---|---|---|
| Concanaco | CIPE | Mexico's leading confederation of business organizations | To improve individual chambers of commerce in their advocacy of the private sector | 1990 | $111,506 |
| Council for Democracy & Convergence of Civic Organizations for Democracy | NDI | Mexican civic organizations focusing on democratization issues | Technical and financial assistance to domestic civic groups observing elections in Sinaloa. Support for efforts at increasing electoral participation, including independent vote count in Chihuahua | 1992 | 156,779 |
| Council for Democracy | Resources for Action | Private organization for electoral reform in Mexico | To expand its program of election observation, "quick counts," publications, and forums | 1992 | 60,000 |
| Civic Front of San Luis Potosí | Resources for Action | Civic group in San Luis Potosí (supported Salvador Nava's campaign) | To support its new civic education school, offering courses on human rights, leadership skills, civic education, and increased women's participation in public affairs | 1992 | 55,000 |

*CIPE—Center for International Private Enterprise. FTUI—Free Trade Union Institute. IRI—International Republican Institute. NDI—National Democratic Institute for International Affairs. NRIIA—National Republican Institute for International Affairs.
SOURCE: NED annual reports, 1985–1992; board meeting minutes and grant documents.

focus. The organization sponsors seminars and produces publications, most of which are critical of the PRI and of the state of democracy in Mexico. These educational forums tend to have relatively few participants and are not aimed at developing a broad social movement. The organization also conducts monthly public-opinion polls in Mexico City. These too, however, are targeted mostly at the middle class, with an average sample size of only four hundred to five hundred people. The relevance and reliability of these polls is limited by class factors, sample size, and the fact that the subjects are all from a single large urban area.

Looking at the above grants suggests that NED's role in Mexico has been conservative, and sometimes even irrelevant. In 1992, however, NED got directly into the electoral arena. The focus of the endowment's grants moved away from actively promoting free-market policies. With the PRI taking on such a promarket mantle since Salinas took office, there is less need for NED to advocate such reforms. Instead NED's recent grants have concentrated more on politics per se than the endowment's earlier grants did.

The organizations receiving NED grants for their election-related activities since 1992 are the Council for Democracy (*Consejo para la Democracia*), the Convergence of Civic Organizations for Democracy (*Convergencia de Organismos Civiles por la Democracia*), and the Civic Front of San Luis Potosí (*Frente Cívico Potosino*).[158] The grants supported training for election monitors, "quick counts" during elections in Sinaloa and Chihuahua, publications, conferences, and some infrastructure development.

The Mexican grantees are known among democracy activists and Mexico-watchers for their solid support for electoral democracy and their opposition to the way politics are currently structured in the country. The Council for Democracy, for example, is an association of prominent Mexicans whose permanent members include journalists, academics, politicians, and political activists from all three major parties. But these people mostly lend their names to the association, which is, in reality, a one-man show headed by Julio Faesler. Faesler, a former member of the PRI, is now linked to the PAN. He is known as a political moderate who tries to stay on good terms with the Mexican government and who is trusted by U.S. organizations like NED and the National Democratic Institute for International Affairs. Although NED's 1992 grant was to help the Council recruit new members, the organization still relies on activists mobilized by other groups to help carry out tasks like vote counts and election observation.

The Convergence of Civic Organizations for Democracy (*Convergen-*

*cia)* is more left-of-center than the Council. Set up by activists in nongovernmental organizations and popular organizations, *Convergencia* is closer to the Party of the Democratic Revolution (PRD) than to any other political party. It represents a coalition of some 136 groups representing 20 Mexican states and the Federal District in Mexico City. Since 1991, *Convergencia* has organized election observations in seven states and in Mexico City. NED, however, has not funded *Convergencia*'s election observations, instead supporting the group's seminars on election monitoring and its trainings for poll watchers.

The Civic Front of San Luis Potosí is the most broad-based of these three grantees. The Civic Front was a creation of Salvador Nava—a leading member of the PAN who, until his death, was recognized as one of the most coalition-minded of Mexico's democracy activists. The group received $55,000 from NED in 1992 to support a school for civic education and to improve its outreach to other civic organizations and political sectors around the country. Nava also helped set up a powerful national network, the Citizens' Movement for Democracy *(Movimiento Ciudadano Democrático)*. Filled with firebrands, the Citizens' Movement for Democracy includes the Civic Front as a regional affiliate and is coalition-oriented in its approach to Mexican politics. Among its members are activists in the PAN and PRD, reformist elements in the PRI, and independent political activists. So far, it has not been a recipient of NED grants.

Despite the broader range of support for groups from various political tendencies, NED's grants still seem to be most favorable toward either the PRI-dominated status quo or toward center-right parties like the PAN. This is most clearly seen by comparing funding levels. Election-related grants for individual organizations since 1992 have averaged around $68,000, with two grants going to Faesler's Council for Democracy, an organization that is closer to the PAN than to other political parties. The other major NED grants since that time have gone to Demos Paz, another center-right critic of the current Mexican government. But the funding picture is not completely black and white. Demos Paz, for example, is not opposed to working with left-of-center political organizations and parties. In fact, for a short time, the Citizen's Movement for Democracy had its national office at the ISCD.

The focus—at least to date—on poll watching and quick counts raises another doubt about the value of NED's grants in Mexico. These are obviously important tasks in Mexico, where fraudulent elections are the norm. But the effectiveness of these activities is limited both because of the size of the country—there are too many polling places to be covered—

and because so much of the fraud and distortion of the political process takes place well before the elections. Biases in the federal electoral commission, for example, make it virtually impossible for opposition parties to get fair treatment of their complaints. Human rights violations, irregularities during voter registration, manipulation of the voter lists, patronage programs, and the government's domination of the Mexican media all contribute to a playing field tilted in the PRI's favor. If these issues remain unaddressed, quick counts and election monitors even risk the chance of validating undemocratic election results in cases where the voting itself was relatively free of overt fraud, but the combined irregularities over time add up to an election climate that is unfair and invalid.

So far, NED's grants have not had the broad agenda suggested by this list of problems. The 1993 proposals to NED, however, reportedly have a wider focus, ranging from supporting pressure for changes in the structure of the electoral commission, to coalition-building and message development among the opposition parties. NED has also been talking with another national citizens' group, the National Accord for Democracy, or ACUDE. ACUDE, like the Citizens' Movement for Democracy, is considered a potent, broad-based organization headed by politically sophisticated activists capable of mobilizing large masses of people. Whether NED will fund these activities or these organizations is not yet clear.

Besides the NED, the other major conduit for U.S. government support to overseas political activities is the Agency for International Development. Even though the AID has made promoting democracy one of the central pillars of its international activities, it has no such programs in Mexico. In fact, its Mexico office stated in its 1991–92 action plan that democracy-building activities would be "counterproductive" in Mexico.[159] Ruling out projects in such areas as legislative procedures, election reform, or encouraging political pluralism, AID/Mexico—after consulting with the U.S. Embassy in Mexico City—instead urged increased support for its "administration of justice" (AOJ) programs in Mexico. A small, interagency AOJ program was run in Mexico for a couple years in the early 1990s, but its focus was not democratization. Instead its projects supported trainings, conferences, and visitor exchanges aimed at Mexico's law enforcement and legal communities, many of which overlapped with antidrug efforts.[160]

Mexico's progress toward democracy depends above all on its own internal processes, but the fact that the United States has chosen not to emphasize democratization as strongly as it has pushed economic liberalization undermines political reforms while shoring up authoritarianism.

Making this observation is not a call for U.S. intervention in Mexico's political affairs. Washington's interference in Mexican politics would not resolve the country's democracy dilemma. Worse, as in countries like Nicaragua, such intervention would indeed violate Mexican sovereignty and is not advocated here.[161]

The new administration in Washington may indeed move questions regarding Mexico's treatment of human and political rights higher on its priority list, although as of mid-1993 the evidence on that possibility is mixed. Whatever the impact of U.S. political aid programs, democratization in Mexico is a crucial issue for the two neighbors. In many ways Mexico and the United States seem bound to a common future. The economic integration of the two countries makes such a common future probable, and partnership in NAFTA will assure it. With the politics and economies of the two countries increasingly intertwined, the state of democracy in each becomes a foreign policy as well as a domestic concern.

# Notes

1. Cathryn L. Thorup, "U.S. Policy-making Toward Mexico: Prospects for Administrative Reform," in *Foreign Policy in U.S.-Mexican Relations,* eds. Rosario Green and Peter H. Smith (San Diego: Center for U.S.-Mexican Studies, 1989), 157.
2. During his tenure Miguel Alemán steered government policies away from the extreme nationalism and populism of previous Mexican presidents. A probusiness conservative supported by financiers and industrialists, he encouraged tourism, commercial agriculture by large-scale private interests, big business, and market policies. He also brought the Mexican Army under civilian control and limited its power, a remarkable achievement in Latin American politics. Like Salinas's, Alemán's policies found favor in Washington, and a warm relationship characterized the period.
3. Interview with Eric Fredell, 28 July 1993.
4. That Clinton basically supports NAFTA as negotiated by Bush and Salinas is not surprising. He hails from the conservative wing of the Democratic party and as governor of Arkansas used many of the same enticements that Mexico uses to attract foreign investment.
5. The labor accord, for example, allows sanctions only for violations of child labor laws, minimum wage guidelines, and health and safety protections. But violations of fundamental worker rights, such as freedom of association and the right to organize, could not result in trade sanctions under the accord. Exempting such protections means that labor suppression—a common problem in Mexico—could continue without recourse under NAFTA. The effect would be downward pressure on wages and working conditions in the United States, as competition between U.S. workers and Mexican counterparts increased under the free trade agreement. Just as worrisome is the fact that omitting protections for worker rights from NAFTA represents a step backward for the United States, which includes provisions protecting internationally recognized worker rights in other preferential trade policies, such as the Generalized System of Preferences.
6. This careful study of the relations between the federal governments in each country does not mean that other relationships—state, local, and nongovernmental—are unimportant. As integration has advanced, linkages between U.S. and Mexican counterparts at these levels have proliferated at a dizzying rate. An extensive array of actors, including government agencies, environmental groups,

426

health care organizations, labor and human rights groups, and community activists have been developing ties with those who share common interests and concerns on the opposite side of the border. With interests and objectives that often compete with those of the national governments, this "citizen diplomacy" is helping shape the bilateral agenda, especially around concerns such as the environment. Two surveys of the expanding ties among U.S. and Mexican organizations are Ricardo Hernández and Edith Sánchez, *Cross-Border Links: A Directory of Organizations in Canada, Mexico, and the United States* (Albuquerque: Inter-Hemispheric Education Resource Center, 1992), and Sevrens, *Environmental, Health, and Housing Needs*. See also Cathryn Thorup, "The Politics of Free Trade and the Dynamics of Cross-Border Coalitions in U.S.-Mexican Relations," *Columbia Journal of World Business* (Summer 1991).

7. Quoted in Norman Gall, "Can Mexico Pull Through?," *Forbes* (15 August 1983), 79.

8. The U.S. State Department promotes the view that the U.S. and Mexican interests are converging. See, for example, the summaries of participant commentaries from its conference on "United States and Mexico: Converging Destinies" (Washington, D.C., 4–5 April 1991). See also William D. Rogers, "Approaching Mexico," *Foreign Policy*, no. 72 (Fall 1988).

9. Bilateral Commission on the Future of United States–Mexican Relations, *The Challenge of Interdependence: Mexico and the United States* (Lanham, MD: University Press of America, 1989), 26.

10. This function as a doorway to Latin America reportedly prompted a large-scale U.S. intelligence presence in the country. The U.S. Central Intelligence Agency (CIA) sent its first agents to Mexico in 1948, only a year after the agency's creation. Press reports, former agents, and former U.S. government officials have indicated that at least in earlier years, the CIA's station in Mexico was among the largest in the world. The agency helped establish a training school for Latin American unionists in Mexico and used the country as a post for keeping watch on Cuba. The Mexican government allowed the CIA to monitor travelers to and from Cuba who came through the airport in Mexico City, and until the early 1970s Mexican authorities permitted the CIA to tap the phones of Cuban diplomats both at the Cuban Embassy and in their Mexican homes. For more on the CIA in Mexico, see Manuel Buendía, *La CIA en México*, 2d ed. (Mexico: Cal y Arena, 1990); Alan Riding, *Distant Neighbors: A Portrait of the Mexicans* (New York: Alfred A. Knopf, 1985), 343, 344, 347, and 355; Philip Agee, *Inside the Company: CIA Diary* (New York: Stonehill Publishing Co., 1975), 385 and 614; and Bob Woodward, *Veil: The Secret Wars of the CIA 1981–1987* (New York: Simon and Schuster, 1987).

11. Address by Carlos Salinas de Gortari to the Joint Session of the Congress of the United States of America, Washington, D.C., 4 October 1989.

12. The signs of what economists and political scientists call U.S. decline are multiplying at a frightening rate. Over the decade of the 1980s the U.S. debt quadrupled. During the mid-1980s the debt was climbing by a staggering twelve billion dollars each month. When totaled, the U.S. foreign and domestic debt equaled about four trillion dollars in the early 1990s—roughly ten times the foreign debt of all the countries in Latin America combined. The United States is now the world's largest debtor, and its borrowing over the decade left behind very little of lasting value, although it did help stimulate the world economy during the worst

of the recession years by letting the dollar become considerably overvalued and running huge budget deficits that prompted U.S. demand for foreign goods. That "orgy of unfunded expenditure," as one historian described it, fueled speculative investments, a consumer spending spree, and a massive military buildup, but little productive investment. Garry Wills, "Can Clinton Close the Vision Gap?", *The New York Times*, 8 November 1992, sec. E, p. 17. See Sherle R. Schwenninger, "Reinvigorating the Global Economy," *World Policy Journal* (Summer 1992), 432, for a discussion of U.S. debt-led growth during the early 1980s.

13. Robert A. Pastor, "The Latin American Option," *Foreign Policy*, no. 88 (Fall 1992).

14. For a concise and readable overview of these problems and their origins, see Schwenninger, "Reinvigorating the Global Economy," 429–48.

15. The need to expand exports in a protected regional market also brought Washington closer to Latin America as a whole, prompting programs like the Enterprise for the Americas Initiative and stimulating trade and investment. In 1991, for example, U.S. exports to Latin America (excluding Mexico), climbed by 20 percent, a rate nearly three times as fast as exports to the world as a whole and four times as fast as exports to the European Community. Latin America/Caribbean Business Development Center and the Agency for International Development, "U.S. Exports to Latin America Show Steady Gain," *LA/C Business Bulletin* II, no. 10 (Washington, D.C.: Government Printing Office, November 1992).

16. Presidential Statement, White House, 12 August 1992.

17. Comments made by Professor Jorge Castañeda, National Autonomous University of Mexico, on the draft of this chapter.

18. Cable from the U.S. Embassy, Mexico, D.F., to all U.S. consulates in Mexico, Cable No. 918868, 17 April 1991.

19. In contrast with this optimistic view, the Commission for the Study of International Migration and Cooperative Economic Development (Asencio Commission) found that an improved economic climate in Mexico would likely lead to increased migration, at least in the short term. The commission, which was established by the Immigration Reform and Control Act, said that the creation of low-paying jobs in Mexico would provide more people with the resources needed to head north for better-paying jobs. It predicted that even if Mexico's economy did improve sharply as a result of NAFTA, it would take at least five years for wages and living standards to rise enough to slow migration to any substantive degree. Commission for the Study of International Migration and Cooperative Economic Development, *Unauthorized Migration: An Economic Development Response* (Washington, D.C., 1990). Also see the research on NAFTA suggesting that migration will increase as a result of disruption in Mexico's agricultural sector. Robinson, *Agricultural Policies*.

20. Cable from the U.S. Embassy, 17 April 1991.

21. Those scars have not all healed. Some sectors of Mexican society—progressive academics and labor groups, for instance—still harbor fears and resentment of U.S. domination. Much of Mexican society, however, had already rejected intense anti-Americanism even before the late 1980s, as revealed by the quick acceptance of pro-U.S. policies and the new rhetoric of cooperation under Salinas. Many authors have written about U.S. intervention in Mexico and the wounds it left on

the relationship. One of the most sensitive treatments by a U.S. observer is found in the chapter on U.S.-Mexico relations in Riding, *Distant Neighbors*.

22. Sally Cowal, speaking at the State Department conference on "United States and Mexico: Converging Destinies."

23. The meeting took place in Mexico City. López Portillo was quoted in Riding, *Distant Neighbors*, 321.

24. Quoted in ibid.

25. For a review of Carter's approach to Mexico, and its contrast with policy-making under Ronald Reagan, see Thorup, "U.S. Policy-making Toward Mexico."

26. Ibid., 150.

27. More information on Mexican foreign policy and its effects on bilateral relations is found in: Tom Barry, ed., *Mexico: A Country Guide* (Albuquerque: Inter-Hemispheric Education Resource Center, 1992), 71–74; Riding, *Distant Neighbors*, 340–363; and Green and Smith, *Foreign Policy in U.S.-Mexican Relations*.

28. Washington's first Mexican bailout occurred in 1976 under Republican President Gerald Ford. The 1982 intervention was much more extensive, however, involving the advance purchase of Mexican oil for the U.S. Strategic Petroleum Reserve, support from the U.S. Treasury and Federal Reserve Bank, rescheduled payments to commercial banks, import credits for grains and basic foods, and a standby agreement with the International Monetary Fund that required Mexico to impose severe austerity measures. See James H. Street, "Mexico's Development Crisis," *Current History* 86, no. 518 (March 1987), and Sidney Weintraub, *A Marriage of Convenience: Relations between Mexico and the United States* (Oxford: Oxford University Press, 1990).

29. From a commentary by John Saxe-Fernandez in *Excélsior*, cited in *Latin America News Update* (November 1990).

30. Quoted in Riding, *Distant Neighbors*, 323.

31. Ibid., 360, and Bruce Michael Bagley, "Interdependence and U.S. Policy Toward Mexico in the 1980s," in Roett, *Mexico and the United States*, 225–26.

32. Negroponte's "confidential" cable was directed to Bernard Aronson, assistant secretary of state for inter-American affairs. It was cited by *Proceso* (Mexico, D.F., 13 and 20 May 1991).

33. One of the major signs of increased cooperation between the two countries was the creation of the U.S.-Mexico Binational Commission (BNC). This cabinet-level commission pulls together all the threads of the U.S.-Mexico relationship. Established in 1981 by presidents Ronald Reagan and José López Portillo, the BNC predated by several years the genial collaboration kicked off under Bush and Salinas. As a matter of fact, the BNC weathered some of the stormiest years in recent U.S.-Mexico relations. Buffeted by the many disagreements of the mid-1980s, the commission lost effectiveness and was nearly scrapped. But as testimony to the U.S. government's interest in maintaining access to Mexican oil, its concerns about Mexico's stability, Mexico's wish to climb out of its economic crisis, and shared interests in stimulating economic ties, Bush and Salinas reinvigorated the BNC. Composed of U.S. cabinet members and their Mexican counterparts, the BNC is cochaired by the U.S. secretary of state and the Mexican foreign secretary. The commission holds annual meetings, while working groups meet throughout the year to discuss topics of concern and devise

joint responses. Among the U.S. agencies that have participated in BNC work groups are the Treasury Department, Justice Department (including the FBI), Immigration and Naturalization Service, Environmental Protection Agency, Drug Enforcement Administration, and the U.S. Information Agency.

34. Quoted in "Trade Zone Prototype?", *National Journal* (29 July 1989), 1924.

35. Statement given in hearings before the Committee on Foreign Relations, Subcommittee on Western Hemisphere and Peace Corps Affairs, *Fiscal Year 1992 Foreign Assistance Request for the Western Hemisphere*, 102nd Cong., 1st sess., 18 and 25 April 1991, 10.

36. There were many important factors besides fear of Mexican competition for U.S. markets that influenced Latin American governments to liberalize their economies. These included conditions attached to loans and other assistance from the United States and the international lending institutions, stagnant growth rates, a stubborn global slowdown, the failures of previous development strategies, and—at least temporarily—the collapse of the Marxist alternative.

37. Cable from the U.S. Embassy, 17 April 1991.

38. Jill Abramson, "U.S.-Mexico Trade Pact Is Pitting Vast Armies of Capitol Hill Lobbyists Against Each Other," *The Wall Street Journal*, 25 April 1991, sec. A, p. 16.

39. The U.S. Council of the Mexico-U.S. Business Committee is a committee of the Council of the Americas and is sponsored by the American Chamber of Commerce of Mexico and the U.S. Chamber of Commerce. Its counterpart in Mexico is the Mexican Business Council for International Affairs (CEMAI).

40. U.S. Council of the Mexico-U.S. Business Committee, "Statement of Purpose: Strategies for 1990–92," n.d.

41. Established to compensate for the fast-track provision written into the 1974 Trade Act, ACTPN is a major voice in trade negotiations and is the only statutory mechanism for including private-sector input in trade negotiations. The Mexican Business Council on Foreign Trade (COECE) served as the private-sector advisory committee on NAFTA for the Mexican government.

42. The 1987 Framework Understanding on Trade and Investment, for example, established a consultative mechanism to help resolve trade and investment issues and to negotiate removal of trade barriers. It acted as a vehicle for hashing out disagreements over trade and investment, providing for annual cabinet-level consultations but permitting more frequent meetings by policy specialists when necessary. In a more ambitious move, the Understanding Regarding Trade and Investment Facilitation Talks of 1989 mandated both a comprehensive negotiation process and joint study groups aimed at resolving disputes and devising agreements on specific issues.

43. John Watling, "State Trade Offices Pave Way for U.S. Businesses," *El Financiero International*, 15 June 1992.

44. Ann M. Veneman, U.S. deputy secretary of agriculture, in a news release on NAFTA, 13 August 1992, and interview with Wendell Dennis, U.S. Foreign Agricultural Service, 4 November 1992.

45. Interview with Wendell Dennis, ibid.

46. Interview with Wendell Dennis, 12 August 1993.

47. Under NAFTA, according to U.S. Deputy Secretary of Agriculture Ann M.

Veneman, the United States expects export gains in meats (including beef, pork, and sausage), grains (such as corn, wheat, and sorghum), poultry, and horticultural products (including fresh apples, pears, peaches, fresh vegetables, and tree nuts). Veneman, news release. Products like these are already being exported in increasing quantities to Mexican markets.

48. According to Wendell Dennis of the U.S. Foreign Agricultural Service, "Europeans are putting out a greater and greater supply [of agricultural products] that is subsidized." There is a "considerable gap" between the U.S. domestic price and the world market price of certain commodities, Dennis said. He explained that the EEP helps compensate for that differential, keeping U.S. businesses competitive. Interview with Dennis, 4 November 1992.

49. U.S. Foreign Agricultural Service, "Export Enhancement Program" (Washington, D.C., June 1992).

50. Congressional studies in 1990 and 1991 found that U.S. government subsidies, credit guarantees, loans, set-asides, infrastructure support, research, marketing services, and other assistance provided a staggering 61.5 percent of the value of U.S. wheat producers' income in 1987. *Agricultural Trade: Government Support Calculations Under the U.S.-Canada Free Trade Agreement* (Washington, D.C.: General Accounting Office, August 1990); and *Agricultural Trade: Determining Government Support Under the U.S.-Canada Free Trade Agreement* (Washington, D.C.: General Accounting Office, February 1991).

51. U.S. Agricultural Affairs Office, "Grain and Feed Annual Narrative" (Mexico, D.F., 1990).

52. Interview with Kathy Anderson, U.S. Foreign Agricultural Service, 1 December 1992; and interview with Dennis, 12 August 1993.

53. Interview with Max Bowser, U.S. Foreign Agricultural Service, 13 November 1990, and interview with Wendell Dennis, U.S. Foreign Agricultural Service, 1 December 1992.

54. Interview with Susan Reed, U.S. Foreign Agricultural Service, 2 December 1992.

55. Interview with Kevin Bernhardt, U.S. Department of Agriculture, 13 August 1991.

56. U.S. Agricultural Affairs Office, "Annual Plan of Work" (Mexico, D.F., 10 March 1988).

57. Among the participants in USDA market development programs in Mexico are the American Embryo Transfer Association, American Quarter Horse Association, Kentucky Distillers Association, National Dry Bean Council, Pillsbury Company, U.S. Mink Export Development Council, and USA Poultry and Egg Export Association. Information provided by the U.S. Foreign Agricultural Service, November 1992.

58. One of the trade associations whose members benefit from U.S.-backed market development programs is the U.S. Feed Grains Council (USFGC). Among other projects the council sponsors demonstration farms in Mexico that work with major Mexican dairy farmers to enhance technology and skills and to encourage them to buy U.S. feed and other supplies. The USFGC has been teaching Mexico's dairy producers how to raise Holstein bull calves as a sideline to their dairy operations. Normally slaughtered within their first three days of life, the calves are being promoted by the council as stock for the Mexican and U.S. beef industries. At the same time, the organization is encouraging the farmers to use

U.S. feed grains for the calves. Ricardo Celma, "Mexico Ranks Among World's Most Promising Markets for U.S. Feed Grains," *AgExporter* (March 1991), 11.

59. The U.S. Food Festival, held in July 1991, was the first food show in Mexico to focus solely on U.S. foods and beverages. It was cosponsored by the Western United States Agricultural Trade Association, the Mid-America International Agri-Trade Council, the Southern United States Trade Association, and the U.S. Foreign Agricultural Service. Reflecting the surge of interest in consumer-ready and high-value products, the show included exporters of frozen yogurt, pizzas, microwaveable foods, and frozen foods, as well as meat, wines, snacks, and other products. Interview with Bobby Richey, Jr., U.S. agricultural attaché, Mexico, D.F., 4 March 1992, and Elizabeth Offutt, "New Trade Festival in Mexico to Spotlight U.S. Food and Beverages," *AgExporter* (March 1991).

60. Figures obtained from Wendell Dennis, 4 November 1992.

61. Interview with Wendell Dennis, 4 November 1992.

62. *U.S.-Mexico Trade: Trends and Impediments in Agricultural Trade* (Washington, D.C.: General Accounting Office, 1990), 34. Conasupo was the principal buyer of corn under GSM-102 as recently as 1991. Interview with Pat Haslach, Commodity Credit Corporation, 13 August 1991.

63. The GSM-102 program, with repayment terms ranging from three to ten years, underwrites transactions on products with longer economic life spans, like breeding livestock. Mexico was allocated ten million dollars in GSM-102 credit guarantees in fiscal year 1992. Interview with Amy Brooksbank, U.S. Department of Agriculture, GSM Program, 4 November 1992.

64. Interviews with Amy Brooksbank, U.S. Department of Agriculture GSM program, 4 November 1992 and 2 August 1993.

65. Interview with Bobby Richey, Jr., 4 March 1992, and Bobby G. Richey and Lynn Reich, "Credit Guarantee Programs Help Open Doors in Mexican Marketplace," *AgExporter* (March 1991).

66. Interview with Bobby Richey, Jr., 4 March 1992.

67. George Anthan, "U.S. Food Programs Cut to Aid Exports," *Des Moines Register*, 20 May 1992, 1.

68. Although minimal in dollar terms, the Trade and Development Program's funding for infrastructure development in Mexico is aimed at "helping U.S. firms get in on the ground floor of projects that offer significant export opportunities" in the long run. It has supported hydroelectric, environmental, mining, and transportation projects in Mexico by providing funding for U.S. firms that carry out feasibility studies, consultancies, and other planning services. *Business America* (4 December 1989); and United States Trade and Development Program, *Congressional Presentation Fiscal Year 1992* (Washington, D.C., 22 February 1991).

69. Japan, for example, provided $805 million in untied credits for equipment and infrastructure to make lead-free gasoline and sulfur-free fuel and diesel oil, as well as to rehabilitate locomotives. Andrea Curaca Malito, "Japanese Assistance in Pollution Control Opens Door for U.S. Business," *Business America* (8 October 1990).

70. American Chamber of Commerce in Mexico, "The Role of Development Banks in U.S.-Mexico Trade," *Review of Trade and Industry*, 2nd quarter, 1992. By 1993, Mexico's percentage of Eximbank's total portfolio had dropped to about 17 percent. Based on figures obtained in interview with Don Schuab, Eximbank, 3 August 1993.

71. Eximbank classifies countries according to the terms of an agreement worked out among members of the Organization for Economic Cooperation and Development. In terms of income level, Mexico is considered an "intermediate" country. This allows interest rates at levels below those of "rich" countries but above those of "poor" countries.

72. U.S. Export-Import Bank, *Export-Import Bank of the United States: An Independent Government Agency That Assists the Financing of U.S. Exports*, pamphlet, November 1990.

73. When loan guarantees and insurance were included, the total for those years exceeded $15.5 billion. U.S. Export-Import Bank, *1987 Annual Report* (Washington, D.C.); interview with Quang Phung, Eximbank, 26 August 1991; and "Eximbank in Mexico," *Business America* (4 December 1989), 17.

74. Despite the large value of the portfolio devoted to Mexico, Eximbank's loans and credits held by Mexican buyers represented only about 10 percent of U.S.-Mexican trade in 1991. John Watling, "Fast Finance: Where Big Banks Fear to Tread," *El Financiero International*, 23 November 1992.

75. Interview with Don Schuab, 3 August 1993.

76. "Eximbank in Mexico," *Business America*.

77. Ironically, Mexican cement industries that have benefited at least in part from Eximbank programs face tariff barriers when they export to the United States because they have been accused of selling their cement below cost. See "Penalties on Cement Exports to Continue," *El Financiero International*, 28 December 1992.

78. The first loan guarantee to Pemex occurred in 1990, igniting a fire storm of criticism in Mexico. The bank guaranteed a $1.5 billion loan to Pemex for offshore exploration projects in the Bay of Campeche. As with other Eximbank programs, the conditions attached to the loan guarantee required Mexico to use U.S. firms to conduct the oil exploration and development projects that were planned. Mexican critics feared that the agreement would provide a back door into the Mexican oil industry, which was protected by provisions in the Mexican constitution. Vindicating the critics, that first agreement did foretell increased U.S. participation in the Mexican oil industry. Although the sector was kept off the table during NAFTA negotiations and foreign investors still may not own Mexican oil reserves, the government's deregulation of many petrochemicals and decentralization of Pemex opened the way for U.S. involvement in petrochemicals, exploration, plant building, and other types of investment. See, for example, Edward Cody, "Oil Loan Touches a Mexican Nerve," *The Washington Post*, 7 December 1990, and Thomas S. Heather, "Private Sector Participation in Petroleum," *Business Mexico* (August 1992).

79. Mexico's sales to the Strategic Petroleum Reserve were discontinued in the late 1980s. From the late 1970s to 1988 Pemex sales to the Strategic Petroleum Reserve totaled 236 million barrels. Interview with John Bartholomew, Strategic Petroleum Reserve, 13 April 1993.

80. Watling, "Fast Finance."

81. The dividing line between explicitly promoting runaways and providing services that may inadvertently encourage such a move is a fine one. Recent press reports about AID programs in Central America, for example, show that the agency helped fund training programs and advertising campaigns aimed at attracting

U.S. companies to El Salvador and Honduras. See Doyle McManus, "U.S. Aid Agency Helps to Move Jobs Overseas," *Los Angeles Times*, 28 September 1992, sec. A, p. 1, and National Labor Committee Education Fund in Support of Worker and Human Rights in Central America, *Paying to Lose Our Jobs* (New York: National Labor Committee, September 1992).

82. For a discussion of the legislation and arguments on both sides, see hearings before the U.S. House of Representatives Committee on Energy and Commerce, Subcommittee on Commerce, Transportation, and Tourism, *Department of Commerce's Program to Promote Relocation of U.S. Industry*, 99th Cong., 2nd sess., 10 December 1986. Also see Michael Moore, "Made in Mexico: Reagan Administration Encourages U.S. Businesses to Move Jobs South of the Border," *Multinational Monitor* (February 1987).

83. Responding to criticism of these programs, one AID official angrily justified the initiatives: "Don't we want these economies to develop? Or do we just want to send sacks of grain, the way we do to Somalia, to keep people alive for another day?" McManus, "U.S. Aid Agency Helps to Move Jobs Overseas."

84. Interview with Art Danart, Agency for International Development, 28 October 1992.

85. Ibid.

86. University of the Americas, "Analisis de la Rotacion de Personal en las Industrias Maquiladoras en Mexico" (proposal submitted to the AID, July 1990).

87. Agency for International Development, *Action Plan for Fiscal Years 1985 and 1986* (Mexico, D.F., October 1984), 24.

88. Ibid., 27.

89. Agency for International Development, *Mexico: Action Plan, FY1991–92* (Washington, D.C.: Government Printing Office, April 1990), 15.

90. Ibid.

91. Interview with Gerard Bowers, Agency for International Development, Mexico, 4 March 1992. The following discussion on NAFTA is taken from this interview.

92. *El Financiero International*, 25 November 1992.

93. *Agence France-Press*, 20 July 1992.

94. Quoted in "Commission Nurtures Export Culture," *El Financiero International*, 30 November 1992.

95. In December 1990, for example, Charles Roh of the Office of the U.S. Trade Representative spoke with Juárez business leaders to promote the proposed free trade agreement. Cable from the U.S. Consulate in Juárez to the U.S. Embassy, Mexico, D.F., Cable No. 901963, 12 December 1990.

96. U.S. Department of Justice, "Pending Foreign Principals" (cumulative list of registered foreign agents for Mexico in the United States, 20 November 1992).

97. For a rough layout of these trends, see ibid. See also Abramson, "U.S.-Mexico Trade Pact"; Peter H. Stone, "In Mexico, Lobbyists Strike Gold," *National Journal* 24, no. 38, 19 (September 1992); Diana Solis, "Mexico Hires Numerous U.S. Lobbyists to Push Passage of Free Trade Accord," *The Wall Street Journal*, 24 September 1992; Herminio Rebollo and Leticia Rodríguez, "Mexico Spent 56 Million Dollars to Promote NAFTA in the U.S.," *El Financiero International*, 19 April 1993; and Tim Golden, "Mexico Tries to Bolster Political Image in U.S.," *The Miami Herald*, 3 January 1992.

98. Rebollo and Rodríguez, "Mexico Spent 56 Million Dollars," ibid. According to this report, which cites the government's public accounts documents, Mexico spent approximately fifty-six million dollars during the 1990–92 period in consulting fees, operation expenses, salaries, media coverage, promotion, and public relations related to the NAFTA negotiations.

99. Brock was retained by Mexico through two separate contracts, one with the Brock Group, of which he is senior partner, and one with Burson-Marsteller, a leviathan in the public relations business. For his services with Burson-Marsteller, Brock received $30,000 a month. To handle public relations for Mexico, Burson-Marsteller was paid $323,000 per month, out of which it took cuts for subcontractors like Brock and the lobbying firm of Gold and Liebengood. Stone, "In Mexico," and U.S. Department of Justice, "Pending Foreign Principals."

100. Stone, "In Mexico."

101. Abramson, "U.S.-Mexico Trade Pact."

102. For a detailed history of these relations, see essays by Jorge A. Bustamante, J. Angel Gutiérrez, and Rodolfo O. de la Garza in *Chicano-Mexicano Relations*, eds. Tatcho Mindiola and Max Martínez (Houston: University of Houston Mexican American Studies Program, 1986).

103. Rodolfo O. de la Garza, "Chicanos and U.S. Foreign Policy: The Future of Chicano-Mexican Relations," *Western Political Quarterly* 33, no. 4 (December 1980), 571–82.

104. Bustamante concluded at the time that the idea of the Mexican government looking to Chicanos as a lobby had been "discarded from the panorama of objectives." Jorge Bustamante, "Relación Cultural con los Chicanos," *Uno Más Uno* (11 October 1982). Also see his "Chicano-Mexicano Relations: From Practice to Theory," in Mindiola and Martínez, *Chicano-Mexicano Relations*, 8–19. However, the creation in 1987 of the Program for Enhanced Relations between the Mexican government and the U.S. Mexican-American Community did indicate continuing sharp interest by the Mexican government in cultivating ties with Mexican Americans. Rodolfo O. de la Garza and Claudio Vargas, "The Mexican-Origin Population of the United States as a Political Force in the Borderlands: From Paisanos to Pochos to Potential Political Allies," in Herzog, *Changing Boundaries*, 89–111.

105. For more information see Secretaría de Relaciones Exteriores and Comunidades Mexicanas en el Exterior, *Programa para las Comunidades Mexicanas en el Exterior: Objetivos, Políticas, Campos de Acción* (September 1990).

106. Interview with Rodolfo O. de la Garza, University of Texas at Austin, 14 April 1993.

107. Southwest Voter Research Institute, "Latino Consensus on NAFTA" (San Antonio: September 1993).

108. U.S. Information Agency, Cable from the U.S. Consulate in Hermosillo to the U.S. Secretary of State, Cable No. 901640, 18 Dec. 1990.

109. This section deals with U.S. development aid, narrowly defined. Much more important to Mexico in dollar terms have been the enormous sums from multilateral lending institutions such as the World Bank and the International Monetary Fund. The seal of approval and financial support from these institutions constitutes an indirect form of U.S. government assistance because of the major influence the United States wields in these forums.

110. Agency for International Development, *Mexico: Action Plan, FY 1991–92*, 53–54 and interview with Babette Prevot, AID Mexico Desk Officer, 29 July 1993. Given overall cutbacks in U.S. aid, along with increasing claims on aid funds from Eastern Europe, and the fact that for several years Mexico has exceeded the cutoff level for aid in terms of per capita income, the level of funding through 1992 was significant. The information that Mexico had exceeded aid cutoff levels was obtained during an interview with Art Danart, Agency for International Development, 28 October 1992.

111. More telling, most of AID's assistance to Mexico came in the form of loans that Mexico was expected to repay. Riding, *Distant Neighbors*, 344, and Agency for International Development, *U.S. Economic Assistance Programs Administered by the Agency for International Development and Predecessor Agencies* (Washington, D.C.: Government Printing Office, 1971), 35.

112. Riding, *Distant Neighbors*; Agency for International Development, *Action Plan for Fiscal Years 1985 and 1986*, 3; and interview with Gerard Bowers, Agency for International Development, Mexico, 26 July 1990.

113. Agency for International Development, *Action Plan for Fiscal Years 1985 and 1986*.

114. Interview with Gerard Bowers, 26 July 1990.

115. The expanding U.S. aid programs in Mexico (and in Central America) were particularly ironic in light of the social service cutbacks being leveled against the U.S. poor during these same years of the Reagan administration.

116. Interview with Samuel Taylor, AID/Mexico, May 1989.

117. Agency for International Development, *Action Plan for Fiscal Years 1985 and 1986*, 7.

118. Assistance in previous years was even higher, averaging $7.5 million in 1988 and 1989. Agency for International Development, *Mexico: Action Plan, FY1991–92*, 5.

119. The AID provided contraceptives—forty million condoms in 1986, for example—surgical supplies, training, equipment, and institutional support. It also promoted "voluntary surgical contraception," such as tubal ligation and vasectomies, and funded media campaigns to popularize birth control among Mexico's public.

    Strong criticisms have been raised against population control programs like these that are promoted by developed countries in poorer countries like Mexico. Critics argue that the problems of global and national poverty are caused by an inequitable distribution of resources, not by overpopulation or scarcity per se. They also point out the classist and racist character of many of these programs, which are most often directed against the poor and the nonwhite. The fact that the Reagan and Bush administrations provided funding for media campaigns around contraception in Mexico while remaining lukewarm to similar programs in the United States—even in the face of the AIDS epidemic—gives strong weight to these criticisms. See Eduardo Galeano, *Open Veins of Latin America: Five Centuries of the Pillage of a Continent* (New York: Monthly Review Press, 1973) for a passionate exploration of the relationship between poverty and the inequitable distribution of resources in the Americas.

120. Agency for International Development, *Mexico: Project Assistance* (Washington, D.C.: Government Printing Office, May 1991), 26. See also Agency for International Development, *Action Plan for Fiscal Years 1985 and 1986*; Agency for

International Development, *Mexico: Action Plan, FY1991–92;* and Catherine Mansell Carstens, "Financing Mexican Microenterprise (Part II)," *Business Mexico* (November 1992).

121. Agency for International Development, *Mexico: Action Plan, FY1991–92,* 3, 20–22, 35, and 51–53.
122. Agency for International Development, *Congressional Presentation Fiscal Year 1989* (Washington, D.C.: Government Printing Office, 1990), 283.
123. Agency for International Development, *Action Plan for Fiscal Years 1985 and 1986,* 4.
124. Until 1972 Mexico received modest levels of support under three U.S. PL480 food assistance programs. With the exception of some PL480 Title II (food donations) commodities provided to the United Nations World Food Program for refugees in Mexico, the country no longer receives any PL480 assistance. See Barry, *Mexico: A Country Guide,* 379–80, n. 36, for a closer look at PL480 programs in Mexico.
125. From 1983 to 1991 Mexico received more than three hundred million dollars in Section 416 aid. Foreign Agricultural Service, "U.S.G. Section 416(b) Assistance to Mexico," 26 August 1991; and Agency for International Development, *Mexico: Action Plan: FY 1991–1992.*
126. David L. Franklin, "Assessment of Section 416 Food Assistance Program to Mexico Summary Report," report prepared for AID/Mexico (Research Triangle Park, N.C.: Sigma One Corporation, September 1990), 8.
127. On the changing role of the Mexican military, including its participation in civic action programs and its increasing involvement in subduing labor and civil disturbances, see David Ronfeldt, ed., *The Modern Mexican Military: A Reassessment* (San Diego: Center for U.S.-Mexican Studies, 1984). For a more recent overview of the Mexican military, see Roderic A. Camp, *Generals in the Palacio: The Military in Modern Mexico* (London: Oxford University Press, 1992).
128. See, for example, "Use of Troops a Cause of Concern in Mexico: Armed Forces Are Sent to Deal with Politics, Labor, and Crime," *The New York Times,* 5 November 1989.
129. U.S. Department of Defense, *Congressional Presentation for Security Assistance Programs,* fiscal year 1992 (Washington, D.C.: 1991), 217.
130. Mexico is the United States' second most important source of strategic raw materials. *Department of State Bulletin,* October 1989.
131. In contrast with other U.S. aid programs, however, U.S. military assistance has been less successful in accomplishing a turn toward the United States. The Mexican military remains extremely nationalistic, with a fairly strong undercurrent of anti-U.S. sentiment.
132. U.S. Department of Defense, *Congressional Presentation for Security Assistance Programs,* fiscal year 1989 (Washington, D.C., 1988), 248.
133. From 1950 to 1978 there were only a few countries in the region that received less military aid from the United States than Mexico did. These included various Caribbean microstates and several small countries such as Costa Rica, Haiti, and El Salvador. Lars Schoultz, *Human Rights and United States Policy Toward Latin America* (Princeton: Princeton University Press, 1981), 215, and Agency for International Development, *U.S. Overseas Loans and Grants and Assistance from International Organizations,* Obligations and Loan Authorizations, July 1, 1945–

September 30, 1981 (Washington, D.C.: Government Printing Office, 1981). On Mexico's military spending, see U.S. Arms Control and Disarmament Agency, *World Military Expenditures*, 1989.

134. A major component of U.S. security aid to Mexico consists of funding for antidrug efforts. These are described in the chapter "The Drug Connection," pages 49–72.

135. Stephen J. Wager, "Basic Characteristics of the Modern Mexican Military," in Ronfeldt, *The Modern Mexican Military*, 100.

136. This discussion of historical ties between the two militaries draws heavily on Wager's study, ibid. For a brief overview of the notion of a U.S.-Mexico "security community," see also Paul Ganster and Alan Sweedler, "The United States–Mexican Border Region: Security and Interdependence," in *United States–Mexico Border Statistics Since 1900*, ed. David Lorey (Los Angeles: UCLA Latin American Center Publications, 1990).

137. During the postwar period Mexico received under fifty thousand dollars in support through the MAP. Agency for International Development, U.S. *Overseas Loans and Grants and Assistance from International Organizations*.

138. Wager, "Basic Characteristics," 101.

139. Quoted in a commentary by John Saxe-Fernandez, *Excélsior* (2 April 1991). Relationships with Latin American militaries forged during such U.S. programs have long been cultivated by the Department of Defense. As Robert McNamara, former secretary of defense, once explained to Congress: "I need not dwell upon the value of having in positions of leadership men who have the first-hand knowledge of how Americans do things and how they think. It is beyond price to make friends of such men." Statement given in hearings before the U.S. House of Representatives Committee on Appropriations, Subcommittee on Foreign Operations Appropriations, *Foreign Operations Appropriations for 1963*, 1962, E59.

140. Agency for International Development, U.S. *Overseas Loans and Grants and Assistance from International Organizations*; and interview with Karen Garvey, Department of Defense, 28 July 1993.

141. These figures are drawn from several sources: Schoultz, *Human Rights*; Carmen Lira, "Desde 1982, México Ha Comprado a EU Más Armas que en los 30 Años Anteriores," *La Jornada*, 30 June 1989, interview with Major Michael González, U.S. Department of Defense, Latin America and Africa Division, 13 September 1991; and interview with Karen Garvey, ibid.

142. Agency for International Development, U.S. *Overseas Loans and Grants and Assistance from International Organizations*, 56; U.S. Department of Defense, *Congressional Presentations for Security Assistance Programs*, 1983–1992; and hearings before a Subcommittee of the U.S. House of Representatives Committee on Appropriations, *Foreign Operations, Export Financing, and Related Programs Appropriations for 1991*, 426.

143. Lira, "Desde 1982," and U.S. Department of Defense, *Congressional Presentations*, ibid.

144. U.S. Department of Defense, *Congressional Presentation*, 1989, 248–50.

145. U.S. Department of Defense, *Congressional Presentation*, 1992, 217.

146. In commenting on this section, Colonel Stephen Wager, a historian and student

of the Mexican military at West Point, said that the Mexican Army grew more uncomfortable with performing police duties during the 1980s. He noted that senior officers complained to Mexican political leaders, who then attempted to curtail such functions. Wager described Salinas's use of the army to control dissenting groups as a "deviation" from the general policy during the 1980s. These observations are important, but the fact that the Mexican government believes the army is available as a reserve police force holds negative implications for human rights nonetheless.

147. During a forum in Mexico City in 1990 Peruvian novelist Mario Vargas Llosa described Mexico as a "perfect dictatorship . . . camouflaged so that it appears not to be a dictatorship." The assessment of Salinas's objectives in emphasizing economic restructuring over democratization is taken from Douglas W. Payne, "Mexico: The Politics of Free Trade," *Freedom Review* (July–August 1991), 26.

148. In mid-1993 the Mexican government proposed a number of electoral reforms that were being considered in the Chamber of Deputies as of this writing. The proposals ranged from setting limits on campaign financing to eliminating the "governability clause," which guarantees majority control of the Congress to any party that wins 35 percent of the popular vote. The proposed reforms did not include changes to the federal electoral commission to make it more impartial, a critical omission in terms of Mexican democratization. See Ted Bardacke, "All the Right Moves," *El Financiero International*, 12 July 1993, 13.

149. For statements about the proclaimed importance of democratization in U.S. hemispheric policies under George Bush, see the testimonies of Bernard Aronson, assistant secretary of state for inter-American affairs, and James H. Michel, assistant administrator for the AID's Bureau for Latin America and the Caribbean, in hearings before the U.S. Senate Committee on Foreign Relations, Subcommittee on Western Hemisphere and Peace Corps Affairs, *Fiscal Year 1992 Foreign Assistance Request for the Western Hemisphere*, 102nd Cong., 1st sess., 18 and 25 April 1991. For detailed information about repression under the Salinas government, see Amnesty International, *Mexico: Torture with Impunity* (London, 1991); Americas Watch, *Human Rights in Mexico*; Americas Watch, *Unceasing Abuses: Human Rights in Mexico One Year After the Introduction of Reform* (New York: 1991); and Alicia Ely-Yamin, "Justice Corrupted, Justice Denied: Unmasking the Untouchables of the Mexican Federal Judicial Police," paper prepared for the Mexico Project of the World Policy Institute (New York: New School for Social Research, 20 November 1992).

150. One blatant example of Washington's support for the PRI and Salinas even in the face of government-sanctioned electoral fraud in Mexico occurred after the November 1990 summit between Bush and Salinas. Just one week before the summit the PRI declared that its candidates had won all thirty-four legislative districts in the state of Mexico, where opposition candidate Cuauhtémoc Cárdenas had beaten Salinas two to one in 1988. Ignoring media analysts, opposition leaders, and other critics who cried fraud, Bush announced a $1.5 billion loan to the Mexican government to be backed by Eximbank.

151. For descriptions of irregularities that favor the ruling party in Mexico's electoral system, see Payne, "Mexico: The Politics of Free Trade"; Andrew Reding, "Mexico: The Crumbling of the Perfect Dictatorship," *World Policy Journal*

(Spring 1991); and Andrew Reding, "Mexico Under Salinas: A Facade of Reform," *World Policy Journal* (Fall 1989).

152. For a close look at the specific question of U.S. support for democratization in Mexico, see Lorenzo Meyer, "Mexico: The Exception and the Rule," in *Exporting Democracy: The United States and Latin America,* ed. Abraham F. Lowenthal (Baltimore, Md.: Johns Hopkins University Press, 1991).

153. In a major show of support President Reagan telegraphed congratulations to Salinas even before the election results were in. He then provided the new Mexican government with a $3.5 billion bridge loan.

154. Established in 1983, the National Endowment for Democracy is a privately incorporated grant-making institution funded by Congress. Active around the world, NED supports foreign political parties, trade unions, business groups, civic organizations, the media, and other important political sectors. For more on this institution, see Beth Sims, *National Endowment for Democracy: A Foreign Policy Branch Gone Awry* (Albuquerque: Inter-Hemispheric Education Resource Center, 1990).

155. NED has four "core" grantees, through which the bulk of its grants are funneled to organizations in other countries. They are the Center for International Private Enterprise, Free Trade Union Institute, International Republican Institute, and National Democratic Institute for International Affairs. These are the international arms of the U.S. Chamber of Commerce, AFL-CIO, Republican Party, and Democratic Party, respectively.

156. Most of this information is drawn from the annual reports, board meeting minutes, and other documents of the National Endowment for Democracy, but also see: Sims, *National Endowment For Democracy,* and Barry, *Mexico: A Country Guide,* 326–27.

157. National Endowment for Democracy, annual reports, 1988–1992; and National Endowment for Democracy, board meeting minutes, 22 January 1993.

158. The following discussion on recent NED grants in Mexico is taken largely from National Endowment for Democracy, board meeting minutes, 1992–93; and grant proposals and grant reports from the recipient organizations to NED.

159. Agency for International Development, *Mexico: Action Plan, FY1991–92,* 8.

160. Interview with Arthur Danart, Agency for International Development, 17 November 1992; Cable from the U.S. Embassy, Mexico, D.F., to the Secretary of State, Attachment D, 25 Oct. 1989; and an information memorandum from Maria Mamlouk to the AID's assistant administrator for the Bureau of Latin America and the Caribbean, 8 March 1991.

161. In Mexico, for instance, there has been nothing comparable to Washington's noisy denunciations of the Nicaraguan government under the Sandinistas, its subsequent insistence that elections there be declared free and fair by international observers, and its massive election-related aid to the opposition. For the best overview of Washington's aid to the main opposition coalition in Nicaragua's 1990 elections, see William I. Robinson, A *Faustian Bargain: U.S. Intervention in the Nicaraguan Elections and American Foreign Policy in the Post–Cold War Era* (Boulder, CO: Westview Press, 1992).

# Conclusion: Crossing the

# Great Divide

So near and yet so far. That's a cliché that always seems appropriate when we stand at the U.S.-Mexico border. As we look over to the other side, there can be little doubt that a great divide still separates the two nations. Notwithstanding official rhetoric about warm relations and all the hype about free trade and economic integration, the challenges of drawing the United States and Mexico together are still immense.

Binational tensions over issues like immigration and narcotics persist, and the socioeconomic gap between the United States and Mexico seems only to have widened. It is true that business relations have improved, and trade and investment have increased. But Mexico remains mired in the development problems of the third world. For its part, the United States seems less intent on building bridges between north and south than on finding ways to bolster its economic hegemony.

At the border the fences seem to get only higher, the customs checks more thorough, and the social and economic divisions more severe. The line drawn through the desert and defined elsewhere by the trickle of the Rio Grande seems not an arbitrary barrier but one established by a timeless order that separates rich from poor, industrialized from underdeveloped, and the powerful from the weak.

But such stark imaginings, while capturing part of the binational reality, may lead one to miss the momentous changes under way that are bringing the two neighbors together. The evolution of national economies into integral elements of an emerging global economy is probably the most important factor in shaping these changes in cross-border relations. In a world where production and marketing are global, international borders are regarded as nuisances rather than essential demarcations. Modern technology—facsimile machines, E-mail, and satellite communications—keeps business, professional, and personal acquaintances in close

441

contact across international boundaries. These advances in communications technology and the steady integration of the regional economy have created the potential for a new kind of international cooperation. The problem is that most of the new bridges being built across the north-south divide are those that primarily serve the interests of international traders and investors.

## Business Leads the Way

Large corporations have been quick to jump on advances in transportation and communications technology to globalize financial and production systems. Between the United States and Mexico, as elsewhere in the world, big business has been the driving force in breaking down nationalist boundaries and promoting economic integration. This process of economic integration has followed a value-free path.

The principles of the free market have provided the ideological underpinnings of global and regional economic integration. During the post–World War II era the transnational corporations that emerged began to define a new world order based on their own production and marketing needs. Defining the specific dimensions and regulations of this global economic order fell to the international financial institutions like the IMF and World Bank and to multilateral trade accords, particularly the GATT.

Following the end of the Cold War, free market triumphalism infected economic strategists around the world. When it appeared that the "West" had won the postwar competition with the Soviet Union, this turn of history sparked a widening consensus in favor of deep structural reform based on market principles. At least for the time being, no other real alternative to market economic strategies seemed to exist anymore for countries like Mexico that wanted to climb from poverty into well-being.[1] Other than opening up its economy to transnationalization, no other path to national development seemed feasible.

Because integration is being defined by a corporate view of free markets and trade, its social and environmental costs have been largely overshadowed by the imperatives of supply, demand, efficiency, and comparative advantage. Production and markets are integrating, while the rights and interests of consumers and workers have been ignored or marginalized.

Crossing the great divide between nations has become increasingly easy for corporate America. In many ways, however, all that economic integration means for most North Americans is that barriers that previously served to protect their livelihoods are crumbling. In fact, escalating the global wage competition has spurred an upsurge of reactionary nationalism among adversely affected sectors. By not addressing such fundamental cross-border issues as immigration, runaway production, and vastly different labor and environmental standards, free trade initiatives are contributing to north-south polarization as well as aggravating class divisions within affected nations.

With free market neoliberals and other members of the political and economic elite making policy in the United States and Mexico, the chances are uncertain that the needs of popular sectors in either country will be met. Pegging Mexican labor at low wage rates will boost the global competitiveness of some Mexican and U.S. businesses, but only at the cost of equity and labor rights. What is more, those costs will not stay confined to Mexico. As U.S. workers are pitted against low-wage counterparts in Mexico, the workers of both countries will find themselves competing for international investment with their own declining standards of living.[2]

Downward harmonization, not only in wages but also in environmental and consumer regulations, is not the sort of integration the United States and Mexico should be looking for. In the short run, even without a formal free trade agreement, Mexico will reap some economic benefits as jobs and investment shift south, and U.S.-based corporations clearly benefit in the short term from a downward leveling of wages and regulations. Already, however, these same corporations are finding that low-paid workers make poor consumers and that the environmental costs of unsustainable business practices are catching up with them. True economic development needs a more solid foundation than flimsy theories about free trade and the magic of the marketplace. If the great divide ever is to be bridged, the upward harmonization of wages and standards represents a better approach toward globalization.

## Transboundary Consciousness

The euphoria generated by the collapse of the Soviet Union and the accompanying enthusiasm for a new capitalist world order have masked the many obstacles and dangers that mark the path toward global economic integration. Obviously the world's governments should not take a step backward toward petty protectionism and reactionary nationalism. Economic integration at the regional and global levels is indeed the way of the future. But it is not at all clear that a globalism guided solely by the dictates of comparative advantage and the perceived needs of the transnational corporations is, as its advocates argue, the most desirable and sustainable kind of economic integration.

In our chapter "Free Trade: The Ifs, Ands & Buts" (pages 287–320), we discuss the alternatives to the dominant concept of free market globalism. We examine the need for control over policy-making to begin to shift to the people affected by policy and away from the corporate and government leaders who profit from it. Widening citizen participation, informed citizen participation, is needed to democratize the decision-making process in both countries. From support for Mexican electoral and human rights reforms to pursuing right-to-know legislation in U.S. and Mexican communities, there are many tasks demanding attention.

The groundwork for such a wide-scale democratic response to what has been a controlled and opaque process has already been laid. Cross-border ties have proliferated over the past decade, linking groups and individuals with similar concerns that are trying to hash out common strategies to respond to their needs. Activist organizations and umbrella networks link environmentalists, labor unions, consumer groups, religious organizations, women, peasants, and community groups. Despite problems like sectarianism and regionalism, despite the everyday complications of too much to do and too few resources, the binational efforts of groups like these have begun to widen the policy debate.

In pointing the way to a new type of transboundary consciousness and international cooperation, equally important are the experiences of less politicized groups that recognize the value of close cross-border relations. Mexican and U.S. communities that face each other across the boundary have for many years been molding their own formal and informal channels of communication and cooperation. Or take the example of the Mixtec and Zapotec communities of southeastern Mexico that have established organizational links with migrant communities in California. In the United States these Indian communities have formed mutual aid societies that work together with peasant organizations back in Mexico to foster the economic development of their ancestral communities.

Institutionalizing the input, insights, and experiences of grassroots advocates is a fundamental step toward broadening the policy-making process and achieving equity. Models for such binational institutions have been proposed by activists involved in community health, environmental, and labor issues. They have called for trinational commissions to include both nongovernmental and government representatives to respond to international concerns. Similarly, border activists have advocated the creation of binational institutions that would respond to the escalating environmental and health problems in the U.S.-Mexico borderlands. These proposed commissions would have the right to raise funds and to allocate them, giving the body real power. Because the nongovernmental participants would be chosen by the community, not appointed by the government, there would be at least a chance that grassroots concerns might be an integral part of the policy process.

Conflict began to give way to cooperation in the bilateral relations between Mexico and the United States in the 1980s. It is hoped that this cooperative spirit will continue through the 1990s. But if this bilateralism is to continue, negotiations between Mexico and the United States will have to address such fundamental issues as immigration flows, runaway production, and the different developmental needs of two neighbors. Both at the grassroots and at the national levels, efforts to establish partnerships must recognize the existing asymmetry of power and wealth while also acknowledging that citizens of both sides should enjoy the same rights to earn a decent income and enjoy a democratic society.

If such issues are ignored in bilateral talks and if the forces of corporate free trade are allowed to determine the economic future of both nations, the tensions that have traditionally marked U.S.-Mexico relations will again come to the fore. The spread of U.S. investment and other foreign influence in Mexico without parallel improvements in socioeconomic conditions could spark a renewal of the nationalist and anti-imperialist sentiments stirred up in the Mexican Revolution. Similarly, if the Mexican government proves incapable of providing decent employment for its citizens, anti-immigrant and anti-Mexican sentiment in the United States could increase.

As with so many other transitions, the ongoing integration of the U.S. and Mexican economies, indeed the world's economies, holds both promise and peril. But there is no turning back. Free trade agreement or not, regional and global integration is a force we need to acknowledge. Shaping the framework of the integration is a crucial task that must include the broadest range of perspectives possible so that the future does not hold promise for a few and peril for the rest.

At either end of the Bridge of the Americas linking El Paso and Juárez, the U.S. and Mexican flags signal the end of one nation and the beginning of another. Here the Americas are joined, but north and south still face off. The transportation links are in place, the communications networks are functioning, and economic integration is proceeding apace. But the great divide remains as important as ever for those seeking to cross the Rio Grande to make a better life for themselves on the other side, and for those who fear that their jobs are slipping south. Clearly, economic globalization has set the stage for U.S.-Mexico relations in the 1990s, but resolving the human consequences of economic restructuring will be the main challenge of the decade.

# Notes

1. Alternatives such as democratic socialism or social democracy along the lines seen in Europe did not challenge the dominance of a market-oriented approach to organizing social relations during the first years after the end of the Cold War. These and other alternatives will undoubtedly be discovered or rediscovered as the negative social effects of strict market approaches generate thorny political repercussions.
2. For a closer look at the dangers to workers everywhere when labor anywhere is weakened, see Sims, *Workers of the World Undermined*.

# Acknowledgments

It is always a pleasure to write the acknowledgments of a book we have recently finished. Not only does it mean that all those long hours are behind us, but it also finally gives us a chance to express our appreciation to the many people and institutions that made this effort possible. We would like to thank the individuals and groups that are working hard in both countries to improve U.S.-Mexico relations and guide both countries along mutually beneficial paths of economic and social development. In writing about the dynamic of cross-border relations, we were continually inspired by the openness, friendliness, and determination of the activists, academics, and community leaders who are every day experiencing the joys and challenges of U.S.-Mexico relations.

Researching and writing a book of this scope would not have been possible without the direct contributions of many friends and colleagues. The staff of the Resource Center formed the foundation that allowed the book to take shape. Although all staff members helped at one time or another, especially important were the research assistance by Jerry Harvey, Rose Hansen, Ricardo Hernández, Wendy Kappy, Erik Leaver, Laura Sheridan, and Steve Whitman; the administrative and personal support offered by executive director Debra Preusch; and the publications skills of production manager John Hawley. Our good friend Christine Jepson contributed much of her time and energy, without which we would still be pushing back deadlines. Vital in detecting errors, correcting misconceptions, and offering important insights were the following area experts who commented on parts of the manuscript and shared their information: Mark Anderson, C. Richard Bath, Fernando Bejerano, Ron Blackwell, David Brooks, Roderic Camp, Jorge Castañeda, John Cavanagh, Richard Craig, James Cypher, Ed Feigen, Paul Ganster, Rodolfo O. de la Garza, Antonio Gonzalez, Michael Gregory, Steve Hecker, Rosemary Jenkins,

Dick Kamp, Geoffrey Land, Thea Lee, Nancy Lowrey, Peter Lupsha, Philip Martin, Oscar Martínez, Mary McGinn, Peter Morici, Stephen Mumme, Wilson Peres, Andrew Reding, Primitivo Rodríguez, Fred Schellenberg, Peter Schey, Steve Wager, Christopher Whalen, and Matt Witt. Perhaps most important, however, was the close working relationship that developed among the three of us that allowed us to shape diverse research focuses, writing styles, and areas of expertise into what we hope is a helpful contribution to the improvement of U.S.-Mexico relations. Finally we gratefully acknowledge the financial support of the John D. and Catherine T. MacArthur Foundation, North Shore Unitarian Universalist Veatch Program, Threshold Foundation, Presbyterian Hunger Program, United Church of Christ, Max and Anna Levinson Foundation, and Mennonite Central Committee for our U.S.-Mexico project and for the general support offered by the Evangelical Lutheran Church in America, National Community Funds, United Methodist Church, and Limantour Fund. Also important were the many individual contributors and patrons of the Resource Center.

# About the Authors

Tom Barry, Harry Browne, and Beth Sims are research associates at the Inter-Hemispheric Education Resource Center in Albuquerque, New Mexico. Barry is the author of numerous books on Central America, including *Central America Inside Out* (Grove Weidenfeld, 1991), and he edited *Mexico: A Country Guide* (Resource Center Press, 1992). Browne and Sims coauthored *Runaway America: U.S. Jobs and Factories on the Move* (Resource Center Press, 1993), and Sims is the author of *Workers of the World Undermined: American Labor's Role in U.S. Foreign Policy* (South End Press, 1992).

# About the Resource Center

The Inter-Hemispheric Education Resource Center is a private non-profit research and policy institute in Albuquerque, New Mexico. Founded in 1979, the Resource Center provides books, policy reports, audiovisuals, and other educational materials about U.S. foreign policy. For more information, please write to the Resource Center, Box 4506, Albuquerque, NM 87196.

DATE DUE  132715

JUN 25 1997